Data Mining in Dynamic Social Networks and Fuzzy Systems

Vishal Bhatnagar
Ambedkar Institute of Advanced Communication Technologies & Research, India

A volume in the Advances in Data Mining and Database Management (ADMDM) Book Series

Managing Director: Lindsay Johnston
Editorial Director: Joel Gamon
Production Manager: Jennifer Yoder
Publishing Systems Analyst: Adrienne Freeland
Development Editor: Christine Smith
Acquisitions Editor: Kayla Wolfe
Typesetter: Erin O'Dea
Cover Design: Jason Mull

Published in the United States of America by
Information Science Reference (an imprint of IGI Global)
701 E. Chocolate Avenue
Hershey PA 17033
Tel: 717-533-8845
Fax: 717-533-8661
E-mail: cust@igi-global.com
Web site: http://www.igi-global.com

Copyright © 2013 by IGI Global. All rights reserved. No part of this publication may be reproduced, stored or distributed in any form or by any means, electronic or mechanical, including photocopying, without written permission from the publisher. Product or company names used in this set are for identification purposes only. Inclusion of the names of the products or companies does not indicate a claim of ownership by IGI Global of the trademark or registered trademark.

Library of Congress Cataloging-in-Publication Data

Data mining in dynamic social networks and fuzzy systems / Vishal Bhatnagar, editor.
pages cm
Includes bibliographical references and index.
Summary: "This book brings together research on the latest trends and patterns of data mining tools and techniques in dynamic social networks and fuzzy systems"--Provided by publisher.
ISBN 978-1-4666-4213-3 (hardcover) -- ISBN 978-1-4666-4214-0 (ebook) -- ISBN 978-1-4666-4215-7 (print & perpetual access) 1. Social networks--Research. 2. Social sciences--Network analysis. 3. Online social networks--Research. 4. Data mining. 5. Fuzzy systems. I. Bhatnagar, Vishal, 1977-
HM741.D384 2013
006.3'12--dc23
2013009733

This book is published in the IGI Global book series Advances in Data Mining and Database Management (ADMDM) (ISSN: 2327-1981; eISSN: 2327-199x)

British Cataloguing in Publication Data
A Cataloguing in Publication record for this book is available from the British Library.

All work contributed to this book is new, previously-unpublished material. The views expressed in this book are those of the authors, but not necessarily of the publisher.

Advances in Data Mining and Database Management (ADMDM)

David Taniar
Monash University, Australia

ISSN: 2327-1981
EISSN: 2327-199X

Mission

With the large amounts of information available to businesses in today's digital world, there is a need for methods and research on managing and analyzing the information that is collected and stored. IT professionals, software engineers, and business administrators, along with many other researchers and academics, have made the fields of data mining and database management into ones of increasing importance as the digital world expands. The **Advances in Data Mining & Database Management (ADMDM) Book Series** aims to bring together research in both fields in order to become a resource for those involved in either field.

Coverage

- Cluster Analysis
- Customer Analytics
- Data Mining
- Data Quality
- Data Warehousing
- Database Security
- Database Testing
- Decision Support Systems
- Enterprise Systems
- Text Mining

IGI Global is currently accepting manuscripts for publication within this series. To submit a proposal for a volume in this series, please contact our Acquisition Editors at Acquisitions@igi-global.com or visit: http://www.igi-global.com/publish/.

The Advances in Data Mining and Database Management (ISSN 2327-1981) is published by IGI Global, 701 E. Chocolate Avenue, Hershey, PA 17033-1240, USA, www.igi-global.com. This series is composed of titles available for purchase individually; each title is edited to be contextually exclusive from any other title within the series. For pricing and ordering information please visit http://www.igi-global.com/book-series/advances-data-mining-database-management/37146. Postmaster: Send all address changes to above address. Copyright © 2013 IGI Global. All rights, including translation in other languages reserved by the publisher. No part of this series may be reproduced or used in any form or by any means – graphics, electronic, or mechanical, including photocopying, recording, taping, or information and retrieval systems – without written permission from the publisher, except for non commercial, educational use, including classroom teaching purposes. The views expressed in this series are those of the authors, but not necessarily of IGI Global.

Titles in this Series

For a list of additional titles in this series, please visit: www.igi-global.com

Data Mining in Dynamic Social Networks and Fuzzy Systems
Vishal Bhatnagar (Ambedkar Institute of Advanced Communication Technologies and Research, India)
Information Science Reference • copyright 2013 • 341pp • H/C (ISBN: 9781466642133) • US $195.00 (our price)

Ethical Data Mining Applications for Socio-Economic Development
Hakikur Rahman (University of Minho, Portugal) and Isabel Ramos (University of Minho, Portugal)
Information Science Reference • copyright 2013 • 359pp • H/C (ISBN: 9781466640788) • US $195.00 (our price)

Design, Performance, and Analysis of Innovative Information Retrieval
Zhongyu (Joan) Lu (University of Huddersfield, UK)
Information Science Reference • copyright 2013 • 508pp • H/C (ISBN: 9781466619753) • US $195.00 (our price)

XML Data Mining Models, Methods, and Applications
Andrea Tagarelli (University of Calabria, Italy)
Information Science Reference • copyright 2012 • 538pp • H/C (ISBN: 9781613503560) • US $195.00 (our price)

Graph Data Management Techniques and Applications
Sherif Sakr (University of New South Wales, Australia) and Eric Pardede (LaTrobe University, Australia)
Information Science Reference • copyright 2012 • 502pp • H/C (ISBN: 9781613500538) • US $195.00 (our price)

Advanced Database Query Systems Techniques, Applications and Technologies
Li Yan (Northeastern University, China) and Zongmin Ma (Northeastern University, China)
Information Science Reference • copyright 2011 • 410pp • H/C (ISBN: 9781609604752) • US $180.00 (our price)

Knowledge Discovery Practices and Emerging Applications of Data Mining Trends and New Domains
A.V. Senthil Kumar (CMS College of Science and Commerce, India)
Information Science Reference • copyright 2011 • 414pp • H/C (ISBN: 9781609600679) • US $180.00 (our price)

Data Mining in Public and Private Sectors Organizational and Government Applications
Antti Syvajarvi (University of Lapland, Finland) and Jari Stenvall (Tampere University, Finland)
Information Science Reference • copyright 2010 • 448pp • H/C (ISBN: 9781605669069) • US $180.00 (our price)

Text Mining Techniques for Healthcare Provider Quality Determination Methods for Rank Comparisons
Patricia Cerrito (University of Louisville, USA)
Medical Information Science Reference • copyright 2010 • 410pp • H/C (ISBN: 9781605667522) • US $245.00 (our price)

www.igi-global.com

701 E. Chocolate Ave., Hershey, PA 17033
Order online at www.igi-global.com or call 717-533-8845 x100
To place a standing order for titles released in this series, contact: cust@igi-global.com
Mon-Fri 8:00 am - 5:00 pm (est) or fax 24 hours a day 717-533-8661

Editorial Advisory Board

Lotfi A. Zadeh, *University of California, USA*
Marenglen Biba, *University of New York, Albania*
B. De Baets, *Ghent University, Belgium*
Xiaohua (Tony) Hu, *College of Information Science & Technology, USA*
Vicenc Torra, *IIIA-CSIC, Campus UAB, Spain*
Karthik P Hariharan, *IBM India Software Labs, Bangalore*
Shao-cheng Qu, *Central China Normal University, China*
Tansel Ozyer, *TOBB Economics and Technology University, Turkey*

List of Reviewers

Sunil Pandey, *I.T.S, Mohan Nagar, India*
Bazar Öztayşi, *Technical University, Turkey*
Anshuman Tripathi, *KEC College, India*
Sachin Malhotra, *IMS Ghaziabad, India*
Manish Kumar, *IIIT Allahabad, India*
Rakesh Mohandas, *IBM, India*
Preeti Gupta, *NTRO, India*
Behrouz Jedari, *Dalian University of Technology, China*
Vineet Kansal, *I.T.S, Mohan Nagar, India*
Partha Banerjee, *Jaypee Institute of Technology, India*
Naveen Dahiya, *MSIT, India*
Dhiraj Murthy, *Bowdoin College, USA*
Vikram Bali, *Rayat Bahra Institute of Engineering and Biotechnology, India*
Munish Trivedi, *Dehradun Institute of Technology, India*
Raju Ranjan, *Ideal College of Engineering, India*
Alessandro Fiori, *Institute for Cancer Research and Treatment, Italy*
Luigi Grimaudo, *Politecnico di Torino, Italy*
Luca Cagliero, *Politecnico di Torino, Italy*
Sapna Sinha, *Amity University, India*
Tarun Srivastava, *Steria, Seaview special Economic Zone, India*

Saurabh Kumar, *IMS Ghaziabad, India*
Sanur Sharma, *GTBIT, India*
Pasi Laukka, *Lappeenranta University of Technology, Finland*
Min-Soeng Kim, *Data Lab, CTO, Republic of Korea*
Sara Moridpour, *School of Civil, Environmental and Chemical Engineering, RMIT University, Australia*
Awadesh Kumar, *Galgotia's University, India*
Amit Rathi, *Jaypee Institute of Technology, Guna (M.P), India*
Shao-cheng Qu, *Department of Information & Technology, Central China Normal University, China*

Table of Contents

Detailed Table of Contents

Section 1
Data Mining in Dynamic Social Networks

This section is primarily focused on the data mining in social network analysis. The chapters are framed considering and assuming that before an in-depth applicative area is dealt, the basic/primary concept of the same is highlighted and focused. The initial chapters focused on the need of the dynamicity in social network and preprocessing to be carried for the in-depth analysis of the social network data by the data mining tools. The emerging tools in the area of data mining are compared in the following chapter to enable the researchers to clearly identify the tool as per there data and patterns to be identified. The subsequent chapter focuses on finding an suitable framework for preserving the privacy of the data pertaining to the users in social network for which conceptual framework is proposed and empirical study is done to validate the saying in this regard. Broadening the discussion, further finding on analyzing the twitter user-generated content changes to find the patterns in the social network data is done by the authors. The application, issues and prospects related to implementation of the data mining in dynamic social network data is dealt in subsequent chapters. The usage of the data mining techniques in social network data is further widened by using the same in Mobile social networks. The optimization of the mobile social network is a must for which cloud based Semantic integrating for Intelligent Cloud Data Mining Platform and Cloud Based Business Intelligence for Optimization of Mobile Social Networks is proposed by the authors in the chapter. The summing of the section is done by finding the real statistical data related to usage of the social media analytics presented by the authors in the chapter.

This chapter describes the basic need of the social media networking sites. The chapter provides an in-depth understanding of as why dynamicity is must in social media networking and also the applications of the social media networking sites. The chapter focuses of the functionality and design issues related to social media networking sites. The evolution, current status, challenges and how data mining and big data can play an effective role is very well presented in the chapter which will definitely help the young researchers to understand and pursue their work in this area.

This chapter identifies key issues which is often missed but is of utmost importance before analyzing the social network data. The chapter presents an insight into as what should be steps carried to preprocesses the data before an analysis can be performed on special network data. The steps would help the researchers as stepping and essential elements which they should consider before analyzing the social network data. The chapter highlights various phases of social network data preprocessing. The chapter particularly focuses on various challenges in each phase. The goal of this chapter is to illustrate the importance of data preprocessing for social network analysis.

This chapter starts with finding the relevance of the data mining tools for the social network data analysis. Then it describes as what are the Formats, Conventions, Utilities, and Languages for the analysis of the social network data. The chapter then presents the features of the existing tools of the data mining for the social networking data analysis. The development of a hybrid system, which builds upon the work of the open-source Web-Harvest framework, for the collection of information from online social networks is presented and discussed named VoyeurServer, attempts to address the weaknesses of tools identified in earlier sections. The chapter is concluded with a case study and subsequent evaluation of the VoyeurServer system itself.

The increase in the privacy issues concerning with a tremendous increase in the number of social networking sites and their users is highlighted by the authors for which an conceptual framework is presented. The authors presented in the chapter conceptual framework to secure the social network data effectively by using data mining techniques to perform in-depth social network analysis before carrying out the actual anonymization process. This proposed framework is basically divided by the authors in three levels which are namely analysis of the social network data, data mining techniques inclusion and then application of the information security measures to safeguard the vital and critical information pertaining to the users. The empirical case study in the end of the chapter validates and strengthens what is said by the authors in the chapter.

In this Chapter authors argued for the continuous evolution of the patterns in the user generated content. They argued for the effective use of the data mining to extract the patterns out of such data. The chapter focuses on a novel data mining system that performs dynamic itemset mining from both the content and the contextual features of the messages posted on Twitter. The presented framework exploits a dynamic itemset mining algorithm, named HiGen Miner, to discover relevant temporal data correlations from a stream of tweet collections. The major stress of the algorithm implementation is to extract compact patterns, namely the HiGens that represent the evolution of the most relevant itemsets over consecutive time periods at different abstraction levels. The authors performed experiments on real Twitter posts showing the effectiveness and the usability of the proposed system in supporting Twitter user behavior and topic trend analysis.

The chapter starts with describing the importance of the dynamic social network data. The author described the uses of various data mining techniques like clustering, association rule mining, link Mining, classification and graph mining in dynamic social network. The chapter is concluded by the author by finding the relevance of the privacy preservation data mining in dynamic social network which is growing importance in modern day era.

The authors had presented in the chapter the basic data mining approaches in the context of the social network data in particular about the dynamic social network. The chapter presented state-of-the-art work concerning the analysis of social data in four real-life application contexts that is recommendation systems, query engines, topic trend detection, and document summarization. In each application context, the social context in which it has been proposed, its main goals, and the most significant experimental results are summarized. The chapter concludes with Future research directions in data mining application in social data.

The chapter provides an in-depth understanding of the prospect in the mobile social network (MSN). The importance of data mining and its prospects in MSN has an enormous potential to handle, manage and extract actionable patterns, which can be beneficial for transformation of the conventional social networks to advance one (MSN). The chapter presents Conceptual descriptions of mobile social network architecture which helps to understanding the basic working in mobile social networks. The authors had shown the growing importance of MSN considering the use of a mobile device which has led to the emergence of dynamic and interactive social networked environment, which is fertile to the use of data mining techniques. The authors described Social networking mapping as a mining prospects and Data structure and mining processing in the chapter. The mining algorithms for the MSN and MSNs data set Bayesian Networking distribution models are presented in the chapter.

The authors proposed Semantic intelligent cloud model for optimization of mobile social networks. The model is vitally necessary to optimize MSNs applications that appropriate for users' desires, which provides efficient data/information distribution and access facilities. It involves intelligent agents cloud components to identify dynamic social networking on users' inputs and contexts. The authors argued in the chapter for Intelligent DM and BI based social cloud which made significant use of social ontologies and collaborative semantic annotations to documents and social resources and knowledge, and to describe the semantics of cloud services.

This chapter aims at providing a data-centric view of online social networks. The growth of the social network over the years is shown using the statistics available over the years. The authors showed Process paradigm and applications of data mining in social media over the years. The authors had considered facebook and had compared the growth of its user over the years to reflect the overall growth in social network users. The recent applications, challenges and opportunities which are created in said field are presented by the authors in the chapter.

Section 2
Data Mining in Fuzzy Systems

This section is based on the usage of the data mining in Fuzzy systems. The basic understanding as how the data is to be before applying the data mining is focused in the initial chapter with finding the critical/essential parameters for fuzzy data mining. The trend and importance of fuzzy clustering especially for the segmentation of the data is focused in subsequent chapter. The usage of data mining techniques for fuzzy lane changing behavior analysis is focused which helps to understand the applicative area of the data mining involving the fuzzy systems. The primary focused is to explain as how the fuzzy system and data mining can provide solution to many unsolved problems in Engineering and scientific fields. The discussion is further broaden by the application of fuzzy clustering to identify the clusters and fuzzy association rule to find new patterns and associations in the application areas like Twitter data and the sports portal.

approach, using Text Mining and Fuzzy Clustering techniques. The proposed approach users self description text is used as an input to the Text Mining process and Fuzzy Clustering technique is used to extract knowledge from data. The authors argued that with this approach, Business users/companies can segment their customers based on their comments, ideas or any kind of other unstructured data on SNSs.

The chapter focuses on the extensive usage of the social network sites for the sharing of the views. The organizations/companies would like to provide the benefits to the customer on the basis of the frequent items sets found and association. Considering this fact the authors in the chapter proposed a fuzzy association rule mining based methodology which will present the potential of using the Fuzzy association rule mining techniques in the field of social network analysis. In order to reveal the applicability, an experimental evaluation of the proposed methodology in a sports portal news feed is presented in which Apriori algorithm is used for finding the association.

Foreword

As never experienced before, in the rapidly growing world of the Internet, social networks, and emergence of the omnipresence of floods of data, arises a genuine and pressing need to make sense of the surrounding digital world, visualize, analyze and acquire knowledge from data. With this regard, we witness a highly visible and undisputed role of knowledge discovery and data mining (KDD). After more than almost two decades, KDD is a vibrant field of research, which every year is confronted with new challenges and opportunities coming from the dynamic environment of cyberspace and a way in which people interact with new media. Social media have revolutionized the world and immensely changed a way people communicate among themselves and with computer systems (being continuously endowed with new functionalities). The role of KDD in this domain is unquestionable: there are tangible benefits to understand human needs, organize resources by comprehending ways in which human interacts, offer a conceptual framework for business intelligence. There is a growing pressure to endow the technology of KDD with methods and tools to deal with the mobility of the environment of social media and address the complex dynamics and interactions.

Human-system interaction is at the heart of intelligent systems. Granularity of information becomes central to the analysis and design of efficient human-system interaction schemes. Granular Computing delivers a broad, well-established platform to cope with granular information, formalize it (quite often resorting here to fuzzy sets or rough sets) and process information granules. KDD has to address the challenges human-centric systems bring into the picture.

This volume offers a comprehensive, well-rounded view at the concepts, methodologies, algorithms, and systems and solutions of data mining in social networks and fuzzy systems. The authors offer a truly remarkable wealth of ideas, identifying issues central to data mining in new challenging environments such as social networks. The organization of the volume highlights the two key focal points of applications in data mining, namely dynamic social networks (Part I) and fuzzy systems (Part II). In the first one, the authors identify main features of social media and social networks and elaborate on the innovative ways in which the crucial problems of data mining arising in this setting could be addressed. Those include data preprocessing, dealing with dynamic facets of processes of interaction, data security, content changes analysis and investigating their impact on data mining processes, studying data mining in mobile environments. Emerging data mining tools for social network analysis are covered. Part II is devoted to data mining in fuzzy systems. Owing to the specificity of these human-centric systems, we encounter interesting issues when exploiting or augmenting classic schemes of data mining. Fuzzy clustering and fuzzy association rules along their analysis play here a pivotal role and their position is well exemplified in this volume through a number of interesting contributions.

The Editor, Dr. Vishal Bhatnagar has to be congratulated for the excellent job. This volume is indeed a highly welcome, timely, and an important publication providing the reader with a very much needed material both of a significant research and applied nature.

Witold Pedrycz
University of Alberta, Edmonton, Canada

Witold Pedrycz *(IEEE- M'88, SM'90, F'99) is a Professor and Canada Research Chair (CRC - Computational Intelligence) in the Department of Electrical and Computer Engineering, University of Alberta, Edmonton, Canada. He is also with the Systems Research Institute of the Polish Academy of Sciences, Warsaw, Poland. He also holds an appointment of special professorship in the School of Computer Science, University of Nottingham, UK. In 2009, Dr. Pedrycz was elected a foreign member of the Polish Academy of Sciences. His main research directions involve Computational Intelligence, fuzzy modeling and Granular Computing, knowledge discovery and data mining, fuzzy control, pattern recognition, knowledge-based neural networks, relational computing, and Software Engineering. He has published numerous papers in this area. He is also an author of 14 research monographs covering various aspects of Computational Intelligence and Software Engineering. Witold Pedrycz has been a member of numerous program committees of IEEE conferences in the area of fuzzy sets and neurocomputing. Dr. Pedrycz is intensively involved in editorial activities. He is an Editor-in-Chief of Information Sciences and Editor-in-Chief of IEEE Transactions on Systems, Man, and Cybernetics - part A. He currently serves as an Associate Editor of IEEE Transactions on Fuzzy Systems and is a member of a number of editorial boards of other international journals. He has edited a number of volumes; the most recent one is entitled "Handbook of Granular Computing." In 2007, he received a prestigious Norbert Wiener award from the IEEE Systems, Man, and Cybernetics Council. He is a recipient of the IEEE Canada Computer Engineering Medal 2008. In 2009, he has received a Cajastur Prize for Soft Computing from the European Centre for Soft Computing for pioneering and multifaceted contributions to Granular Computing.*

Preface

Data mining is finding hidden and unknown information from large databases. The data mining tools and techniques are finding its immense applications in the modern day which needs to be addressed and explained in one book to understand the importance of the data mining applications. The implications of data mining can be understand by the facts that whether it's a public or private sector organization all are taking the advantage of the data mining tools and techniques to reveal the hidden and unknown information from the available data. This has being widened primarily because of the large or can we say terabyte of data which is collected by all the organizations over the year and they are confused as how to use such bulk of the data. The new and emerging areas of data mining techniques have surprised many a researchers and business persons who are actually gaining a lot of hidden and unknown information for increasing their ROI. This will widen the application area and more interest will be created in budding researchers to pursue their research in data mining. The data mining is all about the revealing of hidden and unknown information from the huge available data. The techniques of data mining which are primarily making it happen are:

1. Classification
2. Clustering
3. Association rule mining
4. Neural network
5. Genetic algorithms

These techniques are able to classify the given data on the basis of whether it is supervised or unsupervised learning methodology. In case of supervised learning, the dependent and independent variables are considered. There are set of independent variables on the basis of which the value of the dependent variable is predicted while in the case of unsupervised learning, the useful information is searched by forming the clusters or group. The variables in both the case can be nominal, ordinal, categorical or continuous variables depending upon the available data which enable us to apply the various algorithms of the different techniques discussed above. Considering the vast application area of data mining, book is targeted towards finding the data mining applications in emerging areas. These areas are already hot topics in the research. By the inclusion of the data mining in such areas, the application and usability of all the said areas will be widened.

With the proliferated use of social networks in today's modern era, data mining has found its significant place in social network analysis and its security. Privacy preservation of social networks is a brewing topic of research these days. With large amounts of content being posted on social networks, privacy breach has become one of the prime issues of social networking. Data mining techniques like classification, clustering, and association rule mining has been used extensively for social network analysis and data mining techniques like heuristics based, reconstruction based, and cryptographic techniques that are being applied on social networks for providing desired security. There are also various anonymization techniques like clustering and clustering with constraints that make use of data mining to provide privacy preservation of released social network data. Much less work has been done in the area of dynamic social network security and is a focus of study for various researchers and practitioners. Social networks contain a vast amount of information and such high dimensional data are difficult to be handled by the traditional systems like OLAP. For this, data mining has proved to be a blessing in disguise. Various data mining and statistical techniques find its use in analyzing large amounts of online (Dynamic) social network data, where the interactions among the users of the network are studied to find out interesting patterns and also to find out various outliers in the data. The chapters in the first part of the book aim towards fulfilling the above said aim and finding the wide and emerging current development in the application of data mining in dynamic social network.

The use of fuzzy logic can be intervened with data mining so as to give another dimension to the concept of data mining. The fuzzy logic is used in data mining to create a new concept called the fuzzy data mining which makes data mining more flexible and extends its utility by a large extent in fields such as intrusion detection, approximations of missing values, power plant optimizations, human resource management, cross-selling, detection of quality of water, decision making or medical image processing. Fuzzy theory is useful for data mining systems performing rule based classification. The future prospect of data mining in the field of fuzzy data mining is revealing applications on fuzzy sets. The research is currently focused on finding the utilization of other techniques of data mining in fuzzy systems like genetic algorithms. The focus of the study is also as how more effective results can be drawn on application of data mining on fuzzy systems. The chapters in the second part of the book aim towards fulfilling the above said aim and finding the wide and emerging current development in the application of data mining in fuzzy systems.

The objective of the this edited book is to make aware researchers and other prospective readers with latest trends and patterns in the inclusion of the data mining tools and techniques in the areas which affect the common men so that a better system can be developed with improved and modern techniques of data mining. The mission of the proposed publication was to come up with an edited book which aims at latest and most advanced topic inclusion and simultaneously discussion of contributions of renowned researchers whose work created a revolution in the area.

The development in the area of application of data mining in Dynamic social network and fuzzy system will help and target the researchers and academicians targeting their Doctoral and post Doctoral research and this edited book will act as a stepping stone for grooming of the budding researchers who intend to work in the area of data mining and its applications. The book will target the audiences which would like to work on latest and advanced concepts of data mining inclusions in the applicative areas of Dynamic social network and fuzzy system for the benefit of the society and country. The specific beneficiary will be:

1. The researchers will be able to know the latest application area of the data mining.
2. The business users will get to know how inclusion of data mining can provide added advantages for them in their professions.
3. The common people will get the secure edge for their data which is revealed in the social network analysis.

Intended Audiences:

1. Business users
2. Researchers
3. Common peoples

In my May 2012 call for chapters, I urged and sought for contribution to this book from researchers, IT savvys and young Engineers, across the globe with an aim to extract and accumulate the whole modern day research in the field of data mining in dynamic social network and fuzzy system and gradually I started getting quality and very conceptual, basic and advanced contributions that too from various contributors from different countries. Initially I thought as whether I will be getting any chapters on this topic as it is very new and emerging area, but surprisingly I saw an great response with authors started to respond which encouraged me and motivated me by showing that this area is gaining its importance. After screening through them, my aim and objective was clear, which aimed and concentrated on getting chapters which focused on elementary issues, needs, demand of the data mining in said area and finally on application areas of the data mining in dynamic social networks and fuzzy systems.

The book is a collection of the fifteen chapters which are written by eminent professors, researchers and Industry people from different countries. The chapters were initially peer reviewed by the Editorial board members, reviewers and industry people who themselves span over many countries. The whole book is divided into two sections, namely Section I Data Mining in Dynamic Social Networks and Section II Data Mining in Fuzzy Systems.

SECTION 1: DATA MINING IN DYNAMIC SOCIAL NETWORKS

Chapter 1 by Gurdeep S Hura urged us to felt that there is really an urgent need for the dynamicity in social networking sites considering the data mining perspective. This chapter presents this new emerging technology of social media and networking with a detailed discussion on: basic definitions and applications, how this technology evolved in the last few years, the need for dynamicity under data mining environment. It also provides a comprehensive design and analysis of popular social networking media and sites available for the users. A brief discussion on the data mining methodologies for implementing the variety of new applications dealing with huge/big data in data science is presented. Further, an attempt is being made in this chapter to present a new emerging perspective of data mining methodologies with its dynamicity for social networking media and sites as a new trend and needed framework for dealing with huge amount of data for its collection, analysis and interpretation for a number of real world applications.

In Chapter 2, Preeti Gupta and Dr. Vishal Bhatnagar discussed about the social network analysis which is of significant interest in various application domains due to its inherent richness. Social network analysis like any other data analysis is limited by the quality and quantity of data and for which data preprocessing plays the key role. Before the discovery of useful information or pattern from the social network data set, the original data set must be converted to a suitable format. In this chapter authors present various phases of social network data preprocessing. In this context they discuss various challenges in each phase. The goal of this chapter is to illustrate the importance of data preprocessing for social network analysis.

The analysis of the dynamic network data is a challenge in modern era. In Chapter 3, Dhiraj Murthy, Alexander Gross and Alex Takata identifies a number of the most common data mining toolkits and evaluates their utility in the extraction of data from heterogeneous online social networks. It introduces not only the complexities of scraping data from the diverse forms of data manifested in these sources, but also critically evaluates currently available tools. This analysis is followed by a presentation and discussion on the development of a hybrid system, which builds upon the work of the open-source Web-Harvest framework, for the collection of information from online social networks. This tool, VoyeurServer, attempts to address the weaknesses of tools identified in earlier sections, as well as prototype the implementation of key functionalities thought to be missing from commonly available data extraction toolkits. Authors concluded the chapter with a case study and subsequent evaluation of the VoyeurServer system itself. This evaluation presents future directions, remaining challenges, and additional extensions thought to be important to the effective development of data mining tools for the study of online social networks.

The need of privacy and security in the social network data has increased with more and more dynamicity in social network data. The urge and demand of the growing users of the social network had resulted in contribution from Sanur Sharma and Dr. Vishal Bhatnagar in Chapter 4 that in recent times there has been a tremendous increase in the number of social networking sites and their users. With the amount of information posted on the public forums, it becomes essential for the service providers to maintain the privacy of an individual. Anonymization as a technique to secure social network data has gained popularity but there are challenges in implementing it effectively. In this chapter, authors have presented a conceptual framework to secure the social network data effectively by using data mining techniques to perform in-depth social network analysis before carrying out the actual anonymization process. The framework in the first step defines the role of community analysis in social network and its various features and temporal metrics. In the next step authors proposes the application of those data mining techniques that can deal with the dynamic nature of social network and discover important attributes of the social network. Finally, authors mapped security requirements and findings of the network properties which provide an appropriate base for selection and application of the anonymization technique to protect privacy of social network data.

Chapter 5 by Luca Cagliero, Luigi Grimaudo and Alessandro Fiori argued that User-generated content (UGC) coming from social networks and online communities continuously grows and changes. By analyzing relevant patterns from the UGC, analysts may discover peculiar user behaviors and interests which can be used to personalize Web-oriented applications. In the last several years, the use of dynamic mining techniques has captured the interest of the research community. They are focus on analyzing the temporal evolution of most significant correlations hidden in the analyzed data. However, keeping track of all temporal data correlations relevant for user behaviors, community interests, and topic trend analysts may become a challenging task due to the sparseness of the analyzed data. The authors in this Chapter presents a novel data mining system that performs dynamic itemset mining from both the content and the contextual features of the messages posted on Twitter. Dynamic itemsets represent the evolution of data correlations over time. The framework exploits a dynamic itemset mining algorithm, named HiGen Miner, to discover relevant temporal data correlations from a stream of tweet collections. In particular, it extracts compact patterns, namely the HiGens that represent the evolution of the most relevant itemsets over consecutive time periods at different abstraction levels. Taxonomy is used to drive the mining process and prevent the discarding of knowledge that becomes infrequent in a certain time period. Experiments, performed on real Twitter posts, show the effectiveness and the usability of the proposed system in supporting Twitter user behavior and topic trend analysis.

Chapter 6 by Manish Kumar focused on the application of data mining in dynamic social network analysis. Social Networks are nodes consisting of people, groups and organizations growing dynamically. The growth is horizontal as well as vertical in terms of size and number. Social network analysis has gained success due to online social networking and sharing sites. The accessibility of online social sites such as MySpace, Facebook, Twitter, Hi5, Friendster, SkyRock and Beb offer sharing and maintaining large amount of different data. Social network analysis is focused on mining such data i.e. generating pattern of people's interaction. The analysis involves the knowledge discovery that helps the sites as well as users in terms of usage and business goals respectively. Further it is desired that the process must be privacy preserving. This chapter describes the various mining techniques applicable on social networks data.

Chapter 7 by Luca Cagliero and Alessandro Fiori reviews statistics about past few years which have witnessed the rapid proliferation of Web communities such as social networking sites, wikis, blogs, and media sharing communities. The published social content is commonly characterized by a high dynamicity and reflects the most recent trends and common user behaviors. The Data mining and Knowledge Discovery (KDD) process focuses on discovering and analyzing relevant information hidden in large data collections to support expert decision making. Hence, the application of data mining techniques to data coming from social networks and online communities is definitely an appealing research topic. This chapter presents overviews on most recent data mining approaches proposed in the context of social network analysis. In particular, it aims at classifying the proposed approaches based on both the adopted mining strategies and their suitability for supporting knowledge discovery in a dynamic context. To provide a thorough insight into the proposed approaches, main work issues and prospects in dynamic social network analysis are also outlined.

The demand and essentiality of the mobile device is not hidden from any one of us. The growth of both fields simultaneously that is social network and mobile devices had presented a great potential for the researchers across the world. In Chapter 8 Gebeyehu Belay Gebremeskel, Zhongshi He and Huazheng Zhu explores and argued for Data mining is a key paradigm for Mobile Social Networks (MSNs) in which growing and exciting area of research that has in front of itself a long way to go across many fields, including social networks. With the evolution of the social networking and the rapid adoption of a mobile device's large and unprecedented amount of data generated, which gained significant attention to improve social network's applications easily, and accessible platform for users. However, the traditional social-networking system could not capable and scalable to provide these dynamic applications. The challenges are unable to handle and manage large-scale data, which includes noisiness, unstructured, diversified sources and dynamic in nature, and other functionality challenges. Unable to accommodating new technologies, including social technology, mobile devices and computing are other potential problems, which are significant challenges to social-networking service. The very broad range of such social-networking challenges and problems are demanding advanced and dynamic tools. Therefore, in this chapter, authors introduced and discussed data mining prospects to overcome the traditional social-networking challenges and problems, which led to optimization of MSNs application and performances. Data mining prospects in MSN has an enormous potential to handle, manage and extract actionable patterns, which can be beneficial for transformation of the conventional social networks to advance one (MSN). The proposed method infers defining and investigating social-networking problems using data mining techniques and algorithms based on the large-scale data. The approach is also exploring the possible potential of users and systems contexts, which leads to mine the personal contexts such as the users' locations and situations from the mobile logs. As a result, data mining playing an essential and dynamic role to developing appropriate solutions, visualized the social contexts, users' contexts and others in section 3, 4 and 5. In these sections, they discussed and introduced new ideas on social technologies, data mining techniques and algorithm's prospects, social technology's key functional and performances, which include social analysis, security and fraud detections by presenting a brief analysis, and modeling based descriptions. The approach also empirically discussed using the real survey data, which the result showed how data mining vitally significant to explore MSNs performance and its crosscutting impacts. Finally, this chapter provides fundamental insight to researchers and practitioners who need to know data mining prospects and techniques to analyze large, complex and frequently changing data. This chapter is also providing a state-of-the-art of data mining techniques and algorithm's dynamic prospects. In addition, authors provide insights on future research directions.

Chapter 9 by Gebeyehu Belay Gebremeskel, Zhongshi He and Xuan Jing discusses the Semantic integrating with intelligent cloud data mining platform for optimizing of the Mobile social networks (MSNs). With the evolution of the social-networking in relation to computing development (DM and BI) and the rapid adoption of mobile devices such as cell phones and other handheld devices, social networks, which began as web-based applications, and migrated onto the semantic cloud platform. It is the fundamental knowledge and optimal features of social networks, which helps to manage the human relationship and interaction using semantic intelligent cloud. It revolutionizes how social relationships develop, understand, and secure real value through a social cloud that involving semantic intelligent agents and mobile clouds of the dynamic social networking. However, the current social-networking service has many challenges, including the lack of integrated semantic intelligent agents cloud and mobile devices. The challenges are including less consolidation of social-networking, unable to defining the problem of characterization of social-networking structures towards large-scale data handling and analysis missed the opportunity to bind social context tightly with the intelligent agents cloud system and local context of interacting users. In this chapter, authors focused on optimization of MSNs based on integrating for intelligent DM and BI platforms, which involving mobile devices. The approach is defining the challenges based social network trends and current situation explorations, and then applying the techniques to exploring the social media towards social cloud technology, which focused on creating a scalable, adaptable and optimal social cloud as the users' contexts and IT technologies. The newly proposed method is vigorously significant to develop flexible social networking in relation to the development of IT, which facilitates data/information access, distributions, high availability and a large amount of data analysis and others. Therefore, the techniques this chapter is vitally crucial to improve the performance and use of social networking in a comprehensive and powerful way. Nutshell, this chapter overviews the impetus for the development of intelligent semantic cloud and diversified social-networking in both physical and wireless sectors, which representing a wide aspect of social cloud change, and increasingly appropriate service providing a platform for innovative ideas and technological innovation in the business environment.

Chapter 10 by Dr. Sunil Kr Pandey and Dr. Vineet Kansal presents an in-depth online survey on the growing demand of the social media analytics. In present context, online social media demonstrates a fundamental shift in the way information is being produced, transferred and consumed. Large volume of user generated contents in the form of posting blogs, comments, and tweets establishes a connection between the producers and the consumers of information. It has been observed that sensing and tracking the pulse of social media channels may make possible for companies to gain feedback and detailed insight in how to improve, promote and market their services & products better. For consumers, the wealth of information and opinions from various diversified sources facilitates them tap into the wisdom of crowds, to aid in making more informed decisions. The advent of online social networks has been one of the most exciting events in this decade. It has established itself in such a way that in a business organization, search engine optimization, search engine marketing, social media and e-commerce is now a very small piece of an overall online marketing business plan. More and more companies today are focused on brand protection and understanding how people discuss, comment and share information about their company online. Companies like the New Jersey Devils and Gatorade have created social intelligence command centers that listen and mine data within social media platforms such as Google+, Facebook, LinkedIn and Twitter (Li, Surendran, & Shen, 2005). Companies are mining massive data sets to get a competitive edge on their competition. Data mining is the process of analyzing data from different perspectives and summarizing it into useful information. This type of information that can be used to find out what people are seeking, what type of branding might be working and then be able to react accordingly.

Many popular online social networks such as Twitter, LinkedIn, and Facebook have become increasingly popular (based on Facebook statistics by Country, 2011 and other social media reports, 2011, 2012). In addition, a number of multimedia networks such as Flickr have also seen an increasing level of popularity in recent years. Many such social networks are extremely rich in content, and contain tremendous amount of content and linkage data which can be leveraged for analysis. The linkage data is essentially the graph structure of the social network and the communications between entities; whereas the content data contains the text, images and other multimedia data in the network. The richness of network provides unprecedented opportunities for data analytics in the context of social networks. This significant increase in its usage and increased number of users, there has been trend of a substantial increase in the volume of information generated by users of social media. Irrespective of primary domain in which organization is operating in to, whether it is insurance sector, social media (including facebook, twitter etc), medical science, banking etc. Virtually a large number of varying nature and services of organizations are making significant investments in social media. But it is also true that many are not systematically analyzing the valuable information that is resulting from their investments. This chapter aims at providing a data-centric view of online social networks; a topic which has been missing from much of the literature and to draw unanswered research issues which can be further explored to strengthen this area.

SECTION 2: DATA MINING IN FUZZY SYSTEMS

Chapter 11 by Sinchan Bhattacharya and Dr. Vishal Bhatnagar explored critical parameters for application of fuzzy data mining. Research on data mining is increasing at an incessant rate and to improve its effectiveness other techniques have been applied such as fuzzy sets, rough set theory, knowledge representation, inductive logic programming, or high-performance computing. Fuzzy logic due to its proficiency in handling uncertainty has gained its importance in a variety of applications in combination with the use of data mining techniques. In this chapter we take this association a notch further by examining the parameters which allow fuzzy sets and data mining to be combined into what has come to be known as fuzzy data mining. Analyzing and understanding these critical parameters is the main purpose of this chapter, so as to acquire maximum efficiency in applying the same which impelled the authors to work extensively and find out the crucial parameters essential to the application of fuzzy data mining.

Chapter 12 by Zekai Sen provides a clear idea to trends developing in Fuzzy Clustering. Fuzzy methodologies show progress day by day towards better explanation of various natural, social, engineering and information problem solutions in the best, economic, fast and effective manner. This chapter provides cluster analyses from probabilistic, statistical and especially fuzzy methodology points of view by consideration of various classical and innovative cluster modeling and inference systems. After the conceptual assessment explanation of fuzzy logic thinking fundamentals various clustering methodologies are presented with brief revisions but innovative trend analyses as k-mean-standard deviation, cluster regression, relative clustering for depiction of trend components that fall within different clusters. The application of fuzzy clustering methodology is presented for lake time series and earthquake modeling for rapid hazard assessment of existing buildings.

Chapter 13 by Sara Moridpour analyses the Performance of a Fuzzy Lane Changing Model Using Data Mining. Heavy vehicles have substantial impact on traffic flow particularly during heavy traffic conditions. Large amount of heavy vehicle lane changing manoeuvres may increase the number of traffic accidents and therefore reduce the freeway safety. Improving road capacity and enhancing traffic safety on freeways has been the motivation to establish heavy vehicle lane restriction strategies to reduce the interaction between heavy vehicles and passenger cars. In previous studies, different heavy vehicle lane restriction strategies have been evaluated using microscopic traffic simulation packages. Microscopic traffic simulation packages generally use a common model to estimate the lane changing of heavy vehicles and passenger cars. The common lane changing model ignores the differences exist in the lane changing behaviour of heavy vehicle and passenger car drivers. An exclusive fuzzy lane changing model for heavy vehicles is developed and presented in this chapter. This fuzzy model can increase the accuracy of simulation models in estimating the macroscopic and microscopic traffic characteristics. The results of this chapter shows that using an exclusive lane changing model for heavy vehicles, results in more reliable evaluation of lane restriction strategies.

Chapter 14 by Başar Öztayşi and Sezi Çevik Onar showed User Segmentation Based on Twitter Data Using Fuzzy Clustering. Social Networking Sites, which create platform for social interactions and sharing are the mostly used internet websites, thus are very important in today's world. The vast usage of social networking sites (SNSs) has affected the business world, new business models are proposed, business process are renewed and companies try to create benefit from these sites. Besides the functional usage of SNSs such as marketing and customer relations, companies can create value by analyzing and mining the data on SNSs. In this paper, a new segmentation approach, using Text Mining and Fuzzy Clustering techniques. Text mining is process of extracting knowledge from large amounts of unstructured data source such as content generated by the SNSs users. Fuzzy clustering is an algorithm for cluster analysis in which the allocation of data points to clusters is fuzzy. In the proposed approach, users self description text are used as an input to the Text Mining process, and Fuzzy Clustering is used to extract knowledge from data. Using the proposed approach in this chapter, companies can segment their customers based on their comments, ideas or any kind of other unstructured data on SNSs.

Chapter 15 by Başar Öztayşi and Sezi Çevik Onar defined the factors that Effect User Interest on Social Network News Feeds via Fuzzy Association Rule Mining through the Case of Sports News. Social networking became one of the main marketing tools in the recent years since it's a faster and cheaper way to reach the customers. Companies can use social networks for efficient communication with their current and potential customers but the value created through the usage of social networks depends on how well the organizations use these tools. Therefore a support system which will enhance the usage of these tools is necessary. Fuzzy Association rule mining (FARM) is a commonly used data mining technique which focuses on discovering the frequent items and association rules in a data set and can be a powerful tool for enhancing the usage of social networks. Therefore the aim of the chapter is to propose a fuzzy association rule mining based methodology which will present the potential of using the FARM techniques in the field of social network analysis. In order to reveal the applicability, an experimental evaluation of the proposed methodology in a sports portal will be presented.

The applications of data mining in dyanamic social network and fuzzy system are so vast that it cannot be covered in single book. However with the encouraging research contribution by the researchers in this book, we (contributors) tried to sum the latest development and work in the area. This edited book will serve as the stepping stone and a factor of motivation for those young Researchers and Budding Engineers who are witnessing the every stopping growth in the field of dynamic social network and fuzzy system.

Vishal Bhatnagar
Ambedkar Institute of Advanced Communication Technologies & Research, India

Acknowledgment

No one walks alone on the journey of life. Just where do you start to thank those that joined you, walked beside you, helped you along the way, and continuously urged you. I want to express my deep sense of thanks and gratitude to all those who made this book possible. Apart from the efforts of myself, the success of this work depends largely on the encouragement and guidelines of many others. I take this opportunity to express my gratitude to the people who have been instrumental in the successful completion of this book.

First of all, I would like to extend my special note of thanks to the publishing team at IGI Global Publishing whose contributions throughout the whole process- from submission of the proposal to final publication – have been invaluable. In particular, thanks to Christine Smith, whose continuous suggestions and valuable information kept me motivated for completing the work on time. The most touching was the greeting card and chocolates which symbolize the humbleness and great character of her and really helped me to work for the project for timely completion. Not to forget I would like to extend my thanks to Kayla Wolfe for her initial support and necessary information. I would also like to thank Jan Travers for timely completion of the contract agreement. I would like to thank all other support staff of Idea Group for extending their full support.

The guidance and support received from all the authors who contributed to this project, was vital for the timely and successful completion of the book. I wish to thank all of the authors for their insights and excellent contributions to this book. I am also grateful for their constant support and help in getting the review done of the chapters which was appreciated by all the authors and had made a great change in the structure of the chapter which ultimately provided constructive and comprehensive reviews. I also want to thank a group of anonymous reviewers who assisted me in the peer-review process. I would like to extend my special thanks to Professor Witold Pedrycz for agreeing to write the foreword for the book. I would also like to thank all the EAB members for their support and valuable advice. My special thanks goes to Professor L.A Zadeh for agreeing to be part of the EAB and helping me to find the professor to write Foreword. Many a thanks Sir!

I also take this opportunity to express a deep sense of gratitude to Prof. Ashok Mittal, Principal of my college for his cordial support, valuable information and guidance, which helped me in completing this task through various stages. I would also like to thank my friends and colleagues for providing me advice and support all through this work.

Finally, yet importantly, I would like to express my heartfelt thanks to my beloved parents for their blessings and motivating words that always encourages me to work hard and to remember that "There is no replacement for hard work." Not to forget my life is incomplete without the support and confidence which I always get from my beloved wife who is always standing with me for all help. I sincerely thank her for the same. I would also like to openly admit that I would not have worked hard unless I get positive energy and innocent looks from my son who is always beside me to give love and affection.

Vishal Bhatnagar
Ambedkar Institute of Advanced Communication Technologies & Research, India

Section 1
Data Mining in Dynamic Social Networks

Chapter 1
Need for Dynamicity in Social Networking Sites:
An Overview from Data Mining Perspective

Gurdeep S Hura
University of Maryland Eastern Shore, USA

ABSTRACT

This chapter presents this new emerging technology of social media and networking with a detailed discussion on: basic definitions and applications, how this technology evolved in the last few years, the need for dynamicity under data mining environment. It also provides a comprehensive design and analysis of popular social networking media and sites available for the users. A brief discussion on the data mining methodologies for implementing the variety of new applications dealing with huge/big data in data science is presented. Further, an attempt is being made in this chapter to present a new emerging perspective of data mining methodologies with its dynamicity for social networking media and sites as a new trend and needed framework for dealing with huge amount of data for its collection, analysis and interpretation for a number of real world applications. A discussion is also being provided for the current and future status of data mining of social media and networking applications.

INTRODUCTION

A Social Media Networking Site (SMNS) provides a web-based service over Internet that allows individuals to i) design and maintain a private, public or semi-public profile, ii) share their profiles with their friends through shared connection, and (iii) view and be connected with others. The type of connections and sharing of profilers via shared connections may vary from site to site. The social media networking sites and social media together describe the new concept that works on computer network communication. It offers a unique and interesting service that it not only allows users to make friends, meet, articulate and share with their friends but also allows them to make new friends via this frame and means of communication over the network and hence the name Social Media Networking Site (SMNS).

Social media and networking sites offer a communication and sharing platform to meet and connect with people of varied interests. We can

DOI: 10.4018/978-1-4666-4213-3.ch001

Copyright © 2013, IGI Global. Copying or distributing in print or electronic forms without written permission of IGI Global is prohibited.

choose to develop, shallow, meaningless ad hoc relationships that can be just as easily broken as they are formed or develop real, meaningful and useful relationships with people you feel connected to. We can choose to keep things simple and form virtual relationships that do not require any effort or choose to reach out for the people you care about and develop a long lasting bond (Social Media, n.d.; Social networking service, n.d.; Boyd & Ellison, 2007; Kaplan, 2012; Digital Journalism – How News is Sourced with Social Media, n.d.; Research Survey, n.d.; Laurent, 2011; CBS news, 2010; Social media and social networks, n.d.)

WHAT IS A SOCIAL MEDIA NETWORKING SITE (SMNS)?

The backbone of any social media networking site is based on user-friendly interface for the design and maintenance of individuals' profile that may be created after joining it and answering to typical questions of descriptions like as age, location, interests, personal information, and usually an "about me" section. Most social media networking sites also encourage users to upload a profile photo and allow users to enhance their profiles by adding multimedia content or modifying their profile's look and feel. Some social media networking sites in particular Facebook allows the users to add their application that enhances their profile for the employment opportunities (Facebook Detox, n.d.; Is Facebook making us lonely?, n.d.; Create your own blog, n.d.; People you may know, n.d.; My Space, n.d.; Boyd & Ellison, 2007; Kaplan, 2012; Kaplan & Haenlein, 2010; Kietzmann et al., 2011; Digital Journalism – How News is Sourced with Social Media, n.d.; Research Survey, n.d.; Laurent, 2011; Bloomers joining Social at Record Rate, Social Media and Social Networks, n.d.; Kirkpatrick, 2011; An Internet Patent Magazine, Social Media/Don't steal my avatar!, n.d.; FOMO: The Unintended Effects of Social Media Addiction, n.d.).

It has become a new trend of using these special network sites for providing a sense of community and connection to their users within large companies, universities and small businesses. These types of social networking websites have been used for marketing the business, listing the accomplishments of their users, achieving goals, strategic planning and its impact and so while the brand name SMNSs are primarily been used for social connection with the community. There are two ways of building these sites: i) we can create our own stand-alone social site and ii) we can add or link our site to a corporate site.

Social news media usually provide accurate, can be reported by anyone quickly using different media like TV camera, cell phones, iPads and other mobile devices. Maximum number of letters in a frame are about 149, may be in accurate, reporter's integrity may be compromised. Digital devices used for online news include desktop/laptop (70%), smartphone (51%), and tablet (55%) (Boyd & Ellison, 2007; Digital Journalism – How News is Sourced with Social Media, n.d.; Research Survey, n.d.).

DYNAMICITY IN SOCIAL NETWORKING ENVIRONMENT

One of the essential features of internet services is dynamicity which will make sure that the new internet services are always introduced which in turn requires the professionals to keep reviewing their skills and knowledge base and also industries to be more dynamic and aggressive. One of the examples of dynamicity could be a situation where a company may use consultant to have access to view and modify the confidential policies and procedures and at a later time may terminate the consultant and make all the policies and procedures to be unusable.

The concept of dynamicity has been extended as framework in a number of applications of trust management in particular in Peer-to-peer (P2P) mobile networks. In P2P mobile networks, users receive the same services as on traditional social sites such as forming a group, sharing information, documents, audio, and video files etc. The proposed dynamicity framework uses a light weight model to determine the trustworthy users and isolating the untrustworthy users from the group.

Based on the above discussion on dynamicity and its impact on internet market, collaborative social media and dynamicity considerations has become integral part of companies and also has been accepted by the clients. It is now well known that companies will not be able to meet the market demand if dynamicity is not adopted. Nowadays, companies are more dependent on each other for Internet marketing as they have to communicate and interact with suppliers, clients and also competitors. As such the companies have to adopt dynamicity into their business process management and structured workflow for creating a dynamic environment where market demand and requirements are constantly changing.

The following section presents known applications of SMNSs and various specific sites for different categories of applications. We have collected a lot of known applications of SMNSs from various references as shown below.

APPLICATIONS OF SOCIAL MEDIA NETWORING SITES (SMNSs)

Social Media Networking sites find applications in various groups of society like most high schools, colleges, or workplaces where the internet is filled with millions of individuals who are looking to meet other people, to gather and share first-hand information and experiences about cooking, golfing, gardening, developing friendships professional alliances, finding employment, business-to-business marketing and even groups sharing information about baking cookies etc. The topics and interests are as varied and rich as the story of our universe.

Twentieth century saw a big shift towards television journalism that influenced collective memory and disclosure about national development, public images, and national trauma. There seems to be a decline in journalistic influence on the citizens due to growing acceptance of social networking like Facebook, YouTube and Twitter that are providing an alternative source of news sources for users. Many Americans learn the significance of historical events and political issues through news media, as they are presented on popular news stations. These social networking sites are gradually undermining the traditional voices of news media. American citizens, in general prefer contest media coverage of various social and political events as they see fit, inserting their voices into the narratives about America's past and present, and shaping their own collective memories.

More and more news, stories appearing on social networking are providing needed pressure on the media to consider those for general discussions at national level. The mainstream news media journalists are accepting the importance of social networking that they are now monitoring these sites to inform their reports on news, stories at national level. It is argued that the life of social networking may be short, but they have already proved their effectiveness in helping the American citizens remember historic events and is shaping the value and meanings inscribed in those news, stories and events (Social Media, n.d.; Social Networking Service, n.d.; Pajala, 2010; Myers et al., 2011).

The early 2012 is known as mobile era where people are connected to the web irrespective of their locations and arrivals. A new survey of more than 3,000 U.S. adults conducted in January 2012 as reported finds that people are taking advantage of having access to news in their pockets, on their laps and at their desks: mobile devices appear to be adding to the news experience. Eight in ten who get news on smartphones or tablets, for instance, get news on conventional computers as well.

Richard Edelman in his Trust 2008 survey summarized the following findings (Harris, 2008). Business has opportunity to take on dual mandate of making money while addressing major societal issues: Consider heritage, Communicate peer-to-peer, Align corporate reputation with consumer brands, Media is more important today than ever, corporate communications must incorporate social media, engage the info-entail generation to build a beachhead. In conclusion, as we seem to be heading toward recession, the goal for business should be to maintain their license to operate. This depends on banking trust capital by running a good business, taking on large societal issues in the context of profit making opportunities and presenting the business case in a transparent and convincing manner.

We are living in digital information civilization where nearly half of the population in US is using mobile devices (Laptops, Notebooks, iPods, iPads, Cell phones, Tablets, etc.) for getting the news and nearly half of this population accesses the mobile devices at least four times per week. As such the online revenue in 2012 has surpassed printed newspaper revenue. According to a number of surveys, the social media provides nearly 29% online news source (Facebook->60%, Twitter->20%, YouTube->13%, Google->11% and others 43%), TV provides approximately 60%, Newspaper provides nearly 29%, Radio provides 19%, Printed sources provide nearly 6% while Other sources provide about 11% (Boyd & Ellison, 2007; Investor Relations, n.d.; Create Your Own Blog, n.d.; People You May Know, n.d.; My Space, n.d.; Pajala, 2010; Myers et al., 2011).

- **Social media measurement:** Attensity, Statist, Sysomos, Vocus, Social Flow, Simplify360,
- **Location-based social networks:** Facebook places, Foursquare, Geoloqi, Google Latitude, Go Walla, The Hotlist, Yelp, Inc.,
- **Events:** Eventful, The Hotlist, Meetup.com, Upcoming, Yelp, Inc.,
- **Online Advocacy and Fundraising:** Causes, Jumo, Kick starter, IndieGoGo,
- **Social networking:** ASmallWorld, Bebo, Chatter, Cyworld, Diaspora, Facebook, Google+, Hi5, Hyves, IRC, LinkedIn, Mixi, MySpace, Netlog, Ning, Orkut, Plaxo, Tagged, Tuenti, XING, Yammer, Side Talk, Antsfriend,Bongal, Frucle,
- **Collaboration:** Central Desktop,
- **Content Management Systems:** E107 (CMS), Drupal, Joomla, Plone, Word Press,
- **Diagramming and Visual Collaboration:** Creately,
- **Document Managing and Editing Tools:** Docs.com, Dropbox.com, Google Docs, Syncplicity,
- **Social Media Gaming:** Empire Avenue,
- **Research/Academic Collaboration:** Mendeley, Research Gate, Zotero,
- **Game sharing:** Armor Games, Kongregate, Miniclip, New grounds,
- **Media and entertainment platforms:** Cisco Eos, MySpace, YouTube,
- **Live casting:** blip.tv, Justin.tv, Live stream, oovoo, Open CU, Skype, Stickam, Upstream, YouTube,
- **Music and audio sharing:** Band camp, ccMixter, Groove Shark, The Hype Machine, imeem, Last.fm, MySpace Music, Pandora Radio, ReverbNation.com, ShareTheMusic, Sound click, Sound Cloud, Spotify, Turntable.fm, 8tracks.com,
- **Photography and art sharing:** deviant Art, Flickr, Photo bucket, Picasa, Smug Mug, Zooomr, Web shots, Pinterest,
- **Presentation sharing:** Prezi, scribd, Slide Share,
- **Video sharing:** Daily motion, Metacafe, Nico Nico Douga, Open film, seven load, Viddler, Vimeo, YouTube,
- **Business reviews:** Customer Lobby, Yelp, Inc.,

- **Community Q&A:** ask.com, Askville, EHow, Quora, Stack Exchange, WikiAnswers, Yahoo! Answers,
- **Product reviews:** epinions.com, MouthShut.com,
- **On-line social games:** friends, draw something, Cow Clicker, Jet set, City Ville, Zynga Slots, Parking Frenzy, Weed farmer, The game of the life, Kingdome of Camelot, and others (Ralf & Markus, 2011).

WHO ARE USING SOCIAL MEDIA NETWORKING SITESS (SMNSs)?

A recent survey by Credit Sesame indicates that that 35% of Americans check-in and tweet about their whereabouts and 15% of Americans regularly use social networking websites to tell their friends when they are not home. A recent report from Legal and General Group says that nearly 40% of Facebook users post details of their vacation plans on the website (Venture Beat, n.d.; Time spent on Facebook 700 Percent, but MySpace.com still tops for video according Nielson MySpace connecting and engaging with digital consumers, n.d.; Social Media Revolution Video, n.d.)

Studies show that a large number of robbers/burglars use social networking websites to identify potential properties for burglary. A survey conducted among ex-burglars shows that 78% of ex-robbers/burglars used Facebook, Twitter, and Foursquare to target potential properties and 74% of them used Google Street View to look for potential properties and know more about the location.

Studies have further revealed that a planned, calculated robbery/burglary takes only two minutes on the average for a robber/burglar to break into a home and only about ten minutes to steal everything. Social media networking websites have been used to catch the bad guys.

In February 2007, police nabbed a University of Connecticut student and charged him for hit-and-run by following leads via Facebook. In October 2008, police charged an Alberta based man with first-degree murder charges by monitoring his Facebook activity, which turned out to be an important piece of evidence. Some burglars, bullies, rapists, and miscreants have been caught by the police with the help of social media outlets. As a result, law enforcement agencies use social networking websites as a weapon to catch criminals. The Salt Lake City Police Department, for example, has set up an online community policing program to stay in touch with people and solve crimes (Social Networking Service, n.d.).

According to statistics from Wikipedia.com (Social Media, n.d.) on May 1, 2012, the registered users of SMNS are as follows: Facebook has over 9 million; Google+ has over 170,000,000; Twitter has over 130,000,000 and MySpace has 100,000,000. This does not include some the smaller specific SMNSs. These smaller social networking websites offer a more personalized experience and exposure by focusing on the personal interests of its members rather than trying to build a brand. They are known as specialty networking sites or "niche" social networking sites, and allow the users to move from network to network based on their specific choice of connection and community. The following section describes in details various functionalities and design issues that have been addressed and implemented in various networking sites.

SOCIAL MEDIA ASSOCIATED WITH NETWORKING

Social media is defined as a group of internet-based applications that allow the creation and exchange of user-generated messages, content, profiles or any other private, public or semi-public information. These are used to convert communication into interactive communication among individuals, friends, groups, communities and organizations and these are based on web-based and mobile based technologies.

Different forms of social media have been defined to provide services to different users such as social media magazines, Internet forums, weblogs, social blogs, micro-blogging, wikis, podcasts, photographs or pictures, video, rating and social bookmarking and many others. Using integrated technologies of social media and self-presentations, Kaplan and Haenlein (2010) identified different types of social media for its classification as: Collaborative projects (e.g., Wikipedia), Blogs and micro-blogs (e.g., Twitter), Content communities (e.g., YouTube), Social networking sites (e.g., Facebook), Virtual game worlds (e.g., World of Warcraft), and Virtual social worlds (e.g. Second Life).

A Content Management System (CMS) is a software tool that allows the designers to publish, edit and modifying the content of the document on a web site. It further helps to maintain the document as well. The tool supports both manual and automated procedures. There are three types of CMS in the literature as: Enterprise, Web and Component (Social Media, n.d.; Social Networking Service, n.d.; Boyd & Ellison, 2007; Kaplan, 2012; Kietzmann, Hermkens, McCarthy, & Silvestre, 2011; Digital Journalism – How News is Sourced with Social Media, n.d.; Research Survey, n.d.; Social Media Revolution Video, 2011).

An Enterprise Content Management System (ECMS) allows the designers to organize documents, contacts and records that are related to the processes of the organizations, agencies and others. It supports the framework of enterprise's information content, file formats, management of locations, streamlines accesses, and optimal security and integrity. A Web Content Management System (WCMS) is stand-alone application to create, manage, store and deploy content on Web pages. It supports display and interaction with users for different types of web contents including text, embedded graphics, photos, video, audio, and application code etc. and for displaying that displays content or interacts with the user. A Component Content Management System (CCMS) allows the designers to create documents (maps, images, etc.) from component parts. These components can be reused in other documents or across multiple documents.

Following is a short list of some of the popular Content Management systems. Drupal (free open-source content management system and content management framework written in PHP under GNU General public License), Expression Engine(a content management system and does not require any knowledge of PHP and provides extensive online documentation), Code Igniter (an open source web application framework for building dynamic web site with PHP), Joomla (a free open source content management framework for publishing contents on www, intranets and model-view-controller and written in PHP), Plone (a free open source content management system for blogs, internet sites, web shops and internal websites under GNU General Public License), Word Press (a free and open source blogging tool, content management system based on PHP and MySQL), CodeIgnitor (an open source web application framework for building dynamic web sites with PHP). The following micro blogging are available: Daily Life, Foursquare, Google Buzz, Identi.ca, Jaiku, Nasza-Klass.pl, Plurk, Posterous, Qaiku, Tumblr, Twitter, and Go. For more details about these Content management Systems, please visit their respective websites.

FUNCTIONALITY AND DESIGN ISSUES OF SMNSs

The visibility and availability of social media networking sites are all dependent on their design and implementation policies and usually expect the users to have accounts with them and follow the policy under Terms of Use agreement (TOU). Some sites are being accessed by search engines (Friendster.net, Tribe.net) and as such are available to anyone and not expect the users should have account with them. On other hand, social media networking site like LinkedIn has a control over the framework and may not be available to the users who do not have account with it (Boyd & Ellison, 2007; Kaplan & Haenlein, 2010; Kitzmann et al., 2011; Harris, 2008; Galdwell, 2011; Is Facebook making us lonely?, 2012; Laurent, 2011).

The users have a choice of making their profiles to be public or restricted to their friends only (e.g. MySpace). For similar service, the users can have a choice of using the same network, share the profiles or deny the access of profiles (e.g. Facebook). In general, all the social media networking sites providing the similar service support different categories of relationships like: family, friend, fan, follower and so on which users may choose for individuals with who they want to have social networking connections.

All SMNSs in general include links to user's friends list are included that allow the friends to either accept the invitations or ignore it. Depending on the sites, some sites include the friends list that contains links to each of those friends in the list so that the friends can easily be connected to them when accessing their friends. These sites also allow the users to leave their messages or comments (private: similar to webmail or public) on their friend's profiles. Although all sites support private and, public and semi-public messaging are very popular means of communication, but these features may not be universally available on all sites. Beyond profiles, friends, comments, and private messaging, SMNSs offer different features during the design, maintenance and use for their profiles and messaging.

In general, these sites contain a huge amount of data to be generated, collected, communicated and analyzed over the Cyberspace environment (connected to Internet) for sharing among the friends, users, professionals and all of us. Although many of these social media and networking sites do offer a way to hide personalized information but will not make this feature available to the members to turn it off in the very first place. Also, user's postings may be used by the advertisers who may not only republish or repackage the postings but also may broadcast member's friends who are associated in their social network sites.

The advertisement groups generate revenue of over two billion dollars using these sites globally. It is estimated that Facebook alone has over .7 billion registered members and other sites are also attracting more members (Social Media, n.d.; Social Networking Service, n.d.). The design of social media services includes various functional modules such as identification, interactive conversations, information sharing, online presence, mutual relationships, personal reputation, and mutual groups. These functional blocks help the users understand the systematic method for engagement and communication requirements needs of the social media and networking.

DESIGN AND IMPLEMENTATION OF SMNS

The design of any SMNS depends on its features and type of service and as such may not use all these functional modules. For example, LinkedIn uses identification, personal reputation and mutual relationships. The YouTube use information sharing, interactive conversations, mutual groups and personal reputation. Many companies build their own social containers that attempt to link the seven functional building blocks around their brands. These are private communities that engage people around a more narrow theme, as in around a particular brand, vocation or hobby, than social media containers such as Google+ or Facebook (Harris, 2008; Top 100 Social Media Colleges-Student Advisor, n.d.; Google, n.d.).

The design of social media services includes various functional modules such as identification, interactive conversations, information sharing, online presence, mutual relationships, personal reputation, and mutual groups. These functional blocks help the users understand the systematic method for engagement and communication requirements needs of the social media and networking. The design of any SMNS depends on its features and type of service and as such may not use all these functional modules. For example,

LinkedIn uses identification, personal reputation and mutual relationships. The YouTube use information sharing, interactive conversations, mutual groups and personal reputation.

We need to bear in mind a number of issues like development process and functionality, customized signup for the users, customized methods for photos, videos, e-mail messages, calendars, and appropriate space for describing themselves, expected accomplishments from our site, hosting of our application, legal ownership and intellectual property rights, maintenance (local vs. hired contractor), etc. Further, the maintenance of site is on-going process and need to be updated regularly. In addition to these issues, we need to install security measures to prevent any malicious attacks, unsolicited messages/comments. In summary, a technically knowledgeable administrator will be needed who will implement, manage the running of lots of communication tools, take appropriate actions for users who abuse their memberships, making site a user-friendly and intelligent for exchange of information.

These sites can be searched using standard internet search from hundreds of networking communities to join and depends on your comfort and interest. You may get the following results to choose from: MySpace, Friend Wise, Friend Finder, Yahoo!, 360, Facebook, Orkut, Classmates and many others.

EVOLUTION OF SOCIAL MEDIA NETWORKING SITE (SMNSS)

In this section, we will discuss how the concept of social networking was introduced into existing web sites to make it a friendly and social platform for communication, sharing of personal information, pictures, videos etc. over the internet (Social Media, n.d.; Social Networking Service, n.d.; Boyd & Ellison, 2007; Digital Journalism – How News is Sourced with Social Media, n.d.; Andesron & Technica, 2011; Galdwell, 2011; Kirkpatrick, 2011; An Internet Patent Magazine, Social Media/ Don't Steal My Avatar!, n.d.; The Atlantic, 2012; My Space, n.d.; Social Media Revolution Video, 2011; Laurent, 2011). Figure 1 reproduced from (1) shows how each of web sites containing features of social networking and also how new SMNSs have been launched since 1997.

First Generation of SMNSs

During this generation of network communication, many sites with limited version of profiling capabilities and other features were forced to adopt the SMNS features in one way or the other to make them more acceptable and adoptable sites for personal use of people with view to create means for network connections. Although some community and "dating" sites like AIM, ICQ with profiling capabilities and other features were existing, but based on the definition of Social media and networking site, these sites did not have all the features of creation of profiling, friends lists and were not available to friends. The first full fledge SMNS was introduced in 1998 by SixDegrees.com that allowed combined these features and became very popular among the users to create their personal profiles, list the list of their Friends and, surf the Friends lists.

Another sites Classmates.com allowed people to affiliate with their high school or college and surf the network for others who were also affiliated, but users could not create profiles or list Friends until years later. This is due to the fact that many users did not find any real use of these sites after the friends accept the request and some users felt uncomfortable in making contacts with strangers on-line over internet.

A number of community tools for the design of sites supporting various combinations of profiles and public articulation like Friends, Asian Avenue, Black Planet, MiGente were introduced during 1997-2001 and invariably all these tools support creation of personal profiles, professional and other categories of profiling like dating and

Figure 1. Timeline of the launch dates of many major SNSs and dates when community sites re-launched with SNS features

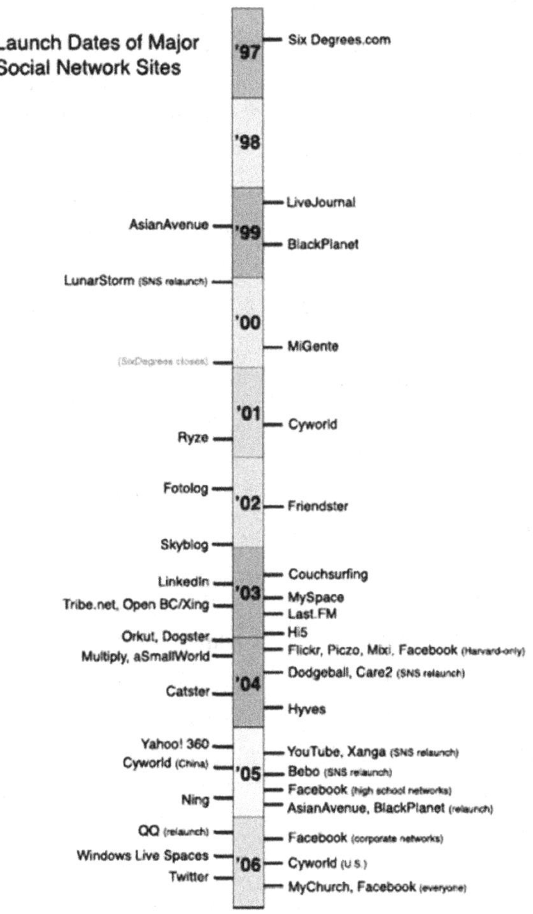

many other related shareable information without seeking any approval for the network connections. A one-directional connection per user page named as Live Journal site was introduced in 1999. This site allowed the users to make friends after instant messaging, and allowed the user to maintain their privacy settings. During the same time, Korean virtual site Cyworld was introduced with added SMNS features and options. A Swedish web community web site Lunar Storm with added SMNS features was introduced in 2000 that contained Friends lists, Guestbook, and diary pages.

Second Generation of SMNSs

The success of SMNSs for personal use of profiling and communication by people provided developers to launch these sites for various scientific and business applications. As a result, Ryze founded a web site Ryze.com: a business-oriented SMNS in 2001 to help people leverage their business networks. Initially, he introduced the site to his friends who were mainly members of the San Francisco business and technology community, including the entrepreneurs and investors behind many future SMNSs. During the same time other sites like Tribe.net, LinkedIn, MySpace, Facebook and Friendster were introduced as social complement to Ryze. The same professionals accepted by these sites and started using them for their future and career enhancements without any competition. All these SNSs have given a new shape and flavor to the business, cultural, and created a new dimension for research opportunities. By the end of 2001, due to the popularity and acceptance of Tribe.net, LinkedIn, Facebook, Friendster sites it became quite clear that majority of the professionals liked it over Ryze site.

Tribe.net created a passionate niche user base while LinkedIn came us as a top business service. Friendster site was in competition with another site Match.com an on-line dating site. The design of Friendster mainly was aimed to provide matching among the romantic partners who are friends of friends while other dating sites were aimed to providing the platform for romantic partners who are strangers with similar interests. It was argued that friends of friends would provide a better and reliable platform for romantic partnerships than meeting strangers. Friendster became very popular amongst bloggers, people attending Burning Man arts festival and gay men and attracted press coverage in 2003. The exponential growth of Friendster on one side attracted many people to use their emails with Friendster, but on other side due to in insufficient technical support and equipment, and collapse in social and culture balance forced the developers of Friendster to restrict its use to only passionate users.

Third Generation of SMNSs

In addition to messaging features, majority of the included features like photo-sharing or video-sharing options, built-in blogging, instant messaging capability, etc. These sites after 2005 were designed, implemented and launched at different times with different applications and basic features. We will mention few of those social networking sites here:

QQ site offers a Chinese instant messaging service, Lunar Storm provides general messaging service to community, Cyworld is a Korean discussion forum tool, and Skyrock (formerly Skyblog) is a French blogging service before adding social networking service. In addition to these sites, other sites like Asian Avenue, MiGente and Black Planet were introduced as ethnic sites with limited Friends functionality and now have been re-launched during 2005-2006 as Social networking sites features and structure. A directory of school affiliated as Classmates.com was launched in 1995 and now supports articulated lists of Friends with SNS features.

With the advent of mobile devices, many of the sites now have developed social media networking sites that are specific to these devices e. g. Dodge ball. Few other web-based social media networking sites such as Facebook, MySpace, Cyworld and others support limited interaction with some mobile devices. Some sites are specific to geographical regions and linguistic groups such as Orkut (introduced in US with English-only interface). Kopyoff was launched in 2004 for Portuguess-speaking Brazilians as a user group. Some sites have been introduced based on ethnicity, religion, sexual orientation, political affiliation, and many other identity-specific categories. It has extended its services to pets as well e.g. Dogster (SNS for dogs), Catster (SNS for cats) and others and is usually managed by their owners.

Current Status OF SMNSs

Different available social media networking websites including Facebook, Twitter, Bebo, MySpace and others are based on a number of technologies such as blogs, picture-sharing, vlogs, wall-postings, email, instant messaging, music-sharing, crowdsourcing, voice over IP and many others. There are now over 250 published applications and 10 patent applications in the area of social media (An Internet Patent Magazine, Social Media/Don't Steal My Avatar!, n.d.; United State Patent and Trademark Office, n.d.).

Recently a number of attempts have been made by scholars to study and measure the impact of social media on different types of uses. A new study from International Center for Media and Public Agenda (ICMPA) at University of Maryland (Students Addicted to Social Media – New UM Study, n.d.) shows that most of the students are not just unwilling but functionally unable to be without their media links to the world (Harris, 2008; Top 100 Social Media Colleges- Student Advisor, n.d.). Similar study by other universities clear conclude that social media services are becoming addictive among the students and are they are being trapped by Fear Of Missing Out (FOMO) (FOMO: The unintended effects of social media addiction, n.d.). Further, it has been observed that Facebook is now the primary method for communication by college students in the U.S. Several colleges have even introduced classes on best social media practices, preparing students for potential careers as digital strategists (Is Facebook making us lonely?, 2012; Berners, 2011; Social Media, n.d.; Social Networking Service, n.d.; Investor Relations, n.d.; Facebook Detox, n.d.; Is Facebook making us lonely?, 2012; Create your own blog, n.d.; People you may know, n.d.; My Space, n.d.).

- Social networking now accounts for 22% of all time spent online in the US.
- A total of 234 million people age 13 and older in the U.S. used mobile devices in December 2009.
- Twitter processed more than one billion tweets in December 2009 and averages almost 40 million tweets per day.
- Over 25% of U.S. internet page views occurred at one of the top social networking sites in December 2009, up from 13.8% a year before.
- Australia has some of the highest social media usage in the world. In usage of Facebook, Australia ranks highest, with over 9 million users spending almost 9 hours per month on the site.
- The number of social media users age 65 and older grew 100 percent throughout 2010, so that one in four people in that age group are now part of a social networking site.
- As of June 2011[update] Facebook has 750 Million users.
- Facebook tops Google for weekly traffic in the U.S.
- Social Media has overtaken pornography as the No. 1 activity on the web.
- IPhone applications hit 1 billion in 9 months, and Facebook added 100 million users in less than 9 months.
- If Facebook were a country it would be the world's 3rd largest in terms of population, that's above the US.
- U.S. Department of Education study revealed that online students out performed those receiving face-to-face instruction.
- YouTube is the 2nd largest search engine in the world.
- In four minutes and 26 seconds 100+ hours of video will be uploaded to YouTube.
- 1 out of 8 couples married in the U.S. last year met via social media.
- 1 in 6 higher education students are enrolled in online curriculum.

The above sections presented basic definitions of SNMS, its applications, categories of application, some useful sites with appropriate applications, functionalities and design issues and the current status of these sites. With the advent of data mining methodologies to integrated social networking and big data to address and solve real world problems, a new integrated approach of designing and using networking sites has been adopted and successfully been implemented in some applications. In spite of these features, the design of social networking still possesses the following problems and challenges as discussed below.

PROBLEMS AND CHALLENGES ASSOCIATED WITH SOCIAL MEDIA AND NETWORKING

One of the main problems and challenges with social media and networking is management and handling of the amount of data usually measured in the range of petabytes and as it contains high signal to noise ratio. Further, the identification of their users among millions of users in any given online over internet is another big challenge that these SMNSs are facing. It has been observed that very little percentage of useful and relevant information is contained in the social media data stream. A number of techniques have been used by these companies identifying their users and currently are using a matching technology based on Artificial Intelligence to identify their users and offers faster and more comprehensive search.

Another problem that most of the companies are facing is the format of data that needs to be transformed from non-useful data to into useful data. Master Data management (MDM) technology provides the mapping between these two types of data. MDM is the process of managing business-critical data, also known as master data (about customers, products, employees, suppliers, etc.) on an ongoing basis, creating and maintaining it as the system of record for the enterprise. MDM is implemented in order to ensure that the master data is validated as correct, consistent, and complete. MDM has been used for more than a decade by companies that want to integrate disparate databases for a 360 degree view of their customers (or product portfolios, for that matter). It is equally effective in integrating social media data into existing CRM systems, and filtering that data for relevance. It provides behavioral data that allows them to more appropriately target segments for better marketing results, personal preferences, and interests to move closer to a true one-to-one relationship with their customers

Another problem associated is with Social media information that is generated through social media networking interactions when users access the social networking sites. There has always been a huge debate on the ownership of the content on social media platforms since it is generated by the users and hosted by the company. Critics contend that the companies are making a huge amount of money by using the content that does not belong to them. Hence the challenge for ownership is lesser with the communicated content, but with the personal data disclosed by the subscribed writers and readers and the correlation to chosen types of content. The security danger beyond is the parasitic conveying, leaking of agglomerated data to third parties with certain economic interest.

The future and current trend in social networking and data mining has seen various attempts to optimize the search engines and social media separately depending on the applications, but now these two attempts have been integrated and being used in new applications as it not only lowers the investment but also provides a better management of resources and allocation of budget.

The effect of the integrated approach of optimization of search engines and social media has shown the effect on the businesses to maintain effective and ethical social work for marketing their products via authentic links. The search engines are promoting the social media incoming links by encouraging their clients to have their presence on social media sites. This approach has been implemented in Google+ in 2011 where users can search and access his social site. Sometimes in 2011, a third party survey and analytics company reported that posting a video on YouTube is very helpful in getting high ranking on search engine. Thus, Internet marketing is helping many small companies due to budget limitations are using social site to promote their brand as opposed to using radio, TV channels, print outlets etc. (Boyd & Ellison, 2007; Digital Journalism – How News is Sourced with Social Media, n.d.; Laurent, 2011; Social Media and Social Networks, n.d.; Andesron & Technical, 2011; Harris, 2008; Pajala, 2010; Myers et al., 2011).

The following section describes one of the most popular publishing services Blog that allows the users to use SNMSs in a better way as it provides interface for posting, image handling and many other features needed in networking sites.

PRIVACY ISSUES AND CONCERNS WITH SOCIAL MEDIA NETWORKING SITES

There are many factors that affect the privacy on social networking sites for example, users may place a lot of personal information, sites may not have adequate steps to protect user privacy, and personal information maintained by third parties on social networks can be used for a variety of purposes. Since the social networks sites have become popular for social interaction but due to their easy access, many posted information and personal information can be reviewed by those users (Social Networking Service, n.d.; Berners, 2011; George, 2006; Kornblum & Marklein, 2006; Auer, 2011; Jones, 2011).

The information managed by medical and scientific researchers is subjected for strict scrutiny by various boards and as such different rules have to be defined and implemented for its access and review. Even if the information may be available, it forms invasion of piracy if somebody republishes the accessed information.

There has been a big privacy issue and concern associated with social media networking services among the users as a large amount of personal information is available with big corporations or government agencies who in turn may misuse the personal information. In particular there is a big danger amongst the users from sexual predators. Also, users of these services need to be aware of data theft or viruses. However, large social media networking services, such as MySpace and Netlog, often work with law enforcement to try to prevent such incidents. Furthermore, there is an issue over the control of data—information that was altered or removed by the user may in fact be retained and/or passed to third parties.

Following plans by the UK government to monitor traffic on social networks schemes similar to e-mail jamming have been proposed for networks such as Twitter and Facebook. These would involve "friending" and "following" large numbers of random people to thwart attempts at network analysis.

BLOG PUBLISHING SERVICES (BLOGGER)

A blog publishing service is also known as Blogger was launched in 1999 and it allows private or multi-user blogs with time-stamped entries. It was launched by created by Pyra Labs, which was bought by Google in 2003 under undisclosed terms. Usually, the blogs are hosted by Google at a subdomain of blogspot.com. During 2004, Blogger went through a major redesign, addition of features such as web standards-compliant templates, individual archive pages for posts, comments, and posting by email in its services. In 2004, Google purchased Picasa; it integrated Picasa and its photo sharing utility Hello into Blogger, allowing users to post photos to their blogs, people you may know.

In 2006, Blogger migrated all of its users to Google servers and added some new features, including interface language in French, Italian, German and Spanish. In 2007, Blogger was completely operated and managed by Google servers. Blogger allowed users to publish blogs on other hosts, via FTP. All such blogs had (or still have) to be moved to Google's own servers, with domains other than blogspot.com allowed via custom URLs. During 2008, Blogger introduced a number of features in its services including label organization, a drag-and-drop template editing interface, reading permissions (to create private blogs) and new Web feed options and still being managed by Google servers. These blogs are updated dynamically, as opposed to rewriting HTML files.

In September 2009, Google introduced other new features like a new interface for post editing, improved image handling, Raw HTML Conversion, and other Google Docs-based implementations. In 2010, Blogger introduced new templates and redesigned its website. The New Design templates known as Dynamic views are introduced such that users can change between different dynamic views. But the other templates can be chosen by blogger.

Blogging services with complete SMNS features became popular in USA. Various blogging tools with SMNS features, such as Xanga, Live Journal, Open Diary, Type Pad, World Press, and Vox, attracted broad audiences. Skyrock reigns in France, and Windows Live Spaces dominates numerous markets worldwide, including in Mexico, Italy, and Spain. Although SMNSs like QQ, Orkut, and Live Spaces are just as large as, if not larger than MySpace, they receive little coverage in U.S. and English-speaking media, making it difficult to track their trajectories.

Following is a list of language that are supported by Blogger: Arabic, Bengali, Indonesia, Bulgarian, Catalan, Chinese (Simplified), Chinese (Traditional), Croatian, Czech, Danish, Dutch, English, Filipino, Finnish, French, German, Greek, Gujarati, Hebrew, Hindi, Hungarian, Indonesian, Italian, Japanese, Kannada, Korean, Latvian, Lithuanian, Malay, Malayalam, Marathi, Norwegian, Oriya, Persian, Polish, Portuguese (Brazil), Portuguese (Portugal), Romanian, Russian, Serbian, Slovak, Slovenian, Spanish, Swedish, Tamil, Telugu, Thai, Turkish, Ukrainian, Vietnamese (Social Media, n.d.; Social Networking Service, n.d.; Create your own blog, n.d.; People you may know, n.d.; Time spent on Facebook 700 Percent, but MySpace.com still tops for video according to Nielson MySpace connecting and engaging with digital consumers, n.d.).

Cyber Harassment

As mentioned above, social media networking sites pose a privacy concerns and issues regarding the sharing of our information that can be distributed worldwide. Once we publish any information (text, pictures, profiles, video or any other something) online, it is in the public domain. It can be redistributed again and again without our permission for years to come. The use of smart phone over internet has caused a considerable harassment to the users worldwide over the internet and has become uncontrollablen adult can probably handle the embarrassment better than a teenager.

Most of the documented suicides caused by Cyberbullying or internet harassment and cybertalking involve teenagers. This is one of the social issues that we all have to deal with unless we want to avoid the internet entirely. Advertising and marketing firms have been taking advantage of this phenomenon for years now and term this as "Viral marketing" (National State Conference of Legislatures, n.d.; US Department of Justice, Information on Cyberstalking, n.d.).

Scientists consider internet privacy (or the lack of it) one of today's serious social issues. Sociologists believe there is a need for legislation concerning social networking privacy and all of the things that we say and do online. The laws would help, but public awareness is just as important. The following paragraphs will describes some of these internet harassment followed by the steps we as users must take to protect our privacy and integrity over the internet while taking the fullest advantages of SMNSs.

Cyberbullying

Another privacy concern scientists are facing is harassment over the internet known as Cyberbullying similar to the harassment people are receiving over internet using smart phones. Unlike bullying in the school yard, a Cyberbully may get friend's online name and send any type of information about friend. For the sake of fun or any other intentional act, Cyberbullies often post damaging information (email messages, videos, images and other forms) on blogs or websites and even secretly record conversations (via cell phone) and then playing back the recording to the friend being talked about. There are bullying stories all over the internet that many users ended up committing suicide as it offers 24 hours a day service.

According to the US National Crime Prevention Council (National State Conference of Legislatures, n.d.), it is when the internet, cell phones or other devices are used in cruelty to others by sending or posting text or images intended solely to hurt or embarrass another person.

Many studies and surveys over years found that approximately 30 percent of students in grades six through eight reported they recently had been cyber bullied or had cyber bullied another person at least once. It further also showed that those girls are about twice as likely as boys to be victims and perpetrators of cyber bullying. Cyber bullying can be implemented using different methods such as: instant messaging, chat rooms, e-mails and messages posted on websites and others.

Cyber Stalking

Cyber stalking is another form of internet harassment where the cyber talker vandalizes a search engine or encyclopedia, to threaten a victim's earnings, employment, reputation, or safety. A repeated pattern of such actions against a target defines cyber stalking. When a person's physical safety is threatened, cyber bullying is illegal. There are tools available to help those who have experienced both cyber bullying and cyber stalking.

The National State Conference of Legislatures lists information about cyberstalking laws for 47 states can be found (National State Conference of Legislatures, n.d.). Two reports from the U.S. Department of Justice provide detailed information on cyber stalking: Stalking and Domestic Violence: Report to Congress and, Cyber stalking: A New Challenge for Law Enforcement and Industry." (US Department of Justice, n.d.).

Polls conducted in 2010 report that most people are more concerned about internet safety now than they were 3 or 4 years ago. Major social networking sites like Facebook have taken steps to help protect user safety. Bullies can be blocked. Threatening messages can be reported. The user's account can be disabled by Facebook (other sites are not monitored that well.) Bullies do not usually participate in public chats, but sometimes they will trick people into visiting private chat rooms. It only takes a moment to upset someone with disgusting photos or violent images.

Published information from the National Crime Prevention Council indicates that half of all American teens are bullied online. Because the disturbing trend seems to be on the rise, celebrities, businesses, parents, teachers and kids have joined together to help teach everyone about internet safety practices. Posting our photos online and revealing too much personal information over social media networking sites may be used by stalkers, sexual predators, identity thieves, scammers, and other such unwanted elements. Some new programs help parents stop cyberbullying without forcing their kids to stay off of their computers (Bullying, n.d.).

Preventive Measures against Cyber Harassment

We should not hesitate to contact the police. The Department of Health and Human Services offers very comprehensive information on bullying at (Bullying, n.d.).

The following is a list of preventive measures that we can take to avoid any damage a bad person can do to us

- We should set the privacy settings on Social Media Networking site so that only our friends should be allowed to see our profile and content.

- We should not accept friend requests from strangers.
- We should not reveal our day-to-day schedule to anyone.
- We should not inform anybody including our friends that that we are not at home.
- We should post anything about our schedule as these sites automatically update our postings on a regular basis.
- We should not post pictures of our family members in particular the pictures of our kids and also the pictures of any expensive items from Do not post photos of your family members (especially kids) or expensive household items like car, TVs, appliances, furniture, etc. However, if we still want to show these on the site, we can request Google Maps to blur the images (as is being done on TV for a number of news clips).

In conclusion, the social media and networking can enhance our experience if we can follow the following three collaborative steps:

- **Listen and respond for help or need:** We should listen for signals from social media for help and needs of existing and potential clients. We can engage proactively by listening at the point of need; as well as reactively: listening for indicators that someone may need help.
- **Cross-reference social and internal customer data:** We can cross-reference people from the social media stream (our own or keyword searching result) to the internal record.
- **Understand context of relationship:** We should use new level of customer intelligence in context of the relationship without revealing that the individual customer is not part of our organizations.

DATA MINING OF SOCIAL MEDIA AND NETWORKING

The thinking about using and managing social media in corporate marketing departments is rapidly evolving. Initially, social media was seen as yet another broadcast opportunity for pushing messages out into the world, and for many companies that view persists. For business marketing, most of the popular social media in general are doing business through third party as PR agency. The social media has been used as a tool to disseminate marketing messages or establish relationships with current or potential customers. However, there is another use of social media which may prove to be more powerful over the long term: listening to the voice of the customer by data mining social networks (Data Mining Curriculum, 2006; Clifton, 2010).

Although there exist a number of definitions for data mining, but in general, researchers consider the data mining as an iterative process that selects, explores, and models a large amount of data to identify meaningful, logical patterns and relationships among key variables. Data mining finds its application to predict future trends and events and assess the merits of various courses of action. Over 10 of the largest social media monitoring companies and over 90% of the Fortune 500 are getting their big data using a very popular Gnip (API) launched in 2008 that is linked to a number of social media web sites for collecting big data. It is the first API aggregation that became a standard toll to build real-time web. By the end of 2009, this service was used for collecting huge volumes of data for analyzing Twitter clients. During the same time period, Gnip launched a Push-API and went through an internal restructuring of resources. In 2010, Gnip introduced new product for data collection over social media as Twitter Streaming API and became very popular among other social media such as Facebook, YouTube, Flicker, Google Buzz, Vimeo and others (Data Mining, n.d.).

WHY DATA MINING BIG DATA IN SOCIAL NETWORKING?

The big data refers to a large amount of data that needs to be collected, analyzed and interpreted. This type of data pertain to different applications which can be grouped into a number of groups such as enterprise (customer relationship management, enterprise resource planning, web transactions, purchase transaction, etc.), Machine-generated/sensor data (Call Detail Records, weblogs, manufacturing sensors, equipment logs, trading systems data, etc.), social data (customer feedback streams, micro-blogging sites like Twitter, social media platforms like Facebook), digital pictures and videos of satellite climate, cell phone GPS data, weather information, medical data, etc. It is estimated through a number of surveys, that we create about 2.5 quintillion bytes of data every day. This data comes from about mentioned groups. It is also further estimated that data volume is growing at the rate of 40% per year in the last three years and will grow at the rate of 45% per year until 2020.

The big data analytics is a process to be used on big data of large amount and a variety of types and extracts hidden patterns, any unknown correlations and any other information from it. This information may be used for a business marketing strategies, enhanced productivity, effective sales and increased revenue. The big data analytics help the companies to strategize the marketing for effective sales and revenue and still be competitive over competitors. The data captured include web server logs, internet clickstream data, social media activity reports, mobile devices, and other information captured by sensors. The big data analytics use various software tools to extract useful information from this captured data for improving the business benefits and decisions.

There has been a tremendous growth in the big data and science due to social networking and data mining. Further, both social media and data mining together are providing to create new technologies in big data and science and data analytics. Over the course of the last few years both areas have experienced a startling rate of growth and reached high levels of sophistication. Some of the material presented below has partially been derived from (Data Mining, n.d.).

Characteristics of Big Data

A big data is characterized by following four attributes:

- **Volume:** This attribute represents all the categories of data are produced in much larger quantities than non-traditional data. This includes the few approximately few terabytes of Tweets created each day; over 350 billion annual meter readings to better predict power consumption, a single jet engine can generate 10TB of data in 30 minutes. With more than 25,000 airline flights per day, the daily volume of just this single data source runs into the Petabytes. Smart meters and heavy industrial equipment like oil refineries and drilling rigs generate similar data volumes, compounding the problem.
- **Velocity:** This attribute correspondence to big data for time-sensitive processes such as catching fraud into enterprise, over 5 million trade events created each day to identify potential fraud, analysis of over 500 million daily call detail records in real-time to predict customer churn faster, etc.
- **Social media data streams:** This attribute does not represent massive data as we see in machine-generated data, but it represents a large data corresponding to influx of opinions and relationships valuable to customer relationship management. Even at 140 characters per tweet, the high velocity (or frequency) of Twitter data ensures large volumes (over 8 TB per day).

- **Variety:** This attribute represents both structured and unstructured data that include text, sensor data audio, video, log files, etc. and these formats are well described and change slowly. As new services are added, new sensors deployed, or new marketing campaigns executed, new data types are needed to capture the resultant information. Some of the example of this data type includes monitoring of live video from surveillance to target, data growth in images, video and documents to improve customer satisfaction, etc.
- **Value or Veracity:** This attribute correspondence to economic value of different types of data that varies significantly and it becomes a big challenge to find useful and good information that is hidden in large body of data and transforming and extracting useful information from this huge amount of data. Further, establishing trust in big data offers another challenge as the types and number of sources grows.

Applications of Big Data

The big data found its applications in areas like sensor networks, social networks, internet text and documents, internet search indexing, atmospheric science, biological, biochemical, Radio Frequency identifier (RFID), medical records, archives, large scale e-commerce, military surveillance, intelligent services, government agencies (President Obama announced Big Data Research and Development Initiative for six departments, the US owns six of ten most powerful super computers in the world), private sectors (Wal Mart handles over 1 million customers per hour and performs equivalent to over 2.5 petabytes of data, Facebook handles over 40 billion of photos of its users) and many other complex systems.

- In the past, the companies have been doing their business decision is based on transactional data stored in relational databases which is well structured. The advent and use of social media, emails, sensor networks, videos, images, weblogs, and many other applications, the companies are more involved in integrating social media with big data to identify the useful information. Companies like, Oracle and other companies are using this concept for the internet marketing.
- All big companies use available tools for acquiring the big data for analyzing the big volume of data generated in different formats. A suitable platform for processing this huge amount of data for further processing (batch, massive parallel or other computational activities) that requires filtering, transformation and sorting before loading into enterprise environment. There exist a number of tools for performing the above operations. The analysis tool can be used to identify much useful information from the stored data and this information can be used for a variety of business and internet marketing.
- The enterprise data can be analyzed along with big data to provide useful information regarding the strategies for enhanced productivity, revenue generation, competition with competitors, etc. Some of the applications of this approach of data analysis could be a delivery of healthcare services where any particular disease or medical problem may be handled by use of monitoring devices based on sensor data, avoidance of frequent office visits and hospital admittance, thus reducing the costs sand still monitor the health of patient.
- Another application could be in manufacturing companies where data from sensors for their products can provide the type of product and services like communications, security, navigations, etc. being provided. Further, the feedback from users like usage, failure rates and other related comments may be used to improve the develop-

ment and assembly costs, improved quality of products and services may be provided.

- The data sent to other sources like mobile devices (both communication and computation like smart phones, iPads, notebooks, etc.), GPS devices can provide very useful means for advertisement, marketing and offering of services to a large number of consumers. The availability of these services provides incentives to new consumers as well. Useful information from the feedback data from consumers can be derived including who buys the product and services, why did not they buy the product and services, reviewer's comments, cots of product and services, need for new services, and many other needed information. This useful information is then used for improving marketing and sale strategies, and also improving the supply chain effectiveness which could not have been done if we would not have social media and web log capabilities in today's e-commerce environment.
- It finds its application in retail sale for market need analysis where it can be used to keep a record of customers who prefer a particular item over another item of same category using association rules within transaction-based data or inexact rules within database. The data mining is very effective tool in the catalog marketing companies. This can identify the pattern of customers from its database that contains history of transactions for a large number of customers that can be used in a variety of applications like bioinformatics, genetics, medicine, education research, software engineering, spatial data mining, Geographic Information System (GIS) – based decision making applications, other engineering disciplines and government records particularly justice system, courts, prisons, etc. (Miller & Han, 2001; Ralf & Markus, 2011).
- Retailers usually know who buys their products. Use of social media and web log files from their ecommerce sites can help them understand who didn't buy and why they chose not to, information not available to them today. This can enable much more effective micro customer segmentation and targeted marketing campaigns, as well as improve supply chain efficiencies.
- The human resource department can make use of data mining for making a profile, characteristics of their employees and may be useful for recruitment, operational decisions, production plans, workforce levels, management etc.
- Credit card companies are already using social media to launch new products e.g. Citi Forward credit card launched in March 2009 on MySpace, in December 2009; American Express launched its new Zync card on social media sites, etc. Business industries like airlines, car companies, hotels, retailers, banks, politicians, even non-profits find it very useful to use this data for finding new customers or targeting products to existing ones. Financial services companies such as banks and lenders are also using the same data mining services for marketing purposes and to make lending decisions. In all these applications, the customer's requirements, data mining methodologies will allow the behavior and needs are used to personalize their experiences for those customers thus providing high level of service, information about the product and their experiences/feedbacks at these sites (Zernik, 2010; Miller & Han, 2001; Karl, Heather, & Paul, 2010; National Research Council, 2008; Dominique, Joel, Abdolreza, Selin, Nicholas, & Heikki, 2003; Ralf & Markus, 2011).

Problems and Challenges with Big Data Associated with Social Networking

Although some companies have used data mining of big data of their respective social network sites, still majority of the industries, organizations, government agencies are facing more challenges dealing with big data as we can access those data using different sources, but we do not seem to have tools to interpret the value from this data as it is usually in semi-structured/unstructured format and some data is in motion and extreme volume. It is really a challenge dealing with big data as we do not have enough knowledge and tools to collect, process, analyze and interpret (Data Mining Curriculum, 2006; Clifton, 2010).

As the amount of data in any application has grown in size and complexity, data analysis using direct "hands-on" and indirect automated data processing have been augmented by a number of new technologies such as neural networks, cluster, generic algorithm, intelligence, machine learning, decision tress, support vector machines, cloud computing and others. In the context of big data, the data mining can play a very crucial role as it applies these methods to determine the hidden patterns in the big data sets. It is important to note that Applied Statistics, Artificial Intelligence, Machine learning, techniques usually provide Mathematical modeling and analysis while the database management provides ways to Model, Store, Data processing, inference and index the data. The data mining actually provides a strong link between these two technologies by executing the actual learning and discovery algorithms more efficiently, allowing such methods to be applied to ever larger data sets with added considerations of complexity, visualization, in-line updating and others. It is also known as Knowledge Discovery in Databases (KDD).

The data mining process can be used to identify multiple groups in the data, which can then be used to obtain more accurate prediction results by decision support systems. Although the steps of data collection, data preparation, interpretation and reporting are not a part of part of the data mining process but belong to the KDD process as additional steps required in its implementation. Other techniques used in data mining like data dredging, data fishing, data snooping provide sampling of large data sets that are too small for reliable statistical inferences.

The data mining methodologies for big data particularly from social media have become a new trend in data science technology. In the last few years, researchers have experienced a tremendous growth and opportunities in levels of sophistication of solving real world problems dealing with huge amount of data. The social media and networking data are becoming very popular for sharing the pictures, personal information and routine schedules and the handling of this huge amount of data over Internet needs data mining practices. The data mining applications of information available on social networking sites like Facebook, Twitter, LinkedIn, My Space, YouTube, etc. become more timely and appropriate as the collected information that will remain on the network can be proceed at a later time. The Computing infrastructure dealing with consumer-oriented services, behaviors and preferences are becoming very crucial aspect of any Business technology initiatives and trends (Data Mining Curriculum, 2006; Clifton, 2010; Bouckaert, Frank, Hall, Holmes, Pfahringer, Reutemann, & Witten, 2010).

Open source tools for data mining like Weka make it possible for big data to be analyzed. Data scientists examine social behavior for social media sites like Google, Facebook, MySpace, Twitter and others. Individuals produce and consume significant amount of information from Internet-based sources each day. Social networking sites represent a growing cluster of information behaviors on Internet, shifting information flow from conventional consumption models through elementary forms of participants like Wikipedia towards an echo of participatory mass media. Social traces of online transaction including discussion, task completion and coordination are main features of social networking (Bouckaert, Frank, Hall, Holmes, Pfahringer, Reutemann, & Witten, 2010).

Association for Computing Machinery's special interest group on Knowledge Discovery and Data Mining (SIGKDD) has been conducting an annual conference and published its proceedings since 1989 and started a biannual academic journal as SIGKDD Explorations in 1999. The following is a list of conferences on data mining (Data Mining Curriculum, 2006; Data Mining, n.d.).

- **CIKM Conference:** ACM Conference on Information and Knowledge Management
- **DMIN Conference:** International Conference on Data Mining
- **DMKD Conference:** Research Issues on Data Mining and Knowledge Discovery
- **ECDM Conference:** European Conference on Data Mining
- **ECML-PKDD Conference:** European Conference on Machine Learning and Principles and Practice of Knowledge Discovery in Databases
- **EDM Conference:** International Conference on Educational Data Mining
- **ICDM Conference:** IEEE International Conference on Data Mining
- **KDD Conference:** ACM SIGKDD Conference on Knowledge Discovery and Data Mining
- **MLDM Conference:** Machine Learning and Data Mining in Pattern Recognition
- **PAKDD Conference:** The annual Pacific-Asia Conference on Knowledge Discovery and Data Mining
- **PAW Event:** Predictialytics World
- **SDM Conference:** SIAM International Conference on Data Mining (SIAM)
- **SSTD Symposium:** Symposium on Spatial and Temporal Databases
- **WSDM Conference:** ACM Conference on Web Search and Data Mining

CONCLUSION AND FUTURE WORK

It has become a new trend of using these social network sites for providing a sense of community and connection to their users within large companies, universities and small businesses. These types of social networking websites have been used for marketing the business, listing the accomplishments of their users, achieving goals, strategic planning and its impact and so while the brand name SMNSs are primarily been used for social connection with the community. There are two ways of building these sites: i) we can create our own stand-alone social site and ii) we can add or link our site to a corporate site. It has been observed through four annual surveys of data miners (Data Mining, n.d.) that people involved in data mining projects come across four main challenges in particular i) amount of data, ii) convincing and training professionals in data mining techniques, iii) access to data and availability of data for data mining. Further, due to large amount of data for any applications ranging from small event (e.g. robbery, accident, etc.) to performance of high level computation of big data (e.g. financial data, stock groups, etc.), the data mining methods may not be concerned with any ethical or social and ethical concerns, legal or any confidentiality or privacy concerns.

Based on the discussions on two integrated technologies of social networking and data mining under privacy and ethical environments, it seems that professional working in these areas need to address the following issues before implementing the projects as: the purpose for data collection for ant data mining applications, the format of data and the suitable data mining methods to use it, individual's expertise to mine the original collected data and its derivatives, security measures for accessing the data, interpretation of data analysis, updating the date without violating its integrity, transporting on different platforms and maintainability.

In Summary, it can be stated that data mining methodologies dealing with big data need to be standardized and customized for a number of future applications on use of social networks. It has already become a business strategy in major corporations, companies, industries and also educational institutions to use the personal information provided by the consumers for buying any products and services as a form or means of big data on social media. It is becoming a backbone for any business model for future and it seems clear that without big data and web logs, the existence of social media such as Facebook, Twitter, LinkedIn, Google+ and others would not be of any use for any business applications, personal interactions and instantaneous news broadcasting.

REFERENCES

An Internet Patent Magazine, Social Media/Don't Steal My Avatar! (n.d.). *Website*. Retrieved August 1, 2012, from http://ipwatchdog.com/

Anderson, N., & Technica, A. (2011, January 14). *Tweeters tyrants out of Tunisia: Global Internet at its best*. Retrieved June 23, 2012, from http://www.wired.com/

Auer, M. R. (n.d.). The policy sciences of social media. *Policy Studies Journal, 39*(4), 709-736. Retrieved May 24, 2012, from http://pa pers.ssm.com/

Auer, M. R. (n.d.). The policy sciences of social media. *Policy Studies Journal, 39*(4), 709-736.

Berners, T. (2011, May 4). *Long live the Web: A call for continued open standards and neutrality*. Retrieved May 24, 2012, from http://www.scientificamerican.com/

Bouckaert, R. R., Frank, E., Hall, M. A., Holmes, G., Pfahringer, B., Reutemann, P., & Witten, I. H. (2010). WEKA experiences with a java open-source project. *Journal of Machine Learning Research, 11*, 2533–2541.

Boyd, D. M., & Ellison, N. B. (2007). Social network sites: Definition, history, and scholarship. *Journal of Computer-Mediated Communication, 13*(1). doi:10.1111/j.1083-6101.2007.00393.x.

Bullying. (n.d.). *Website*. Retrieved May 22, 2012, from http://www.stopbullyingnow.hrsa.gov/

CBS News. (n.d.). *Bloomers joining social at record rate*. Retrieved November 15, 2010, from http://www.cbsnews.com/

Clifton, C. (2010). *Encyclopædia Britannica: Definition of data mining*. Retrieved July 2, 2012, from http://www.britannica.com/EBchecked/topic/1056150/data-mining

Connecting and engaging with digital consumers. (n.d.). *Website*. Retrieved November 15, 2011, from http://www.blog.nielsen.com/

Create your own blog. (n.d.). *Website*. Retrieved May 23, 2012, from http://www.blogger.com/

Data Mining. (n.d.). *Website*. Retrieved June 10, 2012, from http://en.wikipedia.org/wiki/Data_mining

Data Mining Curriculum. (2006, April 30). *Website*. Retrieved August 21, 2012, from http://www.sigkdd.org/curriculum.php

Digital Journalism – How News is sourced with Social Media. (n.d.). *Website*. Retrieved July 5, 2012, from http://www.roymorejon.com

Dominique, H., Joel, D., Abdolreza, E., Selin, S., Nicholas, T., & Heikki, T. (2003). A review of software packages for data mining. *The American Statistician, 57*(4), 290–309. doi:10.1198/0003130032486.

Edelman 2010 Trust Barometer Study. (2010). *Website*. Retrieved June 26, 2012, from http://www.edelman.com/trust/2010/

Facebook Detox. (n.d.). *Website*. Retrieved May 21, 2012, from http://www.facebookdetox.com

FOMO. The unintended effects of social media addiction. (n.d.). *Website*. Retrieved June 29, 2012, from http://www.nbcnetwork.com/

Galdwell, M. (2011, March). Malcolm Gladwell and Clay Shirky on social media and revolution. *Foreign Affairs*. Retrieved June 24, 2012, from http://www.foreignaffairs.com/

George, A. (2006, September 18). Living online: The end of privacy? *New Scientist, 2569*. Retrieved August 29, 2007, from http://www.newscientist.com/channel/tech/mg19125691.700-living-online-the-end-of-privacy.html

Google. (n.d.). *Website*. Retrieved May 21, 2012, from http://www.google.com

Harris, K. (2008). Using social networking sites as student engagement tools. *Diverse Issues in Higher Education*, *25*(18).

Hura, G. S., & Singhal, M. (2001). *Data and computer communications: Networking and internetworking*. CSR Press. doi:10.1201/9781420041316.

Investor Relations. (n.d.). *Website*. Retrieved June 25, 2012, from http://investor.fb.com/

Is Facebook making us lonely? (2012, May). *The Atlantic*. Retrieved July 13, 2012, from http://www.theatlantic.com/

Jones, S. (2005). Facebook: Threats to Privacy. *MIT*. Retrieved May 2012, from http://groups.csail.edu/

Kantardzic, M. (2003). *Data mining: Concepts, models, methods, and algorithms*. John Wiley & Sons.

Kaplan, A. M. (2012). If you love something, let it go mobile: Mobile marketing and mobile social media 4x4. *Business Horizons*, *55*(2), 129–139. doi:10.1016/j.bushor.2011.10.009.

Kaplan, A. M., & Michael, H. (2010). Users of the world, unite: The challenges and opportunities of social media. *Business Horizons*, *53*(1), 59–68. doi:10.1016/j.bushor.2009.09.003.

Karl, R., Heather, A., & Paul, G. (2010). *2010 Data miner survey – Overcoming data mining's top challenges*.

Kietzmann, J. H., Hermkens, K., McCarthy, I. P., & Silvestre, B. S. (2011). Social media? Get serious! Understanding the functional building blocks of social media. *Business Horizons*, *54*, 241–251. doi:10.1016/j.bushor.2011.01.005.

Kirkpatrick, D. D. (2011, February 9). Wired and shrewd, young egyptians guide revolt. *The New York Times*. Retrieved June 23, 2012, from http://www.nytimes.com/

Kornblum, J., & Marklein, M. B. (2006, March 8). What you say online could haunt you. *USA Today*. Retrieved August 29, 2007, from http://www.usatoday.com/tech/news/internetprivacy/2006-03-08-facebook-myspace_x.htm

Laurent, W. (2011). *Business intelligence, governance, and IT strategy*. Retrieved May 21, 2012, from http://williamlaurent.com/biography.htm

Laurent, W. (2011). *Strategic IT planning and business Intelligence*. Retrieved May 23, 2012, from http://williamlaurent.com/

Miller, H., & Han, J. (Eds.). (2001). *Geographic data mining and knowledge discovery*. London: Taylor & Francis. doi:10.4324/9780203468029.

My Space. (n.d.). *Website*. Retrieved May 21. 2012, from http://www.MySpace.com

Myers, O., et al. (2011). On media memory: Collective memory in a new media age. New York: Palgrave MacMillan. Retrieved from http://www.scientificamerican.com/

National Research Council. (2008). *Protecting individual privacy in the struggle against terrorists: A framework for program assessment*. Washington, DC: National Academies Press.

National State Conference of Legislatures. (n.d.). *Issues with cyberbullying and cyber stalking*. Retrieved June 23, 2012, from http://www.Ncsl.org

Pajala, M. (2010). Television as an archive of memory? *Critical Studies in Television, 2010*, 133–145.

People you may know. (n.d.). *Website*. Retrieved May 23, 2012, from http://blog.twitter.com

Ralf, M., & Markus, R. (2011, September/October). Data mining tools. *Wiley Interdisciplinary Reviews: Data Mining and Knowledge Discovery, 1*(5), 431–445. doi: 10.1002/widm.24. Retrieved October 21, 201 1, from http://onlinelibrary.wiley.com/doi/10.1002/widm.24/abstract

Research Survey. (n.d.). *Media Psychology Resource Center*. Retrieved June 24, 2012, from http://mprcenter.org/

Roberto, B., & Mauro, B. (2011, February). *Reactive business intelligence. From data to models to insight*. ISBN 978-88-905795-0-9.

Social Media. (n.d.). *Website*. Retrieved May 22, 2012, from http://en.wikipedia.org/wiki/Social_media

Social Media and Social Networks. (n.d.). *Website*. Retrieved June 17, 2012, from http://www.socialnomics.net/

Social Media Revolution Video. (2011, June 22). *Website*. Retrieved June 24, 2012, from http://www.youtube.com/

Social media-statistic in Australia Facebook, Blogger, MySpace. (n.d.). *Website*. Retrieved May 24, 2012, from http://www.socialmedianews.com.au/

Social Networking Service. (n.d.). *Website*. Retrieved May 23, 2012, from http://en.wikipedia.org/wiki/Social_networking_service

Students Addicted to Social Media – New UM Study. (n.d.). *Website*. Retrieved June, 24, 2012, from http://www.newsdesk.umd.edu/

Time spent on Facebook 700 Percent, but MySpace.com still tops for video according Nielson MySpace connecting and engaging with digital consumers. (2011, November 15). Retrieved from http://www.blog.nielsen.com/

Top 100 Social Media Colleges- Student Advisor. (n.d.). *Website*. Retrieved May 24, 2012, from http://www.studentadvisor.com/

United State Patent and Trademark Office. (n.d.). *USPTO search on published patent applications mentioning, social media*. Retrieved May 29, 2012, from http://appft.uspto.gov

US Department of Justice. (n.d.). *A report to Congress, cyber stalking: A new challenge for law enforcement and industry: Report to congress*.

Venture Beat. (n.d.). *Tech, people, money, digital*. Retrieved April 24, 2012, from http://digital.venturebeat.com/2010/02/10/54-of-us-internet-users-on-facebook-27-on-myspace/trackback/

Zernik, J. (2010). Data mining as a civic duty – Online public prisoners' registration systems. *International Journal on Social Media: Monitoring, Measurement, Mining*, 1, 84–96. Retrieved from http://www.scribd.com/doc/38328591/

Zernik, J. (2010). Data mining of online judicial records of the networked US federal courts. *International Journal on Social Media: Monitoring, Measurement, Mining*, 1, 69–83. Retrieved from http://www.scribd.com/doc/38328585/

Chapter 2
Data Preprocessing for Dynamic Social Network Analysis

Preeti Gupta
Ambedkar Institute of Advanced Communication Technologies & Research, India

Vishal Bhatnagar
Ambedkar Institute of Advanced Communication Technologies & Research, India

ABSTRACT

The social network analysis is of significant interest in various application domains due to its inherent richness. Social network analysis like any other data analysis is limited by the quality and quantity of data and for which data preprocessing plays the key role. Before the discovery of useful information or pattern from the social network data set, the original data set must be converted to a suitable format. In this chapter we present various phases of social network data preprocessing. In this context, the authors discuss various challenges in each phase. The goal of this chapter is to illustrate the importance of data preprocessing for social network analysis.

INTRODUCTION

Social network has become one of the most important communication media. Social network consists of a wide range of social media services which are used by the members for various purposes. The number of members registered with these social media services is huge and is further increasing. Social network analysis has been established as an important area of research due to its increased usage. Social network contains abundant information which is structurally complex, heterogeneous, high dimensional and incremental in nature.

Analyzing the social network data for information mining has the potential of revealing information of great value. Social network analysis provides a systematic method to identify, examine, visualize and support processes of knowledge sharing in social networks (Müller-Prothmann, 2006) such as expert finding and search ranking. Social network analysis plays an integral in

DOI: 10.4018/978-1-4666-4213-3.ch002

Copyright © 2013, IGI Global. Copying or distributing in print or electronic forms without written permission of IGI Global is prohibited.

knowledge extraction from the rich data source. Social network analysis can help in determining various queries such as how the information flows, important members or links and network dynamics. Social network analysis may also help in revealing otherwise unobservable information. Aim of social network analysis is to discover and retrieve useful and interesting patterns from a large dataset. Social network data contains different kind of data such as profile data, log data, structural data, documents, audio and video which could be broadly classified as (Gupta & Bhatnagar, 2012)

- **Profile Data:** Profile data is the data member provides to social network provider for registering itself
- **Posted Data:** The data which is explicitly posted by the members such as messages, comments and blog entries.
- **Derived Data:** The data which is derived or mined by correlating other information.

Social network data could be viewed and modeled as a graph where individuals or groups can be represented by nodes or vertices and relationship or flow between individuals represent links. The social network graph is highly dynamic, very large and sparse in nature. Social network analysis enables mapping of relationships between people, groups and other related information entities. Social network analysis thus helps in understanding and analyzing the social network structure and evolution. Social network analysis is a powerful approach to understand the subtleties of social network. Social network analysis has great utility value due to which it has been applied fields such as community detection, evolution in dynamic social networks, social influence analysis, link prediction, privacy in social networks, data mining and text mining (Aggarwal, 2011).

The major challenge in social network analysis comes in accessing that data and transforming it into something that is usable & actionable for the analysis. The data should be processed to improve the efficiency and ease of the analysis process. The data preprocessing thus plays an important role in social network analysis. In this chapter author has provided various challenges in preprocessing of social network data. These issues will also provide an insight to other researchers for further research in the area of preparation and preprocessing of social network data. This is the motivation for our chapter.

RELATED RESEARCH

There has been an immense growth in the area of social network analysis which brought about the different aspects of data analytics issues in online social networks such as Community Detection, Evolution in Dynamic Social Networks, Social Influence Analysis, Link Prediction, Visualizing Social Networks, Privacy in Social Networks, Data Mining in Social Media, Text Mining in Social Networks (Aggarwal, 2011). Ferguson and Buckingham (2012) have broadly classified social analytics into network analytics, discourse analytics, content analytics, dispositions analytics and context analytics. Social network analysis provides a systematic method to identify, examine, visualize and support processes of knowledge sharing in social networks (Müller-Prothmann, 2006).

The social network is just not the social networking sites such as Facebook or Twitter; it is much more. A social network consists of service provider, user, social media services and third parties. Kaplan and Haenlein (2010) have broadly categorized social media into six parts namely collaborative projects, blogs, content communities, social networking sites, virtual game worlds, and virtual communities. Growth of social media services have made people to use these services for sharing and exchanging the information at an incredible rate and has influenced people in almost every walk of the life. Social network data may be scattered across various sources which needs to be gathered, checked and integrated before a meaningful analysis can take place (Wang, 2010).

The growth in usage of the social media services has also made social networks a rich source of information making social network data publishing and analysis a necessity. Various researchers, academician, analyst and businessman want to take the advantage of social network data in the hope of finding new or interesting patterns. Social network data consist of shared views, values and visions. Social network data could be broadly classified as profile data, posted data and derived data (Gupta & Bhatnagar, 2012).

There are a number of proposals in the literature illustrating algorithms for social network analysis and sentiment analysis to discover, respectively, patterns of relationships between individuals and qualitative aspects in recorded statements (Santos et al., 2012); but just like anything, there are some issues in the analysis of social network analysis. Social network data is so huge and voluminous in nature that even the data from a single site such as Twitter can be difficult to manage (White et al., 2012). For handling the scalability issue the data is reduced into much smaller form which would produce same or almost same output. Various data reduction techniques have been proposed in literature such as compression (Maserrat & Pei, 2010; Hernández & Navarro, 2012). Mosely (2012) pointed out that the social network data is mostly informal in nature containing lots of misspellings and abbreviations which need to be properly handled before the analysis. Analysts may want to remove the unwanted and irrelevant information from the data before the analysis such as elimination of spam. Benevenuto et al. (2010) have presented a machine learning strategy for detection of spam from twitter data. Omitting this extraneous information would result in fast analysis. Missing attributes should also be properly taken care. For example, location unknown attributes could be searched and filled using scripts avoiding the existence of null attributes in the data (Paulo et al., 2012). Haddadi et al. (2012) pointed out that there exists great utility value in social network data but the attackers or adversaries could get or link the information from social network data and may deduce sensitive information and relationship resulting in security breach which needs to be protected before releasing the data. Another most vital factor which needs to be considered for complete and accurate analysis is to consider the dynamic and evolving nature of social network analysis (Macskassy, 2012).

For most analysts, the main aim is to remove the undesirable and unwanted content from the raw data before performing the analysis. This has also motivated us to understand the social network data preprocessing issues in the most imperative way in today's social networking era. These issues will also provide an insight to other researchers for further research in the area of social network data analytics.

RESEARCH METHODOLOGY

The author has adopted an empirical research methodology where the study was done to understand the subtleties of social network analysis and the various data preprocessing issues that needs to be addressed to achieve accurate and effective analysis. The author studied various papers related to social network analysis and its related issues and realized the importance of data preprocessing.

A qualitative research was done across various journals and conference databases to gather the relevant material in the field of social network analysis. The online databases were searched based on the descriptor, 'social network analysis,' 'social network mining and its issues,' 'social network data analytics,' and 'dynamic social network analysis,' which produced various journal and conference papers. The full text of each paper was reviewed to eliminate those that were not actually related to data preprocessing issues for social network data analysis. Each selected paper was carefully reviewed on the various parameters. The process is shown in Figure 1.

The aim of the research was to provide a complete and detailed description of the topic. The researchers have not collected any data from the tool or the service provider of the service for carrying out the particular research. Different data preprocessing challenges were identified in the analysis process of social network using the empirical research methodology. The study provides a good comprehensive base for understanding the importance and need of data preprocessing in the emergent and profound field of social network analysis.

SOCIAL NETWORK ANALYSIS

Social network proliferation has generated a vast database which is expected to grow even more in the future. Richness of social network database has caused an exponential growth in the area of social network analysis. Social network analysis helps in understanding the dynamic and multi-faceted social network. Social network analysis has become an integral part of various application domains such as marketing, health care and sociology. Social network analysis is of significant value to academicians, researchers, policy makers, advertisement agencies, application developers and government or security agencies. The major goal of social network analysis is to effectively handle voluminous social network data, extract relevant information and to perform analysis on it for deducing relevant insight. Social network analysis can expand the researchers' capability of

Figure 1. Selection criterion (adapted from Ngai et al. (2009))

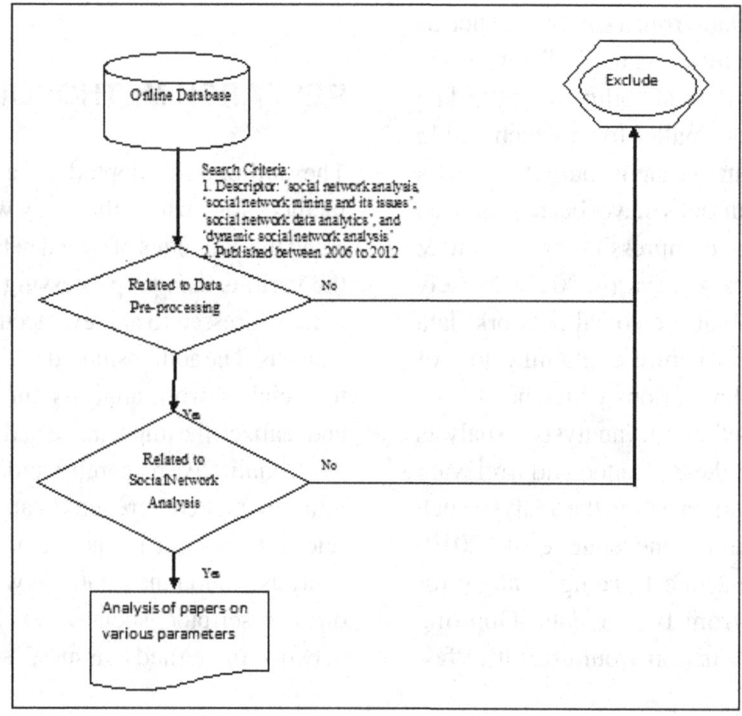

exploring the various social media services and improve and develop innovative opportunities. For example, social network analysis could help in expert finding, search ranking, brand management, target marketing. Social network analysis could also help in understanding the evolution of network and network structure. Social network analysis is a fast growing and multi-disciplinary field that can be used in the development and research in various application domains. Social network analysis could be classified into five broad categories of social learning analytic namely network analytics, discourse analytics, content analytics, dispositions analytics and context analytics (Ferguson & Buckingham, 2012).

Social network analysis depends mainly on the social network data. Social network data contain rich, interrelated, multi-typed data, forming a gigantic, interconnected, heterogeneous information network. The information power contained in the social network data makes the extraction of useful knowledge not otherwise available. However, searching, correlating, and understanding billions of messages is a big problem especially in the case of social network which is so voluminous in nature that data from a single social media site such as Twitter may be difficult to manage (White et al., 2012). The data preprocessing is carried on it to transform the data into suitable format which is easy to analyze.

In a social network, member information may update or change, new members may join, old members may leave, new links may emerge and old links may fade leading to change in social network data with time. This continuous evolving nature of social network makes it important to consider the dynamic updates for achieving better or accurate analysis. Static social network analysis considers the network observed only in one instance of time where as dynamic social network analysis considers multiple releases. In case of dynamic analysis researchers or analysts could be provided with most recent data continuously which would yield better analysis. The major aim of dynamic social network analysis is to study and analyze how a network will evolve, change or stabilize. In case of static social network analysis some of the information may be missing so dynamic analysis is essential in considering the complete scenario before giving incomplete or inaccurate result. Dynamic social network analysis can be useful to model and analyze various potential scenarios and wide range of applications such as tracking covert activities of the terrorist network.

A dynamic perspective is essential for analyzing the dynamic and evolving social network. However, moving from static to dynamic network analysis may help in modeling and simulating various problems, but on the other hand, it may increase various complexities. A major issue is the generation of initial and subsequent data set which could yield good analytical value without any privacy breach. The data set generated should have minimum unnecessary or redundant changes while emphasizing temporal trends or features for dynamic analysis and here data preprocessing plays an important role.

Social network analysis like any other analysis requires preprocessing of data as the first step. The data preprocessing includes data collection, data cleaning, data reduction and data conversion. In social network analysis most of the time and work is spent on obtaining and preparing the data which is discussed in more detail in the next sections.

IMPORTANCE OF DATA PREPROCESSING IN A SOCIAL NETWORK

The goal of data preprocessing is to represent the social network data in a form which could be analyzed efficiently. A mining or the analysis algorithm cannot operate on the raw and messy data. The success of analysis is dependent on the quality of data. The analysis may not provide correct results or may provide misleading results if the underlying data is inadequate or contains redundant and irrelevant information. The raw data must be converted into the format desired by the underlying algorithm. Data preparation and preprocessing of the initial data set gathered from multiple and varied sources involve transformation of the initial data set into a desired data format suitable for analysis. Social network analysis algorithm or tool may not run if the data set is too huge. The quality of data may be more important than its scale for better understanding. Data preprocessing can handle this issue also by using dimensionality reduction technique. The analysis of social media is dependent on many factors. However, the quality of social network data is the most important factor. Social network mining is different from any other kind of analysis in a number of ways such as:-

- Social network data may be scattered across various sources which needs to be gathered, checked and integrated before a meaningful analysis can take place (Wang, 2010).
- Social network data is mostly informal in nature containing lot of misspellings and abbreviations making the need of data preprocessing an important task (Mosley, 2012).
- Social network data is temporal in nature which enables us to analyze the evolution of network adding complexity to the task of data preprocessing (Macskassy, 2012).

In data analysis, the data preparation is the most ignored and time consuming process. However, the effectiveness and correctness of analysis is directly proportional to the data preprocessing to which social network analysis is no exception. The key benefits of data preprocessing are

- Accuracy,
- Better Interpretability,
- Enhancing data quality,
- Better data management,
- Improved analysis,
- Reduced cost in terms of both time and space.

Data preprocessing lays the groundwork for any kind of analysis and is thus constituted a highly important task. Data preprocessing depends on the underlying context to yield valuable associations. Data preprocessing helps in solving various teething issues for social network analysis such as inconsistency, redundancy, noise, and missing values. Accuracy and quality of social network analysis rely mainly on data generated by data preprocessing making data preprocessing an important task. The data produced by data preprocessing is more compact and easily interpretable representation of raw data.

STEPS IN DATA PREPROCESSING

Data preparation is the most crucial step in analysis which involves transformation of the initial data set into required format. It can be divided into four steps namely data collection, data cleaning, data reduction and data conversion as shown in Figure 2. In this section we discuss some of the issues and challenges related to data preparation in social network analysis. While the discussion is in the general context, we are focused especially on the factors related to social network data.

In what follows, is a brief description of various phases involved in data preparation of social network data.

Data Collection

Data collection involves extraction of data from the social network. Social network consists of various social media services. Kaplan and Haenlein (2010) have broadly categorized social media into six parts namely collaborative projects, blogs, content communities, social networking sites, virtual game worlds, and virtual communities.

Figure 2. Data preparation phases of social network data

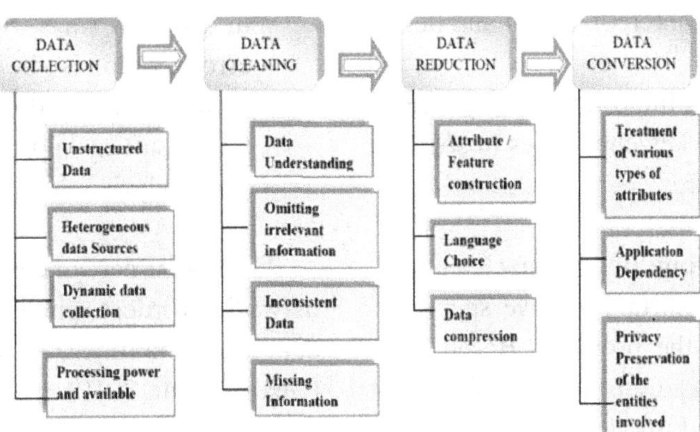

Social network data is usually collected programmatically or through scripts. Some of the social media sites such as Facebook and Twitter also provide APIs for data crawling. Depending on the kind of analysis required and type of mandate with the analysis agency the social network data may be taken from the service providers of these social media services who have the complete overall data of their network.

Some of the key challenges in the social network data collection are:

- **Unstructured Data:** Social network data is highly unstructured in nature containing various types of data rather than plain structured text. Depending on the social media site, the data in a social network could consist of profile data, connections, tags, posted messages, recommendations, communities and the browsing history. The social network data also contain multimedia information such as audio or video over text.
- **Heterogeneous data Sources:** Social network is a very heterogeneous network having varied kind of information networks. Social network contains multiple kinds of nodes and links. Data formats in different social media services are often varied and incompatible. This heterogeneity is an important point in the data collection.
- **Dynamic data collection:** Social networks are highly dynamic and evolving in nature. The dynamic analysis of social networks has recently got the importance which requires dynamic collection of data. Dynamic and incremental data collection from social media services could lead to better analysis and knowledge extraction. However, dynamic data collection requires considering various temporal characteristics such as duration of collection, different time intervals at which data will be collected and rate of collection.
- **Processing power and available storage space:** The proliferation of social network in terms of number of users and posts has caused the exponential growth in social networking data. For handling the huge amount of data there is a need of robust system having high processing power and good storage space.

Data Cleaning

The growth of social media services has resulted in wealth of rich information.However; the information in a social media may also be accompanied by noise or extra information such as spams, banner ads and copyright forms. The purpose of data cleaning is to remove the noise from useful information. Data cleaning is a difficult task to achieve as it is very difficult to demarcate the noise from the gigantic, interconnected and heterogeneous data.

Data cleaning is very important for any kind of analysis, some of the key challenges in social network data cleaning are:

- **Data Understanding:** In order to clean the noise it is very important to have specific knowledge about the problem. Based on the context, the required filtering of noise could be achieved more efficiently and easily.
- **Omitting irrelevant information:** Social network data is fairly detailed but it could not be analyzed directly as the analysis may start focusing on irrelevant information. In social network analysis the kinds of records which are unnecessary and should be removed are graphics, videos, records with the failed HTTP status code, formatting information. Records having extension such as CSS, GIF or FLV in the URL could be removed. Automated programs like web robots, spiders and crawlers should also be removed. Spam/Spammers detection and removal may also be addressed (Benevenuto et al., 2010). Omitting this extraneous information would result in fast analysis.
- **Inconsistent Data:** Social network data could be gathered or crawled from varied and conflicting sources having varied forms of data. The main purpose is to remove inconsistency to derive the most complete and accurate integrated records. The syntactic and formatting differences may exist in the records from various sources. In the social network data there may be the case of ambiguity and synonym issues where different entities may be presented similarly or same information could be presented in different ways. Spelling errors or other errors could also be present which needs to be removed. Removing data inconsistency will result in improvement of data quality and analysis.

The social network is a continuous evolving network. In order to prevent the privacy breach the data should be consistent across multiple releases (Bhagat et al., 2010).

- **Missing Information:** The correct and complete analysis requires the complete and valid data. It may be possible that some information is missing from the data due to various reasons such as inability to extract some attributes or due to lack of content such as non-registration. Depending on the specific context we should try to treat the missing information in the best possible way. The problem and causes of missing observations in social network data have been widely acknowledged by Huisman and Steglich (2008). URL expansion may also be addressed by appending missing pages in the path.

Data cleaning would result in structured and clean records so that a meaningful analysis could be performed.

Data Reduction

A social network data may contain petabytes of data which might take very long to be processed by the analysis tool. The information could be so large that it could even become difficult to extract interested pattern from it or could be difficult to project visually. The goal of data reduction deals with representing the data in the reduced form (with or without a loss of information) that is much smaller in volume, yet produce same or almost same output.

The major aim of data reduction is to maintain the data integrity and consistency of the original data set. The various data reduction strategies for social network data are:

- **Attribute/Feature construction:** Social network data is highly dimensional in nature with thousands of variables and lot of redundancy. This high dimensional data could be represented in a lower dimension by fewer variables. Feature construction deals with keyword identification and to prepare the data for analysis. Selection of keyword, pattern is dependent on the context of analysis of social media. Treating data as a bag of words or a bag of strings is also dealt in this phase. Lee et al.(2011) have used Bag-of-Words approach for text classification. Feature selection results in improving the performance of the analysis and achieving better data understanding. It will also result in data reduction.
- **Data compression:** Data could also be reduced by smaller data representations. Compressing social network can significantly improve the analysis process. Compression of social network should be done in a way that it could be used without decompression for analysis (Maserrat & Pei, 2010). Social network could be represented by compact data structure (Hernández & Navarro, 2012).
- **Language Choice (monolingual or multilingual):** Social media connects people across the various parts of the world. The numbers of members registered with social network are also increasing at a fast rate. The social network data contain multilingual content rather than just English words. Eleta (2012) has identified the characteristics that could enable cross-language information flows. Data reduction can also be achieved by filtering out the languages which are not of interest or are not supported by the tool.

Data Conversion

Data conversion deals with converting a set of values into the format which could be worked upon for analysis and making it suitable for automatic processing. The data conversion could also be done through a separate module in the analysis tool with a suitable interface. Data conversion may involve various operations such as aggregation, generalization; attribute filtering, new attribute addition.

A proper data conversion could result in significant improvement in analysis time, some of the key challenges in social network data conversion are:

- **Treatment of various types of attributes:** Social network data contains categorical as well as continuous variables. It may be the case that some analysis algorithm or tool accepts only categorical variable. Thus, a proper conversion between each kind of variable may be required before analysis.
- **Application Dependency:** Various tools either commercial or open source are available for social network analysis whether it is Twitter, Facebook, YouTube or any other media service. Combe et al. 2010 have provided a comparison between major social network analysis tools. These tools allow performing content, semantic or network analysis on social media data. However, each tool has its own format for input and storing the data. The data needs

to be first converted to the desired format before analysis could begin. Common formats mostly used by various tools are HTML/XML, delimited text, spreadsheets, or JSON. As discussed by Huhtam et al. (2010), each tool has its own strengths but sometime a single tool is not sufficient for covering all the aspects of analysis so it may be required to convert the data into different formats.

- **Privacy Preservation of the entities involved:** Social network users expect a level of privacy and control over their data which has raised various privacy issues. Haddadi et al. (2012) pointed out that there exists great utility value in social network data but the attackers or adversaries could get or link the information from social network data and may deduce sensitive information and relationship resulting in security breach. Hence, the need of protecting the information from the adversaries and maintaining a balance between utility and privacy. The data is converted to obfuscated form to achieve privacy preservation with the help of various techniques such as anonymization.

As social network is an evolving network, the social network data would be dynamic and evolving in nature. The data preprocessing should also be robust enough to handle the dynamicity and multiple releases of social network data.

HYPOTHETICAL CASE STUDY

Social networks are full of rich and valuable information. To elicit valuable information, social network data could be used for trend and pattern mining by the analyst or researchers in various domains and for various purposes. Consider one such company who wants to utilize the social network data for target marketing. Target marketing is about reaching the right customers and offering them products and services. Social network data could be used as an effective way of reaching the right customers by mining the social network data. Some of the benefits of using social network data for target marketing are:

- The great advantage of social networks to marketing is their tendency to propagate information virally.
- Social networks help in the creation of new customers or business associates much easily.
- Social networks allow marketing the products to a large market at no cost and no time.
- Social network could be used for tracking the likes and dislikes of the customers and then marketing them accordingly.
- Social network data could be used by various third parties in tracking and maintain their brand for enhancing their business.

The company decided to perform the social network data analytics. Social network data analytics would help the company to monitor the customer in real time, to monitor how people are viewing their brands and to see what their competitors are doing. Analysis of this would enable the company to understand its market, customers and what the target market is looking for, what people like about their products or services, and what needs to be improved. By gathering demographics of potential customers it would able to identify those that fit into their target market. This also brought many challenges with it. To market effectively using social networks there is a need to analyze the context and campaign properly. Following are some challenges that the company faced:

- Selection of data sources and their data compatibility.
- Ability to handle the large amount of data.
- Ability to handle missing data.

- Ability to perform dynamic data collection and analysis.
- Removing noise from data.
- Preventing the negative effects of social network analysis.

Social network data may be scattered across various sources which needs to be collected. Selecting the various sources is very important as discussed in section 7.1. Collecting data from various sources may also bring the inconsistency issue such as multiple variations of the same value like city, zip code, company, customer or address including multiple abbreviations and types as discussed in section 7.2.3. There is no use in having the data if we do not have enough resources to handle the amount of data as discussed in section 7.1.4. Even if we have enough resources the data quality may be improved by using various data reduction strategies as mentioned in section 7.3. The problem of missing data has been a pervasive problem in data analysis since it may lead to discovering irrelevant information or may not lead to inaccurate analysis as discussed in section 7.2.4. Social network data is temporal in nature which enables us to analyze the data dynamically, thus there is a need to collect and analysis social network data dynamically as discussed in section 7.1.4. It is also very important to remove noise such as spam from social network data as discussed in section 7.2.2. Due to overwhelming benefits of analyzing social network data, we sometimes tend to ignore its negative effects such as privacy preservation of the entities involved as discussed in section 7.4.3

The social network is characterized by an enormous amount of data. However, these data have to be turned into information in order to be useful. To overcome the major challenges, the senior executives of the company decided to pre-process the data before performing the analysis leading to better and accurate analysis. The data analytics of social network data depends on current context; designing an efficient data preprocessing will cater all the needs to a large extent due to which the data preprocessing is a viable and necessary process to achieve effective analysis.

IMPLICATION/BENEFITS OF DATA PREPROCESSING IN A SOCIAL NETWORK

With the advancement of internet based social media services there is a tremendous increase in the area of social network analysis due to the rich wealth of information available to them. Social network analysis like any other data analysis is limited by the quality and quantity of data and for which data preprocessing plays the key role. The major task in data preprocessing is a creation of suitable data to which analysis algorithms could be applied. The widespread application of social network analysis in various fields is justified by the research of the authors which paved way for data preprocessing of social network data. Some of the important implications of our study are:

- Development of tools for social network analysis with dynamic and varied kind of data handling.
- Developing and validating formal models for data processing and analysis.
- The study carried would help to identify the new challenging area in the field of data preparation and preprocessing which is the need of the current era.
- The study would also help the researchers who would like to do deeper research in various applications of social network analysis.

LIMITATIONS OF THE STUDY

Data preprocessing of dynamic social network data is an interesting area of research. The key efficacy of the study is to progress in the area of social network analysis by properly dealing with the challenges of data preprocessing. A number of important limitations that need to be addressed are:

- The study has discussed data preprocessing with a broader perspective and does not focus on a particular model or algorithm that can be applied to data preprocessing of social network.
- The current study was unable to include any real analysis.
- The research provides an insight into this area and can be further evaluated.
- The study discusses data preprocessing for social network analysis and does not discuss other issues related to social network analysis.
- There exists a possibility that some papers are not included, as many of the journals do not have open access.

FUTURE RESEARCH

The chapter contributes to an understanding of data preprocessing of social network data. The future works which we plan to work upon in the field of data preprocessing of social network data are:

- Development of automated tools, modules or plugins for social network data preprocessing to ease the process of data preprocessing.
- Identification of various other challenges in data preprocessing of social network data.
- Proper handling of various kinds of missing or false data and other issues for dynamic social network data.

CONCLUSION

An important task in any kind of analysis is the creation of a suitable data set which could be worked upon for accurate and better analysis. The data preprocessing is often the most time consuming and computationally intensive step in the analysis process and requires the understanding of data and the analysis tool. The author has tried to present the various challenges in the data preprocessing phases of social network data which would provide the valuable insight to the researchers and analysts. The consequences of conducting proper data preprocessing are better and accurate analysis which plays a vital role in social network analysis. A good data preprocessing would also make the analysis tool or algorithm to perform better.

REFERENCES

Aggarwal, C. C. (2011). *Social network data analytics*. New York, NY: Springer. doi:10.1007/978-1-4419-8462-3.

Benevenuto, F., Magno, G., Rodrigues, T., & Almeida, V. (2010). Detecting spammers on Twitter. In Collaboration, electronic messaging, anti-abuse and spam conference. Redmond.

Bhagat, S., Cormode, G., Krishnamurthy, B., & Srivastava, D. (2010). *Prediction promotes privacy in dynamic social networks*. In *Proceedings of the 3rd conference on Online social networks (WOSN)*. CA, USA.

Combe, D., Largeron, C., Egyed-Zsigmond, E., & Grey, M. (2010). *A comparative study of social network analysis tools*. In *International Workshop on Web Intelligence and Virtual Enterprises 2*.

Eleta, I. (2012). *Multilingual use of Twitter: Social networks and language choice. CSCW* (pp. 363–366). Companion.

Ferguson, R., & Buckingham Shum, S. (2012). *Social learning analytics: Five approaches.* In *Proc. International Conference on Learning Analytics & Knowledge* (pp. 23-33). Vancouver, BC.

Gupta, P., & Bhatnagar, V. (2012). Pros and cons of publishing social network data. In *Proceedings of National Conference on Data Mining and Warehousing* (pp. 422-425).

Haddadi, H., Mortier, R., & Hand, S. (2012). Privacy analytics. *Computer Communication Review, 42*(2), 94–98. doi:10.1145/2185376.2185390.

Hernández, C., & Navarro, G. (2012). Compressed representation of web and social networks via dense subgraphs. *Proceedings of SPIRE, 12*, 264–276.

Huhtam, J., Salonen, J., Marttila, J., & Nyk, O. (2010). Context-driven social network visualisation: Case wiki co-creation. In *International Workshop on Knowledge Federation*. Dubrovnik, Croatia.

Huisman, M., & Steglich, C. (2008). Treatment of non-response in longitudinal network studies. *Social Networks, 30*, 297–309. doi:10.1016/j.socnet.2008.04.004.

Kaplan, M., & Haenlein, M. (2010). Users of the world, unite! The challenges and opportunities of Social Media. *Business Horizons, 53*, 59–68. doi:10.1016/j.bushor.2009.09.003.

Lee, K., Palsetia, D., Narayanan, R., Patwary, M. A., Agrawal, A., & Choudhary, A. N. (2011). Twitter trending topic classification. In ICDM Workshops (pp. 251-58).

Macskassy, S. A. (2012). *Mining dynamic networks: The importance of pre-processing on downstream analytics.* Retrieved August 2012, from http://www.research.rutgers.edu/~sofmac/paper/ecml2012-commper/macskassy-commper2012-preprint.pdf

Maserrat, H., & Pei, J. (2010). Neighbor query friendly compression of social networks. In *Proceedings of the 16th ACM SIGKDD international conference on Knowledge discovery and data mining* (pp. 533-542).

Mosley, R. (2012). *Social media analytics:Data mining applied to insurance Twitter posts.* Retrieved August 2012, from http://www.casact.org/pubs/forum/12wforumpt2/Mosley.pdf

Müller-Prothmann, T. (2006). *Leveraging knowledge communication for innovation. Framework, methods and applications of social network analysis in research and development.* (Dissertation).

Ngai, E. W. T., Xiu, L., & Chau, D. C. K. (2009). Application of data mining techniques in customer relationship management: A literature review and classification. *Expert Systems with Applications, 36*(2), 2592–2602. doi:10.1016/j.eswa.2008.02.021.

Rawassizadeh, R., Heurix, J., Khosravipour, A., & Min Tjoa. (2011). LiDSec- A lightweight pseudonymization approach for privacy-preserving publishing of textual personal information, ares. In *Sixth International Conference on Availability, Reliability and Security* (pp. 603-608).

Santos, P., Souza, F., Times, V., & Benevenuto, F. (2012). *Towards integrating online social networks and business intelligence.* In *Proceedings of International Conference on Web Based Communities and Social Media.* Lisbon, Portugal.

Wang, Y. (2010). *SocConnect: A social networking aggregator and recommender*. Retrieved August 2012, from http://library.usask.ca/theses/available/etd-11292010-112405/unrestricted/yuan_thesis.pdf

White, J., Matthews, J., & Stacy, J. (2012). Coalmine: An experience in building a system for social media analytics. In proceedings of SPIE.

ADDITIONAL READING

Boyd, D., & Ellison, N. B. (2007). Social network sites: Definition, history, and scholarship. *Computer-Mediated Communication*, *13*(1), 210–230. doi:10.1111/j.1083-6101.2007.00393.x.

Catanese, S., Meo, P. D., Ferrara, E., Fiumara, G., & Provetti, A. (2011). *Crawling Facebook for social network analysis purposes* (pp. 52–60). WIMS. doi:10.1145/1988688.1988749.

Fan, W. (2012). Graph pattern matching revised for social network analysis. In *Proceedings of the 15th International Conference on Database Theory* (pp. 8-21).

Han, J. (2009). Data mining. In Liu, L., & Tamer, M. (Eds.), *Encyclopedia of database systems* (pp. 595–598). Springer.

Kempe, D., Kleinberg, J. M., & Tardos, É. (2003). Maximizing the spread of influence through a social network. In *Proceedings of KDD* (pp. 137-146).

Kleinberg, J. M. (2007). *Challenges in mining social network data: Processes, privacy, and paradoxes* (pp. 4–5). KDD. doi:10.1145/1281192.1281195.

Korolova, A., Motwani, R., Nabar, S. U., & Xu, Y. (2008). Link privacy in social networks. In *International Conference on Data Engineering (ICDE)* (pp. 1355–1357).

Kumar, R., Novak, J., & Tomkins, A. (2006). *Structure and evolution of online social networks* (pp. 611–617). KDD. doi:10.1145/1150402.1150476.

Leskovec, J., Backstrom, L., Kumar, R., & Tomkins, A. (2008). Microscopic evolution of social networks. In ACM SIGKDD.

Lin, Y., Chi, Y., Zhu, S., Sundaram, H., & Tseng, B. L. (2008). Facetnet: A framework for analyzing communities and their evolutions in dynamic networks. In *Proceedings of WWW* (pp. 685-694).

McKelvey, K., Rudnick, A., Conover, M., & Menczer, F. (2012). Visualizing communication on social media: Making big data accessible. In *Proceedings of CSCW Workshop on Collective Intelligence as Community Discourse and Action.*

Mislove, A., Marcon, M., Gummadi, K. P., Druschel, P., & Bhattacharjee, B. (2007). Measurement and analysis of online social networks. In *Proceedings of the 7th ACM SIGCOMM conference on Internet measurement* (pp. 29-42).

Tanbeer, S., Ahmed, C., & Jeong, B. S. (2010). *Mining regular patterns in data streams* (pp. 399–413). Database Systems for Advanced Applications.

KEY TERMS AND DEFINITIONS

Data Analytics: Science of examining raw data with the purpose of drawing conclusions about that information.

Dynamic Data Mining: Analysis and comparison of the information extracted by different data mining and knowledge discovery sessions scheduled over time.

Social Media: Interactive platforms via which individuals and communities co-create, share, and modify user-generated content.

Social Network: A social network is a social structure made up of a set of actors (such as individuals or organizations) and the ties between these actors. In social network architecture, there are users, social media services, data owner and third party data recipients.

Social Network Analysis: Analysis of the structure of social networks and online communities and mining from social network user-generated content to support the knowledge discovery process.

User-Generated Content: Textual and multimedia content (e.g., photos, videos, posts, tags) published by Web users on social networks and online communities.

Chapter 3
Emergent Data Mining Tools for Social Network Analysis

Dhiraj Murthy
Bowdoin College, USA

Alexander Gross
Bowdoin College, USA

Alex Takata
Bowdoin College, USA

ABSTRACT

This chapter identifies a number of the most common data mining toolkits and evaluates their utility in the extraction of data from heterogeneous online social networks. It introduces not only the complexities of scraping data from the diverse forms of data manifested in these sources, but also critically evaluates currently available tools. This analysis is followed by a presentation and discussion on the development of a hybrid system, which builds upon the work of the open-source Web-Harvest framework, for the collection of information from online social networks. This tool, VoyeurServer, attempts to address the weaknesses of tools identified in earlier sections, as well as prototype the implementation of key functionalities thought to be missing from commonly available data extraction toolkits. The authors conclude the chapter with a case study and subsequent evaluation of the VoyeurServer system itself. This evaluation presents future directions, remaining challenges, and additional extensions thought to be important to the effective development of data mining tools for the study of online social networks.

INTRODUCTION

With the increased pervasiveness of the internet, society has seen exponential growth in digital data that has been made available on global public networks. With this rise of 'Big Data,' researchers have seen the need to identify, organize, collect, and extract this information back out of the system and into useful forms (Hammer, Garcia-Molina, Cho, Aranha, & Crespo, 1997). The fields of data mining and web-content extraction are critical to this process and have remained active areas of re-

DOI: 10.4018/978-1-4666-4213-3.ch003

Copyright © 2013, IGI Global. Copying or distributing in print or electronic forms without written permission of IGI Global is prohibited.

search, as the types and forms of data available on the Web have continued to grow and evolve. The continued growth of information on the Web - due in part to more recent trends of fully online, social, and context aware computing - have made more types of data available, which are of potential use in a highly interdisciplinary range of fields. Many disciplines are looking at 'Big Data' and ways to mine and analyze these data as the key to solving everything from technical problems to better understanding social interactions. For example, large sets of tweets mined from Twitter have been analyzed to detect natural disasters (Doan, Vo, & Collier, 2011; Hughes, Palen, Sutton, Liu, & Vieweg, 2008; Murthy & Longwell, in press), predict the stock market (Bollen & Mao, 2011), and track the time of our daily rituals (Golder & Macy, 2011). As our use of blogs, social networks, and social media continues to increase, so does our creation of more web-based hyperlinked data. The successful extraction of this web-based data is of considerable research and commercial value.

Data mining often goes beyond simple information retrieval and has moved towards a meta-discovery of structures and entities hidden in seas of data. As our social interactions become increasingly mediated by Internet-based technologies, the potential to use web-based data for understandıng social structures and interactions will continue to increase.

Online social networks are defined as 'web-based services that allow individuals to (1) construct a public or semi-public profile within a bounded system, (2) articulate a list of other users with whom they share a connection, and (3) view and traverse their list of connections and those made by others within the system' (Boyd & Ellison, 2008). Individuals interact within online social networks through portals such as Facebook, which create social experiences for the user by creating a personalized environment and interaction space by combining knowledge of one users' online activity and relationships with information about other networked individuals. It is through data mining algorithms that Twitter, for example, determines recommendations for users to follow or topics that may be of potential interest. One way to study social networks is by examining relationships between users and the attributes of these relationships. However, data on a blog, Facebook, or Twitter is not directly translatable into network-based data that would be useful within research praxis, and this is where the ability to perform effective data mining becomes important. Social networks typically only provide individual portal access to one's egocentric network. Put in the language of social network analysis (SNA), the visible network is constructed in relation to ego (the individual being studied) and relations of ego, known as 'alters,' are seen (e.g. Facebook friends). However, in a restricted profile environment, the alters' relationships are not revealed. In order to understand network structure (which is key to a systems perspective), the researcher must use methods like data mining in order to gather information about all users and interactions by iterating over the data. A variety of different types of tools have been developed to collect this web-based information. These tools were created for a wide array of purposes. The majority of these tools have been commercially released. Some of these tools can be used to construct profiles of individuals based on data from multiple sources. Given issues of privacy, ethical uses of these tools should be strictly employed (Van Wel & Royakkers, 2004).

Despite the existence of a variety of tools, their ease-of-use and robustness can vary widely. There are many types of networks and online communities that could qualify as a subject of network-based research. Many of these virtual organizations and networks often share key elements and structures that are common across online social networks. These could include users, groups, communications, and relationship networks between these entities. Also, unlike the simple structured or semi-structured data that is subject of most data mining projects, SNA is not merely focused on generating lists of entities and information. Social networks are more organic in their growth and place emphasis on relational attributes. SNA seeks to understand how individuals and groups within networks (termed 'cliques') are connected together.

The Social Network Innovation Lab (SNIL) is an interdisciplinary research lab dedicated to understanding online social networks, social media, and cyberinfrastructure for virtual organizations. Research at the SNIL often involves the need for tools that are able to extract social network-based data for analysis from varied online social communities. The SNIL currently has projects that require data mining of popular microblogging services, shared interest forums and traditional social networks. We found that many currently available data mining tools were insufficient or poorly suited toward applications in social network research. This led us to begin to investigate the development of our own custom data mining tools. As part of this project, we researched existing tools, developed a conceptual framework for general data mining of online social networks, and tested prototype implementations of these ideas while acquiring data for use in current ongoing projects.

In this chapter, we will consider a variety of common methodologies and technologies for generic data mining and web content extraction. We will highlight a number of features and functionalities we see as key to effective data mining for social network analysis. We will then review several current data mining software tools and their fitness for data mining online social networks. The remainder of the chapter discusses our development of a data-mining framework for online social networks. Specifically, we introduce our work in extending the Web-Harvest 2.0 framework to data mine online social networks. This is followed by a case study of some of our initial results to acquire data from an online virtual community organized around social network technologies. The final sections summarize what we have learned through this process and maps out a course of action for future development in this area.

WEB-CONTENT EXTRACTION TECHNOLOGIES

With online social networking sites, the information and data that constitutes the network and its entities are, by necessity, distributed over a vast array of unique and dynamically generated page instances. Even when only a basic set of common SNS features (user profiles, friend lists, discussion boards) are considered, it is easy to see how the number of pages required to encounter and capture all the activity of the social network could quickly grow exponentially. In order to study the structure and operation of virtual communities within social networks, researchers need to parse and capture this sea of distributed data into formats more appropriate for research and analysis. In the absence of direct access to the database systems that drives a social network or a site-provided API, one must utilize other means to capture SNS data for research.

The majority of information on the Web is circulated in the form of HTML content, which wraps information in a nested set of tags that specify how data needs to be visually rendered in the browser. This is suitable for making data easily read and understood from the screen or through printing, but not as useful when clean organized machine-readable datasets are desired. Most online data extraction tools take advantage of the fact that the HTML is itself a structured data interchange format and leverage the HTML format to create parsers, which can extract the simple content and structure of data on a page in an organized way while discarding the irrelevant material. Generally, most online data extraction technologies can be classified into several categories.

Formats, Conventions, Utilities, and Languages

Technologies in this class are low-level constructs that often derive from some sort of published standard grammar. This grammar may then be implemented in whole or in part by other higher-level programming languages and technologies. They often simply define a way in which data can be ordered, searched, manipulated, or transformed. For instance, the XPath standard defines a format for finding and isolating pieces of information from a structured XML document (Clark & DeRose, 1999). Similarly, regular expressions are a structured format, which are useful for performing advanced searches and manipulation on unstructured strings of characters. XSLT is a language defined to assist in the transformation of one type of structured XML document into another (e.g. transforming an HTML document into a simpler RSS feed or vice-versa) (Clark, 1999). In the absence of well-defined standards for interacting with various types of data, extraction becomes more difficult. However, because of the low level nature of these structures, they present challenges when used in isolation within advanced data extraction projects (without constructing a broader framework for their application to a set of data).

Libraries

Data extraction libraries often perform the job of wrapping one or more lower level data manipulation/extraction constructs into an organized framework within the context of a specific programming language. These libraries then manage the implementation of a given construct within a framework useful for further development within a programming language. Development libraries leave the end goals completely open to the developer. Depending on the time, investment, and goals of the developer, development libraries can be used to create anything from simple one-off scripts to high-level applications with many advanced features.

Application Programming Interface (API)

Web-based APIs provide a standardized abstraction layer for secure portal access to certain Web-based environments. APIs provide serialized access to information from online data ecosystems. APIs allow administrators to enforce restrictions and terms of use on data access. They also obscure and protect proprietary implementation details. Furthermore, they will generally apply and be structured around the content available from one data source (e.g. a particular website, web-enabled technology, or application). A prominent example is Google's OpenSocial API framework (Häsel, 2011). The OpenSocial API is an open standard for a set of API features specific to social networking. Code developed against such frameworks would be potentially adaptable to any social network using the open standard. Other examples include APIs provided by popular social networking sites including Twitter and Facebook.[1]

Applications

The majority of data extraction solutions take the form of applications. Applications often make use of a large set of lower level extraction technologies and development libraries and bundle them into an interface designed around a set of desired functionality. These differing function sets and the varying levels of expertise expected of the user results in the availability of a wide range of different types of data extraction applications. These applications range from self-adapting, learning, fully GUI-based extractors for non-technical users to applications for advanced data extraction that require some in-depth knowledge of programming or data extraction utilities. Many applications fall into this latter category. Some of the most common are Helium Scraper, Djuggler, Newprosoft, Deixto, and Web Harvest.[2]

Enterprise Suites

This class of data extraction solutions is characterized by providing very high level, multi-featured, and advanced software solutions. They are often delivered as a suite of highly specialized applications. The implementations of these software packages are usually not open-source (as the code is often developed from proprietary development libraries). Like many enterprise solutions, these software products are often intricately complex and necessitate special training and/or ongoing technical support from the company itself to effectively use these tools. This support and training usually is an additional cost beyond the original software license. Pentaho[3] and QL2[4] are two examples of enterprise level data extraction and mining solutions that offer custom solutions, training, and support.

Outsourcing, Contracting, and Crowdsourcing

Alternative paradigms that merit mention are outsourcing, crowdsourcing, and freelance contracting. In outsourcing and freelance work, the researcher partners with a company or individual and explains the data extraction project and agrees upon a price and timeline for the delivery of the data. Crowdsourcing uses a slightly different model where a large data mining task might be divided into a large number of small tasks and a small fee may be offered for the delivery of each incremental piece of data delivered. Amazon's Mechanical Turk is a popular platform for streamlining this process and has been successfully deployed (Sheng, Provost, & Ipeirotis, 2008). Individual micro-tasks are constructed such as asking someone to record the tags on an online article or to classify a given webpage. Mechanical Turkers are often offered between 0.01¢ and 0.20¢ for the completion of each microtask. For some researchers, outsourcing works well because the tasks are cost-effectively completed in a short timeframe (Sheng, Provost, & Ipeirotis, 2008). For those who do not regularly need to acquire new data, this one-time fee structure may work well. Crowdsourcing may also be cost and resource effective. This method can bring additional concerns of uncertainty of when the task will be completed and, more importantly, quality control of data as contributors usually vary highly in terms of quality of work (Snow, O'Connor, Jurafsky, & Ng, 2008). These approaches do not represent new technologies for data mining per se, but illustrate new solutions in the absence of tools and expertise for acquiring their own data sets.

CONSIDERATIONS FOR DATA MINING OF ONLINE SOCIAL NETWORKS

The utility of data mining applications for social network research is dependent on what functionalities are most appropriate to the domain. This section explores what functionalities are most valuable in social network research. This discussion is guided and informed by experiences and needs identified through our own research in the study of life science virtual communities of practice as well as work exploring health related communication networks on Twitter.

Input and Output

Data extraction is ultimately about acquiring formatted information from a data source and then translating, manipulating or filtering this information into other formats as appropriate to one's research objectives. In basic online content extraction, the initial input is often a simple web address of the location of the information one seeks to capture. The distributed organization of most social networks means the information you need could be dispersed over a large number of pages. The URLs for these pages may need to be dynamically generated from one or more lists of attributes. Furthermore, one will most likely need to extract information from one location and use the results to identify and locate other pieces of information. This paradigm is best served by tools which allow for the most possible types of automated data extraction and manipulations. Data mining tools should be able to both read from and output to as many potential data formats as possible. Common formats most useful within a data mining tool kit include various kinds of structured text files like HTML/XML, delimited text, spreadsheets, or JSON. Data mining tools can be even more powerful when they include the ability to read and write to database systems, APIs, or even to have the ability execute local system commands to generate input variables. The power and usability of a tool increases as it is able to take input and give output in diverse formats.

Dynamic Query Specification

An important feature to consider when evaluating the utility of a data extraction tool to one's needs is to understand the ways in which the tool allows you to request and gather information. Many basic data mining applications use a GUI to allow one to specify the desired extractions. This will always have certain limitations. Other tools use a command-based query language like SQL to scrape data. In our work with social networks, we often need to traverse a list of forum locations, record all the user names encountered, collect information from each user's unique profile page, and then conditionally acquire extra information about certain users (if they are found in the previous step to have some specific attribute). Queries of this complexity often cannot be defined as a single request without resorting to multiple individual queries managed by a researcher. A query of this sort requires grammar for conditional branching, looping structures, and benefits from the ability to define functions (as well as local and global variables). Tools that implement full programming logic allow complex, dynamic, and context-aware queries to be defined. All the entities from a social network could conceivably be acquired via one request. This frees the researcher from having to micromanage many aspects of complex data mining projects, once the extraction rules and logic of the extraction job have been defined.

Social Network Interfacing

Online social networks often recognize the importance of allowing access to their data. Site developers often provide a programming interface for third parties developers to create value-added applications leveraging this social data (the use of which might further enhance participation in the network by its users). These application programming interfaces (APIs) often provide alternate methods for requesting information from a site beyond simply observing the information in situ. For example, Twitter and Facebook both have well-developed APIs to access vast stores of data. As opposed to simply requesting a page and extracting data from it, APIs allow developers to make a special kind of request to the API and return just the raw data one is looking for. APIs can greatly ease the process of gaining access the information on a social network. Some of the smaller, less well-known, networks we are studying include API-like features. Data mining tools for the analysis of social networks benefit greatly if they allow content extraction from common APIs.

Job Scheduling

In contrast to many common data mining tasks, social network researchers are more likely to be interested in near real-time data. Using the methods already described, one could create a data mining specification which would capture a snapshot of the activity on a social network at the time the extraction was run, but, what about the next day or a month later? The constant use and modification of networks by their user base can cause networks to change greatly in short periods of time. One could simply capture a snapshot once a month, but these snapshots could contain large amounts of redundant information. A more robust solution might involve using programming logic coupled with automated time aware functionality to develop a data extraction request with the power to detect changes within the source network and incrementally update itself over time. In addition, a system of this type would likely require a perpetual extraction process which is able to detect and log changes periodically, and then call appropriate update scripts autonomously as needed. There are several key types of job scheduling attributes that could be associated with data extraction scripts:

- **Now:** This option would immediately execute a job. This is the most basic type of scheduling operation.
- **Later:** This option allows a user to schedule jobs at specific times. This could be useful to extract data from a site during low traffic hours, or for a situation where it is known that new information will be posted or made available at a specified times.
- **Chain:** The ability to chain tasks would allow one job to be scheduled to start once another has completed. This is very useful when one data extraction task is dependent upon the completion of one or more other tasks. With this option, the whole extraction flow for a complex and self updating extraction job could be specified in advance and sent to the mining application as a single project.
- **Recurring:** Recurring jobs are valuable in data mining of online social networks. Social network data presents challenges due to the fact that social networks are often in continuous flux. Most research of online social networks begins by capturing a snapshot of data as it exists at a specified point in time. A robust function for recurring data extraction allows researchers greater control over when to update their data and at what intervals to poll the site for new information.

Concurrency

Most web-content extraction tools acquire data by creating a virtual agent to make automated requests from a web host. This is the same way a web browser works. A browser requests a web site and the host sends a file containing information (i.e. in HTML) needed to display the web page. In data mining, this data is simply grabbed and parsed in a variety of methods to obtain data. Most tools and extraction workflow simply utilize one agent to fetch each required page in sequence. For non-dependent extraction tasks, this process could be streamlined by creating multiple agents to make multiple concurrent requests to the same web host (for different information). For large jobs, this feature places a key role in speeding up the acquisition of data, (as these requests are rarely taxing on local hardware or network speed). Concurrency should be evaluated as a key component of any data mining tool designed for online social networks.

Progress Management

Many of the features we have discussed focus on ways to allow for some level of automation in a data extraction task to be specified in advance (so the researcher is not required to micromanage the numerous aspects of large and complex extraction jobs). Usually, the analysis of social networks requires collecting large amounts of data from a network. In data mining tasks, data extraction is often limited by the speed that the hosting server allows clients to access data. Aside from concurrency, there is often little that can be done if the social network you are mining is slow at returning requested information or is very large. If the network is both, it could take hours or perhaps days to complete certain large data extraction tasks. Our research often involved extracting information from numerous user profiles and forum pages. We noticed that although we could not predict when a job would complete, we could often determine the number of entities that needed to be captured before the process took place. This helped us realize that if we could also keep track of the number of completed entity extractions, we would be able to implement a progress monitor and estimate completion time for all our extraction tasks. We feel this type of progress tracking and management are important features for the data mining of online social networks. Wherever possible, extraction tools should attempt to keep track of the progress of data extraction tasks as well as expected time to completion. This feature will be of great value to researchers responsible for managing one or more large data extraction projects by giving them the information they need to maximize their own productivity and to be prepared in advance as to when data will be ready for post-hoc processing.

Extraction Meta-Behavior

A natural instinct in the design of data extraction tools for large social networks is to find ways to acquire the desired data as quickly as possible. Further consideration reveals an important counter argument to this instinct. The operator of an extraction process tool might be tempted to create large numbers of page request agents, which in turn might generate large amounts of traffic on the hosting site. This not only is considered bad 'netiquette' (Mozry, 2011), but has ethical and legal considerations. If one's data mining project is part of academic research, the relevant Institutional Review Board (IRB) should be consulted to confirm ethical compliance with human subjects. A large volume of page requests with a web host could degrade the quality of the experience of other users of the site. Also it could result in the web host banning all requests from your IP address if the host believes your requests are malicious. Furthermore, many social networking sites have specific policies or Terms of Service (TOS) in place that would dictate how much data can be requested per agent. Whenever possible, it is recommended that permission and guidelines be obtained from the administrators of any site one wishes to extract information from. It is in the best interest of the data extractor to be responsible and follow any appropriate rate-limiting conventions whether explicit, or implicit when extracting data from a host. Having one's IP banned from a site could be potentially catastrophic to a project. Any data mining toolkit for online social networks should implement some standard to protect the user, but also provide the ability to create custom guidelines depending on the known TOS of a web host or for when the user knows it is acceptable to request large volumes of data. These limits should be able to be defined in multiple ways by the number of requests per time unit or staying below some defined throughput or bandwidth measure. The idea is to be able to maximize program efficiency to acquire data as fast as possible, but not so fast that you may be garnering ill-will from a network and its users. In other words, data mining social networks should be - if possible - an open and collaborative process. Often, the social network being studied will also be interested in research results gained from the data that was mined.

Client-Server Paradigm

Extracting data from the web can require significant processing power as well as bandwidth. Many types of data extraction projects may be ongoing and most users do not want their computer constantly running potentially resource expensive scripts. We feel an ideal solution involves tools that use a client server paradigm (where each user simply submits their jobs to a server for handling). That way, the designated server can handle all the heavy processing and high data load while the clients' machine remains free for use. With robust scheduling, concurrency, and progress management in place, the server application just needs to notify the client when the final collected data is available. The use of a client side application gives a lot of flexibility to the user requesting certain extraction jobs. They can use the client to log onto the main server and manage all their running jobs regardless of where they are physically located. The server should provide the client with options such as checking job progress, creating new jobs, aborting running jobs, changing scheduling, and changing the extraction specification. Also, this provides the ability for multiple users with different data extraction needs to utilize one centralized server.

REVIEW OF EXISTING DATA-MINING TOOLS TO MINE ONLINE SOCIAL NETWORKS

Our ultimate goal in this research was to begin development of a custom data mining solution optimized for extracting information from online social networks. Though we began the process with the aim of developing a custom "built-from-scratch" data extraction toolkit, we decided to first evaluate existing tools. As discussed in the previous section, we were interested in whether we could incorporate these existing tools into a hybrid data extraction toolkit which implemented our functionalities. In this section, we present this evaluation of common online data extraction tools. These reviews speak both to a tool's usefulness in social network research and in regard to their ability to be used as the basis for a prototype extraction tool. After the evaluation of several commonly available tools and technologies for online data extraction, we determined that Web-Harvest 2.0 was an ideal choice for the needs of our project goals. Among the tools considered were Helium Scraper, Newprosoft, Happy Harvester, Djuggler, Rapid Miner, Deixto, and Web-Harvest.

Common Data-Mining Tools

Based on our evaluation it was determined that Helium Scraper, Newprosoft, Happy Harvester, and Djuggler were all powerful GUI-based scraping applications. However, these tools also shared the same limitations. All four tools were single operating system applications that only allow scraper configurations to be defined within the context of the application. They also have no ability to be controlled or configured from the command-line. Their source code is not open-source and scripts could not be written against their various executables. When taken in consideration with our project goals (which would require software modifications for large social network scrapes to be conducted with minimal impact on the host), it became clear that these tools could not be leveraged to achieve our desired functionality.

Rapid Miner

Rapid Miner is one of the leading open-source applications for data mining and analytics and has been successfully used in data extraction projects (Graczyk, Lasota, & Trawiński, 2009; Han, Rodriguez, & Beheshti, 2008). Rapid Miner was evaluated as a potential fit for our project's needs. It is open-source, cross-platform, uses XML-based configuration files, which can be developed through the interface or written directly, and the code base can be scripted against both in application wrapper interfaces as well as from the command line. Though Rapid Miner is a powerful tool, it has a steep learning curve and includes a large number of features which would not be needed for our project's needs. Using Rapid Miner would prevent us from being able to develop a fast lightweight utility in a reasonable amount of time.

DEiXTo

DEiXTo (also known as ΔEiXTo) (Kokkoras, Lampridou, Ntonas, & Vlahavas, 2008) is another web extraction technology that was evaluated for our project's needs. DEiXTo is a single platform GUI-based web extraction application built on top of an open source Perl-based scraper utility. DEiXTo also uses an XML based configuration language that potentially allows configurations to be defined outside of the GUI. The Perl module that forms the backbone of DEiXTo's extraction technology could also be scripted against any operating system or code framework that supports the Perl scripting language. The DEiXTo file format (.wpf) is obtuse and the documentation is not easily accessible. Ultimately, most .wpf files must be developed within the GUI application, which is single platform and is not open-source. DEiXTo is also limited in the ways output can be written only to specific file formats and in specific ways. While the features and options available in DEiXTo would allow us to accomplish our project goals, it was determined that tools which were more configurable and more open (in terms of input and output capabilities) would be better suited to our project.

Web-Harvest

Web-Harvest 2.0 is a Java-based open source data extraction tool, which has been successfully used in the data mining literature (Yang, Liu, Kizza, & Ege, 2009). It is a hybrid tool that consists of a GUI based application wrapped around an open-source Java development library. This library, in turn, implements several of the most common and powerful extraction utility formats such as XPath and regular expressions. The Web-Harvest 2.0 platform also defines syntax for defining custom data extraction workflows. This was ideal for several reasons. First, quick start-up of development was possible using the features of the graphical user interface to easily debug, learn, and understand how to develop complex workflows in the Web-Harvest scraper configuration format. In many ways, defining workflows via this format is better than coding library solutions that require workflows to be defined in the context of that codebase. This is because the configuration rules are written in a simple XML-based language, and can be written with any text editor (Nikic & Wajda, 2006). This frees the developer from the additional nuances of any high-level programming language. Furthermore, once tested, these workflows could be easily shared with others and passed to the development package, which could execute the scraper configurations through code. The fact that at the core of Web-Harvest is an open-source data extraction engine allowed for our project to wrap this engine in our own lightweight Java code. Web-Harvest 2.0 was a good fit because of its hybrid nature. Most pure application-based scrapers are not extendable and few define an open configuration format (forcing the developer to work within the confines of what the application allows). Pure development package-based based extraction tools can have a steep learning curve and are often difficult to debug. Relying purely on data extraction utilities and standards like XPath and regular expressions requires that an entire framework be built around them in order to execute complex extraction workflows. This can be time-consuming and resource intensive. Given the remit of our project, Web-Harvest served as an ideal solution in terms of features and the ability to separate between code and UI (which allowed us to quickly develop our own tools using the Web-Harvest engine). Other tools were not found to efficiently allow us to work in this way. See

Table 1. A comparison between data mining tools

	Availabilty	Expertise	Specification Language	Automation	Concurrency
Newprosoft	$, PC	Moderate	No	NA	NA
Helium Scraper	$$, PC	Easy	No	NA	NA
Djuggler	$,PC	Moderate	No	NA	NA
Rapid Miner	Free, Cross	Very High	No	Possible	Possible
Deixto	Free, Cross	High	Yes	Indirect	Possible
Web-Harvest	Free, Cross	High	Yes	No	Possible

Table 1 for a comparison between Web-Harvest and other data mining tools.

Extension of Web-Harvest for Data Mining of Online Social Networks

After a review of existing data mining tools and a consideration of the desired features of data mining for online social networks, we decided to develop extensions and an application wrapper for the open-source Web-Harvest 2.0 data extraction engine to serve as a prototype of a full-fledged social network-centric data extraction engine. As discussed previously, Web-Harvest features a robust query specification language with capabilities to import and export data to a number of important formats including MySQL database integration. We sought to add features important to data extraction for social networks including time-based and repeating jobs, running multiple jobs simultaneously, client-based process and progress management, and server-based execution. Our tool incorporates all of these features by building on top of the open-source Web-Harvest source code.

As discussed in the previous section, Web-Harvest has been used successfully in various studies as a basic scraper. One example is Nagel and Duval's (2010) work, which used Web-Harvest in order to collect large amounts of publication data. For their study, they required a simple web scraper and used Web-Harvest in its original form to mine publication data from Springer, an academic publisher. They used the software to collect data including titles, authors, affiliations, and postal addresses.

Katzdobler and Filho (2009) use Web-Harvest extensively. They combined Web-Harvest with JENA, a tool used to build semantic web applications, as well as an ontology which described what type of information they wanted to extract. The JENA API then accesses the ontology and Web-Harvest extracts the information from the site. However, manual creation of the configuration file and manual startup of Web-Harvest is needed.

TagCrawler is another program written using Web-Harvest and is one of the few cases of Web-Harvest being directly extended (Yin, 2007). The creators of TagCrawler required a web crawling tool which would be able to retrieve information from tagging communities. While the end goal of the project was not related to our project, their use of Web-Harvest as a base and building from it illustrates that this can be a successful model.

Our project, 'VoyeurServer,' uses Web-Harvest's existing functionality, but adds several layers of additional features. The features we identified in Section 3 served as a guide to our development efforts. By extending the Web-Harvest core framework, we were afforded the opportunity to discard the overhead of a GUI in favor of a lightweight command-line interface implemented with a client-server pattern. We were also freed from the limitations placed on the extraction engine by the GUI. We were also able to take advantage of the Java programming language to develop our own features not present in the GUI or the engine itself.

Structure

The implementation of this project using the client-server paradigm required that we split the functionality for extraction into two applications: the VoyeurServer and the VoyeurClient. The latter was developed as a lightweight command line interface to provide users a way to submit and control their individual data extraction projects. It is through the VoyeurClient that users can submit their extraction jobs, manage the job's behavior, as well as monitor the progress of all their running jobs. The VoyeurServer application was designed to run continuously on a special server and to respond to requests from VoyeurClient instances. When the server receives a job from a client, the server creates an instance of the WebHarvest 2.0 extraction engine in its own thread, and manages the execution of the job as directed by users' interaction with the client. Figure 1 shows the relationships and flow of communication between these program entities.

Functionality

In addition to the ability to submit and manage multiple simultaneous extractions, we also sought to develop a set to features to allow for the smart management of extraction behavior and management of job progress. The ability to control and manage this behavior was incorporated into the VoyeurClient and VoyeurServer applications.

Temporal Control

The ability to control the temporal execution of job and recurrent behavior is one of the key features we identified for social network-aware data-extraction. This control allows users to create self-updating scripts as well as control how and when individual jobs will be run. Taking a cue from modern calendar systems, VoyeurServer was designed to allow jobs to be defined as a single event or as a repeating process to be executed in an ongoing manner.

Process Management

VoyeurServer users retain full control over their running and completed jobs. There is some danger that clients might feel they have lost control once their jobs were submitted to the server. In order to combat this, the VoyeurClient provides users with complete control over their running jobs at all times. This functionality includes the ability of users to start, stop, or pause as job at any point during its execution. Additionally users are given the ability to alter or remove a jobs repeating behavior at any time.

Figure 1. Schematic of data flow in Voyeur server

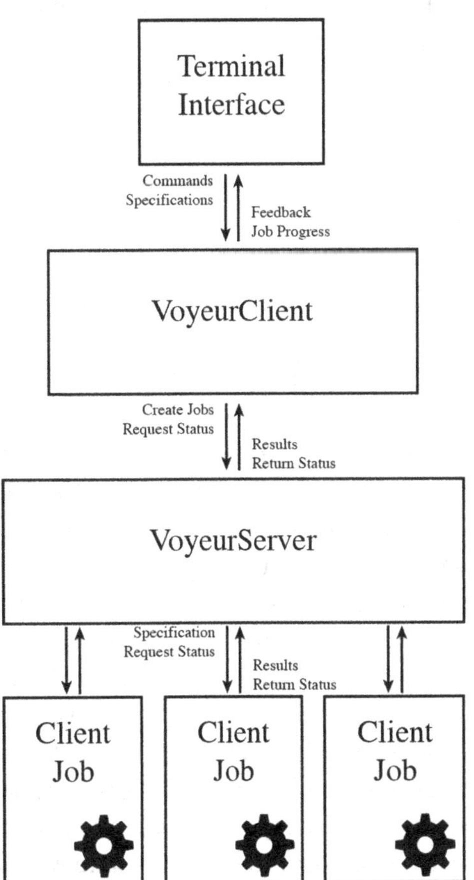

Progress Management

The ability to view and manage the progress of ongoing scrapes is an important feature for users managing large and complex data extraction jobs within online social networks. In order to add this functionality to the existing WebHarvest extraction framework, we developed an extraction specification template for progress aware content extraction jobs. This template adds two requirements to any extraction file. The first requirement is the initial definition of some measure of progress, which is stored in a special progress management database. The second involves having the extraction specification itself update this database regularly (based on its ongoing progress). The addition of these structures to any WebHarvest extraction specification file is sufficient to make the job progress-aware within the VoyeurServer framework. At the user's request, the VoyeurClient application will request and report this information to the user about their progress-aware jobs. Additionally, this feature will report on the start time, current running time, and any important log messages of any running job (regardless of whether it implements the progress-aware framework).

Summary

There a wide variety of valuable tools that can be immediately put to use or be modified to suit the needs of almost any data mining projects. In our case, we found that Web-Harvest 2.0 already incorporates many of the basic functionalities we had previously identified as important in the effective mining of online social networks. Because it is open source, we saw Web-Harvest as an ideal place to begin testing and developing a social network-centric data-mining tool. Our development plan centered on taking the core framework of Web-Harvest 2.0 and wrapping the code base to extend the application to serve as a multithreaded data extraction engine (implemented using a client-server interaction paradigm). Once the base extraction modules were wrapped in this way, we could focus on adding additional management features to the wrapper like task scheduling and process/progress management. Further work to develop and refine these ideas will be important to make this tool available to the broader data mining community.

EXPERIMENTAL RESULTS: A CASE STUDY

We engaged in this exploration of developing data extraction tools better suited towards collecting data for online social networks as part of a NSF funded research project on "Virtual Organization Breeding Environments." A key aspect of this project required us to gather large amounts of data from online life science communities of practice in order to explore the organization and cyberinfrastructure of virtual communities within these networks. As we collected this data, we realized there were ways in which the functionality of existing data extraction tools could be enhanced to streamline our extraction workflows.

The online network we studied had several key features we were interested in capturing. Specifically, we needed to collect over 200,000 user profiles, over 9,000 forums, a blogging ecosystem, and a friendship-based social network. This section details how we were able to use our tool to acquire the information we needed for our research.

Our needs included capturing information about the users within this community and their communications with one another. Our eventual goal is to use this data to study patterns of trust development and of online scientific collaboration. The community we studied did have an API for requesting information about each user's egocentric peer network. However, for all other data we had to rely on traditional web content extraction methodologies.

We were able to use the Web-Harvest query specification language to develop separate workflows to collect each type of information (user data including profile information, forum posts, friend networks). Using the features developed in our VoyeurServer application, we were able to develop a broad automated workflow to simultaneously collect data from these three key areas (while at the same time respecting the bandwidth consumption limits agreed upon by communication with site administrators). Using the workflows and the VoyeurServer tool, we were able to successfully collect user and post information over the course of a week while limiting any daily micromanagement of the process. In this regard, our time aware processes, progress management features, and concurrent extraction jobs were able to prove themselves successful in application. The flexibility of Web-Harvest's I/O framework allowed us to capture data to structured XML as well as directly to a database simultaneously. In our research, we had previously developed an application to assist in the qualitative coding and classification of the community's data in this database. Our VoyeurServer content extraction workflows allowed the data to be integrated directly with our existing downstream research applications. This realized potential represents an extremely powerful and desirable workflow for network analysis. This experiment also helped identify issues that were not addressed by the current version of VoyeurServer. Some of these limitations and potential solutions are discussed in the next section.

FUTURE RESEARCH DIRECTIONS

Despite initial success in using Voyeur Server for mining data from online social networks, there remain further capabilities of Voyeur Server that require further development. We outlined key features for data mining of online social networks. Currently, the VoyeurServer extension of Web-Harvest implements these features at a basic level. Further testing and development would help determine whether this extension has a future as a general research tool or whether it suggests that extending Web-Harvest 2.0 is perhaps less preferable than starting from scratch to develop a data mining toolkit for online social networks. We consider further work in robust data-extraction tools for social networks to be of the utmost importance.

For those considering developing their own custom wrappers for the Web-Harvest 2.0 extraction engine, we suggest considering these suggestions of extended functionality:

- Utilize Web-Harvest's plugin architecture to develop integrated modules for common social network APIs to ease the process of developing extraction specifications for complex APIs (especially those requiring authenticated requests).
- Develop custom plugins for common database tasks. The VoyeurServer and WebHarvest database features rely on raw SQL statements and thus increases the level of expertise required to develop and implement database functionality.
- Develop a specification file for projects as opposed to per file scrapes. Incorporate time-aware functions, extraction meta-behavior, and progress monitoring options into this project specification format. This would allow for integrated individual workflows for large projects.
- Explore automated concurrency as opposed to having to design your individual jobs or projects for concurrency. This would help basic users take maximum advantage of parallel processing possibilities.

Our continued research seeks to address some of the issues and limitations discovered in developing this tool. We seek to further develop VoyeurServer in the following ways:

- Develop further functionality that allows for higher levels of concurrency.
- Investigate the feasibility of a broad-based public research server providing network-structured extraction as a service.

- Investigate high per-thread resources. Experience suggests that VoyeurServer is memory intensive. Our goal would be to reduce the memory overhead to a minimum for each running job. This will make running large numbers of jobs for various projects more efficient.
- Improve the interface for this Web-Harvest extension. Specifically, develop a GUI for the VoyeurServer client application.

We have shared these improvements so that developers can be aware of issues we currently face and some possible solutions. This will enable designers and developers to learn from the development challenges we have faced.

CONCLUSION

This chapter has reviewed various data mining tools for scraping data from online social networks. It has highlighted not only the complexities of scraping data from these sources (which include diverse data forms), but also introduces currently available tools and the ways in which we have sought to overcome these limitations through methodological extensions to existing software. After reviewing currently available data scraping tools, we developed a tool of our own, VoyeurServer, which builds upon the Web-Harvest framework. In this chapter, we outlined the challenges we faced and our specific solutions. We also included future directions of our data mining project. Ultimately, we introduce concrete methods to develop data mining solutions of online social networks using the Web-Harvest framework.

Though this research is preliminary and its remit has not been comprehensive, our experience in developing VoyeurServer tools has been positive and represents an important step towards the further development of this and/or other data mining tools specifically for online social networks. It is important to begin developing these domain specific solutions so that good open source options are available to researchers. Current tools tend to be focused around the domains of marketing and business knowledge. These types of solutions often fall short for use in academic contexts. As social media continues to become increasingly part of our online interactions, methods for data extraction from these networks will continue to remain critically important.

ACKNOWLEDGMENT

This material is based upon work supported by the National Science Foundation under Grant No. 1025428.

REFERENCES

Bollen, J., & Mao, H. (2011). Twitter mood as a stock market predictor. *Computer*, *44*(10), 91–94. doi:10.1109/MC.2011.323.

Boyd, D. M., & Ellison, N. B. (2007). Social network sites: Definition, history, and scholarship. *Journal of Computer-Mediated Communication*, *13*(1), 210–230. doi:10.1111/j.1083-6101.2007.00393.x.

Clark, J. (1999). XSL transformations (XSLT). *World Wide Web Consortium (W3C)*. Retrieved from http://www. w3. org/TR/xslt

Clark, J., & DeRose, S. (1999). XML Path Language (XPath) version 1.0 w3c recommendation. *World Wide Web Consortium (W3C)*. Retrieved from http://www.w3.org/TR/1999/REC-xpath-19991116

Deixto. (n.d.). *Website*. Retrieved from http://deixto.com/

Djuggler. (n.d.). *Website*. Retrieved from http://www.djuggler.com/

Doan, S., Vo, B.-K., & Collier, N. (2011). An analysis of Twitter messages in the 2011 Tohoku earthquake. In P. Kostkova, M. Szomszor, & D. Fowler (Eds.), *Electronic healthcare: 4th International Conference, eHealth 2011* (pp. 58-66). Málaga, Spain, November 21-23, 2011. Berlin: Springer Berlin Heidelberg.

Golder, S. A., & Macy, M. W. (2011). Diurnal and seasonal mood vary with work, sleep, and daylength across diverse cultures. *Science*, *333*(6051), 1878–1881. doi:10.1126/science.1202775 PMID:21960633.

Graczyk, M., Lasota, T., & Trawiński, B. (2009). *Comparative analysis of premises valuation models using KEEL, RapidMiner, and WEKA* (pp. 800–812). Computational Collective Intelligence. Semantic Web, Social Networks and Multiagent Systems. doi:10.1007/978-3-642-04441-0_70.

Hammer, J., Garcia-Molina, H., Cho, J., Aranha, R., & Crespo, A. (1997). Extracting semistructured information from the Web. In *Proceedings of the Workshop on Management of Semistructured Data* (pp. 18-25). Tucson, AZ.

Han, J., Rodriguez, J. C., & Beheshti, M. (2008, December). Diabetes data analysis and prediction model discovery using RapidMiner. In *Future Generation Communication and Networking, 2008. FGCN'08. Second International Conference on* (Vol. 3, pp. 96-99). IEEE.

Häsel, M. (2011). Opensocial: An enabler for social applications on the web. *Communications of the ACM*, *54*(1), 139–144. doi:10.1145/1866739.1866765.

Heliumscraper. (n.d.). *Website*. Retrieved from http://www.heliumscraper.com/

Hughes, A. L., Palen, L., Sutton, J., Liu, S. B., & Vieweg, S. (2008, May). Site-seeing in disaster: An examination of on-line social convergence. In *Proceedings of the 5th International ISCRAM Conference*. Washington, DC.

Katzdobler, F.-J., & Filho, H. P. B. (2009). *Knowledge extraction from web*. Retrieved from http://subversion.assembla.com/svn/iskm/FinalDocumentation/FinalReport.pdf

Kokkoras, F., Lampridou, E., Ntonas, K., & Vlahavas, I. (2008). *Mopis: A multiple opinion summarizer. Artificial Intelligence: Theories* (pp. 110–122). Models and Applications.

Morzy, M. (2011). Internet forums: What knowledge can be mined. In Kumar, A. S. (Ed.), *Knowledge discovery practices and emerging applications of data mining: Trends and new domains* (pp. 315–335). IGI Global Publishing.

Murthy, D., & Longwell, S. A. (in press). Twitter and disasters: The uses of Twitter during the 2010 Pakistan floods. *Information Communication and Society*.

Nagel, T., & Duval, E. (2010, September). Muse: Visualizing the origins and connections of institutions based on co-authorship of publications. In *Proceedings of the 2nd International Workshop on Research 2.0. At the 5th European Conference on Technology Enhanced Learning: Sustaining TEL* (pp. 48-52).

Newprosoft. (n.d.). *Website*. Retrieved from http://www.newprosoft.com/

Nikic, V., & Wajda, A. (2006). *Web harvest: Overview*. Retrieved from http://web-harvest.sourceforge.net/overview.php

Pentaho. (n.d.). *Website*. Retrieved from http://www.pentaho.com

QL2. (n.d.). *Website*. Retrieved from http://www.ql2.com

Sheng, V. S., Provost, F., & Ipeirotis, P. G. (2008, August). Get another label? Improving data quality and data mining using multiple, noisy labelers. In *Proceeding of the 14th ACM SIGKDD international conference on Knowledge discovery and data mining* (pp. 614-622). ACM.

Snow, R., O'Connor, B., Jurafsky, D., & Ng, A. Y. (2008, October). Cheap and fast---but is it good?: Evaluating non-expert annotations for natural language tasks. In *Proceedings of the Conference on Empirical Methods in Natural Language Processing* (pp. 254-263). Association for Computational Linguistics.

Sourceforge. (n.d.). *Website*. Retrieved from http://web-harvest.sourceforge.net/

Twitter. (n.d.). *Website*. Retrieved from https://dev.twitter.com/, http://developers.facebook.com/

Van Wel, L., & Royakkers, L. (2004). Ethical issues in web data mining. *Ethics and Information Technology*, *6*(2), 129–140. doi:10.1023/B.ETIN.0000047476.05912.3d.

Yang, L., Liu, F., Kizza, J. M., & Ege, R. K. (2009, March). Discovering topics from dark websites. In Computational Intelligence in Cyber Security, 2009. CICS'09 (pp. 175-179). IEEE.

Yin, R. M. (2007). Tagcrawler: A Web crawler focused on data extraction from collaborative tagging communities. (Unpublished thesis). University of British Columbia, Canada.

KEY TERMS AND DEFINITIONS

Application Programming Interface (API): These interfaces are often defined within a given programming language or computer-based system to allow the system to communicate with other complex systems without revealing access to proprietary technology, private implementation details, or sensitive information.

eXtensible Markup (XML): A generic semi-structured format for the organization of data. The HTML format which defines how web pages should rendered in a browser is simply and extension of the more generic XML format, defined for a specific purpose. Extensions of the basic XML format are often developed and used to organize large amounts of repetitive structured metadata, like records of books in a library, or the organization of songs information (Album, Artist, Title, etc) within iTunes.

Graphical User Interface (GUI): A graphical user interface is an interface to a technological system that is presented to users through the use of visual widgets often displayed on a screen. These visual elements often make use of metaphors with real world objects to convey how they ought to be used to accomplish tasks in a virtual environment (i.e. virtual buttons, dials, etc.).

HyperText Markup Language (HTML): A standardized semi-structured format for the definition of content for a webpage on the World Wide Web. HTML files tell a browser all the information it needs to render content to the browser window. These files are often the subjects of data mining projects, which attempt to extract important information from the data directly and prior to rendering.

Social Network Analysis (SNA): Broadly, this entails the study of Social Networks and their component entities and transactions. SNA is often focused particularly on analytic and quantitative methods. Examples of SNA include the evaluating of social network maps using graph theory, utilizing machine learning techniques to attempt automatically classify different types of users, or identify sentiment of communications within a social network.

Structured Query Language (SQL): A generic language specification and format to request data from a data archiving system. There are many implementations of SQL, each of which is in use in different database systems. The most common of these is Microsoft SQL (MSSQL) and the widely used MySQL open-source database variant.

Terms of Service (TOS): A form of legal document that stipulates the terms under which a person may utilize a service. They often contain legally binding guidelines regarding what a user of a service may or may not do, as well as what the guidelines for how the service provider will behave (including the transmission and storage of data).

ENDNOTES

1. See Twitter (n.d.).
2. See Heliumscraper (n.d.), Djuggler (n.d.), Newprosoft (n.d.), Deixto (n.d.), and Sourceforge (n.d.).
3. See Pentaho (n.d.).
4. See QL2 (n.d.).

Chapter 4
A Conceptual Framework for Social Network Data Security:
The Role of Social Network Analysis and Data Mining Techniques

Sanur Sharma
Ambedkar Institute of Advanced Communication Technologies & Research, India

Vishal Bhatnagar
Ambedkar Institute of Advanced Communication Technologies & Research, India

ABSTRACT

In recent times, there has been a tremendous increase in the number of social networking sites and their users. With the amount of information posted on the public forums, it becomes essential for the service providers to maintain the privacy of an individual. Anonymization as a technique to secure social network data has gained popularity, but there are challenges in implementing it effectively. In this chapter, the authors have presented a conceptual framework to secure the social network data effectively by using data mining techniques to perform in-depth social network analysis before carrying out the actual anonymization process. The authors' framework in the first step defines the role of community analysis in social network and its various features and temporal metrics. In the next step, the authors propose the application of those data mining techniques that can deal with the dynamic nature of social network and discover important attributes of the social network. Finally, the authors map their security requirements and their findings of the network properties which provide an appropriate base for selection and application of the anonymization technique to protect privacy of social network data.

DOI: 10.4018/978-1-4666-4213-3.ch004

Copyright © 2013, IGI Global. Copying or distributing in print or electronic forms without written permission of IGI Global is prohibited.

INTRODUCTION

Social Network can be defined as a collection of people that form groups or communities based on similar interests or features. In a social network structure, the individuals or the members of the group are represented by nodes and the relationship among them is represented by edges that join any number of nodes together. Backstrom et al. (2006) address some important issues regarding group formation and evolution, and discussed them in detail.

There are different kinds of users in a social network like creators, critics, collectors, joiners, spectators and inactives (Li, 2007).

- **Creators:** Creator is a person who creates a social media and publicises it to the world. It includes creation of a web page, blog, uploading videos and other information.
- **Critics:** Critic is a person who responds to the information posted by others by posting his/her ratings, reviews about the product or services and updates on the social media.
- **Collectors:** Collectors are the ones who use the content for themselves as well as for others by using RSS feeds. They vote for websites online and add tags to web pages.
- **Joiners:** Joiners are people who join different social networking sites and maintain and update their profiles. They generally have multiple profiles on various social networking sites.
- **Spectators:** Spectators include people who read blogs, view user generated content and check for products with user ratings and reviews.
- **Inactives:** Inactives are people who do not participate in any social networking activity but are members of the social network.

Social network analysis is the study of such networks where users exist in the form of groups or communities and analysis of the network is done to find out interesting relationships and patterns. Social network analysis is not limited to finding patterns and relationships but it also provides valuable information like strong relationships in the graph, degree, density, power and centrality. This information can be used for evaluation of critical parameters and evolution of social network with time which can further serve as an important base for application of anonymization technique to achieve the desired level of privacy with minimum possibility of any security breach. Social networks inherently appear in groups that change and evolve with time. Community analysis is one of the major parts of social network analysis that is used to study the structure, evolution and behaviour of the social network. Our framework proposes the use of community analysis by using data mining techniques that can track the dynamic nature of social network. To study the temporal nature of social networks we found dynamic clustering technique to be the most appropriate and our framework proposes to use the same. Dynamic clustering techniques provide an in depth analysis of changes that occur in social networks with time and are also consistent with the previous releases of data. These techniques will provide all the necessary information about the network that can be very critical from security point of view. This information will hence, serve as an important base for application and selection of the correct anonymization technique. Our framework provides the mapping of the parameters provided by social network analysis with the security requirements that will prove as the deciding factor for the selection of correct anonymization technique to achieve better security.

This chapter is organized as follows: Section two presents the related research and motivation. Section three outlines the research methodology adopted for designing the framework. Section four introduces the conceptual framework for social network data security, its requirement and detailed design. Section five presents an empirical case study that discusses the application of the framework. Section six discusses the research implication of the proposed conceptual framework. Section seven discusses the advantages of the study followed by section eight pointing the limitations of the work and finally section nine conclude by presenting some direction for future research in the area of social network data security.

RELATED RESEARCH AND MOTIVATION

There has been a considerable increase in the use of social media with the advances in the field of virtual networking that has brought about various privacy issues in the social networking media. A lot of research has been devoted to social network security and many anonymization techniques have been proposed to achieve the desired level of privacy but most of these techniques have failed to provide privacy and are consistently prone to attacks. The major reason that has been found behind the lack of privacy is improper analysis of social networks. This motivated us to design a framework that provides proper analysis of the social networks before applying any security measure on the social network data. Our proposed framework provides an approach that points out how social network analysis can be used to understand and find out the intricate and critical information about social network which when used before applying any security measure will provide better privacy as compared to the existing security techniques.

A lot of work has been proposed in the area of social network analysis. Jamali and Abolhassani (2006) have discussed a few social network models for analysis of social networks. These include statistical models for social network analysis, using graphs to represent social relations, using matrices to represent social relations and other descriptive methods. Mitra et al. (2007) have proposed an object relational graph model for social network applications. This model represents common structural and node based properties and has also defined new structural operators for different social network applications. There are various data mining techniques that have been proposed for social network analysis like classification, clustering and association rule mining. To deal with the dynamic nature of social networks, various dynamic clustering techniques have been proposed. Chakrabati et al. (2006) proposed the concept of evolutionary clustering to deal with the temporal nature of data. Several variants of this approach have been proposed and are discussed in detail in the next sections.

In social networks, there are basically three types of disclosures: identity disclosure that includes revelation of individual's identity, link disclosure that includes revelation of sensitive relationships and content disclosure that includes revelation of sensitive information about nodes and links (Liu & Terzi, 2008; Liu et al., 2008). To prevent all such disclosure of information, the concept of anonymization was introduced. Anonymization prevents information disclosure by hiding data in such a way that an unauthorized party cannot infer anything from the published data. The need of anonymization originated when the service providers of the social network data started releasing the data to third parties for their profit, and so in order to preserve user's data anonymization was introduced in social networks. Sweeney (2002) first introduced the concept of K-anonymity by which individual sensitive information in the published data cannot be uniquely identified from k-1 other individuals in that published data. Sharma et al. (2012) have presented a literature review and classification of various disclosures and the anonymization techniques that have been proposed so far for privacy preservation of social networks. The anonymization techniques that have been proposed so far in literature cover only some of the background knowledge like k-candidate anonymity (Hay et al., 2007), k-degree anonymity (Liu

& Terzi, 2008) and k-neighbourhood anonymity (Zhou & Pei, 2008; Liu et al., 2008). Some other anonymization techniques include l-diversity (Machanavajjhala et al., 2006; Zhou & Pei, 2010) and p-sensitivity (Sun et al., 2011). Another issue with the anonymization techniques is that they majorly cover the static nature of social network data and little research has been done in the area of dynamic anonymization of social networks.

Backstrom et al. (2007) have presented two types of attacks on anonymized social networks: active attacks and passive attacks. Active attacks are those attacks by which an adversary enters a social network by creating a fake profile and appears on the network before it is anonymized and when the social network is released after anonymization then he tries to figure out hidden patterns and data using this information. Passive attack on the other hand does not require an adversary to create a fake profile, but the attacker simply utilizes the background information to launch an attack.

Bhatnagar and Sharma (2010) have identified various challenges that an anonymization technique has to face in order to achieve privacy. These challenges include but are not limited to ensuring structural stability, maximizing coverage of background knowledge, striking a balance between privacy and utility and handling noise.

RESEARCH METHODOLOGY

A qualitative research methodology was adopted by authors wherein the problem identification was done by studying various research works scattered across several journals and conference databases in the field of social network security. It was found that there is a high need of privacy preservation of social network data, which when released by the service provider to third parties, lead to various privacy issues. It was found that most of the anonymization techniques fail to provide the desired level of privacy to the social network data. Consequently, the authors adopted a research strategy and approach to solve the problem by proposing a conceptual framework for securing released social network data by using dynamic data mining technique for analysis which reveals critical and important information about social networks, which accordingly serve as base for the selection of appropriate anonymization approach. The authors have tried to provide an insight to the use of social network analysis from security point of view by using a social network analysis tool. The study provides a good comprehensive base for understanding the importance of social network analysis and its application via data mining techniques before performing anonymization on data.

CONCEPTUAL FRAMEWORK FOR SOCIAL NETWORK DATA SECURITY

Need of the Framework

The challenges in securing social network data are primarily due to lack of proper understanding of the network structure and analysis. If the social network is properly comprehended and analysed before applying any security measure or anonymization technique, it will provide reasonably important information about the network structures that will help to better anonymize the social network data and provide better security from various breaches. The analysis of social network looks into the relationships among individuals, their location, flows and other connected information to find out the strong connections, nodes which are powerful and active, reveal more information or can be critical for the entire network, group or community. All this information can be very vital from the security point of view but is ignored by most anonymization techniques as they do not perform complete social network analysis, leading to security breaches. This highlights the need for examining the social network data on security parameters before applying any of the anonymization techniques. The framework that we present caters to this need of developing a sound base for the application of anonymization techniques.

Anonymization techniques like k-anonymity, l-diversity and p-sensitivity are all relational techniques that have been applied on social networks quiet effectively, but, in case the attacker possesses some background knowledge, these anonymization techniques fail to provide the desired level of privacy. On the other hand relational techniques when applied to databases, do not suffer from background knowledge attacks because in relational data there are a set of attributes which serve as quasi-identifiers and associates multiple tables. Anonymization techniques therefore can provide a much higher level of privacy to relational data by working with these quasi-identifiers only. In social networks, however, there are multiple pieces of information like vertices, relationships, neighbourhood properties and sub-graph properties that can be used by an attacker which these anonymization techniques fail to cover properly. This happens because of the complex nature of the social network, improper understanding of the network and lack of analysis of the network. It has been seen that a small change in the network can cause a considerable effect on the entire network. A proper understanding and structural analysis is required in order to identify the critical values, nodes, links and other properties of the network and this can be achieved by social network analysis. Our framework provides an approach that will help in removing all such issues by applying data mining techniques for social network analysis in the initial phase and then perform anonymization on the social network data. Data mining techniques for analysis will handle large, high dimensional and complex social network data effectively and will help in providing the intricate and crucial information about the social network so that appropriate security measures can be applied effectively after the analysis.

Another important aspect of social network is its evolution with time which is known as the dynamic nature of social networks. Not much work has been done in the area of dynamic anonymization which is an open problem for researchers and practitioners. There are various dynamic anonymization techniques that have been proposed for relational data but there application on social networks is still in its infancy. The complex and dynamic nature of social networks pose a great problem for the application of these relational anonymization techniques on social network. Dynamic social network analysis is required to meet the changing needs of social network. There are some very effective dynamic data mining analysis techniques that have been proposed more recently for social network, which considers the evolving nature of social network and effectively handles noisy and historical data. Our framework therefore presents the use of such dynamic data mining techniques like evolutionary and incremental clustering for performing analysis on social network data. This will track the evolving data, providing necessary information in the initial phase itself and eliminating the effort of handling dynamic social network data separately during anonymization, resulting in an effective overall approach.

Building the Conceptual Framework

To track the evolution of social networks with time, dynamic techniques are being adopted for which data mining techniques are majorly used. In this chapter we present a general framework by which we link the social network analysis to information security via data mining techniques. Figure 1 presents in general the three main levels of the framework as analysis of social network, data mining technique inclusion and information security measure

Level 1 of the framework presents the role of social network analysis that can be used for identification of important and critical factors of the social network which can be helpful while performing anonymization of the social networks. Social network analysis includes ego centric network analysis, socio-centric network analysis and open system network analysis (Kadushin, 2012). Social network properties that can be critical for anonymization of social networks include network density, centrality and power. There are various temporal metrics which describe the social network evolution and reveal important information about the network structures and groups. These temporal metrics will help in forming the base for selection and implementation of anonymization techniques.

Level 2 of the framework presents the inclusion of the data mining technique which can be used for social network analysis. Data mining techniques provide the best means to understand and analyse the social network as social networks contain large volumes of high dimensional data that traditional methods like OLAP are unable to handle properly. The time evolving nature of social networks makes its analysis quite complex and this is where the dynamic data mining techniques will help provide the correct picture of the network. There are various data mining techniques that can be used for analysis of social networks like classification, clustering and association rule mining. To track the dynamic changes of the network, dynamic clustering is one of the data mining techniques that effectively analyses the social network.

Figure 1. Levels of the framework

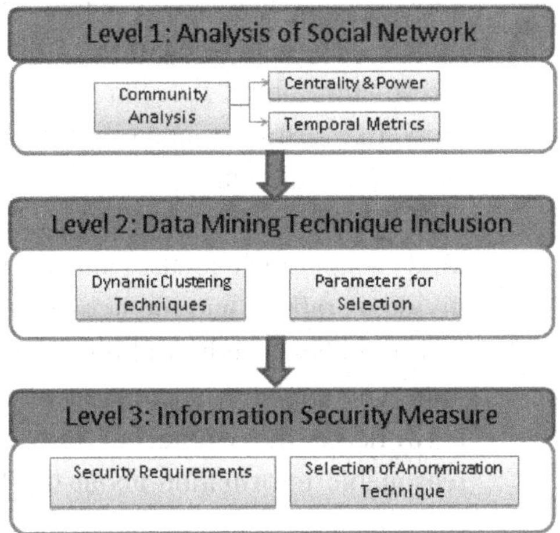

Level 3 of the framework presents the information security measure that can be applied on the social network based on the analysis that has been done in the previous level. Information security measure will include the application of the various anonymization techniques on the social network data. The selection of the anonymization technique will be based on the analysis which is done in the previous levels. The analysis will provide a base for selection of the anonymization technique depending upon the various privacy parameters. It has been seen that anonymization techniques are applied without any proper analysis which is the major cause of the security breach.

The next section discusses the framework in detail where every level is elaborated and its functions are explained.

Detailed Framework for Social Network Data Security

The detailed framework explains the complete process adopted to achieve security of social network data and specifies how each layer is connected with the other. The various steps involved are:

Step 1: The first step includes the analysis of social network that will depend on the type of network. Community analysis is found to be most efficient, as individuals usually appear as part of a group in a network and community analysis provides a complete view of the network and tracks the evolution of network effectively.

Step 2: The next step includes the application of data mining techniques for community analysis. Data mining techniques like classification, clustering and association rule mining can be used for community analysis, but for temporal evolution of social networks dynamic clustering fits well. There are two types of dynamic clustering techniques for social network analysis- evolutionary and incremental clustering. The clustering technique provides the critical and significant information about the network and its data. It helps in the identification of intricate and susceptible areas of the network.

Step 3: The third step marks the selection of the dynamic approach based on the various parameters that define the purpose and usability of the technique. It includes the following parameters- Snapshot, history, Efficiency, accuracy, time slice, noise, scalability and cluster consistency.

Step 4: The fourth step involves mapping of the clustering results with social network analysis metrics which provide critical and sensitive information about the network that needs to be considered by the anonymization techniques in accordance with the various privacy parameters.

Step 5: The fifth step defines the various security requirements for the social network data security and evaluates the privacy parameters based on the sensitive information that is provided from the previous step. This step identifies and maps the critical and sensitive information of the network according to the security requirements

Step 6: The final and the most important step marks the selection of the anonymization technique based on the information provided by all the previous steps. The selection of anonymization techniques will rely on the privacy parameters.

Figure 2 presents the conceptual framework in detail where each layer is sub divided into various parts and functioning of each part is discussed.

Social Network Analysis

Social network analysis is the mapping and measuring of relationships, flow of information among individuals, group, organizations or any other connected entities. Social networks are generally represented by a graph where the node or vertices represent the individuals or members in a network and the links represents the relationships or flow of information among the nodes. Social network analysis has gained a lot of prominence due to its proliferated use in various applications. One of the stimulating and major tasks of social network analysis is to develop ways of analysing communities and groups known as community analysis. Individuals in a social network usually tend to appear in groups and sub-groups and information about them can reveal important structural information and behaviour of the entire network.

Social network analysis can be done on the basis of the centralities of the network. According to Kadushin (2012), social scientists have studied three types of networks: ego centric, socio centric and open system networks explained.

- **Ego Centric Networks:** Networks that are connected with a single node or individual are known as ego centric networks. Hanneman and Riddle (2005) discuss two types of ego centric networks:
  - **Ego centric with alter connections:** In these types of networks a node is selected and all nodes that are connected to that node are identified. The nodes that are identified in the first stage are then checked to find out which of them are interconnected to one another. This kind of approach provides a reliable picture of the networks and their local neighbourhoods. They can sometimes provide information about the complete network like distance, centrality, reciprocalities and cliques.
  - **Ego centric with ego only:** This kind of approach focuses on the individuals rather than the networks as a whole. This method although provides incomplete information of the network on the whole but provides reasonable information about the local structures or neighbourhoods.

Figure 2. Detailed framework for social network data security

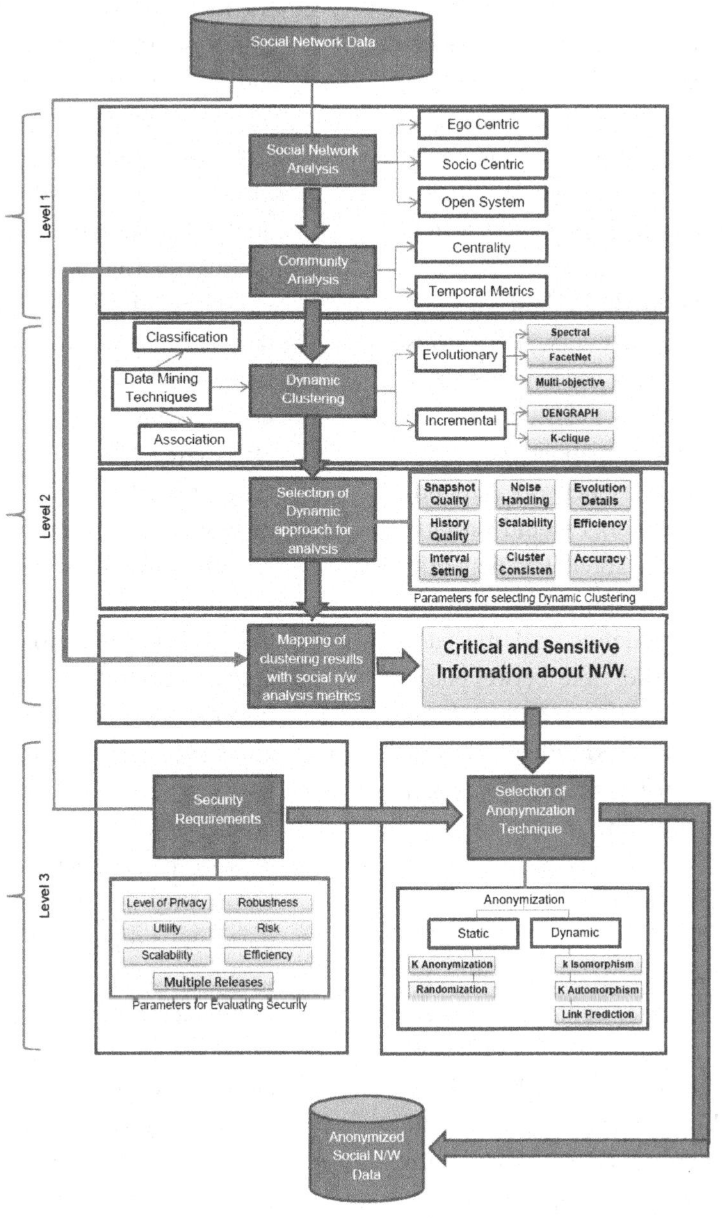

- **Socio Centric Networks:** These are the closed system networks and provide information about fine points of the network. For analysis of socio centric networks snowball method can be used. According to Hanneman and Riddle (2005), snowball method begins with a focal node or set of nodes and all nodes connected with them are found and then there ties are further found and the process continues till no new nodes are left to be identified. This method is used to track down particular groups or sub-groups that are mixed with large number of others. The author has discussed two problems of this network. First, this method is unable to detect the isolates in the network that can be an important feature for some analytic purposes. Second, there is no definite way to find all connected nodes in the network. If the snowballing method is not started from the correct node or nodes, there are chances that it could miss an entire sub set of connected nodes, which were not attached from the starting points.

- **Open System Networks:** These are the networks where the network boundaries are not clearly defined. These are the most stimulating networks for analysis. In these networks the information about each node with all other nodes in the network is found. Analysis of such networks would provide complete information about the network. Full network data is required for network analysis to properly define and measure the structural properties like betweenness (Hanneman & Riddle, 2005). Full network data is also expensive and difficult to collect which further makes the study of open system networks difficult.

Social Network Properties

There are various properties of social networks that include density, degree, centrality, power, distance, group size, modularity and clustering coefficients. Hanneman and Riddle (2005) have discussed properties like maximum flow, Hubbell and Katz cohesion, centrality and power which are explained below: Some of the major properties that are useful for social network analysis are:

1. **Maximum Flow:** The property of maximum flow finds all the possible number of paths from the source node to the target node and not just the efficient ones. The flow approach suggests that the strength of ties lies in the maximum number of alternatives that the source has towards the destination than the weakest link in the chain of connections. The weakest links are the ones with lack of alternatives. This property stresses on the idea that number of pathways are more important than their lengths for connecting individuals in a network. This property also helps in classifying actors more or less similar to one another in terms of patterns of their relations with other actors. Cluster analysis is one of the major techniques which is used for finding group of actors having similar relationships with other actors in the network also known as community identification which is discussed in detail in the next section.
2. **Hubbell and Katz Cohesion:** The maximum flow property focuses on the vulnerability or redundancy of connection between pair of actors whereas the Hubbell and Katz cohesion considers the strength of all links as defining connections, but it would not be appropriate to select a path of length 10 as important as a path of length 1. The Hubbell and Katz approach counts total connections between actors and assign weights to each connection. The greater the length, the weaker the connection will be considered.
3. **Centrality and Power:** Power is the fundamental property of social network, and centrality and power are closely interrelated to one another. In social network analysis, measures of centrality are used than measures of power. Centrality measures provide a comprehensive view into various roles, grouping and relationships among the actors in a network. Below are explained the various measures of centrality:
   a. **Degree Centrality:** It is used to measure the network activity for a node. It is defined as the number of links that a node has with other nodes in a network. It is generally considered that having more connections have high influence in a network, but this is not always true. There might be nodes with less number of connections but still they might be more important from connectedness

point, as they may have connections with different groups or clusters.

b. **Betweenness Centrality:** It is a measure that defines the influence of those nodes in the network that act as brokers or are the point of failures. They are the critical components which upon their removal can isolate nodes or group of nodes.

c. **Closeness Centrality:** It is used to measure the length of the paths to other nodes in a network. It includes those nodes which might have less number of connections but would be able to form paths to all nodes in a network.

4. **Temporal Metrics:** Traditional methods of social network analysis revolve around only the static nature of the social network. Static networks are those which do not change over a period of time. More recently a lot of work has been started in the area of dynamic networks, as social networks change with time there are a lot of properties that consider the dynamic aspect of social networks. One such property is the temporal metrics which define all the properties related to the dynamic evolution of social networks. Following are various temporal metrics that are inherent for social network analysis:

   a. **Temporal Distance:** Santoro et al. (2011) defines temporal distance to be symmetric to temporal view and is defined as the sequence of temporal sub graphs that reflects how close in time or in hops the node tends to move. Tang et al. (2009) have defined temporal path and temporal distance as shown below:

      i. Given two nodes i and j temporal path is defined as () to be set of paths from i to j that pass through the nodes . . . where is the time window that node n is visited and h is the max hop within the same window t.

      ii. Given two nodes i and j shortest temporal distance: (to be the shortest temporal path length. Starting from, this can be thought as the number of time windows it takes for information to spread from a node i to node j. here h indicates the maximum number of nodes with in each time window which information can be exchanged.

   b. **Temporal Centrality:** The centrality measure as explained above is one of the most important properties of social network and evolution of centrality measures will provide information about powerful nodes that tends to emerge in a network. Tang et al. (2010) have explained temporal betweenness and temporal closeness mentioned below:

      i. **Temporal betweenness:** Temporal betweenness centrality of a node is defined as the fraction of temporal shortest path between all pair of nodes that pass through that node. It not only includes the number of shortest path which pass through that node but also the length of time for which a node along that path retains the message before forwarding it to the next node.

      ii. **Temporal Closeness:** Temporal closeness centrality of a node can be defined as a temporal shortest path length to all other nodes in the network. It measures how early a node can deliver message to all other nodes in a network.

   c. **Evolution of Density:** The evolution of density can be measured by calculating the closeness of graph to a complete one by observing it at a sequence of time steps (Sontoro et al., 2011).

d. **Evolution of Modularity:** The evolution of modularity can be measured by determining how a graph can be decomposed into sub parts over a period of time. It quantifies the quality of a given network division into communities. For community identification, high values of modularity are characterized by intra module and inter module connections (Sontoro et al., 2011).

e. **Evolution of Clustering Coefficient:** Clustering coefficient of a node is defined as a measure of how close a cluster is to its neighbourhood. Its value is measured at different time steps and an increasing or decreasing value will indicate the formation or division of communities in a social network (Sontoro et al., 2011).

All the above mentioned properties of social network form a major base for community identification and analysis and will serve as a support for anonymization techniques. Below we discuss the network segmentation and group formation in social networks.

Network Segmentation/ Community Identification

Analysis of smaller Subgroups within a social network can help analyse the entire network on a whole. Each smaller group has its own attributes like number of nodes and the relationship between them. These attributes may be common to all nodes within a group but may have no similarity at all with nodes of other groups. If there exist, nodes in two sub groups, having some common attributes, it facilitates easy diffusion across the network. The major task of social network analysis is to find ways to analyse these sub groups or clusters. There are various methods for analysis of social network structures that provides information about the dense connections and helps in developing larger clusters and groupings.

Kadushin (2012) has defined principles of network segmentation which state how the networks can be segmented on the basis of density and structural similarity, are discussed below:

1. **Density:** The process of finding cohesive groups is a complex task, as finding regions in the network that are denser in sociological terms is difficult. It has several considerations like the density of connections in the group. It includes the number of direct and indirect connections. Secondly the connections can be mutual and reciprocal and multiplicity of ties is possible which adds to the complexity. Lastly, an increase in density of group will increase the level of believability. If a rumour was spread and if one heard the same rumour from multiple sources due to multiple connections in the network then it will be more believable.
2. **Structural Similarity:** The networks can also be segmented on the basis of patterns of relationships with other nodes. The nodes that have similar patterns of relationships with other nodes can grouped together to form clusters.

The groupings and subgroupings of the social networks can be done in several ways. There are different types of clusters that can be formed during segmentation of networks. Following are the three major types of network clusters that can be formed.

1. **Cliques:** The simplest definition of clique is that the nodes in the sub structure have all possible connections among themselves. N-clique can be defined as the nodes in the group that are connected to every other node in the group at a maximum distance of N. The path length can include connections with all other nodes.
2. **N-Clans:** N-clans poses a restriction on N-cliques whereby the nodes in the group are connected to other nodes in the group

at a maximum distance of N and the path length will only include the nodes of the same group or clique.

3. **k- Plexes:** k-Plexes can be defined as the group of nodes having N members, out of which the node has direct ties with n-k nodes of the group.

Data Mining Technique Inclusion

Recently there has been a rapid increase in the use of data mining techniques for social network analysis. Social networks contains large amount of high dimensional and complex data which brought about the need of data mining for analysis and visualization of the data. Data mining techniques have been used extensively for finding trends and patterns from the network data. For social network analysis, network segmentation and community identification is one of the major tasks and data mining techniques can perform such tasks very effectively and efficiently. There are several data mining techniques that can be used for analysis of social networks like classification, clustering and association rule mining.

Social networks are those networks which evolve with time, that is, new nodes and edges are added in the networks, some nodes leave the networks and edges and relationships keep on changing with time. This evolution of social network is known as the dynamic nature or dynamic social networks. More recently data mining has also found its place in the dynamic world of social networks and to track these dynamic changes various data mining techniques are been used. One such efficient data mining technique is dynamic clustering which tracks every change in the dynamic social networks and helps in performing community analysis and community identification which is the major aspect of social network analysis.

Our framework uses the dynamic clustering techniques for performing the analysis of social networks and specifically performs analysis of community structures and there evolution with time.

There are two major types of dynamic clustering which are used to detect communities in social networks and to study the evolution of these structures over time as discussed below.

1. **Evolutionary Clustering:** Evolutionary clustering is a type of dynamic clustering in which the clustering at any point in time should remain faithful to current data and at the same time should not deviate much from the previous releases of data. Chakrabati et al. (2006) proposed the first evolutionary clustering method. They defined evolutionary clustering for problems of processing time stamped data and used graph cut metrics for measuring community structures and evolution of these structures. In this type of technique, a sequence of clustering is carried out at each time step and each clustering should be similar to the clustering at previous time step and should accurately reflect the data arriving at that time step. The important property of this type of clustering is that it provides a trade-off for benefit of consistent clustering with the cost of representation of accuracy of current data. This type of clustering basically takes a snapshot of the graph at particular intervals of time. Evolutionary clustering techniques are based on the graph model based approach and the problem with this type of clustering technique is the setting up of the time intervals. There are various variants of this type of clustering that have been proposed so far. Some of the major types of evolutionary clustering are as follows:
    a. **K-means and Agglomerative Hierarchical Clustering with Evolutionary Setting:** Chakrabati et al. (2006) have given a general framework discusses the evolutionary version of the two most commonly used data mining clustering algorithms. These algorithms are converted into

evolutionary versions in two steps. In the first step the standard algorithms are applied at particular time intervals and in the second step they are merged together based on the similarity matrix. The similarity measures forms the base of clustering which captures the history of data to some extent. These algorithms can be applied on dynamic networks, though they are not very effective when dealing with large and complex data.

b. **Evolutionary Spectral Clustering:** Evolutionary spectral clustering is used in various dynamic applications where the data is not expected to change very rapidly. Chi et al. (2009) proposed two frameworks based on the evolutionary spectral clustering. Their works showed that evolutionary spectral clustering provided stable and consistent clustering results that are less sensitive to noises and were adaptive to long term cluster drifts. This type of clustering also provides temporal smoothness between clusters in successive time steps. Spectral clustering is based on eigenvectors of matrices derived from similarity matrix of data points and algorithms based on spectral clustering gives good performance. These algorithms are used for solving graph partition problems where different graph based measures are required to be optimized. Chi et al. (2009) have proposed their algorithms based on this observation and have proposed two frameworks for evolutionary spectral clustering that provide temporal smoothness to the overall clustering quality. This algorithm is proposed for dynamic applications and can be extended for application on social networks.

c. **FacetNet:** Lin et al. (2008) have proposed FacetNet which is a framework for analysing communities and their evolutions in dynamic networks. Their approach deviates from the traditional two-step process by which the communities are first detected at each time slice and then compare to determine various communication and relationships. These traditional methods generate high temporal variations which in turn induces undesirable evolutionary characteristics. The proposed FacetNet algorithm provides temporal smoothness and is based on matrix factorization, where communities and their evolutions are factorized in a unified way.

d. **Particle and Density Based Evolutionary Clustering:** This is another variant of the basic evolutionary clustering which was proposed by Kim and Han (2009). The authors have discussed three major problems of the previous clustering techniques, first is that those methods consider only fixed number of communities over time, second they do not allow arbitrary start stop of community over time and third these methods are not scalable to large network size. This method removes these problems by using the concept of nano community that captures the evolution of dynamic networks over time at particle level and models the community as a dense subset of nano communities forming an l-clique by clique topology. For this, a density based clustering method is used which efficiently finds the local clusters of high quality using a cost embedding technique and optimum modularity. This method was proposed for dynamic networks and as social network is a type of dynamic network, this algorithm can be effectively implemented on social network data for community analysis.

e. **Multi-objective Evolutionary Clustering:** In dynamic social networks deciding the number of clusters in advance is not possible as the network keeps on changing with time and it is also very difficult to determine the number of clusters during the evolutionary process when there are multiple criteria for selection. This is where multi-objective evolutionary clustering can be used. Kim et al. (2010) have proposed this method for dynamic social networks which is based on the approximation of pareto front where by multiple objectives can be achieved.

2. **Incremental Clustering:** Incremental clustering is based on the change stream model by which the dynamics of social networks are captured with every small change in the network. In this type of clustering, every change in the network with node addition, deletion, swapping of nodes or links is tracked. Incremental clustering removes the problem of setting up of time intervals as in evolutionary clustering methods. An important property of this type of clustering is that it tracks the changes in a network in a sequential manner and captures every minute detail and so it discovers a lot of interesting information and details about the social network. Some of the variants of incremental clustering are discussed below:

   a. **Incremental DENGRAPH Clustering:** Falkowski et al. (2008) have proposed the DENGRAPH, an incremental clustering algorithm which is based on incremental DBSCAN algorithm. DENGRAPH is a density based algorithm which is used to deal with noisy and evolving network data. In this type of clustering, the updates in the network are done based on edge changes from one interval to other. These changes may include creation of a new cluster, removal of an existing cluster, and absorption of a new node, reduction of a node, merging of two or more clusters and splitting of clusters in to two or more. This type of clustering is an efficient procedure for large networks which can handle high proportion of noisy data and frequent updates with time.

   b. **Incremental k-clique Clustering:** Duan et al. (2011) have proposed an algorithm based on k-clique clustering which incrementally updates the changes in a social network and also removes the parameter setting problem which the evolutionary clustering faces. K-clique clustering allows multiple cluster membership for nodes in which a member can be a part of more than one cluster which is an important aspect of social networks. K-clique clustering provides consistent clusters and the value of k maintains the certainty in the clustering process. The incremental k-clique algorithm outperforms the incremental spectral clustering algorithms in terms of efficiency and time complexity. The incremental k-clique clustering algorithm is based on local DFS forest updating technique. This algorithm captures all the evolving details of the clusters which the snapshot based models miss.

Our framework is based on these dynamic clustering techniques for social network analysis as dynamic clustering tracks the social network data very effectively and all these techniques are specifically used for community analysis and detection, which is the major task of social network analysis. Community analysis provides a better view of the social networks on the whole as well as all the important information which would be required and will act as the deciding factor for application of the various anonymization techniques. The next section forms the basis for the selection of the dynamic technique based on the parameters that are helpful in evaluation and selection of the technique.

Selection of Dynamic Approach for Analysis

This stage of the framework marks the selection of the appropriate dynamic approach for community analysis based on the various parameters that define the nature and evolving details of the network.

Incremental techniques track every change in the network and can be considered better where every minute change is critical whereas evolutionary techniques would be more apt where the network does not change very frequently. The selection amongst these two will be based on the nature and evolution of the network. Various parameters are identified by the authors which forms the basis for the selection of the suitable dynamic approach for analysis.

Following are the various parameters that can be used for the selection of the dynamic clustering techniques:

1. **Snapshot Quality:** Snapshot Quality parameter captures the evolving details of the cluster. It measures how well the cluster is represented at a particular timestamp.
2. **History Quality:** The history quality parameter defines how well the cluster at the current timestamp drifts from the cluster at a previous timestamp.
3. **Parameter/Interval Setting:** Interval setting can be defined as a measure which specifies the time intervals at which the clustering time window is divided. It defines the division of the time window into predefined time slices.
4. **Noise Handling:** The nodes that are not members of any community in a network are known as noisy data. Noisy data basically represents the links among the nodes that seem to be part of the community but in actual are the expedient ones. Consistent clustering provides greater robustness against noisy data as the consistent clustering takes in to account the previous clustering results.
5. **Scalability:** Scalability is the measure that defines the ability of the dynamic approach to handle large amount of high dimensional data. Social network data usually contains high dimensional and large amounts of data, so scalability parameter will include how effectively the dynamic approach is able to handle what amount or number of communities with time. This is one of the important parameters that cannot be ignored.
6. **Cluster Consistency:** Consistency is one of the significant parameters for selection because if the cluster at one stage is not familiar with the cluster at a previous stage then the stability of the social network is hampered considerably.
7. **Evolution Details:** Evolution Details is another parameter which can be considered as a deciding factor while selection of the dynamic approach for analysis. It includes important evolution details about the network like smoothing property that presents smooth transitions of the views of the evolving network. This parameter will also check that whether any technique misses out any evolution detail which is important for selection of the technique.
8. **Efficiency:** Efficiency is one parameter which checks for the running time of the algo-

rithms that are used for dynamic clustering. This parameter measures the performance of the algorithm in terms of time and space complexity.

9. **Accuracy:** Accuracy is a parameter which is based on the clustering result of the algorithm. The clustering algorithm is considered to be accurate if the updated clustering results are consistent with the static ones and if the algorithm maintains a balance between the temporal noise and drift.

Based on all the above mentioned parameters, a dynamic clustering technique is selected for community analysis of the social network data. These parameters form the base for the selection of the appropriate approach.

Mapping of Clustering Results with Social Network Analysis Metrics for Network Security

In this stage, the clustering results are mapped with the social network analysis metrics, based on which the important critical and sensitive information about the network is derived which will form a base for application of the anonymization technique. Results of this stage will provide all the critical information from security point of view, which needs to be considered by the anonymization techniques in accordance with the various privacy parameters, discussed in the next section.

Clustering results in creations of subgroups, each having at least one node which is highly sensitive or defines the network. Such nodes if removed during anonymization can distort the network structure reducing the end utility of the data set. At the same time these subgroups also give us an indication of such nodes which can be good candidates for replacement/removal in the anonymization technique. Certain isolated nodes as clusters can also be removed if classified as noise/outliers. There are different attributes of a node that can be effectively measured from cluster analysis. Some of these metrics include centrality measures, clustering coefficients, Hubbles and Katz cohesion, reciprocity measures, Bonacich Power.

Centrality measures provide information about nodes and links which are central to the network like nodes with high degree have more connections with respect to others and can be vital for propagation of information to the entire network, nodes with high betweenness value are sensitive to the network structure, as they are considered to be the brokers, nodes with high closeness value are more central to the network and is based on the distance of a node to all other nodes in the network. Eigen vector on the other hand also finds the nodes that are central to the network, but they identify actors globally and not locally as in case of closeness measure.

Hubbell and Katz cohesion is another measure which defines the strength of the connection between the nodes. Every connection in the network is assigned a weight according to its length, which determines the strong and weak connections in the network. This information is very vital from security point of view, as strong and weak connections should be preserved in accordance with the privacy and utility of the network.

Bonacich power is a measure that identifies powerful nodes which are not only based on the direct connections but more importantly the connections of the neighbourhood nodes that an actor has. High value of this measure provides nodes which are not only central but are also powerful in the network and act as the one on which the other node rely for connections. So while anonymization, if such nodes are removed from the network then this might lead to structural information loss and might also distort the entire network.

Clustering Coefficient measure defines the probability that a neighbourhood of the node knows each other. This measure can also be used to indicate the association and disassociation of nodes or groups. Higher value of clustering coefficient will indicate strong connections amongst the neighbours of the node such that the nodes have multiple paths for connectivity and do not solely rely on one node, whereas smaller values will indicate that the neighbours of the node will have high dependency on that node and while anonymization, such nodes if removed can completely isolate those nodes from the network that were solely relying on the removed node.

Reciprocity measure defines the connectedness of the nodes. If two nodes equally and frequently respond to each other than such nodes will have high values of reciprocity and higher value will define strong interactions among them, which is vital information about the nodes stating their activeness, closeness and chances of sharing important information amongst them. Therefore such nodes having high value of reciprocity should be considered sensitive from adversary's point of view and should be considered for anonymization.

All this information is derived cluster wise which makes the analysis easy and efficiently identifies sensitive nodes and relationships that are present in the cluster which in turn affects the entire network. For maintaining the security of the network all this information should be considered prior to the application of anonymization technique.

Evaluating the Network on Security Parameters

This stage of the framework includes the security requirements of the social network data, which defines the various security parameters that the authors have identified in their previous works also. These parameters mark the basis of selection of the anonymization techniques. Before the selection of anonymization technique, it is necessary to understand how well the analysis technique will map with the security parameters which are not considered by the various anonymization techniques and is one of the major issues which lead to inference and other identification attacks on social networks.

This part of the framework discusses the security requirements and evaluates the sensitive information obtained from the cluster analysis in context with the privacy parameters. It identifies and maps the critical and sensitive information of the network according to the security requirements. The security requirements rely on the privacy parameters which revolve around the notion of privacy. The notion of privacy in social network relies on three major things: the level of privacy, utility of the released social network data and the background knowledge that is possessed by an adversary. It has been stated by researchers that a balance needs to be maintained between the privacy and utility of data, but we feel that this factor should not be the sole basis on which the anonymization techniques are applied. In our previous works we have identified various privacy parameters that would help in determining which among the available anonymization technique fulfils the privacy requirements. Following are the various parameters that were identified by us (Gupta et al., 2011):

1. **Level of privacy:** The level of privacy varies from situation to situation due to the evolving nature of social networks. The privacy level is based on factors like entity or node privacy, privacy of observed and future edges and privacy of sensitive information. All these factors will help in deciding the amount of privacy to be achieved.
2. **Robustness:** Robustness defines the strength of the technique to fight against the background knowledge attacks and is based typically on the structural properties of the networks which are largely ignored. The structural properties include features like average path length, clustering coefficient, distribution of node degree, group size and density.
3. **Utility:** Utility defines how useful the social network data will be after anonymization, as anonymization leads to information loss.

This parameter measures the information loss that occurs due to anonymization and the effort user expends to re-identify information from anonymized data.

4. **Risk:** Risk includes the assessment of privacy breach which might occur due to disclosure of information. In social networks there is a large amount of data which changes dynamically and makes the social network susceptible to higher risk of privacy breach. Ying et al. (2009) have quantified two risk measures which are prior and posterior risk measure.
5. **Efficiency:** The efficiency measure relies on two metrics which are total cost metric and space and time complexity of the anonymization techniques.
6. **Scalability:** Scalability defines the capability of the anonymization technique to handle large amounts of high dimensional data.
7. **Multiple Releases:** This parameter includes the adaption of the anonymization technique to dynamic social network data due to its changing needs with time. This parameter also includes various temporal metrics which are already discussed in the previous sections. Multiple releases consist of two categories of releases which are as follows:
    a. Subsequent release of the same data where the earlier anonymized data is again published.
    b. Republication of data.

All the above mentioned privacy parameters are mapped with the sensitive information provided by the dynamic cluster analysis approach. The clustering technique, when applied to social network for analysis, provides important information about the network like which nodes hold strong position in the network and have maximum or minimum links. It tells about the sensitive relationships and nodes, and how their evolution will affect the network. The evolution would include the dynamic changes that occur in the network upon addition, deletion or swapping of nodes and relationships. All this information is significant for the selection and application of the anonymization technique. The results provided by the clustering technique are analyzed on the security parameters and based on these results and their analysis, the selection of the anonymization technique is done.

The next section finally explains the selection and application of the anonymization technique based on the mapping and evaluation of the parameters that are used for the analysis technique and the privacy parameters.

Selection and Application of Anonymization Techniques

This stage of the framework includes the selection and application of the anonymization technique based on the community/cluster analysis which provides all the important structural and sensitive information which the anonymization techniques usually miss out on owing to lack of analysis of the social network data.

Anonymization refers to hiding of data in such a way that an unauthorized party cannot infer anything from the published data whereas the authorized party can perform analysis on the same published data without any privacy breach.

There are basically two kinds of anonymization techniques that can be applied on social network data which are discussed below:

1. **Static anonymization techniques:** Static anonymization techniques are those techniques which anonymize the data in a static fashion and consider only static nature of social networks. These techniques are useful for networks where the social network data is to be released only once. These techniques consider only single instance of the network and apply techniques for privacy preservation of social network data. Sharma et al. (2012) have discussed in detail various static ano-

nymization techniques that are proposed so far. These techniques are mentioned below:

a. **K- Anonymity:** K-anonymity can be defined as a technique by which an individual is in distinguishable from k-1 other individuals in the released data (Sweeney, 2002). This technique was initially proposed for relational data but was later extended to social network data. There are various variants of K-anonymity on social network data like: K-candidate anonymity, k-degree anonymity, k-neighbourhood anonymity.

There are two other techniques which were derived from k-anonymity were: l- Diversity, p-sensitivity and t-closeness.

b. **Randomization:** Randomization is another type of static anonymization technique in which the nodes and edges are added, deleted and swapped according to the nature and structure of social network. Ying and Wu (2008) proposed two randomization techniques for privacy protection of social network: Random add/del technique and Random Switch Edges.

2. **Dynamic anonymization techniques:** Dynamic anonymization techniques consider the evolving nature of social network and anonymize the data dynamically. Dynamic anonymization techniques works on the problem of repeatedly publishing of anonymized data due to the dynamic nature of social networks. Bhagat (2010) has proposed work on dealing with problems of multiple releases of social networks and the major problem with dynamic anonymization is that every release of the anonymized data should be consistent with the previous releases in order to prevent the identification and other attacks. Work in the area of dynamic anonymization is still in its nascent stage as there are not many efficient techniques to handle this problem. Some of the techniques that have been proposed for dynamic anonymization are as follows:

a. k- isomorphism,
b. k- automorphism,
c. Link prediction,
d. k^w structural diversity anonymity and many more.

We see that this framework provides a necessary link between the social network analysis and the anonymization techniques to achieve better privacy of social network data

EMPIRICAL CASE STUDY

In today's realm, social networking is one of the most brewing and emerging area in social media. It has gained importance because of its widespread use for establishment of communication across boundaries without being physically present. With this, social networking has opened a big platform for business and marketing. To meet the increasing and widespread use of social networks, there has been an immense increase in the number of various social networking sites.

Considering one such social networking site where users create their profiles, become members of various groups, join communities, interact with other members, post messages, create blogs and share all sorts of information with each other. This offering is given by, what we call a service provider. The service provider of the site contains all the information about the users registered with this site. The users of this site at the time of joining it provide all the personal details to the service provider and it is the duty of the service provider to keep this sensitive information secure from any privacy breach. The service provider for earning profit may sometimes sell the user's data to third parties like advertisers, researchers and analysts. The biggest issue for the service provider is that he cannot release the user's data in its original form, as it will lead to revelation of user's sensitive data which is a threat to user's privacy. The service provider first anonymized the data by applying an anonymization technique and then released this data to the third parties.

The applied anonymization technique, however, did not provide complete security to the social network user data, as it considered only some of the background knowledge. Following are the problems that the anonymization technique faced:

1. It was unable to cover all the structural properties of the network and considered only some fixed background knowledge.
2. It was unable to meet the changing needs of the social network.
3. It was unable to handle spurious and noisy data.
4. Due to the evolving nature of the communities and groups of this social networking site, the applied anonymization technique was unable to handle this dynamic evolutionary data.
5. The applied technique considered only some of the temporal metrics for analysis which were insufficient for complete security.
6. The service provider increased the privacy level by repeatedly applying anonymization techniques in order to achieve better security, but this decreased the utility of the data considerably.
7. The anonymization technique was unable to handle the historical data, as the service provider distributed multiple releases of the social network data and the anonymization technique could not provide consistency among the different releases of data.
8. Another issue that came up with the applied anonymization technique was scalability. It was unable to handle the increasing network size of this social networking site.

All these above mentioned problems and issues led to various kinds of active and passive attacks which lead to disclosure of the user's identity, relationships and attributes. The major cause of these privacy issues with the anonymization technique was lack of proper analysis of the networking site's data before applying anonymization.

Our proposed framework resolves all such privacy issues and problems by providing an in depth analysis of the social network data before applying any anonymization technique. Figure 3 explains how the framework can be applied on this site's network data. There are various kinds of users that are registered with this site like creators, collectors, critics, spectators, joiners and inactives. Privacy settings for all users are by default set to private. Users can change them according to their needs. There are various access control policies that can be applied by the users in the network to ensure the privacy of their content and relations. A lot of attacks occur due to user's negligence and lack of knowledge about the access policies. The attacks on network data from this angle can be handled by various access control policies and our proposed framework does consider this aspect of security but is inclined towards more grave problems that occur with the privacy of user's data about which the user is unaware and neither can he/she control it.

Our proposed framework is inclined towards the security of the user's sensitive data that lies with the service provider. The service provider gives the data to the security expert to first analyse it by using appropriate data mining techniques and then apply anonymization techniques to the data.

It was seen that the users in this networking site usually appear in groups, so community analysis is the best way for the analysis of the network on whole. It was also found that this site had dynamic

Figure 3. Application of framework through an empirical case study

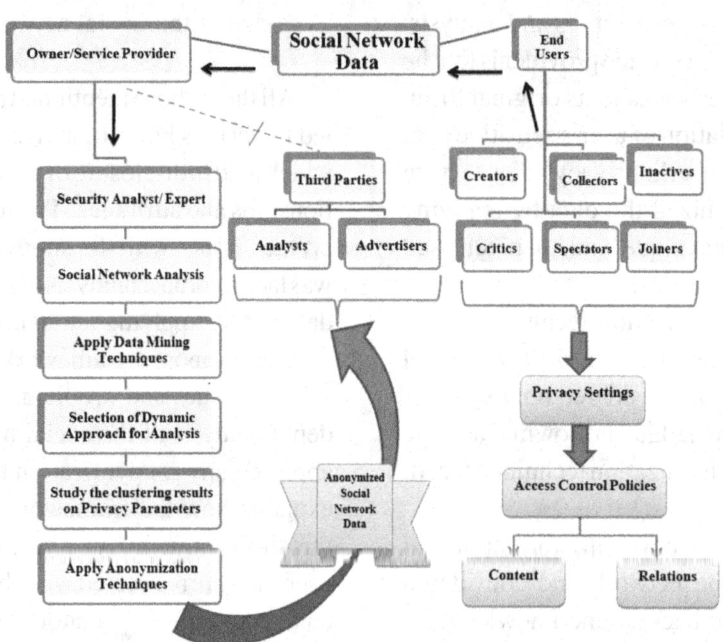

nature as there were various users who joined and left the site daily or even changed their community and group relationships. For this kind of evolving network, dynamic clustering was found to be the best technique, of which incremental clustering fits well as it tracks complete changes of the network. Every single change in the network is tracked by the clustering technique and it provides consistent results also. The incremental clustering algorithm was hence used to deal with most of the above mentioned problem of this site. This clustering technique tracked the dynamic nature of data and handled noisy data very well. The incremental clustering considers the temporal metrics of the social network data like temporal centrality, clustering coefficients and the new releases of the data matched very well with past releases and provided consistent results. The incremental approach considered all the network properties and provided crucial information about the network like strong relationships, nodes with high density, closeness and betweenness which act as the deciding factors for application of anonymization techniques. The incremental approach also matched some of the security parameters like scalability, adaption to multiple releases and provided critical structural information. Based on this information the selection of appropriate anonymization technique can be made which can then meet the remaining security parameters very well and will provide better security and will also eliminate the use of repeated anonymization.

Social network analysis provides important information about the structure of the social network which forms the basis of the application of the anonymization technique. To explain the use of social network analysis, we have used a small network consisting about 12 nodes and have analysed it using a social network analysis tool: UCINET 6 with Net Draw. Social network may contain any number of nodes and therefore it can be applied to larger datasets and accordingly can be analysed based on the clustering results. We have taken a smaller network to show better understanding of our framework and larger network will not affect our proposed framework.

UCINET matrix spread sheet editor was used to design the network matrix as shown in Figure 4 and net draw used to design the graph network shown in Figure 5.

This network is analysed for various social network metrics like centrality measures which includes measures like degree, closeness, betweenness and Eigen vectors, Hubbles and Katz cohesion, Bonacich power, reciprocity, information centrality and clustering coefficients. Table 1 and Table 2 provide values of all the above mentioned metrics for our sample network.

After we have obtained all these values, a clustering algorithm based on tabu search is applied, which performs clustering based on the correlation measure. Clustering is done based on the similarity matrix, where similarity among nodes is found based on all the above mentioned

Figure 4. Matrix representation of the network

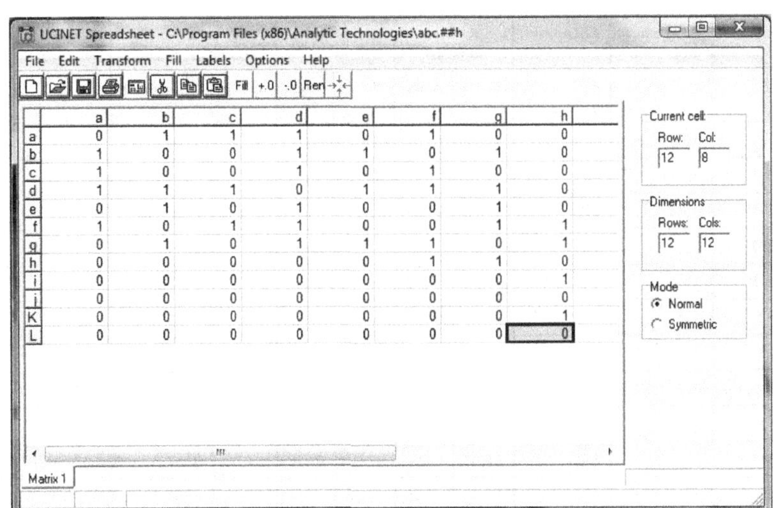

	a	b	c	d	e	f	g	h
a	0	1	1	1	0	1	0	0
b	1	0	0	1	1	0	1	0
c	1	0	0	1	0	1	0	0
d	1	1	1	0	1	1	1	0
e	0	1	0	1	0	0	1	0
f	1	0	1	1	0	0	1	1
g	0	1	0	1	1	1	0	1
h	0	0	0	0	0	1	1	0
i	0	0	0	0	0	0	0	1
j	0	0	0	0	0	0	0	0
K	0	0	0	0	0	0	0	1
L	0	0	0	0	0	0	0	0

Figure 5. Graphical representation of a sample network

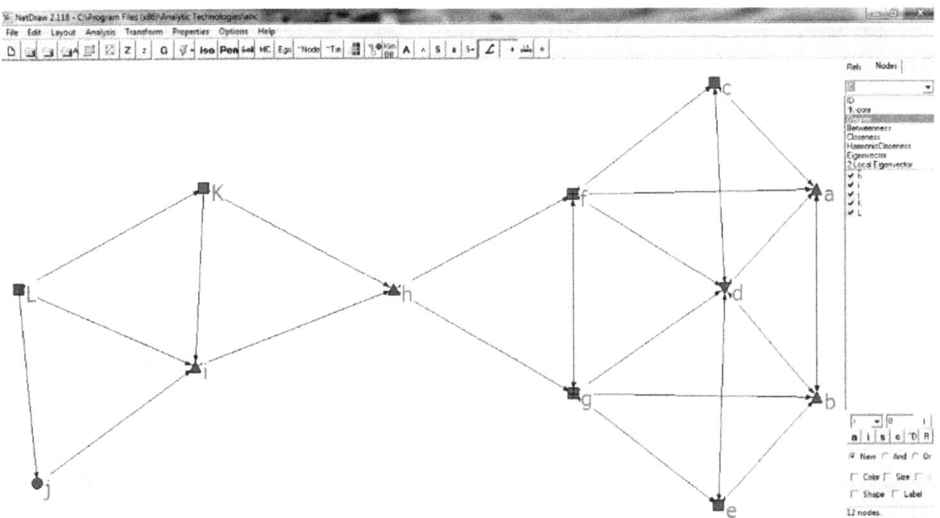

analysis metrics. In Figure 6 we can see the clustering results which have predicted 4 clusters for our sample network. The first cluster includes nodes h, i and j, the second cluster includes nodes k and l, the third cluster has a, c, d and f nodes and finally the fourth cluster includes nodes b, e and g. Now, according to these clusters, we find the nodes which have high values of all the analysis metrics and low values for the clustering coefficient measure. As already discussed in previous sections, how high and low values of these measures provide us information about nodes, links and their attributes that could be sensitive and critical for privacy of social networks. Now examining the results, we can see that in first cluster out of the 3 nodes node h has the higher value of centrality measures, power, reciprocity, Hubbles and Katz cohesion, information central-

Table 1. Values of social network analysis metrics

S.No	Node	Degree	Closeness	Betweenness	Eigenvector	Hubbles Influence		Katz Influence		Bonacich Power		Reciprocity	Information Centrality	Clustering Coefficient
						RowS	ColS	RowS	ColS	Power	Normalized Value			
1	a	0.333	0.531	0.031	0.35	1.107	1.107	0.107	0.107	4	1.069	1	1.146	0.667
2	b	0.333	0.531	0.031	0.35	1.107	1.107	0.107	0.107	4	1.069	1	1.146	0.667
3	c	0.25	0.515	0.016	0.284	1.081	1.081	0.081	0.081	3	0.802	1	1.048	1
4	d	0.5	0.567	0.091	0.477	1.158	1.158	0.158	0.158	6	1.604	1	1.284	0.533
5	e	0.25	0.515	0.016	0.284	1.081	1.081	0.081	0.081	3	0.802	1	1.048	1
6	f	0.417	0.63	0.157	0.399	1.132	1.133	0.132	0.133	5	1.336	1	1.336	0.5
7	g	0.417	0.63	0.157	0.399	1.132	1.133	0.132	0.133	5	1.336	1	1.336	0.5
8	h	0.25	0.63	0.22	0.2	1.079	1.105	0.079	0.105	3	0.802	0.75	1.356	0.25
9	i	0.167	0.5	0.074	0.054	1.05	1.1	0.05	0.1	2	0.535	0.5	0.993	0.333
10	j	0.083	0.415	0	0.017	1.025	1.051	0.025	0.051	1	0.267	0.5	0.712	0.5
11	K	0.25	0.548	0.139	0.07	1.076	1.024	0.076	0.024	3	0.802	0.333	0.963	0.5
12	L	0.25	0.447	0.121	0.022	1.075	1.024	0.075	0.024	3	0.802	0.333	0.83	0.5

Table 2. Values of centrality measures

S.No	Node	Flow Betweenness	nFlow Betweenness	In Degree	Out Degree	NrmOutDegree	NrmInDegree	inCloseness	outCloseness	Betweenness	nBetweenness
1	A	23.633	21.485	4	4	36.364	36.364	45.833	26.829	42	38.182
2	B	5.633	5.121	4	4	36.364	36.364	45.833	26.829	21.667	19.697
3	C	2.8	2.545	3	3	27.273	27.273	44	26.19	21.667	19.697
4	d	9.3	8.455	6	6	54.545	54.545	50	28.205	20.5	18.636
5	e	2.8	2.545	3	3	27.273	27.273	44	26.19	7.333	6.667
6	f	15.633	14.212	5	5	45.455	45.455	57.895	28.947	4	3.636
7	g	15.633	14.212	5	5	45.455	45.455	57.895	28.947	1.667	1.515
8	h	47.2	42.909	3	4	27.273	36.364	61.111	28.205	1.667	1.515
9	i	22	20	2	4	18.182	36.364	47.826	24.444	0.5	0.455
10	j	0	0	1	2	9.091	18.182	34.375	20.755	0	0
11	K	0	0	3	1	27.273	9.091	9.091	45.833	0	0
12	L	0	0	3	1	27.273	9.091	9.091	35.484	0	0

ity and lowest value of clustering coefficient. From this we can derive that node h is very central and critical for this cluster and should be taken in to account before applying any anonymization technique. It should be noted that removal of such a node will affect the network and accordingly it should be seen that how this node has to be anonymized without disturbing the structural properties of the network and still maintaining the desired level of privacy and utility.

In the second cluster, there are two nodes k and l and it can be seen that they do not have very high values of the analysis metrics and at the same time have same values. From this we can derive that these nodes are not very active in the network and can be anonymized directly. In the third cluster of nodes a, c, d and f, it can be seen that node d has high value of degree centrality, eigen vectors based centrality and Bonacich power, and node f has high values of closeness, betweenness, Hubbles and Katz influence, information centrality and low value of clustering coefficient. So nodes d and f are the critical ones where both being the central actor of the network and node f is being more powerful in the structure. Therefore while anonymizing it is important to note that how these nodes affect the network upon removal and the strength of the relationships that they have, might also get affected drastically. In the fourth cluster it was found that node g has higher value of all the analysis metrics and therefore is sensitive and holds strong position in the network.

It has been seen that clustering results provide important information that can be used for identification of important and critical nodes and relationships in the network and based on these measures, anonymization techniques can be applied to provide better privacy. Another important aspect is to analyse the network at different time stamps and to see how the network evolves and to evaluate the differences in results at each timestamp. The clustering results at each time stamp should be consistent with the previous results so that when anonymization technique is applied and the data is released it is also consistent with the previously released data. It has been seen that major cause of security breach is due to the multiple releases of the anonymized data which is studied by the adversary to re-identify the data by linking the data from previous releases. Dynamic clustering techniques are therefore very efficient in this kind of scenario, where the dynamicity of the data is considered on all possible parameter, which we have already discussed in our previous sections.

We finally conclude from our analysis that the various metrics provided by social network analysis are very critical from security point of view and should be considered before applying any anonymization technique. These metrics will serve as the selection criteria for the most appropriate anonymization technique.

RESEARCH IMPLICATIONS

Our extensive study in the area of securing social network data before its release led us to understand the issues that arise in privacy preservation of social networks and the need of anonymization in social network data. Most of the anonymization techniques fail to cater the changing needs and the desired privacy level in social networks. It was found that the major reason for this incompetence of techniques is due to the lack of proper analysis of social network. Our proposed conceptual framework provides the use of proper dynamics of social network analysis before application of anonymization techniques. Social network analysis provides all the useful and required information about the network beforehand so as to understand the network structures and their evolution, in order to provide a proper base for selection of the anonymization techniques. This study will help the researchers to gain better understanding of the role of social network analysis in securing social network data and will provide a prospective direction for future research. The researchers who are already working in this direction will be benefited from our work and will get a good comprehensive base to work in the field of social network security.

ADVANTAGES OF THE FRAMEWORK

Every research work has some pros and cons. The proposed conceptual framework will provide better security of the released social network data. Below are some of the projected advantages of the framework:

1. The framework will cater to the need of development of a sound base for the application of the anonymization technique by performing social network analysis in the initial phase itself.
2. The framework handles the most important issue of social network and that is its temporal evolution that most anonymization techniques fail to cover.
3. Our framework projects the use of social network analysis from the security point of view and thus the analysis technique will track all the important structural properties of the social network.
4. Use of dynamic clustering, a data mining technique for analysis will handle large and multidimensional data and will understand the complexities of the network very well.

LIMITATION OF THE FRAMEWORK

Although the proposed framework provides some decent advantages and works towards achieving better privacy conforming to the utility of released data, but contains some limitations that need to be addressed.

1. The framework induces the use of social network analysis in the initial phase which is

Figure 6. Clustering results

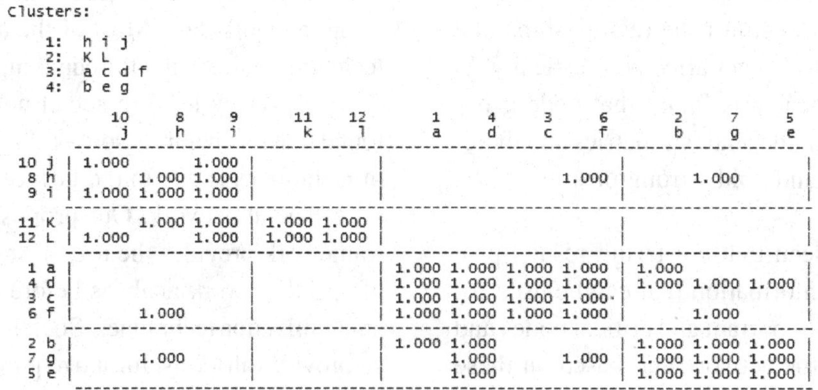

```
Clusters:

   1:  h i j
   2:  K L
   3:  a c d f
   4:  b e g

        10     8     9      11    12       1     4     3     6       2     7     5
         j     h     i       k     l       a     d     c     f       b     g     e
      ------------------------------------------------------------------------------
 10 j | 1.000       1.000 |             |                         |                   |
  8 h |       1.000 1.000 |             |                   1.000 |       1.000       |
  9 i | 1.000 1.000 1.000 |             |                         |                   |
      ------------------------------------------------------------------------------
 11 K |       1.000 1.000 | 1.000 1.000 |                         |                   |
 12 L | 1.000       1.000 | 1.000 1.000 |                         |                   |
      ------------------------------------------------------------------------------
  1 a |                   |             | 1.000 1.000 1.000 1.000 | 1.000             |
  4 d |                   |             | 1.000 1.000 1.000 1.000 | 1.000 1.000 1.000 |
  3 c |                   |             | 1.000 1.000 1.000 1.000 |                   |
  6 f |       1.000       |             | 1.000 1.000 1.000 1.000 |       1.000       |
      ------------------------------------------------------------------------------
  2 b |                   |             | 1.000 1.000             | 1.000 1.000 1.000 |
  7 g |       1.000       |             |       1.000       1.000 | 1.000 1.000 1.000 |
  5 e |                   |             |       1.000             | 1.000 1.000 1.000 |
      ------------------------------------------------------------------------------


Density Table

           1     2     3     4
       ----- ----- ----- -----
   1   0.667 0.000 0.083 0.111
   2   0.667 1.000 0.000 0.000
   3   0.083 0.000 1.000 0.417
   4   0.111 0.000 0.417 1.000

Partition saved as dataset ClusterID
```

quiet extensive in it and therefore will make the entire process a bit time consuming.

2. This framework though provides a beneficial insight into this area but can be further extended and evaluated considering the real dynamic data which will be accumulated over time and forming time slice to evaluate the sensitive node for better security of the critical node.

CONCLUSION AND FUTURE WORK

The application of security techniques like anonymization on dynamic temporal networks is a challenging research problem as lots of issues arise due to the complex and changing nature of social networks. It has been seen that most of the anonymization techniques miss out important structural properties of the network which lead to security breaches. We believe that if the social networks are properly analysed before applying anonymization techniques, it would result in better privacy of the social network data. In this chapter we propose a conceptual framework to secure the social network data effectively by using data mining techniques to perform in-depth analysis of dynamic social networks, which would provide important structural information about the network, before carrying out actual anonymization process. Our framework provides a base for the selection of appropriate anonymization approach. The framework is evaluated on network data and presents various results depicting the analysis of network data and predicting critical and sensitive information about the network which, further helps in the selection of appropriate anonymization technique for social network security.

There are still some interesting works left for future research and can include:

1. Finding feasibility of collaboration of various anonymization techniques for achieving better privacy than the existing techniques.
2. Inclusion of new parameters which will add new dimension to the work which can be continued for future enhancement in the already existing algorithms.
3. The dynamic nature of the networks can be further explored to uncover hidden problems which can be overcome by the incremental or evolutionary clustering algorithms.
4. Implementation of the framework on dynamic data sets of social networks.

REFERENCES

Backstrom, L., Dwork, C., & Kleinberg, J. (2007). Wherefore art thou r3579x? Anonymized social networks, hidden patterns, and structural steganography. *International Conference on World Wide Web (WWW)*.

Backstrom, L., Huttenlocher, D., Kleinberg, J., & Lan, X. (2006). Group formation in large social networks: Membership, growth, and evolution. *KDD'06: Proceedings of the 12th ACM SIGKDD International Conference on Knowledge Discovery and Data Mining* (pp. 44-54). New York, NY.

Bhagat, S., Cormode, G., Krishnamurthy, B., & Srivastava, D. (2010). Prediction promotes privacy in dynamic social networks. In *Workshop on Online Social Networks (WOSN)*.

Bhatnagar, V., & Sharma, S. (2010). Challenges in anonymization of social network. *International Conference on Facets of Business Excellence (FOBE)* (pp. 388-396). Delhi, India.

Chakrabarti, D., Kumar, R., & Tomkins, A. (2006). Evolutionary clustering. In *Proceedings of the 12th ACM International SIGKDD Conference on Knowledge Discovery and Data Mining* (pp. 554–560).

Chi, Y., Song, X., Zhou, D., Hino, K., & Tseng, B. L. (2009). On evolutionary spectral clustering. *ACM Transactions on Knowledge Discovery from Data, 3*(4), 17:1-17:30.

Duan, D., Li, Y., Li, R., & Lu, Z. (2011). Incremental K-clique clustering in dynamic social networks. *Artificial Intelligence Review*, 1–19.

Falkowski, T., Barth, A., & Spiliopoulou, M. (2008). Studying community dynamics with an incremental graph mining algorithm. In *Proc. of the 14th Americas Conference on Information Systems (AMCIS)*. Toronto, Canada.

Gupta, G., Sharma, S., & Bhatnagar, V. (2011). Critical parameters for privacy preservation through anonymization in social networks. *International Journal of Networking and Virtual Organisation, 11*(2), 156–172. doi:10.1504/IJNVO.2012.048327.

Hanneman, A., & Riddle, M. (2005). *Introduction to social network methods*. Retrieved January 15, 2012, from http://faculty.ucr.edu/~hanneman/

Hay, M., Miklau, G., Jensen, D., Weis, P., & Srivastava, S. (2007). *Anonymizing social networks*. University of Massachusetts Technical Report.

Jamali, M., & Abolhassani, H. (2006). Different aspects of social network analysis. In *Proceedings of IEEE/WIC/ACM International Conference on Web Intelligence*. Washington, DC, USA.

Kadushin, C. (n.d.). *Introduction to social network theory*. Retrieved January 15, 2012, from http://www.communityanalytics.com/Portals/0/Resource_Library/Social%20Network%20Theory_Kadushin.pdf

Kim, K., Mckay, R., & Moon, B. R. (2010). Multiobjective evolutionary algorithms for dynamic social network clustering. In *Proceedings of the 12th annual conference on Genetic and evolutionary computation.*

Kim, M. S., & Han, J. (2009). *A particle and density based evolutionary clustering method for dynamic networks*. Lyon, France: VLDB.

Kleinberg, J. M. (2007). *Challenges in mining social network data: Processes, privacy, and paradoxes* (pp. 4–5). KDD. doi:10.1145/1281192.1281195.

Krishnamurthy, B., & Wills, C. E. (2008). Characterizing privacy in online social networks. In *Proceedings of the Workshop on Online Social Networks in conjunction with ACM SIGCOMM Conference* (pp. 37–42). ACM.

Li, C. (2007). Forrester's new social technographics report. *Forrester Research*. Retrieved January 15, 2012, from http://forrester.typepad.com/groundswell/2007/04/forresters_new_.html

Lin, Y. R., Chi, Y., Zhu, S., Sundaram, H., & Tseng, B. L. (2008). Facetnet: A framework for analyzing communities and their evolutions in dynamic networks. In *Proceeding of WWW '08 Proceedings of the 17th international conference on World Wide Web* (pp. 685-694).

Liu, K., Das, K., Grandison, T., & Kargupta, H. (2008). Privacy preserving data analysis on graphs and social networks. In *Next Generation of Data Mining* (pp. 419–437). CRC Press. doi:10.1201/9781420085877.ch21.

Liu, K., & Terzi, E. (2008). *Towards identity anonymization on graphs*. SIGMOD.

Machanavajjhala, A., Gehrke, J., Kifer, D., & Venkitasubramaniam, M. (2006). l-diversity: Privacy beyond k-anonymity. *International Conference on Data Engineering (ICDE).*

Mitra, S., Bagchi, A., & Bandyopadhaya, A. K. (2007). Design of a data model for social network applications. *Journal of Database Management, 18*(4), 51–79. doi:10.4018/jdm.2007100103.

Santoro, N., Quattrociocchi, W., Flocchini, P., Casteigts, A., & Amblard, F. (2011). *Time-varying graphs and social network analysis: Temporal indicators and metrics*. Retrieved August 1, 2011, from http://arxiv.org/abs/1102.0629

Sharma, S., Gupta, P., & Bhatnagar, V. (2012). Anonymisation in social network: A literature survey and classification. *International Journal of Social Network Mining*, *1*(1), 51–66. doi:10.1504/IJSNM.2012.045105.

Sun, X., Sun, L., & Wang, H. (2011). *Extended k-anonymity models against sensitive attribute disclosure. Presented at* (pp. 526–535). Computer Communications.

Sweeney, L. (2002). k-anonymity: A model for protecting privacy. *International Journal on Uncertainty, Fuzziness and Knowledge-based Systems*, *10*(5), 557–570. doi:10.1142/S0218488502001648.

Tang, J., Musolesi, M., Mascolo, C., & Latora, V. (2009). Temporal distance metrics for social network analysis. *WOSN*, *2009*, 31–36. doi:10.1145/1592665.1592674.

Tang, J., Musolesi, M., Mascolo, C., Latora, V., & Nicosia, V. (2010). Analysing information flows and key mediators through temporal centrality metrics. In *Proceedings of the 3rd Workshop on Social Network Systems*. ACM.

Ying, X., Pan, K., Wu, X., & Guo, L. (2009). Comparisons of randomization and k-degree anonymization schemes for privacy preserving social network publishing. *The 3rd SNA-KDD Workshop* (pp. 1–10).

Ying, X., & Wu, X. (2008). Randomizing social networks: A spectrum preserving approach. *SIAM International Conference on Data Mining (SDM)* (pp. 739–750).

Zheleva, E., & Getoor, L. (2007). Preserving the privacy of sensitive relationships in graph data. PinKDD (pp. 153–171).

Zhou, B., & Pei, J. (2008). Preserving privacy in social networks against neighborhood attacks. *IEEE 24th International Conference on Data Engineering* (pp. 506–515).

Zhou, B., & Pei, J. (2010). *The k-anonymity and l-diversity approaches for privacy preservation in social networks against neighborhood attacks. Knowledge and Information Systems*. London: Springer-Verlag.

ADDITIONAL READING

Aggarwal, C. C. (2011). *Social network data analytics*. Springer. doi:10.1007/978-1-4419-8462-3.

Aggarwal, C. C., & Yu, P. S. (2008). Privacy-preserving data mining: Models and algorithms. Advances in Database Systems, 34, 10–32. New York, NY: Springer.

Backstrom, L., & Leskovec, J. (2011). Supervised random walks: Predicting and recommending links in social networks. *WSDM 2011, Proceedings of Fourth International Conference on Web Search and Data Mining* (pp. 635–644).

Cormode, G., & Srivastava, D. (2009). Anonymized data: Generation, models, usage. *Proc. SIGMOD Conference* (pp. 1015–1018).

Folino, F., & Pizzuti, C. (2010). A multiobjective and evolutionary clustering method for dynamic networks. *International Conference on Advances in Social Networks Analysis and Mining* (pp. 256–263). IEEE.

Greene, D., Doyle, D., & Cunningham, P. (2010). *Tracking the evolution of communities in dynamic social networks. Advances in Social Networks Analysis and Mining* (pp. 176–183). Odense: ASONAM.

Gupta, M., Aggarwal, C. C., Han, J., & Sun, Y. (2011). *Evolutionary clustering and analysis of bibliographic networks* (pp. 63–70). ASONAM. doi:10.1109/ASONAM.2011.12.

Ning, H., Xu, W., Chi, Y., Gong, Y., & Huang, T. (2010). Incremental spectral clustering by efficiently updating the eigen-system. *Journal of Pattern Recognition Society*, *43*(1), 113–127. doi:10.1016/j.patcog.2009.06.001.

Saha, B., & Mitra, P. (2006). Fast incremental minimum-cutbased algorithm for graph clustering. In *Sixth IEEE International Conference on Data Mining Workshops ICDMW06* (pp. 207–211).

Zhou, B., Pei, J., & Luk, W. S. (2008). A brief survey on anonymization techniques for privacy preserving publishing of social network data. *SIGKDD Explorations*, *10*(2), 12–22. doi:10.1145/1540276.1540279.

KEY TERMS AND DEFINITIONS

Dynamic Clustering: One of the efficient data mining techniques is dynamic clustering which tracks every change in the dynamic social networks and helps in performing community analysis and community identification which is the major aspect of social network analysis.

Dynamic Social Network: Social networks are those networks which evolve with time, that is, new nodes and edges are added in the networks, some nodes leave the networks and edges and relationships keep on changing with time. This evolution of social network is known as the dynamic nature or dynamic social networks.

Evolutionary Clustering: Evolutionary clustering is a type of dynamic clustering in which the clustering at any point in time should remain faithful to current data and at the same time should not deviate much from the previous releases of data.

Incremental Clustering: Incremental clustering is based on the change stream model by which the dynamics of social networks are captured with every small change in the network. In this type of clustering every change in the network with node addition, deletion, swapping of nodes or links is tracked.

Social Network Analysis: Social network analysis is the mapping and measuring of relationships, flow of information among individuals, group, organizations or any other connected entities. One of the stimulating and major tasks of social network analysis is to develop ways of analysing communities and groups known as community analysis. Individuals in a social network usually tend to appear in groups and sub-groups and information about them can reveal important structural information and behaviour of the entire network.

Social Networks: Social Network can be defined as a collection of people that form groups or communities based on similar interests or features. In a social network structure the individuals or the members of the group are represented by nodes and the relationship among them is represented by edges that join any number of nodes together.

Chapter 5
Analyzing Twitter User-Generated Content Changes

Luca Cagliero
Politecnico di Torino, Italy

Luigi Grimaudo
Politecnico di Torino, Italy

Alessandro Fiori
Institute for Cancer Research at Candiolo, Italy

ABSTRACT

User-generated content (UGC) coming from social networks and online communities continuously grows and changes. By analyzing relevant patterns from the UGC, analysts may discover peculiar user behaviors and interests which can be used to personalize Web-oriented applications. In the last several years, the use of dynamic mining techniques has captured the interest of the research community. They are focused on analyzing the temporal evolution of most significant correlations hidden in the analyzed data. However, keeping track of all temporal data correlations relevant for user behaviors, community interests, and topic trend analysts may become a challenging task due to the sparseness of the analyzed data.

This chapter presents a novel data mining system that performs dynamic itemset mining from both the content and the contextual features of the messages posted on Twitter. Dynamic itemsets represent the evolution of data correlations over time. The framework exploits a dynamic itemset mining algorithm, named HiGen Miner, to discover relevant temporal data correlations from a stream of tweet collections. In particular, it extracts compact patterns, namely the HiGens, that represent the evolution of the most relevant itemsets over consecutive time periods at different abstraction levels. A taxonomy is used to drive the mining process and prevent the discarding of knowledge that becomes infrequent in a certain time period.

Experiments, performed on real Twitter posts, show the effectiveness and the usability of the proposed system in supporting Twitter user behavior and topic trend analysis.

DOI: 10.4018/978-1-4666-4213-3.ch005

Copyright © 2013, IGI Global. Copying or distributing in print or electronic forms without written permission of IGI Global is prohibited.

INTRODUCTION

In recent years, social networks and online communities have become a powerful source of knowledge. Social network users are used to publish and continuously update multimedia resources, posts, blogs, etc. Actions undertaken by Web users reflect their habits, personal interests, and professional skills. Hence, the analysis of the user-generated content coming from social networks has received an increasingly high attention in several application contexts. For instance, data mining techniques have already been applied to recommend personalized services and products based on social annotations (Wang et al., 2010; Shepitsen et al., 2008; Xue et al., 2009), organize and make social knowledge accessible (Kasneci et al., 2009), and perform email spamming based on social networks (Lam et al., 2007). In particular, data mining from UGC published on the popular Twitter microblogging Website has achieved promising results in the analysis of most notable user behaviors (Li, Guo, & Zhao, 2008; Mathioudakis & Koudas, 2010) and topic trends (Cheong & Lee, 2009).

Twitter user-generated content consists of a large collection of short textual messages (i.e., the tweets) posted by Web users and their contextual information (e.g., publication time and date). Since the Twitter user-generated content and contextual data continuously evolve over time, a relevant research issue is the application of data mining techniques to discover most significant pattern changes. Dynamic itemset mining (Agrawal & Psaila, 1995) entails discovering itemsets that (i) frequently occur in the analyzed data, and (ii) may change from one time period to another. The history of the main itemset quality indexes reflects the most relevant temporal data correlation changes. However, the sparseness of the analyzed data makes dynamic itemset mining from UGC a challenging task. In fact, potentially relevant itemsets discovered at a certain time period are likely to become infrequent (i.e., their support value becomes lower than a given threshold) in at least another one. Hence, the information associated with the discovered itemsets may be lost, unless lowering the support threshold and mining a huge amount of other (potentially redundant) itemsets.

This chapter presents the TwiChI (Twitter Change mIner) system that aims at supporting experts in the analysis of Twitter UGC changes targeted to user behavior and topic trend analysis. TwiChI exploits the Twitter Application Programming Interfaces (APIs) to retrieve both tweet textual contents and their contextual features (i.e., publication date, time, place). Data crawling is continuously executed using the Twitter Public stream endpoint to track the temporal evolution of the frequent itemsets occurring in the analyzed data. The retrieved data is analyzed by the proposed HiGen Miner algorithm (Cagliero, 2011), which discovers compact patterns, named the History Generalized Patterns (HiGens). HiGens represent the evolution of frequent itemsets across consecutive time periods. To avoid the discarding of rare but potentially relevant knowledge, itemsets that become infrequent in a certain time period with respect to the minimum support threshold are generalized at a higher level of abstraction by exploiting a taxonomy (i.e., a set of is-a hierarchies built on data items). A generalized version of a traditional itemset is an itemset that represents the same knowledge at a higher level of aggregation according to a given taxonomy (Agrawal & Srikant, 1995). Hence, the knowledge associated with itemsets that rarely occur at certain time periods is still maintained by replacing the low level itemset versions with their frequent generalizations with least abstraction level.

Consider, for instance, tweet messages and related contextual information (e.g., publication time, geographical location) retrieved in the period January and February 2012. The tweet collection may be partitioned into two distinct monthly time periods. Analyzing the two sub-collections, the TwiChI framework may discover the HiGens reported in Table 1. Suppose that

{(Keyword, Obama), (Place, New York City)} is the reference itemset under analysis. Since it occurs frequently in January 2012 according to the enforced minimum support threshold (i.e., a minimum frequency of occurrence in the source data), then it is reported for the corresponding time period as is. Instead, since in February 2012 the reference itemset becomes infrequent, it is generalized by exploiting an analyst-provided taxonomy. In particular, item *(Keyword, Obama)* is generalized as the corresponding government role and the corresponding high level version of the reference itemset *{(Keyword, President of USA), (Place, New York City)}* is reported. Note that by generalizing the reference itemset at a higher level of abstraction, its associated information becomes frequent with respect to the support threshold and is kept instead of the infrequent version.

Experiments, performed on real Twitter datasets show the applicability of the proposed system to real-life use-cases. For instance, the HiGen reported in Table 1 may be used to discover which Twitter message topics (e.g., politics) are more likely to be matter of contention in certain time slots. The achieved experimental results show that TwiChI is particularly suitable for supporting domain expert analysis targeted to user behavior analysis and topic trend detection. Usability and functionality of the proposed system are thoroughly evaluated in Section "Experimental results."

This Chapter is organized as follows. Section "Related works" compares our work with recent related approaches. Section "The TwiChI System" presents the architecture of the TwiChI framework and describes its main blocks. Section "Experimental validation" assesses the capability of the proposed system in supporting knowledge discovery from Twitter user-generated data. Section "Future research directions" presents future development of this work, while Section "Conclusions" draws conclusions.

RELATED WORKS

This section overviews main state-of-art approaches related to (i) generalized itemset mining, (ii) dynamic data mining, and (iii) data mining from user-generated content.

Generalized Itemset Mining

Frequent itemset mining is a widely exploratory data mining technique that allows the identification of hidden and interesting correlations among data. Introduced in the context of market basket analysis, this mining activity nowadays finds applications in a wide range of different contexts (e.g., network traffic characterization (Baldi et al., 2005), context-aware applications (Baralis et al., 2009)). However, the suitability of data mining approaches for business decisions strictly depends on the abstraction level of the analyzed data. Traditional frequent itemset mining algorithms (e.g., Apriori (Agrawal & Srikant, 1994), FP-Growth (Han, Pei, & Yin, 2000)) are sometimes not effective in mining valuable knowledge, because of the

Table 1. Example of HiGens extracted by enforcing the minsup = 10%

Timestamped Tweet Dataset	Itemset	Support (%)
$D_{Jan\ 2012}$	{(Place, New York City), (Time, 3.45 p.m.)}	20%
	{(Keyword, Obama), (Place, New York City)}	10%
$D_{Feb\ 2012}$	{(Place, New York State), (Time, from 3 to 6 p.m.)}	50%
	{(Keyword, President of USA), (Place, New York City)}	16%

excessive detail level of the mined information. In fact, to make the mining process computationally tractable a minimum support threshold is commonly enforced to select only the patterns that frequently occur in the analyzed data. Hence, rare but potentially relevant knowledge is discarded.

Generalized itemsets (Agrawal & Srikant, 1995) are patterns that represent high level correlations among data. By exploiting a taxonomy (i.e., a set of is-a hierarchies) that aggregates data items into upper level generalizations, generalized itemsets are generated by combining items belonging to different abstraction levels. Generalized itemsets may allow better supporting the expert decision process than traditional ones, because they provide a high level view of the analyzed data and also represent the knowledge covered by their low level infrequent descendants.

The first generalized association rule mining algorithm, namely Cumulate, was presented in Agrawal and Srikant (1995). It is an Apriori-based algorithm that generates generalized itemsets by considering, for each item, all its parents in the hierarchy. One step further towards a more efficient extraction process for generalized association rule mining was based on new optimization strategies (Han & Fu, 1999; Hipp et al., 1998). In Hipp et al. (1998), a faster support counting is provided by exploiting the TID intersection computation, which is common in rule mining algorithms designed for the vertical data format. Differently, in Han and Fu (1999) an optimization based on top-down hierarchy traversal and multiple-support thresholds is proposed. It aims at identifying in advance generalized itemsets that cannot be frequent by means of an Apriori-like approach. To further increase the efficiency of generalized rule mining algorithms, in Pramudiono et al. (2004) a FP-tree based algorithm is proposed, while in Sriphaew and Theeramunkong (2002) both subset-superset and parent-child relationships in the lattice of generalized itemsets are exploited to avoid generating meaningless patterns. More recently, in Baralis et al. (2010), authors propose an algorithm that performs support-driven itemset generalization, i.e., a frequent generalized itemset is extracted only if it has at least an infrequent (rare) descendant.

This work focuses on analyzing the temporal evolution of generalized itemsets mined from Twitter data. The mining algorithm integrated in TwiChI (Cagliero, 2011) extends the generalization procedure first proposed in Baralis et al. (2010) to a dynamic context. However, unlike Baralis et al. (2010), it does not extract all frequent generalizations of an infrequent low level itemset, but considers only the ones characterized by minimum abstraction level.

Dynamic Data Mining

Traditional itemset and association rule mining approaches do not take the temporal evolution of the extracted itemsets/association rules into account. Instead, dynamic data mining focuses on tracing the evolution of the main itemset and/or association rule quality indexes to figure out the most significant temporal changes.

The problem of discovering relevant changes in the history of itemsets or association rules has already been addressed by a number of previous works (Agrawal & Psaila, 1995; Baron, Spiliopoulou, & Gunther, 2003; Bottcher et al., 2007; Liu et al., 2001; Tao & Tsu, 2009; Cagliero, 2011). For instance, active data mining (Agrawal & Psaila, 1995) has been the first attempt to represent and query the history collection of the discovered association rule quality indexes. Rules are mined from datasets collected at consecutive time periods and evaluated based on well-known quality indexes (e.g., support, confidence). Then, the analyst is in charge of specifying a history pattern in a trigger which is fired when such a pattern trend is exhibiting. The history patterns are exploited to track most notable pattern index changes. More recently, other time-related data mining frameworks tailored to monitor and detect changes in rule quality measures have also been proposed (Baron et al., 2003; Bottcher et al., 2007; Tao & Tsu, 2009). For instance, in Bottcher et al. (2007), patterns are evaluated and pruned based on both subjective and objective interestingness measures, while in Baron et al. (2003) authors focus on monitoring pattern mining with a limited computational effort. To this aim, new patterns are observed as soon as they emerge, while old patterns are removed from the rule base as soon as they become extinct. Furthermore, at one time period a subset of rules is selected and monitored, while data changes that occur in subsequent periods are measured by their impact on the rules being monitored. Similarly, the work proposed in Tao and Tsu (2009) also addresses itemset change mining from time-varying data streams. Differently, in Liu et al. (2001), authors deal with rule change mining by discovering two main types of rules: (i) stable rules, i.e., rules that do not change a great deal over time and, thus, are likely to be reliable and could be trusted, and (ii) trend rules, i.e., rules that indicate some underlying systematic trends of potential interest.

Since all the above-mentioned approaches do not consider itemsets/rules at different abstraction levels, their ability in capturing relevant data correlation changes may be biased by the support threshold enforcement. In fact, some relevant trends may be discarded, because the underlying recurrences become infrequent at a certain time period. To overcome this issue, in Cagliero (2011) a dynamic itemset mining approach has recently been proposed. It discovers History Generalized Patterns, which represent a sequence of generalized itemsets extracted in consecutive time periods. Each HiGen is mainly focused on a reference itemset, whose support index values are traced in the consecutive time periods. In case an itemset becomes infrequent in a certain time period, its generalization with least abstraction level is maintained to avoid discarding potentially relevant knowledge. This chapter proposes a data mining system that discovers History Generalized Patterns from Twitter UGC and exploits them to drive the knowledge discovery process.

Data Mining from User-Generated Content

The proliferation of the UGC, posted by Web users in different data formats (e.g., posts, tags, videos), has increased the attention of the research community in developing new methods to manage and analyze this huge amount of information. The UGC coming from social networks and online communities is a powerful resource of information which can be analyzed by means of different data mining approaches. Even if the most significant research efforts have been devoted to improving the performance of recommendation and categorization systems, in the last several years the analysis and the identification of the evolution of the UGC content, user behaviors and interests have been received more and more attention by the research community. In particular, the proposed approaches are mainly addressed to (i) improve the knowledge discovery processes from online resources, (ii) discover topic trends of the news published online and (iii) understand the dynamics behind social networks and online communities.

One of the main research directions is the discovery of most relevant online community user behaviors (Benevenuto et al., 2011; Guo et al., 2009). For instance, in Benevenuto et al. (2011) common user activities (e.g., universal searches, message sending, and community creation) are discovered by means of clickstream data analysis. Differently, Guo et al. (2009) study the UGC lifetime by empirically analyzing the workloads coming from three popular knowledge-sharing online social networks, i.e., a blog system, a social bookmark sharing network, and a question answering social network.

The UGC published on social networks, such as Facebook and Twitter, can be very useful for profiling user behaviors and discovering patterns valuable for further analysis. In particular, several new approaches have been proposed to support knowledge discovery from Twitter by means of data mining techniques. For instance, TwitterMonitor (Mathioudakis & Koudas, 2010) is focused on the detection of topic trends from Twitter streams. This system first identifies and clusters the "bursty" keywords (i.e., keywords that appear in tweets at unusually high rate), and then performs contextual knowledge extraction to compose an accurate description of the identified trends. Trend patterns can also be exploited to support decision-making and recommendation processes. For instance, Cheong and Lee (2009) analyze the trend of the topics and the demographics of the sets of Twitter users who contribute towards the discussion of particular trends to support decision-making activities. Differently, Phelan et al. (2011) combine RSS news and UGC coming from microblogs into a news recommendation system. In particular, they mine Twitter message content to identify emerging topics and breaking events. The RSS stories have been ranked based on a weighted score that takes the Lucene tf-idf score of each article term and the information provided by tweets into account.

Similarly, this chapter also presents a data mining system to perform knowledge discovery from messages posted on Twitter. Unlike previous approaches it exploits both the content and the contextual information associated with Twitter posts to perform user behavior and topic trend analysis. To this aim, it extracts generalized dynamic patterns that represent the evolution of the most relevant patterns over consecutive time periods at different abstraction levels.

THE TWICHI FRAMEWORK

The TwiChI (Twitter Change mIner) is a data mining system aimed at supporting the discovery of dynamic patterns that represent the historical evolution of the most valuable correlations among textual content and publication context of messages posted on Twitter (tweets). The extracted patterns can represent the changes in user behaviors and/or topic trends. In Figure 1 the TwiChI framework architecture is shown, while the main blocks of the system are briefly described in the following.

Twitter data crawling and representation: This block aims at retrieving and preprocessing user-generated messages (tweets) posted on Twitter. Tweets are partitioned in a sequence of collections according to their publication date. For each collection, the main tweet features are modeled into two different representations: (i) a relational data schema, and (ii) a taxonomy model. The relational data schema includes both content (i.e., the message words) and contextual (e.g., the geographical location) features. The taxonomy model is composed of a set of hierarchies built over the tweet contextual and content features and is generated by a semi-automatic process. In particular, aggregation functions based on hierarchical models are exploited to aggregate values of lower level features (e.g., the GPS coordinates) into their higher level aggregations (e.g., cities and regions). Aggregation functions may be generated by exploiting either established knowledge bases (e.g., WordNet) or Extraction, Loading, and Transformation (ETL) processes.

History Generalized pattern mining: This block focuses on discovering History Generalized patterns (HiGens) from the sequence of timestamped tweet collections by exploiting the recently proposed HiGen Miner algorithm (Cagliero, 2011). HiGens represents the most signifi-

Figure 1. The TwiChI framework

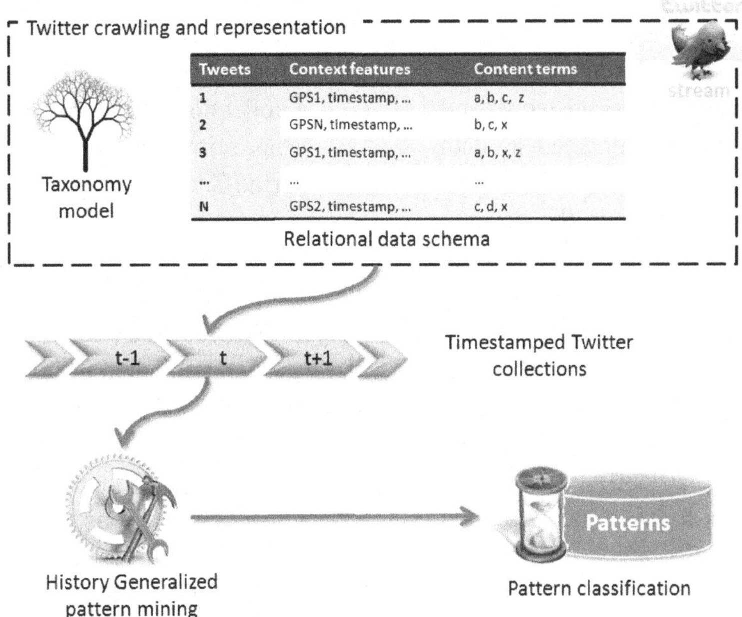

cant data correlation changes by also considering knowledge at different abstraction levels.

Pattern classification: The last block focuses on categorizing the extracted HiGens based on their main characteristics to ease the expert in-depth analysis. HiGens are classified as (i) stable HiGens, (ii) monotonous HiGens, and (iii) oscillatory HiGens, according to the time-related trend. In particular, the evolution trend of the abstraction level at which patterns are represented within each time period is considered as discriminative feature.

In the following sections, a more detailed description of the main TwiChI framework blocks is given.

Twitter Data Crawling and Representation

This block addresses the retrieval and preprocessing of the tweets posted on Twitter (http://twitter.com). User-generated tweets are at most 140 characters long and publicly visible by default. Moreover, they are enriched by several contextual features (e.g., publication location in terms of GPS coordinates, date, and hour) which are peculiar characteristics of the context in which tweets are posted. Since data retrieved by Twitter Stream APIs (Application Programming Interfaces) is not suitable for being directly analyzed by a dynamic miner, an ad-hoc crawling procedure and a preprocessing phase are needed. In the following, the data representation and the Twitter crawler of the TwiChI system are presented.

Twitter Data Representation

Given a collection of retrieved tweets, we define two different data representations which will be exploited by the subsequent TwiChI mining step: (i) a relational data schema, and (ii) a taxonomy model. In the following each data representation is better formalized.

Relational data schema: Tweets belonging to a retrieved collection are composed of the textual message and a set of contextual features (e.g. publication date, time, location). To represent tweets into a relational schema both message words and contextual feature values are modeled as data items, where an item (l_i, v_i) is a couple (attribute, value) and the value v_i belongs to the discrete domain attribute of the attribute l_i.

When coping with continuous attributes, the value range is discretized into intervals and the intervals are mapped to consecutive positive integers. Items represent either the textual message content, (e.g., text word "travel"), or a contextual feature value (e.g., Date, 2012-07-28). A tweet could be represented as a set of items, called record, as stated in the following.

Definition 1: Record. Let $L=\{l_1, l_2, \ldots, l_n\}$ be a set of attributes and $\Omega=\{\Omega_1, \Omega_2, \ldots, \Omega_n\}$ the corresponding domains. A record *r* is a set of items that contains at most one item for each attribute in *L*. Each record is characterized by a time stamp *t*.

The time stamp *t* is defined by the analyst during the crawling process and may represent the tweet publication date or time. A set of records (tweets) whose time stamps belong to a fixed time period *T* is called timestamped relational tweet collection.

Definition 2: Timestamped relational tweet collection. Let $L=\{l_1, l_2, \ldots, l_n\}$ be a set of attributes and $\Omega=\{\Omega_1, \Omega_2, \ldots, \Omega_n\}$ the corresponding domains. A relational tweet collection D_T is a collection of records, where each record *r* has a time stamp that belongs to the time period *T*.

For instance, when considering as timestamp the tweet publication date and as time period *T* = [July 1st 2012, July 31st 2012] each crawled tweet that has been published in July 2012 is included in the timestamped tweet collection relative to *T*.

To enable the dynamic mining process, tweets are organized in a sequence of timestamped relational tweet collections relative to consecutive time periods. For instance, tweets crawled in the first trimester of the year 2012 may be partitioned in a sequence of three timestamped collections, each one related to a distinct monthly time period.

Taxonomy model: Semantic relationships between attribute values belonging to a tweet collection are usually not defined in the relational data schema. To drive the generation of generalized itemsets we define a taxonomy, which is a hierarchical model that represents the is-a relationships holding between data instances (i.e., the data items) relative to the same concept (i.e., the attributes). To aggregate attribute values into higher level concepts, we introduce the notion of

Figure 2. Examples of aggregation trees

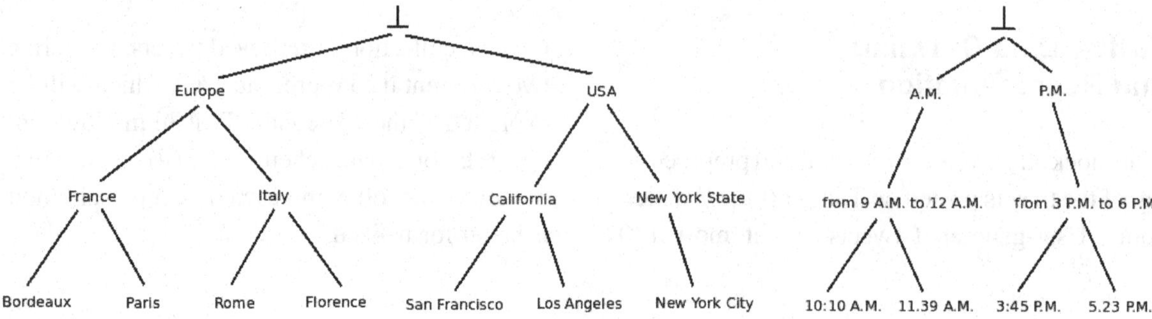

aggregation tree, i.e., an aggregation hierarchy built on the domain of one attribute of the relational tweet collection.

Definition 3: Aggregation tree. Let l_i be an attribute and Ω_i its domain. An aggregation tree A_i is a tree representing a predefined set of aggregations over values in Ω_i. A_i leaves are all the values in Ω_i. Each non-leaf node in A_i is an aggregation of all its children. The root node $\perp$ aggregates all values for attribute l_i.

Figure 2 reports two examples of aggregation trees built on the *Place* and *Time* attributes, respectively.

We define a taxonomy as a set of aggregation trees built over distinct data attributes.

Despite a taxonomy may potentially include many aggregation trees over the same attribute, for the sake of simplicity in the following we exclusively consider taxonomies that contain at most one aggregation tree $A_i \in \rho$ per attribute $l_i \in L$. Given a taxonomy Δ, we formalize the concept of generalized item as an item (l_i, e_i) such that e_i is a non-leaf node in some $A_i \in \Delta$.

Definition 4: Generalized item. Let l_i be an arbitrary attribute, Ω_i its domain, and A_i an aggregation tree built on values in Ω_i. A generalized item (l_i, e_i) assigns the value e_i to attribute l_i. e_i is a non-leaf node in A_i which defines an aggregation value over values in Ω_i. leaves(e_i) $\subseteq \Omega_i$ is the set of items whose values are leaf nodes descendant of e_i in A_i.

The support of a generalized item (l_i, e_i) in a relational tweet collection d_t is the (observed) frequency of *leaves(e_i)* in D_T.

For instance, if the words "Boots" and "Tennis Shoes" occur, respectively, in half and one third of the tweets of a collection, their supports are 50% and 33%. If "Boots" and "Tennis Shoes" are the only descendants of the common generalization "Shoes," according to a given taxonomy, the support of "Shoes" is 50%.

The two data representations are generated by the Twitter crawler described in the following, which also partitions the retrieved data into collections based on the publication timestamp.

Twitter Crawler

Twitter APIs are general-purpose tools that allow the efficient retrieval of tweets from the Web. However, tweets inherent to the submitted queries are retrieved disregarding the temporal and semantic relationships among their content. Moreover, tweets are provided in a data format which is commonly unsuitable for further analysis. For instance, the tweet geographical provenance is provided as a couple of GPS coordinates, but the related city, region, and/or state are usually missing. Furthermore, it may be not easy to differentiate between tweets published in close time periods (e.g., during the last 12 hours) from the ones that are rather far from (e.g., the tweets published the day before).

Since our system addresses the analysis of the dynamic data correlation changes that occur in the messages posted by the community, we exploit a tweet crawler that automatically collects and organizes timestamped relational tweets relative to a sequence of given time periods. To this aim, *D* is defined as the original set of tweets collections and D_T is a collection of tweets whose time stamps are contained in the time period *T*. The tweet crawler has the following parameters: (i) the sequence of time periods whereby tweets are partitioned, and (ii) a set of filtering parameters. Filtering parameters include all the parameters provided by Twitter APIs, such as the selection of keywords and the geographical radius used to select the tweets of interest from the Public stream. The crawler continuously monitors the stream and retrieves tweets according to the search parameters. At the end of a given time period, a new collection D_T is defined according to the predefined time scheduling.

Since data is retrieved in the JSON format, a preprocessing step is applied to suit tweets to the two-way data representation (see Section "Twitter data representation"). The relational data schema is generated by a data cleaning process which discards useless and redundant information and correctly manages missing values. For each tweet, the textual message is tailored to the Bag-of-Word (BOW) representation. It includes only the terms selected by a stemming algorithm. The stemming method integrated in the TwiChI system discards noisy data such as stopwords, numbers, and links. The relational data schema, composed of the set of distinct terms belonging to the BOW representation, is then enriched with the set of contextual information (e.g., GPS coordinates, publication date, Twitter username) provided by the Twitter APIs.

To build a taxonomy over the Twitter relational data distinct aggregation trees are built over each tweet feature (e.g, spatial information, and message words). To properly manage data associated with distinct attributes, the aggregation values used for generalizing low level item values are extracted by means of semi-automatic procedures called *aggregation functions*. In particular, we exploit a set of ad-hoc aggregation functions tailored to each attribute domain. To prevent discarding useful information and enrich the tweet features, the aggregation functions can exploit established semantics-based models, such as controlled vocabularies or lexical/domain-specific databases. For instance, an aggregation function that accesses a geographical database is used to define the relationship between the GPS coordinates and their corresponding region or state. Similarly, the WordNet lexical database (http://wordnet.princeton.edu) is queried to retrieve the most relevant semantic relationships holding between tweet term couples. More specifically, we focus on the hyponyms (i.e., is-a-subtype-of relationships). Terms belonging to these relationships are considered as generalizations of the original term. Consider, as an example, the term "dog" since the semantic relationship <dog> is-a-subtype-of <domestic animal> is retrievable from the WordNet database, then the term "domestic animal" is selected as the upper level generalization of the term "dog." To enrich the aggregation tree built over textual features, the database querying process is deepened to find all the possible upper level aggregations (e.g., <dog> is-a-subtype-of <animal>). If no semantics-based model is available for a given attribute, the aggregation functions may extract is-a relationship by simply parsing the corresponding attribute domain values, by exploiting an approach similar to the Extraction, Transformation and Load (ETL) processes used in data warehousing (Kimball et al., 2002). Consider, for instance, the "Date" attribute and its high level aggregation "Semester." The corresponding mapping may be simply derived by parsing the lower level "Date" domain values (e.g., 2012-07-28) and generating upper level concepts (e.g., 2nd Semester 2012) according to the corresponding aggregation function (i.e., Date → Semester). The generalization hierarchies extracted by means of the above-mentioned aggregation functions are combined in a taxonomy, which will be used to drive the dynamic generalized itemset mining process, as described in the following.

History Generalized Pattern Mining

This block aims at discovering from the collection of timestamped relational tweet collections dynamic patterns, namely the History Generalized patterns (HiGens) that represent the evolution of the most notable data correlation changes.

Correlations among the tweet content and context collected within each time period are represented in the form of *generalized itemsets*. A formal definition of generalized itemset follows.

Definition 5: (Generalized) itemset. Let L be a set of attributes, Ω the corresponding domains, and Δ a taxonomy defined on values in Ω. An itemset I is a set of items (l_k, e_k) in which each attribute $l_k \in L$ may occur at most once. A generalized itemset is an itemset that includes at least a generalized item (t_k, e_k) such that $e_k \in \Delta$.

For instance, {(Place, New York), (date, October 2010)} is a generalized itemset of length 2 (i.e., a generalized 2-itemset).

A (generalized) itemset covers a given record (tweet) with timestamp t if all its (possibly generalized) items $x \in X$ are either contained in r or ancestors of items $i \in r$ (i.e., $i \in leaves(x)$, $i \in r$). The support of a (generalized) itemset X in a timestamped relational tweet collection D_T is given by the number of tweets $r \in D_T$ covering X divided by the cardinality of D_T.

The generalization level of a (generalized) itemset is affected by the highest generalized item level according to the given taxonomy.

Definition 6: (Generalized) itemset level. Let $X=\{(l_1, e_1), \ldots, (l_k, e_k)\}$ be a (generalized) k-itemset. Its level $L[X]$ is the maximum item generalization level by considering items in X, i.e., $L[X] = max_{1 \leq j \leq k} L[(l_j, e_j)]$.

It follows that the level of a not generalized itemset is 1.

A descendant of an itemset represents part of its knowledge at a lower aggregation level.

Definition 7: (Generalized) itemset descendant/ancestor. Let Q be taxonomy. A (generalized) itemset X is a descendant of a generalized itemset Y if (i) X and Y have the same length and (ii) for each item $y \in Y$ there exists at least an item $x \in X$ that is a descendant of y with respect to Q. If X is a descendant of Y then Y is an ancestor of X.

Consider the generalized itemset {(Place, New York State), (date, from 3 to 6 p.m.)}. According to the taxonomy reported in Table 1, its level is 2 because (Place, New York) and (date, from 3 to 6 p.m.) have levels 2. Furthermore, it is an ancestor of {(Place, New York City), (date, 3.45 p.m.)}. If {(Place, New York State), (date, from 3 to 6 p.m.)} covers half of the tweets contained in the analyzed timestamped collection, its support is 50%.

The generalized itemset mining task entails discovering all itemsets (generalized and not) that satisfy a minimum support threshold *minsup*, i.e., the itemsets whose frequency of occurrence is above or equal to *minsup*. Itemsets satisfying the above constraint are said to be *frequent.*

To analyze changes in the evolution of the extracted itemsets in consecutive time periods, TwiChi discovers the dynamic patterns, namely the History Generalized patterns (HiGens), proposed in Cagliero (2011).

Definition 8: HiGen. Let $D=\{D_1, \ldots, D_n\}$ an ordered sequence of timestamped relational tweet collections, Δ a taxonomy built on D, it a not generalized itemset, named *reference itemset*, and *minsup* a minimum support threshold. A HiGen HG_{it} relative to it is an ordered sequence of generalized itemsets g_1, …, g_n such that:

- If it is frequent in $D_i \in D$ then $g_i = it$
- Else g_i is an frequent ancestor characterized by minimal generalization level with respect to Δ among the frequent ancestors of it

Each HiGen is associated with a (not generalized) reference itemset and describes its evolution, in terms of its main quality indexes, from one time period to another. Notice that, by Definition 8, each not generalized itemset may be associated with one or more HiGens. In case the considered reference itemset becomes infrequent with respect to the support threshold in a given time period, it is substituted by its generalization(s) with minimal level. Hence, the knowledge covered by the considered pattern is still maintained at a higher level of abstraction for this time period.

For instance, the HiGens, reported in Table 1, may represent the evolution of the reference itemset {(Place, New York City), (Time, 3.45 p.m.)} over two example timestamped relational tweet collections $D_{Jan\ 2012}$ and $D_{Feb\ 2012}$, retrieved in two consecutive monthly time period (January and February 2012, respectively), by enforcing a minimum support threshold equal to 20% and by exploiting the taxonomy reported in Figure 2. Since the reference itemset, which is frequent in $D_{Jan2012}$, becomes infrequent in $D_{Feb2012}$ with respect to the support threshold its frequent generalization (Place, New York State), (Time, from 3 to 6 p.m.)} is kept in place of it.

A brief description of the algorithm exploited to extract HiGens is given in the following.

The HIGEN MINER Algorithm

Given a sequence of timestamped relational tweet collections, a taxonomy, and a minimum support threshold, HiGen Miner discovers all HiGens, according to Definition 8.

To avoid extracting HiGens as a postprocessing step that follows the traditional generalized itemset mining phase, HiGen Miner exploits an Apriori-based support-driven generalized itemset mining approach in which the generalization procedure is triggered on infrequent itemsets only. The generalization process does not generate all possible ancestors of an infrequent itemset at any abstraction level, but it stops at the generalization level in which at least a frequent ancestor occurs. Furthermore, the taxonomy evaluation procedure over a pattern is postponed after its support evaluation in all timestamped collections to avoid multiple (computationally expensive) evaluations.

A pseudo-code of the HiGen MINER is reported in Algorithm 1. At an arbitrary iteration *k*, HiGen MINER performs the following three steps: (i) *k*-itemset generation from each timestamped collection in *D* (line 3), (ii) support counting and generalization of infrequent (generalized) *k*-itemsets of increasing level (lines 6-37), (iii) generation of candidate itemsets of length *k+1* by joining *k*-itemsets and infrequent candidate pruning (line 39). After being generated, frequent *k*-itemsets are included in the corresponding HiGens contained in the *HG* set (line 9), while infrequent ones are generalized by means of the taxonomy evaluation procedure (line 17). Given an infrequent itemset *c* of level *l* and a taxonomy, the taxonomy evaluation procedure generates a set of generalized itemsets of level *l+1* by applying, on each item the corresponding generalization hierarchy. All the itemsets obtained by replacing one or more items in *c* with their generalized versions of level *l+1* are generated and included into the *Gen* set (line 21). Finally, generalized itemset supports are computed by performing a dataset scan (line 26). Frequent generalizations of an infrequent candidate c, characterized by level *l+1*, are first added to the corresponding HiGen set and then removed from the *Gen* set when their lower level infrequent descendants in each time period have been fully covered (lines 27- 32). In such a way, their further generalizations at higher abstraction levels are prevented. Hence, the taxonomy evaluation over an arbitrary candidate of length *k* is postponed when the support of all candidates of length *k* and generalization level *l* in each timestamped dataset is known. The sequence of support values of an itemset that is infrequent in a given time period is store and reported provided that (i) it has at least a frequent generalization in the same time period, and (ii) it is frequent in at least one of the remaining time periods. The generalization procedure stops, at a certain level, when the *Gen* set is empty, i.e., when either the taxonomy evaluation procedure does not generate any new generalization or all the considered generalizations are frequent in each time period and, thus, have been pruned (line 30) to prevent further knowledge aggregations. The algorithm ends the mining loop when the set of candidate itemsets is empty (line 40).

Pattern Classification

Domain experts are usually in charge of analyzing the results of the data mining process to discover patterns valuable for targeted analysis. TwiChi provides to the experts a selection of dynamic generalized patterns, i.e., the HiGens, which represents potentially valuable Twitter data correlation changes. However, the amount of the discovered patterns may be large, especially when low support threshold values are enforced. Hence, a preliminary pattern classification is desirable to ease the knowledge discovery process.

TwiChi categorizes the extracted HiGens based on their time-related trend in the sequence of timestamped relational collection. In particular, to better highlight the temporal evolution of the knowledge associated with the HiGen reference itemset, HiGens are classified as: (i) stable HiGens, i.e., HiGens that include generalized itemsets belonging to the same generalization level, (ii) monotonous HiGens, i.e., HiGens that include a sequence of generalized itemsets whose generalization level shows a monotonous trend, and (iii) oscillatory HiGens, i.e., HiGens that include a sequence of generalized itemsets whose generalization level shows a variable and non-monotonous trend.

Since a generalized itemset of level l may have several generalizations of level l + 1 and taxonomies may have unbalanced data item distributions, stable HiGens are further partitioned in: (i) strongly stable HiGens, i.e., stable HiGens, in which items contained in its generalized itemsets and belonging to same data attribute, are characterized by the same generalization level, and (ii) weakly stable HiGens, i.e., stable HiGens in which items contained in its generalized itemsets and belonging to the same attribute, may be characterized by different generalization levels.

In Table 2 a HiGen example relative to each category is reported. HiGens have been extracted from an example sequence of tweet collections by enforcing a minimum support threshold equal to 20% and by exploiting the taxonomy reported in Figure 2. For each HiGen, the corresponding reference itemset is also reported. Notice that the itemsets contained in the strongly and weakly stable HiGens are all characterized by the same generalization level (i.e., 1 and 2, respectively) while for the monotonous HiGen the level of the reported itemsets increases from 1 to 3 from January to March 2012. Finally, for the oscillatory HiGen the generalization level varies with a non-monotonous trend.

Examples of HiGens mined from a real-life Twitter dataset are reported in Section "Expert validation."

EXPERIMENTAL VALIDATION

In the previous sections, we introduced and thoroughly described the TwiChI framework. To assess the effectiveness of the devised approach, in this section we report and describe a set of experiments we performed on real datasets coming from Twitter.

This section is organized as follows. Section "Evaluated datasets and taxonomy" describes the main characteristics of the analyzed datasets and the corresponding taxonomy. Section "Characteristics of the mined patterns" analyzes the characteristics of the patterns generated by TwiChi and their corresponding categories. Finally, Section "Real-life use-cases" presents two real-life use-cases of the proposed system.

All the experiments were performed on a 3.2 GHz Pentium IV system with 8 GB RAM, running Ubuntu 12.04.

Evaluated Datasets and Taxonomy

The TwiChi frameworks exploits a crawler to effectively access to Twitter's global stream of Tweet data. We monitored the *public streams* endpoint offered by the Twitter API, covering the time period from 2012-07-07 to 2012-07-23 and track-

Algorithm 1. The HiGen miner algorithm

```
Input: ordered sequence of timestamped relational tweet collection D=D_1, D_2,.., D_g, minimum support threshold minsup, taxonomy Δ
Output: set of HIGENs HG
k = 1//Candidate length
HG = HiGen set;
C_k = set of distinct k-itemsets in D
repeat
        for all c in C_k do
                scan all D_i in D and count the support of c in D_i
        end for
        L^i_k = itemsets c in C_k that satisfy minsup for any D_i
        HG = update HIGEN set(L^i_k, HG)
         l = 1//Candidate generalization level
         Gen = generalized itemset container
         repeat
                 for all c in C_k of level l do
                         D^inf_c = {D_i in D | c is infrequent in D_i}
                         if D^inf_c is empty then
                                 gen(c) = set of new generalizations of itemset c of level l+1
                                 gen(c) = taxonomy evaluation(c, Δ)
                                 for all gen in gen(c) do
                                         gen.desc = c
                                 end for
                                 Gen = Gen ∪ gen(c)
                         end if
                 end for
                 if Gen is not empty then
                         for all gen 2 Gen do
                                 scan all D_i in D^inf_gen.desc and count the support of gen in D_i
                                 for all gen frequent in any D_i in D^inf_gen.desc do
                                         HG = update HIGEN set(gen, HG)
                                         if gen is frequent in all D_i in D^inf_gen.desc then
                                                 remove gen from Gen
                                         end if
                                 end for
                         end for
```

continued on following page

Algorithm 1. Continued

```
                    C_k = C_k ∪ Gen
               end if
               l = l + 1
          until Gen is empty
          k = k + 1
          C_{k+1} = candidate_generation(C_k)
until C_k is empty
return HG
```

Table 2. HiGen examples (minsup = 20%)

Collection	Itemset	Support (%)
Strongly Stable HiGen **Reference itemset: {(Place, New York City), (Time, 3.45 p.m.)}**		
$D_{Jan\ 2012}$	{(Place, New York City), (Time, 3.45 p.m.)}	20%
$D_{Feb\ 2012}$	{(Place, New York City), (Time, 3.45 p.m.)}	50%
$D_{Mar\ 2012}$	{(Place, New York City), (Time, 3.45 p.m.)}	25%
Weakly Stable HiGen **Reference itemset: {(Place, New York City), (Time, 4.00 p.m.)}**		
$D_{Jan\ 2012}$	{(Place, New York State), (Time, from 3 to 6 p.m.)}	27%
$D_{Feb\ 2012}$	{(Place, New York City), (Time, from 3 to 6 p.m.)}	21%
$D_{Mar\ 2012}$	{(Place, New York State), (Time, from 3 to 6 p.m.)}	25%
Monotonous HiGen **Reference itemset: {(Place, New York City), (Time, 5.00 p.m.)}**		
$D_{Jan\ 2012}$	{(Place, New York City), (Time, from 5.00 p.m.)}	28%
$D_{Feb\ 2012}$	{(Place, New York City), (Time, from 3 to 6 p.m.)}	25%
$D_{Mar\ 2012}$	{(Place, New York City), (Time, p.m.)}	21%
Oscillatory HiGen **Reference itemset: {(Place, New York City), (Time, 6.00 p.m.)}**		
$D_{Jan\ 2012}$	{(Place, New York City), (Time, from 6.00 p.m.)}	20%
$D_{Feb\ 2012}$	{(Place, New York City), (Time, from 3 to 6 p.m.)}	24%
$D_{Mar\ 2012}$	{(Place, New York City), (Time, from 6.00 p.m.)}	21%

ing a selection of keywords ranging over different topics (e.g., weather, finance, sport). The crawler establishes and maintains a continuous connection with the stream endpoint to collect and store the Twitter data. As described in Section Twitter crawler, the tweets are preprocessed to represent the data into the relational data format and extract the taxonomies over content and context features.

In our crawling session, we collected 5047 tweets over 13 consecutive days in the time period [07/07/2012, 23/07/2012] posted by 708 distinct users located in 101 different GPS coordinates. To build the taxonomy model over the tweet textual content, we used the semantic generalizations of 3-levels Wordnet hyponym (i.e., is-a-subtype-of). Similarly, over the spatial attribute, a geographical hierarchy, which aggregates single locations into larger regions (province, region, state, continent) was built as well.

Since the tweets contain only the GPS coordinates from which tweet are posted, we mapped the coordinates to the nearest location (i.e., city). Finally, the twitting date and time are analyzed by the aggregation functions to derive a hierarchy over the corresponding attributes (i.e., time, day, period).

Characteristics of the Mined Patterns

TwiChi analyzes sequences of timestamped tweet collections to discover the most significant pattern changes. We analyzed the characteristics of the patterns generated by TwiChi by setting two different temporal configurations: the former configuration, denoted in the following as *Configuration A*, aggregates tweets relative to the 13 considered time periods as follows: [2012-07-07, 2012-07-12], [2012-07-13, 2012-07-17], [2012-07-18, 2012-07-23]. The latter configuration (*Configuration B*) aggregates tweets based on the following time periods: [2012-07-07, 2012-07-09], [2012-07-10, 2012-07-13], [2012-07-14, 2012-07-18], [2012-07-19, 2012-07-23].

Figure 3 reports the number of HiGens mined from the real-life collections by varying the minimum support threshold in the range [0.5%, 5%] and by setting Configurations A and B. The number of mined HiGens increases more than linearly when lowering the support threshold due to the combinatorial increase of the number of generated combinations. To have a deep insight into the achieved results, we also analyzed the per level distribution of the itemsets contained in the mined HiGens. When rather low support thresholds (e.g., 0.5%) are enforced, many HiGens (53%) exclusively contain level-1 (not generalized) itemsets representing the reference itemset in each considered time period. When increasing the support threshold, the reference itemset becomes infrequent in some time periods. Hence, it is generalized by exploiting the given taxonomy and upper level itemsets are also included in the mined HiGens. For instance, at medium support thresholds (e.g., 1%) at least two out of three HiGens contain a generalized itemset and the percentage of level-2 itemsets contained in the mined HIGens is rather high (66%). When high

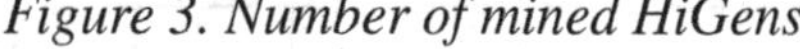

Figure 3. Number of mined HiGens

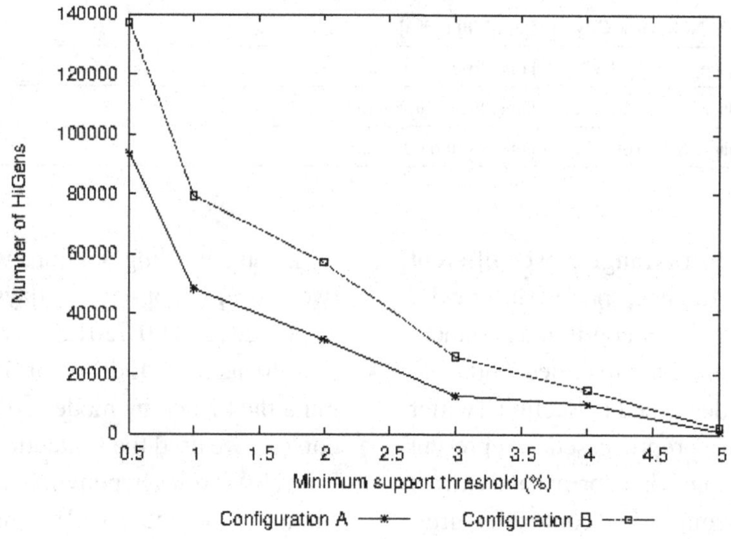

support thresholds are enforced (e.g., 5%) most of the mined HiGen (78%) exclusively contain generalized itemsets and the number of itemsets with level higher than 2 becomes significant (39%). Notice that the high level information covered by the generalized itemsets is representative of the one associated with the low level reference itemset discarded due to the support threshold enforcement.

Since TwiChi classifies the extracted dynamic patterns based on their temporal trends (see Section "Pattern classification"), we also analyzed the per category distribution of the extracted HiGens. Table 3 reports the percentages of HiGens classified as strongly stable, weakly stable, monotonous, and oscillatory mined by enforcing three different support thresholds, i.e., 0.5%, 1%, and 5%.

When low support thresholds are enforced, the majority of the extracted patterns are stable because, in many cases, the knowledge covered by the reference itemset remains frequent in all the considered time periods. Differently, when medium and large support thresholds are enforced, the number of monotonous and oscillatory HiGens increases due to the higher selectivity of the support threshold. At high support thresholds (e.g., 5%) the number of stable HiGen still slightly increases because some of the extracted HiGens contain (possibly generalized) itemsets with the same level in all the considered time periods. The percentages of extracted monotonous and oscillatory HiGens are also affected by the number of considered time periods, as comes out from the comparison between Configuration A (3 time periods) and B (4).

Real-Life Use-Case Study

In this section, we present two real use-cases for the TwiChi system targeted to user behavior and topic trend analysis. Examples of the discovered HiGens are also given.

Weather Forecasting Service Profiling

Consider an application scenario for the TwiChi system in which experts are interested in discovering peculiar user behaviors in order to shape service provisioning to the actual user interests and needs. Through the TwiChi system, analysts may automatically retrieve tweet collections posted by users coming from different cities in consecutive time periods and figure out the most relevant data correlation changes.

Consider, as an example, the real-life collections and taxonomy described in Section "Evaluated datasets and taxonomy." By setting the configuration A (see Section "Characteristics of the mined patterns") and the minimum support threshold to 1% the HiGens 1 and 2 reported in Table 3 are extracted. Users coming from Los

Table 3. HiGen per category distribution

Configuration	Minsup (%)	Number of Stable HiGens (%)			Number of Monotonous HiGens (%)	Number of Oscillatory HiGens (%)
		Weak	Strong	Total		
A	0.5%	15	41	56	18	26
	1%	23	14	37	27	36
	5%	30	11	41	24	45
B	0.5%	13	46	59	11	30
	1%	27	9	36	21	43
	5%	35	8	43	13	44

Angeles (California, USA) frequently posted weather information during the analyzed time period. Hence, they may be likely to be interested in receiving automatic weather forecasting information. Similarly, people from Philadelphia frequently posted information about daily temperatures. The information may be deemed useful for profiling weather forecasting services to actual user needs. Notice that the interest about temperature information decreases in the second and third time periods. However, the weather topic, which is a generalization of the former one, remains of interest in the considered city.

Service Shaping

Consider again the previous application scenario. Suppose that analysts are now interested in shaping the bandwidth of an online weather forecast service to improve the efficiency of the provided service. Analysts may focus on the HiGens that show a monotonous or oscillatory trend to figure out which user groups, coming from specific cities or regions, are less used to request for weather forecasts.

Consider, for instance, the HiGen 3 reported in Table 3. It turns out that the interest in the weather service in the New York State becomes rather low in the second and third time periods. In fact, the location is generalized as USA, because the correlation with the New York State remains infrequent in the considered time periods. Indeed, the discovery of the reported HiGen may prompt service bandwidth reallocation in order to optimize resource usage.

FUTURE RESEARCH DIRECTIONS

In the last years, social network analysis has attracted the attention of different research communities, including database, information retrieval, pattern recognition, and data mining. Many research efforts have significantly contributed to improve the applicability of data mining techniques to social network and online community analysis.

Table 4. HiGen selection (configuration A; minsup = 1%)

Time Period	Itemset	Support (%)
Strongly Stable HiGen 1 **Reference itemset: {(Place, Los Angeles), (Word, Rain)}**		
[07-07, 07-12]	{(Place, Los Angeles), (Word, Rain)}	1%
[07-13, 07-17]	{(Place, Los Angeles), (Word, Rain)}	1.3%
[07-18, 07-23]	{(Place, Los Angeles), (Word, Rain)}	1%
Monotonous HiGen 2 **Reference itemset: {(Place, Philadelphia), (Word, Temperature)}**		
[07-07, 07-12]	{(Place, Philadelphia), (Word, Temperature)}	1.2%
[07-13, 07-17]	{(Place, Philadelphia), (Word, Weather)}	1.6%
[07-18, 07-23]	{(Place, Philadelphia), (Word, Weather)}	1%
Monotonous HiGen 3 **Reference itemset: {(Place, New York City), (Word, Weather)}**		
[07-07, 07-12]	{(Place, New York State), (Word, Weather)}	1%
[07-13, 07-17]	{(Place, USA), (Word, Weather)}	2.1%
[07-18, 07-23]	{(Place, USA), (Word, Weather)}	1.8%

In particular, the analysis of the dynamics behind the evolution of social network data is becoming an appealing research issue. To address this issue, this chapter proposes a novel data mining system that entails generating and analyzing dynamic generalized patterns in the presence of taxonomies.

The proposed approach could be extended in a number of directions, among which (i) the automatic generation of taxonomies suitable for driving the generalization process, (ii) the pushing of user-provided constraints to reduce the amount of extracted patterns, and (iii) the application of the proposed framework to perform context-aware user profiling and shaping of social network services.

The taxonomies exploited to generalize items are usually provided by a domain expert. Since the taxonomy generation process is a complex task, automatic or semi-automatic taxonomy generation algorithms should be developed and integrated in the proposed system. Some existing techniques already addressed the inference of meaningful ontologies (Hamasaki et al., 2009; Lau et al., 2009; Cagliero et al., 2011). Their application to drive the dynamic data mining process from Twitter UGC is a promising research direction.

Although the enforcement of a minimum support threshold significantly reduces the amount of discovered patterns, in some cases the number of the mined HiGens may still remain unmanageable by domain experts. To overcome this issue, the enforcement of user-provided constraints about either the content or the schema of the discovered patterns may further reduce the cardinality of the mined set.

Finally, the discovered patterns may be also deemed suitable for performing social network service shaping. In particular, based on the context in which the user has published the UGC, the proposed system may suit service provision to the actual user needs.

CONCLUSION

This chapter presents TwiChi, a data mining system that addresses Twitter user-generated content mining targeted to user behavior and topic trend analysis. A dynamic data mining algorithm is exploited to mine patterns which represent the evolution of most significant correlations among data in consecutive time periods. To avoid discarding relevant patterns that suddenly become infrequent in a certain time period, a taxonomy is used to generalize patterns at a higher level of abstraction and represent their associated knowledge at the proper generalization level.

TwiChi performance has been evaluated on real-life Twitter datasets. The usability and functionality of the proposed system have been validated in different use cases, among which topic trend detection and user behavior analysis. The discovered HiGens have shown to be particularly suitable for supporting the experts in the analysis of the Twitter UGC, because they may be exploited to drive domain experts in performing a number of different targeted actions.

REFERENCES

Agrawal, R., & Psaila, G. (1995). *Active data mining*. In *First International Conference on Knowledge Discovery and Data Mining* (pp. 3-8). ACM press.

Agrawal, R., & Srikant, R. (1994). *Fast algorithms for mining association rules in large data-bases*. In J. B. Bocca, M. Jarke, and C. Zaniolo (Eds.), *International Conference on Very Large Data Bases* (pp. 487-499). Morgan Kaufmann.

Agrawal, R., & Srikant, R. (1995). *Mining generalized association rules*. In *International Conference on Very Large Data Bases* (pp. 407-419). Morgan Kaufmann.

Baldi, M., Baralis, E., & Risso, F. (2005). *Data mining techniques for effective and scalable traffic analysis*. In Proceedings *International Symposium on Integrated Network Management* (pp. 105-118). IEEE press.

Baralis, E., Cagliero, L., Cerquitelli, T., D'Elia, V., & Garza, P. (2010). *Support driven opportunistic aggregation for generalized itemset extraction*. In Proceedings *The 2010 IEEE Conference on Intelligent Systems* (pp. 102-107). IEEE press.

Baralis, E., Cagliero, L., Cerquitelli, T., Garza, P., & Marchetti, M. (2009). *Context-aware user and service profiling by means of generalized association rules*. In Proceedings *Conference on Knowledge and Engineering Systems* (pp. 50-57). Springer.

Baron, S., Spiliopoulou, M., & Gunther, O. (2003). Efficient monitoring of patterns in data mining environments. In Kalinichenko, L., Manthey, R., Thalheim, B., & Wloka, U. (Eds.), *Advances in Databases and Information Systems* (*Vol. 2798*, pp. 253–265). Lecture Notes in Computer Science Springer Berlin Heidelberg. doi:10.1007/978-3-540-39403-7_20.

Benevenuto, F., Rodrigues, T., Cha, M., & Almeida, V. (2011). Characterizing user navigation and interactions in online social networks. In Information Sciences.

Bottcher, M., Nauck, D., Ruta, D., & Spott, M. (2007). Towards a framework for change detection in data sets. In Bramer, M., Coenen, F., & Tuson, A. (Eds.), *Research and development in intelligent systems XXIII* (pp. 115–128). Springer London. doi:10.1007/978-1-84628-663-6_9.

Cagliero, L. (2011). Discovering temporal change patterns in the presence of taxonomies. [PrePrints] [. IEEE press.]. *IEEE Transactions on Knowledge and Data Engineering*, 99.

Cheong, M., & Lee, V. (2009). Integrating web-based intelligence retrieval and decision-making from the twitter trends knowledge base. In *Proceedings of the Second ACM Workshop on Social Web Search and Mining* (pp. 1-8). ACM press.

Guo, L., Tan, E., Chen, S., Zhang, X., & Zhao, Y. E. (2009). Analyzing patterns of user content generation in online social networks. In *Proceedings of the 15th ACM SIGKDD international conference on Knowledge discovery and data mining* (pp. 369-378).

Hamasaki, M., Matsuo, Y., Nishimura, T., & Takeda, H. (2009). Ontology extraction by collaborative tagging. In World Wide Web (pp. 427-437).

Han, J., & Fu, Y. (1999). Mining multiple-level association rules in large databases. *IEEE Transactions on Knowledge and Data Engineering*, *11*(5), 798–805. doi:10.1109/69.806937.

Han, J., Pei, J., & Yin, Y. (2000). Mining frequent patterns without candidate generation. In *Proceedings ACM-SIGMOD International Conference Management of Data* (pp. 1-12). ACM press.

Hipp, J., Myka, A., Wirth, R., & Guntzer, U. (1998). A new algorithm for faster mining of generalized rules. In *Proceedings of the 2nd European Symposium on Principles of Data Mining and Knowledge Discovery* (pp. 72–82).

Kasneci, G., Ramanath, M., Suchanek, F., & Weikum, G. (2009). The YAGO-NAGA approach to knowledge discovery. [ACM press.]. *SIGMOD Record*, *37*(4), 41–47. doi:10.1145/1519103.1519110.

Kimball, R., Ross, M., & Merz, R. (2002). *The data warehouse toolkit: The complete guide to dimensional modeling*. Wiley.

Lam, H. Y., & Yeung, D. Y. (2007). A learning approach to spam detection based on social networks. In *Proceedings of the Fourth Conference on Email and Anti-Spam* (pp. 81-94). AIDAA.

Lau, R. Y. K., Song, D., Li, Y., Cheung, T. C. H., & Hao, J. (2009). Toward a fuzzy domain ontology extraction method for adaptive e-learning. *IEEE Transactions on Knowledge and Data Engineering*, *21*(6), 800–813. doi:10.1109/TKDE.2008.137.

Li, X., Guo, L., & Zhao, Y. E. (2008). Tag-based social interest discovery. In *Proceeding of the 17th international conference on World Wide Web* (pp. 675-684). ACM press.

Liu, B., Ma, Y., & Lee, R. (2001). Analyzing the interestingness of association rules from the temporal dimension. Proceeding of the International Conference on Data Mining (pp. 377-384). IEEE press.

Mathioudakis, M., & Koudas, N. (2010). TwitterMonitor: Trend detection over the twitter stream. In *Proceedings of the 2010 International conference on Management of data* (pp. 1155-1158). ACM press.

Phelan, O., McCarthy, K., Bennett, M., & Smyth, B. (2011). Terms of a feather: Content-based news recommendation and discovery using Twitter. In Advances in Information Retrieval (pp. 448-59).

Pramudiono, I., & Kitsuregawa, M. (2004). FP-tax: Tree structure based generalized association rule mining. In *Proceedings ACM SIGMOD workshop on Research issues in data mining and knowledge discovery* (pp. 60-63). ACM press.

Shepitsen, A., Gemmell, J., Mobasher, B., & Burke, R. (2008). Personalized recommendation in social tagging systems using hierarchical clustering. In *Proceedings of the ACM Conference on Recommender Systems* (pp. 259-266). ACM press.

Sriphaew, K., & Theeramunkong, T. (2002). A new method for finding generalized frequent itemsets in association rule mining. In *Proceedings of the VII International Symposium on Computers and Communications* (pp. 20-26). ACM press.

Tao, Y., & Tsu, M. (2009). Mining frequent itemsets in time-varying data streams. In *Proceedings of the XVIII Conference on Information and Knowledge Management* (pp. 1521-1524). ACM press.

Wang, J., Li, Q., Chen, Y. P., & Lin, Z. (2010). User comments for news recommendation in forum-based social media. In *Information Sciences* (pp. 4929–4939). Elsevier.

Xue, Y., Zhang, C., Zhou, C., Lin, X., & Lin, Q. (2009). An effective news recommendation in social media based on users' preference. In *International Workshop on Education Technology and Training* (pp. 627-631). IEEE Computer Society.

ADDITIONAL READING

Cagliero, L., & Fiori, A. (2011). Knowledge discovery from online communities. In Social Networking and Community Behavior Modeling: Qualitative and Quantitative Measures, 123.

Cerquitelli, T., Fiori, A., & Grand, A. (2011). *Community-contributed media collections: Knowledge at our fingertips*, 21.

Cheng, J., Ke, Y., & Ng, W. (2008). A survey on algorithms for mining frequent itemsets over data streams. *Knowledge and Information Systems*, *16*(1), 1–27. doi:10.1007/s10115-007-0092-4.

Cunha, E., Magno, G., Comarela, G., Almeida, V., Gonçalves, M. A., & Benevenuto, F. (2011). Analyzing the dynamic evolution of hashtags on Twitter: A language-based approach. *ACL HLT*, *2011*, 58.

Eisenstein, J., O'Connor, B., Smith, N. A., & Xing, E. P. (2010). A latent variable model for geographic lexical variation. *Proceedings of the 2010 Conference on Empirical Methods in Natural Language Processing*, 1277-1287.

Han, J. (2009). Data mining. In Liu, L., & Tamer, M. (Eds.), *Encyclopedia of Database Systems* (pp. 595–598). Springer.

Ienco, D., & Meo, M. (2008). Towards the automatic construction of conceptual taxonomies. In *Proceedings of the 10th international conference on Data Warehousing and Knowledge Discovery* (pp. 327-336). Springer-Verlag.

Java, A., Song, X., Finin, T., & Tseng, B. (2007). Why we Twitter: Understanding microblogging usage and communities. *Proceedings of the 9th WebKDD and 1st SNA-KDD 2007 workshop on Web mining and social network analysis* (pp. 56-65).

Jiang, N., & Gruenwald, L. (2006). CFI-Stream: Mining closed frequent itemsets in data streams. *Proceedings of the 12th ACM SIGKDD international conference on Knowledge discovery and data mining* (pp. 592-597).

Kwak, H., Lee, C., Park, H., & Moon, S. (2010). What is Twitter, a social network or a news media? *Proceedings of the 19th international conference on World wide web* (pp. 591-600).

Lee, C., Kwak, H., Park, H., & Moon, S. (2010). Finding influentials based on the temporal order of information adoption in Twitter. *Proceedings of the 19th international conference on World wide web* (pp. 1137-1138).

Lee, C. H., Wu, C. H., Yang, H. C., & Wen, W. S. (2012). *Computing event relatedness based on a novel evaluation of social-media streams* (pp. 697–707). Future Information Technology, Application, and Service. doi:10.1007/978-94-007-4516-2_74.

Li, H. F., Huang, H. Y., & Lee, S. Y. (2011). Fast and memory efficient mining of high-utility itemsets from data streams: With and without negative item profits. *Knowledge and Information Systems, 28*(3), 495–522. doi:10.1007/s10115-010-0330-z.

Li, H. F., & Lee, S. Y. (2009). Mining frequent itemsets over data streams using efficient window sliding techniques. *Expert Systems with Applications, 36*(2), 1466–1477. doi:10.1016/j.eswa.2007.11.061.

Manerikar, N., & Palpanas, T. (2009). Frequent items in streaming data: An experimental evaluation of the state-of-the-art. *Data & Knowledge Engineering, 68*(4), 415–430. doi:10.1016/j.datak.2008.11.001.

Mislove, A., Marcon, M., Gummadi, K. P., Druschel, P., & Bhattacharjee, B. (2007). Measurement and analysis of online social networks. *Proceedings of the 7th ACM SIGCOMM conference on Internet measurement* (pp. 29-42).

Neshati, M., & Hassanabadi, L. S. (2007). Taxonomy construction using compound similarity measures. In *Proceedings of the 2007 OTM Confederated international conference on the move to meaningful internet systems* (pp. 915-932). Springer-Verlag.

Qamra, A., Tseng, B., & Chang, E. Y. (2006). Mining blog stories using community-based and temporal clustering. *Proceedings of the 15th ACM international conference on Information and knowledge management* (pp. 58-67).

Rodrigues Barbosa, G. A., Silva, I. S., & Zaki, M. Meira Jr., W., Prates, R.O., & Veloso, A. (2012). Characterizing the effectiveness of Twitter hashtags to detect and track online population sentiment. *Proceedings of the 2012 ACM annual conference extended abstracts on Human Factors in Computing Systems Extended Abstracts* (pp. 2621-2626).

Sakaki, T., Okazaki, M., & Matsuo, Y. (2010). Earthquake shakes Twitter users: Real-time event detection by social sensors. *Proceedings of the 19th international conference on World wide web* (pp. 851-860).

Tan, P., Kumar, V., & Srivastava, J. (2002). Selecting the right interestingness measure for association patterns. In *Proceedings ACM SIGMOD International Conference on Knowledge Discovery and Data Mining* (pp. 32-41). ACM press.

Tanbeer, S., Ahmed, C., & Jeong, B. S. (2010). *Mining regular patterns in data streams* (pp. 399–413). Database Systems for Advanced Applications.

Wang, E. T., & Chen, A. L. P. (2011). Mining frequent itemsets over distributed data streams by continuously maintaining a global synopsis. *Data Mining and Knowledge Discovery*, *23*(2), 252–299. doi:10.1007/s10618-010-0204-8.

Woon, W., & Madnick, S. (2009). Asymmetric information distances for automated taxonomy construction. [ACM press.]. *Knowledge and Information Systems*, *21*(2), 91–111. doi:10.1007/s10115-009-0203-5.

KEY TERMS AND DEFINITIONS

Data Mining and Knowledge Discovery: The Data mining and Knowledge Discovery (KDD) is the process of extracting patterns from data and exploiting them to support analyst decision making.

Dynamic Data Mining: Analysis and comparison of the information extracted by different data mining and knowledge discovery sessions scheduled over time.

Frequent Itemset Mining: Frequent itemset mining is an exploratory technique to discover relevant correlations hidden in the analyzed data.

Generalization Process: The generalization process is the process of aggregating concepts into higher level ones. Concept generalization is typically performed by climbing up a taxonomy stepwise.

Social Network Analysis: Analysis of the structure of social networks and online communities and mining from social network user-generated content to support the knowledge discovery process.

Taxonomy: A taxonomy is a representation of a set of is-a relationships between concepts in a knowledge domain.

User-Generated Content: Textual and multimedia content (e.g., photos, videos, posts, tags) published by Web users on social networks and online communities.

Chapter 6
Applications of Data Mining in Dynamic Social Network Analysis

Manish Kumar
IIIT, Allahabad, INDIA

ABSTRACT

Social Networks are nodes consisting of people, groups and organizations growing dynamically. The growth is horizontal as well as vertical in terms of size and number. Social network analysis has gained success due to online social networking and sharing sites. The accessibility of online social sites such as MySpace, Facebook, Twitter, Hi5, Friendster, SkyRock and Beb offer sharing and maintaining large amount of different data. Social network analysis is focused on mining such data i.e. generating pattern of people's interaction. The analysis involves the knowledge discovery that helps the sites as well as users in terms of usage and business goals respectively. Further it is desired that the process must be privacy preserving. This chapter describes the various mining techniques applicable on social networks data.

INTRODUCTION

Social network is a network made up of a set of nodes consisting individuals, groups, organizations and systems that share relationship such as contacts, friends, group participation and many others. Social networks are self-organizing and complex with the incremental property in terms of size such that it can generate a global pattern from the local interaction which constitutes system (Newman et al., 2006). Due to the increase in network size, patterns become more apparent. The research components in social networks involves at two levels; micro-level and macro level. At the micro level, research associated with small group of people related with particular social context whereas macro level focuses on outcomes of group interaction and transfer of resources over large groups. The social network creates platform to analyze the structure of entire complex social entities (Wasserman et al.,1994). These structures generate local and global patterns

DOI: 10.4018/978-1-4666-4213-3.ch006

Copyright © 2013, IGI Global. Copying or distributing in print or electronic forms without written permission of IGI Global is prohibited.

from social entities and it also examines the social network dynamics. Social networks analysis is an interdisciple research activity which involves social psychology, information science, biology, political science, statistics, data mining and graph theory (Wasserman et al., 1994; Scott, 2000). Social network analysis becomes now a major paradigm in social and formal sciences. However, a global network analysis is very much difficult and contains so much uninformative information. Mathematically, social network (Nam et al., 2011) is modeled as a graph G = (V, E) where V denotes vertices of individuals and E denotes edges of interaction. Dynamic social networks deals with dynamic interactions i.e. changes over time are considered for the mining purposes. To model the dynamic social network (Jiangtao et al., 2011; Takafoli et al., 2010), let $G_d = (V_d, E_d)$ be a graph network depending on time i.e. instances are recorded at time t. Let V_e and E_e be the sets of vertices and edges to be inserted or deleted at time t and hence Ge = (V_e, E_e) is the modified graph after the changes at time t. The sequence of network changes over time: $G_0, G_1, G_2 \ldots\ldots G_m$ creates a dynamic social network. The application of data mining in social networks is a major area of research which involves identification of different pattern of online community. Dynamic Social networks are represented as complex networks which require modeling and new techniques to evaluate the system and methods to interpret the information from the networks. Dynamic social network provides important methods for analyzing the friendship graphs (Catanese et al., 2010) i.e. relationship dynamics. Various models and statistical algorithms have been proposed for identifying the actor nodes, groups and relationships for friendship graph networks. Now, social networks are useful to predict the organizational relationships and interpersonal relationship. The Figure 1 depicts the different modes of dynamic social network.

Clustering

Clustering is unsupervised learning that forms clusters of the data points. Clustering may be applied on numerical as well as categorical data with transformation in suitable data types. The clustering in social network analysis is different

Figure 1. Social networks (source: Jiangtao et al., 2011)

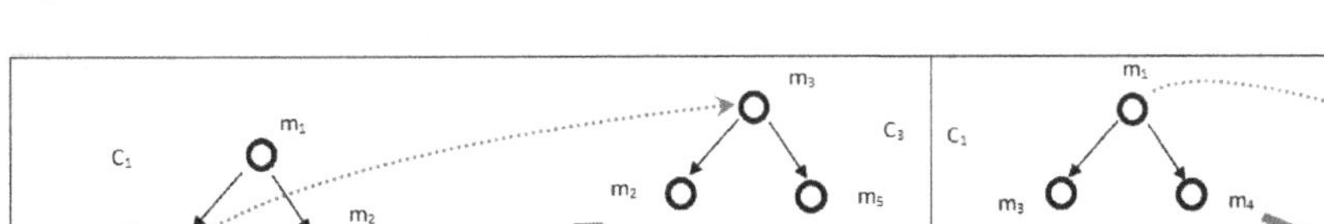

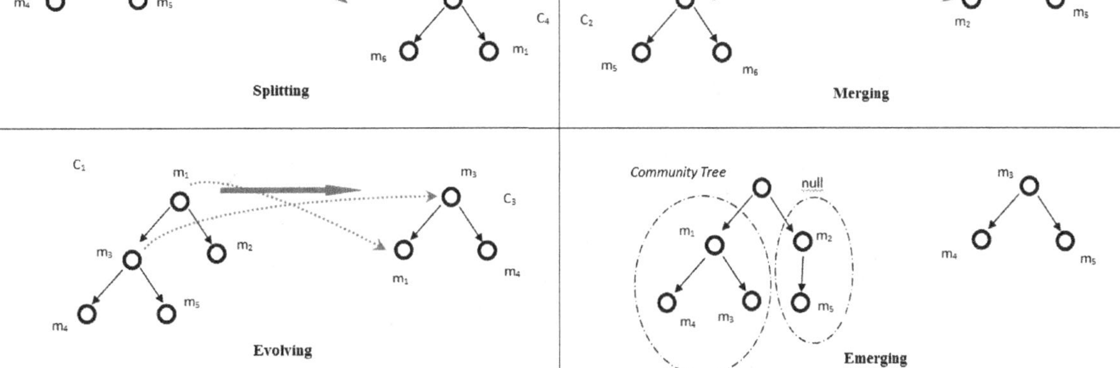

from traditional clustering. It requires grouping objects into classes based on their links as well as their attributes. While traditional clustering algorithms group objects only based on object's similarity and it can't be applied to social network analysis directly.

Keehyung et al. (2010) proposed an effective framework for Multi-Objective Evolutionary Algorithms (DMOEA) for dynamic social network clustering growing with time. This work is dependent on Multi-objective Evolutionary Algorithms and Immigrant Schemes in Dynamic Optimization algorithms and combined the two approaches to perform dynamic clustering in social network analysis. Multi-objective evolutionary algorithms are used to find a population of solutions. Thus it is important to track a variety of elite individuals, while single objective algorithms need only find one best individual. A typical social network tends to expand over time, with newly added nodes and edges being incorporated into the existing graph. Since social networks change continuously, the immigrant schemes effectively used in dynamic optimization. Evolutionary algorithms is used for the above is Genetic algorithm (GA). Modified algorithm follows the same general procedure as GA, only differing in how the child population P is generated. In modified algorithm, part of P is generated by crossover and mutation from original population P just as in GA; the remainder is introduced by an immigration scheme. Thus we have two proportions of population P, Q_1 and Q_2 refer to the proportions immigrants in population P and proportion generated by crossover and mutation. Keehyung et al. (2010) uses a locus-based adjacency representation as shown in Figure 2. Consider the graph representation, each individual g consists of |V| genes and each gene g(i) can take an integer value j between 1 and |V|. A value j assigned to the gene g(i)is interpreted as a link from vertex i to j. After decoding the genotype, we can determine the cluster structure as shown.

Selection operator: When choosing a parent from population P, two individuals are selected, and compared. Depending on probability, one parent is finally chosen from them. Crossover operator: Uniform crossover is chosen because it is unbiased with respect to the ordering of genes, and can generate any combination of solutions from the two parents. Fitness function: Min-max cut is used as a fitness score calculator.

Fuzzy Sequential Patterns: Romsaiyud et al. (2012) proposed algorithm that combines Apriori algorithm with Fuzzy set concepts focusing factors

Figure 2. Cluster structure

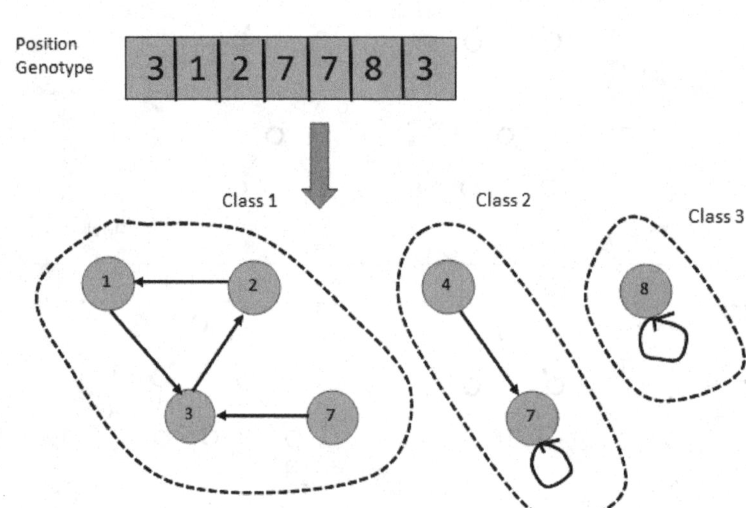

for leadership in social network. One node acts as a central node and treated as opinion leader. This algorithm generates association rules and results interesting sequential patterns by transforming posting messages into quantitative values. The algorithm considers three factors activity, links and closeness. It measures and map invisible links between people considering above three factors. Attributes values are transformed in transactions and then generate the sequential pattern by applying modified Apriori algorithm.

An example has been discussed such as some entity always uses slang and abbreviations to express their contents on online social network all the time. Based on previous transactions, prediction is performed using fuzzy sequential pattern sets applying natural language processing that will increase the user's decision making for association.

Gong (2007) proposed a clustering algorithm based on Business System Planning (BSP) clustering algorithm. The algorithm can group objects in a social network into different classes based on their links, and it can also identify the relations among classes. Gong (2007) describes the algorithm as

- Generate edge creation matrix and edge pointed matrix.
- Calculate one-step reachable matrix between objects.
- Calculate multi-steps reachable matrix between objects.
- Calculate reachable matrix.
- Calculate mutual reachable matrix and generate clusters.

Association Mining

Association mining is a task to find the strong relationship between entities based on minimum support and minimum confidence criteria (Han et al., 2011). The support and confidence of association between items A1 and A2 is defined as

Rule 1: Support, *Sup (A1=>A2) =P (A1 U A2)*
Rule 2: Confidence, *Conf(A1=>A2) =P (A2/A1) =P (A1 U A2)/P (A1)*

Many traditional algorithms were developed such as Apriori algorithm, frequent pattern growth and their variations. These algorithms are applicable in social networks in many ways like finding pattern within the social networks, classification of entities or nodes and relationships or links and generating clusters as groups with similar properties. A frequent pattern (Agrawal et al., 1993) is defined as a subset that frequently associated according to user's specified support threshold. Different authors have extended the idea of frequent pattern with respect to the temporal changes as the case in dynamic social networks. The original Apriori algorithms is varied in a way that can be applied in particular for frequent pattern mining and subsequently algorithms have also been proposed.

Coenen et al. (2001) proposed algorithm that extends Apriori and named as TFP (Total from Partial) that is used for the purpose of trend mining. Trend mining plays an important role in finding patterns in dynamic social networks (Puteri et al., 2012) and is defined as a sequence of support values over a sequence of timestamp referred as epoch $\{e_1, e_2 \ldots e_m\}$ associated with a specific pattern. A set of values $\{v_1, v_2 \ldots v_n\}$ collected where n is the number of timestamp in the epoch constitutes trend t. t_i is a trend of a associated pattern i and t_{ik} is k[th] value in a trend t_i. Identifying the changes in the trends patterns and aim is to compare trends over multiple epochs (Khan et al. (2010)). T= $\{t_1, t_2 \ldots t_m\}$ as sequence of trends where m is the number of epochs obtained by the sequence. Trend mining (Puteri et al., 2012) is applied for frequent pattern trend generation and second stage involves trend clustering formation and lastly trend cluster analysis is done as depicted in Figure 3.

Figure 3. Trend mining tasks (source: Puteri et al., 2012)

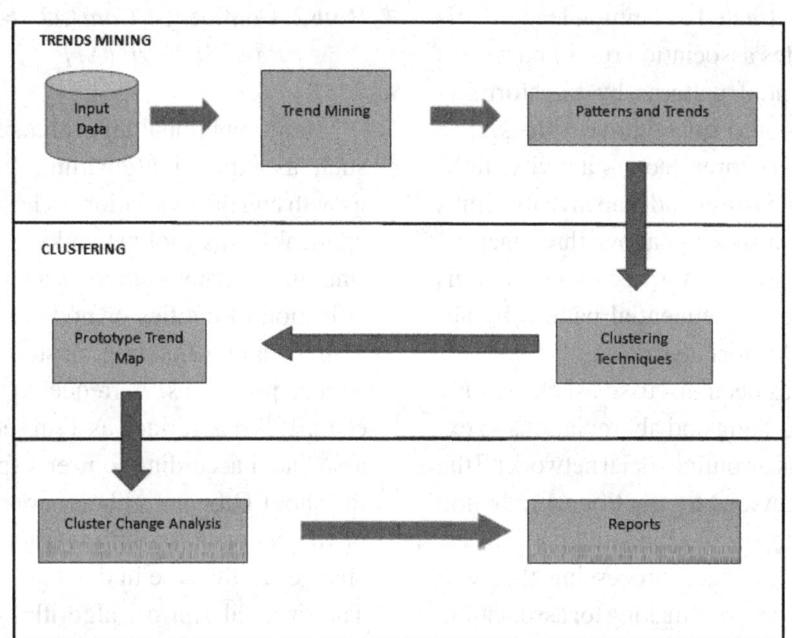

TFP algorithm (Coenen et al., 2001) is a frequent pattern trend mining algorithm and unable to address the temporal aspect of frequent pattern trend. The TFP is extended called TM-TFP (Trend Mining TFP) to include the temporal aspect as required in dynamic social networks (Puteri et al., 2012; Khan et al., 2010) so that a sequence of data sets could be processed and the frequent patterns would be stored allowing differentiation between individual time stamps and epochs. TFP uses two data structures, that is, a P-tree and T-tree. P-tree is used to encapsulate the input data and generate a partial pattern and T-tree to store interesting patterns.

Classification

Standard techniques are available for classification like decision tree classification, Bayesian classification, artificial neural network based classification and many classifiers developed for the accuracy testing. Dynamic social networks associated with organizations, groups and individuals can be used to generate patterns and community structure. Pattern classification was proposed for social network analysis mining tasks (Richard et al., 2001).

Pattern Classification: Pattern classification (Richard et al., 2001; Thayne et al., 2004) is method of observing features about an object of interest and classify them into a number of categories. The task automated pattern classification approaches is a field of research. The steps involved are

- Select training and testing sets from the observed data.
- Select a set of interesting features to classify.
- Start training phase.
- Accuracy checking by testing datasets.

Bayesian Classifier: It classifies on a particular feature set. Given that

- x is a true entity of one of m category i.e. x € $\{x_1, x_2 \ ...x_m\}$.
- The prior probability $P(w_i)$ of each category w_i.
- The conditional transition probabilities of class $p(y / x_i)$ for observed metrics given that the entity or node is in a given class.

A posteriori probability (Bayes' theorem) of the class x_i given set of feature values y is

$$P\left(\frac{x_i}{y}\right) = \frac{P\left(\frac{y}{x_i}\right)p\left(x_i\right)}{p\left(y\right)}$$

y is assigned to the class x_i iff

$$P\left(\frac{x_i}{y}\right) > P\left(\frac{x_j}{y}\right), for\, all\, j! = i$$

This is a maximization problem for the classification and minimization problem in terms of the total cost of misclassification. The classification methods applied on social network is discussed in link and graph mining as well.

Link Mining

In data mining, link mining explores predictive (or descriptive) models of the linked data. Link mining (Ted et al., 2005; Geetor, 2005) tasks include ranking of objects, group detection, classification, link prediction and subgraph detection. The purpose of the link mining is to classify the data for known interesting pattern, generate new pattern and detect noisy data that create problem for known pattern. Link Prediction is used to extract features from the structure of social network for the link classification, prediction of hidden links and addition of new links dynamically. Figure 4 illustrates the link prediction tasks.

Link prediction is performed by supervised as well as unsupervised techniques. Binary classifier can be used for link prediction between a given pair of nodes whereas link existence can be detected using methods such as decision tree, K-nearest neighbors or other classification methods. Subgraph discovery is an example of graph classification and used in link mining. Akihiro et al. (2000) proposed an Apriori-based algorithm that generates subgraphs in a graph with minimum support criteria. Kuromachi et al. (2004) presents the improvement using an adjacency representation of the graph data and formulating a new approach for optimizations in substructure generation. Due to the heterogeneity and complex structure of dynamic social network, link mining becomes challenging task. Moreover, it also provides opportunities for researchers due to presence of enormous information in the structure of linked data. Other link mining tasks (Lise et al., 2004;

Figure 4. Link prediction task (source: Link Prediction in Social Networks, Project by Svitlana Volkova)

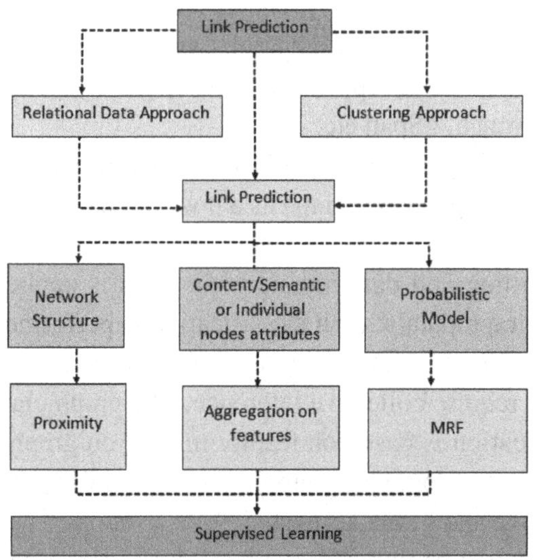

Geetor, 2005) are object ranking, object classification and group detection. Lise et al. (2004) proposed link-based object ranking (LBR).This algorithm uses structural link of a graph to establish the object ranking within the graph. The other algorithms used in this category are PageRank and HITS algorithms that are application in web information retrieval. Link based object classification (LBC) labels the members of set objects connected through links in a data graph. Most challenging job is to design the classification algorithm and throws tasks for research community. The task of group detection is to cluster the nodes groups that share common properties. Various techniques have presented to address this problem such as statistical block modeling (Wolfe et al., 2004), spectral graph partitioning, stochastic block modeling, pair-dependent stochastic block model etc.

Graph Mining

Graph mining and link mining is closely interrelated and share common theory. Subgraph discovery in link mining is graph mining task. Graph mining (Jiawei et al., 2011) attempts to find interesting subgraphs in a set of graphs and referred as graph classification (Akihiro et al., 2000; Kuromachi et al., 2004; Kudo et al., 2004; Coffman et al., 2004). The different methods for generating frequent subgraphs were proposed like Apriori based approach, pattern growth graph approach, gSpan etc.

Graph classification is a supervised learning that categorizes a graph as a positive or negative instance of a concept. The concept of machine learning and data mining techniques is applied to graph data. Graph classification is performed on independently generated graphs and does not require collective inference. The graph classification is based on feature mining on graphs, inductive logic programming (ILP) as discussed above and graph kernels.

Feature mining is usually performed by generating frequent substructures in the graph instances. These substructures further transformed into data stored in a single table and then instances are classified using efficient traditional classifiers. Graph kernels are based on a measure of the walks on the graphs whereas another approach counts walks with equal initial and terminal labels.

Cluster Analysis Using Graph Patterns: Cluster analysis can be applied on mined graph patterns. The grouping of set of graphs that share high similarity properties should be grouped into similar clusters. To adjust the clusters frequency, the minimum support threshold can be applied. Thus outlier analysis plays an important role for those graphs which are not falling in any category. The efficiency can be improved with proper threshold selection and by applying efficient graph clustering algorithms.

Probabilistic Model for link prediction: Wang et al. (2007) presented simple probabilistic models for link prediction. Using topological structure of the network, neighborhood set is identified for two nodes and MRF model has been used to learn the local neighborhood. This method uses link probability from the resulting model and classifies the nodes using supervised learning algorithm. The classifier improves while combining the topological and semantic features. Detail methodology can be studied from Wang et al. (2007).

Privacy Preserving Data Mining

Various work have been carried out on privacy preserving of social networks treating them as a graph made up of entities and relationship between these entities. Such networks contains large amount of private information that need to be protected. Privacy preservation of such large amount of private information leads to the requirement of confidentiality and security techniques to be developed for dynamic social networks. The dynamic nature of social networks adds complexity in this requirement as network structures are changing with time. Figure 5 illustrates the various components of privacy preserving data mining in social networks.

Figure 5. Privacy preserving data mining in social networks (source: Maximilien et al., 2009)

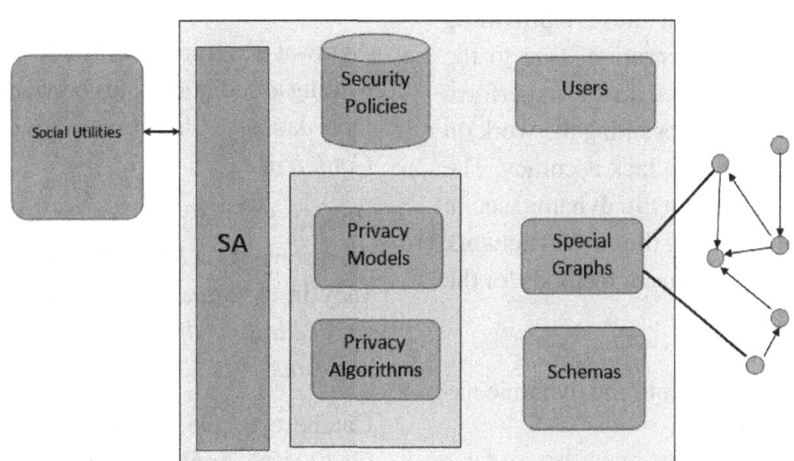

Kin et al., (2009) discussed the privacy issue of a user's identity in context of the user's perspective. Author proposed a framework that calculates an estimated privacy score for each user. Using this score, the privacy risk in real time can be monitored. The position of the user is decided while comparing the score with the rest of the population. The system is able to recommend the types of privacy settings requirement of a user based on the social neighbor's information. The privacy score mainly depends on the two factor visibility and sensitivity of the information.

Privacy score is computed using partial privacy scores of each individual's profile items and transforming the information in a m × n response matrix. This matrix data shows the privacy settings of n users and m profile items.

Kin et al. (2009) computes the sensitivity of item i∈{1, . . ., m} is denoted by βi that depends on the item itself. For the profile items that are more sensitive by nature than others. The visibility of a such profile item i that belongs to user j is denoted by S(i, j). These computations are done using item response theory. Privacy risk is thus calculated using

$$Pr\left(i,j\right) = \beta_i \left(operator\right) S\left(i,j\right)$$

where operator stands for any arbitrary combination function used.

$$Pr\ (j)=\sum Pr\ (i,j)=\sum \beta_j \times S(i,j)$$

Anonymity in social network is put into two categories as follows (Bhagat et al., 2010).

Clustering-based approaches: A clustering-based method clusters vertices and edges into groups and anonymizes a subgraph into a super-vertex. In such a way, the details about individuals can be hidden properly. *Graph modification approaches:* A graph modification method anonymizes a graph by modifying (that is, inserting and/or deleting) edges and vertices in a graph.

Lian et al. (2009) mainly focuses on a social network which maintains the utility of the shortest paths while hiding the actual cost between a pair of entities. The edge between two nodes is often associated with a quantitative weight that reflects the strong relationship between the two entities.

Research Methodology

Large number of research papers has been published in the area of data mining application in dynamic social networks. A section of researchers presented the work using static data collected from email and social sites. Social sites are providing the data with privacy preservation. Due to the privacy issues, researchers are unable to perform the tasks on real data and presenting the work on simulated data and therefore lack accuracy. The research issues in data mining in dynamic social network require investigating the current network status and deriving algorithms or methods for the following

- New architecture for handling dynamic nature of social networks.
- Incremental group cluster formation of dynamic social networks.
- Analyzing the friendship graph.
- Link-based object classification of networks.
- Link Prediction algorithms.
- Subgraph generation methods.
- Graph Classification algorithms.
- Generating Graphs Models etc.

CONCLUSION

Dynamic social network is evolving rapidly with high increase in numbers of users. Data mining provides the techniques to analyze the networks in many directions. The need of efficient algorithms in different category always throws challenge to researchers. This work investigated about the data mining task in dynamic social network and its application in rich network information mining.

ACKNOWLEDGMENT

I would like to acknowledge and extends my thanks to all the authors of research paper and books whose contents are part of this work.

REFERENCES

Agrawal, R., Imielinski, T., & Swami, A. (1993). Mining association rules between sets of items in large databases. In *Proceedings of ACM SIGMOD Conference*.

Bhagat, S., Cormode, G., Krishnamurthy, B., & Srivastava, D. (2010). Prediction promotes privacy in dynamic social networks. In *WOSN'10 Proceedings of the 3rd conference on Online social networks*.

Catanese, S., De Meo, P., Ferrara, E., & Fiumara, G. (2010). *Analyzing the Facebook friendship graph*.

Coenen, F. P., Goulbourne, G., & Leng, P. (2001) Computing association rules using partial totals. Principles of data mining and knowledge discovery. []. SpringerBerlin/Heidelberg.]. *LNCS*, *2168*, 54–66.

Coffman, T., Greenblatt, S., & Marcus, S. (2004). Graph-based technologies for intelligence analysis. *Communications of the ACM*, *47*(3), 45–47. doi:10.1145/971617.971643.

Coffman, T. R., & Marcus, S. E. (2004). Pattern classification in social network analysis: A case study. In *Proc. of IEEE Aerospace Conference*.

Duda, R., Hart, P., & Stork, D. (2001). *Pattern classification* (2nd ed.). New York: John Wiley & Sons.

Duncan, J. (1999). *Watts, small worlds. The dynamics of networks between order and randomness*. Princeton: Princeton University Press.

Getoor, L. (2005). Link-based classification. Advanced methods for knowledge discovery from complex data (pp. 189-207).

Getoor, L., & Diehl, C. (2005). Link mining: A survey. *SIGKDD Explorations*, *7*(2), 3–12. doi:10.1145/1117454.1117456.

Han, J., Kamber, M., & Pei, J. (2011). *Data mining: Concepts and techniques* (3rd ed.). Morgan Kaufmann.

Inokuchi, A., Washio, T., & Motoda, H. (2000). An Apriori-based algorithm for mining frequent substructures from graph data. In *Proceedings of the 4th European Conference on Principles of Data Mining and Knowledge Discovery* (pp. 13-23).

Khan, M. S., Coenen, F., Reid, D., Tawfik, H., Patel, R., & Lawson, A. (2010). A sliding windows based dual support framework for discovering emerging trends from temporal data. Research and Development in Intelligent Systems XXVIl (pp. 35-48).

Kim, K., McKay, R., & Moon, B. (2010). *Multiobjective evolutionary algorithms for dynamic social network clustering* (pp. 1179–1186). GECCO. doi:10.1145/1830483.1830699.

Kudo, T., Maeda, E., & Matsumoto, Y. (2004). An application of boosting to graph classification. *Advances in Neural Information Processing Systems*, *17*, 729–736.

Kuramochi, M., & Karypis, G. (2004). An efficient algorithm for discovering frequent subgraphs. *IEEE Transactions on Knowledge and Data Engineering*, 1038–1051. doi:10.1109/TKDE.2004.33.

Liu, K., & Terzi, E. (2009). *A framework for computing the privacy scores of users in online social networks*. ICDM. doi:10.1109/ICDM.2009.21.

Liu, L., Wang, J., Liu, J., & Zhang, J. (2009). *Privacy preservation in social networks with sensitive edge weights* (pp. 954–965). SDM.

Maximilien, E. M., Grandison, T., Sun, T., Richardson, D., Guo, S., & Liu, K. (2009). Enabling privacy as a fundamental construct for social networks. The *Proceedings of the Workshop on Security and Privacy in Online Social Networking (SPOSN09) at the 2009 IEEE International Conference on Social Computing (SocialCom-09)*. Vancouver, Canada.

Newman, M., Barabâsi, A. L., & Watts, D. J. (2006). *The structure and dynamics of networks (Princeton Studies in Complexity)*. Oxford: Princeton University Press.

Nguyen, N., Dinh, T., Xuan, Y., & Thai, M. (2011). *Adaptive algorithms for detecting community structure in dynamic social networks* (pp. 2282–2290). INFOCOM. doi:10.1109/INFCOM.2011.5935045.

Nohuddin, P., Coenen, F., Christley, R., Setzkorn, C., Patel, Y., & Williams, S. (2012). Finding "interesting" trends in social networks using frequent pattern mining and self organizing maps. *Knowledge-Based Systems*, *29*, 104–113. doi:10.1016/j.knosys.2011.07.003.

Qiu, J., & Lin, Z. (2011). A framework for exploring organizational structure in dynamic social networks. *Decision Support Systems*, *51*(4), 760–771. doi:10.1016/j.dss.2011.01.011.

Romsaiyud, W., & Premchaiswadi, W. (2012). Applying mining fuzzy sequential patterns technique to predict the leadership in social networks. *9th International Conference on ICT and Knowledge Engineering (ICT & Knowledge Engineering)* (pp. 134-137).

Scott, J. P. (2000). *Social network analysis: A handbook* (2nd ed.). Thousand Oaks, CA: Sage Publications.

Senator, T. E. (2005). Link mining applications: Progress and challenges. *SIGKDD Explorations*, *7*(2), 76–83. doi:10.1145/1117454.1117465.

Srinivasan, A., King, R. D., Muggleton, S. H., & Sternberg, M. J. E. (1997). Carcinogenesis predictions using ILP. In *Proc. of the 7th International Workshop on Inductive Logic Programming* (vol. 1297, pp. 273–287). Springer-Verlag.

Takaffoli, M., Sangi, F., Fagnan, J., & Za¨ıane, O. (2010, September). A framework for analyzing dynamic social networks. *Applications of Social network Analysis (ASNA)*.

Wang, C., Satuluri, V., & Parthasarathy, S. (2007). Local probabilistic models for link prediction. In *Data Mining, 2007. ICDM 2007. Seventh IEEE International Conference on* (pp. 322-331).

Wasserman, S., & Faust, K. (1994). *Social network analysis in the social and behavioral sciences. Social network analysis: Methods and applications* (pp. 1–27). Cambridge University Press. doi:10.1017/CBO9780511815478.

Wolfe, A. P., & Jensen, D. (2004). Playing multiple roles: Discovering overlapping roles in social networks. In *ICML-04 Workshop on Statistical Relational Learning and its Connections to Other Fields*.

Yu, G. (2007). Social network analysis based on BSP clustering algorithm. *Communications of the IIMA, 7*(4).

ADDITIONAL READING

Adriaans, P., & Zantinge, D. (1998). *Data mining. Addison- Wesley. Dasu, T., & Johnson, T. (2003). Exploratory data mining and data cleaning*. Wiley.

Agrawal, R., & Srikant, R. (1994). *Fast algorithms for mining association rules*. VLDB.

Breiman, L., Friedman, J., Olshen, R., & Stone, C. (1984). *Classification and regression trees*.

Brin, S., & Page, L. (1998). The anatomy of a large-scale hypertextual Web search engine. In WWW-7.

Cios, K., Pedrycz, W., & Swiniarski, R. (1998). *Data mining methods for knowledge discovery*. Kluwer. doi:10.1007/978-1-4615-5589-6.

Freund, Y., & Schapire, R. E. (1997). A decision-theoretic generalization of on-line learning and an application to boosting. *Journal of Computer and System Sciences, 55*(1), 119–139. doi:10.1006/jcss.1997.1504.

Groth, R. (1997). *Data mining: A hands-on approach for business professionals*. Prentice-Hall PTR.

Han, J., Pei, J., & Yin, Y. (2000). *Mining frequent patterns without candidate generation*. SIGMOD.

Han & Kamber. (2000). *Data mining concepts and techniques*. Morgan Kaufmann.

Hand, D. J., & Yu, K. (2001). Idiot's bayes: Not so stupid after all? *International Statistical Review, 69*, 385–398.

Kantardzic, M. (2003). *Data mining: Concepts, models and algorithms. IEEE-Wiley. Groth, R. (1998). Data mining: A hands-on approach for business professionals*. Prentice Hall.

Kennedy, R. et al. (1998). *Solving data mining problems through pattern recognition*. Prentice-Hall PTR.

Kleinberg, J. M. (1998). *Authoritative sources in a hyperlinked environment*. SODA.

MacQueen, J. B. (1967). Some methods for classification and analysis of multivariate observations. In *Proc. 5th Berkeley Symp. Mathematical Statistics and Probability*.

McLachlan, G., & Peel, D. (2000). *Finite Mixture Models*. New York: J. Wiley. doi:10.1002/0471721182.

Pei, J., Han, J., Mortazavi-Asl, B., Pinto, H., Chen, Q., Dayal, U., & Hsu, M.-C. (2001). PrefixSpan: Mining sequential patterns efficiently by prefix-projected pattern growth. In ICDE.

Pujari, K. (2001). *Data mining techniques. Universities Press. Chakrabarti, S. (2003). Mining the web*. Morgan Kaufman.

Quinlan, J. R. (1993). *C4.5: Programs for machine learning*. Morgan Kaufmann.

Srikant, R., & Agrawal, R. (1996). Mining sequential patterns: Generalizations and performance improvements. In *Proceedings of the 5th International Conference on Extending Database Technology*.

Vapnik, V. N. (1995). *The nature of statistical learning theory*. Springer-Verlag. doi:10.1007/978-1-4757-2440-0.

Wadsworth. Hastie, T., & Tibshirani, R. (1996). Discriminant adaptive nearest neighbor classification. *TPAMI, 18*(6).

Weiss, S., & Indurkhya, N. (1998). *Predictive data mining: A practical guide*. Morgan Kaufmann.

Witten, I. H., & Frank, E. (2000). *Data mining: Practical machine learning toolsand techniques with java implementations*. Morgan Kaufmann.

Yan, X., & Han, J. (2002). gSpan: Graph-based substructure pattern mining. In ICDM.

Zhang, T., Ramakrishnan, R., & Livny, M. (1996). BIRCH: An efficient data clustering method for very large databases. In SIGMOD.

KEY TERMS AND DEFINITIONS

Association: Generate for relationships between data objects. It creates rules that describe how often events have occurred together. Example: "When customer buy PC, also buy CD. Such relationships are typically expressed with a support and confidence interval.

Classification: It generates model that describe and distinguish classes or concepts for future prediction. Example: classify an e-mail as "legitimate" or as "spam". Prediction is type of classification and it is the task to predict some unknown or missing numerical values.

Clustering: It is the task to maximize intra-class similarity & minimizing interclass similarity. Class label is unknown. It groups data to form new classes. Example: cluster friends to find interest patterns.

Graph Mining: Graph mining involves detection in social networks, malicious program analysis in computer security and structural analysis in chemical compounds. It investigates the modeling and mining of graphs or networks in social networks. Example: generating subgraph from large scale social network graph.

Link Mining: Link mining is emerging research area that involves intersection of the work in link analysis, web mining, relational learning, inductive logic programming and graph mining.

Outlier Detection: The identification of unusual data records that might be interesting or data errors and possibility to create new class. Data object that does not comply with the general behavior of the data. Example: Such analysis is useful in fraud detection, intrusion and rare events analysis.

Regression: Generate a function which models the data with the least error.

Summarization: It provides representation of the data set including visualization and also can generate reports.

Trend Mining: It involves trend detection, trend recognition and trending analysis. It detects emerging product from interest pattern analysis in social network or to detect the trends based on numeric data analysis for stock exchange. Example: regression analysis.

Chapter 7
Dynamic Social Network Mining:
Issues and Prospects

Luca Cagliero
Dipartimento di Automatica e Informatica, Politecnico di Torino, Italy

Alessandro Fiori
IRC@C: Institute for Cancer Research at Candiolo, Italy

ABSTRACT

The past few years have witnessed the rapid proliferation of Web communities such as social networking sites, wikis, blogs, and media sharing communities. The published social content is commonly characterized by a high dynamicity and reflects the most recent trends and common user behaviors.

The Data mining and Knowledge Discovery (KDD) process focuses on discovering and analyzing relevant information hidden in large data collections to support expert decision making. Hence, the application of data mining techniques to data coming from social networks and online communities is definitely an appealing research topic.

This Chapter overviews most recent data mining approaches proposed in the context of social network analysis. In particular, it aims at classifying the proposed approaches based on both the adopted mining strategies and their suitability for supporting knowledge discovery in a dynamic context. To provide a thorough insight into the proposed approaches, main work issues and prospects in dynamic social network analysis are also outlined.

INTRODUCTION

During recent years, the steadfast popularity increase of social networks and online communities has caught the attention of the data mining research community. Since their introduction, social network sites have attracted millions of users, many of whom have integrated these sites into their daily practices. The possibility to easily share multimedia content, thoughts, and electronic documents opens room to a novel form of communication and gives access to a huge amount of shared information.

DOI: 10.4018/978-1-4666-4213-3.ch007

Copyright © 2013, IGI Global. Copying or distributing in print or electronic forms without written permission of IGI Global is prohibited.

Since social data coming from social networks, blogs, twikis, and bookmarking sites has become a powerful source of knowledge, the in-depth analysis of both the social network structure and the published content may trigger many insightful actions. For instance, the study of common social user behaviors may significantly improve the effectiveness of e-commerce services. Moreover, the analysis of the annotations made by Web users may drive product recommendation as well as ease Web resources' retrieval.

The application of Data mining and Knowledge Discovery (KDD) techniques to social data has become more and more attractive for research purposes. For instance, Heymann et al. (2008) discovered relevant tag associations to model the metadata associated by Web users to public resources. The discovered tag associations are also used to drive the annotation process of partially annotated resources. In parallel, social tagging systems have also been used to classify videos and photos in order to improve the performance of search engines (Yin et al., 2009). At the same time, Wikipedia content has been used to infer semantics-based models, such as ontologies and taxonomies (Suchanek et al., 2008).

Data mining approaches entail either modeling peculiar characteristics of the analyzed data or predicting the label/value to assign to a given object/variable given a set of labeled data. The large variety of different data mining techniques which may be applicable to social data prompts the need of better understanding (i) the objective of the most recently proposed algorithms, (ii) their suitability for being applied in dynamic contexts, and (iii) the usefulness of the discovered knowledge for in-depth analysis. Peculiar aspects that should be taken into account by data mining analysts are, for instance, the algorithm efficiency in terms of computational time, the average prediction accuracy, and the succinctness and readability of the generated models. Since these properties actually depend on the social context under analysis, choosing the most suitable data mining approach is a challenging task. Furthermore, since social data continuous evolve over time, data mining algorithms are often required to be easily adaptable to dynamic contexts.

Interested readers may look into the large body of survey papers or books regarding social network analysis and mining (Liu, 2007; Scott & Carrington, 2011; Bonchi et al., 2011). They describe the characteristics of real-life social Web systems (Scott & Carrington, 2011), the applicability of intelligent data mining and information retrieval techniques (Liu, 2007), as well as they provide an in-depth insight into the most challenging research directions in social data analysis (Bonchi et al., 2011). However, a systematic classification and overview of the most recent data mining approaches applied to data coming dynamic social networks and online communities are still missing.

This chapter focuses on overviewing recently proposed data mining approaches in the context of social network and online community analysis. Unlike previous overviews (e.g. Liu, 2007; Scott & Carrington, 2011; Bonchi et al., 2011), this work provides a detailed overview of state-of-the-art approaches from a data mining perspective. In particular, it aims at better clarifying the scope of recent data mining research in social network analysis, highlighting the issues encountered by the most renewed data mining systems, and discussing prospects of the data mining research on social networks. Hence, a particular attention has been paid to the mining methods applied to perform social network mining and analysis. Furthermore, a relevant effort has also been devoted to better understanding the ability of data mining research in capturing the evolution of the underlying social networks through the analysis of the most recurrent trends. To achieve this goal, an analysis of the most established data mining applications oriented to dynamic social network analysis is presented.

This chapter is organized as follows. Section "Data mining techniques" outlines fundamentals of five among the most established data mining techniques, i.e., classification, clustering, association rule mining, dynamic data mining, and graph mining, as well as discusses their applicability to data coming from social networks and online communities. Section "Dynamic social network analysis" presents state-of-the-art approaches focused on the analysis of the dynamics behind the underlying structures of social networks and online communities. In particular, to clarify the key role of dynamic systems in social data analysis, main data mining approaches devoted to the study of the evolution of both social groups and individual user activities are presented. Section "Data mining application" overviews state-of-the-art work concerning the analysis of social data in four real-life application contexts (i.e., recommendation systems, query engines, topic trend detection, and document summarization) in which effective data mining solutions have been proposed. For each presented approach, the social context in which it has been proposed, its main goals, and the most significant experimental results are summarized. Finally, Section "Future research directions" presents future research directions of data mining from social data, while Section "Conclusions" draws survey conclusions.

DATA MINING TECHNIQUES

This section discusses the applicability of four among the most established data mining techniques, i.e., classification, clustering, association rule mining, dynamic data mining, and graph mining, to social data and presents the most relevant related approaches.

Classification

Classification is the task of assigning unlabeled objects, belonging to a test set, to one or several categories, called classes (Tan et al., 2006). The class assignment is driven by a model, called classifier, which is built from a set of labeled data, called training set.

Since social tags and user-generated content may be exploited to improve the representation of Web resources like documents, Web pages, photos, and videos, they may be also useful for improving classification system performance. For instance, in Schőnhofen (2009) a new classification model based on Wikipedia was proposed. It identified and ranked all Wikipedia categories related to the analyzed document by matching Wikipedia articles titles with the words present in the document. The retrieved categories are then ranked according to their relevance statistics. Experimental results on Wikipedia article body and the well-known news corpora, showed that the best performance were achieved by combining Wikipedia categorization with the top terms identified by tf-idf statistics.

Wikipedia can be also employed to augment the bag-of-word (BOW) representation of a document. Wang et al. (2009) proposed to enrich the BOW representation by means of a thesaurus automatically extracted using redirect and disambiguation pages and the hyperlink graph of Wikipedia. The thesaurus is employed to identify synonyms, hyponyms, and correlations among entities cited in the document. In such a way, documents related to the same topic that involve few co-occurred terms are shifted closer to each other in the new representation. The effectiveness of BOW representation enriched with Wikipedia related terms was empirically demonstrated on different document collections by means of a linear Support Vector Machine (SVM) (Tan et al., 2006). The micro-average and the macro-average of the precision-recall break-even point (BEP) were used to compare classification performance with respect to the baseline approach (i.e., the bag-of-word representation without enrichment). Against the baseline method, the proposed approach yielded an average improvement of 2-5%. Similarly, Sriram et al. (2010) enrich the BOW representation with additional features extracted from the authors' profiles to classify the short messages posted on microblogging websites (e.g., Twitter).

Unlike Wikipedia articles, social tags associated by the users with Web resources can be directly employed to categorize Web objects (e.g., Web pages, products). Social tag prediction has been first addressed in Heymann et al. (2008). The goal is to assign the most pertinent tag to partially annotated resources by exploiting associative classification. Similarly, the work presented in Yin et al. (2009) focused on modeling the relations between Web objects and social tags provided by del.icio.us as graphs, an optimization framework has been proposed to assign the correct category associated with tags. A comparison with SVM and harmonic Gaussian classifiers, which used the title and the tags associated with each Web resource as feature space, was performed. The proposed approach outperformed the other classifiers in terms of F-measure (Tan et al., 2006). Thus, the authors concluded that social tags are effective features in the Web object classification as they allow propagating the category information of training samples from one domain to another.

Clustering

Clustering is a well-established descriptive data mining technique that aims at grouping objects belonging to large collections in homogenous subsets (i.e., the clusters) based on a given distance measure (Tan & al., 2006). The objective is to minimize the distance between couples of objects belonging to the same cluster and to maximize the one between objects associated with different clusters. In the social network analysis field, clustering is exploited to evaluate the structure of the communities and their evolutions. For instance, in Chen et al. (2009), the authors present a hierarchical clustering algorithm exploiting a new measure, i.e., Max-Min Modularity, to detect communities in networks. This metric considers both connected pairs and criteria defined by domain experts in finding communities. Results on synthetic and real world networks show the approach robustness against to noise and the capability of finding the community structures similar to the real structures are already known.

Clustering algorithms also allows improving the performance of classification and recommendation systems. For instance, Becker et al. (2011) exploit an incremental, online clustering algorithm to identify events from a stream of messages posted on Twitter. The resulting clusters are then analyzed to extract features which describe the event. Finally, these features are used to train an event classifier which predicts which clusters correspond to events at any point in time and the probability that a cluster contains event information. Differently, DuBois et al. (2009) adopted a clustering approach on a trust network of users to improve recommendation accuracy. It defined a metric space based on a trust function over which a variant of correlation clustering algorithm is applied. The users that belong to the same cluster show a high level of agreement for recommended items. This approach has been integrated into two basic recommendation algorithms. Experimental evaluation showed the proposed system achieves a statistically significant accuracy improvement against state-of-the-art competitors.

Association Rule Mining

Association rule mining is a widely used exploratory technique to discover valuable correlations among data. It has been introduced in Agrawal et al. (1993) in the context of market basket analysis. To focus on patterns that are relatively strong, e.g., the one occurring frequently and holding in most cases, several quality indexes, such as support and confidence, have been introduced. The mining task is typically performed by following a two-step process: (i) frequent itemset mining, driven by a minimum support threshold, and (ii) rule generation from the previously mined frequent itemsets, driven by a minimum confidence threshold.

A relevant research issue is the selection of frequent patterns (i.e., frequent itemsets or association rules) based on the strength of the correlations among their items (Aggarwal & Yu, 1998; Brin et., 1997; Barsky et al., 2011; Savasere et al., 1998). For instance, Brin et al. (1997) propose measuring significance of an association rule via the chi square test for correlation. A mining algorithm that exploits the upward closure of the chi square measure to discard some of candidate itemsets early has also been proposed. Since negative data correlations are usually characterized by an averagely low support, their extraction is a challenging task (Tan et al., 2006). To overcomes this issue, in Aggarwal and Yu (1998) and Savasere et al. (1998), itemset correlation is evaluated by the collective strength and support expectation measures, respectively, which may enable discovering negative associations among data indirectly (Tan et al., 2005). However, since the measures proposed in Aggarwal and Yu (1998), Brin et al. (1997), and Savasere et al. (1998) are not null-invariant, their selectivity depends on the dataset size. In Wu et al. (2010), the authors first investigate the use of null-invariant correlation measures (Hilderman & Hamilton, 2001) for evaluating the interestingness of positively correlated itemsets. More recently, the approach proposed in Barsky et al. (2011) focuses on exploiting the null-invariant Kulczynsky measure to discover flipping correlations among data supplied with taxonomies. Flipping correlations are itemsets whose correlation flips from positive to negative (or vice versa) when items are generalized to a higher level of abstraction for every generalization step.

A parallel research effort has been devoted to discovering generalized itemsets and rules (Agrawal & Srikant, 1995). Generalized itemsets are patterns that represent high level correlations among data. By exploiting a taxonomy (i.e., a set of is-a hierarchies) that aggregates data items into upper level generalizations, generalized itemsets are generated by combining items belonging to different abstraction levels. Generalized itemsets may allow better supporting the expert decision process than traditional ones, because they provide a high level view of the analyzed data and also represent the knowledge covered by their low level infrequent descendants. The first generalized association rule mining algorithm, namely Cumulate, was presented in Agrawal and Srikant (1995). It is an Apriori-based algorithm that generates generalized itemsets by considering, for each item, all its parents in the hierarchy. Many optimization strategies have been proposed to address generalized pattern mining efficiently (Han & Fu, 1999; Hipp et al., 1998; Pramudiono et al., 2004; Baralis et al., 2010). Among them, in Baralis et al. (2010) the authors propose an algorithm that performs support-driven itemset generalization, i.e., a frequent generalized itemset is extracted only if it has at least an infrequent (rare) descendant.

Frequent itemset and association rule mining algorithms have also been applied to perform knowledge discovery from data coming from social networks and online communities. For instance, in Hotho et al. (2006) the exploitation of association rules in the analysis of the structure of folksonomies is addressed. In particular, they discussed how the semantics behind the mining results can be used for supporting ontology learning and demonstrated that their approach scales well on a large dataset stemming coming from an online system. The approach proposed by Heymann et al. (2008) analyzed social tag associations. The analysis of the extracted rules allowed both characterizing the past annotation set and effectively supporting the process of additional tag recommendation of partially annotated Web resource. Similarly, in Cagliero, Fiori, and Grimaudo (in press), the authors propose a Flickr tag recommendation system. Given a partially annotated photo available at the photo sharing system Flickr, the system automatically proposes additional pertinent tags by exploiting generalized rules mined from the past history annotations. Since, due to the lack of controlled vocabularies, the real-world annotation set are intrinsically sparse, discovering high level data correlations improves recommender system performance substantially compared to traditional rule-based approaches. Cagliero and Fiori (in press) (a) addressed generalized association rule mining from Twitter. To counteract the excessive level of detail of the underlying social data associations, the authors propose to also analyze high correlations among Twitter data, i.e., the generalized rules. To perform generalized association rule mining from Twitter data, a taxonomy is exploited to aggregate data items into higher level concepts. Both the tweet content and their publication context are evaluated and exploited to perform user behavior analysis. The achieved results show that generalized rules provide to expert actionable knowledge hardly inferable traditional association-based approaches.

Dynamic Data Mining

Traditional itemset and association rule mining approaches do not take the temporal evolution of the extracted itemsets/association rules into account. Instead, dynamic data mining focuses on tracing the evolution of the main itemset and/or association rule quality indexes to figure out the most significant temporal changes.

The problem of discovering relevant changes in the history of itemsets or association rules has already been addressed by a number of previous works (Agrawal & Psaila, 1995; Bottcher et al., 2007; Liu et al., 2001; Tao & Tsu, 2009; Cagliero, 2011). For instance, active data mining (Agrawal & Psaila, 1995) has been the first attempt to represent and query the history collection of the discovered association rule quality indexes. Rules are mined from datasets collected at consecutive time periods and evaluated based on well-known quality indexes (e.g., support, confidence). Then, the analyst is in charge of specifying a history pattern in a trigger which is fired when such a pattern trend is exhibiting. The history patterns are exploited to track most notable pattern index changes. More recently, other time-related data mining frameworks tailored to monitor and detect changes in rule quality measures have also been proposed (Bottcher et al., 2007; Tao & Tsu, 2009). For instance, in Bottcher et al. (2007), patterns are evaluated and pruned based on both subjective and objective interestingness measures. To this aim, new patterns are observed as soon as they emerge, while old patterns are removed from the rule base as soon as they become extinct. Furthermore, at one time period a subset of rules is selected and monitored, while data changes that occur in subsequent periods are measured by their impact on the rules being monitored. Similarly, the work proposed in Tao and Tsu (2009) also addresses itemset change mining from time-varying data streams. Differently, in Liu et al. (2001) authors deal with rule change mining by discovering two main types of rules: (i) stable rules, i.e., rules that do not change a great deal over time and, thus, are likely to be reliable and could be trusted, and (ii) trend rules, i.e., rules that indicate some underlying systematic trends of potential interest.

Since all the above-mentioned approaches do not consider itemsets/rules at different abstraction levels, their ability in capturing relevant data correlation changes may be biased by the support threshold enforcement. In fact, some relevant trends may be discarded, because the underlying recurrences become infrequent at a certain time period. To overcome this issue, in Cagliero (2011) a dynamic itemset mining approach has recently been proposed. It discovers History Generalized Patterns, which represent a sequence of generalized itemsets extracted in consecutive time periods. Each HiGen is mainly focused on a reference itemset, whose support index values are traced in the consecutive time periods. In case an itemset becomes infrequent in a certain time period, its generalization with least abstraction level is maintained to avoid discarding potentially relevant knowledge. This chapter proposes a data mining system that discovers History Generalized Patterns from Twitter UGC and exploits them to drive the knowledge discovery process.

Graph Mining

The structure of online social networks is usually modeled as a graph whose nodes represent the online community actors, i.e., Web users, while edges the connections among them, e.g. friendship, chat messages, etc. Many studies exploit this representation to understand the structure of online social networks, shape the user behavior and analyze the evolution of the connections among community members.

For instance, Kumar et al. (2010) analyzed graph features, such as in-degree, out-degree, strongly connected components, to study the evolution of the blogosphere. Similarly, Palla et al. (2007) analyze community evolution of a co-authorship network and a mobile phone network. Their approach, based on the clique percolation method, allowed identifying some interesting characteristics, such as community sizes, ages and their correlation, community autocorrelation. Differently, Sun et al. (2007) proposed the GraphScope method to mine time-evolving graphs where the Minimum Description Length principle is employed to extract communities and to detect community changes.

A comparison of graph models has been conducted by Mislove et al. (2008). The authors studied the link formation process that drives the growth of Flickr online social networks by comparing empirical observations with the predictions of statistical models. The authors collected data covering three months of growth from Flickr, encompassing 950,143 new users and over 9.7 million new links. The analysis was focused on the ways in which new links are formed. The results highlighted that links tend to be created by users who already have a large neighborhood and users usually create a connection with other users already close in the network. Moreover, users tend to respond to incoming links by creating links back to the source. The overall links formation process followed the well-known preferential attachment model, but that global mechanisms alone are insufficient to explain the observed proximity between link sources and destinations.

Mining social network graphs also allows improving online services, such as recommendation systems and email services. For instance, Yoo et al. (2009) proposed a method based on the extraction of the main features from a graph model to improve the performance of a personalized email prioritization system. In particular, they analyzed the network to capture user groups and to obtain rich features that represent the social roles from the viewpoint of a particular user. The combination of these features with the ones extracted from the messages allowed increasing the performance of a baseline system in terms of micro- and macro-average accuracy.

DYNAMIC SOCIAL NETWORK ANALYSIS

Since online communities evolve under different aspects during consecutive time periods, many studies have been devoted to analyzing their dynamic features. Models based on graph representation are usually exploited to analyze the community structure in a given moment. The analysis of graph models extracted on different time period allow extracting information about time-evolving community structures, user behaviors and changing community interests. For instance, Backstrom et al. (2006) analyzed friendship link evolution on both LiveJournal and DBLP communities. The authors performed an insight analysis on group evolution within online communities by exploring principles by which groups develop and evolve in large-scale social networks. They found that a reasonable performance estimation can be obtained based purely on the structural properties of the group as a subgraph in the social network. As with group membership, relatively subtle structural features are crucial in distinguishing between groups likely to grow rapidly and those not likely to. For example, groups with a very large number of triangles (i.e., consisting of three mutual friends) grow significantly less quickly overall than groups with relatively few triangles. Thus, the framework is able to identify the most "informative" group of features that can be interpreted in terms of the underlying sociological considerations.

Other approaches have been focused on extracting models which represent the community's structure and their evolutions. For instance, the FacetNet method relies on formulating the problem in terms of maximum a posteriori (MAP) estimation, where the community structure is estimated both by the observed networked data and by the prior distribution given by historic community structures (Lin et al., 2009). Experimental results, achieved on both synthetic and real datasets, show that this method discovers meaningful communities and provide additional insights with respect to traditional methods. Differently,

Greene et al. (2010) proposed a method which involves matching communities found at consecutive time steps in the individual snapshot graphs. Unlike other approaches, this method allows aggregating information from either disjoint partitions or overlapping groupings of nodes.

The analysis of sub-group evolutions in online communities has also been addressed by many research studies. For instance, in Chakrabarti et al. (2006) an evolutionary clustering framework has been proposed to integrate into the objective of the clustering process both current and historic information. According to this objective function, the cluster membership for a node at time t depends both on its relationship with other nodes at time t and on its cluster membership at time t-1. Dynamic variants of common partitional and agglomerative clustering algorithms suitable for feature-based data have also been proposed. Differently, Spiliopoulou et al. (2006) proposed the MONIC framework to model and monitor cluster transitions over time. The authors defined a set of external transitions such as survive, split, disappear, to model transactions among different clusters and a set of internal transitions, such as size and location transitions to model changes within a community.

APPLICATIONS

Data coming from dynamic social networks and online communities represent powerful sources of knowledge. The application of data mining techniques may allow experts to figure out relevant data correlations which may be used to personalize service provision, improve resource shaping, perform data segmentation, or analyze common user behaviors and activities. For example, many commercial websites exploit recommender systems to either suggest new products to their customers (e.g., books, CDs, movies) or enhance the quality of the offered services. These recommender systems are usually targeted on the customer behavior and preferences of the customer. Furthermore, query engines can take advantage of folksonomies and ontologies extracted from UGC. In parallel, textual data analysis is commonly focused on extracting salient from potentially large Web document collections retrieved from online community websites.

This section overviews three among the most relevant data mining applications related to social data analysis, discusses their issues, and presents their prospects.

Recommender Systems

Recommender systems are commonly used Web systems, which are focused on providing information about items that are likely to be of customer's interest. To figure out the most interesting items, recommender systems usually exploit detailed user profile knowledge and other correlated pieces of information provided by the online community. The most renewed Web sites and portals commonly integrate advanced recommendation systems. For instance, the most popular news Web services often integrate recommender systems to provide breaking news to their users according to their personal interests. In the last several years, recommender systems also find application in supporting user-generated content creation. In this context, recommending potentially inherent tags to Web resources published on a social network site may improve the accessibility of the published content. However, since users may express the same concept with different tags, recommender systems may allow improving the quality and the coherence of the added annotations. Recommender systems may be categorized in two different categories: (i) content-based systems and (ii) collaborative filtering systems.

Content-based filtering aims at creating a profile for each user and product to be recommended. Profiles are used to associate users with matching items, by also comparing the personal user knowledge with the one associated with similar users. An overview of the kind of approaches is given in Herlocker et al. (2004).

Collaborative filtering methods analyze the information about user's behaviors, activities, or preferences to predict what users will like based on their similarity to other users. They assume that similar users share similar tastes. For instance, to incorporate user trust ratings coming from the social network, in Golbeck and Hendler (2006) a collaborative filtering approach is adopted to compute the similarity between user profiles and recommended movies. Users are requested to assign a trust rating to each friend of their social network. Moreover, the website allows users to assign rating to films and provide comments. Consider a movie m and a set of raters R, where each rater r has an associated trust rate t_r. The recommended movie rating is computed by considering all the ratings for the movie m weighted by the trust value t_r assigned by the user to each rater r. The results obtained by this approach show a significant improvement in terms of accuracy with respect to simple recommendation approaches based on ratings assigned to movies and Pearson similarity measure between user profiles. Unfortunately, collaborative filtering methods suffer from the *cold start* problem due to their inability to draw any inference for users or items about which they have not gathered sufficient information yet. On the contrary, they are, on average, more accurate than content filtering approaches because they consider a broader range of different aspects. Moreover, the power law distribution in user rating could negatively affect the recommendation system performance. Typically, a few users rate for most of available resources while the majority of the users do not apply any rating. Recent technologies focused on coping with data sparseness. For instance, Koren et al. (2009) presented a matrix factorization technique to map both users and items to a joint latent factor space. Unlike Koren et al. (2009), in Cagliero et al. (in press) the authors exploit generalized association rules to discover high level data correlations useful for supporting tag recommendation. In particular, to avoid discarding rare, but potentially useful tag associations the proposed personalized tag recommendation systems exploits a taxonomy to aggregate individual tags into higher level concepts.

According to data information employed in selecting most relevant items, we may categorize social recommender systems in two main classes: (i) news recommendation and (ii) tag recommendation. In the following, for each category the most recently proposed approaches are presented.

News Recommendation

These systems focus on recommending news of topical interest to Web users by exploiting the individual profile. News recommendation by means of collaborative filtering methods is challenged the hardness in matching user profiles with recent news content. Often, a limited user information is given and the resource content is not enough informative to well discriminate between recommendable news.

Some approaches that aim at improving the quality of recommended news have been proposed in literature. For instance, in Xue et al. (2008) the authors proposed a system that also takes into account the opinion of readers to enrich news content information. For each news discussion thread posted on a social bookmarking site, a topic profile is built. The computation of the topic profile relies on the following considerations: (i) comments with a high number of votes are typically the most interesting ones and (ii) most recent comments are representative of the current topic trend. Based on the assumptions, the system retrieves the most relevant news by evaluating, for each news, its relevance according to the topic profile, the popularity, and the timeliness.

The Buzzer system proposed by Phelan et al. (2009) is instead focused on the identification of the current trend in a social community. The recommendation system gathered public and private posts published on Twitter to build a Lucene index. This index is then employed to compare the content of the news provided by the RSS (Really Simple Syndication) sources selected by the user. The systems were tested by analyzing the behavior and the preferences of a pool of ten participants.

Unlike Xue et al. (2008), Wang et al. (2010) proposed to exploit a graph-based model to represent the content similarity between comments and logic relationships among them. Thus, the relevance of comments and their relationships are used to compute the topic profile. Moreover, the authors introduced a novel approach to suggest to the reader the relationships between the recommended news. The approach is based on the analysis of the set of keywords that represent the news topic. A manual evaluation of a pool of judgers has been performed. The proposed system achieved better performance in terms of precision and novelty than baseline recommendation systems (e.g., Okapi method). More recently, user comments have been exploited to perform news recommendation (Li et al., 2010). The idea behind is to figure out recommendable news based on the content of posts published by users of forum-based social systems. The experimental results demonstrate system effectiveness on data coming from a real-life context.

Tag Recommendation

Tags are metadata which may be assigned to Web resources (e.g., photos, videos) published on online communities and social networks. They allow improving the retrieval and the interpretability of the resource content. Tags highlight the main user's interest and, thus, may represent a useful knowledge about the UGC. However, tag collections are typically very sparse and affected by noise, because of the lack of a controlled vocabulary. In fact, the same concept can be described by many different keywords and the same keyword can be associated with different resources covering different contexts. Recommendation systems may improving the quality of tag recommendation process by suggesting most pertinent based on the past tag annotation history. Tag recommendation may be also driven by the interests of either the user who is annotating the resource and the social community. For example, in Basile et al. (2007) a classification system is exploited to maps documents with tags that are likely to be of user interest. More recently, in De Meo et al. (2010) a query expansion method is proposed to build and maintain user profiles. When a user submits a query, the system automatically enriches the query with further "authoritative" tags matching with user needs and desires.

Shepitsen et al. (2008) focused its attention on the problem of tag redundancy and ambiguity. To overcome this issue, it exploits a hierarchical clustering algorithm to identify the correlations among groups of tags. The system was tested on two popular bookmarking systems, delicious and

Last.fm, by evaluating the raking of a resource based on tf-idf score. The results showed that the system achieves a significant performance improvement with respect to state-of-the-art competitors.

Other approaches focus on modeling the interaction between different objects in social tagging systems to cope with tag noise and sparseness. For instance, in Wu et al. (2006) a probabilistic generative model is presented. Social tagging system entities are mapped to a common multi-dimensional vector, where each dimension corresponds to a knowledge category. Unlike Wu et al. (2006), in Kashoob et al. (2009) Latent Semantic Analysis (LSA) is exploited to tackle the tag recommendation problem in large-scale systems, such as Flickr and Delicious. Krestel et al. (2009) also proposed an approach based on Latent Dirichlet Allocation (LDA). Latent topics are elicited from resources equipped with a fairly stable and complete tag set to recommend topics for new resources with only a few tags. Similarly, in Symeonidis et al. (2008) a 3-order tensor is exploited to represent the three main entities of a social tagging system. On the tensor-based representation, a latent semantic analysis and dimensionality reduction is performed by using the Higher Order Singular Value Decomposition (HOSVD) technique.

To recommend additional pertinent tags to users who are annotating Flickr photos, Sigurbjőrnsson and van Zwol (2008) proposed a method based on two steps. Given a photo with user-defined tags, an ordered list of candidate tags is first provided for each photo, based on co-occurrence measure. The co-occurrence between two tags is computed by summing the photos in which both tags are used in the annotation. Both symmetric and asymmetric measures were exploited. Then, the lists of candidate tags are aggregated to generate a ranked list of recommended tags according to two different ranking strategies. Experimental results show that, for almost 70% of the photos, the system suggested a good descriptive tag at the first position of the ranked list, and, for 94%, a good tag is provided among the top 5 ranked tags.

Differently, authors in Garg and Weber (2008) evaluated different approaches to improve Flickr tag recommendation systems. They consider the history of tags selected by both the single users and the community. In particular, a set of promising groups is first identified by analyzing both individual users and group profiles. Then, for each group, a ranked list of suggested tags is generated according to the tag frequency and the previously inserted tags. Experimental results showed that the proposed hybrid approach achieved good accuracy performance. The best results were achieved by pictures characterized by a higher number of tags. More recently, in Hassan et al. (2010) a tag recommender system for social bookmarks is presented. It exploits a clustering-based approach, which groups pertinent tags and bookmarks in homogenous clusters to drive the annotation process. The achieved results show that the system outperforms state-of-the-art collaborative filtering techniques.

In Guan et al. (2009), the authors addressed tag recommendation by exploiting graph-based model. Specifically, graph index is exploited to rank most popular tags based on the pertinence to the resource under exam. Similarly to Guan et al. (2009), Song et al. (2011) propose a tag recommender system that exploits the information provided by the underlying social network structure to provide pertinent tag recommendations. In particular, a graph-based model that combines users, tags, and Web resources is analyzed in order to highlight most accurate personalized tag recommendations for a given resource. The applicability of the proposed system in a real-life use-case is evaluated as well.

Topic Trend Detection

The analysis of the User-Generated Content published on social networks, such as Facebook and Twitter, may be targeted to topic trend detection and analysis. For instance, several new approaches have been proposed to support topic trend analysis from Twitter data by means of data mining techniques. For instance, TwitterMonitor (Mathioudakis & Koudas, 2010) is focused on the detection of topic trends from Twitter streams. This system first identifies and clusters the "bursty" keywords (i.e., keywords that appear in tweets at unusually high rate), and then performs contextual knowledge extraction to compose an accurate description of the identified trends. Trend patterns can also be exploited to support decision-making and recommendation processes. Unlike Mathioudakis and Koudas (2010), Cheong and Lee (2009) analyze the trend of the topics and the demographics of the sets of Twitter users who contribute towards the discussion of particular trends to support decision-making activities.

The work presented in Cagliero and Fiori (in press) (a) also addresses topic trend detection and user behavior analysis from Twitter data. However, it analysis both tweet content and contextual information to support expert in-depth analysis.

Query Engines

Knowledge coming from social networks and online communities may be particularly useful for improving the performance of query engines. Main works that integrate the UGC coming social networks in query engines is presented in the following.

In Bender et al. (2008), the authors proposed a framework that considers user interests in evaluating query results. The social relationships between the users and the correlation among tags associated with media resources (e.g., photos, bookmarks) are represented into a unified graph-based model. The resulting graph is composed of different types of nodes, which represent different elements of the online community, and links, whose weights depend on the type of relationships between nodes. For example, the weight associated with a link between two users can reflect the mutual interest overlap or can be in inverse proportion with the total number of friends of the user. A scoring model is introduced to evaluate the correlation between the keywords query and the relations in the graph model. Different search strategies are exploited to take into account different relationships between query terms, users, and documents. Experiments performed on dumps of the social communities del.icio.us and Flickr showed good precision results according to the interest of the user that performed the query.

In Schenkel et al (2008), the unified graph-based model is exploited to build an efficient query engine. The proposed approach, named ContextMerge, combines a top-k algorithm with dynamic tag expansion, by considering the semantic relationships between tags and dynamic social expansions according to the strength of the relations among users. The effectiveness of the method is evaluated by computing the precision and the normalized discounted cumulative gain (NDCG) on two out of three different datasets crawled from del.icio.us, Flickr and LibraryThing. On average, the precision achieved by different experimental settings is around 36% on del.icio.us and 55% on LibraryThing. Instead, the NDCG score is on average 0.41 and 0.66 for, respectively, Flickr and LibraryThing. Interesting results are also the efficiency performance in term of the cost measure, wall-clock runtimes and abstract cost in terms of the disk accesses. ContextMerge is up to an order of magnitude faster than the standard baseline method of processing inverted list.

The problem of integrating knowledge coming from online communities in online new search engines has been investigated in Abrol and Khan (2010). In particular, they exploited Twitter messages to retrieve keywords that are highly correlated with the user query. To this aim, they consider the geographical content of Twitter message to determine which messages are most relevant according to the user query. From the retrieved messages a set of keywords is selected by also considering the semantic relatedness among them. The system has been tested on three different news events and compared with the document retrieved by original query. A significant accuracy improvement has been achieved for all the considered events.

TwitterMonitor (Mathioudakis & Koudas, 2010) is focused on the detection of topic trends from Twitter streams. This system first identifies and clusters the "bursty" keywords (i.e., keywords that appear in tweets at unusually high rate), and then performs contextual knowledge extraction to compose an accurate description of the identified trends. Trend patterns can also be exploited to support decision-making and recommendation processes. For instance, Cheong and Lee (2009) analyze the trend of the topics and the demographics of the sets of Twitter users who contribute towards the discussion of particular trends to support decision-making activities. Differently, Phelan et al. (2011) combine RSS news and UGC coming from microblogs into a news recommendation system. In particular, they mine Twitter message content to identify emerging topics and breaking events. The RSS stories have been ranked based on a weighted score that takes the Lucene tf-idf score of each article term and the information provided by tweets into account.

Document Summarization

Document summarization focuses on generating concise summaries that describe the content of a single document or a collection of textual documents. Based on the type of generated summaries, summarizers may be classified as sentence-based or keyword-based. The *sentence-based* approach consists in partitioning the document(s) into sentences and selecting the most informative ones to include in the summary (e.g. Carenini et al., 2007; Goldstein, Mittal, Carbonell, & Kantrowitz, 2000; Wang & Li, 2010; Wang et al., 2011). The *keyword-based* approach focuses on detecting salient keywords that effectively summarize the document content by adopting, for instance, co-occurrence measures (Lin & Hovy, 2003) or latent semantic analysis (Dredze, Wallach, Puller, & Pereira, 2008).

In the last several years, some attempts to convey the user-generated content into document summarization process have been performed. For instance, Wikipedia content has been exploited to identify relevant concepts in document collections and analyze their semantic correlations (Gong et al., 2010; Miao & Li, 2010). In particular, in Gong et al. (2010) the authors make use of Wikipedia, currently the world's largest online encyclopedia, to catch the semantic meaning under words. Most peculiar document features are extracted for sentence selection, based on both disambiguated Wikipedia concepts and their first paragraphs in Wikipedia articles. Similarly, in Miao and Li (2010) the WikiSummarizer is presented. It enriches sentence representation with concepts coming from Wikipedia. By examining sentences in the feature space of Wikipedia concepts, sentence similarity is shown to be consistent with human judgment.

Query-based summarization systems that rely on UGC to evaluate document terms have also been proposed (Nastase, 2008; Tang, Yao, & Chen, 2009; Sharifi, Hutton, & Kalita, 2010). For instance, in Nastase (2008) user queries are expanded using encyclopedic knowledge in Wikipedia. The expanded queries are then linked with their associated documents through spreading activation in a graph that represents words and their grammatical connections in these documents. The topic expanded words and activated nodes in the graph are used to produce an extractive summary. The method effectiveness has been validated on the DUC'04 summarization data. Since the analyzed documents often cover more than one topic, the approach proposed in Tang, Yao, and Chen (2009) focused on multi-topic based query-oriented summarization. To overcome the limitations of the existing methods a probabilistic approach is used to generate accurate summaries tailored to the given queries. In parallel, Sharifi, Hutton, and Kalita (2010) addressed the problem of automatic summarization of Twitter topics. To address this issue, a semantics-based algorithm to identify, collect, and summarize post phrases relative to specific trends is proposed and evaluated on real-life data.

Knowledge provided by social annotations has also been adopted in graph-based summarization to better discriminate among document sentences (Zhu et al., 2009). In particular, social knowledge coming Web annotations is integrated in a graph-based summarization system, which associates to social network user appropriate tags in order to personalize the generated summaries. The proposed system is shown to significantly outperform traditional tf-idf-based approaches. Similarly, in Cagliero and Fiori (in press) (b) the authors focus on integrating the analysis of Twitter messages of topical interest (i.e., the toptweets) in multi-document summarization. The proposed system, namely NeDocS, combined the use of an itemset-based model with established information retrieval measures to generate concise yet informative summaries. System effectiveness has been evaluated against a large number of competitors on both the DUC'04 benchmark collections and real-life news collections retrieved from the most renewed newspapers. Finally, the use of supervised approaches in social-driven summarization has also been investigated. In Yang et al. (2011), the authors focus on training a unified graph-based model that convey knowledge coming from UGC by exploiting a dual-wing factor graph (DWFG) to learn the prediction model from Web documents and social networks.

FUTURE RESEARCH DIRECTIONS

The large applicability of data mining approaches to social data makes room to several future research directions. Firstly, the integration of Web portals and online systems with social networks is expected to further increase in the following years. Hence, data mining systems must adapt their mining results to the actual social interests and influences. For instance, online classification systems should become context-aware and social-aware, i.e., they must adapt class prediction to the current contextual and social situation.

Secondly, the development of complex applications based on data mining and information retrieval approaches (e.g., recommender systems, query engines, text processing tools) may evolve towards a more interactive and real-time use. For instance, document summaries generated by state-of-the-art summarizers should dynamically adapt their results based on the preferences of social network users, the news of topical interests published on the most renewed newspapers, and the presence of domain-specific dictionaries which may be used to drive the sentence evaluation process.

Lastly, the analysis of social network structures may also consider the effect of real-life events on Web user actions. For instance, combining the analysis of the context of recent news articles with the study of the evolution of modern social networks analysts may discover potentially relevant correlations between user activities in the social network context and real-world user activities. This may ease the understanding of unexpected changes in the social network graph.

Finally, an open issue remains the validation of the achieved experimental results. Whilst many quality measures have been proposed for addressing specific validation problems, establishing an agreed validation benchmark is still a challenging task. Overcoming this issue may relevantly improve the ability of researchers in comparing their proposed solutions with the existing approaches and, thus, show the usefulness and the effectiveness of their research.

CONCLUSION AND SUGGESTED READINGS

Data mining techniques have largely been adopted to discover relevant patterns from social data collections. They enable the integration of intelligent Web applications and the analysis of the evolution of social networks and online communities. An exhaustive overview of the most established data mining techniques is given in Tan et al. (2006). Their applicability to data coming from the Web is addressed in several research works. Interesting classifications of Web data mining approaches are reported in Bonchi et al. (2011) and Liu (2007). In parallel, a significant research effort has been devoted to analyzing social network structure and evolution (Kumar et al., 2010; Palla et al., 2007). Hence, the integration of the knowledge coming from dynamic social network analysis in modern data mining systems has become a promising research direction (Heymann et al., 2008; Lin et al., 2009; Song et al., 2011).

This chapter overviews main contribution of recent works regarding social network mining and analysis as well as the most appealing data mining applications oriented to knowledge discovery from online communities. It focuses on providing a classification of most established data mining techniques applied to social network data as well as a categorization of the most renowned data mining social applications.

The applications described in this chapter highlight the key role of data mining techniques in improving the understanding of social data and the performance of Web data mining systems. For instance, user behavior patterns and social interests published on social network websites are very useful for improving system performance and usability in real-world applications. For these reasons, we believe that their use in future intelligent Web applications and social networks will become more and more established. Furthermore, the dynamicity of the analyzed online communities is a peculiar aspect. Hence, future applications should monitor the evolution of online community structures (Palla et al., 2007) and Web user interests (Mathioudakis & Koudas, 2010; Nastase, 2008) in order to thoroughly analyze the huge amount of information published on social network websites and promptly react to changes in common user needs and habits.

REFERENCES

Abrol, S., & Khan, L. (2010). TWinner: Understanding news queries with geo-content using Twitter. *Proceedings of the 6th Workshop on Geographic Information Retrieval* (pp. 1-8).

Aggarwal, C. C., & Yu, P. S. (1998). A new framework for itemset generation. In *Proceedings of the seventeenth ACM SIGACT-SIGMOD-SIGART symposium on Principles of database systems* (PODS '98) (pp. 18-24). ACM.

Agrawal, R., Imielinski, T., & Swami, A. (1993). Mining association rules between sets of items in large databases. [ACM press.]. *SIGMOD Record*, *22*(2), 207–216. doi:10.1145/170036.170072.

Agrawal, R., & Psaila, G. (1995). *Active data mining*. In *First International Conference on Knowledge Discovery and Data Mining* (pp. 3-8). ACM press.

Agrawal, R., & Srikant, R. (1995). *Mining generalized association rules*. In *International Conference on Very Large Data Bases* (pp. 407-419). Morgan Kaufmann.

Asur, S., Huberman, B. A., Szabo, G., & Wang, C. (2011). Trends in social media: Persistence and decay. In *Proceedings of the Fifth International AAAI Conference on Weblogs and Social Media* (pp. 434-437). AAAI press.

Backstrom, L., Huttenlocher, D., Kleinberg, J., & Lan, X. (2006). Group formation in large social networks: Membership, growth, and evolution. *Proceedings of the 12th ACM SIGKDD international conference on Knowledge discovery and data mining* (pp. 44-54). ACM press.

Baralis, E., Cagliero, L., Cerquitelli, T., D'Elia, V., & Garza, P. (2010). *Support driven opportunistic aggregation for generalized itemset extraction*. In Proceedings of *The 2010 IEEE Conference on Intelligent Systems* (pp. 102-107). IEEE press.

Barsky, M., Kim, S., Weninger, T., & Han, J. (2011). *Mining flipping correlations from large datasets with taxonomies*. In *Proceedings of the Very Large DataBase Conference* (VLDB'12) (pp. 370-381). Morgan Kaufmann.

Basile, P., Gendarmi, D., Lanubile, F., & Semeraro, G. (2007). Recommending smart tags in a social bookmarking system. Bridging the Gap between Semantic Web and Web (pp. 22-29).

Becker, H., Naaman, M., & Gravano, L. (2011). Beyond trending topics: Real-world event identification on Twitter. In *Proceedings of the Fifth International AAAI Conference on Weblogs and Social Media*. AAAI press.

Bender, M., Crecelius, T., Kacimi, M., Michel, S., Neumann, T., Parreira, J. X., et al. (2008). Exploiting social relations for query expansion and result ranking. *IEEE 24th International Conference on Data Engineering Workshop,* 2, (pp. 501-506). IEEE press.

Bonchi, F., Castillo, C., Gionis, A., & Jaimes, A. (2011). Social network analysis and mining for business applications. ACM Transactions on Intelligent Systems Technologies, 2(3), 22:1-22:37. ACM press.

Bottcher, M., Nauck, D., Ruta, D., & Spott, M. (2007). Towards a framework for change detection in data sets. In Bramer, M., Coenen, F., & Tuson, A. (Eds.), *Research and Development in Intelligent Systems XXIII* (pp. 115–128). Springer London. doi:10.1007/978-1-84628-663-6_9.

Brin, S., Motwani, R., & Silverstein, C. (1997). Beyond market baskets: Generalizing association rules to correlations. [ACM press.]. *SIGMOD Record, 26*(2), 265–276. doi:10.1145/253262.253327.

Cagliero, L., & Fiori, A. (in press) (a). *Generalized association rule mining from Twitter. Intelligent data analysis*. IOS press.

Cagliero, L., & Fiori, A. (in press). (b). News document summarization driven by user-generated content. In *Social media mining and social network analysis: Emerging research*. IGI Global.

Cagliero, L., Fiori, A., & Grimaudo, L. (in press). Personalized tag recommendation based on generalized rules. *Transactions on Intelligent Systems and Technology*. ACM press.

Carenini, G., Ng, R. T., & Zhou, X. (2007). Summarizing email conversations with clue words. In *World Wide Web Conference Series* (pp. 91–100).

Chakrabarti, D., Kumar, R., & Tomkins, A. (2006). Evolutionary clustering. In *Proceedings of the 12th ACM SIGKDD international conference on Knowledge discovery and data mining* (pp. 554-560). ACM press.

Chen, J., Zaiane, O. R., & Goebel, R. (2009). *Detecting communities in social networks using max-min modularity* (pp. 978–989). SDM.

De Meo, P., Quattrone, G., & Ursino, D. (2010). A query expansion and user profile enrichment approach to improve the performance of recommender systems operating on a folksonomy. *User Modeling and User-Adapted Interaction, 20*(1), 41–86. doi:10.1007/s11257-010-9072-6.

Dredze, M., Wallach, H. M., Puller, D., & Pereira, F. (2008). Generating summary keywords for emails using topics. In *Proceedings of the 13th international conference on Intelligent user interfaces* (pp. 199-206).

DuBois, T., Golbeck, J., Kleint, J., & Srinivasan, A. (2009). *Improving recommendation accuracy by clustering social networks with trust*. Recommender Systems & the Social Web.

Garg, N., & Weber, I. (2008). Personalized tag suggestion for flickr. In *Proceeding of the 17th international conference on World Wide Web* (pp. 1063-1064).

Golbeck, J., & Hendler, J. (2006). Filmtrust: Movie recommendations using trust in web-based social networks. In *Proceedings of the IEEE Consumer communications and networking conference*, 42, 43-44. IEEE press.

Goldstein, J., Mittal, V., Carbonell, J., & Kantrowitz, M. (2000). Multi-document summarization by sentence extraction. In *Proceedings of the ANLP/NAACL Workshop on Automatic Summarization* (pp. 40-48).

Gong, S., Qu, Y., & Tian, S. (2010). Summarization using Wikipedia. *Proceedings of Text Analysis Conference.*

Guan, Z., Bu, J., Mei, Q., Chen, C., & Wang, C. (2009). Personalized tag recommendation using graph-based ranking on multi-type interrelated objects. In *Proceedings of the 32nd international ACM SIGIR conference on Research and development in information retrieval* (pp. 540-547).

Han, J., & Fu, Y. (1999). Mining multiple-level association rules in large databases. [IEEE press.]. *IEEE Transactions on Knowledge and Data Engineering*, *11*(5), 798–805. doi:10.1109/69.806937.

Herlocker, J. L., Konstan, J. A., Terveen, L. G., & Riedl, J. T. (2004). Evaluating collaborative filtering recommender systems. [TOIS]. *ACM Transactions on Information Systems*, *22*(1), 5–53. doi:10.1145/963770.963772.

Heymann, P., Ramage, D., & Garcia-Molina, H. (2008). Social tag prediction. *Proceedings of the 31st annual international ACM SIGIR conference on Research and development in information retrieval* (pp. 531-538). ACM press.

Hilderman, R. J., & Hamilton, H. J. (2001). *Knowledge discovery and measures of interest.* Kluwer Academic Publishers. doi:10.1007/978-1-4757-3283-2.

Hipp, J., Myka, A., Wirth, R., & Guntzer, U. (1998). A new algorithm for faster mining of generalized rules. In *Proceedings of the* 2nd *European Symposium on Principles of Data Mining and Knowledge Discovery* (pp. 72–82). Springer.

Hotho, A., Jäschke, R., Schmitz, C., & Stumme, G. (2006). BibSonomy: A social bookmark and publication sharing system. In *Proceedings of the Conceptual Structures Tool Interoperability Workshop at the 14th International Conference on Conceptual Structures* (pp. 87-102).

Hotho, A., Jäschke, R., Schmitz, C., & Stumme, G. (2006). Mining association rules in folksonomies. In *Data Science and Classification* (pp. 261–270). Springer Berlin Heidelberg.

Kashoob, S., Caverlee, J., & Ding, Y. (2009). A categorical model for discovering latent structure in social annotations. In *Proceedings of the International AAAI Conference on Weblogs and social media* (pp. 27-35).

Koren, Y., Bell, R., & Volinsky, C. (2009). Matrix factorization techniques for recommender systems. *Computer*, *42*(8), 30–37. doi:10.1109/MC.2009.263.

Krestel, R., Fankhauser, P., & Nejdl, W. (2009). Latent Dirichlet allocation for tag recommendation. *Proceedings of the 3rd conference on Recommender systems* (pp. 61-68).

Kumar, R., Novak, J., & Tomkins, A. (2010). Structure and evolution of online social networks. Link mining: Models, algorithms, and applications (pp. 337-357).

Li, Q., Wang, J., Chen, Y., & Lin, Z. (n.d.). User comments for news recommendation in forum-based social media. *Information Sciences. Elsevier.*.

Lin, Y. R., Chi, Y., Zhu, S., Sundaram, H., & Tseng, B. L. (2009). *Analyzing communities and their evolutions in dynamic social networks. ACM Transactions on Knowledge Discovery from Data, 3(2)*. ACM press.

Liu, B. (2007). *Web data mining*. Springer.

Liu, B., Ma, Y., & Lee, R. (2001). Analyzing the interestingness of association rules from the temporal dimension. *Proceedings of the International Conference on Data Mining* (pp. 377-384). IEEE press.

Mathioudakis, M., & Koudas, N. (2010). TwitterMonitor: Trend detection over the Twitter stream. In *Proceedings of the 2010 international Conference on Management of data* (pp. 1155-1158). ACM press.

Miao, Y., & Li, C. (2010). WikiSummarizer - A Wikipedia-based summarization system. In *Proceedings of Text Analysis Conference.*

Nastase, V. (2008). Topic-driven multi-document summarization with encyclopedic knowledge and spreading activation. In *Proceedings of Conference on Empirical Methods on Natural Language Processing* (pp. 763-772).

Palla, G., Barabasi, A. L., & Vicsek, T. (2007). Quantifying social group evolution. *Nature*, *446*(7136), 664–667. doi:10.1038/nature05670 PMID:17410175.

Phelan, O., McCarthy, K., & Smyth, B. (2009). Using twitter to recommend real-time topical news. *Proceedings of the third ACM conference on Recommender systems* (pp. 385-388). ACM press.

Pramudiono, I., & Kitsuregawa, M. (2004). FP-tax: Tree structure based generalized association rule mining. In *Proceedings ACM SIGMOD workshop on Research issues in data mining and knowledge discovery* (pp. 60-63). ACM press.

Savasere, A., Omiecinski, E., & Navathe, S. B. (1998). Mining for strong negative associations in a large database of customer transactions. In *Proceedings of the Fourteenth International Conference on Data Engineering* (ICDE '98) (pp. 494-502). IEEE Computer Society.

Schenkel, R., Crecelius, T., Kacimi, M., Michel, S., Neumann, T., Parreira, J. X., & Weikum, G. (2008). Efficient top-k querying over social-tagging networks. In *Proceedings of the 31st annual international ACM SIGIR conference on Research and development in information retrieval* (pp. 523-530). ACM press.

Schőnhofen, P. (2009). Identifying document topics using the Wikipedia category network. *Web Intelligence and Agent Systems*, *7*(2), 195–207.

Shepitsen, A., Gemmell, J., Mobasher, B., & Burke, R. (2008). Personalized recommendation in social tagging systems using hierarchical clustering. In *Proceedings of the 2008 ACM conference on Recommender systems* (pp. 259-266). ACM press.

Sigurbjőrnsson, B., & van Zwol, R. (2008). Flickr tag recommendation based on collective knowledge. In *Proceedings of the 17th international conference on World Wide Web* (pp. 327-336).

Song, Y., Zhang, L., & Giles, C. L. (2011). Automatic tag recommendation algorithms for social recommender systems. [ACM press.]. *ACM Transactions on the Web*, *5*(1), 1–31. doi:10.1145/1921591.1921595.

Spiliopoulou, M., Ntoutsi, I., Theodoridis, Y., & Schult, R. (2006). Monic: Modeling and monitoring cluster transitions. In *Proceedings of the 12th ACM SIGKDD international conference on Knowledge discovery and data mining* (pp. 706-711). ACM press.

Sriram, B., Fuhry, D., Demir, E., Ferhatosmanoglu, H., & Demirbas, M. (2010). Short text classification in twitter to improve information filtering. In *Proceeding of the 33rd international ACM SIGIR conference on research and development in information retrieval* (pp. 841-842). ACM press.

Suchanek, F. M., Kasneci, G., & Weikum, G. (2008). Yago: A large ontology from wikipedia and wordnet. *Web Semantics: Science. Services and Agents on the World Wide Web*, *6*(3), 203–217. doi:10.1016/j.websem.2008.06.001.

Sun, J., Faloutsos, C., Papadimitriou, S., & Yu, P. S. (2007). GraphScope: Parameter-free mining of large time-evolving graphs. In *Proceedings of the 13th ACM SIGKDD international conference on Knowledge discovery and data mining* (pp. 687-696). ACM press.

Symeonidis, P., Nanopoulos, A., & Manolopoulos, Y. (2008). Tag recommendations based on tensor dimensionality reduction. In *Proceedings of the ACM conference on Recommender systems,* pp. 43-50.

Tan, P. N., Kumar, V., & Srivastava, J. (2000). Indirect association: Mining higher order dependencies in data. In *Proceedings of the 4th European Conference on Principles of Data Mining and Knowledge Discovery* (PKDD'00) (pp. 632-637). Springer-Verlag.

Tan, P. N., Kumar, V., & Srivastava, J. (2002). Selecting the right interestingness measure for association patterns. In *ACM SIGKDD International Conference on Knowledge Discovery and Data Mining* (KDD'02) (pp. 32-41). ACM press.

Tan, P. N., Steinbach, M., & Kumar, V. (2006). *Introduction to data mining*. Pearson Addison Wesley.

Tang, L., & Liu, H. (2009). Relation learning via latent social dimensions. In *Proceedings of the 15th ACM SIGKDD international conference on Knowledge discovery and data mining* (pp. 817-826).

Tang, L., & Liu, H. (2010). Toward predicting collective behavior via social dimension extraction. *IEEE Intelligent Systems*, *25*(4), 19–25. doi:10.1109/MIS.2010.36.

Tao, Y., & Tsu, M. (2009). Mining frequent itemsets in time-varying data streams. In *Proceedings of the XVIII Conference on Information and Knowledge Management* (pp. 1521-1524). ACM press.

Wang, D., & Li, T. (2010). Document update summarization using incremental hierarchical clustering. In *Proceedings of the 19th ACM international conference on Information and knowledge management* (pp. 279–288). ACM press.

Wang, D., Zhu, S., Li, T., Chi, Y., & Gong, Y. (2011). Integrating document clustering and multidocument summarization. ACM Transactions on Knowledge Discovery from Data, 5(3), 14:1-14:26. ACM press.

Wang, J., Li, Q., Chen, Y. P., Liu, J., Zhang, C., & Lin, Z. (2010). News recommendation in forum-based social media. In *Proceedings of the Twenty-Fourth AAAI Conference on Artificial Intelligence* (pp. 1449-1454). AAAI press.

Wang, P., Hu, J., Zeng, H. J., & Chen, Z. (2009). Using Wikipedia knowledge to improve text classification. *Knowledge and Information Systems*, *19*(3), 265–281. doi:10.1007/s10115-008-0152-4.

Wu, T., Chen, Y., & Han, J. (2010). Re-examination of interestingness measures in pattern mining: A unified framework. [ACM press.]. *Data Mining and Knowledge Discovery*, 21.

Wu, X., Zhang, L., & Yu, Y. (2006). Exploring social annotations for the semantic web. *Proceedings of the 15th International Conference on the World Wide Web* (pp. 417-426).

Xue, Y., Zhang, C., Zhou, C., Lin, X., & Li, Q. (2008). An effective news recommendation in social media based on users' preference. In *Proceedings of the 2008 International Workshop on Education Technology and Training & 2008 International Workshop on Geoscience and Remote Sensing,* 1, 627-631.

Yang, Z., Cai, K., Tang, J., Zhang, L., Su, Z., & Li, J. (2011). Social context summarization. *International ACM SIGIR Conference on Research and Development in Information Retrieval* (pp. 255-264). ACM press.

Yin, Z., Li, R., Mei, Q., & Han, J. (2009). Exploring social tagging graph for web object classification. *Proceedings of the 15th ACM SIGKDD international conference on Knowledge discovery and data mining* (pp. 957-966). ACM press.

Yoo, S., Yang, Y., Lin, F., & Moon, I. C. (2009). Mining social networks for personalized email prioritization. *Proceedings of the 15th ACM SIGKDD international conference on Knowledge discovery and data mining* (pp. 967-976). ACM press.

Zhu, J., Wang, C., He, X., Bu, J., Chen, C., Shang, S., et al. (2009). Tag-oriented document summarization. *Proceedings of the 18th international ACM conference on World Wide Web Conference* (pp. 1195—1196). ACM press.

ADDITIONAL READING

Agrawal, R., & Srikant, R. (1994). Fast algorithms for mining association rules in large data-bases. *Proceedings of the 20th International Conference on Very Large Data Base* (pp. 487-499). Morgan Kaufmann.

Aleman-Meza, B., Nagarajan, M., Ramakrishnan, C., Ding, L., Kolari, P., Sheth, A. P., et al. (2006). Semantic analytics on social networks: Experiences in addressing the problem of conflict of interest detection. *Proceedings of the 15th international conference on World Wide Web* (pp. 407-416). ACM press.

Anagnostopoulos, A., Kumar, R., & Mahdian, M. (2008). Influence and correlation in social networks. *Proceeding of the 14th ACM SIGKDD international conference on Knowledge discovery and data mining* (pp. 7-15). ACM press.

Anyanwu, K., & Sheth, A. P. (2003). P-Queries: Enabling querying for semantic associations on the Semantic Web. *Proceedings of the 12th international conference on World Wide Web* (pp. 690-699). ACM press.

Auer, S., Bizer, C., Kobilarov, G., Lehmann, J., Cyganiak, R., & Ives, Z. (2007). Dbpedia: A nucleus for a web of open data. *The Semantic Web*, *4825*, 722–735. doi:10.1007/978-3-540-76298-0_52.

Baralis, E., Cagliero, L., Fiori, A., & Jabeen, S. (2012). *Multi-document summarization exploiting frequent itemsets*. In *ACM Symposium on Applied Computing* (SAC' 12) (pp. 782-786). ACM press.

Baron, S., Spiliopoulou, M., & Gunther, O. (2003). Efficient monitoring of patterns in data mining environments. In Kalinichenko, L., Manthey, R., Thalheim, B., & Wloka, U. (Eds.), *Advances in databases and information systems* (*Vol. 2798*, pp. 253–265). Lecture Notes in Computer Science Springer Berlin Heidelberg. doi:10.1007/978-3-540-39403-7_20.

Bonhard, P., & Sasse, M. A. (2006). 'Knowing me, knowing you' - Using profiles and social networking to improve recommender systems. *BT Technology Journal*, *24*(3), 84–98. doi:10.1007/s10550-006-0080-3.

Cha, M., Mislove, A., & Gummadi, K. P. (2009). A measurement-driven analysis of information propagation in the flickr social network. In *Proceedings of the 18th international conference on World Wide Web* (pp. 721-730). ACM press.

Chi, X., Song, D., & Zhou, K. Hino, & Tseng, B. (2007). Evolutionary spectral clustering by incorporating temporal smoothness. In *Proc. 13th ACM SIGKDD International Conference on Knowledge Discovery and Data Mining* (pp. 162). ACM press.

Christakis, N. A., & Fowler, J. H. (2007). The spread of obesity in a large social network over 32 years. *The New England Journal of Medicine*, *357*(4), 370–379. doi:10.1056/NEJMsa066082 PMID:17652652.

Crandall, D., Cosley, D., Huttenlocher, D., Kleinberg, J., & Suri, S. (2008). Feedback effects between similarity and social influence in online communities. In *Proceedings of the 14th ACM SIGKDD international conference on Knowledge discovery and data mining* (pp. 160-168). ACM press.

Ereteo, G., Buffa, M., Gandon, F., Grohan, P., Leitzelman, L., & Sander, P. (2008). State of the art on social network analysis and its applications on a semantic web. In *Proceedings of the 7th International Semantic Web Conference.*

Gabrilovich, E., & Markovitch, S. (2007). Computing semantic relatedness using Wikipedia-based explicit semantic analysis. In *Proceedings of the 20th International Joint Conference on Artificial Intelligence* (pp. 6-12).

Ghita, S., Nejdl, W., & Paiu, R. (2005). *Semantically rich recommendations in social networks for sharing, exchanging and ranking semantic context* (pp. 293–307). The Semantic Web - ISWC. doi:10.1007/11574620_23.

Greene, D., Doyle, D., & Cunningham, P. (2010). Tracking the evolution of communities in dynamic social networks. In *Proceedings on the International Conference on Advances in Social Networks Analysis and Mining (ASONAM'10)* (pp. 176-183).

Guo, L., Tan, E., Chen, S., Zhang, X., & Zhao, Y. E. (2009). Analyzing patterns of user content generation in online social networks. In *Proceedings of the 15th ACM SIGKDD international conference on Knowledge discovery and data mining* (pp. 369-378). ACM press.

Hassan, M. T., Karim, A., Javed, F., & Arshad, N. (2010). Self-optimizing a clustering-based tag recommender for social bookmarking systems. In *Proceedings of the 2010 Ninth International Conference on Machine Learning and Applications* (pp. 601-606).

Hu, X., Zhang, X., Lu, C., Park, E. M., & Zhou, X. (2009). Exploiting Wikipedia as external knowledge for document clustering. In *Proceedings of the 15th ACM SIGKDD international conference on Knowledge discovery and data mining, 16*(7), 389-396. ACM press.

Java, A., Song, X., Finin, T., & Tseng, B. (2007). Why we twitter: Understanding microblogging usage and communities. In *Proceedings of the 9th WebKDD and 1st SNA-KDD 2007 workshop on Web mining and social network analysis* (pp. 56-65).

Jung, J. J. (2008). Query transformation based on semantic centrality in Semantic Social Network. *Journal of Universal Computer Science, 14*(7), 1031–1047.

Jung, J. J., & Euzenat, J. (2007). Towards semantic social networks. In *Proceedings of the 4th European conference on The Semantic Web* (pp. 267-280).

Kumar, R., Novak, J., & Tomkins, A. (2010). *Structure and evolution of online social networks. Link Mining: Models* (pp. 337–357). Algorithms, and Applications.

Kuramochi, M., & Karypis, G. (2004). An efficient algorithm for discovering frequent subgraphs. [IEEE press.]. *IEEE Transactions on Knowledge and Data Engineering*, *16*(9), 1038–1051. doi:10.1109/TKDE.2004.33.

Lam, H. Y., & Yeung, D. Y. (2007). A learning approach to spam detection based on social networks. *4th Conference on Email and Anti-Spam (CEAS)*.

Lau, R. Y. K., Song, D., Li, Y., Cheung, T. C. H., & Hao, J. (2009). Toward a fuzzy domain ontology extraction method for adaptive e-learning. [IEEE press.]. *IEEE Transactions on Knowledge and Data Engineering*, *21*(6), 800–813. doi:10.1109/TKDE.2008.137.

Lerman, K. (2007). Social networks and social information filtering on Digg. In *Proceedings of International Conference on Weblogs and Social Media*.

Li, X., Guo, L., & Zhao, Y. (2008). Tag-based social interest discovery. In *Proceedings of the 17th international conference on World Wide Web* (WWW '08) (pp. 675-684). ACM.

Lu, C., Hu, X., Chen, X., Park, J. R., He, T., & Li, Z. (2010). The topic-perspective model for social tagging systems. In *Proceedings of the 16th ACM SIGKDD international conference on Knowledge discovery and data mining* (pp. 683-692). ACM press.

Matsuo, Y., Mori, J., & Hamasaki, M. (2006). POLYPHONET: An advanced social network extraction system from the web structure and evolution of online social networks. In *Proceedings of the World Wide Web Conference* (pp. 262-278). ACM press.

Michalski, R. S., & Stepp, R. (2009). Automated construction of classifications conceptual clustering versus numerical taxonomy. IEEE Transactions on pattern analysis and machine learning, 4, 396-410. IEEE press.

Mihalcea, R., & Csomai, A. (2007). Wikify!: Linking documents to encyclopedic knowledge. In *Proceedings of the sixteenth ACM conference on Conference on information and knowledge management*, 7, 233-242. ACM press.

Mika, P. (2005). Social networks and the semantic web: The next challenge. [IEEE press.]. *IEEE Intelligent Systems*, *20*(1), 82–85.

Mika, P. (2007). Ontologies are us: A unified model of social networks and semantics. *Web Semantics: Science* [ACM press.]. *Services and Agents on the World Wide Web*, *5*(1), 5–15. doi:10.1016/j.websem.2006.11.002.

Mislove, A., Marcon, M., Gummadi, K. P., Druschel, P., & Bhattacharjee, B. (2007). Measurement and analysis of online social networks. In *Proceedings of the 7th ACM SIGCOMM conference on Internet measurement* (pp. 29-42).

Passant, A., Hastrup, T., Bojars, U., & Breslin, J. (2008). Microblogging: A semantic and distributed approach. In *Proceedings of the 4th Workshop on Scripting for the Semantic Web*.

Rowe, R., & Creamer, G. (2007). Automated social hierarchy detection through email network analysis. *Proceedings of the joint 9th WEB-KDD and 1st SNA-KDD conference* (pp. 109-117).

Sharifi, B., Hutton, M. A., & Kalita, J. (2010). Automatic summarization of Twitter topics. *National Workshop on Design and Analysis of Algorithms*.

Shen, H. T., Shu, Y., & Yu, B. (2004). Efficient semantics-based content search in P2P network. [IEEE press.]. *IEEE Transactions on Knowledge and Data Engineering*, *16*(7), 813–826. doi:10.1109/TKDE.2004.1318564.

Specia, L., & Motta, E. (2007). Integrating folksonomies in the Semantic Web. The semantic web: Research and applications (pp. 624-639).

Szomszor, M., Cattuto, C., Alani, H., O'Hara, K., Baldassarri, A., Loreto, V., & Servedio, V. D. P. (2007). Folksonomies, the semantic web, and movie recommendation. *4th European semantic web conference, bridging the gap between semantic web and web,* 2.

Tang, J., Sun, J., Wang, C., & Yang, Z. (2009). Social influence analysis in large-scale networks. In *Proceedings of the 15th ACM SIGKDD international conference on Knowledge discovery and data mining* (pp. 807-816). ACM press.

Tang, J., Yao, L., & Chen, D. (2009). Multi-topic based query-oriented summarization. *SIAM International Conference Data Mining*.

Tang, J., Zhang, J., Yao, L., Li, J., Zhang, L., & Zhoung, S. (2008). ArnetMiner: Extraction and mining of academic social networks. *International conference on Knowledge discovery and data mining* (pp. 990-998).

Tao, L., & Sarabjot, S. A. (2009). Exploiting domain knowledge by automated taxonomy generation in recommender systems. In *Proceedings of 10th International Conference on E-comemerce and Web Technologies* (pp. 120-131).

Walter, F. E., Battiston, S., & Schweitzer, F. (2008). A model of a trust-based recommendation system on a social network. *Autonomous Agents and Multi-Agent Systems, 16*(1), 57–74. doi:10.1007/s10458-007-9021-x.

Yu, L. (2011). OWL: Web Ontology Language. A Developer's Guide to the Semantic Web (pp. 155-239).

KEY TERMS AND DEFINITIONS

Association Rule: An association rule is an implication in the form A → B, where A and B are sets of data items, which represent correlations hidden in a source dataset.

Cluster: Group of objects with similar properties and having different characteristics with respect to objects outside the cluster.

Collective Behavior: Behaviors of groups of individuals who are exposed in a social network environment.

Data Mining and Knowledge Discovery (KDD): The process of extracting hidden information from large data collections.

Social Bookmarking: Social bookmarking web services allow users to share, organize, search, and manage bookmarks of web resources.

Social Influence: The phenomenon that the action of individuals can produce their friends to act in a similar way.

Social Network: Social networks are Web platforms that allow users to define a profile, build a network with other users (friends), and share information or user-generated media content with their friends.

User-Generated Content: User-generated content (UGC) refers to various kinds of publicly available media content that are produced by Web users, such as document, photos, and videos.

Chapter 8
Data Mining Prospects in Mobile Social Networks

Gebeyehu Belay Gebremeskel
Chongqing University, China

Zhongshi He
Chongqing University, China

Huazheng Zhu
Chongqing University, China

ABSTRACT

Unable to accommodating new technologies, including social technology, mobile devices and computing are other potential problems, which are significant challenges to social-networking service. The very broad range of such social-networking challenges and problems are demanding advanced and dynamic tools. Therefore, in this chapter, we introduced and discussed data mining prospects to overcome the traditional social-networking challenges and problems, which led to optimization of MSNs application and performances. The proposed method infers defining and investigating social-networking problems using data mining techniques and algorithms based on the large-scale data. The approach is also exploring the possible potential of users and systems contexts, which leads to mine the personal contexts such as the users' locations and situations from the mobile logs. In these sections, we discussed and introduced new ideas on social technologies, data mining techniques and algorithm's prospects, social technology's key functional and performances, which include social analysis, security and fraud detections by presenting a brief analysis, and modeling based descriptions. The approach also empirically discussed using the real survey data, which the result showed how data mining vitally significant to explore MSNs performance and its crosscutting impacts. Finally, this chapter provides fundamental insight to researchers and practitioners who need to know data mining prospects and techniques to analyze large, complex and frequently changing data. This chapter is also providing a state-of-the-art of data mining techniques and algorithm's dynamic prospects.

DOI: 10.4018/978-1-4666-4213-3.ch008

Copyright © 2013, IGI Global. Copying or distributing in print or electronic forms without written permission of IGI Global is prohibited.

1. INTRODUCTION

These days, researches in Mobile Social Networks (MSN)s are at the forefront of innovation in data mining (Bonchi et al., 2011) and prevalent on the Internet, which becomes a hot research topic attracting many professionals from a variety of fields. The reason is that all entities (such as friends, devices, or systems) in this world are related to one another in one way or other. Thus, social network mining is a growing research field. It aims at bringing researchers together from different fields, which includes machine learning, artificial intelligence, optimization, graph theory, mobile computing and other fields with the goal of solving fundamental problems that the rise of social networks has brought into the scientific arena (Bonchi et al., 2011; Park & Cho, 2010). MSNs are a matured level of the traditional social networking, which is advancing to location-acquisition and mobile communication technologies empower people to use location data with existing online social networks. The dimension of location helps bridge the gap between the physical world and on-line social-networking services. As mobile devices are the most essential components of MSNs, which users are capable of access social service as their own locations, able to know who are there, and many other benefits. These also give a chance to collect record and store large data sets, which can be significant to further analysis of MSNs applications and performances.

The rapid growth of collected and stored MSNs data are an interacting research issue as challenges and opportunities or prospects of the social network applications, which is demanding powerful tools processing (Shen & Ma, 2008). The issue of mining large data set is exciting research topic in which enters the center stage of data exploration. Social network analytics involves the rapid analysis of user-generated system content (for example, blogs, tweets, microblogs, etc.), which the social businesses can enjoy dynamic social networking that could handle the implicit user feedbacks related to services or other social media resources, events, and society. The spread of information via social media challenges, users' knowledge of network science and information distribution, and issue of new opportunities and its understanding is the growing challenges of social network's applications and dynamisms (Shim et al., 2011). At the same time, mobile computing towards social networking is truly becoming pervasive in the everyday lives, which poses other additional challenges for research on social network's access and computing, activity recognition and intention detection, and other problems (McLennan & Howell, 2010).

Currently, the demands of social networking and data generated from its services have exceeded the dimensions, which is invisible to perform thorough and accurate analysis with traditional data manipulation methods. Since, the conventional data analysis method is not networked to accommodate the newly developing social-networking applications. Therefore, in this chapter, we introduce data mining prospects and discussed its successful opportunity to overcome the challenges, which is also significant to optimize MSNs performance and applications (Ploderer et al., 2010). The data mining prospects refer to the ability to explore and learn from past trends, and current status concatenates to the future predictions. The approach is searching the possible options for the challenges based on extracted knowledge or data explorations with the involvements of mobile and computing technologies. It is an advanced machine learning tool to develop patterns from large data sets, which is essential to handle MSNs multi function. Thus, data mining prospects or applications in MSNs arise in several ways, including social groups' speech processing, social interconnection's machine translation, mobile technologies, and visual processing. Machine learning at MSNs raises deep scientific and engineering challenges (Domingos & Richardson, 2001).

The goal of data mining prospects in the field of social networking is multi dimensional outcomes, which include developing acceptable solutions of challenges and problems, data handling, managing and exploring towards optimization and perdition of MSNs applications as the systems and users' contexts. The methods are first, defining the research issues or challenges of traditional social networking, formulate and explore them. Based on the data exploration and interpretations predict the way to optimize of MSN applications and their performances. Through these prospects' techniques and algorithms, we discussed the detail procedures and functionality of MSNs including its future directions and dynamisms. The approach is also essential to understand the entail users in social networks (for example, vast blogosphere), identify hidden groups in a social-networking site, notice user perceptions or sentiments from users' contexts, such as locations, current situations, and others. Therefore, the approaches to the data mining process are handling large-scale data, extract actionable patterns, and gain insightful knowledge, which the social networking is widely used for various purposes, such as decision making, efficient social media access, and others. Data mining in social service, therefore, viewed as an extension through the use of a decision support system (Shim et al., 2011; Daskalaki et al., 2003), which is extremely designed to address the problem associated with maintaining a strong social network infrastructure and the need to maximize network reliability, and minimizing risks. Within a huge amount of data usually lies hidden knowledge of strategic importance, which the natural ability cannot analyze unless with powerful tools (Bose & Mahaptra, 2001). Thus, a deep understanding of the knowledge hidden in MSNs data is vital to the successful application and performance of competitive position and decision making.

The rest of the chapter organized as section 2, is the related work of data mining prospects and scopes in MSNs, and also the dynamism of social networks. In section three, we discussed mobile social networks mining in details in terms of social network mapping, data structure, social enhancement and privacy. In section four, we discussed data mining algorithms and components including social unobtrusive assessments, mining algorithms, MSN data intelligence and mining process. Section five discussed performance evaluation and model development of the basis of surveying real data and the last section conclusion and future research directions followed by acknowledgment and reference, which are cited throughout this chapter.

2. RELATED WORKS

Data mining research has successfully produced various methods, tools, and algorithms for handling large amounts of data to solve real-world problems (Ngai et al., 2011; Shim et al., 2011). Modern data mining has become an integral part of many application domains, including Mobile Social Networks (MSN), data warehousing, predictive analytics, and decision support systems. MSN is a companion's mobile technology and technology in social science as a network service, platform, or site (Kayastha et al., 2011). MSNs are real and/or virtual relationships of people that focusing on building and reflecting of social networks or social relations among them. Those who have common interests and/or activities are interacting and making relations with someone else having common interests with somewhat, backgrounds and/or activities develop their own communities (Backstrom et al., 2006). It is conceptual interactions and relationships that the concept of social networking started among the people who have a common interest to form networks. People under the network could be secure many socialized, helped each other whenever they had difficulty, and thus, social networking helped them to make life stable (Aarthi et al., 2011; Min &

Cho, 2011). Therefore, data mining of MSNs can expand researchers' capability of understanding new phenomena due to the use of social networks and improve social media to provide better services and develop innovative opportunities.

Research in MSNs from the prospects of data mining provides many significant, including detecting the structural patterns of social networks. Data mining playing a role of understand the inertial social objects in the vast blogosphere, which includes knowing implicit groups in the systems or sites, sense user perceptions for analysis of users' behavior analysis and others. These tasks ranging from accessing social services to make new friends, understanding network development and changing entity relationships, which includes protect user privacy, build and strengthen trust among users or between users and entities. Therefore, data mining refers to the process of extracting new knowledge from a huge amount of data (Nair & Sarasamma, 2007). It is the use of mining algorithms for extracting patterns from large data, which is capable of discover the past success and failures and predict what happen in the future and achieve its popularity through time in relation to World Wide Web (Rahman et al., 2010). Data mining techniques used to analyze human interactions and relationships or social networks system to optimizing social-networking service (Jensen & Neville, 2002), which is useful in any field where there are large data to extract meaningful patterns and rules (Bonchi et al., 2011). The social network's data is always so dynamic and heterogeneous large that manual analysis of the data is practically impossible (Barbier & Lui, 2011), which requires the data mining techniques that promised solution to analyze, distribute and access large data sets of the social-networking services (Guo et al., 2011). It is also essential to pattern development and predicting techniques, which made a better of social services and resource's access and gives an insightful multidimensional data analysis to understand the behaviors of users (Pushpa & Shobhag, 2012; Hullermeier, 2005) in the networks.

Mobile device's activities are flourishing in diversified branches of social-networking endeavor, despite numerous hurdles inflicting on their ways that are truly cross-sectoral (Yang et al., 2010). That is mobile utilization of social-networking platforms increases the structural interaction and interrelationships of the social members. Since the mobile devices are used in dynamically varying situations, many researchers have tried to find complex contexts with advanced approaches, which researches on extracted the landmarks from individual logs such as the user's position, emotion, and events by using modular Bayesian Networks (Park & Cho, 2010; Wang & Man, 2009). There are also studies focused on the user's physical activity such as walking, resting, and sleeping by using data mining based pattern recognition techniques with the integrated mobile accelerometer or a group of wearable sensors connected to a mobile phone (Shen & Ma, 2008). Therefore, the advent of cell phones and handmade computers is making universal access to the large volume of data possible, which advanced analysis of data for extracting useful knowledge that the next logical step with the world of ubiquitous computing (Ziv & Mulloth, 2006).

3. MOBILE SOCIAL NETWORK MINING PROSPECTS

Data mining approaches social data Analysis are focusing on the social, structural, and behavioral aspects of users' interactions and relationship of the networks (Min & Cho, 2011). Social networking is a social media, which serves the communities as the roadmap of data/information access and distributions. The contents of traditional social networking are the evolutions undergoes consistence metamorphosis, which studied by sociologists, physiologists, anthropologists and other researchers of the past decades. The growths of social networks are characterized as human confident, trust, resource's access and sharing formation and other common interests between the groups. These relations and structural union influence the behavior and performance of almost all the real world social entities (Jensen & Neville, 2002), which always growing in competitive and complement ways by having a huge volume of data. The advent of social-networking development is making universal access to large data possible, which demanding advanced analysis of data for extracting applicable information and/or knowledge. Data mining is, therefore, useful to extract meaningful patterns and rules (Shim et al., 2011) from such data sets.

Data mining in social networking is an essential tool, which is performing routinely tasks, accessing, sharing, and distributing tremendous amounts of data. The advent of data mining prospects promised solution to social-networking challenges, such as the challenges of dimensionality, social media problems (accessing and distributing), information/knowledge diffusion, users and/or activity's recognitions, handling pervasive data manipulations and others. Data mining prospects in MSN have tremendous contributions, which includes handling, managing and exploring large data, extraction of valuable information to expand a suitable technology with enormous potential and users' contexts. Thus, data mining techniques are capable, dynamic and adaptable to investigate heterogeneous and multi-relational data set, which graphic represented human interactions and relationships among the network nodes. MSNs are not only defining the behavior of social entities but also help to understand different relations among them. In principle, a social network is a structure of entities (e.g., individuals, organizations, and systems) that are connected one to other individual or group members through their own interdependencies interests for which significant prospects for data mining applications (Figure 1). These interdependencies could be shared values, physical contacts, social feelings, perceptions, sentiments or onions, group participations, etc. using mobile or wearable devices through the network, via the internet. The concept of social networks used the context of information and communication technologies of MSNs, which provides efficient data exchange, share, and delivers effective and productive social services.

Data Mining Techniques for Social Networking

These days, social networking has become a pervasive medium, which is growing dynamically and perhaps necessary means to access, share and distribute information and knowledge throughout the world. The ever growing of the social network and its tremendous functionality are generating vast volumes of data, which needs to analysis, the continuum of social-networking activities. The data mining techniques have the capability of analyzing these massive data and providing relevant answers to questions on the base of social networks and users' contexts. Using the techniques of data mining support the growing social media business, which is vitally significant to handling and managing the collected, stored and distributed large data in dynamic and systematic ways. It is

Figure 1. Conceptual descriptions of mobile social network architecture

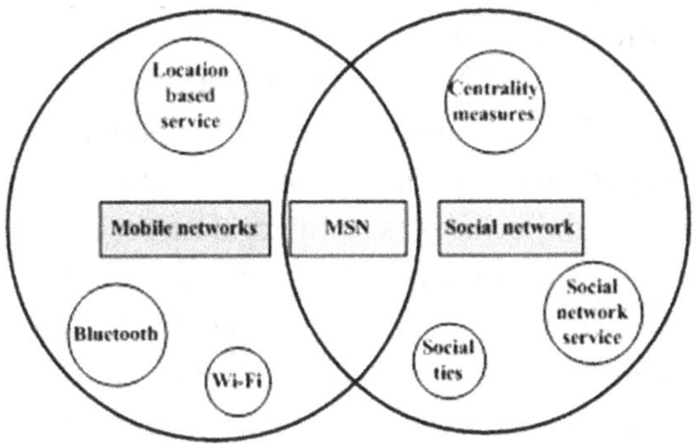

also playing pivotal roles to facilitate the active inter connectivity, interact to many research opportunities and as a result, essential to develop diversified network systems (Pentland, 2007). Social networks are providing a different way for individuals to the organization communicate digitally, which form communities of hypertexts links allow for the sharing of information and ideas of an old concept placed in a digital environment. For example, OLAP (online analytical processing) is one of the analytical tools that focus on providing multidimensional data analysis to specify the user's hypotheses (Bose & Mahaptra, 2001). Data mining prospects can, therefore, essential to expand researchers' capability of understanding and new phenomena on social networking, which improve MSN applications to provide better services and develop innovative opportunities (Dokoohaki & Matskin, 2008; Chang et al., 2007).

The techniques of data mining are, therefore, useful in any field, including social networking to extract meaningful patterns and rules from large data (Ngai et al., 2011; Skillicorn & Talia, 2002), which gives insights to learn about MSN application and performance and predict its future optimizations. Data mining technique in MSNs is a powerful application because social networks routinely generate and store a tremendous amount of data. The quantity of data is always so large that manual analysis of the data is practically impossible. The advent of data mining technology promised solution to these challenges, which gives a possibility to handle, manages access and distribute data in a proper and users' desire ways. Data mining techniques have different features that make them suitable for analyzing large quantity of data. The techniques are mainly used for simplifying and supporting interactive data analysis. Some of the techniques and algorithms focused in this chapter are clustering, classification, regression methods, prediction, association rule, and visualization, which are playing decisive roles for analyses and exploration of large data towards of knowledge extractions in the process of social networks prediction and description (Ngai et al., 2011; Shim et al., 2011; Fei-Yue et al., 2007; Dustdar et al., 2005; Bose & Mahaptra, 2001).

Clustering: It is a technique involves identifying a limited set of clusters to describe a set of data items of unstructured data as the basis of their similarities, which breaks a large database into different subgroups or clusters to ascertain global distribution pattern and correlations among data attributes. The clusters could consist of a richer representation, which could be partition or hierarchical or overlapping clusters. Classification method can also be used for effective means of distinguishing groups or classes in the object, but it becomes costly. So that, clustering can be used as preprocessing approach for attribute subset selection and classification. Clustering differs from classification because there are no predefined classes. The clusters put together based on similarity to each other, but it is up to the data miners to determine whether the clusters provide any useful insight. For example, social data explorations to determine which things are also relevant and applicable throughout the system. It is a form of clustering; which supports social media analysis of relationships and interactions records reveal that information flows.

Classification: It is the most commonly applied technique used to predict group membership for data instance to predict the main factor, which helps to find a rule or formula for organizing data into classes. This approach frequently employs decision tree or neural network-based classification algorithms. The data classification process involves learning and classification, which is remarkably efficient when working with categorical data or a mixture of continuous numeric and categorical data. It is also capable of processing a wider variety of data with output that is much easier to interpret. For example, in social media users can classify based on their interactions as strong, medium or lose. A classification technique is powerful to learning the training data and also applying to evaluate the accuracy of the classification rules using test data. Therefore, if the accuracy is acceptable, the rules can be applied to the new data tuples, such as for fraud detection, this would include complete records of both fraudulent and valid activities determined on a record-by-record basis.

Regression: It takes a numerical data set and develops a mathematical formula that fits the data. That is, for a set of data, regression technique predicts attribute value automatically for a new data depending on the dependency of an attribute on another. This technique is highly efficient when working with categorical data where the order is not necessary. Regression as data mining techniques is applying to use values of one or more explanatory variables to explain or predict an outcome. For example, social network's security risk analysts use regression method to estimate the average risk value as a function of variables such as the service quality or access (explanatory variables). These explanatory variables often called rating factors, so-called because they used by secure the systems as required (Hullermeier, 2005).

Association rule: It is usually to find a frequent item to set findings among large data sets. This finding helps social media to make easy access, such as index design, social and user behavior, sentiments and perception's analysis. Association Rule algorithms need to be able to generate rules with confidence values less than one. However, the number of a possible association rules for a given data set is large, and a high proportion as the rules is usually of little (if any) value.

Prediction Techniques: Prediction is fascinating mining technique, which born in mind that it can easily overlap with classification and regression process. The forecasting of MSNs optimization and performance when using social media service bears, the potential of facilitating the improvement of virtual networking environments in general. A methodology to improve the performance of developed social networking through adaptation and analysis, which can be used to model the relationship between one or more independent and dependent variables. In data mining, independent variables are attributes already known, and response variables are what we want to predict. Unfortunately, many real-world problems are not simply prediction. For example, human perception, opinion, sentiments and trust lose failure rates are all difficult to predict because they may depend on complex interactions of multiple predictor variables. Therefore, more complex techniques (e.g., logistic regression, Hidden Markova Model, frequent emerging pattern, or neural nets) are necessary to forecast the hidden interconnectivity of the social networks. The same model types can often be used for both regression and classification. For example, the CART (Classification and Regression Trees) decision tree algorithm can be used to build both classification trees (to classify categorical response variables) and regression trees (to forecast continuous response variables). Thus, social media data stored in databases could be mined by group members using evolutionary algorithms to develop meaningful relationships and patterns, with the target of discovering relationships between users' skills levels.

Visualization Techniques: It is the most prominent mining process, which support to data exploration through visualization methods. Visualization was understood within the context of social network analysis adapted to collaborative mobile devices, where the cohesion of social groups. The cohesion computed in several ways in order to highlight isolated people, active subgroups and various roles among the members within the group communication structure.

Data Mining Prospect Description of Social Networking

The descriptions of social networking allow conceptualizing the components and the entire functions of MSN, which is essential to data mining applications. Conceptual MSNs architecture showed the combination of mobile networks and social networks and applied to the social network services. The architecture is the structures and ties between the users in which the users and the system can use the knowledge of the relationship to improve efficiency and effectiveness of network services (Chou et al., 2011). Mobility has become an integral part of the human society, which generating large data and can be handling and exploring using data mining techniques (McLennan & Howell, 2010).

The human relationship graph is typically dynamic and large in which different groups and/or individual nodes corresponding to social objects and edges to relations or interactions between them (Backstrom et al., 2006). Data mining process is computer armed mining algorithm, which is given the task of mining the MSN's links and behavioral data sets for useful knowledge (Cao, 2010). The MSNs data sets are describing by various social attributes such as links or interactions in terms of Wi-Fi, Bluetooth, social groups or ties, and others (Nair & Sarasamma, 2007). These interactions functioning to access, share, distribute or other tasks based on user's desires of social data records as a group and/or individual based social service, which needs to be the analysis to extract data and meaningful information to visualize MSNs applications and performances. Data mining is also playing an important role to define the social groups as a clustering and modeling formations of their interaction, including the strength of the relationships (section 5.1). The techniques of data mining are considering actors or entities of the social network, which are persons or other social objects significant to analyze the content and applications of the MSNs media services (Daskalaki et al., 2003).

Furthermore, the rapid growth of mobile technology is providing a wealth of social network data collection, access and distributions (Yang et al., 2010). The use of a mobile device has led to the emergence of dynamic and interactive social networked environment, which is fertile to the use of data mining techniques. As the rapid growth of mobile technology in related to IT technologies, including data mining, the social networks extend to social-networking mobility, which is scalable, capable and useable to access the services on-demand. The performance and application of MSN also optimizing by involving expansions and interactions of many other entities, leading to extensive social information networks with tremendous business potential (Bonchi et al., 2011). MSN can be further classified as homogenous and heterogeneous social networks (Pushpa & Shobhag, 2012). The later classification (heterogeneous MSN) is most related to the contexts of the real world social networking, which representing several kinds of relationship between users of multi-relational social networks that demanding the prospects of data mining.

Therefore, data mining technique is playing a significant role to address the intra and inter communities and organization groups of people with similar profiles that could have relationships among them. This mining process is also essential to understand the location and context of the current user, which is the solution of 'who is that?' and the different relations that exist in the network (Jensen & Neville, 2002). Each relation can be modeled as a social graph. Depending on the information someone wants to obtain analyze one of the relations to be more relevant for a better analysis of MSNs prediction, which is essential to select and analyze the weight of connectivity of the social networks (Ploderer et al., 2010). For example, cell phone calling social networks is social networks where two nodes (caller and receiver) are considering connected if they have social relationships, in this contest the duration of voice calls, and its frequency, etc. that exchanged during a certain period. These networks are more complex as their relationships require different types of collaboration or interaction (Hine, 2011).

Social Networking Mapping as a Mining Prospects

Social network's mapping is a graphic representation of human interactions and relationships via IT device, including mobile and the internet for which developing MSNs applications. The users inter connectivity's are different ways in which supporting various data exchange, share, deliver, and to other functionalities of data mining (Pentland, 2007), which clearly showed the data origin and its flows to a define attributes or domain ontology. It is appropriate to select the significant entities and relationships in the interpretation of mining results to make the system better aligned with MSNs application and understanding. The graphic or mapping prospect is a connection and/or communications system, which characterized the social relationship of centralized or distributed or hybrid MSN structure that can be modeling by data mining technique. These architectures support users can access, share, and distribute data in a mobile environment by exploiting the social relations at their locations. The ubiquitous availability of mobile devices (such as smart phones) (MSN) can fully take advantage of human interaction and physical mobility to achieve efficient and effective data delivery services (Shen & Ma, 2008). An MSN can be established on any existing centralized or distributed mobile network given, which the interdependency of mobile devices can be exploited using social network analysis methods for providing better quality of service. Therefore, social-networking architecture is a fundamental to the mining process in considerations of social observations and contexts (Backstrom et al., 2006). Context inference module adopts Bayesian Networking to extract the user's profiles, including time, locations and other social information Table 1. An architecture design of social-networking components could have different subgroups or individuals and the Smartphone in which serving as the interface of access of MSNs in relation to the intelligent data mining process (Figure 2). On the other hand, the deployment of social-networking platforms is perhaps the most widespread contribution of mapping social networks (Chang et al., 2007).

The activities that occur under the umbrella of social networking could be viewed as separate from analysis and mining social-networking, which we foresee many research opportunities. The basic tools built using the data mining techniques described within this chapter could support many of the social-networking activities and have significant business impact.

As it showed on Figure 2, the component of MSN consists of three main categories, including Smartphone features, social (user) networks. MSNs conceptual network infrastructures, including the social content provider's servers. Smartphone features are the content of log collections, context inference and recommendation, which build the functionality of personal digital assistance with a mobile phone (Chou et al., 2011). User's networks are the interactions and relationships between people in groups and/or individuals access and transfer social data with other users through social network interactions (Aarthi et al., 2011). The groups could be families, friends, lovers, colleagues, and others, within the groups' individuals or user interactions, and relationships could also vary as we differentiate into different colors. Network infrastructures are used to transfer data from a source (such as social content provider or servers) to a destination (mobile user). The network architectures can be identified within the context such as namely, centralized and opportunistic network architectures. The content provider can be a fixed dedicated server (e.g., news server and web-based MSN server) connected to the Internet which injects its content or data to a group of mobile users through the network infrastructure.

Data Structure and Mining Processing

Social data sets are genuinely large, complex and heterogeneous, and also having a large amount of replications at the level of what the social network is dynamic and diversified (Bonchi et al., 2011). Social data contents or descriptions, contexts and status are core strictures of data for

Table 1. Social data structure

Type	Description	Context	States
General	User's current state directly gained from the preprocessed logs	Time	{*morning, afternoon, night, down*}
		Day of week	{*workday, weekend*}
		Location	{*home, workplace, others*}
Personal	User's current state inferred by using Bayesian Networking (BN)	Emotion	{*angry, sad, comfort, joy*}
		Busyness	{*busy, idle*}
		Stress	{*high, low*}
		Activity	{*move, work, rest, play, others*}
Social	Historical information between the user and a subject inferred by BN	Related activity[1]	{*move, work, rest, play, others*}
		Relation type[2]	{*public, private*}
		Closeness[3]	{*close, distance*}
		Relationship	{*family, partner, friend, colleague, acquaintance, others* }

An activity that the user normally shared with the subject
Whether the relationship between the user and the subject is public or private
Whether the user has contact with the subject closely or not

Figure 2. Social networking graphic representation overview

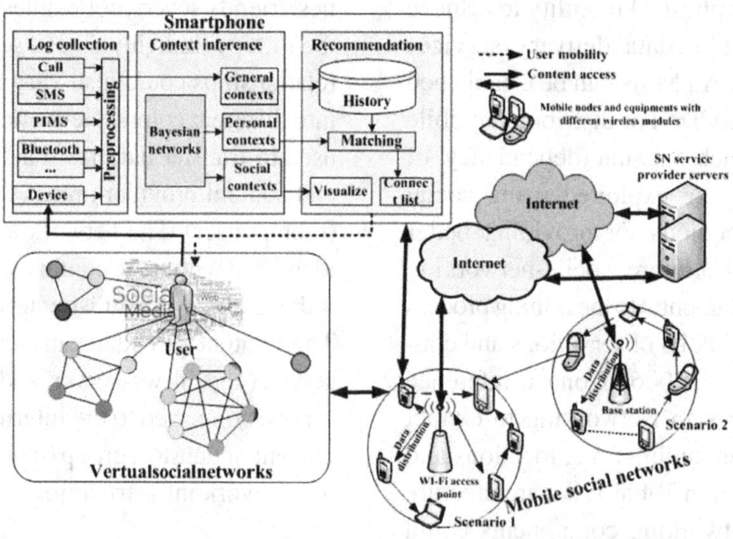

which significant to mining algorithms for a given social network's data (Table 1). The structure on the data includes details of attributes such as user name, address, age, user ID, sex, etc. under user profile or records. Such data sets are large enough for developing predictive models, which can handle valid types of data heterogeneity. The pattern of responses of human behavior seems likely to remain broadly similar as one move from one location to another. Therefore, from a mining perspective, pre-understanding of data structure as classification or clustering vitally significant to effective assessment and predictive of the MSNs performances (Howison et al., 2011).

Social data may be organized as structured, unstructured or semi-structured formats, which are significant to explore social data towards optimization of MSNs applications (Shen & Ma, 2008). In the case of structured data, data mining approach targeted for predefined mining process, whereas, unsupervised or unstructured data structure requires pre processing to clustering the data according to their similarity. The advantage of unstructured data structuring is essential to perform heuristic mining algorithms, which is pertinent to visualize the whole description and performance of MSN. Therefore, the successful mining and structuring process is depending on the understanding, handling and managing the data, which is core potential of data mining. Such data records are including social connectivity's and relationships correlations weights, human behavior (emotion, stress, interactions and others), time (when and for how long), activities, and others as described on Table 1.

Thus, data generated on social networks are heterogeneous from conventional attribute's value, which are user generated content on social media. The data also characterized as noisy, distributed, unstructured, dynamic and vast, which are challenging to simple analysis tools. Therefore, data mining is capable to processing such data of extract new information or knowledge. These dynamic mining process or pattern developments are passing sequential steps from data cleaning to the final knowledge extractions (see Figure 4). The steps begin from a data set organizing and selection, including data cleanup for preprocessing step, then pass through other subsequent steps until verification and validation of the outcomes. The clean data then mined for unusual patterns by computer algorithms, and the patterns interpreted to generate new knowledge.

Data structure and mining prospects visualize the explicit interactions correlate with actions, which can prove to establish the known actors of the networks and gives insight to understand the nature of these interactions. From the point of view of mining and analysis of social networks, it is also necessary to develop effective sampling methods, which is a basic task of data mining in tractable and uniform approaches (Wang & Man, 2009). This is important if a representative sample of strong social networks is needed in order to provide a practical estimation of the properties of the social network (Yang et al., 2010). The two approaches for analyzing the social network, i.e. collecting accurate data and sampling the network, are both essential for a thorough analysis of the properties of the network and mining interesting patterns as the basis of implicit connection of the social network (Rangaswamy & Cutrell, 2012). The inherent connections can be discovered from user's activities by analyzing extensive and repeating interactions between users. For example, in social media sites commenting items from a user or set of users, repeated interactions between individuals, which supports such as cell phone call networks, repeated calls or SMS between individuals can be extracted from call-detail records and interpreted as relationships (Ziv & Mulloth, 2006).

Data structure and mining prospects also characterized in terms of network size, connectivity, data type, data tasks and others. The size of social network data is continuous to grow as people understand the hidden values of social networking, which is the most obvious methods of characterizing a relational data set, such as data proximity. This growth could be enlarging in size aspect of web grounded social networks and would not stop and as many have predicted and data fusion (Rangaswamy & Cutrell, 2012). The semantic web based development of the social network leads to a strong and growing demand for combination of the data from different social networks as social networks, which many interested in sharing their profiles while others are interested to merging their data from multiple networks. The degree of connectivity among unusual portions of the data graph is also another key aspect of interaction data sets, which support to visualize the data types that

Figure 3. Data mining approach social networks node description

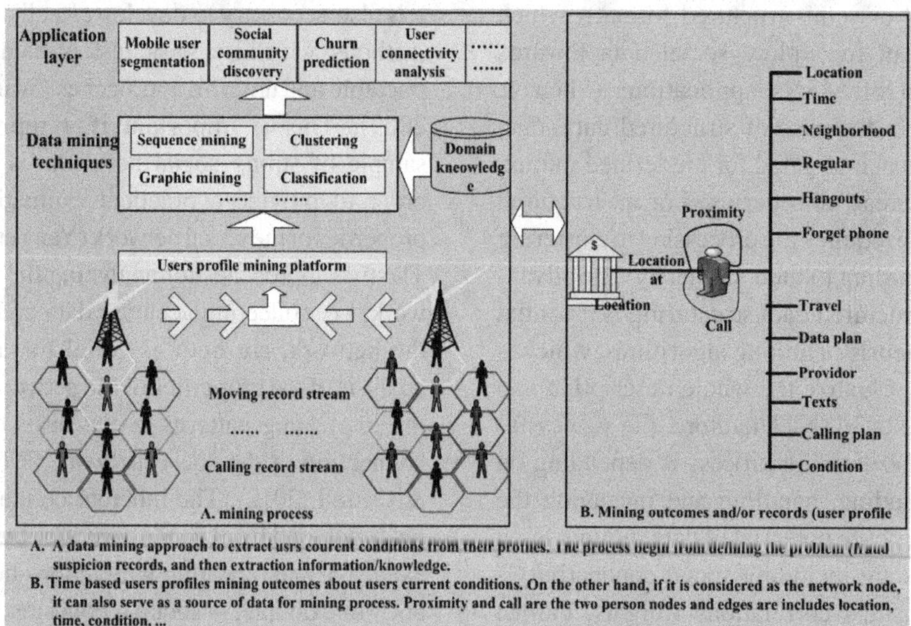

Figure 4. An iterative social data mining process

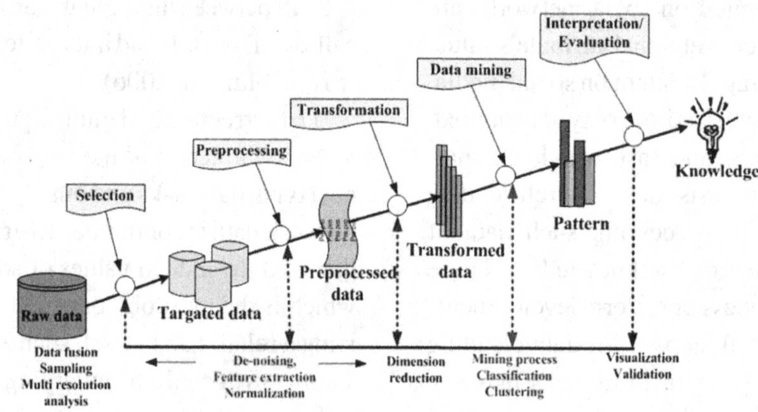

help to analyze the relational strength or weight assumes the data consist of homogeneous and diversified social objects. Such social networks include sets of cell phone records, persons, movies, and others within the social network. Social network data task includes data relational dependence, task type, level determinism, location inference and others (Chang et al., 2007; Jensen and Neville, 2002).

Mining Prospects in Social Enhancement and Privacy

Mining prospects is vitally essential to examine the aspect of social networks, such as the use of hyperlinks between linked pages and to outside sources of information. The simple aspect of social network probes into the personal traits of an individual nationality, political affiliation, thinking orientation and others are social network users' style. The variety of posts, the comments that follow can help in identifying and classifying the like minded people and also in reasoning their interpretations. Ranking the social networks members of the basis of in-and-out links or group of likes can be used to enhance and determine users, which is the significance in the MSNs Sphere. Based on these facts, there is a need of standards for information retrieval, which includes predefined ways to convey information or guarantee the authenticity of data. The privacy policies and settings in MSNs social media paramount to secure and easy data access to social-networking sites is pushing users to classify their profile as individual while this certainly improves privacy, which is a challenge to optimize MSNs performance. Therefore, research on the social network always versatility and intrigue researchers and give scope for innovations and algorithms for data mining (Domingos & Richardson, 2001).

Furthermore, the virtual social networking conceptual modeling is important to handling, managing and accessing data, information and services, which considering the interactions among people, organizations and automatic systems of the networks. In this conceptualization modeling, there are interlinked between social objects, which are not visible but considering in the process of mining prospects. For example, the map of actual human responses how close or far is from the reality can always be a subject of managing the hidden functionality and interactions of the networks. Therefore, data mining prospect is playing a significant role to managing the unseen interactions and connectivity of the social network data, which is not easy addressing by other tools. It is an opportunity of the social media's affluence in features and patterns, gives rise to, and an orientation towards the infinite scope of exploring, analyzing and channelizing the output in the desired direction the social networks services (Rahman et al., 2010). For example, users can run Google MapReduce search jobs to analyze such invisible data for insight and factors of new relationships. For example, we may use Google Prediction API bases for pattern matching and recognition approach to generate and clarify social data. It gives a set of the data train, which can create applications that can perform many tasks. (i) It gives a user's past viewing habits, predict what other services or relationships or even the social media that could the users like. (ii) It helps to categorize the sites or blogs to spam or non spam. (iii) Analyze posted comments about MSNs to determine whether they have a positive or negative tone, and others.

Data mining techniques are powerful, capable enough, scalable and adaptable to handle MSN performance as the basis of social-networking contexts and user's desires. Its enormous tasks and techniques are opportunities to explore the data and its functionality involving the required devices or components, such as mobile devices, which are necessary to the success in the analysis of social networks towards optimizations. Thus, it is a key approach to manage the complexity and dynamism of social interactions, which based on user desires and social contexts (Kemp et al., 2012). Therefore, the advantages of data mining application in MSNs are its dedication to predicting the MSNs, which develop relationships among entities in a social network that can be directly or indirectly connected (Bonchi et al., 2011). Mining dynamic behavioral patterns is a highly interesting task in social networks due to its relevant business value. Understanding the behavior of users in a social network might lead powerful channels towards marketing products in a more personalized manner. However, most of the time, social interactions correspond to infrequent and hard-to-detect interaction patterns, which at the same time also show meaningful features. From a data mining and computational point of view, this is equivalent to discovering periodic or near-periodic sub graphs in flexible social networks. Efficient, effective and scalable methods are required to solve this social interaction problem, and these require contributions from areas that have long dealt with the analysis of dynamic networks.

In the data mining prospects, social network defined as a group of actors (or social objects, or nodes, or points) and one or more relationships (or links, or edges) between pairs of actors. Data mining based techniques are proving to be useful for analysis of social network data, especially for large data sets that cannot be handled by traditional methods. Social network analysis is the mapping and measuring of relationships and flows between people, groups, organizations, computers or other information/knowledge processing entities (Cao, 2010; Wang & Man, 2009). Data mining based social network analysis is a method for visualizing social interactions and relationship dimensions, leading to understand how users can interconnect to share knowledge. On the other hand, the challenges of MSNs research could be defined as social network for analysis and mining from a business perspective, and given an overview of the technical areas that we consider most relevant to future business impact. The data mining playing a crucial role to managing data preparation (large-scale data management) and presentation, improving network dynamism and reputation, users' trust, and expertise, data propagations, evaluation and other's activities. Users' understanding and social challenges are also essential issues of the inherent mining process, which require an interdisciplinary approach at every network hierarchy level. Such fundamental task's challenge includes cultural factors, privacy expectations, legal and ethical issues, and community structure (Barbier & Lui, 2011).

4. DATA MINING PROSPECTS AND ALGORITHMS

Algorithms and prospects of data mining in MSNs are vitally significant in many ways. It plays predicting roles in optimization of MSNs applications and performances, which users' contexts and activities are likely to default on analysis and explorations MSNs data sets patterns. Such fundamental tasks are data mining unobtrusive assessment, mining algorithms and components prospects, MSNs data intelligence, social data mining process, and others. Information gained from data mining techniques, and algorithms can be used for application ranging from knowing the individual's context to optimization of MSN applications. In additions to these, it gives an insightful interpretation from past trend analysis to future predictions. Therefore, the data mining benefits to overcoming the challenges of MSN by exploring the trends and current situations and also making reliable predictions about social service performances (Kemp et al., 2012; Bose & Mahaptra, 2001).

MSN is dynamic in nature, which requires advanced and capable techniques and mining algorithms. Currently, the ever growing of mobile devices and warless network applications gives an opportunity to be collected, recorded and stored large amount of MSNs data. These data sets are more complex, sensitive and heterogeneous, which are challenging to extract valuable information and knowledge from it. Therefore, data mining algorithms are vitally significant to handle, manage and analysis and obtain useful information/knowledge. The prospect of data mining in MSN is the possibility to use different techniques and algorithms as discussed in section 3.1 and below from 4.1 to 4.5. Data mining in social networking is playing intelligent roles, which support the rapid growing and popularity of social networks (YongYeol et al., 2007). Data mining techniques are vitally significant to analyze the social behavior and relationships of users, which applying and interpreting the large data sets from leading mining algorithms to the distributed links and end nodes' contexts. Thus, data mining application visualized on location-based service and data handling of MSNs, which is the demanding optimization power of social-networking services. For example, the data mining based facilities of wearable services, health care services, Geographic Information Sciences or Systems (GIS) and Remote Sensing (RS) data, and others. Besides to these, data mining is also significant to investigate or assess the performance and impacts of social-networking application, for example, unobtrusive approaches of MSN impact assessment (Bin, 2011; Kayastha et al., 2011).

Unobtrusive Data Mining Based Assessment of Social Networks

Optimization of MSNs needs and thorough and unobtrusive assessment seeks to harness the full power of computing to a deep analysis of social media. A data mining technique of unobtrusiveness is a method to visualize the performance of MSNs in terms of efficiency, effectiveness, cost, or other factors, which could visualize the problems in a continuous assessment. Unobtrusive approach is a measure of non-reactive behavioral attention of users, the historical investigation of the social services, network content analysis. It is a principle of data mining approaches, which agglomerates an understanding of the past trends and theory of social networks, including its strengths and weaknesses in the performance of MSNs. Therefore, unobtrusive social-networking approach is a systematic and comprehensive to characterize and content analysis of MSNs. Careful researching of MSN is the issue of privacy social networking study considering inconspicuous methods provide a strong critique of continuous assessment, which the notion that truths can be determined about the social world by scientific computation (Howison et al., 2011).

One can unobtrusively collect social network's data in social media sites, communication and other ways. From such sources, users can obtain records such as a file (friend lists) and then checks to see who on this list also tied to each other. Therefore, unobtrusive data collection is useful when examining social network's performances, which requires the documentation of actual social data rather than self-reported behavior. It is the method of repeatable assessment results, which support easier access to data and the fact that permission from subjects is not always necessary. Unobtrusive methods are relatively inexpensive and are appropriate for longitudinal studies that follow activities over a long period. That is unobtrusive social-networking methods is uninterrupted, time efficient, and secure to sensitive or potentially distressing social information (Hine, 2011).

Mining Algorithms and Components Prospects

Data mining algorithm is an essential to in constructing mining algorithms for knowledge discovery, which includes model representation, evaluation and search. Model representation refers to the language used to represent patterns that could be graphically identified. The model presentation must not be too scanty otherwise no amount of illustration will generate an accurate model of the data. Model evaluation focused on either accuracy or interpretability, but recent algorithms try to combine these two features (Yang et al., 2010). Model evaluation criteria are, therefore, a quantitative evidence of how well a specific pattern meets the goal through a knowledge discovery process. In model evaluation criteria, different rules could be applied to remove redundancy, which usually appears as overlapping fuzzy set (Hullermeier, 2005). Similarity driven rule base simplification is a method that uses a similarity measure to quantify the redundancy among fuzzy sets in the rule base. This method is useful in reducing the number of fuzzy sets from a model, making it understandable and yet powerful. Multi-objective function for genetic algorithm (GA) based identification is another rule based method that improves the classification capability, GA by applying optimization method where cost function is based on the model accuracy measured in terms of the misclassifications (Ahn et al., 2011). Orthogonal transforms for reducing the number of rules are also vital. It evaluates the output contribution of the rules to obtain a prominent ordering. Search methods are made up of parameter and model search. As soon as the model representation and evaluation set, the problem scaled to an optimization task of finding the models and parameters that optimize the evaluation criteria. Model search occurs as a loop over the parameter search method.

Data mining prospects are predicting MSNs future trends, which users are likely to optimizing the services and identifying of new MSNs patterns. It is essential to detect fraudulent activities (Gebremeskel et al., 2012), improving service quality, resource utilization and facilitating multidimensional data analysis to improve access and distributions of information (Nair & Sarasamma, 2007). For example, fraud detection in the traditional method of data analysis is long and complex processes that deal with different domains and skills, which is quantitative and statistical data characteristics to gain better insights on the processes behind the data. However, data mining techniques are going beyond the conventional way of data analysis systems, which can be equipped with a substantial amount of background knowledge, and be able to perform reasoning tasks involving that knowledge, and the data provided. This is a novel source of ideas that data mining techniques can be described as turning background knowledge, such as data (input) into knowledge (output), which helps to discover meaningful patterns, data turns into information (Jensen & Neville, 2002). From this continuous mining process, the systems will be benefits feedbacks that promote the effectiveness of mining tasks, which determines the existence of issues, such as fraud risks to trigger an alert. The techniques of data mining are, therefore, a key to assist in detecting fraud by identifying and storing events. For example, telephone call services records, including location, time, user current conditions vitally crucial to investigate fraud towards time and place (Figure 3) (Ahn et al., 2011).

Social media content and contexts are the most data-intensive sources, which demanding the data mining techniques to assist in generating users desired information from the social network's services. The techniques are using to find recurrent patterns to create a rule-based user's safety and acceptable solutions to the challenges, such as fraud problems (YongYeol et al., 2007). As it showed on (Figure 3) of data mining techniques vitally essential to recognize a coherent call node on its location based, which the profile mining platform a social network can be constructed using calls between users and the calling frequencies, including other detail records. It is ontology of the heterogeneous social network, which includes user, location, time, conditions and others about the user descriptions (Dokoohaki & Matskin, 2008). Users' information is a key to optimizations of MSNs and also to develop other strategies, which targeted for MSNs applications develop sequential patterns on social data streams (Cao, 2010).

Data mining technique analysis of MSNs data set is a systematic way of developing mining algorithm to mine and incrementally maintain on fast social data streams closed sequent patterns, which are a non-redundant representation of social patterns. An effective social network data structure designed to keep close sequential patterns in memory, which various strategies performed to prune the search space aggressively. Based on the experiments on both real and synthetic databases, the data mining algorithm outperforms the best existing algorithms by a large margin. For example, in mobile communication business, the social relationship between users often plays a significant role during a business process. A social network among users constructed in which users represented by a node in the network. An edge is drawn to connect two users or social objects if they call each other over a certain number of times of currently sliding window. A social community in the network is a set of nodes such that they are relatively well connected to each other and much less connected to the other nodes in the network (Min and Cho, 2011). In this application, the connection weights on edges in graphs should be considered.

MSNs Data Intelligence

Among many prospects of data mining, data intelligence, network intelligence, social intelligent, MSNs domain intelligence and others are the fundamentals to visualize performance impacts of social networks. It is the efficient techniques to improve MSNs and deliver services business-friendly, which supports decision-making rules and actions that are of also solid technical aspects of the social process (Min & Cho, 2011). Therefore, data mining caters for the effective involvement of ubiquitous intelligence surrounding analysis of MSNs data sets knowledge discovery and problem solving.

Social network's data intelligence tells interesting stories or uncovers indicators about a social media problem hidden in the data (Korolova et al., 2008). The intelligent system is complicated in which demanding dynamic and intuitive tools such as intelligent data mining to overcome the computational challenges. Therefore, data mining is the key to mainstream complex social data streams focusing on fundamental investigation of various data for interesting hidden patterns or knowledge that could be scalable and adaptable to solve the real-world data and surroundings problems. Basic underpinnings for dealing with social network's data complexities consist of data quality enhancement to improve data quality and readiness for pattern mining, data matching and integration to match/integrate data from multiple heterogeneous data sources. Intelligent data mining also applicable to handle and play coordination roles through central processing to access numerous data sources through coordination techniques. The dynamic functional or techniques of data mining are a multivalent coordination feature extracting and representing features mixing semi structured or ill-structured data with structured data, aligned computing for processing multiple sources of high frequency data in parallel, collective intelligence of data systems. This centralized processing of social-networking data agglomerates data intelligence, which identified in individual data sources, dimension reduction to reduce the number of dimension's level and space mapping such as social mapping. Therefore, the data mining approaches of computational complexity of social data are involving dynamic stochastic computing for more efficient computation and data policy such as privacy and security processing to develop social data pattern and protect sensitive information from disclosure, and so on (Fei-Yue et al., 2007).

Network intelligence emerges from social semantic web intelligence and broad-based network intelligence such as information and resource's distribution, linkages among distributed objects, hidden communities and groups, information and resources from the network and in particular, the semantic web, information retrieval, searching, and structural from distributed and textual data. The information and facilities from the networks surrounding the target social problem either consist of the problem constituents or can contribute to useful information for actionable knowledge discovery (Aarthi et al., 2011). Domain intelligence emerges from domain factors and resources that not only wrap a problem and its target data but also assist in problem understanding and problem solving. Domain intelligence involves qualitative and quantitative aspects. These are instantiated in terms of aspects such as domain knowledge, background information, prior knowledge, expert knowledge, constraints, organization factors, social service's process, and workflow, as well as network system intelligence, social media or service expectation, and interestingness (Pentland, 2007). Social intelligence refers to the intelligence that lies behind group interactions, behaviors, and corresponding regulation. Social intelligence is also covering both human social intelligence and animate/agent-based social intelligence. Human social intelligence is related to aspects such as social cognition, emotional intelligence, consensus construction, and group decision. Animate/agent-based social intelligence involves swarm intelligence, action selection, and the foraging procedure. Both sides also engage social network intelligence and collective interaction, as well as business rules, law, trust, and reputation for governing the emergence and use of social intelligence (Dokoohaki & Matskin, 2008).

Social Data Mining Process

Data mining is an iterative process concerned with uncovering patterns, associations, anomalies, and statistically significant structures and events in MSNs data. The prospects of data mining in MSNs are not only extracting the implicit knowledge, but also useful to enhancing the understanding of social interaction and relationships phenomena, such as defining the human interaction or social pattern. Social pattern developing is the key step in data mining to discover and characterize social patterns from the given social data that can be text, numeric and/or image and others in high-dimensional processing rate (Kemp et al., 2012). A pattern in this chapter is an arrangement or an ordering of social data in which network system organization of the underlying structure can be existed. Patterns in data identified using measurable features or performance impacts of social attributes that extracted from the data (Figure 4). A mining structure can be processed together with all dependent models, or separately. Processing a mining structure separately from models can be useful when some models expected to take a long time to process the given data, which demands to defer that operation.

As it showed on Figure 4, data mining is an iterative and interactive process, which includes preparation or selection, pre-processing, data transformation or exploration, model building or pattern development, and interpretation and evaluation of the process result.

The sequential steps are the possible refinement to the process based on input from the domain raw data to knowledge extraction. Mining process of the raw data is also supporting by the feedback process that comes from the high level of the mining process. The pre-processing of the data is a basic and time-consuming, critical and first step, which include the tasks of de-noising, feature selection and normalization of the data to the subsequent process. It is often domain and application dependent; however, various techniques developed within the context of one application or domain can be applied to other applications and domains too. Data transformation or exploration is the process of dimension reduction for data mining process. Model building or pattern development is the fundamental task of data mining based on reduced dimensions of the data sets. At this step, process is independent of the domain that is the social network contexts or application. Pattern or model deployment is following by interpretation and validation in association to the domain real contexts.

Large-scale MSNs data mining is a newly emerging and interactive research issue, which is significant to other fields of study. Since, MSN is a cross-cutting field, which is valuable to optimize the performance of other fields, for example, marketing or business, security or fraud detections, and others. Therefore, data mining based MSNs research issue is vitally significant to make it fundamental source of a number of open research problems. In order to extend data mining techniques to large-scale social network's service data, several barriers must be overcome (Jensen

& Neville, 2002). The extraction of key features from large, multidimensional, complex data is a critical issue that must be addressed first, prior to the application to the pattern of mining algorithms. The features extracted must be relevant to the problem, insensitive to small changes in the data, and invariant to scaling, rotation, and translation.

Therefore, data mining is the prospect of advancing the existing or traditional mining algorithms or design new ones that are scalable, robust, accurate, and interpretable, which can be applied effectively and efficiently to complex, multidimensional data. It is dynamic mining algorithms that can be adaptable to large-scale multiprocessor systems. So that scientists can be applied an interactively explore and analyze of the data process of mining algorithms. Nutshell, data mining is a dynamic and well advanced tool, which automation is essential to huge data sets of social network data sets. Data processing in a large spreadsheet is not an acceptable way to analyze any data than data mining processing (Barbier & Lui, 2011). The trick is to find effective ways to combine the computer's power to process data with the human eye's ability to detect patterns. The techniques of data mining are designed for and work best with, large data sets. Thus, data mining prospects in MSNs can perform a number of tasks, some of which described as *section 3.1*.

Social Networks Users Analysis

Social network's users or community is formed by individuals or users as linked such that those within a group interact with each other more frequently than those outside the group. Based on the context, a community also referred to as a group, cluster, cohesive subgroup, or module. Communities can be observed via connections in social networks, which allow people to develop social links online (Dustdar et al., 2005). Social networks allow people to join friends and find new users with similar interests, which found in social media that broadly classified into explicit and implicit groups. Explicit groups are formed by user subscriptions, whereas implicit groups emerge spontaneously through interactions. Therefore, social network users' analysts are generally faced with issues such as user detection, formation, and evolution. Users' detection often refers to the extraction of implicit groups within a network. MSN is highly dynamic. Users can expand, shrink, or dissolve in scalable networks. Users' evolution aims to develop the patterns of a user over time in the presence of dynamic network interactions.

Social Networks Users Perceptions Analysis

Social network's users' perception analysis essential to extract users' opinions expressed in the user-generated content, which is significant to understand users' interactions and relationships in relation to business and other fields. This approach helps users to identify social media services opinions or sentiments on a global scale. Perception mining and analysis are hard, but also it plays a significant role to improve MSN performing as the users' desires. Therefore, finding relevant documents, social groups, overall perceptions, quantifying perceptions and aggregating all to a form an overview is the possible way of the analysis MSNs.

Privacy, Security and Trust Analysis

Privacy and security issues are vitally essential in MSN application optimizations. Pervasive use of social media gives rise to concerns on user privacy and safety issues, which is challenging to users opposing needs: on one hand, a user would like to have as many friends and share as much as possible, and, on the other hand, a user would like to be as private as possible when needed. However, being gregarious is requiring openness and transparency review significant to

MSN application optimization, but also being private constricts one's sharing. In addition, a social-networking site has its business needs to encourage users to easily fiend each other and expand their friendship networks as widely as possible. Hence, social media pose new security challenges to fend off security threats to users and organizations. For example, for the various reason users' profiles or information disclosed, individuals may put themselves and members of their social networks at risk for a variety of attacks. Social media has been the target of numerous passive as well as, active attacks, including stalking, cyber bullying, malvertizing, phishing, social spamming, scamming, and clickjacking. Furthermore, social trust depends on many factors that cannot be easily modeled in a computational system. It is because different versions of definition of trust are proposed in the literature (McLennan & Howell, 2010; Fei-Yue et al., 2007; Dustdar et al., 2005). Therefore, Trust between any two people observed to be affected by many factors, including past experiences, opinions expressed, actions taking, contributions to spreading rumors, influence by others' opinions, and motives to gain something extra.

Data Mining Based Social Networks Risk Detections and Protection

Social network risk detection and protection in data mining techniques are to develop patterns of social services and activity, which support to determine the set of groups, indicate an attack. Thus, in social network security, threat identification and prevention system is the act of detecting activity or events that attempt to compromise the confidentiality, integrity or availability of a social resource. Social risk prevention techniques, such as user authentication and information protection encryption have been used to protect computer systems is the act as first line of defense. To improve MSNs service accuracy and security, data mining techniques are used to analyze assessment data and extract features that can distinguish normal activities from intrusions (Gebremeskel et al., 2012; Ngai et al., 2011). Therefore, the purpose of data mining as social-networking risk management and protection is to discover new patterns in data for the purpose of optimization and predictions. To identify patterns of MSNs protection, data mining application analyzed large amount of records or data, which are generating monitors, which watches user's behavior with respect to one pattern of fraud.

5. PERFORMANCE EVALUATION

Social networking technologies have added a new sense of urgency and layers of complexity to the existing debates among scientists and philosophers about computer and informational privacy. For example, the potential availability of users' data to third parties for commercial, surveillance, security, or other purposes and processing social data time to time become more challenging than ever. This challenge is opportunities to the emerging of data mining in this dynamic domain, which support to overcome these challenges and also playing significant roles to predict the services and users' access, understanding, etc. The other prospects of data mining are, its scalability, adaptability and capability to evaluate the performance of MSNs in relation to IT growth, including mobile device developments. IT and mobile device's advancement are facilitating location-based social-networking service for potential users, which could be able to accessing or distributing social resources through their mobile and other wearable devices.

Therefore, data mining prospects are playing prominent roles to generate dynamic concepts and techniques, which investigating social services, users' interactions and access, user's contexts and behaviors. It is also essential to optimization and prediction purpose of MSN based on its historical data explorations. It is the leading deal of scholarly interest from researchers and scientists in details about the contents and its various applications or services of MSNs by having implicit knowledge, which extracted from social data sets. The fundamental of such approaches are essential to visualize the dynamism of the MSNs in consideration to the traditional social-networking services to transfer in its advancing application that is MSNs, which allowing to efficient and effective its performances. Data mining approaches of social data exploration gets the point that user or human behavior to predict social networks as the context of social and users' factors. Social network users and their connectivity are systematic and intelligence's ways, which gives web, based social resource's access via the internet or web browsers. MSNs prospects are mining process of exploring and understanding the social-mobile data. All the data transformed into relational data and presented as social networks, which to handle the sheer number of observed activities, and an interactive of the social agents incorporated for social-networking services.

Model Development

Modeling approach exploration of data mining prospects is vitally significant to visualize MSNs dynamism and applications in which considering the interactions and correlations of social entities. To explore this, we use *Princeton Survey Research Associates International for The Pew Research Center's the Internet & American Life Project Winter Tracking 2012 survey* real social network's data, which had 43 surveying questions and 123 attributes or activities. From this large data set, we use sample data and selected attributes, which are significant to visualize the social networks. The attributes selected based on their relevance to this research issue, which have been high weighted values among others. The selected attributes and their correlation values showed on Table 2. With regardless of the locations and entities' size (from individuals to a different group size), we can build various mobile social networks (fig, 5) showed to visualize the performance of MSN towards user's desires and its dynamisms.

The social networking graphic visualization (Figure 5) developed based on Table 2 attribute's correlation absolute values, which showed the networks connectivity's and their relationship strengths. As the attributes weighted absolute correlation values closed to 1, their interaction is strong, whereas, their values, which are close to 0 are losing interactions. For example, '*emlacc*' and '*intus*' attributes had an absolute value of 0.788, which showed its strong relationships. Whereas '*educ*' with '*celpho*' had an absolute value of 0.004, which had loss relationships between the two attributes. The attributes' data or correlation values do not tell us what comes next

Table 2. Correlation matrix of SMNs sample data set

Attributes	intuse	emlacc	homintuse	Celpho	SNSU	Inter_purpo...	Inter_target	educ	emplnw
intuse	1	0.788	-0.621	-0.095	-0.339	-0.454	-0.563	-0.340	0.186
emlacc	0.788	1	-0.529	-0.075	-0.321	-0.396	-0.500	-0.392	0.168
homintuse	-0.621	-0.529	1	0.088	0.256	0.435	0.518	0.227	-0.124
Celpho	-0.095	-0.075	0.088	1	0.037	0.092	0.071	-0.004	-0.012
SNSU	-0.339	-0.321	0.256	0.037	1	0.196	0.226	0.192	-0.118
Inter_purpos	-0.454	-0.396	0.435	0.092	0.196	1	0.440	0.184	-0.088
Inter_target	-0.563	-0.500	0.518	0.071	0.226	0.440	1	0.277	-0.116
educ	-0.340	-0.392	0.227	-0.004	0.192	0.184	0.277	1	-0.120
emplnw	0.186	0.168	-0.124	-0.012	-0.118	-0.088	-0.116	-0.120	1

respondent ID, gender (female =1, and male =2), internet use (intuse), email account (emlacc), home internet use (homintuse), cell phone use (cellpho), Social network use (NSSU) such as face book twitter, Google, blog, … , internet use purpose (int_pur), internet use target (int_targ), education status (educ), and employment status (empl)

or for predictions about the MSNs performance. Therefore, the data mining prospects are applying different techniques, including modeling approach support to extract valuable information and implicit knowledge from such large data, which support to visualize attribute's connectivity and interactions (Figure 5).

As it showed on Figure 5, graphic representation of social data sets connectivity in 5 clustering groups based on Table 3, which created significant social interconnections. Among the 5 clustering, groups $\mathbf{C_4}$ since the group members are small and the respective graphic representation is not visible. Clustering based explorations of the data provides a basic understanding of the social entities through their networks.

Bayesian networking of social data sets distributions graphic representation visualize both females and males having proportional social networking uses including their internet use purpose and targets (Figure 6).

Visualization of Mining Process Prospects

Data mining techniques have successfully produced numerous modeling and algorithm tools, which handling large social networking data sets to solve real social-networking problems. As it showed on Figure 5 and Figure 6, data mining has become an integral part of many applications to visualize the social-networking capabilities, which gives insight the mining process how effectively handle large-scale social data, extract actionable patterns, and gain insightful knowledge. As social media are widely used for various purposes, vast amounts of user-generated data exist and can be made available for data mining. Furthermore, the modeling representation provides in which data mining of social media can expand the social researchers' capability of understanding new phenomena due to the use of social media and improve social networks to provide better services and develop innovative opportunities.

As the result, data mining gives social users an easy-to-use way to communicate and network with each other on an unprecedented scale and at rates unseen in traditional social media. Data mining prospect vitally important to popularize of social media continues to grow exponentially, resulting in evolution of social networks. It is also significant to understand a social user's behavior, social contexts, and security modules of the social media services. Thus, data mining technique is a systematic and dynamic approach inevitable to perform the social trends and future prediction social network performances. So that, data mining is the techniques to analysis the past trend check-ins provide rich information about social media real problem, which is significant to predict social-networking analysis to support and visualize the social dynamism and IT including mobile technology concatenating towards optimization of MSNs performances. In addition, social correlation theory suggests considering users' social ties since human movement is usually affected by their social events, such as visiting friends, go-

Figure 5. Graphic visualizations of MSNs data set correlations

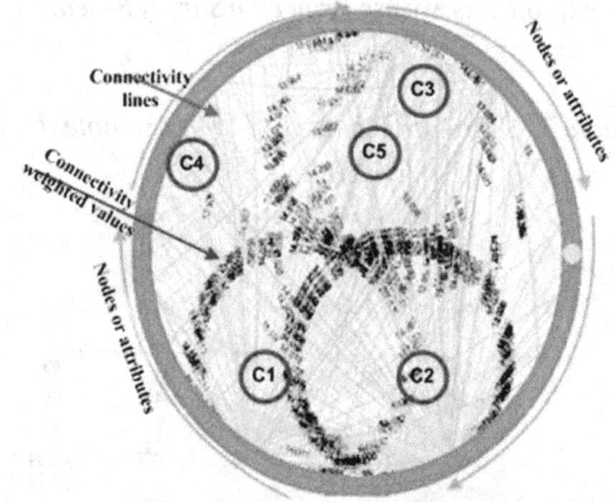

ing out with colleagues, and so on. These social relationship ties can shape the social user's check-in experience on MSNs, which gives insights to optimize MSNs applications.

CONCLUSION AND FUTURE RESEARCH DIRECTIONS

The issues discussed in this chapter could answer several open research questions of social networking challenges and also introducing a novel approaches to optimize MSNs applications, which includes the possible ways of improving social media access and security in relation to users' desires and system contexts. Data mining prospects in social network has made impressive strides toward learning highly accurate models of large relational data. Therefore, in this chapter, we discussed and introduced new ideas how data mining provides many advantages for the better performance of MSN. The research on data mining prospect towards MSNs is a systematic approach to explore the complex and heterogeneous social data to optimize MSNs performance. Data mining visualizing the dynamism of MSN as discussed

Table 3. Clustering model centroid table

Attribute	cluster_1	cluster_2	cluster_3	cluster_4	cluster_5
intuse	2.042	1.069	1.017	1.022	1.031
emlacc	2.038	1.097	1.068	1.067	1.157
homintuse	0.002	1.005	1.063	1.067	1.213
Celpho	1.335	1.476	1.563	1.578	1.590
SNSU	0	0.646	4.384	1.578	0.910
Inter_purpos	0.002	1.259	1.374	8.111	1.563
Inter_target	0.002	1.783	1.819	2.622	1.866
educ	2.826	5.934	5.292	5.444	2.805
emplnw	3.121	2.447	2.304	2.378	2.444

Figure 6. MSNs data set Bayesian Networking distribution models

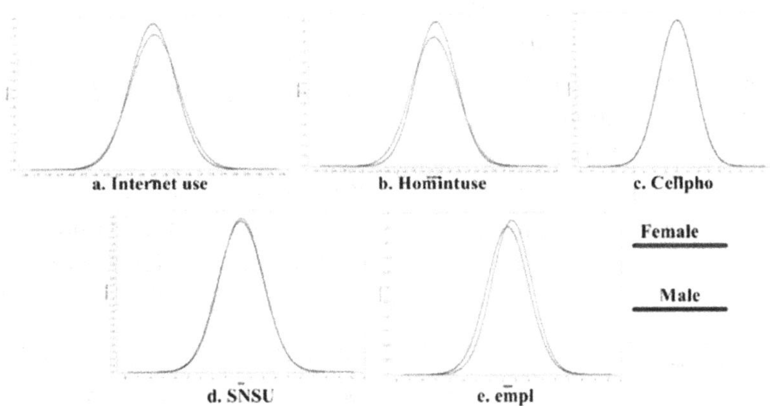

in section 3, 4 and 5, which showed the implicit mining algorithms, graphic representations, social data structuring, and others. All these prospects give a chance to efficient and effective approach of MSNs applications. It also visualized the users who are parts of the MSN could have efficient accessing of the social services, how to improve the services of the MSN as users can be used to optimize data exchange, sharing, and delivery to meet the requirements of the services and applications and others. Data mining as the issue of MSNs prospects would be a key issues towards the applications and advents of data mining in social network analysis and computational analysis, which is fundamental and cross-disciplinary efforts and joint research efforts should be encouraged to promote rapid development and dissemination of useful mining algorithms and data representations. Prospects and scopes of data mining use quite simple data exploring techniques, which is highly sophisticated data analysis.

However, there are also still many issues, which need further research to optimize the efficiency and effectiveness of the MSN that enable to accommodate new applications and services. Such as (i) the issue of the MSNs interoperability such as mobile and desktop interactions platform and mining process are a significant challenge. (ii) The issue of studying the standards of data distributions and contexts awareness in MSNs and connectivity protocol. (iii) The challenges of MSNs future generation information exchanges as the controversy of improving human daily life and privacy, security (safety), are some important points which are identifying for further research issues.

ACKNOWLEDGMENT

We are very thanks to the anonymous reviewers for their useful comments, and the works is supported by the project of Chongqing University Postgraduates' Innovative Team Building under the No. 200909C1011, and the Science and Technology Project of Ministry of Transport under Grant No. 2011318740240.

REFERENCES

Aarthi, S., et al. (2011). Predicting customer demographics in a mobile social network. *International Conference on Advances in Social Networks Analysis and Mining, IEEE Computer Society* (pp. 553 – 554).

Ahn, H. et al. (2011). Facilitating cross-selling in a mobile telecom market to develop customer classification model based on hybrid data mining techniques. *Expert Systems with Applications*, *38*, 5005–5012. doi:10.1016/j.eswa.2010.09.150.

Backstrom, L. et al. (2006). Group formation in large social networks: Membership, growth, and evolution. *ACM KDD*, *06*, 44–54.

Barbier, G., & Liu, H. (2011). *Data mining in social media. Springer Science+Business Media, LLC* (pp. 327–352). Social Network Data Analytics.

Bonch, F. (2011). Influence propagation in social networks: A data mining perspective. *IEEE Intelligent Informatics Bulletin*, 12(1).

Bonchi, F., et al. (2011). Social network analysis and mining for business applications. *ACM Transactions on Intelligent Systems and Technology*, *2*(3), Article 22.

Bose, I., & Mahaptra, R. (2001). Business data mining: A machine learning prospective. Elsevier. *Information & Management*, *39*, 211–225. doi:10.1016/S0378-7206(01)00091-X.

Boyd, D. M., & Ellison, N. B. (2007). Social network sites: Definition, history, and scholarship. *Journal of Computer-Mediated Communication*, *13*(1). Retrieved from http://jcmc.indiana.edu/vol13/issue1/boyd.ellison.html doi:10.1111/j.1083-6101.2007.00393.x.

Cao, L. (2010). Domain-driven data mining: Challenges and prospects. *IEEE Transactions on Knowledge and Data Engineering*, *22*(6). doi:10.1109/TKDE.2010.32 PMID:21373375.

Chang, Y. J. et al. (2007). *A general architecture of mobile social network services* (pp. 151–156). IEEE Computer Society. doi:10.1109/ICCIT.2007.132.

Chou, L.-D. et al. (2011). Mobile social network services for families with children with developmental disabilities. *IEEE Transactions on Information Technology in Biomedicine*, *15*(4), 585–593. doi:10.1109/TITB.2011.2155663 PMID:21606040.

Daskalaki, S. et al. (2003). Data mining for decision support on customer insolvency in telecommunications business. Elsevier. *European Journal of Operational Research*, *145*, 239–255. doi:10.1016/S0377-2217(02)00532-5.

Dokoohaki, N., & Matskin, M. (2008). Effective design of trust ontologies for improvement in the structure of socio-semantic trust networks. *International Journal on Advances in Intelligent Systems*, 1st (1942-2679): 23–42.

Domingos, P., & Richardson, M. (2001). Mining the network value of customers. *ACM KDD*, *01*, 57–66.

Dustdar, S. et al. (2005). Mining of ad-hoc business processes with TeamLog. Elsevier. *Data & Knowledge Engineering*, *55*, 129–158. doi:10.1016/j.datak.2005.02.002.

Fei-Yue, W. et al. (2007). Social computing: From social informatics to social intelligence. IEEE. *Journal of Intelligent Systems*, *2*, 79–83.

Gebremeskel, G. B., et al. (2012). The paradigm integration of computational intelligence performance in cloud computing towards data security. *IEEE Computer Society, 5th International Conference on Information and Computing Science* (pp. 19 – 22).

Guo, B., et al. (2011). Living with Internet of things: The emergence of embedded intelligence. *IEEE Computer Society, International Conferences on Internet of Things, and Cyber, Physical and Social Computing* (pp. 297 – 304).

Hine, C. (2011). Internet research and unobtrusive methods. *Social research update*, Issue 61. University of Surrey. Retrieved from http://sru.soc.surrey.ac.uk

Howison, J. et al. (2011). Validity issues in the use of social network analysis with digital trace data. *Journal of the Association for Information Systems*, *12*(12), 767–797.

Hullermeier, E. (2005). Fuzzy methods in machine learning and data mining: Status and prospects. Elsevier. *Fuzzy Sets and Systems*, *156*(3), 387–406. doi:10.1016/j.fss.2005.05.036.

Jensen, D., & Neville, J. (2002). *Data mining in social networks, symposium on dynamic social network modeling and analysis. National Academy of Sciences*. Washington, DC: National Academy Press.

Kayastha, N., et al. (2011). Applications, architectures, and protocol design issues for mobile social networks: A survey. *IEEE*, 99(12), pp. 2031-2158.

Kemp, D. et al. (2012). Corporate social responsibility, mining and "audit culture." Elsevier. *Journal of Cleaner Production*, *24*, 1–10. doi:10.1016/j.jclepro.2011.11.002.

Korolova, A. et al. (2008). Link privacy in social networks. *ACM, CIKM*, *08*, 1–10.

McLennan, A., & Howell, G. (2010). *Social networks and the challenge for public relations* (*Vol. 11*). Asia Pacific Public Relations Journal.

Min, J.-K., & Cho, S.-B. (2011). Mobile human network management and recommendation by probabilistic social mining. *IEEE Transactions on Systems, Man, and Cybernetics. Part B, Cybernetics*, *41*(6), 761–771. PMID:21172755.

Nair, P., & Sarasamma, S. T. (2007). *Data mining through fuzzy social network analysis* (pp. 251–255). IEEE Community Society. doi:10.1109/NAFIPS.2007.383846.

Ngai, E. W. T. et al. (2011). The application of data mining techniques in financial fraud detection: A classification framework and an academic review of literature. Elsevier. *Decision Support Systems, 50*, 559–569. doi:10.1016/j.dss.2010.08.006.

Park, H.-S., & Cho, S.-B. (2010). Building mobile social network with semantic relation using Bayesian network-based life-log mining. *IEEE Computer Society, International Conference on Social Computing/IEEE International Conference on Privacy, Security, Risk and Trust* (pp. 401-40).

Pentland, A. (2007). Automatic mapping and modeling of human networks. Elsevier. *Science Direct. Physica A, 378*, 59–67. doi:10.1016/j.physa.2006.11.046.

Ploderer, B. et al. (2010). Collaboration on social network sites: Amateurs, professionals and celebrities. *Computer Supported Cooperative Work*. doi:10.1007/s10606-010-9112-0.

Pushpa & Shobhag, G. (2012). An efficient method of building the telecom social network for churn prediction. [IJDKP]. *International Journal of Data Mining & Knowledge Management Process, 2*(3).

Rahman, A. et al. (2010). Building dynamic social network from sensory data feed. *IEEE Transactions on Instrumentation and Measurement, 9*(5), 1327–1341. doi:10.1109/TIM.2009.2038307.

Rangaswamy, N., & Cutrell, E. (2012). Resourceful networks: Notes from a mobile social networking platform in India. *Pacific Affairs, 85*(3), 587–606. doi:10.5509/2012853587.

Shen, Z., & Ma, K.-L. (2008). MobiVis: A visualization system for exploring mobile data. IEEE. *Visualization Symposium, PacificVis. 08*, pp. 175 – 182.

Shim, J. P. et al. (2011). Past, present, and future of decision support technology. Elsevier. *Decision Support Systems, 33*, 111–126. doi:10.1016/S0167-9236(01)00139-7.

Skillicorn, D., & Talia, D. (2002). Mining large data sets on grids: Issue and prospects. *Computing and Informatics, 21*, 347–362.

Wang, W., & Man, H. (2009). Exploring social relations for the intrusion detection in ad hoc networks. *Proc. of SPIE*, Vol. 7344.

Yang, X., et al. (2010). K-means based clustering on mobile usage for social network analysis purpose. IEEE. *Advanced Information Management and Service 6th International Conference Proceeding, MPI QMUL Inf. Syst. Res. Centre.*

YongYeol, et al. (2007). Analysis of topological characteristics of huge online social networking services. *ACM*, pp. 835 – 844.

Ziv, N. D., & Mulloth, B. (2006). An exploration on mobile social networking: Dodgeball as a case in point. *IEEE Computer Society, Proceedings of the International Conference on Mobile Business (ICMB'06).*

ADDITIONAL READING

Cao, L. (2010). Domain-driven data mining: Challenges and prospects. *IEEE Transactions on Knowledge and Data Engineering, 22*(6), 755–769. doi:10.1109/TKDE.2010.32.

Castro, F. et al. (2007). Applying data mining techniques to e-learning problems. [SCI]. *Studies in Computational Intelligence, 62*, 183–221. doi:10.1007/978-3-540-71974-8_8.

Cheun, D. W., et al. (2011). A practical framework for comprehensive mobile context visualization. *IEEE Compunity Society, 8th International Conference on e-Business Engineering* (pp. 201 – 206).

Chlamtac, I. et al. (2003). Mobile ad hoc networking: Imperatives and challenges. Elsevier. *Ad Hoc Networks*, *1*, 13–64. doi:10.1016/S1570-8705(03)00013-1.

Donath, J. (2007). Signals in social supernets. *Journal of Computer-Mediated Communication*, *13*(1), 12. Retrieved from http://jcmc.indiana.edu/vol13/issue1/donath.html doi:10.1111/j.1083-6101.2007.00394.x.

Folasade, I. O. (2011). Computational intelligence in data mining and prospects in telecommunication industry. [JETEAS]. *Journal of Emerging Trends in Engineering and Applied Sciences*, *2*(4), 601–605.

Gil, Y., et al. (2009). Leveraging social networking sites to acquire rich task structure. In *Proceedings of the User-Contributed Knowledge and Artificial Intelligence: An Evolving Synergy (WIKIAI 2009).*

Gundecha, P., et al. (2012). *Mining social media: A brief introduction, tutorial in operational research.*

Hsu, J. (2005). *Data mining trends and developments: The key data mining technologies and applications for the 21st Century*. Retrieved from http://www.proc.isecon.org/2002/224b/ISECON.2002.Hsu.pdf

Hsu, W.H., & Taiwan, T. (2012). Emerging challenges and opportunities in exploiting mobile photos and videos. *ACM IMMPD'12.*

Kempe, D. et al. (2003). *Maximizing the spread of influence through a social network* (pp. 137–146). ACM.

Licoppe, C., & Smoreda, Z. (2005). Are social networks technologically embedded? How networks are changing today with changes in communication technology. Elsevier. *Social Networks*, *27*, 317–335. doi:10.1016/j.socnet.2004.11.001.

Musolesi, M., & Mascolo, C. (2006). Designing mobility models based on social network theory. *ACM, Mobile Computing and Communications Review, 11*(3).

Naaman, M. (2010). Social multimedia: Highlighting opportunities for search and mining of multimedia data in social media applications. *Multimedia Tools and Applications*, 1–26.

Nan, L. et al. (2010). *Mobile takes social computing beyond Web 2.0* (pp. 12–19). Tao Business, Win-win.

Onnela, J.-P. et al. (2007). Structure and tie strengths in mobile communication networks. *National Academy*, *104*(18), 7332–7336. doi:10.1073/pnas.0610245104 PMID:17456605.

Pietiläinen, A. K. (2009). *MobiClique: Middleware for mobile social networking* (pp. 49–54). ACM.

Preibusch, S. et al. (2007). *Ubiquitous social networks – opportunities and challenges for privacy-aware user modeling*. Berlin, Germany: DIW Berlin.

Rana, J. (2009). An architecture in mobile social networking application. *The 1st International Conference on Computational Intelligence, Communication Systems and Networks* (pp. 241 - 246).

Richter, Y., et al. (2010). Predicting customer churn in mobile networks through analysis of social groups. In *Proceedings of the 2010 SIAM International Conference on Data Mining (SDM 2010)* (pp. 732 – 741).

Rosa, P., et al. (2012). An ubiquitous mobile multimedia system for events agenda. IEEE. *Wireless Communications and Networking Conference: Mobile and Wireless Networks*, pp. 2103-2107.

Srinivasan, S. et al. (2011). Multi-agent based decision support system using data mining and case based reasoning. *IJCSI International Journal of Computer Science Issues*, *8*(4), 340–349.

Ting, H. I. et al. (2012). *Social network mining, analysis, and research trends: Techniques and applications*. USA: IGI Global.

Wang, T. et al. (2009). *MobileMiner: A real world case study of data mining in mobile communication. SIGMOD'09*. ACM.

Wil, M.P., & van der Aalst. (2007). Exploring the CSCW spectrum using process mining. Elsevier. *Advanced Engineering Informatics*, *21*, 191–199. doi:10.1016/j.aei.2006.05.002.

Zhao, C., & Liu, B. (2010). Finding gold in intranet data: A comparison of mined and surveyed social networks. In *Proceedings of the Fourth International AAAI Conference on Weblogs and Social Media* (pp. 379-382).

Zheng, L. et al. (2011). *Applying data mining techniques to address disaster information management challenges on mobile devices* (pp. 283–291). ACM. doi:10.1145/2020408.2020457.

Chapter 9
Semantic Integrating for Intelligent Cloud Data Mining Platform and Cloud Based Business Intelligence for Optimization of Mobile Social Networks

Gebeyehu Belay Gebremeskel
Chongqing University, China

Zhongshi He
Chongqing University, China

Xuan Jing
Chongqing University, China

ABSTRACT

In this chapter, the authors focused on optimization of MSNs based on integrating for intelligent DM and BI platforms, which involves mobile devices. The approach is defining the challenges based social network trends and current situation explorations, and then applying the techniques to exploring the social media towards social cloud technology, which focused on creating a scalable, adaptable and optimal social cloud as the users' contexts and IT technologies. The newly proposed method is vigorously significant to develop flexible social networking in relation to the development of IT, which facilitates data/information access, distributions, high availability and a large amount of data analysis and others. Therefore, the techniques this chapter is vitally crucial to improve the performance and use of social networking in a comprehensive and powerful way. Nutshell, this chapter overviews the impetus for the development of intelligent semantic cloud and diversified social-networking in both physical and wireless sectors, which representing a wide aspect of social cloud change, and increasingly appropriate service providing a platform for innovative ideas and technological innovation in the business environment.

DOI: 10.4018/978-1-4666-4213-3.ch009

Copyright © 2013, IGI Global. Copying or distributing in print or electronic forms without written permission of IGI Global is prohibited.

1. INTRODUCTION

Mobile Social Networks (MSN) is a dynamic and extensible social platform that enables users to gain more access of information, resources, services and other benefits through social end nodes. It is the technological communication and interaction between people using integrated intelligent agents and a communication device from their destinations, via the internet and/or mobile device. All the components of the network systems are representing as social objects[1] (Kayastha et al., 2011), which are significant to make easy humans' day-to-day life, and natural paradigm shifts of friend's interactions and relationships. These are the verge and popularity of social networking that started exploring new opportunities and applications over the traditional social media. The advanced social systems allowing users to stay connected to their favorite social networks, which are pertinent social-networking technologies and converge on communication tools that lead to a rise in user-generated content and contextual information such as, personal profiles, their existing location, availability, interests and moods. In these dynamic activities, large data are collected, recorded and stored, which are essential to explore trends, current situations and predict future optimal performance. To these facts, searching and introducing new tools and approach are paramount to extract valuable information/knowledge from the data repositories, which insight to integrate social semantic clouds that initiating and allowing on-demand services and be as ephemeral as the user interests themselves.

Therefore, integrating for semantic intelligent clouds and communication devices are essential that enhance MSNs performance in scalable cloud facilities to access and share social resources and applications. By semantic cloud, we focused on the relation of signifiers and/or technologies that enable the collaborative movement or interactions of intelligent agents in a given standard and form of a generic virtual model called social cloud. The term intelligent and/or intelligent agents are software involving entities, which perform on behalf of users with some degree of independency or autonomy called intelligent Data Mining (DM) and Business Intelligence (BI) (*see more in 1.2*). Thus, intelligent agent in a social cloud is also a clear and high level of understanding of the context and content of the social networking in an abstraction functional system using certain actuators. Communication devices such as, mobile technology towards social-networking services is the key component and more dynamic, which demanding the paradigm integrating for intelligent agent tools to handle, investigate, distribute and secure MSNs data on considerations of the trends and current status and business (companies) structures (Domingue et al., 2011). However, traditional social network's service and applications are not capable of handle these complex performances as users' desires.

Thus, the motives and research issues of this chapter are focusing on the challenges of traditional social networking, on the basis of the following formulated and defined research questions.

Q1: Poor performance of traditional social-networking service to handle social member's data/information need, un able to consolidate with the current advancements, such as the integrating for intelligent DM, BI and mobile technologies,

Q2: The traditional social-networking service missed the opportunity to bind the rich social context tightly with the local context of interacting person, which is un able to answer the question of 'who is that?' to extend the Web interface of the social network among the service users or members, and fewer user interactions,

Q3: In the past, many research works have been done on the social networks that none technological aspects and social networks within the context of human interactions or relationships. However, the need of standard services in related to IT development paramount what we introduce in this chapter, which could provide proper and efficient social media services,

Q4: The issue of social-networking service classifications, which is the newly emerging of the integrating for semantic intelligent agents and mobile device (technologies). That is, the need of clear boundaries of the static and dynamic social-networking categories in terms of interoperability,

Q5: The need of characterization of the structure and interaction of MSNs to elucidate the social behaviors of individuals and/or group's role in the social networks, for example, for suspicion or fraud detections.

Optimization of MSNs application is the other way of overcoming the challenges and problems of traditional social networking, which demanding efficient, dynamic and integrating tools towards the optimal functional of social networks by gaining implicit knowledge of the social service. The research approaching as, first, we defined the weakness and challenges of conventional social-networking services based on literature reviews and trends of social media in relation to Information Technologies (IT). Second, we explore the loads of existing social-networking challenges towards its functions and adaptability of flexible and advance social semantic cloud. Third, exploring the proposed approach towards dynamic social networking, which visualize and understanding how optimization could be made on the current social network services. Therefore, based on the research issues and methodologies, we introduced and discussed on Intelligent Cloud Data Mining (ICDM), and Cloud Based Business Intelligence (CBBI) to overcome the social network's challenges' and problems. It is a systematic and innovative approach to optimize the social-networking performances and search the possible potentials. The approach is capable and also allows to science and engineering and business data processing, handling, distributing and extracting new pattern or knowledge that is the refraction of MSNs towards technological advancement and human interactions' contexts in a dynamic way and full flag integration of semantic intelligent agents (Miluzzo et al., 2008). In this intensive work, MSN dynamism explored in terms of cloud computing techniques and semantic integrating of intelligent agents involving the mobile device and technology.

1.1 Contribution of the Chapter

The main contributions of the chapter are to provide a basic knowledge on the techniques of semantic intelligent cloud, which involves DM, BI and Mobile device towards optimization of MSNs performance. It is a dynamic development of cloud computing based on integrating intelligent agents cloud systems, which is driving the current social web services by enabling users to view and easily accessing social media. On the other hand, undertaking and intensively exploring on semantic integrating for intelligent agents cloud involving a mobile device to optimize the MSN, which make effective, scalable and powerful social-networking services. Therefore, the main contributions of this chapter are:

- Based on the research issues (Q_1 and Q_2), we undertook intensive exploration works on traditional social networking that insight the existing real situations and its trends towards introducing new and novel approaches to optimize MSNs. The readers would gain a clear understanding on social network contents, research methodology, and the newly introducing approaches, which is generic proposed model (Figure 8) that designed as a refined four layers of the architecture to users as a single reference model[2].
- Based on the social-networking theory and empirical analysis (Q_2, Q_3 and Q_4), we visu-

alize and validate the proposed approach to overcome the traditional social-networking challenges. We also proposed a single and cohesive MSN semantic cloud structure that embedded in people daily activities and technologies. As MSN platforms take center stage, we could foresee its application scope an indispensable component of users' offline experiences. Readers could gain a technical and basic understanding how intelligent agents are involving in the cloud systems.

- We would also touch the emerging mobile social computing applications (Q_4 and Q_5) as the new dimension of the MSN by considering connecting experiences without geographic barriers or distance, time, and/or any other physical constraints. It could use as a reference and insight mobile technology research works.
- We made an intensive and interactive research work on the newly initiative research issue (Q_5), which could give basic and fundamental techniques and approaches to the readers and decision makers.

The rest of the chapter is organized into eight sections. Section 2 is a discussion on related work of MSN, and semantic intelligent agents cloud. In section 3, we present the philosophical overview of semantic intelligent cloud based MSNs application including the need of optimization of MSNs, applications, its semantic analysis and mobility modeling, and conceptual representation of context aware. In section 4, we discussed the semantic integration of intelligent agent cloud for MSNs and its architecture, layer representations, data warehouse and semantic enhancement in details. Section 5 discussed the proposed social cloud model for optimization of MSNs applications and its components. Section 6 is for pattern and principles of MSNs models, including modeling and structure of social networking. In section 7, we discussed the potential performance of the proposed MSNs architecture in details, and finally conclusion and further research works followed by acknowledgement and references.

2. BACKGROUND AND RELATED WORK DISCUSSION

In this chapter, we provide innovative concepts and methodologies for the newly innovated approach of the semantic integrated intelligent cloud platform to optimize MSNs applications. We intensively discussed from the defining pertinent research issues in the performance evaluation of the proposed method. The details of the research work are supported by well described models, which are essential to represent clear and understandable information and knowledge about the topic. The work also supported by concepts and ideas of other literatures related to the chapter, which have been done the last two decades. The rationale and an overviewed of related literature works discussions are presented as the following two sub sections.

2.1 Rationale of the Chapter

In this chapter, we use intelligent agents as intelligent Data Mining (DM) and Business Intelligence (BI). DM as an intelligent agent cloud is the platform of dynamic information sources, filtering, system automation and collections and so on, and the invisible functionality or operation of mining data from the repositories. BI is also intelligent as a service of the process of applications, information filtering, navigation, recommender systems and agents, reputations, resource intermediary and monitoring mechanisms of social cloud process using modeling and architectural techniques (Sopchoke & Kijsiridul, 2011; Rama et al., 2009; Yao et al., 2001). Therefore, an integrating for semantic Intelligent Cloud, ICDM_CBBI approach is a systematic and dynamic interaction and interrelation of social networks, which is prominent more understand and expand the social cloud services and make it adaptable, flexible and scalable systems to available and provide capable social services. This approach allows to, not only optimize the MSN performance but also to interact in a digital or physical real-world framework, in the systems. The paradigm of MSN is widely adoptions, fast growth technological collaborative and universal design patterns or principles for social computing within a business process framework (Ding et al., 2012).

Therefore, ICDM_CBBI leverages MSNs semantic clouds techniques are newly innovative way, which is essential to optimize social-networking application's performance based on real user interests and finds potential matches for the social activities. Our approach is fundamental to concatenate the previous trend, current status and future opportunities of social networking to improve the existing and next-generation CC and communication technologies to manage and make accessible to the human life and also enhancing the real-time social groups' interactions and interrelationships. However, in the past decades, semantic cloud based social-networking research did not touch or limited. There are few researchers, which have been done focusing on the problems and challenges of social-networking service's assessment based on Cloud Computing (CC) techniques (Ioannidis et al., 2009) and service limitations (Rosa et al., 2012; Bonchi et al., 2011; Zhang et al., 2011), and on defining the social context's services (Beach et al., 2009). All approaches lacked integrating semantic intelligent agents cloud components to maintain the efficient and effective social cloud as the context of social media.

Intelligent DM and BI based social semantic cloud platform are the newly emerging technology, which demanding to expand its application in the cloud computing environments by involving mobile devices and technologies, which is pertinent to social mobility applications (Beach et al., 2008). The mobile device uses as the users' mobility interface and computing, where as intelligent DM and BI uses as extending the service in efficient, effective and scalable performance via the MSNs cloud. I.e. the semantic integrating of intelligent agents and mobile devices are a fundamental task to optimize the social networking in its advance level (Niyato et al., 2010). Intelligent agent cloud based infrastructure of social networking involving mobile cloud gives a possibility of data collection, storage, exploration, distribution, and sharing application. The data could be personal profiles, text analysis, image recognition and feature selection and sensor application. The availability of massive amounts of MSNs data and the way of access has given a driving action towards a scientific and statistically robust study of the field of social networks.

The MSNs data exploration or analytic and distributions are an attractive area of intelligent DM, which emerging as semantic data and storage clouds. The MSNs data-centric as the data cloud impetus has led to a significant amount of research, which has been unique and challenging in its statistical and computational focus in analyzing large amounts of data (IEEE COMSOC MMTC, 2012). In additions to this, the most current approaches toward integrating social networks with mobile devices have also missed the opportunity to bind social context tightly with the intelligent agents cloud system and local context of interacting users. The challenges are driven forces to the rising of intelligent DM and BI, which experienced a startling rate of growth and reached lofty levels of sophisticated data modeling (Cao, 2010; Mobasher, 2007), which could be adaptable and scalable to make global inter connected and interacted social-networking services. Complex data modeling and handling are ever challenging for dynamic social-networking (Barbier & Liu, 2011), which should be addressed by applying an intelligent semantic cloud.

In this chapter, we introduced the approach is essential to mine rich sources of information in the context of social networks that is the intelligent agents' pertinent task, which provides useful and actionable information in a wide variety of fields such as, social cloud, defense, science and engineering, and others (Apayden et al., 2010). In additions, the volumes of data are a challenge in many cases such as efficiency social-networking and security. Thus, the traditional social-networking services could not be capable, scalable and adaptable, which need to transform integrated semantic technology to perform efficiently as the social members desired. Therefore, the proposed method is a key issue to promulgate optimization of MSNs performance as users' interest in relation to ÍT technology and business dynamism. It is prominent at visualize or foresee MSNs paradigm application and scope to fast development and efficient cloud service, which become indispensable of users' unrestricted access as users and vendors. It also gives a clear insight how to overcome the limitation of traditional social network's services, including defining 'who is that' by considering human contexts. Intelligent DM and BI as a service provides the principle of technology, the implementation process, and constraints the key issues of development prospects of MSNs. ICDM_CBBI based semantic cloud system served as behavior infers user on demand and change service resources for conceptualization resources, which is high reliability social cloud applications.

2.2 Related Work Discussion

The social network involves man and machine distributed across semantic integrating intelligent agents DM and BI) co-coordinating and collaborating with each other. Semantic social cloud via the internet is the inter connection and interaction of people to various applications, such as accessing resources and services (Domingue et al., 2011). Social connectivity is usually based on direct interaction or search for users according to their interests. Searching approaches simply extend the web interface of the social network to the mobile device CC, by providing a view of the user's social network on their mobile phone. However, integrated social networks with mobile devices have more challenges to define social opportunities such as social contexts (Beach et al., 2008), which is important to the advancing of social networking. The platform is the means of enlargement of the members as visitors and vendors to the systems (Chen & Qi, 2011) and relevant to map virtual connections between friends and/groups (Humphreys, 2008). Therefore, connection or communications among members could be based on their own interests and devices such as an instant message (Niyato et al., 2010), which leads the group members to their closed age, culture and other behavioral factors (Zhenyu et al., 2010). Such interest based interrelationships created long lasting connections and pertinent opportunities to debates the issues they like. It is a static and traditional media, which need to transfer to a dynamic service (MSN service) as a semantic integrated intelligent agent cloud that paid much attention science and engineering and business (Gartrell et al., 2010).

Traditional social network is not allowing full or on-demand access of data/information to the public or to the members: typically, users can choose the level of visibility of their personal data through privacy management mechanisms (Ding et al., 2012). Therefore, the need of dynamic social systems considering the advanced computing technology, business diversity and large data accumulations vitally significant, which demanded integrating for mining process, semantic intelligent agent's architecture and a systematic analysis or exploration of social-networking challenges (Chang et al., 2007). The involvement of mobile technology is also an essential component to define the location and existing situations of users and mobility (Rosa et al., 2012). Moreover, the intelligent cloud system besides mobile technology is a roadmap upon social networks that facilitate and make for the interaction and interrelation of social members (Bonchi et al., 2011; Licoppe & Smoreda, 2005) anywhere, anytime and anything. Cloud system architecture and the collaborative intelligent agents' components are made mild to access and dynamic to users as they desired (Janjua et al., 2012). That is, the development of basic cloud collaborations systems allowing users to discover friends, information and other resources dynamically and friendly in their vicinity through their mobile device (Apayden, 2010; Šikšnys et al., 2010).

The proliferations of social networks have created a large demand for social information contents as well as an effective semantic for cloud information retrieval techniques involving DM, BI, and mobile device's technologies. These bode well for social network services that significantly focused on integrated intelligent DM and BI cloud system. For example, information on Facebook, Twitter and Linked in MySpace (Kayastha et al., 2011; Humphreys, 2008, Grob et al., 2009) are confounding for users regularly and living by the mantra and remain unaware (Rama et al., 2009; Li & Chen, 2009) and other problems. Therefore, the need of ICDM_CBBI is paramount to overcome these challenges and problems of the traditional social networking in consideration static social media, information access and dissemination on demand, which gives opportunities to group focusing, business effectiveness and success, time and so on (Chang et al., 2007). BI based computing infrastructure is a flexible and hierarchical based structuring of MSNs forward looking to the dynamism and technological advancements integrating to the group contexts, which is a fundamental to accessing, disseminating, and sharing information and resources on the CBBI cloud system among the groups on the extreme DM techniques (Barbier & Liu, 2011).

3. PHILOSOPHICAL OVERVIEW OF SEMANTIC INTELLIGENT CLOUD BASED MOBILE SOCIAL NETWORK

The philosophical phenomena of the evolution and convergence of electronics, communication, computing and semantic cloud technologies have empowered the users of today's social network with all pervasive and ubiquitous networking defined with location, time and subject restrictions (Kim et al., 2011). The interaction and interrelation model has transcended from one to one, machine to machine to many to many, user to user, in terms of intra group and inter group linkages. Such an abstraction was possible because of the transparency provisioning in terms of location, contents, and others. Moreover, the characteristics of individuals using the network are rapidly declining and the users evolving into a community is increasing very fast. Such communities do have a societal impact by the communication within a social network and communication across a social network. In today's context, it is not farfetched to say that 'user' means 'a social network'. The concept of semantic social network is coined the cognitive of social networks as a form of represent semantically structured knowledge of human behaviors in ideal positions to make semantic social clouds (Kayastha et al., 2011).

The human behavior extends the network of the user readable system (such as web pages) by integrating intelligent systems and collaborative technologies, which gives a possibility of users' preferences based on the social cloud contexts (Li & Chen, 2009). The semantic social cloud effort is an ideal interoperable by providing standards to support data access and distributions and interoperability between social applications enable users and members to collaborate in the process (Domingue et al., 2011; Sheth & Ranabahu, 2010) by involving communication devices. Mobile devices are ubiquitous computing devices, which are pertinent to access data/information on the MSN cloud around the world anytime, anywhere and anything. Since mobile phones are widely deployed, have powerful microprocessors and are networked with other cell phone devices and existing communication infrastructure, they can be a useful platform for connecting in ways other than through voice communication.

Therefore, MSNs technologies are to map effective connections between people without geographic barriers. MSNs semantic cloud built upon intelligent DM and BI cloud towards social networks highly significant to members (users) that correlate the virtual or artificial social network with its real-world counterpart (Mobasher, 2007). The traditional social network services are not efficient to access data/information and also existing implementations of social networks are difficult to explore when they should be at their most useful – in friendly situations. For example, in the bar, in the park or in the movies, and so on ICDM_CBBI integrating mobile MSNs cloud allows users to discover friends and friends of friends in their vicinity, which make the explicit connections that people mapped out using social network technologies more interesting for the abstracting physical world to virtualization in a social semantic cloud. Virtualization of the network system provides flexibility in the use of social-networking resources (Kim et al., 2011). The semantic integrating for intelligent DM and BI involving the mobile devices are key components and collaborative technologies' most useful and significant techniques in virtualization of social semantic cloud. For virtualization of intelligent agents computing environment requires technologies support various systematic arrangements of the intelligent agents' interactions and relations, enabling automated agents to access the intelligent cloud and perform key tasks on behalf of users (Zhong, 2003; Berendt et al., 2002). Thus, it leads to dynamic social-networking services those insights to optimize social semantic cloud applications, which are extremely wide in contents, and typically contain a tremendous amount of social content and linkage data that could be leveraged for analysis (IEEE COMSOC MMTC, 2012; Ioannidis et al., 2009). The integration of this intelligent system is essentially the newly extended graphic structure of the MSNs, and communications between intelligent agents and the content data are the text, images, and other data/information in the vigorous contents of MSNs (Niyato et al., 2010).

Intelligent DM and BI based semantic cloud application leading to the MSNs cloud creating an efficient network of interlinked and semantically rich knowledge, which concatenate applications and public features that the social network knowledge representation language and formats from the intelligent agent clouds (Figure 1). The Semantic approaches for integrating ICDM and CBBI envisioned as a system that intelligent agents are capable of interact, interrelate, understand and respond to complex human requests based on their social networks (Licoppe & Smoreda, 2005). Such dynamic processes, including searching the implicit knowledge require that the relevant information sources be logically structured MSNs contents. The semantic integrating for ICDM regarded as an integrator across different social content, information applications and systems of CBBI is the process of optimization of MSNs service. Optimization of MSNs is the solution of social network's challenges addressing as collective relationship's description framework, web ontology language and extensible markup language that describe documents and links between intelligent systems (Apayden, 2010; Bhogal et al., 2007). The technologies of an extensive markup language are combined in order to provide descriptions that supplement or replace the content of Web documents. Thus, social content manifests itself as descriptive data stored in the cloud data storage and cloud system standards as the aim of reducing of uncertainty social-networking services (Chen & Qi, 2011).

As it showed on Figure 1, the MSNs new content is created by the provider, which stored in the queue of the collective base station with a maximum capacity of the contents (Zhong, 2003). Then, it releases the other content to the nodes in its coverage area that the child social-networking content broadcasted to the users in the coverage area of the circle. The MSNs nodes with the latest content from the social station can move and meet other nodes in the same community. The fresh content transferred between the meeting nodes if the newly created content is newer than that in other nodes. In this MSN model, the benefit of willing provider is a non-decreasing function of the number of nodes receiving the contented. In addition, since the nodes have to register for the content and its provider can keep track of the current number of nodes with invigorated content. In the model, optimization of semantic cloud formulation develops to maximize the number of MSN nodes having the extended fresh pleased (Kim et al., 2008). The semantic intelligent clouds as social documents are data and applications created by the end users from the various social interactions. Semantic cloud technology is an intelligent DM and BI as services to support semantic web data by being the sources of users voluntarily connecting together, which is the semantic integrating of an intelligent agent system with MSNs full cloud potential. This integrating cloud focus on using social cloud technologies to model social data using the ontologies of DM and BI, which social data could be represented as shared, and common models. This approach leveraging the wisdom of the semantic integrating of intelligent cloud services can give a head start towards creating generic of MSN semantic cloud (Niyato et al., 2010; Ioannidis et al., 2009).

3.1 The Need of Optimization and Social Model Conceptual Framework

The social semantic cloud is the representation of the dynamic social platform that allowing one to create, access and/or disseminate data to share with the groups. The usage of a mobile device in a social cloud is vitally significant to envision data portability to each user (Domingue et al., 2011). Therefore, optimization of social networking is a key factor to the development and conceptual understanding of social semantic cloud applications (Rosa et al., 2012). The issue of optimization is fundamental to provide increasing significance of communication or connection towards social media access among the members. This increasing connection between the friendly groups is pertinent to the success of business and other fields (Humphreys, 2008). That is the communication and connections of members involving cell phone service, which are defined distributes location-based information of users, via the cloud intelligent system. The ICDM, (such as data cloud, storage cloud), and BI as a service (such as SaaS, DaaS, ...) within the social-networking site allows users to set up dynamic mobile cloud computing, which leads to optimize MSNs of the social networking that they can distribute, access and share, resources from their locations with any group members (Šikšnys et al., 2010). Such

Figure 1. Social semantic cloud architecture

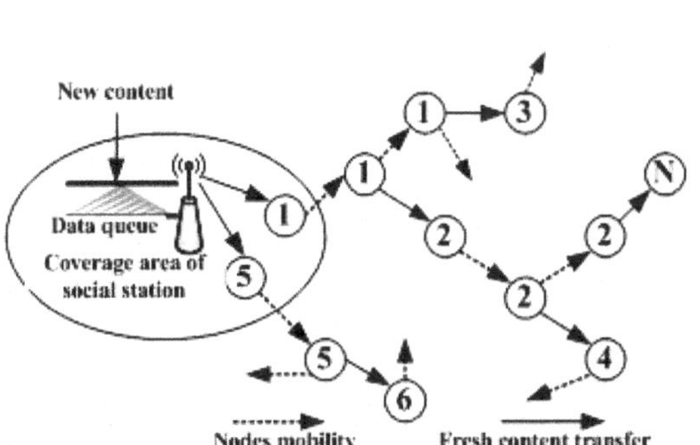

dynamism is an essential to create the new social network media platform for detail exploration of social behaviors and communicative practices. Furthermore, the optimization of MSNs is also vitally significant to intelligent DM for more efficient online data collection on a large scale, pre processing and data storage (cloud data storage) on the context of organization and/business, including individual users desires based on the BI as a service.

The conceptual framework of MSNs semantic model has many inter linked intelligent agents, including mobile agent social network's norms, social space, methods and others (Humphreys, 2008). The concept of MSNs is people or social network members enable to be in touch based on publish subscribe for model in which the service users subscribe to the content provider to access or share information in the social media. Therefore, the conceptual framework is the architecture of MSNs ad hoc transient network to provide contented delivery for users (Pietilainen et al., 2009). The architecture of MSNs is semantic integrating for intelligent agents and mobile internet services, which leads to dynamic social-networking systems that can be broadly used in a current intelligent cloud system. In this case, the traditional social network service is an essential and basic framework to maintain the flexible social media, which made strong relationships than other systems. It is an open intelligent system, which information could easily propagate through the network according to users' profiles and interests.

Therefore, MSNs application is multi dimensional and inter relationships of a group of social networking, which provides diversified group activities as services, such as people, service sites, and others, for example, Facebook, Myspace (Grob et al., 2009; Kamilaris & Pitsillides, 2008). Multi dimensionality of social network service insights to recover a virtual society, which the real situations reflecting and perform various autonomy and intelligent system interactions, activities of social ability and mobility that dynamically lead to the optimization of MSN services (Kim et al., 2011). MSN cloud service is the tailored and dynamic version of social media or services, which integrating intelligent agents cloud with mobile devices via wide access of information and intelligent cloud social resources in general. This dynamism reveals the status of social networking and integrating of semantic intelligent agents. Thus, the traditional or static social network service and MSNs variations clearly defined as summarized on Table 1. Characterization of the two broad categories of the social networking is vitally significant to analyze the features of components based on activities,

Table 1. Basic difference of traditional social network and mobile social networks services

Descriptions or Factors	Their Differences	
	Social Network Service	Mobile Social Network Service
Typical platform, architecture design	Facebook, myspace Ex. Figure 1	Twitter Ex. Figure 2
Service access	Wired network	Wireless network
Services	Traditional desktop, social network service	Location based social network service Basic social network service
Application scenario	static	dynamic
Clients	Desktop browser	Mobile browser/specific client
personalized	limited	abundant
Open API	Yes ex. Facebook API	Yes, ex. Twitter API

contexts, an architecture design, and others (Barbier & Liu, 2011) as showed on Figure 2.

Based on these facts, MSN as a cloud system takes into account the mobile devices, which enlarges the social network platform. This platform gives an access to different kinds of activities in social-networking service scenarios to deliver social services; context generates and collects using mobile devices, which leads to enrich the traditional social network services to intelligent and dynamic social service, such as service on-demands (Banerjee et al., 2010). The intelligent systems are capable of mobile devices to provide effective services as the users' desires. In addition to these, MSNs provide open APIs to develop ICDM and CBBI based MSNs cloud system to connect and access resources in the intelligent system that efficient of insight the social context towards defining 'who is that' (Šikšnys et al., 2010) based on users' contexts. The semantic integrating of ICDM and CBBI enhances the fundamental features, which include activity based, mobility and context based, rely on mobile devices and powerful MSNs platform to optimize services (Ioannidis et al., 2009). MSNs semantic cloud system will involve many new features, which are inevitable the system architecture. The architecture of MSNs is carefully designed to reach the goal and optimization of the current social network systems. I.e., the MSNs architecture should involve a mobile device into consideration, scalable and flexible, refers to SaaS model (Gebremeskel et al., 2012).

The architecture of MSNs as an intelligent cloud system commonly classified as Client/Server (C/S), and Browser/Server (B/S), which includes Widget/server (W/S) (mobile widget as the new type of mobile application platform (Al-Khalifa & Al-Subaihin, 2012; Deinert & Magedanz, 2010) using standard cloud technologies. These three MSNs architecture design features are presented as Table 2, which involves these three features as below.

Mobile widgets are the package interactive design that provides an access to integrate with semantic intelligent agents clouds system. For example, from the detail descriptions of architecture design features of MSNs on Table 2, we can

Figure 2. Components of mobile social networks architecture

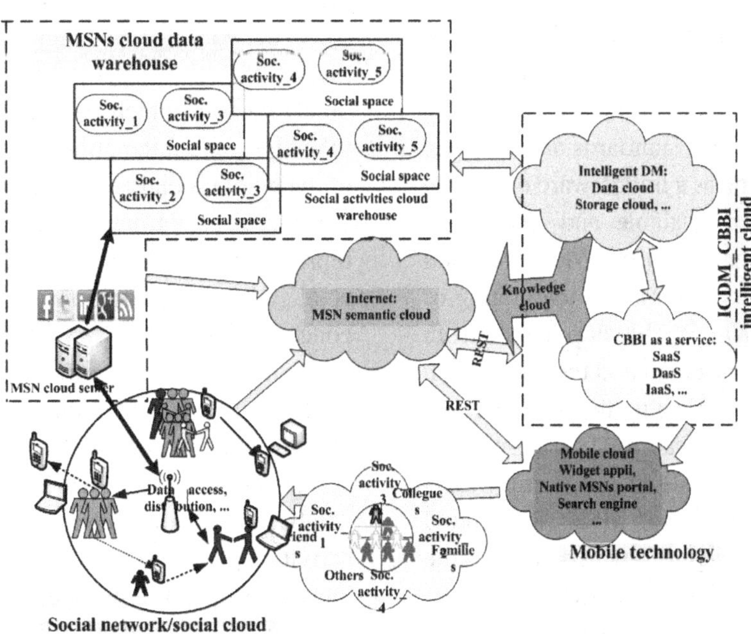

Table 2. MSNs architecture design features behavior in terms of different attributes

MSNs Attributes	MSNs Architecture Design Features		
	C/S	B/S	W/S
Clients	Specific, Symbian/JavaME	Mobile browser	Specific Widget
Application form	Symbian/JavaME	WAP	Mobile widget
Mobility support	Yes	No	Yes
Open API	Feasible	Feasible	Feasible
Scalability	Weak	Strong	Medium
Flexibility	Low	High	Medium
Dynamic context	Rich	Little	Rich
Accessing internet resources	Not easy	Easy	Easy
Cost to develop applications	High	low	low
Common platform	Twitter	Facebook	none

easily understand which browser is more efficient and give a possibility of semantic cloud as integrating of an intelligent system to optimize the service and more exploration of MSN in a dynamic performance (Janjua et al., 2012). Among these three MSNs architecture features, W/S more preferred platform and also compatible architecture to optimize MSNs services based on ICDM and CBBI platforms. The possible reasons are adaptability and integrating mobile application of the designs with intelligent cloud systems (DM and BI). Therefore, mobile widget as a server could invoke local capability of mobile devices such as location, contact lists, etc. considerations, which can support cloud standards and flexible, mobile widget engine as a middleware of mobile operating systems to scalable and extend the services (Miluzzo et al., 2008). Moreover, and vitally significant to the semantic integrating of ICDM and CBBI, W/S capable of pull data from multiple sources in the cloud and the application is easy in terms of technical matter, and less cost demanding than other features, which gives a chance to advance and made more dynamic MSNs systems. The architecture of MSNs conceptual model is depicted on Figure 2, which includes the four major components of the systems.

The classical concepts of MSNs are the concepts of combining two disciplines, which are social network (from social concept) and mobile communications networking. However, as the dynamic natures of MSNs semantic intelligent agents are the fundamental components, which has been introducing in this chapter. Therefore, as showed on Figure 2, the conceptual framework described as four distinctive components, which includes the data warehousing (social activities and server), intelligent agent clouds (intelligent DM and clouds based BI, Mobile device and technologies, social networks (physical social and cloud social networking). Social network and cloud are the set of social structure of members or social object's actors, which gives a clear understanding to analysis the interaction and interrelationships of the whole social entities. It is the platform that focusing on user's interactions and relations, which representing users or actor's interest (Kayastha et al., 2011). In additions, social cloud is the conceptual model of designing web applications, which develop cloud contents based on the social contexts. The data warehousing is the storing and sharing database, which stored on the social cloud server and/or activity, which is fundamental to a database used for content analysis. The data or activities pass through a preprocessing data and then store for additional operations before they are used for analysis and other user needs. Therefore, the typical ETL based data warehouse use staging, integration and access layers in the cloud system is key functions.

Semantic intelligent agents are the third and newly introducing components, which are vitally significant to understand and make easy access of the MSNs applications based on cloud contexts that considering data/information about people, objects, and surrounding, and so on. Such data are infrastructure based context data, personalized context data, social context data, and others (Goggins et al., 2010). The significant of ICDM_CBBI based MSNs cloud is easy access, scalability and adaptability of the cloud systems with the newly advanced technologies such as a mobile device. The intelligent DM integrating to the data cloud, storage cloud, and semantic knowledge cloud, where as CBBI application includes SaaS, DaaS, PaaS, and others as a service. The semantic integrating for intelligent agent cloud optimizes the MSNs cloud through REST, which is a dynamic and large scale of social networking architectural design to a distributed system framework that uses web protocols and technologies. REST used to capture cloud data through interpreting extensible markup language or web page files with the desired data, which includes client and server, cacheable and layered systems (Fielding & Taylor, 2002). The fourth and core components of MSNs are the mobile technology that made the social networks more accessible such as anywhere and anytime, adaptable, which could involve updated technologies. The significant of mobile devices is the involvement of new technology such as widget engine application, which is the core service of mobile device facilitating people or social object interrelationships and interactions each other as a common Representation State of Transfer (REST) design pattern (Deinert & Magedanz, 2010).

The dynamic MSN pattern is the basics of the modern cloud architecture, which provides the guiding principles by which flaws in the existing social-networking architecture could be identified, and extensions validated prior to social media deployment. Thus, MSNs services of semantic intelligent agent cloud and mobile application such as the widget engine are the core module of terminal side to provide socializing capability of integrating services from intelligent cloud and mobile service using REST soft modeling. The intelligent cloud system builds up as a cloud environment and cross platform of mobile middleware for dynamic application of MSNs, which represent social activities for users accessing on demand (Yao et al., 2001). The MSNs services of widget engine drives form mobile widget engine that extended with the MSNs services manager, a plug-in social network service's lib and Native MSNs service's portal. MSNs manager could provide APIs to gather user information and context's information from local mobile devices by invoke their own specific interfaces, which provides embedded interfaces to user/application authentication and other services. Plug-in social network service's lib is a suite of wrapped APIs, which provide basic socializing functions for mobile widget application. The Native MSNs service's portal is also embedded into mobile devices with MSNs services Wideget engine, which provides a foreground user interface to manage MSNs service's application (Licoppe & Smoreda, 2005).

The vigorous and advanced MSNs application's architecture has a key potential to involve social computing engine (Zhang et al., 2009), and mash up engine (Deinert & Magedanz, 2010), which is the various social network service platform to manage large data by retrieving data from and updating to the social sites. These facilities give access to manage different open APIs on the cloud, dynamic social computing as the context of reasoning (Goggins et al., 2010). Therefore, the role of integrating for intelligent DM and BI and mobile device are optimizing the application's performance of the potential relationships among social network members and modeling business process as the form of users' interest (Yeh et al., 2009). The diverse application of MSNs cloud provides many applications that represented different social activities organized as SaaS model, which are managed by activity management service as a software/application. An intelligent cloud form of MSNs refers as open social services as the set of REST architecture of APIs that built prominent application in many websites. Google OpenSocial is an excellent example, which supports social networks as Myspace and others. Intelligent cloud is vitally essential to develop an application for social networks that hosted by other sites. The advantage of REST full APIs is to connect the social network service site to 3rd party to develop dynamic applications. Nutshell, the advance features of MSN cloud systems characterized as capability, scalability and adaptability of the social-networking models to handling forwarding user's interest and access in related to the current technologies. Moreover, the MSNs applications are also capable of retrieve and transfer user interest data into the system as the context of social networking and computing engine server to reason context, mining relationships and research potential user's forward access to 3rd party social application server to execute service logics. The developed system could implement as a registration/authentication server for 3rd party social applications to register into the platform.

3.2 Semantic Based Analysis and Mobility Modeling

Semantic analysis and design of a mobility model of social network are the basic understanding,

Figure 3. Architecture of the social relationships and its correlation models

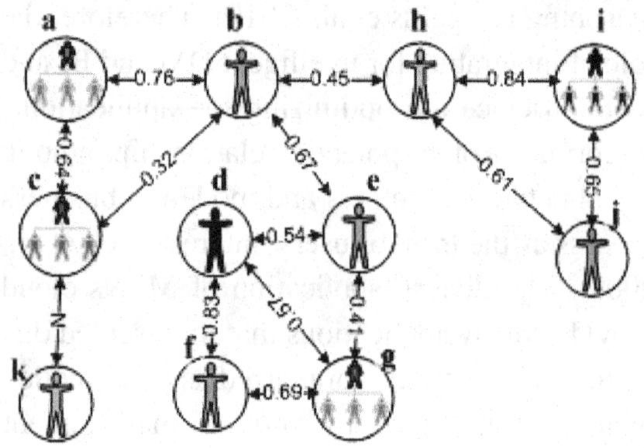

structural graph analysis, and algorithms of social networks (Chen et al., 2009). It is a systematic approach to explore MSNs advancement and performances as the network's entities or nods, time and contexts how it differs from the traditional social networking service. Therefore, mobility model components of the networks (as users, activities, resources), tracing the activity over time (as who is doing what, where), and the possible for understanding of the global activities, which the cloud in terms of identifying acquaintance networks, measuring the amount of social implicit knowledge that is being input in the shared resources and spotting the key members of the social networks (West et al., 2011; Le Grand et al., 2009). Design a mobility modeling is a graphic representation of social networks in terms of one-to-one, one-to-many and many-to-many relationships. The most significant of modeling is to have a clear visualization of the networks and to insight how we use the social networks as input of the mobility model, establishment of the model of the social networks and to define the social link including graphic characteristics, and describing the algorithms of the model as the basis of the dynamic of the nodes of the social networks (Figure 3). The algorithms of the models are the process to detect the links or structures, roles and positions of the nodes of the interactions to describe the MSNs cloud technologies (Gartrell et al., 2010; Licoppe & Smoreda, 2005).

As we showed on Figure 3, the social relationship model or graph represented by letters (a, b …) and the corresponding DM modeling based plot graph are users who made links to their interest of individuals or groups. The way to made interaction from one to another that is the arrows, and the strength of interaction, which represented by weighted value. Therefore, the interaction strength of a to b is 0.76, and algorithms of the model determined the relationships between the nodes such as, a to b and c, which had being strong weighted value as it closed to 1. Whereas, as the weighted value closed to 0 the relationships or interactions between the two entities are weak or null. Thus, the absolute weighted values of interaction defined as (x) '10 x 10' and its corresponding binary semantic matrix of (c) 10 x 10 are defined in Box 1.

Based on Figure 3 users or entities interactions visualized by matrix X, which we analyzed the absolute weighted values of users links. The social interaction strength algorithms defined as the interaction value is greater than a threshold value (0.33)[3] and close to 1, which has strong relations, otherwise 0 or weak or null relationships. Therefore, from matrix X, we generate a binary matrix C where 1 is placed as an entry C_{ij} iff X_{ij} is greater than the defined threshold t (0.33), and the corresponding matrix (C) developed.

3.3 Contextual Modeling and Representation of Knowledge

MSN is a pile of diversified cloud systems, which includes semantic intelligent agent's cloud, knowledge cloud and mobile cloud in integration bases, which could access anywhere and anytime from a variety of interaction points, including a Web browser, Outlook application, or Mobile and Tablet devices as showed on Figure 3. In the context of semantic knowledge cloud, Intelligent DM and BI rely on a multitude set of applications, technologies and methodologies, which promote access to an analysis of social information in order to manage, exploit, and optimize

Box 1.

$$X = \begin{bmatrix} 1 & 0.76 & 0.64 & 0.11 & 0.05 & 0 & 0 & 0.12 & 0.15 & 0 \\ 0.67 & 1 & 0.32 & 0 & 0.67 & 0.13 & 0.23 & 0.45 & 0 & 0.05 \\ 0.64 & 0.32 & 1 & 0.13 & 0.25 & 0 & 0 & 0.15 & 0 & 0 \\ 0.11 & 0 & 0.13 & 1 & 0.54 & 0.83 & 0.57 & 0 & 0 & 0 \\ 0.05 & 0.67 & 0.25 & 0.54 & 1 & 0.2 & 0.41 & 0.2 & 0.23 & 0 \\ 0 & 0.13 & 0 & 0.83 & 0.2 & 1 & 0.69 & 0.15 & 0 & 0 \\ 0 & 0.23 & 0 & 0.57 & 0.41 & 0.69 & 1 & 0.18 & 0 & 0.12 \\ 0.12 & 0.45 & 0.15 & 0 & 0.2 & 0.15 & 0.18 & 1 & 0.84 & 0.61 \\ 0.15 & 0 & 0 & 0 & 0.23 & 0 & 0 & 0.84 & 1 & 0.65 \\ 0 & 0.05 & 0 & 0 & 0 & 0 & 0.12 & 0.61 & 0.65 & 1 \end{bmatrix}$$

$$C = \begin{bmatrix} 1 & 1 & 1 & 0 & 0 & 0 & 0 & 0 & 0 & 0 \\ 1 & 1 & 0 & 0 & 1 & 0 & 0 & 1 & 0 & 0 \\ 1 & 0 & 1 & 0 & 0 & 0 & 0 & 0 & 0 & 0 \\ 0 & 0 & 0 & 1 & 1 & 1 & 1 & 0 & 0 & 0 \\ 0 & 1 & 0 & 1 & 1 & 0 & 1 & 0 & 0 & 0 \\ 0 & 0 & 0 & 1 & 0 & 1 & 1 & 0 & 0 & 0 \\ 0 & 0 & 0 & 1 & 1 & 1 & 1 & 0 & 0 & 0 \\ 0 & 1 & 0 & 0 & 0 & 0 & 0 & 1 & 1 & 1 \\ 0 & 0 & 0 & 0 & 0 & 0 & 0 & 1 & 1 & 1 \\ 0 & 0 & 0 & 0 & 0 & 0 & 0 & 1 & 1 & 1 \end{bmatrix}$$

the social-networking services. This practical approach is a leading task to understand what is going on, and extend the limits, inward looking of capacity of existing social-networking services, and so on (Coben & Adams, 2009). Intelligent DM techniques and applications are collecting, organizing and exploring of data and covering basic knowledge within an intelligent BI cloud system to optimize social-networking services. BI is also used to monitor the internal and external system operations (Zhong, 2003). Therefore, the semantic integrating of intelligent DM and BI as an agent system is a proud approach to synthesis social networking data as the content of the social behavior.

Knowledge cloud is a key component of MSNs, which is providing knowledge as a service for social cloud users without place, time and subject restriction. The services are accessing through wearable and cell phone, which empowered using integrated DM and BI as dynamic processes. This knowledge semantic cloud makes heavy use of domain ontologies, to attach semantic intelligent agents' annotations to social documents, including information resources that describe the semantics of social cloud services (Zhong, 2003; Berendt et al., 2002). Social ontologies facilitate the creation of knowledge cloud services, which can be used by other parties in different knowledge-driven methods and applications (Bèrnstein et al., 2005). On the context of social cloud, knowledge services necessary to enable users to set up ontology-based knowledge bases, which store and manage domain knowledge (e.g., concepts, semantic relations, evidence, patterns, and rules), are vitally significant to access and reasoning about the MSNs cloud contents (Le Grand et al., 2009). Therefore, it is conceptual understanding of the cloud, which includes social ontology,[4] social network resources,[5] knowledge service[6] and application[7] as independent and distinct layers (Ochoa et al., 2009; Bhogal et al., 2007).

3.4 Security in Mobile Social Network

Security for MSNs is more challenging and crucial issue, which is a grant to all activities and services, including cloud computing system and the hardware. MSNs potentially contain much private and sensitive data, which need to be safe, secure and available to the various users (Zhang et al., 2011). MSNs semantic cloud security issue is always in consideration when the intelligent cloud extended, and information is spread into new contexts. Therefore, intelligent agents of semantic cloud virtualizations and physical environment made cloud systems are significant approaches, which is essential to address the challenges, which is considerable across the MSNs cloud scheme of the intimate nature of intelligent semantic ontologies technology. DM ontology and its techniques in each processing step risk is substantial tasks; BI also playing vital roles on system design and monitoring functionality to avoid risks, which make the application is relevant to addressing the security. I. e. MSNs cloud security could improve due to centralization of data to implement a corporate and security system that collaborative to nodes of the MSNs cloud (Ochoa et al., 2009). Thus, it gives broad opportunities to have a strong, and manageable security system that would be extremely difficult to track someone "snooping" information if not validate, authenticate or allow users. The fact that the semantic intelligent agents have a potential to secure the services that would broadcast continually between nodes in integrating and validating ways. The MSNs cloud security issues would occur at all times and possibly in all connections. For example, user cell phone (Geser, 2006) services follow the user with the availability of virtual or intelligent agent services in safe and effective performances (Yao et al., 2001).

AS the issue of protection of MSNs cloud, the proposed approaches require multiple advantages, including security boundaries indicate that different trust boundaries of semantic could be present in any communications of the social networks (Nitti et al., 2012; West et al., 2011). In additions, intermediary applications, such as firewalls, also integrated to assess the application interactions and prevent those outside the security policy of the MSNs from being acted upon the system. The participants in an application's interaction should either assume that any information received is entrusted, or require another additional authentication, authorization and validation before trust can be given. This requires that ICDM_CBBI base MSNs cloud architecture be capable of communicating authentication data and authorization controls (Fielding & Taylor, 2002).

4. SEMANTIC INTEGRATION OF INTELLIGENT CLOUD AGENTS FOR MOBILE SOCIAL NETWORKS

Semantic integrating for intelligent cloud agents is newly emerging scientific and soft simulations of targeted social activities of semantic cloud languages. These are Cloud Resource Description Framework (CRDF), CRDF Schema (CRDFS), Web Ontology Language (WOL) and SPARQL (SPARQL Protocol and RDF Query Language), together with a rich set of practical tools, which allow a mass of data with semantic cloud (Figure 4). This smart based integration for DM and BI is intense research issue, which play effective roles to optimization MSNs performance, and also scalable to different domains, including cognitive science. Therefore, intelligent agent cloud structure is the promotion of social networking, which exploring the possibility of integrating intelligent technologies into cloud computing to develop a reliable MSNs cloud system (Kim et al., 2008; Berendt et al., 2002). It is the active social networking and also the integration of mobile cloud that enables to optimize the social services. The principal of semantic cloud stacks steps include defining a common syntax for machine understandable statement and establish shared vocabularies, integrating to logical language and using the language for exchange proofs (Lal & Mahanti, 2010).

As we showed on Figure 4, the cloud stack is the set, structuring and improvement of linked intelligent data that enabled by technologies, which require a proper description of social concepts, terms, and relationships within a knowledge domain (Rama et al., 2009). MSNs cloud technologies have the potential to overcome the challenges and ontologies use to simplify retrieving and interrelating background data for social-networking applications, which is crucial to identify users, discover contents, rank rate contents and present semantic information agent. Therefore, semantic cloud is appropriate to use integrating intelligent agents involving a mobile device that makes efficient the MSNs cloud to provide long term existing storage to large data sets that are managed as distributed index files (Berendt et al., 2002).

Mobile cloud computing is also a newly emerging intelligent cloud system design to extend the service to the edge of social networks, which includes numerous mobile IT, including mobile

Figure 4. Social semantic cloud stack conceptual model

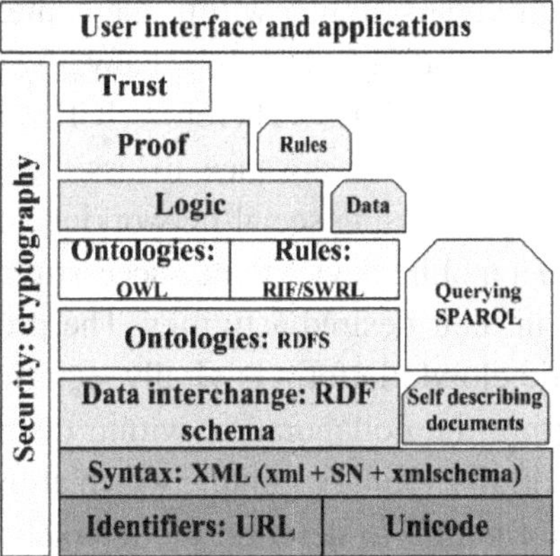

devices that are closely associated with their users. Therefore, MSNs services have a potential to revolutionize the field of social networking by integrating intelligent cloud systems, which is enabling fully context aware (Goggins et al., 2010; Beach et al., 2008) inference in ubiquitous CC environments (Miluzzo et al., 2008; Choudhury et al., 2008). Context aware computing systems in the case of MSNs consist of collaborations of intelligent agents, and mobile technology integrated computing, which communicate and collaborate on behalf of users (Rosa et al., 2012). Such semantic web-based technology allowing to users can directly connect in many cloud activities that enhance the cloud boundaries into the entire social network system (Janjua et al., 2012). On the other hand, intelligent cloud agents are essential components of optimization of the MSNs, which allow diversifying the services in efficient and effective ways. The knowing of semantic integrating of intelligent cloud agents (DM and BI) with mobile cloud to scalable and useful the functionality of MSNs systems to serve as the interconnection of information sources appear both intelligent cloud domains and to a knowledge center to optimize the services to assist the users' access on demands (Ding et al., 2012; Zhong, 2003).

Moreover, semantic integrating of intelligent cloud agents motivated by the observation of the development of social networks, such as mobile Smartphone's and sensor networks provides a thorough understanding within the context surrounding an individual in almost any given location (Rama et al., 2009). Therefore, ICDM_CBBI based MSNs cloud advance to assist users in effectively accessing social-networking services through a mobile device to be successful and efficient in their desired activities. The proposed semantic cloud platform is vitally significant to supporting the collaboration within distributed and multi disciplinary groups, which allow data and information to describe the interaction and relationships among the groups. Semantic MSNs cloud functionality characterized using shared intelligent DM ontologies such as automation personalization (Mobasher, 2007), and to model various aspects of the social activities, including service interfaces, service's messages and interaction and interrelations structures, which allow the discovery, composition and invocation of services in an automatic and ad hoc manner (Pietilainen et al., 2009). Such CBBI as a service will have multiple real-world advantages, including authentication and authorization technologies. It facilitates cloud users to access and retrieve relevant social data and information, including context aware recommendation, recognizes social knowledge from the data.

4.1 System Architecture

Mobile social networks have gained the attention of researchers and business men such as m-commerce through the promotion of social-networking applications. Despite the pragmatic convention social network, architectural advances of intelligent DM, BI and mobile technologies promoted new forms of social relations allowing the maintenance of large distributed networks of contacts (Rosa et al., 2012). In a static (traditional social networking) social media, the services are either complement or change a face–to–face meetings of the social group members, which are using the social software, such as an e-mail, Instance Message (IM) and others, maintain interpersonal or group communication. These tools are limited and inefficient and also not allowing the use of new technologies, which is essential characteristics of traditional social networks that remain often either invisible (e–mail) or private (buddy list). In this chapter, we introduce ICDM and CBBI cloud system to overcome these challenges and get more advancing or optimizing social networking, which allows dynamic and scalable architecture offering access to functional built around the interconnection of user profiles. The proposed issue also insights the necessity of change of traditional social software into modern and mobile location-based software, which is reliable for the dynamic demanding cloud resource access and security.

Modern and location-based MSNs (mobile cloud) applications provide users share social-networking media and have proven successful tools for expanding its applications based on users' contexts, which allows the extensive use of social-networking applications from mobile devices (Rama et al., 2009). The MSNs system architecture consists of four main components: the client devices (smart phones and other wearable devices), the wireless access network (API and gateways), the Internet and its host (MSNs applications or social media) and the server side (HTTP, matching logic, privacy control, etc., which accommodates database and application-specific servers required to MSNs system). Smart mobile applications can be designed to take advantage of context from the different sources, which provide a key access to influence MSNs be adapting to the users' current situation and simplifying communication. This increases the effectiveness and applicability of social-networking applications and enables them to react in a more automated manner. To support this application's semantic and integrated intelligent cloud is essential and interactive systems, which are also prominent for building flexible and innovative MSNs services that can accommodate unique systems to mobile settings. Semantic intelligent social cloud is fundamental at mobility and social media, which can enable a distributed and interoperable architecture to develop smart and efficient MSNs applications, regardless of variations of mobile device's platforms and social-networking applications.

Figure 5. MSN intelligent agent cloud based generic architecture framework

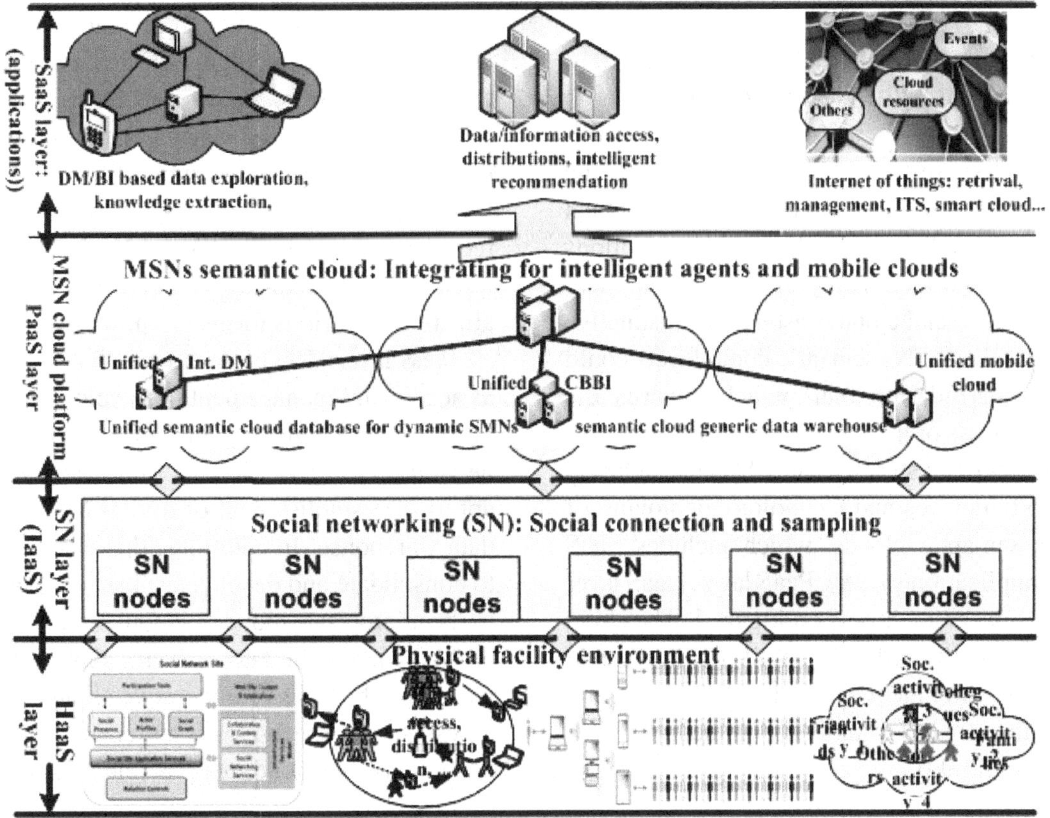

The purpose of MSNs system architecture is the establishing and/or optimizing the traditional social networking into modern semantic integrated intelligent cloud technologies, which have the potential to overcome the challenges in social media applications and services (Zhao & Okamoto, 2008). Use of ICDM and CBBI cloud playing crucial roles to simplify retrieving and correlating context data for social-networking application, which is important to use the semantic mobile for better integration between social networks and mobile software. More specifically semantic social clouds capable to identify friends, discover contents, rank and rate contents and will represent the information in the machine-readable form. Intelligent DM and BI based involving mobile devices based social systems are efficient, scalable and adaptable to collect heterogeneous content (user data and context data) from a different source (sensor, web) and publish these contents to social-networking applications depending on the context data and user interest.

4.2 Integration of Intelligent Agents Cloud and Layer Representation

The architecture of MSNs semantic cloud is the components of various intelligent clouds, which defined as intelligent cloud layer segmentations based on their functionality and semantic applications of the social cloud. Based on its distinctive activities the MSNs semantic could layers could be categorized into four, which governs the whole process of the social-networking services. This conceptual structure of MSNs cloud layers is mobile devices and technology deploying of MSNs semantic clouds, which includes SaaS layer (application's layer), PaaS layer, HaaS layer and IaaS layer as showed on Figure 5. The cloud architecture showed the overall architecture of the MSNs intelligent agent cloud platforms and their functionality towards social media (Coben & Adams, 2009).

SaaS or applications layer: This layer provides software as service applications for the access to social cloud resources on intelligent bases of social domain ontologies. These are enabling social objects or intelligent engineering and management in a virtual organization. It is the key layer to achieve collective intelligence across the social-networking organizations and comprehensive intelligent agent's design tasks. The semantic intelligent agents based MSNs cloud structure contains powerful and fundamental tasks, which are intelligent DM and BI data analysis and/or knowledge extraction, access and distributions of cloud resources, intelligent recommendations, and the internet of things (Nitti et al., 2012). These facilities fetch MSNs structure could provide higher layers with a coherent social service. The significant of ICDM_CBBI based MSNs cloud is the capability, scalability and adaptability of the social clouds, which could represent in various intelligent formats that are translated into semantic cloud web languages such as OWL, and are integrated together in incremental steps. This layer implements intelligent applications through the composition of knowledge services, which contains personalized agents that transform a user's query to machine languages and problem-solving requirements through a series of service requests against lower layers. It also provides interactive mechanisms for navigation and visualization of various forms of knowledge.

PaaS layer: The layer of unified components as access and management of the cloud applications. In these segmentations, managing the connections of merged semantic cloud databases are apt to the establishment of a vital MSNs cloud data warehouse. In additions, this layer enables to consolidate and develop a subset of databases to the appropriate cloud components such as the unified intelligent DM, BI and mobile cloud, which are the basis of integrative cloud resource access, knowledge discovery and create a machine-understandable cloud in a scalable manner.

IaaS layer: this layer wraps formal social-networking service node's connectivity and reasoning capabilities, which provides essential resources to other higher-level layers. In this segmentation, the social cloud service offers computational resources, storage facilities and communications in the social-networking nodes. HaaS layer: is the layer of the actual physical environments or layer, which switches that from the core of the cloud of MSNs. It is a huge IT requirement, including personal communications, which is significant to improve the state of social media, and also it allows to access of remote hardware devices that are distributed over multiple social nodes. Therefore, the HaaS layer could facilitate creating powerful connections between the local and the individual distant social nodes.

The Intelligent agents cloud is being used actively in the field of cloud computing, which is the newly emerging cloud technology that fostering to the development of automation systems. Such automation network service is vitally relevant to exploring and exploiting the social cloud application based on location-based services of the social networks' agent components (Bonchi et al., 2011; Apayden, 2010). Multi agent has a knowledge base for learning users' behavior, and function to infer purposes according to the social network services (Banerjee et al., 2010). Intelligent agents cloud has four features: autonomy, intelligent, mobility and social potential, which conduct message passing or shared memory techniques using agent communication language, transmits messages and procedure using knowledge query and manipulation language (Ding et al., 2012). In additions, the integrations of intelligent agents cloud with mobile cloud computing environments are an interactive and the next-generation issue of cloud technologies that incorporate knowledge cloud based on social-networking contexts, such as social data, user's location information, and so on (Ochoa et al., 2009).

4.3 Mobile Social Networks Data Warehouse

MSNs data is dynamic and vitally crucial to implement the flexible, scalable and high-performance database, which promote social semantic cloud infrastructure, design and composition to generate large data center. Implementation of dynamic data center, automated social media management and provisioning of intelligent tools are the basic requirements of MSNs data warehouse. MSNs data is the agglomeration of social activities and data/information about all social Medias including connections between people, which are vitally significant to investigate aspects of human dynamics and social interactions and also sources of information to members of social network when they are mobile (Nitti et al., 2012). Therefore, the importance of such data is not engaging only for mathematical modeling but also for social investigation, which provides deep insights to science and engineering, and business users (Yeh et al., 2009).

Social data characterizations and data handling are relevant for interaction designers as the contexts of the social groups, which integrating to the semantic intelligent agent clouds towards the existing cloud system. A pattern of such data can identify, track and standardize cloud system, which support social policy-driven configuration using intelligent DM among social infrastructure and BI applications as the principal cloud service that empowers the value of MSNs data warehouse. It is vitally significant to a better performance of data/information storing, accessing, distribute and secure in the semantic cloud and provide tangible benefits for enriching the members' experience by using ETL tools (Chang et al., 2007). As of the in depth technical convergences of ICDM and CBBI with mobile technology of MSNs data warehouse, the mathematical and social traditions in the study of social networks become a more powerful, scalable and sound way (Janjua et al., 2012).

4.3.1 Data Characterization

MSNs data usually consists of attributes, which include name, ID, links, gender, location and so on from different sources, which can be broadly classified as social-networking data from MSNs, mobile data from Smartphone's and sensor data from fixed sensor networks (Pietilainen et al., 2009). These data handling and management require semantic intelligent tools such as DM and BI to analysis, and other tasks that need support from the sources. That is the MSNs data as data streams generated or use the standard APIs provided the data source to collect the relevant as and when needed. Mobile data provides significant contextual information of users as well as groups of users as their locations, which include site, accelerometer, image, digital compass, and other data about the respective user. Whereas, data from sensors are embedded in the local smart space such as temperature, humidity and infrared sensors with microphones, which forwards to MSN data center in given intervals (Geser, 2006).

The fundamental tasks of MSNs data characterizations are to specify which attributes are unique identifiers (for example, ID), quasi-identifiers (such as locations, genders …) and sensitive attributes (such as birthday, calendar applications). Thus, social network data are the data present throughout the user profile, mostly related to demographics and individual preferences used for connecting with other users (Kamilaris & Pitsillides, 2008). In MSNs applications, personal and contextual information is managed by reliable procedures that collect and analyze large amounts of data and return higher-level knowledge of the user (Licoppe & Smoreda, 2005). A group of social algorithms could deal with aspects of relationships, facilitating the establishment of new relational ties or maintenance of existing ones. Social algorithms are a generalization of current collaborative filtering systems (Sopchoke & Kijsiridul, 2011), which are typically used in MSN platform. That is, large amounts of data need to analyze towards past behavioral network trends among users' interactions with the goal of presenting social recommendations. In the context of MSNs software social algorithms could exploit well–known conceptual frameworks to improve interactions (Gartrell et al., 2010; Chen et al., 2009).

4.3.2 Data Usage

MSNs data are large and heterogeneous from independent and non interactive design as a database, which includes unique and sensitive data or data attributes. Such behavior of MSNs data could not apply for many applications and need a set of applications. Social data built using the Data Representation and Integration Framework (DRIF) of the social services, which designed to maintain large quantities of data to a form that is valuable to the end user both for immediate inspection and the use of various kinds of analytics. Social data handling characterized as representations of source data artifacts and their contents within the social-networking services, which includes primary and secondary or drive form of data. The conceptual framework of data usage could be represented in specific categories as showed Figure 6. In the levels of social data support a comprehensive approach to integration that allows understanding of the multiple views of the original and derived data and of the associated data semantics and metadata, which arise, for example, as a result of the workings of many different sorts of analytical tools.

The way to integrating intelligence data starts with source artifacts consisting of basic data across a variety of presentation procedures. The initial data integrated into the sense that indexes provided to support unambiguous (string-based) data search across all essential intelligent agents. The data comes with their social nodes of network's configuration, which aim to be scalable, dynamic and flexible through DM technique's analytical processing (Goggins et al., 2010). The

Figure 6. Social data usage conceptual framework

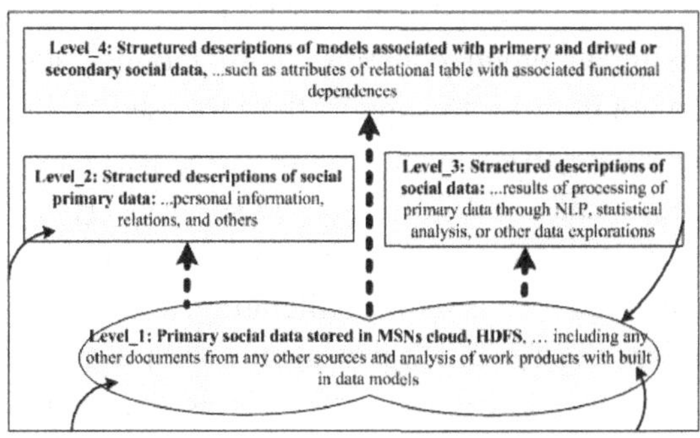

following is BI based cloud storage design and integration step, which is addressing to the unified cloud warehouse of the structured data to support complex search across both primary and derived intelligent data (Pietilainen et al., 2009). Importantly, integrating the diversity of domain-specific data-models employed throughout the Intelligence Community while at the same time reaping benefits from an approach that the data model visualizing the facts of the system. Therefore, the unified representation provided by the data representation, which allows analytic processing of data in really diverse primary artifacts associated to different social data models to be used as targets of cross semantic analytics.

As it showed on Figure 6, the use of data conceptual framework organized as level_1 a repository of primary data, including documents, personal information, analysis of social vetted for re-use as input for further processing. The physical implementation of level_1 can be such that all data stored internally, or it can be distributed. Then after, the source of data could be either contained in the social cloud stored externally to the nodes that referenced in the MSN cloud storage. Social primary data vary widely by nature and have different structures (such as a relational database), which could be unstructured[8] and in different documentation procedures or modalities.[9] Level_2 data categories include primary of personal information and registration data as well as specifications of relations between data (such as nesting of the social model within a document, or extension of one document to another). Level_3 also includes data pertaining to each derived data of level_2, which derived from primary social data of level_1. Level_3 stores the structured data that either already present in original or derived there from through systematic processing resting on DM modeling techniques, which represented in level_4. The top and final step is Level_4, which stores the descriptions of the data used in level_3. These data descriptions include database schemas, message formats, or XML schemas, which stored in level_1 and registered in level_2.

4.4 Semantic Mobile Social Networks Enhancement

Semantic MSNs enhancement focused on optimal access of social services based on ICDM_CBBI cloud. It is the data representation technique, which represents the basic types of data integration, access, distribution and securities in the cloud. MSNs Semantic Enhancement (SE) conceived as a lightweight and dynamic solution, which leverages the richness of the social source data and of any local semantics associated with these data without adding storage and processing weight (Le Grand et al., 2009). MSNs SE is a procedure used to improve social media usage and handling of the enormous heterogeneity of data content, which focusing on building a flexible and extensible framework of hierarchically organized, controlled structured taxonomies of different areas of relevance to intelligence analysis. The social framework enhancement pattern on reusing the existing data or resources and collaboration semantic clouds in the creation of the new structure, which could be used in an incremental process of Annotation (or tagging) of those social concepts, and predicates already identified in data models within the social media (Kim et al., 2008). The MSNs semantic enhancement taxonomies or ontologies as showed on Figure 7 is the representation of the real and narrowly defined social domain.

The approach is the representation of social data without losing or distorting in the social media as it exists prior to SE.

MSNs Semantic enhancement approach is highly flexible, which represents a "pay-as you-go" method for the understanding that payments can be made only on-demand services or access resources that according to existing social media (Hua et al., 2010). It is characterized as the sense that if a given group of annotations for a given subset of the source data model, which could develop as needed. It also enables users to enrich data by characterizing the structure of social connections, strategic positions, and the way information flows. From semantic enhancement, taxonomic structure (Figure 7) person and facility are the main classes of the macro MSNs generic concepts. Whereas, the other sub nodes of the social networks are used for annotations of source of data, which are the attributes of the systems. Such semantic enhancement fusion of MSN model is vitally significant to personalized frameworks of data, which combines the clustering and hidden topic models (Kayastha et al., 2011).

5. PROPOSED SEMANTIC INTELLIGENT CLOUD MODEL FOR OPTIMIZATION OF MOBILE SOCIAL NETWORKS

Semantic cloud for social resources is rules based intelligent cloud agent virtualization, which supporting social network services. The proposed semantic intelligent cloud is vitally necessary to optimize MSNs applications that appropriate for users' desires, which provides efficient data/information distribution and access facilities. The architecture involves intelligent agents cloud components to identify dynamic social networking on users' inputs and contexts. This ICDM_CBBI semantic cloud platform is involving a mobile device that can perform capable and scalable activities in the MSNs semantic clouds, which help to manage social resources of intelligent cloud computing in real time and reconfiguring the social services according to users' behavior (Yao et al., 2001). Intelligent cloud combines with mobile cloud service in order to support the proposed model, to provide efficient and secure MSNs services as users' time and location-based services (Hua et al., 2010). However, such optimization of MSNs semantic cloud is more challenging, and demand integrating for intelligent agents with a mobile device to address the problems as the content and context of the social-networking services. For example, user context data, which is a core task of integrating of agents and cell phones, to describe the current user situations. The mobile agents and intelligent agents perform to record and manage location information of users as log files, which contain personal information, service history and desire signal for accessing location service systems. Based on this information we can be able to know 'who is that' (Šikšnys et al., 2010), which essential to optimization and secure MSN performance regardless of time and location or cloud contents.

The proposed model assumed to offering dynamic social cloud services, which is a solution of traditional social-networking service problems and challenges and to be capable processing large amount of social data in hand devices in real time. The semantic intelligent agents monitored by the server, where as mobile agents perform providing user context information (locations, log files, and other information) and also checking services as of Figure 8.

The architecture of intelligent cloud as it showed on Figure 8 is an optimization MSNs cloud model, which consists of various system or agent components, including semantic intelligent agents, and mobile agent, distributed agents, virtualization resister, agent manager and system resource managers. To address the challenges with recording user context data, and processing large amounts of data in hand devices in real time, collaborative agents except for mobile agents are managed on the server. Whereas the mobile agents perform to record and manage location informa-

Figure 7. MSN semantic enhancement taxonomic structure

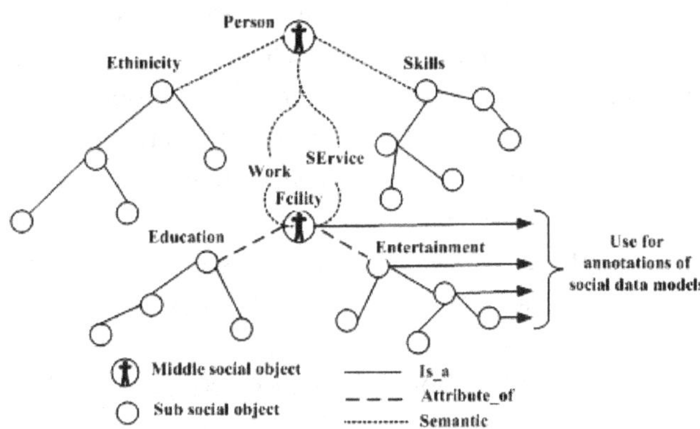

Figure 8. Proposed semantic intelligent cloud for MSNs service optimization

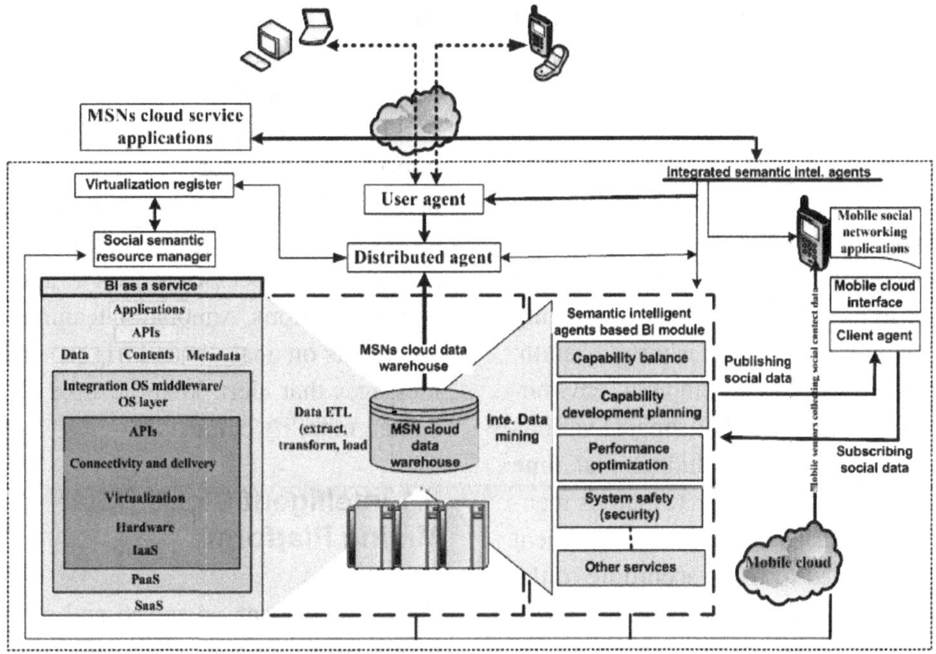

tion of users as well as log files, which contain personal information, service history and request signal for accessing the cloud service system. User agent is an agent used to receive information generated from users or nodes, which pass to the distributed agent to analyze service types and access types of services. Access type can be analyzed via user location and data transfer rate, whereas, service types can be seized through applications of social media service based on user contexts. The integrated information with system state information created from the agent manager is applied to intelligence virtualization rules. In order to maintain an appropriately allocate system resources according to intelligence virtualization rules, the results sent to the distributed agent.

Distributed agent is the fundamental tasks of distributes social cloud resource connection between users and services. It also carried out intelligent virtualization of service resources by constantly learning services requested by users and state information. That means, to virtualize service's resources of the system, distributed agent adopts multilayer perception, which includes a virtualization module that verifies and processes information regarding service resources. The information processed then transfer to the distributed agent to virtualizes service resources consists of user context information transmitted, which the user agent and system context information transmitted through the system resource manager. Virtualization register records and manages virtualization information of social resources that are distributed by distributed agent, which is vitally significant to provide flexibility in the use of computing resources to simplify complex computing environments and improve distributing job process and management efficiency (Gebremeskel et al., 2012).

The two broad categories of virtualization are server, desktop, embedded and mobile virtualization this divide by system size. The most useful and significant techniques in MSNs cloud computing fields, especially mobile cloud, is virtualization. Mobile virtualization in cloud computing environment requires technologies that support various services and applications, including real time characteristics. Social semantic resources manager has a function that controls the management of resources provided to users according to the correlation information in the lists of virtualization resister. Then after, the administrators can obtain distributing state monitored by the system resource manager and can directly or indirectly control network resources. The structure of a resource manager is composed of system usage rate of the analysis domain, context management domain, level analysis domain, resource classification domain and management information of the MSNs data warehouse. It is also monitoring and managing physical and logical resources of the cloud computing system.

Therefore, the proposed MSNs cloud is the generic and users easily working together integrated and intelligent cloud platform, which could be gained more success and quality performance in all users desire. This is the remarkable significance of the proposed cloud model, which offers a chance to integrating for intelligent DM and BI and mobile device to optimize the efficient and performance of social networking. Thus, social cloud users are easily interacting on social cloud sites through their Smartphone or other IT devices such as computers, and wise users already are exploring how to harness this propensity for business purposes. This does not mean that IT will have to support Facebook on mobile devices. However, the social-networking model has conditioned users to a free-flowing collaboration, which implications for their desired activities. For example, business innovative and organizations are considering MSNs applications to support business collaboration tools, which produce information and analysis that provide power for their activities. BI as service capabilities to support the decision-making process, including workflow and approval processes as well as tracking social communications. Annotation features can enable comments on analysis and trigger such as email messages that alert others to take action as the human mobility contexts.

5.1 Intelligent Cloud Data Mining Platform

Data mining is an advanced and powerful tool, which is useful to handle large data in solving real-world problems. It is the process of extracting meaningful and implicit knowledge from given data sets that are not readily apparent and not always easily accessible. The intelligent cloud ubiquitously uses of social-networking services, semantic cloud having massive data, which could be beneficial in many fields of study, including sociology, business, politics, and so on (Mobasher, 2007). Therefore, applying intelligent DM to the field of social networking can generate notable prescriptive of human behaviors and interaction's analysis. The intelligent DM can be used for better understanding of the data and user's opinions about a subject, identifying groups of people in the network, and so on, which gained increasing attention with the significant improvement of flexible social-networking services (Barbier & Liu, 2011; Lal & Mahanti, 2010). The intelligent DM as clouds are the sources and providers of cloud resources and services using web browsers. The cloud technology is the logical approaches to access the social-networking resources and services on demand, which users have a chance to gain more understanding and implicit knowledge from the cloud data. For example, customer based design smart cloud structure is the frontline solutions of cloud service challenges, which demanding an appropriate layout of ICDM platform. Architecture of ICDM platform gives numerous advantages, which includes the cloud service capability and efficiency that allow to be scalable e-business, e-commerce, m-commerce and other services. Other significant of ICDM platform is the architecture design and principles of intelligent data cloud and workflow of the corporate or global cloud services or CC as a whole. The basic principles of these ICDM systems are prime considerations of data confidentiality, integrity, and availability to the better performance cloud service and use or system interoperability of the CC. Therefore, ICDM is the roadmap of empowering optimization of cloud resources and environment monitoring and cloud system conduct towards customers or users need, the CC, such as the principles of cloud security in an intelligent cloud is the task of making guarantees to its service capability and user's satisfactions (Teneyuca, 2011).

An ICDM platform technology has also increased computing effectiveness by providing centralized services such as Software as a Services (SaaS), Platform as a Service (PaaS), Infrastructure as a Service (IaaS) and Data storage as a Service (DaaS) so as to provide efficient and effective data/ information access (Dikaiakos et al., 2009). The cloud structure as showed on Figure 8 it provides IT capabilities to business companies and other organization's dynamic and powerful services. The feature of CC is a driven of economy's scale because of a pool of virtualizes and dynamically scalable computing power, storage facilities, platform and services on demand to the users. It is a new paradigm of CBBI as a service operation, which procures, deliver and support infrastructure, platform as GUI, application and business process capabilities (Buyya et al., 2009).

5.2 Cloud Based Business Intelligence Platform

Cloud Based Business Intelligent (CBBI) refers to the use of data to facilitate decision making, which understood the functioning and anticipating actions for well informed steering of the users. BI as a service (cloud system) is enabling users (social members) to obtain a better understanding of information access, which could gain from various sources and make better-informed and faster decisions on it. The intelligent information retrieved from the semantic intelligent cloud, which supplied with diverse data extracted from multiple sources using ETL (Extract, Transform and Load) tools, i.e., extracting data from different sources, cleaning them up and loading them into a data warehouse. Once an application reserved for technically adept business analysts, BI platform becomes much easier to use in response to the demands of regular users from the lines of social media that actionable information to track pertinent information sources and access as user desires. For example, business companies' member of MSNs cloud, BI as a service supports intelligent information sources, which could apply to company's production, plan marketing, deploy the sales force and manage customer service, among other core activities.

BI technologies provide historical, current, and predictive views of business operations, which include OLAP, analytics, business performance management, and others (Yeh et al., 2009). CBBI applications focused on MSNs using the rapid growing of mobile technology to scale and expand social network services, which need the semantic integrating for intelligent DM and BI, such as network management, signaling monitoring system and others. Intelligent system of social network managing signal exploration and mining is monitoring using BI systems, which used to support MSNs optimization and failure analysis. The dynamic of MSNs involves mobile device and mobile internet accessing logs, which used to support personalized the social network system as users on demand (Xu et al., 2009).

Enlarging of scale and rising of complexity of social-networking as an intelligent cloud system could generate analysis and access large amount of data, which supported by intelligent DM systems. The increasing demand of the intelligent system for MSN is the result of high computing complexity, storage capacity to IT platform and the diversity of social networks, which requires an increasing of intelligent cloud structure as a semantic cloud system. The traditional social net platform is often provides lees and effective information access in a centralized form, which is low scalability and huge cost to optimize the services of social networks. Semantic integrating of intelligent clouds approach and mobile technologies are mainstreaming the challenges to optimize MSNs services based on CBBI as services. With the increasing of semantic intelligent cloud, large-scale social-networking data and computation of cloud computing offering large data access, dissemination, and storage through the dynamic social network centers (Sheth & Ranabahu, 2010). CBBI data centers provide IT supporting infrastructure of cloud data services and resource's allocation on the cluster server based. A new semantic integrating ICDM and CBBI architecture design are useful to scale up, efficient and effective at the MSNs services in its optimal level.

The organization of semantic ICDM_CBBI and the mobile agents (Figure 8) has exclusive layers to promote the social network services, which helps to achieve cloud computing functional towards MSNs services. Therefore, the application and/or SaaS layer serves as the implementation of intelligent DM and BI applications to optimize social network services in efficient and powerful performances. The ICDM_CBBI layer functions for data extract and load module supporting heterogeneous data formats. It includes data-management modules for data management and remote access control, data processing module and parallel DM module present capacity of processing large-scale data sets and visualization module presenting BI as a service to users. The bottom or hadoop platform layer consists of data file structure Map reduces and Large Table. For example, Google's file system is typically underlying the Map reduces means that can provide an efficient and reliable distributed data storage and data-management services as needed. Remote data transformation, data extract parallel data process parallel DM, data management, visualization and workflow managements are the key features of the ICDM_CBBI cloud system, which are vitally crucial to optimize MSNs services as intelligent cloud systems (Lal & Mahanti, 2010).

Optimization of MSNs based on the intelligent cloud system is to maximize the performance of social networks in terms of its capacity, scalability, performance and efficiency across the networks. The ultimate goals of the proposed approach and its significance are: on the one hand, to secure on demand users' social web services access, and increasing the intelligent nodes numbers. On the other hand, to develop a better strategy of social interaction and interrelation can support the success of business, which considering intelligent DM and BI algorithms to achieve higher performance of MSNs services. Furthermore, user access and data access authority are also significant to implement security systems as data privacy processing and encryption protection approaches.

5.3 Mobile Semantic Agents Services Platform

Mobile agent integrated with intelligent DM and BI as a service is the principal component of MSNs of intelligent agents, which are a paradigm of models and tools to analyze structures, roles and positions of social agent association of social cloud. It is the newly emerging technology, which have become an abundantly interactive field in most science, such as sociology that the study of resources and person linked by one or more human relationships as a semantic cloud based communities and hosted services. It is web engineering to describe the distributed collaborations and easy access to social resources by such diverse communications and computing devices (Domingue et al., 2011). These relationships are more effective and successful as the involvement of intelligent agent systems and IT devices (Choudhury et al., 2008). The increasing proliferation and affordability of intelligent cloud enabled devices such as computers, mobiles and other IT hardware innovations as semantic clouds (internet tablets) are the fundamental and convolute garner of ICDM and CBBI platforms. This semantic integrating of intelligent cloud promulgates and optimizes MSNs as a cloud system to optimize social network as the context of social-networking services and social mobility (Berendt et al., 2002). Therefore, semantic integrating of intelligent agents based of social network functionality can be applied to understand social interactions with physical or conceptual entities. On the other hand, the rapid growth of semantic intelligent cloud within MSNs open opportunities for synergy between social network services and mobile computing, which supporting social-networking applications without time and geographic location restrictions (Kim et al., 2011). For example, mobile phone calls and text messages already have had a profound impact, providing the possibility of being in perpetual contact between the group (Humphreys, 2008; Chang et al., 2007) and breaking the traditional time and space boundaries of the social network services (Licoppe & Smoreda, 2005) that optimize the dynamic and benefits of MSNs.

6. PATTERN AND PRINCIPLES OF MOBILE SOCIAL NETWORKS

MSNs cloud pattern is an architectural modeling of social objects of the social network effects, and services use algorithms, which maximize the performance, and also to develop social software that automatically gets better when more people use it. Intelligent DM and BI playing key roles to facilitate user's network access and innovate to new opportunities and experience such as widget search engine issue (Al-Khalifa & Al-Subaihin, 2012), which is leading to comprehension one or more platform for users. For example, Facebook social cloud approach platform allows any third party applications based on rapidly tap into an enormous social network, which employed a BI cloud, based service that is a widget search engine in place. This optimal pattern of cloud service can go beyond traditional social-networking service using mobile devices, which provide social services considering rich user experiences. The structure is considering the real time responsiveness of desktop application, which is ease of use of mobile web applications and rich sensory inputs of Smartphone (Hua et al., 2010; Beach et al., 2008). The use of the mobile device gives opportunities of the wider, powerful and adaptive personalization cloud system that can be enabled to optimize the experience of each user and increase both users' reliability and social media benefit option. MSNs cloud service vitally significant to capture niche social media benefits within optimal effort and efficiency to access the services via the internet.

Traditional social-networking pattern design is a one-to-many web publishing and communication models, whereas, MSNs semantic cloud is dynamic and many-to-many connections, which involves intelligent DM, BI and mobile technologies. Thus, MSNs pattern is the outcome of integrating for intelligent agents cloud and mobile technology, which considering the principles of social services and the existing technologies in relation to the desire of users and business dynamism. It allows accessing the service or social media from global (centralized level) to the individual users or nodes towards their location in effective and effective ways. It gives users unprecedented potential for accessing, participation, collaboration and ultimately impact on the promotion of social media.

6.1 Modeling Social Relationships

Modeling social relationship is an interactive and concern of human ethical information of online friendship reflects to some degree of the real-world counterpart of the social networks, which users have common interests close geographic location's people belong to the traditional social circles (Chen et al., 2009). Therefore, modeling social relationship is an intuitive understanding of the social network-s contexts, which include the structural properties such as nodes of level of distributions of connections with the other attributes. Social network-s contexts and social interaction modeling based approaches use similarity matrices, which show the distance between two users as of the ratio metric that can be incorporated the correlation of all users' preferences to create an optimal social networks model (Sopchoke & Kijsiridul, 2011).

Furthermore, modeling social relationships could also create an automated tool that recommends on new people for the user to connect with a structure, which makes broad social networks with dynamic status updates that be able to cover various intelligent agent clouds and mobile devices. It is vitally significant to understand the interaction and interrelations of the social networks over time, to be capable of identify, scalable and improve the current and active members in the networks.

6.2 The Dynamics of Mobile Social Networks Pattern

MSNs have two broad categories of social network's usage patterns, which are strengthening the connection of social members like friends and making new connections or members (friends) (Li & Chen, 2009). Strengthen of user's connections such as, sharing or access data/information through status updates as a location-based service, which users are sharing share where they are with the mobile devices' localization capability. The dynamic structure of MSNs is also essential to make modern connections such as friends based on their common interests and location based, which allows making potential new friends based on geographic proximity involving intelligent agents. Therefore, intelligent DM cloud and BI as services optimize the application of MSNs to be more capable and compatible with mobile devices and technology to strengthen and diversified MSNs.

7. PERFORMANCE DISCUSSION OF SEMANTIC INTELLIGENT CLOUD SYSTEMS

In this section, we discussed potential of the proposed semantic intelligent cloud of ICDM_CBBI towards optimization of MNSs services. MSNs semantic cloud as a service provides and service users, including SaaS, IaaS and PaaS, which is relevant to social-networking services, including access of social media as the user needs, (i.e. on-demand access), pay-as-you-go (anytime and anywhere) and utility-social computing (intelligent computing, including mobile cloud). The essence of intelligent DM and BI as a cloud is the augmentation of traditional social media to the dynamic, adaptable and scalable MSN cloud scene. The applications are involving data parallel with high social computing to communication performances and knowledge semantic cloud to the generic structure of MSNs, which considering semantic social media cloud processing, search, data mining and BI as a service (Zhang et al., 2011).

These day's technologies become more advanced. Businesses are more complex and competitive. In parallel, social networking is growing in dynamic and diversified ways (from social service providers to end users). People have their own point of view, thoughts and desires, and so on. These and others are challenging of the traditional social media, which demanded the stability and optimal tools to overcome such challenges and provide proper prospective directions of social-networking applications. That is the need of a smart and dynamic tool, which gives insight from the past and present to the future predictive analytics. The proper solution is intelligent DM or DM as a service. DM as an intelligent agent is playing a driven role for social networks, which extracting and providing implicit knowledge to optimize MSNs applications. The vigorous nature of DM is its confluence to many tools, including data warehouse (database) technology, statistics, machine learning, etc. to develop a proper pattern from large social data sets, which is essential to deliver effective, accurate, scalable and adaptive dynamic MSNs applications. Therefore, the right approaches of CBBI based optimization of MSNs applications are the systematic way of intelligent DM as: (i) defining social-networking goal and success criteria from its trends, (ii) identifying social resources required for successful social semantic could services by developing patterns. (iii) Format and integrating social data and (iv) design and developing MSNs semantic cloud models for a better performance of social media by generating and providing implicit knowledge from a large database.

Cloud based BI or BI as a service is the innovative approach to maintain proper and optimal communication and access social cloud resources from various sources, which allows for the predictive modeling of social networking based on social information that users already on social networks. It integrates seamlessly into existing social networking to provide real-time social cloud applications, which aggregate and integrate information from multiple data sources. BI is also a fundamental technique, which insights semantic cloud designing and monitoring tasks to the continuity and completeness of MSNs cloud applications. Therefore, BI as a service towards optimization of MSNSs applications made the cloud capable, scalable and adaptable across other fields. The fundamental significant of CBBI defined as: (i) BI provide to optimize the generic MSNs cloud platform, such as OLAP, analysis, reporting. (ii) Application specific-offering, for example, web analytics, fraud analysis, risk analysis. (iii) Facilitate on-demand BI as services and BI is to enhance the application platform as a service to optimize social media access. (iv) BI technique is pertinent to optimization of MSN applications. It includes cloud service vendor operational practices, security policies, integration interfaces, flexibility of system architectures and customer references. (v) It provides proper data distributions access into and out of the BI as a service offering and that a shared tenancy model without any limitations, and so on.

Based on these facts, ICDM_CBBI plays key roles to optimize MSNs application as at bridging intelligent and social cloud of the advancement of MSNs technology and applications as the context of social environments. The performance could be revealed as: on the one hand, the proposed approach showed as social semantic cloud approaches be supported by semantic intelligent agents cloud or cloud frameworks. On the other hand, it could improve and propose application and additional inferences and intelligent behavior of MSNs interactions with users. For example, folksonomy-based representations and processing and ontology-based representations and processing are key roles on the development social networking services (Gasevi et al., 2011; Cantador et al., 2011). Therefore, the development of social networks for accessing large and heterogeneous data has created an enormous amount of personal information that drives new types of applications, which accounts to location and other contextual information to enhance the friendly relations and individual information provided by social cloud networks. The association of real-time real information with social network design highlights just how independent or confidential the data used by social network applications can be, which includes real association of the details of physical contact with one's social network profile. ICDM and CBBI based of MSNs semantic cloud is remarkably effective in a distributed and multidisciplinary features of social-networking service. It allows efficient and scalable approach, analysis and distribution of data/information of social-networking services, which involving integrating intelligent way of the two technical approaches, including the mobile devices and technology. ICDM_CBBI based semantic cloud characterized the use of shared ontologies, such as intelligent DM, BI and mobile cloud service modeling. The various aspects of social cloud services are including service interfaces, service messages, and service structures, which enables the discovery, composition, and invocation of MSNs cloud services in an automatic and ad-hoc manner. ICDM_CBBI method of MSNs provides diversified and flexible advantages, including social-networking service security (authentication and authorization), mining algorithms and BI as a service (Gebremeskel et al., 2012).

Furthermore, the proposed approach advocated the importance of social cloud technologies both on MSNs CC, which focuses on the vision of communication and computational capacity of the network and storage as a utility, the focuses on the sharing data/information and reuse of knowledge. The social cloud is involving the notion of Knowledge cloud can synthesize data through mining algorithms and BI system structuring methods, which enable search engines to get references, easy access of data/information, and draw conclusions from the social-networking database. Therefore, the performance of MSNs semantic cloud applies in many social domains such as culture, and others. ICDM_CBBI based cloud is characterizing by providing intelligent DM and BI semantic cloud as a service for web users anytime, anywhere, and via any device. The dynamic MSNs application is empowering by intelligent cloud and mobile device based on all users' knowledge and data from the social cloud, which incorporates semantic cloud technologies. Intelligent DM and BI based social cloud made significant use of social ontologies and collaborative semantic annotations to documents and social resources and knowledge, and to describe the semantics of cloud services. Social ontologies also facilitate the establishment of general knowledge services, which can be used by other parties in diverse social media and service, including knowledge-driven research applications.

The potential of semantic cloud discussed based on three main categories, which include intelligent DM, BI and mobile technology. Intelligent DM is the practice of data distributions and knowledge mining algorithms. BI system is also a method to facilitate cloud users to set up intelligent DM ontology-based knowledge bases, which collect and organize social databases (such as concepts, semantic relations, evidence, patterns, and rules). The third key element is the mobile device and technology to access the service regardless of geographic barriers, time and other restrictions. Therefore, MSNs applications are efficient and effective to access the cloud resources on demand, which can be broadcasted through the social networks. Intelligent agents and mobile device integrations support the semantic cloud and localization, and signal triangulation based making MSN applications access.

Moreover, the possible and reliable advent of the semantic intelligent agents based MSNs application is the component of dynamic and advanced intelligent tools tagging and folksonomies, which are essential to organize share resources on the social cloud brought promising opportunities to help communities of users express their knowledge. Therefore, ICDM_CBBI based MSN is a proper framework to alleviate the challenges of lack of semantics variations between tags social objects for browse and review the social data. ICDM_CBBI approaches of optimization of MSNs applications aim at extending the social network analysis to intelligent ontology-based representations of users, communities, links and relationships. The proposed cloud architecture is the future generation semantic CC system, which represents an analysis of extending social network application based on social-networking inferences to recognize and motivate communities of interest. Semantic integrating of intelligent agents is opportunities of exploit intelligent agents to support new algorithms for discovering and monitoring a group's interest. The ultimate goal is to support exchange fostering functional using agents and mobile device to obtain feedback from traditional to drive the evolution of interrelationships. ICDM_CBBI would also consider reifying and discovering the historic growth of cloud systems in relation to the dynamic role of agents in the lifecycles of communities' interconnections.

CONCLUSION AND FUTURE RESEARCH WORK

In this chapter, we discussed and explored in detail DM and BI as an intelligent agent's semantic cloud towards optimization of social-networking applications, which involving mobile cloud computing. Semantic integrating for intelligent agents based MSNs cloud is the most significant paradigm shift of social networking in generation, which increasing the fundamental value of MSNs applications. Intelligent DM and BI framework of the cloud system within the mobile technology are the newly approach that support to optimize MSNs services. ICDM and CBBI platform involving the mobile device are a practical and demanding system to optimize efficient, scalable and reliable networks, which allows to large data access, disseminate, store, and secure in advancing and capable ways. Integrating for intelligent agents and mobile devices are noteworthy components of the advancement of social networks, which offering optimal social services the opportunities to have basic social network's transformation towards users' interest, for example, cloud services access on demand. Therefore, the proposed intelligent cloud approach can provide intelligent virtualization, and rule based intelligent agent's cloud, which involves mobile devices cloud computing environment to optimize social network services. It is also worth analyzing user context, the state of the system, and social resources in real time and learning user context, and the corner stone of future generation CC focuses.

However, there are many works needed to efficient and successful implementation of ICDM_CBBI based MSNs intelligent clouds. ICDM_CBBI is the newly emerge smart approach, which is dynamic, practicable and scalable, capable and reliable components of CC in relation of science and engineering and business competitions. Therefore, the development of ICDM_CBBI based social cloud computing standards, mobile widget engine and an intelligent agent's cloud system, which support new functional, design and employment REST architecture of social cloud of APIs, and automatic modeling MSNs based business process to service mash up are defining for further research works. In addition to this, the significant use semantically of ubiquitous intelligent cloud computing in the MSNs is a reliability issue and rich context's problems modeling, which is pertinent to the common framework for universal computing and social-networking research issue.

ACKNOWLEDGMENT

We are very thanks to the anonymous reviewers for their useful comments, and the works is supported by the project of Chongqing University

Postgraduates' Innovative Team Building under the No. 200909C1011, and the Science and Technology Project of Ministry of Transport under Grant No. 2011318740240.

REFERENCE

Al-Khalifa, H. S., & Al-Subaihin, A. A. (2012). *Introducing mobile widgets development in an advanced web technologies course* (pp. 1–4). ACM. doi:10.1145/2380552.2380569.

Apaydin, A., et al. (2010). Semantic image retrieval model for sharing experiences in social networks. *IEEE, Computer Society, 34th Annual IEEE Computer Software and Applications Conference Workshops* (pp. 1–6).

Banerjee, N. et al. (2010). Virtual compass: Relative positioning to sense, mobile social interactions. Springer-Verlag Berlin Heidelberg. *Pervasive, LNCS, 6030*, 1–21.

Barbier, G., & Liu, H. (2011). *Data mining in social media. Social Network Data Analytics*. Springer.

Beach, A. et al. (2008). WhozThat? Evolving an ecosystem for context-aware mobile social networks. *IEEE Network, 22*(4), 50–55. doi:10.1109/MNET.2008.4579771.

Beach, A., et al. (2009). Solutions to security and privacy issues in mobile social networking. *IEEE, Computer Society, International Conference on Computational Science and Engineering.*

Berendt, B. et al. (2002). Towards semantic web mining. Springer-Verlag Berlin Heidelberg. *ISWC 2002. LNCS, 2342*, 264–278.

Bernstein, A. et al. (2005). Toward intelligent assistance for a data mining process: An ontology-based approach for cost-sensitive classification. *IEEE Transactions on Knowledge and Data Engineering, 17*(4), 503–519. doi:10.1109/TKDE.2005.67.

Bhogal, J. et al. (2007). A review of ontology based query expansion. Elsevier. *Information Processing & Management, 43*, 866–886. doi:10.1016/j.ipm.2006.09.003.

Bonchi, F. et al. (2011). Trajectory anonymity in publishing personal mobility data. *ACM SIGKDD Explorations Newsletter, 13*(1), 30–43. doi:10.1145/2031331.2031336.

Buyya, R. et al. (2009). Cloud computing and emerging IT platforms: Vision, hype, and reality for delivering computing as the 5th utility. Elsevier. *Future Generation Computer Systems, 25*, 599–616. doi:10.1016/j.future.2008.12.001.

Cantador, I. et al. (2011). Categorising social tags to improve folksonomy-based recommendations. Elseiver. *Web Semantics: Science. Services and Agents on the WWW, 9*, 1–15. doi:10.1016/j.websem.2010.10.001.

Cao, L. (2010). Domain-driven data mining: Challenges and prospects. *IEEE Transactions on Knowledge and Data Engineering, 22*(6), 755–769. doi:10.1109/TKDE.2010.32.

Chang, Y. J., et al. (2007). A general architecture of mobile social network services. *International Conference on Convergence Information Technology, IEEE Computer Society* (pp. 151 – 156).

Chen, D., et al. (2009). An efficient algorithms for overlapping community detection in complex networks. *Intelligent Systems GCIS 09 WRI Global Congress*, 1, pp. 244-247.

Chen, G., & Rahman, F. (2008). Analyzing privacy designs of mobile social networking applications. Embedded and ubiquitous computing. *IFIP International Conference*, Vol. 2, pp. 83-88.

Chen, L., & Qi, L. (2011). Social opinion mining for supporting buyers' complex decision making: Exploratory user study and algorithm comparison. *Social Network Analysis Mining, 1*, 301–320. doi:10.1007/s13278-011-0023-y.

Choudhury, T., et al. (2008). The mobile sensing platform: An embedded activity recognition system. *IEEE CS, Activity based Computing, Pervasive computing*.

Coben, P., & Adams, N. (2009). Intelligent data analysis in the 21st century. Springer, Verlag Berlin Heidberg. *LNCS, 5772*, 1–9.

Deinert, F., & Magedanz, T. (2010). Introducing widget-based IMS client applications. Springer. *Mobile Networks and Applications, 15*, 845–852. doi:10.1007/s11036-010-0239-5.

Dikaiakos, M. D. et al. (2009). *Cloud computing distributed internet computing for IT and scientific research* (pp. 10–13). IEEE Computer Society. doi:10.1109/MIC.2009.103.

Ding, Z. et al. (2012). *SeaCloudDM: A database cluster framework for managing and querying massive heterogeneous sensor sampling data*. Springer Science Business Media. doi:10.1007/s11227-012-0762-1.

Domingue, J. et al. (Eds.). (2011). *Handbook of semantic web technologies* (pp. 468–506). Springer-Verlag Berlin Heidelberg. doi:10.1007/978-3-540-92913-0.

Fielding, R. T., & Taylor, R. N. (2002). Principled design of the modern web architecture. *ACM Transactions on Internet Technology, 2*(2), 115–150. doi:10.1145/514183.514185.

Gartrell, M., et al. (2010). Enhancing group recommendation by incorporating social relationship interactions. *ACM GROUP' 10, Proceeding of the 6th ACM International Conference on Supporting group work*, pp. 97 – 106.

Gasevi, D., et al. (2011). An approach to folksonomy-based ontology maintenance for learning environments. *IEEE Transactions on learning technologies, 4*(4), 301-314.

Gebremeskel, G. B., et al. (2012). The paradigm integration of computational intelligence performance in cloud computing towards data security. *IEEE Computer Society, 5th International Conference on Information and Computing Science* (pp. 19 – 22).

Geser, H. (2006). Is the cell phone undermining the social order?: Understanding mobile technology from a sociological perspective. *Knowledge, Technology & Policy, 19*(1), 8–18. doi:10.1007/s12130-006-1010-x.

Goggins, S. P., et al. (2010). Social intelligence in completely online groups: Toward social prosthetics from log data analysis and transformation. *IEEE International Conference on Social Computing/IEEE International Conference on Privacy, Security, Risk and Trust* (pp. 500-507).

Grob, R. et al. (2009). *Cluestr: Mobile social networking for enhanced group communication* (pp. 81–90). ACM. doi:10.1145/1531674.1531686.

Hu, J., & Liu, Y. (2006). Designing and realization of intelligent data mining system based on expert knowledge. *IEEE, Management of Innovation and Technology International Conference*, Vol.1, pp. 380 – 383.

Hua, Z. Y., et al. (2010). Discussion of intelligent cloud computing system. IEEE. *Computer Society, International Conference on Web Information Systems and Mining* (pp. 319-322).

Humphreys, L. (2008). Mobile social networks and social practice: A case study of dodge ball. *Journal of Computer-Mediated Communication, 13*, 341–360. doi:10.1111/j.1083-6101.2007.00399.x.

IEEE COMSOC MMTC. (2012). E-Letter. IEEE Communication Society, 7(5).

Ioannidis, S., et al. (2009). Optimal and scalable distribution of content updates over a mobile social network. IEEE. Communications Society subject matter experts for publication in the IEEE INFOCOM 09 proceedings (pp. 1422-1430).

Janjua, N.K., et al. (2012). Semantic information and knowledge integration through argumentative reasoning to support intelligent decision making.

Kamilaris, A., & Pitsillides, A. (2008). Social networking of the smart home. *IEEE 21st International Symposium on Personal Indoor and Mobile Radio Communications.*

Kayastha, N. et al. (2011). Applications, architectures, and protocol design issues for mobile social networks: A survey. *IEEE Computer Society. Proceedings of the IEEE, 99*(12). doi:10.1109/JPROC.2011.2169033.

Kim, H. K. et al. (2008). Social semantic cloud of tag: Semantic model for social tagging. Springer-Verlag Berlin Heidelberg. *KES-AMSTA, LNAI, 4953*, 83–92.

Kim, M. J. et al. (2011). An intelligent multi –agent model for resource virtualization: Supporting social media service in cloud computing. Springer – Verlag Berlin Heidelberg. *Computer Network Systems and Industrial Eng. SCI, 365*, 99–111.

Lal, K., & Mahanti, N. C. (2010). A novel data mining algorithm for semantic web based data cloud. [IJCSS]. *International Journal of Computer Science and Security, 4*(2), 149–164.

Le Grand, B. et al. (2009). Semantic and conceptual context-aware information retrieval. Springer-Verlag Berlin Heidelberg. *SITIS 2006. LNCS, 4879*, 247–258.

Li, N., & Chen, G.L. (2009). Multi-layered friendship modeling for location based mobile social networks. *Mobile and Ubiquitous Systems Networking, and Services, 6th International* 10.4108/ICST *MobiQuitous2009,* 6828, pp. 1-10.

Licoppe, C., & Smoreda, Z. (2005). Are social networks technologically embedded? How networks are changing today with changes in communication technology. Elsevier. *Social Networks*, 317–335. doi:10.1016/j.socnet.2004.11.001.

Miluzzo, E. et al. (2008). *Sensing meets mobile social networks: The design, implementation and evaluation of the cenceme application.* ACM. doi:10.1145/1460412.1460445.

Mobasher, B. (2007). Data mining forweb personalization. Springer-Verlag Berlin Heidelberg. *The Adaptive Web, LNCS, 4321*, 90–135. doi:10.1007/978-3-540-72079-9_3.

Musolesi, M., & Mascolo, C. (2006). Designing mobility models based on social network theory. *ACM, Mobile Computing and Communications Review, 11*(3).

Nitti, M., et al. (2012). A subjective model for trustworthiness evaluation in the social internet of things. *Personal indoor and mobile radio communications (PIMRC), 2012 IEEE 23rd International Symposium on* (pp.18-23).

Niyato, D. et al. (2010). *Optimal content transmission policy in publish-subscribe mobile social networks.* IEEE, Communications Society. doi:10.1109/GLOCOM.2010.5683085.

Ochoa, S. et al. (2009). Understanding the relationship between requirements and context elements in mobile collaboration. Springer-Verlag Berlin Heidelberg. *Human-Computer Interaction, Part III, HCII. LNCS, 5612*, 67–76.

Pietiläinen, A. K. et al. (2009). *MobiClique: Middleware for mobile social networking* (pp. 49–54). ACM.

Rama, J., et al. (2009). An architecture for mobile social networking applications. IEEE Computer Society, 1st International Conference on Computational Intelligence, Communication Systems and Networks.

Rosa, P. M. P., et al. (2012). An ubiquitous mobile multimedia system for events agenda. IEEE. *Wireless Communications and Networking Conference: Mobile and Wireless Networks* (pp. 2103 – 2107).

Sheth, A., & Ranabahu, A. (2010). *Semantic modeling for cloud, computing, part 1: Semantic and service* (pp. 81–83). IEEE Computer Society.

Šikšnys, L., et al. (2010). Private and flexible proximity detection in mobile social networks. *IEEE, Computer Society, 11th International Conference on Mobile Data Management.*

Sopchoke, S., & Kijsirikul, B. (2011). A step towards high quality one-class collaborative filtering using online social relationships. *Advanced Computer Science and Information System (ICACSIS), International Conference on* (pp. 243-248).

Teneyuca, D. (2011). Internet cloud security: The illusion of inclusion. Elsevier. *Information Security Technical Report*, *16*, 102–107. doi:10.1016/j.istr.2011.08.005.

West, A. et al. (2011). *Trust in collaborative web applications: Future generation computer systems.* Elsevier.

Xu, M. et al. (2009). Cloud computing boosts business intelligence of telecommunication industry. Springer Verlag Berlin Heidelberg, *CloudCom. LNCS*, *5931*, 224–231.

Yao, Y. Y. et al. (2001). Web intelligence (WI) research challenges and trends in the new information age. Springer-Verlag Berlin Heidelberg. *WI 2001. LNAI*, *2198*, 1–17.

Yeh, P. Z. et al. (2009). *Towards a technology platform for building corporate radar applications that mine the web for business insight* (pp. 477–484). IEEE. doi:10.1109/ICTAI.2009.106.

Zhang, H., et al. (2009). Personalized intelligent search engine based on web data mining. *Proceedings of the 2009 International Workshop on Information Security and Application* (pp. 584-587).

Zhang, X. et al. (2011). Towards an elastic application model for augmenting the computing capabilities of mobile devices with cloud computing. Springer. *Mobile Networks and Applications*, *16*, 270–284. doi:10.1007/s11036-011-0305-7.

Zhao, X., & Okamoto, T. (2008). A device-independent system architecture for adaptive mobile learning. *8th IEEE International Conference on Advanced Learning Technologies* (pp. 23-25).

Zhenyu, W., et al. (2010). Towards cloud and terminal collaborative mobile social network service. IEEE. *International Conference on Social Computing, on Privacy, Security, Risk and Trust.*

Zhong, N. (2003). *Toward web intelligence. Springer -Verlag Berlin Heidelberg. AWIC* (pp. 1–14). LNAI.

ADDITIONAL READING

Albus, J. (1992). *Project reports RCS: A reference model architecture for intelligent control* (pp. 56–59). IEEE.

Banerjee, N., et al. (2009). R-U-In? - Exploiting rich presence and converged communications for next-generation activity-oriented social networking. *IEEE Computer Society, 10th International Conference on Mobile Data Management: Systems, Services and Middleware* (pp. 222-231).

Castells, M., et al. (2004). *The mobile communication society: Across cultural analysis of available evidence on the social use of wireless communication technology.*

Cheun, D. W., et al. (2011). A practical framework for comprehensive mobile context visualization. *IEEE International Conference on e-Business Engineering*, pp. 201-206.

Chlamtac, I. et al. (2003). Mobile ad hoc networking: Imperatives and challenges. Elsevier. *Ad Hoc Networks*, *1*, 13–64. doi:10.1016/S1570-8705(03)00013-1.

Ding, L., et al. (2011). Semantic stream query optimization exploiting dynamic metadata. IEEE. *ICDE Conference* (pp. 111-122).

Domingue, J., Fensel, D., & Hendler, J. A. (Eds.). (2011). *Handbook of Semantic Web Technologies*. Springer-Verlag Berlin Heidelberg. doi:10.1007/978-3-540-92913-0.

Domnori, E., et al. (2011). Designing and implementing intelligent agents for e-health. *IEEE Computer Society, International Conference on Emerging Intelligent Data and Web Technologies* (pp. 78-85).

Gill, A. Q., et al. (2011). An empirical analysis of cloud, mobile, social and green computing. *IEEE Computer Society, 9th International Conference on Dependable, Autonomic and Secure Computing*, pp. 697-704.

Hu, J., & Liu, Y. (2011). *Designing and realization of intelligent data mining system based on expert knowledge* (pp. 380–383). IEEE.

Kemelmacher-Shlizerman, I., & Basri, R. (2011). 3D face reconstruction from a single image using a single reference face shape. *IEEE Transactions on Pattern Analysis and Machine Intelligence*, *33*(2), 394–405. doi:10.1109/TPAMI.2010.63 PMID:21193812.

Li, N., et al. (2012). The construction of cloud data analysis platform and its application in intelligent industrial park. IEEE. ICACT2012 (pp. 860-863).

Li, N., & Zhong, N. (2006). Mining ontology for automatically acquiring web user information needs. *IEEE Transactions on Knowledge and Data Engineering*, *18*(4), 554–568. doi:10.1109/TKDE.2006.1599392.

Lin, C. C. (2006). Optimal web site reorganization considering information overload and search depth. *European Journal of Operational Research*, *173*, 839–848. doi:10.1016/j.ejor.2005.05.029.

Liu, J., et al. (2012). CCRA: Cloud computing reference architecture. *IEEE Ninth International Conference on Services Computing* (pp. 657-665).

Maedche, A., & Staab, S. (2001). Ontology learning for the semantic web. *IEEE Intelligent Systems*, 72–79. doi:10.1109/5254.920602.

Metzler, J. (2011). *The 2011 cloud networking report*. Retrieved from http://www.webtorials.com/content/index.html

Nan, L. et al. (2010). *Mobile takes social computing beyond Web 2.0*. Win-win, Tao of Business.

Perkowitz, M., & Etzioni, O. (2000). Towards adaptive web sites: Conceptual framework and case study. Elsiver. *Artificial Intelligence*, *118*, 245–275. doi:10.1016/S0004-3702(99)00098-3.

Pietiläinen, A. K. et al. (2009). *MobiClique: Middleware for mobile social networking* (pp. 49–54). ACM.

Rish, I. et al. (2005). Adaptive diagnosis in distributed systems. *IEEE Transactions on Neural Networks*, *16*(5), 1088–1109. doi:10.1109/TNN.2005.853423 PMID:16252819.

Savla, N., & Roto, V. (2009). *Research topics for optimizing social networking services for mobile use*. ACM.

Simoff, S., & Maher, M. L. (2006). *Ontology-based multimedia data mining for design information retrieval*. Key Centre of Design Computing.

Sun, H., et al. (2012). SOAC-Net: A model to manage service-based business process authorization. *IEEE Computer Society, 9th International Conference on Services Computing*, pp. 376-383.

Wang, F. et al. (2011). *Cloud computing based business intelligence platform and its application in the field of intelligent power consumption* (pp. 3612–3616). IEEE. doi:10.1109/ICECC.2011.6066291.

Wang, S., et al. (2011). Web service selection in trustworthy collaboration network. *8th IEEE Computer Society, International Conference on e-Business Engineering* (pp. 153-160).

Wlodarczyk, T., et al. (2010). DataStorm - An ontology-driven framework for cloud-based data analytic systems. *IEEE Computer Society, 6th World Congress on Services,* pp. 123-127.

Xiao, K., et al. (2011). Extracting semantic relationships for web services based on Wikipedia. *IEEE Computer Society, International Conference on Cloud and Service Computing* (pp. 71-76).

Xu, L. et al. (2012). *Multi-objective optimization based virtual resource allocation strategy for cloud computing* (pp. 56–61). IEEE Computer Society.

Yeh, P. Z., et al. (2009). Towards a technology platform for building corporate radar applications that mine the web for business insight. *IEEE 21st IEEE International Conference on Tools with Artificial Intelligence* (pp. 477-484).

Zheng, J. et al. (2009). Cloud computing based internet data center. Springer-Verlag Berlin Heidelberg. *CloudCom 2009. LNCS, 5931*, 700–704.

ENDNOTES

1. Social objects: Contain records from a social or business application or business process that referred to as system-of-record that are mapped into MSN.
2. A reference model is a model or conceptual framework that is efficient and dynamic essentially to serve as blueprints for modern MSNs cloud systems, which can be referenced as many external representations of the users or readers want that allow them to establish and explain various solutions from the model. Therefore, single reference model is specialized into several functions according to the needs of the users' use of the given domain.
3. We consider the interaction between families of three people, with one child. During the days, when the child is at school and the parents at their workplaces for 8 hours of a day, therefore, their social interaction is weak (i.e., represented with low values in the matrix). Out of that time, they will have a chance to meet and have strong social ties (i.e. 2/3 of the total hours in a day and have high value in the matrix). On the other hand, the social interactions between the office colleagues are the reveres of the families (i.e. 1/3 strong and 2/3 weak).
4. Which provides various social services.
5. The integration and retrieval of knowledge resources.
6. Which provides self explained and reusable services.
7. Semantic intelligent cloud
8. Unstructured social data is a relational data bases which includes free text, audio or video files.
9. The modalities of social data also cells of a relational database, audio sequences, assertions of an analyst.

Chapter 10
Social Media Analytics:
An Application of Data Mining

Sunil Kr Pandey
Institute of Technology and Science, India

Vineet Kansal
Institute of Technology and Science, India

ABSTRACT

Many popular online social networks such as Twitter, LinkedIn, and Facebook have become increasingly popular. In addition, a number of multimedia networks such as Flickr have also seen an increasing level of popularity in recent years. Many such social networks are extremely rich in content, and contain tremendous amount of content and linkage data which can be leveraged for analysis. The linkage data is essentially the graph structure of the social network and the communications between entities; whereas the content data contains the text, images and other multimedia data in the network. The growth of the usage and penetration of social media in the recent years has been enormous and unprecedented. This significant increase in its usage and increased number of users, there has been trend of a substantial increase in the volume of information generated by users of social media. Irrespective of primary domain in which organization is operating in to, whether it is insurance sector, social media (including facebook, twitter etc), medical science, banking etc. Virtually a large number of varying nature and services of organizations are making significant investments in social media. But it is also true that many are not systematically analyzing the valuable information that is resulting from their investments. This chapter aims at providing a data-centric view of online social networks; a topic which has been missing from much of the literature and to draw unanswered research issues which can be further explored to strengthen this area.

DOI: 10.4018/978-1-4666-4213-3.ch010

Copyright © 2013, IGI Global. Copying or distributing in print or electronic forms without written permission of IGI Global is prohibited.

INTRODUCTION

The explosion of the digital data generated as a by-product of the increasing adoption of social media means that the social sciences are flooding with data that promises to revolutionise research, but which the research community is presently not equipped to exploit. While the sheer volume of such data presents challenges for the social sciences, such data is now being routinely analysed by industry for its own purposes. Where, in the past, academic social science was an obligatory point of passage for those wanting to learn about social phenomena, there is now a danger that social scientific research is simply bypassed by powerful actors with access to vast datasets. The amount of data in our world has been exploding, and analyzing large data sets—so-called big data—will become a key basis of competition, underpinning new waves of productivity growth, innovation, and consumer surplus. (Research reports from MGI and McKinsey's Business Technology). The increasing volume and detail of information captured by enterprises, the rise of multimedia, social media, and the Internet of Things will fuel exponential growth in data for the foreseeable future (Manyika, Chui, Brown, Bughin, Dobbs, Roxburgh, & Byers, 2011).

Regardless of where one looks at, one can see an explosion in the use of social media. Online communities have developed that focus on both personal and professional lives. Groups have been formed that focus on every potential area of interest, including food, sports, music, parenting, scrapbooking, and actuarial issues. It is estimated that there are over 900 social media sites on the internet. Some of the more popular platforms are Facebook, Twitter (Mosley, 2012), LinkedIn, Google Plus, and YouTube. To help understand the explosion in the use of social media, consider the statistics in Figure 1 which were compiled (Brown, 2011) at www.dannybrown.me.

Figure 1. Some factual perspectives

Exhibit-1 (As per Jan, 2012)

- People spend over 500 billion minutes per month on Facebook.
- There are 200 million registered Twitter accounts.
- There are more than 70 million users of LinkedIn worldwide.
- YouTube receives more than 2 billion viewers per day.
- Seventy-seven percent of internet users read blogs.
- There are **71% male** users and **29% female users in India**

Table 1 depicts the exponential growth in the user community joining the social media networks and amount of data that is being produced may be just imagined. The majority of the population is using social media in some form or another. In other words the substantial increase in the use of social media, there is a significant amount of information that is being generated. As seen in the same sources referenced above, the volume of this content is staggering:

- More than 30 billion pieces of content are shared each month on Facebook.
- Every minute, 24 hours of video is uploaded to YouTube.
- As of December 2010, the average number of tweets sent per day was 110 million.
- There are currently 133 million blogs listed on leading blog directory Technorati.

So not only are people joining and accessing social media sites, but they are also spending time engaging in social media and creating a significant amount of content. As a result of this time spent on social media and the information being generated, businesses have taken notice and are attempting to leverage the power of social media to help them succeed.

The growth of the "Social Web" and the corresponding rise in available "emotional text" (through on-line social network platforms such as Facebook and blogging platforms such as BlogSpot) over the past few years has led to an increased interest in sentiment analysis (Surma & Furmanek, 2011) and this is depicted in Figure 2. Research that makes use of such analysis primar-

Table 1. World-wide chronological growth of users on Facebook

Timeline	No of Users (Millions)	Timeline	No of Users (Millions)
December-04	1	February-10	450
December-05	5.5	July-10	500
December-06	12	September-10	550
April-07	20	January-11	600
October-07	50	February-11	650
August-08	100	June-11	750
January-09	150	September-11	800
February-09	175	February-12	845
April-09	200	April-12	901
July-09	250	July-12	955
September-09	300		
December-09	350		

ily focuses on extraction of text fragments that contain a particular viewpoint – to subsequently support the development of recommendation systems based on data acquired from a large user community. Aggregating the outcome of such an analysis with demographic information enables a better understanding of how a particular community "feels" at a given point in time. This therefore provides a very powerful, automated, research tool for social scientists, to better understand how a community responds to a particular geo-political event.

BACKGROUND AND MOTIVATION

The Social Data Mining has placed itself well and now is considered to be an industry in its own. This is neither a surprise nor new but is mature enough to have some experts to remember its old heritage. There are numerous examples which exhibit that there are certain organizations who have entered in to the business of social media network through their specific sites and in a very short span of time, they have established themselves well financially and otherwise too. One of such companies is 33Across which was founded in

Figure 2. World-wide chronological growth of users on Facebook

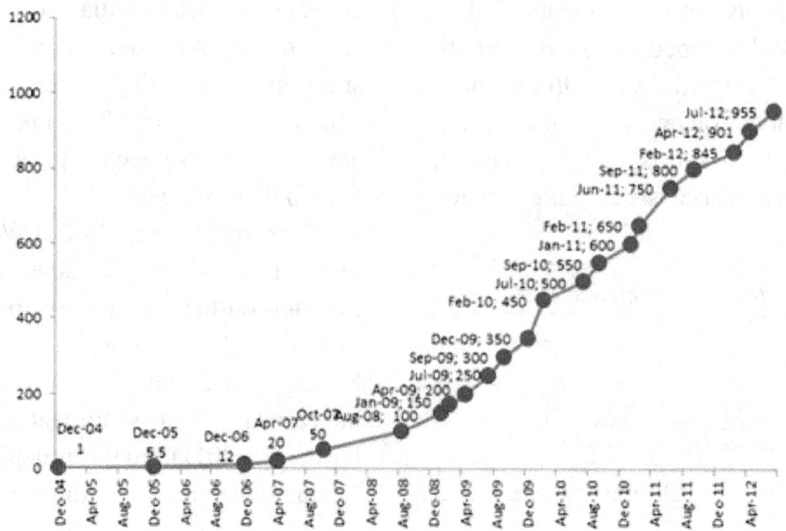

2007. This organization has employed 85 persons and also has risen funding of about $13 millions. This company has recently acquired Tynt, a tool that allows the publishers to see whenever their contents are copied and pasted anywhere on the web. This organization has claimed to have data on 1.25 billion web users that it can mine to find brand affinities based on social connections and interest similarities with users classified as "brand loyalists." Their list of clients includes big giants including AT&T, American Express, eBay and Macy's. Tynt brought 1 billion of those users, and the balance came from sources like content-sharing and messaging platforms, Twitter apps and photo-sharing sites (Mosley, 2012; Delo, 2012; Brown & Danny, 2011; Browne & Sean, 2010).

The company can deliver ads with inventory from exchanges and real-time bidding platforms. Likewise another example in this category Meteor Solutions gets its data from brands and publishers. This company, which was launched in 2009, now works with demand-side platforms to deliver ads to audience segments developed based on how content has been shared. Working with a telecom business, for example, Meteor would embed some code in a web page with a product video, designed to be engaging, that introduces a phone, and would then track how and where it's shared to inform the advertising. This Seattle-based company has 15 employees and is a profit-making company, with a client list including Microsoft, AT&T and NBC Universal. (Delo, 2012).

Table 2 shows that voluminous presence of users on social media networks also opening doors and new opportunities for the businesses to flourish and grow. This is not restricted in any single part of any specific country (Figure 3) but the trends are visible across the world. One of the companies in this list most widely associated with social targeting has publicly renounced that part of its business; Media6Degrees has $24 million in funding and clients such as American Express, Disney and AT&T. It was founded in 2007 on the premise that people who act alike online are apt to have similar brand preferences, but the thinking originally was that the strongest signals should come from social media. It initially bought data about MySpace users from apps operating on the platform, but exchanges and real-time bidding platforms have since become the primary data source. Media6Degrees officially recast its business from "social targeting" to "prospect targeting" last year.

It would not be inappropriate to mention a plan to study data mining of social-networking sites which was funded by one of the largest credit-reporting agency of Germany' which provoked infuriate after internal documents about the project were pour out to German media outlets. As per study reports of Spiegel Online the data gathered from LinkedIn, Twitter, facebook, other social networks and even Google Street View could be used for identifying and evaluating the prospects and threats along with determining the current opinions of a person. According to a new Consumer Reports study, nearly 13 million Facebook users either don't know how to manage their privacy settings or don't even realize they exist (Giannotti & Pedreschi, 2008). Only 37% have altered their privacy settings to control what third-party apps can see and learn about them — which

Table 2. Comparative chart of users

Country	Year 2011 (Millions User)
China	256.5
US	147.8
India	30.2
Brazil	66.2
Indonesia	34.4
Russia	32.1
Japan	39.5
Maxico	23.7
Germany	25.7
UK	23.9
South Korea	20.7
France	19.9
Italy	15.8
Spain	13.3
Canada	16.1
Argentina	14.1
Australia	8.8

Figure 3. Growth of social media users world-wide

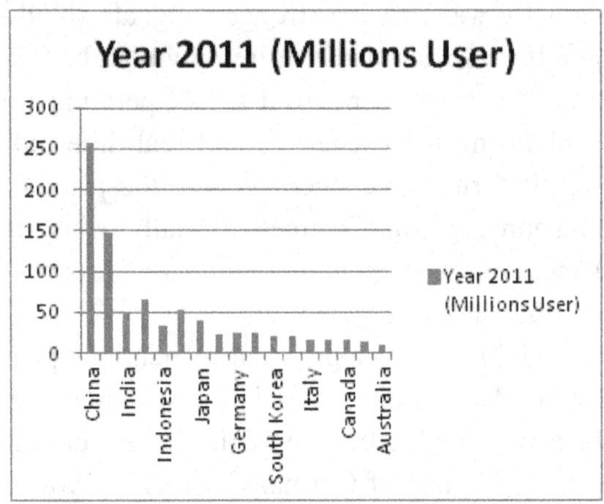

they have the ability to do in some cases based on the activity of a user's friend. Right now companies collect tons of information about our online habits, probably more than most of us realize. For instance, the same reports also mentions that if one visits a Web page that has a Like option, Facebook knows one have been there — even if one doesn't like the page. Increasingly, social-network users are burdened with changes to privacy policies that expose more data by default, putting the onus on the individual to secure their information. So far, all this data is sliced and diced primarily with the goal of selling us stuff. That can be annoying and a little creepy, but it's pretty benign compared with the potential use of that type of information to determine our creditworthiness.

PROCESS PARADIGM AND APPLICATIONS OF DATA MINING IN SOCIAL MEDIA

The increased reach of the social web have added a new dimension in the evolution of the web by technology shift. But, as interesting as the technology shift, has been the *cultural* shift that has accompanied it, where activities that were traditionally considered private have increasingly become public. People who had previously used to pen their thoughts and exploration in a journal, used to store their family photo albums, and used to talk to their known people by phone or e-mail are now increasingly sharing their thoughts through posting on blogs, placing their photos on public photo sharing sites, and having conversations via public wall posts on social networks. Because of all these changes the result of this is that the web has become home to a mass archive of human communication and sentiment, containing large amounts of valuable information that are not well handled by traditional methods of retrieval and presentation. While the data is now available to answer queries like "how did one felt when one got life-time achievement award?" search engines don't, generally, handle queries like this well. The area of research in this direction involves extraction and visualization of sentiment data from the social web, and in building interfaces for real-time querying, analysis, and presentation of social and emotional data.

There are number of data mining techniques that have been developed recently for relational data include probabilistic relational models (PRMs) (Friedman, Getoor, Koller, & Pfeffer, 1999), Bayesian Logic Programs (BLPs) (Kersting & de Raedt, 2000), First-Order Bayesian Classifiers (Flach & Lachiche, 1999), and Relational Probability Trees (RPTs) (Jensen & Neville, 2002). In each of these cases, both the structure and the parameters of a statistical model can be learned directly from data, easing the job of data analysts, and greatly improving the fidelity of the resulting model. Older techniques include Inductive Logic Programming (ILP) (Muggleton, 1992; Dzeroski & Lavrac, 2001) and Social Network Analysis (Wasserman & Faust, 1994).

Social Media networks are contributing in huge growth of data stores designed for the purpose by storing the user's data. This is undoubtedly a large data store (Figure 4) which contains lots of useful information about the demographic behavior of users and this can be used in framing policies and strategies to increase the profitability of the organizations. This is evident from Table 3 that in just a span of almost one and half year, the numbers of users are grown with a pace of more than 300%. Extracting data and finding out the patterns in such a large volume cannot be possible by conventional approaches. And this is the reason why the Data Mining applications make use of various available tools for data analysis. The objective of these tools is to identify novice patterns and relationships in large datasets. It is obvious that the applications based on data mining principles use classification, clustering, prediction, Association rule mining (Hipp, Guntzer, & Gholamreza, 2000) pattern Recognition and Pattern Analysis (Ziegler, Farkas, & Lorincz, 2009).

The applications of data mining have found virtually in every area where social networks play a vital role. Social networks have shown their presence everywhere in today's world. It has become a mean to share information among people all over the world. There are many social networks in on-line mode exist, which include Orkut, Facebook, Frienster, Myspace etc. Among all these Facebook has gained prominence over others because of large number of usage among its users with almost 845 million active users as of February 2012. Not only this but also more than 845 million active users around the world, Facebook is today's most popular and used social networking medium to connect with diversified category of users, including friends, family, coworkers, constituents, and consumers. These connections occur not just through Facebook features but through applications ("apps") developed by third parties over Facebook Platform. The application of data mining on the data store containing the history of social media activity is now commonplace in business intelligence circles. Over last few years, the stream of Business Intelligence has experienced a startling rate of growth and reached disdainful levels of sophistication. Just a few years ago, consumer-oriented businesses were stuck in the world of static "focus groups" and paper-based surveys. But not even the most forward-looking of these organizations could ever have dreamt of present-day scenario, where newly fictitious chunks of data about consumer behavior and preferences wait to be mined by state-of-the-art business intelligence computing infrastructure.

While studying the patterns in users community present on social media networks, there are very interesting patterns are found. When we specifically attempted to study the present user's community on facebook, it was found (Table 4) that around 48% of the facebook users are in the range of age group 18 to 24 years and about 28% of users are from age group of 25 to 34 yrs. This is clear from Figure 5 that about 83% users of Facebook social media site are within the age group of 18 years to 44 years, whereas only 5% users of the facebook are with age having greater than 45%. The other interesting pattern seen has been around 12% users are under 18 years of age group.

Likewise, according to Pew Internet and American Life Project, as shown in Figure 6, depicts the growth of user on another popular social media site, Twitter. Such data values provide representation of major adult population which has the ability to think, use and apply. Their demographic behavior may be of interest for the businesses.

Figure 4. Comparative chart of user growth

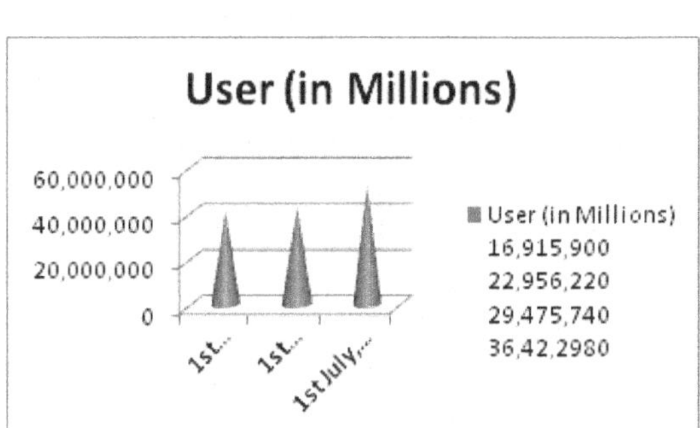

DATA MINING TECHNIQUES

Classification

Classification is the process of formation of groups based on the certain pre-conceded ideas, identified and established norms and well lay down process. The outcome of the classification process is predictive. It is an approach which is a most important and frequently used technique in data mining. It is a process of finding a set of models that describe and distinguish data classes or concepts. The derived model may be represented in various forms such as classification (IF-THEN) rules, decision tree, neural networking, etc. A decision tree is a flowchart like tree structure when each node denotes a test on an attribute value where each branch represents an outcome of the test, and tree leaves represent classes. Decision trees can be easily converted to classification rules. A neural network when used for classification is typically a collection of neuron-like (Han & Kamber, 2006).

While learning classification rules, the system has to find the rules that predict the class from the prediction attributes. So firstly the user has to define conditions for each class, the data mine system then constructs descriptions for the classes. Once classes are defined the system should infer rules that govern the classification. Therefore the system should be able to find the description of the each class. The description should only refer to the prediction attributes of the training set so that the positive examples should satisfy the description. A rule is said to be correct if its description covers all the positive examples and none of the negative examples of a class.

Table 3. Penetration of users on social media since January, 2011 to July, 2012

Timeline	User (in Millions)
1st January, 2011	16,915,900
1st April, 2011	22,956,220
1st July, 2011	29,475,740
1st October, 2011	36,42,2980
1st January, 2012	41,402,420
1st February, 2012	43,497,980
1st July, 2012	53,712,660

Clustering

On contrary to this Clustering is a process of formation of groups which is not based on pre-conceded norms or procedures rather based on certain commonality of attributes such groups are self formed and sustained. Many a times such groups are of interested while analyzing the data and identifying hidden patterns, processing units with weighted connections between the units (Han & Kamber, 2006). The concept of clustering has been around for a long time. It has several applications, particularly in the context of information retrieval and in organizing web resources. The main purpose of clustering is to locate information and in the present day context, to locate most relevant electronic resources. The research in clustering eventually led to automatic indexing --- to index as well as to retrieve electronic records. Term clustering is a method, which groups redundant terms, and this grouping reduces, noise and increase frequency of assignment. If there are fewer clusters than there were original terms, then the dimension is also reduced. However semantic properties suffer. There are many different algorithms available for term clustering. These are cliques, single link, stars and connected components. The particular choice of clustering algorithms depends on the desired properties of the final clustering, e.g. what are the relative importance of compactness, parsimony, and inclusiveness? Other considerations include the usual time and space complexity. A clustering algorithm attempts to find natural groups of components (or data) based on some similarity. The clustering algorithm also finds the centroid of a group of data sets. To determine cluster membership, most algorithms evaluate the distance

Table 4. Demographic distribution of Facebook users age

Age Group (in years)	Population (Percentage)
18 – 24	48
25 – 34	28
16 – 17	08
35 – 44	07
13 – 15	04
45 – 54	03
55 – 64	01
65 – 0	01

between a point and the cluster centroids. The output from a clustering algorithm is basically a statistical description of the cluster centroids with the number of components in each cluster.

Traditionally clustering techniques are broadly divided into hierarchical and partitioning. Hierarchical clustering is further subdivided into agglomerative – which start with the points as individual clusters and, at each step, merge the most similar or closest pair of clusters. This requires a definition of cluster similarity or distance and divisive – which starts with one, all-inclusive cluster and, at each step, split a cluster until only singleton clusters of individual points remain. In this case, we need to decide, at each step, which cluster to split and how to perform the split. The result of a hierarchical clustering algorithm can be graphically displayed as tree, called a dendogram. This tree graphically displays the merging process and the intermediate clusters.

Association Rule Mining

Association analysis is the discovery of association rules sharing attribute-value (Hipp, Guntzer, & Gholamreza, 2000) conditions that occur frequently together in a given set of data. It is widely used in the context of analysis of "transaction data." Association rules are of the form (3)

X => Y

i.e. A1 ^ A2 ^ … ^ Am => B1 ^ B2 ^ B3 … Bn, where Ai (for i {1, 2, …m}) and BJ (for j { 1, 2, 3, …n}) are attribute-value pairs. This rule is interpreted, as "database tuples that satisfy the conditions in X are also likely to satisfy the conditions in Y."

An objective measure for association rules of the form x => y is rule support, representing the percentage of transactions from a transaction database that the given rule satisfies; i.e. P (X ∪Y), where X ∪ Y indicates that a transaction contains both X and Y – the union of items sets X and Y (in the context of set theory it is X ∩ Y). Another objective measure for association rules is confidence, which assesses the degree of certainty of the identified association, i.e., P (Y|X) – probability that a transaction containing X also contains Y. Thus, support and confidence are defined as:

$$\text{support } (X \Rightarrow Y) = P(X \cup Y)$$

$$= \frac{No\,of\,tuples\,containing\,both\,A\ \&B}{Total\,No\,of\,Tuples}$$

$$\text{confidence } (X \Rightarrow Y) = P(X \mid Y)$$

$$= \frac{No\,of\,tuples\,containing\,both\,A\ \&B}{No\,of\,Tuples\,containing\,A}$$

Figure 5. Growth of Facebook in India

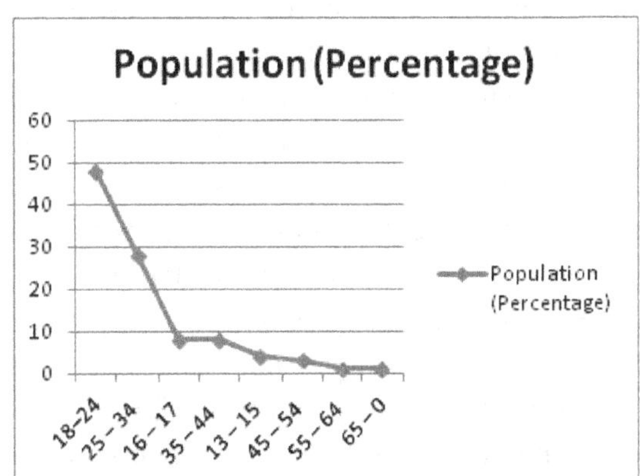

Figure 6. Growth of Twitter account holders

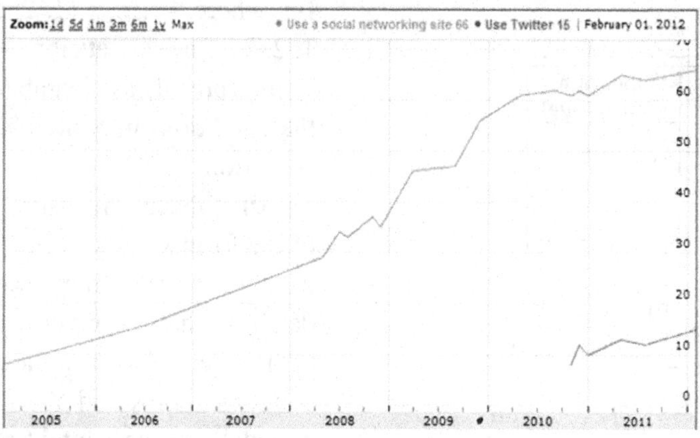

Source: Pew Internet and American Life Project

NEXT GENERATION DATA MINING TECHNIQUES

Last two decades have witnessed tremendous change and continuous & focused research in this direction gave birth to various competent mining techniques. These are specially used in mining, analyzing and interpreting the large data stores generated by social media applications. These techniques can be used for either discovering new information within large databases or for building predictive models. Though the older decision tree techniques such as CHAID are currently highly used the new techniques such as CART are gaining wider acceptance.

Ross Quinlan propounded a decision tree algorithm named ID3 in the late 1970s, which was one of the first decision tree algorithms. In the beginning, this was used for tasks such as learning good game playing strategies for chess end games. Since then, ID3 has been applied to a wide variety of problems in both academia and industry and has been modified, improved and borrowed from many times over. ID3 was later enhanced in the version called C4.5. C4.5 improves on ID3 in several important areas including predictors with missing values can still be used, predictors with continuous values can be used, pruning is introduced and rule derivation.

In addition, to above newer techniques including Neural Networks, Nearest Neighborhood, Decision Trees, Artificial Intelligence and Genetic Algorithms are the approaches (Han & Kamber, 2006) which are very rigorously researched and incorporated in creation of newer, efficient and more accurate pattern identification and analysis techniques.

SOME RECENT APPLICATIONS

- The use of social media sites has grown significantly, and this fact is being recognized by businesses of virtually every domain, including insurance companies.
- In response, insurance companies and other businesses are investing significant time and resources into establishing and maintaining a social media presence. All of these are feeding into the exponential increase in the amount of data and information that is being generated. This then raises a significant question. What are companies in general, and insurance companies specifically, doing with all of this information? Every Facebook post, every Tweet, every blog entry, every connection with social media generates:

- A new data point,
- A new bit of information that may be of value to insurance companies. This information might help an insurance company service a policyholder better,
- Connect with a potential new customer, identify a need or concern in the marketplace, or uncover a competitive issue they may be facing,
- Social media platforms provide opportunities for consumers to share their thoughts with a broader audience, and in understanding how customers are feeling or what they are facing, insurers can better interact with consumers.

- Crowdsourcing technology is exciting, particularly since it can provide granular localized data to peacekeepers, foreign services and development agencies. But without a solid understanding of the operating environment and well developed local partnerships, we end up with a pile of data that can slow the analytic process right when aid workers, diplomats and peacekeepers need information as quickly as possible.
- Since 2006, the industry, private sector in particular, has been using social media and SMS text messaging to crowdsource consumer behavior and trends. Using available efficient and dedicated data mining and mass communication tools, it has now become possible to aggregate social media and text message data from thousands of people in real time, analyze market dynamics and instantaneously communicate a micro-targeted response using SMS, Twitter, Facebook or other online platforms.
- All the ministries, except Ministry of Defense, Govt. of India, senior diplomats, foreign services and peacekeeping operations are beginning to integrate these tools into their e-diplomacy and population engagement strategies, recognizing the vital foreign policy insights that crowdsourced data can provide on rapidly changing dynamics at the local level.

CHALLENGES AND OPPORTUNITIES

- The current growth of users on social media networks and their projected growth (refer Table 5) are enormous. Table 5 represents comparative chart of current state of affair and projected number of users in next 03 years down the line and result is very interesting.
- The table depicts that major growth in number of users are expected in China, India and Indonesia whereas comparatively the growth rate in terms of number of users are stagnant in developed countries including US, UK. Japan, Germany, Russia etc.
- The above-mentioned trends are indicating that there is paradigm shift from the developed countries to the developing countries and majorly in Asia Pacific. This is opening new opportunities and to exploit these opportunities, one needs to trap the demographic behavior, buying pattern of users, their interest and accordingly take appropriate measures to deal with such situations.
- The developed countries may have highly developed policies on e-diplomacy and technology to exploit the benefits of these without having minimum impact on existing system for the development; there are specific technical and organizational issues which need to be considered while designing and implementation of crowdsourcing maneuvers.
- The first issue deals with the technical dimension and comprised of access to the system (hardware) and managing data se-

curity. The other dimension is how to make crowdsourced data flows controllable for responding agencies.

- Access to technology in the Asia Pacific is becoming less of a hurdle as mobile phone penetration increases and security risks are better understood. According to the Mobile and Development Intelligence program, GSM mobile phone penetration in the region is beyond saturated in many countries. These communication tools have significant implications for diplomatic and political engagement strategies.
- The rapid dissemination of false rumours in recent past via Facebook and Twitter, in our countries, highlights the increasing potential of mobile technologies to significantly impact diplomatic relations within the region almost instantaneously. However, while mobile phones are ubiquitous within the Asia Pacific, internet access is not.
- The nature of state surveillance also poses data security problems. As Syrian government hacking of online content has demonstrated, open data is often insecure, particularly SMS text messages. In recent past even in India, the usage of Social media sites, Facebook in particular, was questioned for its role in spreading the messages on viral effect among the common public and resulted in escaping of north-east people to their home state which lead to a situation where Govt. of India was thinking on banning such sites.

Any collection process supported by government agencies or the private sector must account for the potential for screening by local intelligence organs. This brings us to the institutional challenge. There is a way to deal with this and which is looking to trusted local NGOs running crowdsourcing initiatives. Using cleaned and verified data from local partners such as these can make the mass of digital information more manageable for large agencies and can improve the technical capacity on the ground vital to correcting false rumours, coordinating tangible responses to diplomatic and humanitarian crises and collecting accurate data on aid and development projects.

Among the issues which needs attention, are that for many sites, in social media specifically, the Terms of Service are clear and to the point: If one posts his/her contents to the site, he or she actually gives permission to the site for its usage for any purpose they think suitable. This is true that these sites are different in their bindings and perpetual right to use and reproduce the information posted by the members in their posts; it is wise to slip-up on the side of caution. Irrespective of the level of privacy one deems the content, privacy controls usually only go so far - the demarcation between private and public information remains fuzzy at best. In some cases, once contents are submitted, it may instantaneously become the intellectual property of social networking site, even if one delete or purge the submission in its entirety.

DISCUSSIONS

It is evident from discussion in this chapter that in recent years in almost last eight years, the social media has grown at a large pace and showing significant growth in terms of its usage and continuous increase in number of users. This continuous increase of users at a fast pace on the social networking sites are contributing in creating a large data sets. These data sets are the repository of wealth of information which can immensely contribute in strategic result oriented decisions. There is a trend in increase in number of users on the social media networks which needs to be understood and find out the ways and means to exploit their benefits for the organizational benefits. There could be the study of behavior of users visiting such social media sites and the information they are using or sharing on the web.

Table 5. Projections of users on social media

Country	Year 2011	Year 2014
China	256.5	414.5
US	147.8	170.7
India	50.2	129.3
Brazil	66.2	90.7
Indonesia	34.4	79.2
Russia	52.1	69.3
Japan	39.5	50.7
Mexico	23.7	37.2
Germany	25.7	34.7
UK	23.9	29.4
South Korea	20.7	25.9
France	19.9	25
Italy	15.8	21.3
Spain	15.5	21.2
Canada	16.1	18.5
Argentina	14.1	17.9
Australia	8.8	11.6

This creates rich source of information which can yield very useful and crucial information to the organizations.

Today we have different social media and wide variety of social media mediums with us to network and communicate in our groups, and thus generating large amount of data to deal with before us. This poses different types of challenges before us in accessing that large data set and converting them into something that is novice, interesting, usable and actionable. In general, organizations wish to use the social media data to understand the needs and behavior of their customers, potential customers or specific targeted groups of individuals with respect to the organizations' current or future products or services. In fact there are three major methods to visualize the social media – channel reporting tools, overview score-carding systems and predictive analytic techniques (primarily text mining) (Francis & Louise, 2006). Each of these has their different useful aspects and at the same time they do have certain limitations as well. There is also a fourth dimension to and this is – using a predictive analytic environment that includes not only text mining, but network analysis and other predictive techniques such as clustering to overcome not only the limitations of the previous techniques, but generate new fact based insight as well. This approach was first used at a major European Telco. Also Abstract representations (such as clusters from latent analysis) that lack linguistic counterparts are hard to learn or validate and tend to lose information (Halevy, Norvig, & Pereira, 2009).

FUTURE DIRECTIONS

Recent research projects in two closely related areas of computer science — machine learning and data mining — have developed methods for constructing statistical models of network data. Examples of such data include social networks, networks of web pages, complex relational databases, and data on interrelated people, places, things, and events extracted from text documents. Such data sets are often called "relational" because the relations among entities are central (e.g., acquaintanceship ties between people, links between web pages, or organizational affiliations between people and organizations). These algorithms differ from a substantially older and more established set of data mining algorithms developed to analyze propositional data. Propositional data are individual records, each of which can be represented as an attribute vector and each of which are assumed to be statistically independent of any other. For example, a propositional data set for learning medical diagnostic rules might represent each patient as a vector of diagnostic test results, and analysis would assume that knowing the disease of one patient tells you nothing about another patient. In contrast, analysis of a relational representation of the same data would retract this latter assumption and add information about familial relationships, workplace contacts, and other relationships among patients that might influence their medical status.

This new fact-based insight provides a foundation for applying other types of investigative

Figure 7. Comparative list of growth of social media

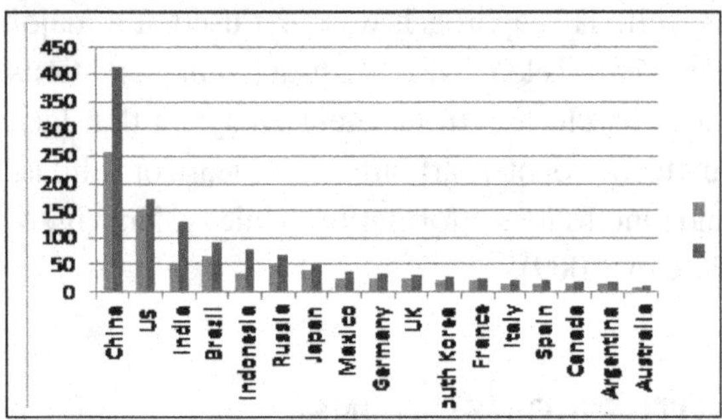

analytic, segmentation, predictive, and machine learning techniques. The ability to group individuals into clearly defined social media segments has of course a strong relevance for all companies that already use data mining and customer intelligence techniques within their organization. In fact, a good understanding of the social media segments can provide an invaluable contribution on the decision about how to invest and shape the company's social media and marketing strategies.

IMPLICATION OF THE WORK AND FUTURE RESEARCH DIRECTIONS IN ANALYSIS OF DATA FROM SOCIAL MEDIA

There are, of course, great benefits are derived and value gained by analyzing the social media data, however, a number of issues and challenges are also associated with this and requires further exploration and analysis.

- One of the challenges we encounter while analyzing the social media data is actually accessing and storing this information. As we discussed earlier, there are applications available which will allow companies to begin collecting and analyzing social media data, and companies may also have the ability to build internal programs that do this. The key is to make sure that the data is being collected in a consistent and complete matter, and that it is easily accessible for analysis.
- Other challenge is to analyze social media data as it relates to analyzing text data (Nancy & Ramani, 2011), which relates to the context. It may appear number of times that when a Facebook post or a tweet is simply a response to another post or tweet. It may be difficult to keep track of responded messages and how the user may be is responding. To the extent that it is not available, this creates a challenge for the analysis to understand exactly what this information means and in case of availability of this information, the issue becomes connecting the right set of social media data together to be able to understand the broader context of a conversation. However, this is not a trivial exercise, and there are still lots of work required to be done for improving the analytics in this respect.
- Another challenge towards social media analysis is the understanding the sentiments of customers. Words in a tweet are simply that, words and these do not carry the normal emotion that is present in a face-to-face conversation, in which case the listener could detect happiness, sadness, sarcasm, etc. Depending on the forum being analyzed, there are a number of understood rules that communicate different things, such as changing the font color to indicate sarcasm. While this analysis focused on the words being used, to understand sentiment would require a more thorough investigation into the ways that users communicate sentiment, and then attempting to capture those sentiments within the data in a structured way. This is another challenging area where there is still work to be done.
- Another challenge which is inherited in such data stored of social media arises from the fact that social media data is unfiltered. There are no system edits that ensure

the social media data that was captured is accurate, and this may result in false information and statements that are driven by pure emotion rather than fact.

- Typical actuarial predictive modeling analyses are based on historical data that is usually at least three months old and could be at least a year old. Also, typical actuarial predictive analyses are repeated relatively infrequently. Therefore, the analysis may require to be automated such that it can be updated quickly and the results reviewed in a timely manner.
- This should be noted that the social media is not only meant for those who use the English language. This is especially true for the organizations those are operating at international level across various countries speaking and using different languages. If a company has social media data which includes information in multiple languages, the differences in the languages will necessitate at least a separate initial analysis. This analysis could then be combined later if it is possible to translate the words and sentiments into one language.

CONCLUSION

The data stores created by the social media sites are becoming ready-made source of valuable information for any business organization or even individual. But extracting meaningful information from such a rich and large data stores is not an easy task and requires specialized mechanism and method to achieve this. The combination of text mining and network mining reveals new heterogeneous insights into social media customer behavior, which would not have been possible by using either technique on its own. Combining sentiment analysis from online forum posts together with reference structures from the quotation network has allowed us to position negative and positive users in context with their relative weight as influencers or followers in the underlying discussion forum.

This chapter provided brief discussion on, through the use of specific examples, the significance and tremendous growth in the size of data stores and how data mining and text analytics can be applied to social media to identify key themes in the data with providing inputs on the significance of social media data and its applications importance in prediction and strategic decision making. The chapter also discussed the application of correlation, clustering, and association analyses to social media. The outcomes of the analysis can help in finding out specific keywords and concepts in the social media data. These have the potential to help in facilitating the application of this information by primary users. As users of different levels in their organization analyze this information and apply the results of the analysis in relevant areas, they will be able to proactively address potential market and customer issues more effectively.

REFERENCES

Aggarwal, C. (2011). *Social network data analytics*. Kluwer Academic Publishers. doi:10.1007/978-1-4419-8462-3.

Banking.com. (n.d.). *Social media statistics: By-the-numbers, January, 2011*. Retrieved by http://www.banking2020.com/2011/01/24/social-media-statistics-by-the-numbersjanuary-2011 part-ii/

Brown, D. (2011). *52 Cool facts about social media*. Retrieved October 08, 2012, from www.dannybrown.me

Browne, S. (2010). *Statistics: Social networks will receive 11% of online ad spending in 2011*. Retrieved on August 22, 2012, from http://dannybrown.me/2010/07/03/cool-facts-about-social-media/

Castro, F., Vellido, A., Nebot, A., & Mugica, F. (2007). *Applying data mining techniques to e-learning problems. Studies in Computational Intelligence* (pp. 183–221). Springer-Verlag Berlin Heidelberg.

Delo, C. (2012). *Startups mining social data take on Facebook AT&T, AmEx, Macy's, Purina warm up to companies targeting ads across the web*. Retrieved by http://adage.com/print/233932

Dzeroski, S., & Lavrac, N. (Eds.). (2001). *Relational data mining*. Berlin: Springer. doi:10.1007/978-3-662-04599-2.

Francis, L. A. (2006, Winter). Taming text: An introduction to text mining. *Casualty Actuarial Society Forum*, pp. 51–88. Retrieved from http://www.casact.org/pubs/forum/06wforum/06w55.pdf

Giannotti, F., & Pedreschi, D. (2008). *Mobility, data mining and privacy: Geographic knowledge discovery* (p. 410). Springer. doi:10.1007/978-3-540-75177-9.

Halevy, A., Norvig, P., & Pereira, F. (2009). The unreasonable effectiveness of data. *Communications of the ACM*, *24*(2), 812.

Han, J., & Kamber, M. (2006). *Data mining: Concepts and techniques. University of Illinois at Urbana-Champaign*. Morgan Kaufmann.

Hipp, J., Guntzer, U., & Gholamreza, N. (2000). Algorithm for association rule mining: A general survey and comparison. *ACM SIGKDD*, *2*(1), 58. doi:10.1145/360402.360421.

Jacobs, A. (2009). The pathologies of big data. *ACM Queue; Tomorrow's Computing Today*, *7*(6). doi:10.1145/1563821.1563874.

Jensen, D., & Neville, J. (2002). *Data mining in social networks. National Academy of Sciences*. Washington: DC, National Academy Press.

Lauw, H. Ee-Peng, Teck, L., Pang, T.T. (2007). Mining social network from spatio-temporal events. *ACM SIGKDD International Conference on Knowledge Discovery and Data Mining*.

Li, Y., Surendran, A. C., & Shen, D. (2005). Data mining and audience intelligence for advertising pp. (96-99). *SIGKDD Explorations*, *9*(2).

Manyika, J., Chui, M., Brown, B., Bughin, J., Dobbs, R., Roxburgh, C., & Byers, A. (2011). *Big data: The next frontier for innovation, competition, and productivity*. McKinsey Global Institute.

Mosley, R., Jr. (2012, Winter). Social media analytics: Data mining applied to insurance Twitter posts, casualty actuarial society. *E-Forum, 2,* pp. 1-36. Retrieved September 10, 2012, from www.casact.org/pubs/forum/12wforumpt2/Mosley.pdf

Nancy, P., & Geetha Ramani, R. (2011). A comparison on performance of data mining algorithms in classification of social network data (pp. 47-54). *International Journal of Computers and Applications*, *32*(8).

Nancy, P., & Geetha Ramani, R. (2012). Frequent pattern mining in social network data (pp. 531-540). *European Journal of Scientific Research*, *79*(4).

Surma, J., & Furmanek, A. (2011). Data mining in on-line social network for marketing response analysis. *IEEE International Conference on Privacy, Security, Risk, and Trust, and IEEE International Conference on Social Computing*.

Wassermann, S., & Faust, K. (1994). *Social network analysis: Methods and applications*. Cambridge: Cambridge University Press. doi:10.1017/CBO9780511815478.

Ziegler, G., Farkas, C., & Lorincz, A. (2009). A framework for anonymous but accountable self-organizing communities. *Information and Software Technology*, *48*, 726–744. doi:10.1016/j.infsof.2005.08.007.

ADDITIONAL READING

Awadallah, A. (2009). How hadoop revolutionized data warehousing at Yahoo and Facebook. *CTO, Cloudera Inc.* Retrieved by http://www.slideshare.net/awadallah/how-hadoop-revolutionized-data-warehousing-at-yahoo-and-facebook

Browne, S. (2010). Statistics: Social networks will receive 11% of online ad spending in 2011. Retrieved on August, 22 2012, from http://dannybrown.me/2010/07/03/cool-facts-about-social-media/

Dean, J., & Ghemawat, S. (2004). MapReduce: Simplified data processing on large clusters. *Proceedings of the 6th Symposium on Operating System Design and Implementation* (pp. 137 – 150).

Ediger, D., Jiang, K., Riedy, J., Bader, D. A., & Corley, C. (2010). *Massive social network analysis: Mining Twitter for social good.* Paper presented at the International Conference on Parallel Processing (ICPP '2010).Ohio State University, Ohio.

Han, J., & Kamber, M. (2006). *Data mining: Concepts and techniques. The University of Illinois at Urbana-Champaign.* Morgan Kaufmann Publishing Company.

Hipp, J., Guntzer, U., & Gholamreza, N. (2000). Algorithm for association rule mining: A general survey and comparison. *ACM SIGKDD*, *2*(1), 58. doi:10.1145/360402.360421.

Killian, T., Kötter, T., Berthold, M., Silipo, R., & Winters, P. (2012). *Creating usable customer intelligence from social media data: Network analytics meets text mining* (pp. 1-17). Retrieved September 9, 2012, from http://knime.org/files/knime_social_media_white_paper.pdf

Kossinets, G., & Watts, D. J. (2006). Empirical analysis of an evolving social network. *Science*, *311*(5757), 88–90. doi:10.1126/science.1116869 PMID:16400149.

Kumar, R., Novak, J., Raghavan, P., & Tomkins, A. (2004). Structure and evolution of Blogspace. *Communications of the ACM*, *47*(12), 35–39. doi:10.1145/1035134.1035162.

Larose, D. T. (2006). *Data mining methods and models.* New York: Wiley Publications.

Laurent, W. (2011). *The realities of social media data mining*. William Laurent Inc. Retrieved from http://www.dashboardinsight.com/articles/new-concepts-in-business-intelligence/the-realities-of-social-media-data-mining.aspx

Manus, A. M., & Kechadi, M. T. (2004). *Scalability issue in mining large data sets. Data Mining V: Data Mining, Text Mining and Their Business Applications* (pp. 189–199). WIT Press.

McGlohon, M., & Faloutsos, C. (2008). *Graph mining techniques for social media analysis*. Paper presented at International Conference on Weblogs and Social Media, Carnegie Mellon, Seattle, USA.

Nasraoui, O., & Krishnapuram, R. (2002). A new evolutionary approach to web usage and context sensitive associations mining. *International Journal on Computational Intelligence and Applications –Special Issue on Internet Intelligent Systems, 2*(3), 339–348.

Surma, J., & Furmanek, A. (2011). Data mining in on-line social network for marketing response analysis. *IEEE International Conference on Privacy, Security, Risk, and Trust, and IEEE International Conference on Social Computing, 3*(11), 537 - 540.

Ting, H., Hong, T.-P., & Wang, L. (2011). *Social network mining, analysis and research trends: Techniques and applications*. IGI Global. doi:10.4018/978-1-61350-513-7.

Tsytsarau, M., & Palpanas, T. (2012). Mining subjective data on the web. *Data Mining and Knowledge Discovery*, *24*(3), 478–514. doi:10.1007/s10618-011-0238-6.

Wasserman, S., & Faust, K. (2009). *Social network analysis. Methods and applications*. Cambridge University Press.

Yates, D., & Paquette, S. (2011). Emergency knowledge management and social media technologies: A case study of the 2010 earthquake. *International Journal of Information Management*, *31*(1), 6–13. doi:10.1016/j.ijinfomgt.2010.10.001.

KEY TERMS AND DEFINITIONS

Classification: Classification is the process of formation of groups, based on certain predefined processes and rules.

Clustering: Clustering is the process of formation of groups, without having clear process and rules. Generally such groups are formed over the time based on some common attribute. Generally these groups are self formed groups.

Machine Learning: While suggesting probable solutions, sometimes exact solutions may not be found and system may be required to produce some other solutions through existing solutions. If such a solution is created, this becomes the part of the existing knowledge base. That's how system adds the created new paths, solutions to use in future. This learning is called machine learning.

Pattern Analysis: It is the process of automated detection of patterns and predictions from the same data source.

Social Data Mining: Social Data Mining refers to process of mining the data gathered from Social Media Networks, viz., Facebook, Twitters, facebook etc, to study the demographic behavior of the users.

Social Media Networks: Social media Networks are the application that create an environment for enabling communication, collaboration; sharing the information among the individuals, groups and communities.

Text Mining: This is process of mining the Text data to identify certain novice, interesting and useful pattern from a Text data Store.

Section 2

Data Mining in Fuzzy Systems

Chapter 11
Critical Parameters for Fuzzy Data Mining

Sinchan Bhattacharya
Maharaja Agrasen Institute of Technology, India

Vishal Bhatnagar
Ambedkar Institute of Advanced Communication Technologies & Research, India

ABSTRACT

Research on data mining is increasing at an incessant rate and to improve its effectiveness other techniques have been applied such as fuzzy sets, rough set theory, knowledge representation, inductive logic programming, or high-performance computing. Fuzzy logic due to its proficiency in handling uncertainty has gained its importance in a variety of applications in combination with the use of data mining techniques. In this chapter we take this association a notch further by examining the parameters which allow fuzzy sets and data mining to be combined into what has come to be known as fuzzy data mining. Analyzing and understanding these critical parameters is the main purpose of this chapter, so as to acquire maximum efficiency in applying the same which impelled the authors to work extensively and find out the crucial parameters essential to the application of fuzzy data mining.

INTRODUCTION

"Data mining is the analysis of observational data sets to find unsuspected relationships and to summarize the data in novel ways that are both understandable and useful to the data owner" (Hand et al., 2001). Ranjan (2008) provided an alternative view to this concept as he dined data mining as a technology that has been developed for investigation and analysis of large quantities of data to discover meaningful patterns and rules, facilitating the selection procedure.

Fuzzy logic is a multivalued logic that allows intermediate values to be defined between predictable values such as true and false, yes and no or high and low, concepts which are unclear or have value out of index or do not have a distinct value, can be formulated mathematically and processed by computers, so as to facilitate programming in computers (Zadeh, 1984). The main character-

DOI: 10.4018/978-1-4666-4213-3.ch011

Copyright © 2013, IGI Global. Copying or distributing in print or electronic forms without written permission of IGI Global is prohibited.

istic of fuzzy logic is that it allows us to define values without specifying a precise value which is not possible with classical logic, upon which computer development has been, based so far (Aroba et al., 2007).

Data mining is applied in various fields where hidden information or a pattern is to be extracted or where the data is insufficient. Data mining is of a more explanatory nature, and patterns discovered in a data set are usually of a descriptive rather than of a predictive nature (Hüllermeier, 2005). This provides the scope for application of fuzzy logic in the mining system. Fuzzy logic imparts a skeleton to handle uncertainty. Application of the data mining techniques is a fast emerging trend in the modern world. This amalgamation gives wings to the concept of data mining extending its utility and flexibility.

It is quite discernable that the combination of these two concepts is not uncomplicated. There have to be certain rules and restrictions while applying the concepts of fuzzy sets in data mining systems and vice versa.

The chapter is organized as follows: Section I, presents a brief review of literature on fuzzy data mining. Section II provides a glimpse of all the application areas that have been exploited so far. Section III discusses the need for these critical parameters which essentially elaborates on the problems faced by the application of fuzzy data mining and the facility these parameters can bring. Section IV discusses the research methodology adopted in the formulation of the work. Section V presents the critical parameters for the application of fuzzy data mining. In Section VI discussion is done on the research in this area of fuzzy data mining. It also suggests the prospects of fuzzy data systems in the future while section VII presents the limitations of the study carried out by the authors. Finally, the chapter is concluded in section VIII by urging the researchers to use fuzzy data mining in various business purviews.

BACKGROUND

The concept of data mining was introduced in the late 1980's and since then it has been a blooming field of research. In his work, Kruse et al. (1999) defined, data mining as a set of tasks (Fayyad et al., 1996; Nakhaeizadeh, 1998) which include segmentation, classification, concept description, prediction, deviation analysis, and dependency analysis.

The foundations of fuzzy logic were laid in the year 1965 by Lofti, A. Zadeh. He stated that, "In a narrow sense, fuzzy logic is a logical system which is an extension of multivalued logic and is intended to serve as logic of approximate reasoning but in a wider sense, fuzzy logic is more or less synonymous with the theory of fuzzy sets, that is, a theory of classes with unsharp boundaries" (Zadeh, 1994).

Fuzzy data mining methods denote the approaches to analyze fuzzy data based on the data mining techniques available in order to predict a trend or a pattern from the available fuzzy data (Feil & Abonyi, 2008). The fuzzy logic theory brings a paradigm in work with the graduation, uncertainty and ambiguity described by linguistic expressions derived from the operations of data mining which uses knowledge that does not have clearly defined boundaries.

Research has been done in surfeit in the separate fields of fuzzy logic and data mining, and combination of these two fields is gradually gaining recognition. It was Hüllermeier (2005), who discovered the potential of combining fuzzy sets and data mining techniques. In his work in the year 2005, he stated the potential contributions of fuzzy logic in data mining. Pedrycz in 1998 and Baraldi and Blonda in 1999 independently established that data mining and fuzzy logic can be used to find various patterns only if the data is such that it can be of assistance in formation of such patterns.

Many other discoveries were made related to the application areas of fuzzy data mining which gradually led to certain rules. Au Keith and Chan in 1999 and Simha and Iyengar in 2006 realized that the linguistic variables used in fuzzy should not lose its significance while it is applied in the data mining systems. The data fed in the fuzzy data mining should be such that it should be able to express the results in a human understandable form. Wang, (2010) noticed the disadvantages of association rules, and he proposed another method in which he introduced the concept of multidimensional mining association rules to improve the efficiency of the algorithm. A new fuzzy-genetic analytical model was presented for the problem of project team formation (Strnad & Guid, 2010). Recently, Su et al. (2011) concocted an algorithm which adopted the incremental mining of fuzzy association rules from network traffic, in which membership functions of fuzzy variables were optimized by a genetic algorithm. Kumar (2011) went a step further as he proposed to combine random projections and fuzzy k-means clustering for reducing dimensionality of the data. Chang et al. (2011) presented a fuzzy k-means clustering algorithm using the cluster center displacement between successive iterative processes to reduce the computational complexity of conventional fuzzy *k*-means clustering algorithm. Chen et al. (2012) extended the existing fuzzy mining approach for handling time- series data to find linguistic association rules.

Need of the Critical Parameters

The employment of fuzzy sets and data mining techniques in various systems has proved efficacious due to certain favorable conditions in the input and the desired output which promote their application. Most data mining algorithms require the setting of many input parameters (Keogh et al., 2004). Though it is a risky task of setting parameters for the input variables, it also imposes prejudices and presumptions of the authors on the problem at hand (Keogh et al., 2004). Data mining techniques cannot be applied directly to the resulting data set obtained after the fuzzy set theory, in any scenario. Kim et al. (2000) derived fuzzy control logic with control table approach and stated that, a large part of the parameters defining the fuzzy logic control, should be fixed at an early stage in order to provide flexibility to fuzzy logic control. There are some obstacles to the application of fuzzy data mining. This predicament motivated the authors to conduct a research on identifying the critical parameters for the application of fuzzy data mining. While applying the process of fuzzy data mining, the researchers do not have to apply the process of 'hit and trial' or random guessing, they can simply look upon these pre-defined parameters discussed in this chapter, whether the data set is satisfying these parameters and then based on the results, the researchers can apply the technique of fuzzy data mining. Another need for developing these critical parameters is to understand a problem, gather data and model it.

For successful implementation of fuzzy data mining to various systems, it is essential to understand these parameters which facilitate the application of fuzzy logic and data mining. Identification of these parameters will lead the area of fuzzy data mining gain momentum.

Applications of Fuzzy Data Mining

Previously, application areas of data mining and its techniques have been identified by many researchers across the globe. Bhattacharya and Bhatnagar (2012) classified the applications of fuzzy data mining on the basis of the data mining techniques being used. The application of data mining tools in fuzzy systems is an emerging trend in current world. These techniques are namely association rules, classification and clustering which were further analyzed on the basis of algorithms used in order to implement the concept of fuzzy data mining, for association rule mining, Apriori algorithm is used, for classification, neural method and decision tree are used and lastly for clustering, K-mean clustering and C-mean clustering methods are used (Bhattacharya & Bhatnagar, 2012). To make the representation of data more comprehensible for the user and make the reasoning process more transparent, fuzzy logic is being increasingly applied to various data mining and decision support systems such as in:

- Intrusion detection
- Approximations of missing values
- Power plant optimizations
- Improving water quality
- Hydrocracking
- Resource planning
- Detecting cancer
- Modeling agility in supply chains
- Human resource management by aiding in personnel selection
- Cross-selling
- Cardiac state diagnosis
- Decision making
- Pattern recognition
- Discriminating between faults and switching
- Coffee rust warning
- Finding cavities in insulating materials
- To detect the severity of Scoliosis
- To reduce data dimensionality
- Medical image processing

Determination of the Parameters

Firstly a thorough review of the literature on the application areas of fuzzy data mining was done. Then the applicative areas of the two key fields mentioned in this chapter were analyzed separately. Conditions which induced the application of these two fields were further scrutinized. In other words, the following issues were considered as to why do the use of data mining and fuzzy set theory became indispensable in their respective application areas? What was common to the fields in which fuzzy data mining is applied, such as, the input parameters, the type of databases or the desired output? After inspection, a few factors responsible for their interplay were jotted down on the basis of these applications. Then finally the parameters were listed out of which some made it to the list of critical parameters for the application of fuzzy data mining. Figure 1 describes this process of determining the parameters in a pictorial representation. It shows the two branches of our study namely Data mining and fuzzy logic interweaving and resulting in a new field called fuzzy data mining.

SETTING UP THE CHAPTER

The aim of this study is to understand the critical parameter on basis of which fuzzy logic can be applied to data mining or the vice-versa. The merging of the two concepts namely, fuzzy logic and data mining began in the early 1990's, as a result of which the research in this area is relatively fresh. To accomplish the study, various journals were examined, all of which are related to fuzzy data mining and its application. Due to the novelty and diversity of this area of research, journal articles are scattered across a range of journals, and for that reason, a literature search was conducted using the following electronic databases to provide a comprehensive bibliography regarding the same.

Figure 1. Process of determining the parameters in a pictorial representation

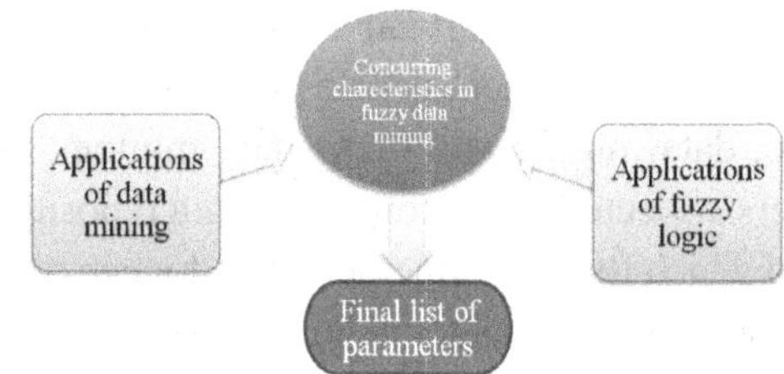

- IEEE
- Springer
- Science Direct
- Wiley
- Emerald Group publisher
- Inderscience
- IGI Global

Every article that was retrieved through the search process was carefully reviewed. This research serves as a comprehensive base for applying the concept of fuzzy data mining. The research methodology expansively involves five steps (see Figure1) which are identifying the scope of the problem and collecting the relevant materials, review and categorizing the papers, recognizing the application areas of fuzzy data mining, identifying the critical parameters from the categorized papers and final evaluation of the papers based on the parameters described by the authors. Initially, both the researchers worked on the problem at hand independently and sorted out as many parameters as possible. If there was any difference in the selection of the two researchers, then the article in question was discussed until an agreement was reached as to whether to include it in the final set of the parameters or not. After this selection process, a total of fourteen parameters were brought into the limelight. This methodology is depicted in a flow diagram presented in Figure 2.

Identifying Scope of the Problem and Collecting Relevant Materials

This is the most basic yet an important step in the research methodology as in this step, the description to the problem in hand was found. It includes downloading and collection of all the relevant and pertinent articles relating to fuzzy logic, data mining and fuzzy data mining. The papers collected were stored in a data repository upon which further refinement was done in order to propose a solution to the problem.

Reviewing and Categorizing the Papers

This is the most time consuming process as it requires extensive study and understanding of each and every paper collected. These papers were then grouped together according to their utility and some other factors. This process facilitates organization and management of the vast pool knowledge which had been gathered after the scope of the problem was decided.

Recognizing the Application Areas of Fuzzy Data Mining

The papers which were categorized were then refined on the basis of the application areas of fuzzy data mining. This allowed the authors to study the parameters which were essential for the application of the same and thus decide the parameters which were quintessential for fuzzy data mining. This also proposed a meaningful question, whether there were some constraints of the data sets in the particular application area which expedites the application of fuzzy sets and data mining in synergy.

Identifying the Critical Parameters from the Categorized Papers

In this step, both the authors worked individually and, extensively studied each and every application area and derived the critical parameters for application of fuzzy data mining. This was a very tedious step which required maximum effort from the authors' perspective.

Final Evaluation of the Chapter Based on the Parameters Described by the Authors

The authors combined their parameters they collected during the previous steps. Any discrepan-

Figure 2. Flow diagram

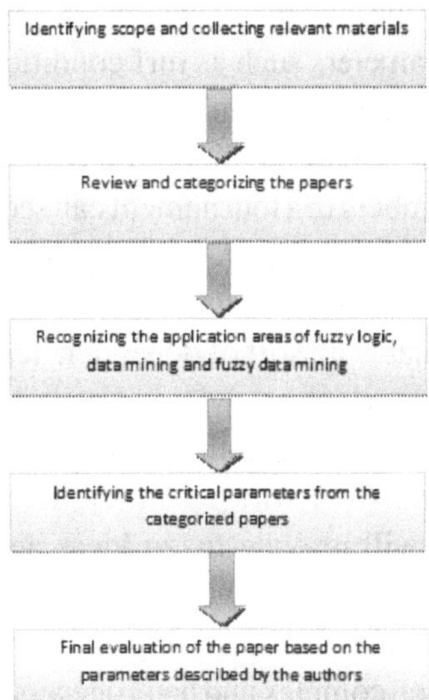

cies among the authors were sorted out during the discussion sessions and in this fashion, the parameters were reduced down to the critical parameters.

CRITICAL PARAMETERS FOR APPLYING FUZZY DATA MINING

There are a number of parameters which are essential for the application of fuzzy data mining in a variety of fields. In a nutshell, these parameters are expressed in Figure 3. The inner most layer is comprised of the fuzzy sets which are surrounded by the various techniques of data mining to depict equal accessibility by each technique to all fuzzy sets. The circular boundary of the diagram depicts of all the parameters which are exhaustive to the application of fuzzy data mining. These parameters are explained in this section.

Uncertainty

The uncertainty is a key parameter for the fuzzy data set. The data needs to be approximated every time whenever there is a need for application of data mining or fuzzy logic. Fuzzy logic is the logic underlying modes of reasoning which are approximate rather than exact, which may be viewed as an extension of classical logical systems, providing an effective conceptual framework for dealing with the problem of knowledge representation in an environment of uncertainty and imprecision (Zadeh, 1989). Data mining predominantly deals with prediction and description. The element of uncertainty is always introduced, where ever there is prediction. Since data mining deals with finding various correlations and patterns, uncertainty is inseparable from data mining. Due to their closeness to human reasoning, solutions obtained using fuzzy approaches are easy to understand and to apply and because of this, fuzzy systems are used, if linguistic, vague, or imprecise information is to be modeled (Kruse et al., 1999). Additionally, the data presented to mining algorithms is imprecise, incomplete or noisy most of the time, a problem that can badly mislead a learning procedure, but even if observations are perfect, the generalization beyond that data, the process of induction, is still afflicted with uncertainty (Hüllermeier, 2005). Data uncertainty is an inherent property in various applications due to reasons such as outdated sources or imprecise measurements and when data mining techniques are applied to these data along with fuzzy systems, their uncertainty has to be considered to obtain high quality results (Chau et al., 2012). The vagueness or uncertainty in data is the key factor which propels the application of fuzzy logic to obtain paramount results, subsequently in its absence the sole purpose of combining fuzzy logic and data mining is rendered useless and may not lead to favorable outcomes.

Heterogeneity

Data is said to be homogenous if properties of one set identical to the data of the other data sets is in the same metric. Partitioning the database into a homogenous groups or clusters is the elementary operation of any data mining algorithm. Homogeneity ensures predictability of data where, data mining is concerned with the analysis of large but homogeneous data (Kruse et al., 1999). Mining of heterogeneous data has posed serious challenges for data mining although it may help disclose high level data regularities in heterogeneous databases (Chen et al., 1996). As different kinds of data and sources may require distinct algorithms and methodologies and there is poor reliability of sources, traditional data mining techniques cannot be used efficiently to mine heterogeneous data. For example, if one is provided with the database of a basketball team, he or she still cannot predict what the outcome would be for the matches in future accurately enough. But the probability of predicting the accuracy would be enhanced if certain parameters such as turf conditions, home ground, injuries and so on, are fed to the data mining system. A basketball team having the same playing numbers in a tournament can score 98 and yet loose a match whereas in the very next match they score 70 and yet win the match. Here, it is observed that is no sort of dependencies between the variables which are winning and scoring and as a consequence data mining cannot be applied to these data sets with accuracy. Even if it is applied, it will provide fuzzy ideas and results. However, modifying the concept of data mining to produce information mining can carry out the operations on complex and heterogeneous sources

Figure 3. Critical parameters for applying fuzzy data mining

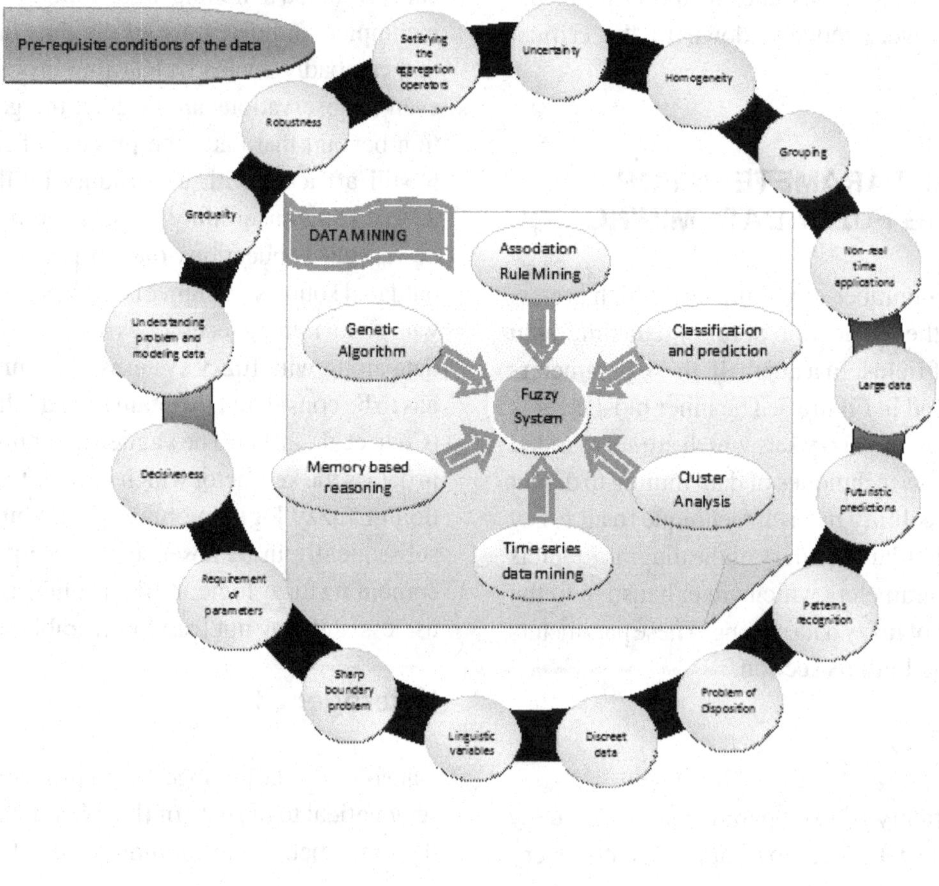

of information (Kruse et al., 1999). Kruse et al. (1999) defined the analysis of heterogeneous information sources with the prominent aim of producing comprehensible results as information mining. Fuzzy set theory means to model the "fuzzy" boundaries of linguistic terms by introducing gradual memberships (Kruse et. al, 1999) is capable to represent miscellaneous data in a synthetic way (Bouchon-Meunier et al., 2007), and its proficiency in handling imperfect, imprecise data makes it a suitable candidate for mining heterogeneous databases. Techniques which belong to the unsupervised learning framework, i.e. they consider that each data point is associated with a category, like fuzzy decision trees and fuzzy prototypes are employed in mining heterogeneous values. Further, techniques like fuzzy clustering which belong to the unsupervised learning framework, i.e. no a priori decomposition of the data set into categories is available, are used to partition large data sets in homogeneous and distinct groups.

Large, Multidimensional and Noisy Data

Keim (2001), claimed that, advanced technology has resulted in the generation of about one million terabytes of information every year in which ninety-nine percent of this is available in digital format from which collecting information is no longer a problem, but extracting value from information collections has become progressively more difficult. Various search engines have been developed to make it easier to locate information of interest, but these works well only for a person who has a specific goal and who understands what and how information is stored, but this is not the case in a data mining application, where the outcome is unknown information, consequently data mining tools can be applied only on those data which have abundant knowledge and from which useful or strategic information can be recovered easily (Keim, 2001). For accurate prediction, the data should be large so that the instability to one data set would not lead to drastic alteration in the result. For example during clustering, more the number of instances better would be the cluster, in association rule, more the number of data sets, more would be the support factor and better would be the accuracy of the algorithm. In today's world with such abound research works going on in parallel, the amount of data is increasing exponentially, in which all the data is not important. Irrelevant attributes are noisy or unimportant and can be removed to reduce the data size for more efficient clustering which reduces the noise and helps in data storage, collection, and processing (Singh et al., 2010). As a result, fuzzy sets are used on large data sets only while working with fuzzy data mining because the fuzzy sets are particularly suitable to model imprecise and noisy data, while association rules are very appropriate to deal with high dimensionality data (Lopez et al., 2009). This requirement of large and multidimensional data set is one of the major requirements for application of fuzzy data mining so as to ensure better accuracy and predictability of data.

Historical Data Considerations

Past data plays an important role in forecasting. The accuracy of forecasts is influenced both by the quality of past data and the method selected to forecast the future (Bouqata et al., 2000). Data mining can facilitate in predicting future values from a given database. The combination of fuzzy logic with data mining can drastically improve the accuracy of the predictions. The if-then rules formed in fuzzy logic by (Sheta, 2006) have vague predicates in their antecedent part while the consequent part is a linear or quadratic combination of the antecedent variables and as the consequent parts of rules are crisp values rather than vague and fuzzy ones, there is no need to defuzzify the output, this characteristic of the objective fuzzy modeling technique favors it over several other fuzzy modeling techniques and is utilized to improve the prediction efficiency (Vaidehi et al., 2008). Fuzzy data mining has its importance in variety of fields in predicting events which are to occur in the future such as breast cancer detection, cardiac state diagnosis, time series prediction and many more. For example various commerce companies require information to predict future trends of the stock market so that they can prepare themselves for the inevitable risks that might come, thereby promoting efficient growth of the organization. The companies require systems that can provide them with strategic information for that. Fuzzy logic has to be applied to these systems in order to remove all the imprecise values as well as to provide with accurate values to all the vague uncertain variables which are then mined with various data mining tools to obtain this tactical knowledge. In order to apply fuzzy logic in data mining systems, the data should contain historical information along with the amalgamation of present data, so as to provide strategic information after the application of fuzzy set theories and data mining techniques.

The Problem of Disposition

Ghosh and Mukhopadhyay (2011) defined disposition as "a proposition which is preponderantly, but not always necessarily, true (Kandel et al., 1985; Zadeh, 1984)." Fuzzy logic is effective when the solutions need not be precise and/or it is acceptable for a conclusion to have a dispositional rather than categorical validity (Zadeh, 1989). A disposition may be viewed as a quantified fuzzy proposition with or without suppression such as most, almost or always almost all (Ghosh & Mukhopadhyay, 2011). Ghosh and Mukhopadhyay (2011) stated that fuzzy logic provides a basis to inference from disposition through the use of fuzzy syllogistic reasoning (Zimmerman, 1985) which is an extension of classical syllogistic reasoning with fuzzy predicates and fuzzy quantifiers. Data mining techniques such as decision trees can be used to deal with the problem of disposition. Data mining in fuzzy systems are applied only if the fuzzy logic can help in deciphering information from the disposition over the data set and this problem of disposition as a result becomes a major parameter in application of fuzzy logic in data mining or vice-versa.

Discrete Data

Fuzzy logic extends the power of expression of traditional two-valued logic, making possible developing real life knowledge-based systems (Ghosh & Mukhopadhyay, 2011). Fuzzy logic cannot be applied over continuous data which are data that change its value with every change per unit time. This is because fuzzy logic can only provide user with precise, well defined and clear-cut values such as either 0 or 1 or 'good' or 'bad' but no intermediate values. Static discrete method cannot follow the change of behavior of the data set, which causes appalling business meaning due to immoderate discrete data and this calls for the adoption of fuzzy clusters to solve this problem and combine subtractive cluster method to improve transaction capability and self-adapt, which overcome the shortage of incorrect hierarchy (Li, 2009). Data mining methods also typically handle discrete data and use symbolic structures, giving results and explanations that may be easier to understand for users but are less suitable for statistical analysis (Onkamo & Toivonen, 2006). Data mining algorithms such as clustering and decision trees are used to predict one or more discrete variables based on other sets of attributes in the databases making it one of the critical parameters for the data to be discrete for the application of fuzzy data mining.

Need for Modeling

Before the process of fuzzy data mining is applied, it is of utmost importance to know the domain upon which work is being done. The first step of any methodology or algorithm is to understand a problem. Once the problem has been apprehended, data needs to be gathered and then finally modeling needs to be done. Fuzzy set-based modeling techniques provide a convenient tool for making expert knowledge accessible to computational methods and hence, to incorporate background knowledge in learning process (Hüllermeier, 2005). According to Kruse et al. (1999),

In addition, background domain and meta knowledge about the data are required to be gathered, in these phases, fuzzy set methods can be used to formulate the background domain knowledge in vague terms, but still in a form that can be used in a subsequent modeling phase. In the data preparation step, the gathered data is cleaned, transformed and maybe properly scaled to produce the input for the modeling techniques. In this step fuzzy methods may, for example, be used to detect outliers, e.g., by fuzzy clustering the data (Bezdek et.al, 1999; Hoppner et.al, 1999) and then finding those data points that are far away from the cluster prototypes. The modeling phase, in which models are constructed from the data in order, for instance, to predict future developments or to build classifiers, can, of course, benefit most from fuzzy data analysis approaches. These approaches can be divided into two classes. In the evaluation phase, the usefulness of fuzzy modeling methods becomes most obvious. Since they yield interpretable systems, they can easily be checked for plausibility against the intuition and expectations of human experts.

Pattern Recognition

The concept of data mining can be intermingled with the concept of fuzzy systems when there is a need of recognizing abstruse patterns or relations from a given set of data but this concept can only be used when the patterns can be extracted from the given data set. This makes pattern recognition another important parameter for application of fuzzy data mining. Futuristic data may or may not be known forehand, and this is where the use of fuzzy systems takes control. Data mining is the application of specific algorithms for extracting understandable patterns from data (Fayyad et al., 1996). Data mining is known as the knowledge discovery of data in which, the use of fuzzy logic can help in providing deft values to entities which are not known. Models or techniques such as association rules, link analysis or affinity analysis are useful in finding patterns between different entities. For instance, in a shop selling shoes, the confidence and support factors calculated by the owner suggests that after buying a leather shoe, the customer probably buys a shoe shiner. This suggests that there is an explicit link or pattern between the leather shoe and the shiner. Such extraction of patterns from the given data set is of utmost importance without which fuzzy data mining cannot be applied fruitfully. Fuzzy models can be said to represent a prudent and user-oriented shifting of data, qualitative observations and calibration of commonsense rules in an attempt to establish meaningful and useful relationships and patterns between system variables (Pedrycz, 1998). A thoughtful integration of neural network and fuzzy theory is one such hybrid paradigm which is most visible that allowed incorporation of advantages of artificial neural networks and fuzzy logic-like massive parallelism, robustness, learning, and handling of uncertainty and impreciseness, into one system.

Use of Linguistic Variables

According to Zadeh (1975), a linguistic variable is a variable whose values are words or sentences in a natural or artificial language. An application of fuzzy systems in data mining is the induction of fuzzy rules in order to interpret the underlying data linguistically and to describe a fuzzy system completely one needs to determine a rule base structure and fuzzy parameters for all variables (Kruse et al., 1999). Many data mining algorithms require the conclusions of rules to be crisp and hence quantitative values cannot be inferred from those rules (Au Keith & Chan, 1999). Although these linguistic descriptions are not precise, they provide important information about the system (Wang, 1995). Temperature can be considered as a linguistic variable if its values provided are 'cold', warm' or 'mild' instead of specifying the numerical values like 27°C or 80°F.The use of linguistic variables provides the ability to allow some interesting patterns to be more easily discovered and expressed but in case of quantitative variables, the resulting intervals are not too meaningful and are hard to understand (Simha & Iyengar, 2006). This allows the rules that are discovered as a result of mining techniques in a database to be presented in such a manner which is very easily understood. Consequently, representation of linguistic variables is one of the prime parameters for application of data mining techniques in fuzzy systems where categorical variables are of more importance.

Sharp Boundary Problem

The sharp boundary problem in binary algorithms deals with the ignorance or overemphasizing the elements near the boundary of the intervals present in the quantitative association rule mining (Verlinde et al., 2006). Clusters and associations do not have crisp boundaries and overlap considerably. In data mining, all the patterns and relations found are not useful and the patterns of interests are often vague and have boundaries that are non-sharp in the sense of fuzzy set theory (Hüllermeier, 2005). For example, in a diving institute in Miami, a gap between 'deep' and 'shallow' depths had been divided. In this database available, it is considered that any depth less than 100 meters as shallow, anything over 100 meters as deep. So 200 meters and 500 meters both come under the category of 'deep', but we cannot have an idea of how much deep they are as compared to each other. This problem is handled using fuzzy logic which designs a membership function for each data set depending upon which problem of sharp boundary problems are resolved. Data sets which show signs of sharp boundary problems can easily be mined with the help of fuzzy sets as they soften the effect of sharp boundaries.

Decisiveness

Data mining is one of the most useful techniques when it comes to taking decisions. Mateou et al. (2005) stated that the best-known representation language for decision problems is the decision tree. The importance of fuzzy logic derives from the fact that there are many real world applications which fit these conditions, especially in the realm of knowledge-based systems for decision-making and control (Zadeh, 1989). The data mining techniques can be applied over the fuzzy systems when the data sets are responsible for taking some decisions. One such mechanism proposed by Mitra et al. (2002) comprised of a judicious integration of the merits of neural and fuzzy approaches, enabling one to build more intelligent decision-making systems. A practical example can be of a company providing loans to its customers. Data mining and fuzzy logic are interleaved to identify customer profiles, his history, his loyalty and his ability to repay the loan. Fuzzy decision trees can be used to plan the course of action by the loan providing companies according to the aptitude of the customer for that reason.

Graduality

The ability to represent gradual concepts and fuzzy properties in a thorough way is one of the key features of fuzzy sets which coincidentally are of primary importance in the context of data mining (Hüllermeier, 2005). Properties such as tall, short, hot, cold or hard are usually vague or fuzzy. Fuzzy logic can then be used to gradually characterize these properties using various logics and algorithm. This avoids any sudden fluctuations in data. In data mining, the patterns of interest are often vague and have boundaries that are non-sharp or vague in the sense of fuzzy logics

(Hüllermeier, 2005). For applying data mining in fuzzy systems, the data should be able to represent itself in a measured or steady manner and is one of the many parameters for applicability of fuzzy data mining.

Robustness

Due to the enormity of the data sets, presence of bad exemplars or outliers, incomplete and noisy data cannot be ruled out. Typical data mining algorithms do not take this issue into account. This makes the data mining systems susceptible to fragileness and flabbiness. As fuzzy sets present a more human understandable form because of the linguistic terms used, the process becomes more intuitive. For example, there is a clear distinction between the ages as 'old' and 'young', anyone who is greater than 60 years of age can be considered as old. As a result, a child of 12 years and a man of 55 years both are considered to be young. But according to human perception, this might be different for different viewers. This distinction between young and old is made intuitively than figuratively. This error can be decimated using fuzzy set so as to provide the hybrid concept of fuzzy mining rules. Fuzzy sets are known to provide natural, vague boundaries. Due to these inherent properties of fuzzy set theory, the fuzzy systems are considered to be more robust than the non fuzzy systems. Fuzzy logic is very useful in this matter because of its capability to represent miscellaneous data in a synthetic way, its robustness with regard to changes of the parameters of the user's environment, and obviously its unique expressiveness. Many robust mining algorithms have been developed which are insensitive to noise and outliers in data. It is clear that for the new class of applications of data mining, several new challenges exist that will demand the development of new techniques for robust fuzzy clustering as well as other fuzzy data mining techniques that can handle noisy, uncertain, vague, and incomplete information (Joshi & Krishnapuram, 1998). Subsequently, for applying data mining over fuzzy systems the appropriate degree of robustness of data should be taken into consideration.

Satisfying the Aggregation Operators

Most data mining techniques make use of the aggregation operators. Aggregation operators are useful in situations when all the information handled is not equally significant. It makes use of fuzzy linguistic and weighted variables. Most common aggregation method is the ordered weighted averaging operator introduced by Yager (1988), which provided a parameterized family of aggregation operators that includes, special cases as the maximum, the minimum and the average criteria but this operator could only be used with the assumption that the available information is in exact numbers or in singletons, but this may not be the real situation found in the decision making problem (Jose & Casanovas, 2012). The available information is vague or imprecise and it is not possible to analyze it with exact numbers and as a result, it is necessary to use another approach that is able to assess the uncertainty such as the use of fuzzy numbers with which the best and worst possible scenario and the possibility that the internal values of the fuzzy interval will occur can be analyzed (Jose & Casanovas, 2012). The basic use of these operators is to make the systems more flexible and therefore for enhancing the utility of the system, the data set should support the generalized aggregation operators to render its applicability in fuzzy data mining. In one such prevalent scenario, fuzzy aggregation operators are used along with clustering to evaluate military system performance.

DISCUSSION AND RESEARCH IMPLICATIONS

In various fields, when it is desired to discover hidden and predictive information from the real data set, the use of fuzzy data mining comes in the frame. This is evident from our chapter which revealed that fuzzy logic and data mining go hand in hand and complement each other in many possible ways. Various scenarios occur where the need of data mining arises in presence of uncertainty in data. In this situation fuzzy logic might be applied to enhance the accuracy. The research in the field of data mining is now at mature stage and inclusion of fuzzy set theory in it will create new areas of research and will definitely help the common man and society. The important aspect of this research is that it provides us with various dimensions which need to be considered in order to implement fuzzy data mining. This might aid future researchers in discovering further applicative areas which are not confined to the fields mentioned earlier in the chapter. Another aspect where the researches can further work upon is the application of fuzzy data mining in real time applications and upon heterogeneous data. Where fuzzy decision trees can be handle heterogeneous data, fuzzy clustering cannot be used in the same. Researches can concoct algorithms and procedures regarding the same.

LIMITATIONS OF THE STUDY

The study on any topic will always encounter some limitations which are hurdles for a quality research work. All the work mentioned in the chapter is derived from collected work of eminent researchers in the field but could also lead to various scalability issues such as:

- The main constraint of fuzzy data mining is that it cannot be feasibly or effectively be applied to real time systems. In real-time control applications, devices such as programmable logic controllers and loop controllers are commonly used, which do not usually possess an additional function of the fuzzy logic control but if these devices possess a function of fuzzy logic control, it will be very helpful for wider applications (Kim et al., 2012). General fuzzy logic control has a long computation time as it performs fuzzification, inference, and defuzzification processes in determining control inputs and it is difficult for control inputs of general fuzzy logic control to be computed within the sampling time of any real time application which generally strive for good average case performance (Kim et al., 2012). Since databases upon which the data mining algorithms are to be applied has a huge number of data sets the computational time would be enormous which cannot be predicted beforehand. The time to compute the response may or may not be known in advance, whereas for execution of real time systems it is very important to specify the time domain of the operation. Owing to these restrictions, fuzzy data mining cannot be used directly in any real time applications.
- The extent of the search for the various articles pertaining to fuzzy data mining was confined to a few publishers which can be considered to be the prime limitation of our research. However, although this means that the review is not exhaustive but it is believed to be comprehensive.
- All the parameters need not be satisfied for the application of fuzzy data mining. It will vary from application to application.
- All non-English publications were excluded in this study. But it is believed that research regarding the same has also been discussed and published in other languages as well.
- Use of specific algorithm for specific data set will vary and will give different result and accuracy.

CONCLUSION AND FUTURE RESEARCH

The application of data mining in fuzzy systems in the various business areas is an emerging trend in the many modern industries. It is observed that fuzzy data mining is easily understood and more robust. From the above discussion, it is obvious that substantial potential contributions have already been made. Fuzzy data mining has drawn the attention of various academicians and researchers to carry quality and innovative research. The parameters stated by the authors will provide a stepping stone for new research in the field of fuzzy data mining and will help in developing an efficient business system. In this work, the authors have identified certain thumb rules which are required for the application of fuzzy data mining. The practitioners will be able to use this work as an analogy for implementing the same in their setup as per business requirement for effective and better business prospects. Though, it is also thought that much scope for further development is yet to be made and for that, it is assumed that this chapter is essential for the researchers. Some of the future researches that can be done are:

- Various new and different fuzzy data mining applications can be discovered and put into practice.
- The already applicative areas of fuzzy data mining can have upgraded results by better accuracy and robustness.
- Not only the results are upgraded, and improved methodology can be adopted by comparing various techniques.
- This chapter would aid in burgeoning the applicative areas of fuzzy data mining concurrently improving the efficiency and mitigating all the ambiguities regarding the same.

REFERENCES

Arroba, J., Grande, J. A., Andujar, J. M., De La Torre, M. L., & Riquelme, J. C. (2007). Application of fuzzy logic and data mining techniques as tools for qualitative interpretation of acid mine drainage processes. *Environmental Geology*, *53*(1), 135–145. doi:10.1007/s00254-006-0627-0.

Au Keith, W. H., & Chan, C. C. (1999). FARM: A data mining system for discovering fuzzy association rules. *Fuzzy Systems Conference Proceedings, 1999. FUZZ-IEEE '99*, 3, 1217-1222.

Baraldi, A., & Blonda, P. (1999). A survey of fuzzy clustering algorithms for pattern recognition—Part I. *IEEE Transactions on Systems, Man, and Cybernetics. Part B, Cybernetics*, *29*(6), 778–785. doi:10.1109/3477.809032.

Bezdek, J. C., Keller, J. M., Krishnapuram, R., & Pal, N. (1999). *Fuzzy models and algorithms for pattern recognition and image processing. The Handbooks on Fuzzy Sets*. Dordrecht, Netherlands: Kluwer.

Bhattacharya, S., & Bhatnagar, V. (2012). Fuzzy data mining: A literature survey and classification framework. *International Journal of Networking and Virtual Organisations*, *11*(3/4), 382–408. doi:10.1504/IJNVO.2012.048925.

Bouchon-Meunier, B., Detyniecki, M., Lesot, M. J., Marsala, C., & Rifqi, M. (2007). Real-World Fuzzy Logic Applications in Data Mining and Information Retrieval. Fuzzy Logic. *Studies in Fuzziness and Soft Computing*, *215*, 219–247. doi:10.1007/978-3-540-71258-9_11.

Bouqata, B., Bensaid, A., Palliam, R., & Gomez Skarmeta, A. F. (2000). Time series prediction using crisp and fuzzy neural networks: A comparative study. *Computational Intelligence for Financial Engineering, 2000. (CIFEr), Proceedings of the IEEE/IAFE/INFORMS 2000 Conference*, 170-173.

Chang, C. T., Lai, J. Z. C., & Jeng, M. D. (2011). A fuzzy k-means clustering algorithm using cluster center displacement. *Journal of Information Science and Engineering*, *27*(3), 995–1009.

Chau, M., Cheng, R., Kao, B., & Ng, J. (2012). *Uncertain data mining: An example in clustering location data*. Retrieved January 13, 2012, from http://www.techrepublic.com/whitepapers/uncertain-data-mining-an-example-in-clustering-location-data/386583

Chen, C. H., Hong, T. P., & Tseng, V. S. (2012). Fuzzy data mining for time-series data. *Applied Soft Computing*, *12*(1), 536–542. doi:10.1016/j.asoc.2011.08.006.

Chen, M. S., Han, J., & Yu, P. S. (1996). Data mining: An overview from a database perspective. *IEEE Transactions on Knowledge and Data Engineering*, *8*(6), 866–883. doi:10.1109/69.553155.

Fayyad, U., Piatetsky-Shapiro, G., & Smyth, P. (1996). From data mining to knowledge discovery in databases. *AI Magazine*, *17*(3), 37–54.

Fayyad, U., Piatetsky-Shapiro, G., Smyth, P., & Uthurusamy, R. (1996). *Advances in knowledge discovery and data mining*. MIT Press.

Feil, B., & Abonyi, J. (2008). *Introduction to fuzzy data mining methods*. Retrieved November 30, 2011, from http://www.igi-global.com/viewtitlesample.aspx?id=20349

Ghosh, J., & Mukhopadhyay, S. (2011). Studies on fuzzy logic and dispositions for medical diagnosis. *International Journal Computer Technology and Applications*, *2*(5), 1235–1240.

Hand, D., Mannila, H., & Smyth, P. (2001). *Principles of data mining*. MIT Press.

Hoppner, F., Klawonn, F., Kruse, R., & Runkler, T. (1999). *Fuzzy cluster analysis*. J. Wiley & Sons.

Hüllermeier, E. (2005). Fuzzy methods in machine learning and data mining: Status and prospects. *Fuzzy Sets and Systems*, *156*(3), 387–406. doi:10.1016/j.fss.2005.05.036.

Jose, M. M., & Casanovas, M. (2012). *Generalized aggregation operators and fuzzy numbers in a unified model between the weighted average and the OWA operator*. Retrieved May 15, 2012, from http://gandalf.fcee.urv.es/sigef/english/congressos/congres15/039_Merigo_Casanovas.pdf

Joshi, A., & Krishnapuram, R. (1998). Robust fuzzy clustering methods to support web mining. In *Proc. Workshop in Data Mining and Knowledge Discovery, SIGMOD*, 1998, 15, 1-8.

Kandel, A., Gupta, M. M., Bandler, W., & Kıszka, J. B. (1985). Approximate reasoning. [Elsevier.]. *Expert Systems: International Journal of Knowledge Engineering and Neural Networks*, 745–765.

Keim, D. A. (2001). Visual exploration of large data sets. *Communications of the ACM*, *44*(8), 39–44. doi:10.1145/381641.381656.

Keogh, E., Lonardi, S., & Ratanamahatana, C. A. (2004). Towards parameter-free data mining. In *Proceedings of the 10th International Conference on Knowledge Discovery and Data Mining (KDD'04)* (pp. 206-215). ACM Press.

Kim, Y. H., Ahn, S. C., & Kwon, W. H. (2000). Computational complexity of general fuzzy logic control and its simplification for a loop controller. *Fuzzy Sets and Systems*, *111*(2), 215–224. doi:10.1016/S0165-0114(97)00409-0.

Kruse, R., Borgelt, C., & Nauck, D. (1999). Fuzzy data analysis: Challenges and perspectives. *Proc. 8th IEEE International Conference on Fuzzy Systems (FUZZ-IEEE'99, Seoul, Korea)*. IEEE Press.

Kruse, R., Nauck, D., & Borgelt, C. (1999). *Data mining with fuzzy methods: Status and perspectives*. Retrieved December 1, 2011, from http://borgelt.net/papers/dm_fuzzy.pdf

Kumar, A. (2011). Reducing data dimensionality using random projections and fuzzy k-means clustering. *International Journal of Intelligent Computing and Cybernetics*, *4*(3), 353–365. doi:10.1108/17563781111160020.

Li, Q. (2009). An algorithm of quantitative association rule on fuzzy clustering with application to cross-selling in telecom industry. *Computational Sciences and Optimization, 2009. CSO 2009. International Joint Conference*, 1, 759-762.

Lopez, J. F., Cuadros, M., Blanco, A., & Concha, A. (2009). Unveiling fuzzy associations between breast cancer prognostic factors and gene expression data. *Database and Expert Systems Application, 2009. DEXA '09. 20th International Workshop*, 338-342.

Mateou, N. H., Hadjiprokopis, A. P., & Andreou, A. S. (2005). Fuzzy influence diagrams: An alternative approach to decision making under uncertainty. *Computational Intelligence for Modelling, Control and Automation, 2005 and International Conference on Intelligent Agents, Web Technologies and Internet Commerce* (1, pp. 58–64).

Mitra, S., Pal, S. K., & Mitra, P. (2002). Data mining in soft computing framework: A survey. *IEEE Transactions on Neural Networks*, *13*(1), 3–14. doi:10.1109/72.977258 PMID:18244404.

Nakhaeizadeh, G. (1998). *Knowledge discovery in databases and data mining. An overview in data mining: Theoretical aspects and applications.* Heidelberg: Physica-Verlag.

Onkamo, P., & Toivonen, H. (2006). A survey of data mining methods for linkage disequilibrium mapping. *Human Genomics*, *2*(5), 336–340. doi:10.1186/1479-7364-2-5-336 PMID:16595078.

Pedrycz, W. (1998). Fuzzy set technology in knowledge discovery. *Fuzzy Sets and Systems*, *98*(3), 279–290. doi:10.1016/S0165-0114(96)00377-6.

Ranjan, J. (2008). Data mining techniques for better decisions in human resource management systems. *International Journal of Business Information Systems*, *3*(5), 464–481. doi:10.1504/IJBIS.2008.018597.

Sheta, A. (2006). Software effort estimation and stock market prediction using takagi-sugeno fuzzy models. *IEEE International Conference on Fuzzy System*, pp. 171-178.

Simha, J. B., & Iyengar, S. S. (2006). Fuzzy data mining for customer loyalty analysis. *Information Technology, 2006.ICIT '06. 9th International Conference*, pp. 245–246.

Singh, P. K., Rajput, D. S., & Bhattacharya, M. (2010). An efficient dimension reduction and optimal cluster center initialization technique. *Computational Intelligence and Communication Networks (CICN), 2010 International Conference*, pp. 503–508.

Strnad, D., & Guid, N. (2010). A fuzzy-genetic decision support system for project team formation. *Applied Soft Computing*, *10*(4), 1178–1187. doi:10.1016/j.asoc.2009.08.032.

Su, M. Y., Lin, C. Y., Chien, S. W., & Hsu, H. C. (2011). Genetic-fuzzy association rules for network intrusion detection systems. *Fuzzy Systems (FUZZ), 2011 IEEE International Conference*, 2046–2052.

Vaidehi, V., Monica, S., Mohamed Sheik, S., Deepika, M., & Sangeetha, S. (2008). A prediction system based on fuzzy logic. *Proceedings of the World Congress on Engineering and Computer Science 2008 WCECS 2008.*

Verlinde, H., De Cock, M., & Boute, R. (2006). Fuzzy versus quantitative association rules: A fair data-driven comparison. *IEEE Transactions on Systems, Man, and cybernatics—Part-B. Cybernatics*, *36*(3), 679–684.

Wang, F. (2010). Application of multidimensional association rule techniques in manufacturing resource planning system. *Fuzzy Systems and Knowledge Discovery (FSKD), 2010 Seventh International Conference,* 3, 1433–1437.

Wang, L. X. (1995). Design and analysis of fuzzy identifiers of nonlinear dynamic systems. *IEEE Transactions on Automatic Control, 40*(1), 11–23. doi:10.1109/9.362903.

Yager, R. R. (1988). On ordered weighted averaging aggregation operators in multi-criteria decision making. *IEEE Transactions on Systems, Man and Cybernetics. Part: B, 18,* 183–190.

Zadeh, L. A. (1975). The concept of a linguistic variable and its application to approximate reasoning-I. *Information Sciences, 8*(3), 199–249. doi:10.1016/0020-0255(75)90036-5.

Zadeh, L. A. (1984). A computational theory of dispositions. *Proceedings of the 22nd annual meeting on Association for Computational Linguistics*, pp. 312-318.

Zadeh, L. A. (1984). Making computers think like people. *IEEE Spectrum Magazine, 8,* 26–32.

Zadeh, L. A. (1989). Knowledge representation in fuzzy logic. *IEEE Transactions on Knowledge and Data Engineering, 1*(1), 89–100. doi:10.1109/69.43406.

Zadeh, L. A. (1994). Fuzzy logic: Issues, contentions and perspectives. *Acoustics, Speech, and Signal Processing, 1994. ICASSP-94., 1994 IEEE International Conference*, 6, 183.

Zimmerman, H. J. (1985). *Fuzzy set theory and its applications*. Boston: Kluwer Nijhoff Publishing.

FURTHER READING

Bhattacharya, S., & Bhatnagar, V. (2012). Fuzzy data mining: A literature survey and classification framework. *International Journal of Networking and Virtual Organisations, 11*(3/4), 382–408. doi:10.1504/IJNVO.2012.048925.

Hüllermeier, E. (2005). Fuzzy methods in machine learning and data mining: Status and prospects. *Fuzzy Sets and Systems, 156*(3), 387–406. doi:10.1016/j.fss.2005.05.036.

Kruse, R., Nauck, D., & Borgelt, C. (1999). *Data mining with fuzzy methods: Status and perspectives*. Retrieved December 1, 2011, from http://borgelt.net/papers/dm_fuzzy.pdf

Nakhaeizadeh, G. (1998). *Knowledge discovery in databases and data mining. An overview in data mining: Theoretical aspects and applications* (pp. 1–33). Heidelberg, Germany: Physica-Verlag.

Zadeh, L. A. (1975). The concept of a linguistic variable and its application to approximate reasoning-I. *Information Sciences, 8*(3), 199–249. doi:10.1016/0020-0255(75)90036-5.

Zadeh, L. A. (1984). Making computers think like people. *IEEE Spectrum Magazine, 8,* 26–32.

KEY TERMS AND DEFINITIONS

Data Mining: Data mining is a descriptive analysis of finding patterns and other relationships among data. There are several techniques of implementing the same such as association rule mining, clustering, classification, genetic algorithm, time series data mining and so on.

Fuzzy Data Mining: This concept combines fuzzy logic and the data mining process. This technique includes mining techniques which are fuzzy as well. The chief advantage of using this technique is that it enhances the flexibility and the utility of both the mentioned topics.

Fuzzy Sets: These are a set of conventions of if-then rules which are implemented to predict uncertain values. Fuzzy logic enables user friendly results and outputs which can be understood by all.

Heterogeneous Databases: These databases not only have predictable data but also operation time on these databases cannot be calculated. Owing to these properties simple data mining techniques cannot be applied to these databases. It is hence combined with fuzzy logic or other options available to mine the heterogeneous data.

Linguistic Variables: Linguistic variables represent crisp information in a form and precision appropriate for the problem which is in human understandable form. These are used in daily ordinary conversations. These variables allow for a more descriptive way of understanding the data.

Parameters: These are the characteristics or properties of an element that defines a system and determine its behavior and are varied in an experiment. Usually parameters limit the boundaries and guidelines.

Sharp Boundaries: It is an anomaly face while using the techniques of data mining in which one tends to over- or under- emphasize the data values near the boundaries.

Chapter 12
New Trends in Fuzzy Clustering

Zekâi Şen
Istanbul Technical University, Turkey

ABSTRACT

Fuzzy methodologies show progress day by day towards better explanation of various natural, social, engineering and information problem solutions in the best, economic, fast and effective manner. This chapter provides cluster analyses from probabilistic, statistical and especially fuzzy methodology points of view by consideration of various classical and innovative cluster modeling and inference systems. After the conceptual assessment explanation of fuzzy logic thinking fundamentals various clustering methodologies are presented with brief revisions but innovative trend analyses as k-mean-standard deviation, cluster regression, relative clustering for depiction of trend components that fall within different clusters. The application of fuzzy clustering methodology is presented for lake time series and earthquake modeling for rapid hazard assessment of existing buildings.

INTRODUCTION

Our social deeds including economy, administration, management, engineering, medicine and science take place in complex world where complexity arises from uncertainty in the form of ambiguity, vagueness, incompleteness, skepticism, blurriness, etc. Complexity and ambiguity are ubiquitous features that dominate most social, economic and even technical problems. The most effective way for computers to deal with complex and ambiguous issues is through fuzzy logical (FL) system analyses, which affect many disciplines and provide technological developments in diverse areas, especially in the intelligent industrial manufacture productions. The number of fuzzy consumer products and FL applications involving new patents are increasing rapidly.

It is the main goal of this chapter to introduce first briefly basic conceptual requirements for FL reasoning, systems, control and problem solving through clustering techniques. Clustering approaches have many interests among qualitative and quantitative studies by scientists for description, identification and prediction purposes. Visual inspection of low dimensional data (2D or

DOI: 10.4018/978-1-4666-4213-3.ch012

Copyright © 2013, IGI Global. Copying or distributing in print or electronic forms without written permission of IGI Global is prohibited.

3D) gives qualitative and subjective impressions about the clustering leading to linguistic, fuzzy numerical or qualitative inferences.

This chapter will try to present the fundamental principles of trend analysis through uncertainty methods and especially fuzzy approaches with several applications.

Preliminary content can be summarized with the following sayings in a rough framework, which may also be elaborated under the light of explanations later in the chapter.

All traditional logic habitually assumes that precise symbols are being employed. It is, therefore, not applicable to this terrestrial life but only to an imagined celestial existence (Russell, 1948).

As the complexity of a system increases, our ability to make precise and yet significant statements about its behavior diminishes until a threshold is reached beyond which precision and significance (or relevance) become almost mutually exclusive characteristics (Zadeh, 1973).

UNCERTAINTY, IMPRECISION AND FUZZINESS

As far as the process of revealing "nature's best secrets" never stops, what "we think we knew" yesterday inevitably changes today, and new vistas "whose splendor we had not even come close to imagining" constantly open to those who are thirsty for knowing. The fuzziness of knowing never ceases to exist. This is a paramount characteristic of the human knowing, which challenges humanity and constantly propels its search for truth and understanding the secrets of reality (Dimitrov, 2000).

There is not even a single event that does not include uncertainty due to our ignorance, vagueness, imprecision and chance of occurrence. Uncertainty and imprecision were digested in the logical reasoning of early philosophers and rational thinkers without mathematical formulations. Observations were the prime sources of information, and accordingly, philosophers deduced rational statements about the phenomenon concerned. A set of assumptions helped to eliminate uncertainties. It is possible to summarize the early studies as having their foundations on philosophical and linguistic logical bases.

Today almost in all branches of science, there are uncertainty ingredients and many scientific deterministic foundations take into consideration uncertainty and fuzzy ingredients. With the advancement of numerical uncertainty techniques such as probability, statistics and stochastic principles scientific progresses even in qualitative sciences (geology, sociology, physiology, etc.) had rapid developments, but still leaving aside the linguistic (verbal) data sources and information, which can be tackled by the FL principles only.

Any natural, social, economic and political phenomena have certain and uncertain information, which can be considered fewer than two types as random and fuzzy (imprecise, vague) (see Figure 1).

Figure 1. Information parts

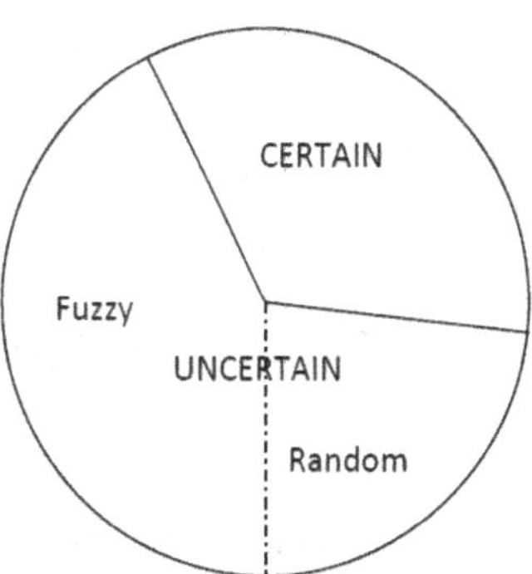

Uncertainty training enables one with FL principles, which are not easy to forget and fuzzy rules are the bases of any systematic algorithm, equation, formulation or software. Fuzzy sets provide a mathematical formalism to represent vagueness in humanistic expert views and inferences. For instance, an experienced staff can warn the local people against flood inundation risk either when the rainfall intensity reaches 110 mm per hour or when rainfall intensity becomes 'close' to this figure. In the first advice, there is a crisp and exact order, but the second alternative provides more freedom to different staff members, because it has fuzziness. Vague terms and imprecise information are used in order to deal with situations of risk (or chance), where probability principles are warranted (Şen, 2011a). The uncertainty of information is indicated in the 'confidence' component. It relates the 'truth' or conformity to reality. Qualifiers such as 'probable' and 'possible' can describe uncertainty as, 'necessary,' 'plausible,' 'credible,' and 'likely' as described by Dubois and Prade (1988).

Mathematical implications based on mental thinking processes might seem exact, but at each stage of modeling there are uncertain ingradients, if not in the macro scale, at least in the micro scales. It is clear today that conceptualization and idealization leading to satisfactory mathematical structure of any physical actualitiy are often an unrealistic requirement. As Einstein stated:

So far as the law of mathematics refer to reality, they are not certain. And so far as they are certain, they do not refer to reality.

SETS AND SYSTEM MODELING

At the very elementary stages of mental thinking, objects are thought as members or non-members of physically plausible clusters. This brings into consideration sets, which include possible outcomes of the phenomenon concerned. In formal sciences such as physics, earth sciences, etc., invariably and automatically, objects are considered as either completely members of the set or outside the same set. The crisp (two-valued) logic clusters elements into either 1 or 0; + or -; yes or no; black or white; etc. groups. Crisp logic (CL) categorizes everything into two mutually exclusive clusters, which are numerically represented by 1 and 0. Zadeh (1965) suggested that instead of crisp clustering why not consider membership degrees between 0 and 1, inclusively. Hence, fuzzy sets take the role of crisp sets, which play plausible philosophical basis at every stage of the mental activity.

Complex interactions among the natural phenomena give rise to spatial and temporal evolutions, which must be tackled in a scientific manner so as to render the consequences into beneficial forms for human activities. In general, future predictions are based on the historical observations with the assumption that they will be repeated indistinguishably on the same pattern in future, but this assumption has several drawbacks.

1. The historical records will not reappear in the same sequence in future,
2. The statistical correlation structure will not have the same pattern,
3. The magnitude of the extreme past values will not be the same in the future.

After 1950s with the use of computers simple modeling ideas became more involved by generation of statistically indistinguishable replicates from the historical records through random number generators. Later stochastic process modeling has become fashionable among researchers (Box & Jenkins, 1970). A system modeling has three components as input and output; and in-between the converter of the inputs into outputs, which is called the inference engine (system) (see Figure 2).

In general, there are three types of system modeling as prediction, identification and filtration as shown in Figure 3 (Gelb, 1974). If two of

Figure 2. Simple model components

the components are known then the third one can be obtained by a convenient modeling such as the fuzzy methodology. The literature is full of analytic, probabilistic, statistical, and stochastic or empiric crisp logic approaches. For the system identification, since the last three decades expert systems including FL modeling started to take place effectively.

Many modeling studies in different disciplines (physics, engineering, chemistry; atmospheric, earth, astronomic, social sciences; medicine and economy) are for predictions. Such a system modeling needs knowledge about the input variable data with inference engine so that the output can be predicted (Figure 3a). Another frequently useful modeling technique is the identification where the search is for inference engine, which translates inputs into output (Figure 3b). The least necessary alternative of system modeling is the smoothing procedure where inference engine and output information are known in search for input features. As for the identification many deterministic (analytical) and uncertainty (probability, statistics, stochastic, chaos) approaches are used for many decades. If the real mechanism is not cared for in the model of Figure 2, then it is called as "black-box" modeling based on the CL. The major key for "gray-box" modeling goes through the FL principles and rules, where linguistically the relationship between the input and output variable can be expressed in terms of logical propositions, which constitute the fuzzy rule base.

For any successful modeling the following implementations must be taken into consideration.

1. General behavior of the phenomenon considered must be explained from different angles first in linguistic terms (philosophical level), which indicate the significance of verbal knowledge and information in the planning and preliminary solution of the problem,
2. The causative (input) effects on the problem must be identified with all detail and verbal attachments to each variable. These verbal information must be categorized into different clusters mentally in the best possible manner according their significance,
3. Among the causative effects, a single variable of interest is depicted as the subject of the problem, and hence, its relationship is searched with the object (output) variable. It may be very helpful first to consider crisp logical relationships between these variables. Even though the relationships might be very primitive, it may indicate direct or inverse proportionalities in addition to existing cluster structures in the input and output variables. Such considerations provide initial logical propositions in a rather fuzzy but useful manner,
4. Each variable may be clustered (Sub-categorization) preferably into three or more classes. This is the stage where the variable names are attached with suitable adjectives, such as "low," "medium" and "high" or alike. In this manner, each variable is rendered into fuzzy variable with various sub-categories (clusters),
5. Logical propositions include premises among the sub-categories of causative (subject) variables, and subsequently, each one of the premises is attached with sensible, rational and logical consequent parts (clusters) of the object (output) variable. In this manner, the linguistic structure of innovative FL principles is complete.

Three most important stages in human thinking, namely, imagination, description and generation help to provide a sound basis for the scientific studies, and especially, fuzzy conceptions about

Figure 3. Different uncertainty problems a) prediction, b) identification, c) filtration

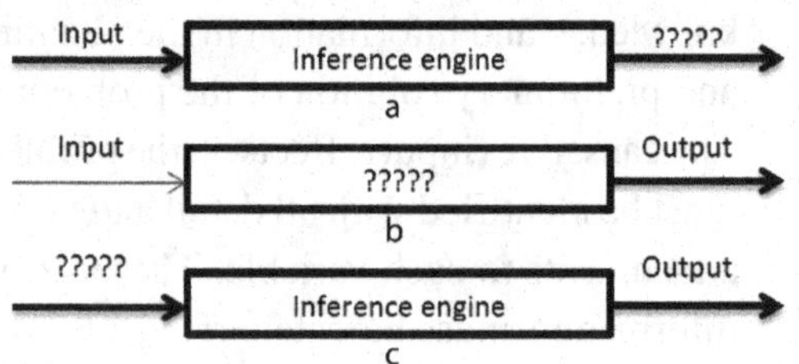

the event logical basis. The relations among stages are not crisply and objectively definable, but vary from individual to others even though different ideas, views and thoughts may overlap, and may have fuzzy relationships. These stages play significant role in the foundation of rational reasoning that leads to FL principles and inferences. The outcome of each stage appears either as silent or loud linguistic expressions, which include knowledge, information and logical statements. The verbal (linguistic) identification and categorization of the statements help to establish the basis of the FL approach more than any other methodology. In order to introduce someone with the basic philosophical principles, generation of verbal knowledge and information these stages must be understood and applied properly in any problem solution. In the scientific philosophical thinking and for technological achievements the three essential steps are shown in Figure 4. Especially, the imagination part is essentially significant, because it provides complete freedom in thinking.

Although initially subjectivity plays dominant role at the imagination stage but as one enters the description domain, the subjectivities decrease and at the final stage since the ideas are exposed to other individuals for criticism, the objectivity starts to take over with reduced uncertainty (vagueness, incompleteness, missing information, etc.) including also fuzzy contents. On the other hand, in the classical and mechanical approaches uncertainty and fuzzy contents are deleted artificially by idealizations, isolations, simplifications and assumptions.

LOGICAL CONCEPTS

Logic is the most essential element in different disciplines as the study of truth. It helps to end up with inferential rational conclusions based on clusters of available knowledge and information. Logic also tries to systemize the rules of thought and it is essentially concerned with language. Language has a variety of uses, such as to express emotions, to give commands, and to ask questions. It is the most effective means to convey information.

In rational thinking and inferences whatever are the linguistic or numerical data, knowledge and information sources cannot lead to valid deductions without logical principles. The fundamentals of inference mechanisms are linguistic and logical rule sets that relate input information to output as in Figure 2. In any study linguistic relationship search must occupy the first stage prior to crisp formulations or rules. Logic has five frequently used words that are ignored by many researches, especially in numerically based disciplines such as engineering, whereas without these words even the crisp formulations and equations cannot have

Figure 4. Reasoning stages

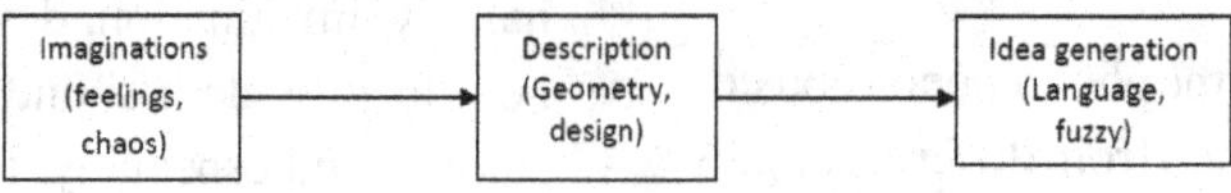

meaningful interpretations and proper uses. These five words are "AND," "NOT," "OR," "IF," and "IF AND ONLY IF," which are referred to collectively as "logical connectives."

Crisp Logic (CL)

Each word has uncertainty ingredient in terms of etymology and epistemology in the forms of fuzziness. Since propositions and logical inferences are composition of words, they also include vagueness and uncertainty which are reflections of thinking, understanding, and explanations. Any inference cannot be absolutely true or false. However, whatever the uncertainty types are, they are rounded artificially to crisp truth or falsity. This is the basic of CL with two alternatives, without any place in the middle; therefore it is also referred to as the exclusion of the middle logic. This CL categorizes logical inferences into two mutually exclusive crisp clusters as "true" and "false." In this manner all skepticism, vagueness and uncertainty are driven outside the thinking domain. This way of classification excludes middle cases, which are cared for in the FL principles. CL is holistic, deductive and tries to separate the whole into meaningful and relational connections. For instance, one may deduce the relationship between rainfall and runoff as directly proportional and even may give its graphical form as in Figure 5.

In this graph, both variables "rainfall" and "runoff" are holistic, and hence the CL seeks for relationships without and specific distinction in the variability domain. The relationship in Figure 5 is valid whatever the clusters whether "small," "medium" or "high." In the FL concept such clusters play dominant roles in search for relationship through a set of reliable logical rules. The CL depends on the "Law of the Excluded Middle." Is the statement 'the traffic is good' completely true or completely false? Probably neither of them is true or false. How about the traffic density? This can be true or false, but how about traffic on most of the routes? Or the road conditions are poor?

Fuzzy Logic (FL)

As explained before the CL relies on something as either true or false, where mutually exclusiveness property is relevant for clustering or sets, which are crisp in the sense that each element within the cluster or set has equal degree of belongingness or non-belongingness.

The FL broadens the definition of sets by considering different belongingness values, which are referred to as the membership degrees (MD) and they are collectively called as the membership functions (MF) (Zadeh, 1965). Such sets are fuzzy, where an object is allowed to belong partially to many sets with MDs between 0 and 1 inclusively. For instance, an element can have a MD of 0.3, which implies that it belongs to that set partially at 30% level. Unlike CL, which requires a deep but certain understanding of a system through exact equations and precise numeric values, FL incorporates an alternative way of thinking, which allows complex system modeling using a higher level abstraction originating from relevant real knowledge and experience.

FL offers a better way of representing reality. It also allows expression of this knowledge with subjective multiple clusters such as 'small,' 'bright red,' and 'long time.'

The FL will attribute degrees even to scientific beliefs (degree of verification or falsification) that assume values between 0 and 1, inclusively. Verifiability of scientific knowledge or theories by

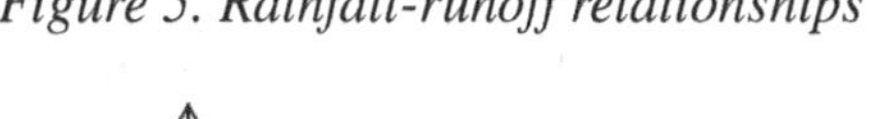

Figure 5. Rainfall-runoff relationships

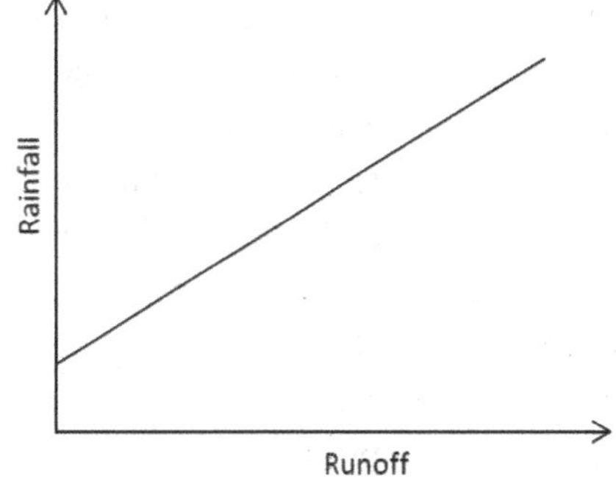

logical positivists means on the classical grounds that the demarcation of science concerning a phenomenon is equal to 1 without giving room for falsification of Popper (1952). The conflict between verifiability and falsifiability of scientific theories includes philosophical grounds that are fuzzy but many scientific philosophers concluded the case with CL, which weakens the nature of scientific reasoning. Although many science philosophers tried to resolve this problem by bringing into the argument the probabilistic and at times the possibility demarcation of the scientific knowledge and development. So far the "fuzzy philosophy of science" has not been introduced into the literature (Şen, 2011a).

CLUSTER METHODOLOGIES

Clustering can be considered as the most important unsupervised learning problem, which deals with finding a structure in a collection of unlabeled data. A loose definition of clustering could be "the process of organizing objects into groups whose members are similar in some way." A cluster is, therefore, a collection of objects, which are "similar" or "dissimilar" to the objects belonging to other clusters (Şen, 2012a).

Even human daily life is full of many arguments among which there are propositions, which relate a set of input words to output word. For instance, in "high speed leads to accident" proposition the input word is "speed" and output word is "accident." This sentence gives the impression that there is a rational relationship, between these words. In general, the cluster of high speeds with many members can be mapped onto a set of accidents so as to visualize the qualitative (non-numerical) relationship. If one questions the sentences that s/he uses in daily life then s/he will be able to come across with many cluster relationships. This mental and qualitative relationship in words can be expressed in terms of fuzzy principles even though numerical data (measurements) are not available; but these relationships may remain rather vague and ambiguous with useful information. In case of numerical data, many researchers depend on the so called objective methods such as correlation coefficient (Pearson or any other type), and finally, reach to a numerical positive or negative value and then onwards bases his/her argument with interpretation of the numerical value according to present crisp rules and regulations, which are questionable as for their validity from FL point of view. One should not forget that any formulation or equation is not without assumptions. For instance, the correlation coefficient requires that the numerical data should accord with Gaussian distribution; provides only linear relations (what about non-linear relations? do the researchers sense or logically think about such non linearity possibilities or blindly apply the ready equations?), the data must be trend and periodicity free, etc. It is advised in this chapter that prior to any mechanical and blind use of formulations one should care for logical possibilities and types of qualitative relationships, whether it is haphazard (independent, without any relationship) (Şen, 2010).

Classical Relationships

Another comparison of CL and FL propositions can be effectively observed and grasped on the basis of Cartesian coordinate system displays. Let us consider classically that the groundwater storage, S; increases with porosity, P, and this can be represented in the CL graphically as in Figure 6. Formally, the holistic CL proposition tells that 'IF porosity increases THEN storage increases' and there are no adjectives (clusters) in this statement. Any CL statement does not tell whether the relationship is linear or non-linear.

On the other hand, in case of FL categorization, storage and porosity can be specified by three clusters (adjectives as "high, h," "medium," m and "small, s") on the two axes of the Cartesian coordinate system (Figure 7).

Comparison of these four alternatives with Figure 6 indicates that after the fuzzy partitioning there are now nine clusters (sub-domains) each corresponding to a specific relationship between the two variables. Hence, more detailed and logical interpretations can be given with ease. There are three sources of information for the identification of valid clusters for the problem at hand. These are,

1. Logical deductions, which may be preliminary work of a non-specialist,
2. Detailed rational and logical deductions by experts (expert view),
3. Data based deductions provide that there are measurements or records.

Education systems today train students on the third step whereas the first and second steps are grossly overlooked. In any innovative education system, last point must be left to students more than the first two steps, which constitute the fundamentals of creative thinking. Logical deductions should furnish the basis for tackling any problem. The classical and systematic training renders the thinking capability of students into molds with definite boundaries. For instance, if asked about the Newton's law, the ready answer is that F = ma or force equals to the multiplication of mass by acceleration. Each variable, force or mass, is thought as having single values not as a cluster of values. Instead of formulation, if someone state the Newton's law linguistically as,

The force is directly and linearly proportional with acceleration,

then s/he considers "force" and "acceleration" as holistic variables as in the CL. The same saying can be put into a formal proposition as,

IF acceleration increases THEN force increases.

The same law can be expressed from the FL point of view by clustering with the force and acceleration categories as "low," "moderate" and "high." Similar to Figure 7 there will be 9 clusters (sub-domains) but not all of them are valid logically. Rational and logical thinking without any expertise or data exposition will invalidate 6 of these clusters which are, "low acceleration- moderate force," "low acceleration- high force," "moderate acceleration- low force," "moderate acceleration- high force," "high acceleration- moderate force," and finally, "high acceleration- moderate force." Three logical statements remain valid, namely, "low acceleration- low force," "moderate acceleration- moderate force," and "high acceleration- high force." The graphical representations of these three clusters are shown in Figure 8.

In this figure, black and white sub-domains are still indicators of CL, because they are all mutually exclusive i.e. there are sharp boundaries. However, in FL clustering such sharp boundaries are not allowed and hence mutually exclusiveness principle is no longer valid. Such a clustering system leads to grey areas where blackness fades away from the center towards the edges as shown in Figure 9.

Mental and Visual Clustering

This section discusses first the uncertainty concepts and then classical and fuzzy clustering methods. An innovative trend analysis is presented with final fuzzy clustering results and applications. Clustering approaches have many interests among qualitative and quantitative studies for description, identification and prediction purposes. They are helpful in data mining studies where there may not be objective correlation or even clear relationships. Quantitative (numerical) data may not yield

Figure 6. CL domain

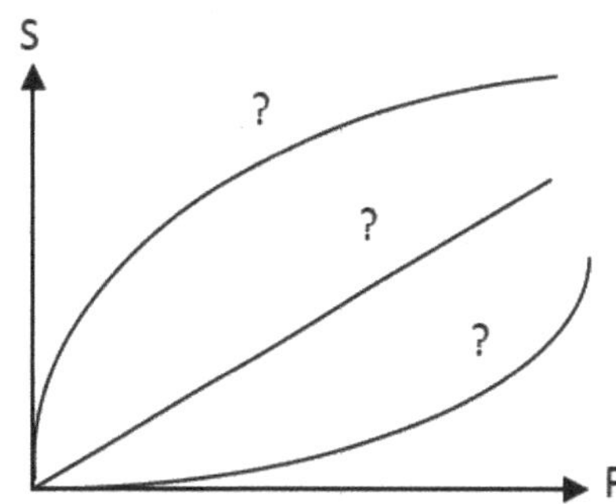

Figure 7. Fuzzy logic domains

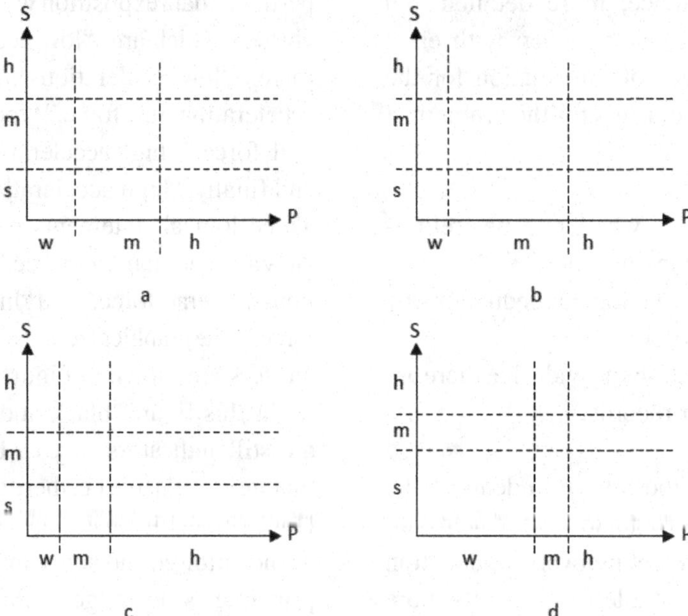

Figure 8. Acceleration-force sub-domains (fuzzy logic)

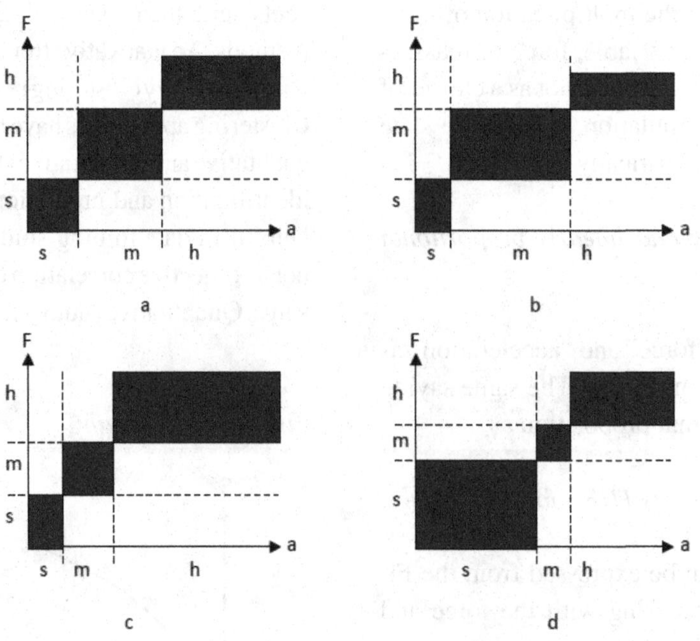

Figure 9. Fuzzy partitioning of sub-domains

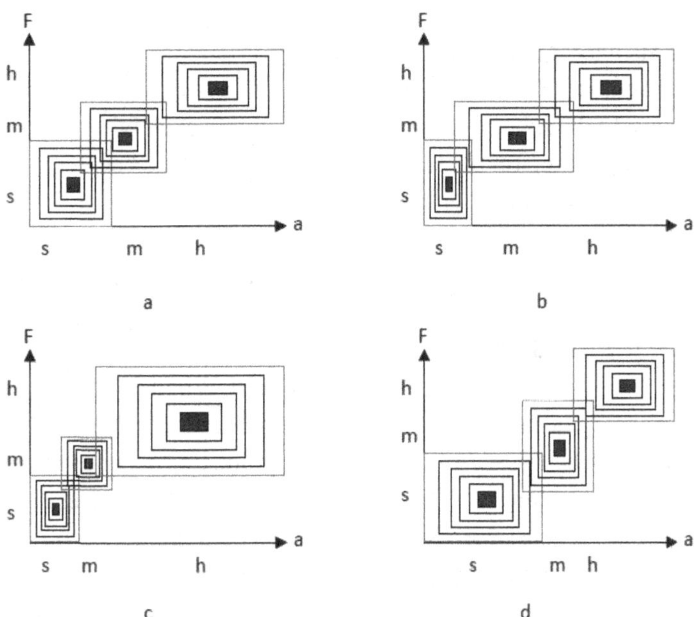

to classical statistical, stochastic or probabilistic approaches due to different reasons such as absence of meaningful dependence existence, vagueness, incompleteness, uncertainty, etc. whereby cluster approach enters the circuit for exposition of useful features linguistically in addition to numerical descriptions. Visual inspection of low dimensional data in 1D, 2D or 3D's gives qualitative and subjective impressions about the clustering leading to linguistic or fuzzy rule base inferences. Such descriptions constitute qualitative fundamentals even for the numerical methodologies, which are, after all, based on science philosophy leading to the final deductions on logical bases. Researchers, especially in the numerical sciences, seek ready formulations (symbolic logic), algorithms and software to solve their problems deterministically. This may be due to the fact that they may not have been trained in effective philosophical thinking manner leading to verbal (linguistic) logical rules (propositions), which may thereafter be converted into formulations, algorithms or software writings.

It is possible to look at the visual inspection of given data for cluster studies through either mental data processing of the observations or in the form of scatter diagrams without any methodology application. The simplest form of mental or visual clustering is through a graph on 1D or 2D spaces. Mental clustering requires inspiration, thinking, understanding, conceptualization and idea generation. For instance, if one thinks about human age then s/he may classify it into three clusters as "young," "middle" and "old," which overlap as shown in Figure 10.

Figure 10. Age clusters

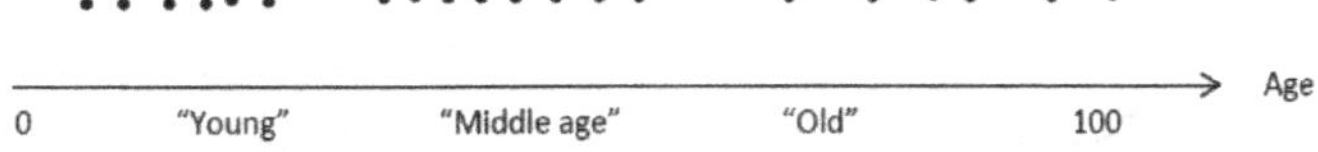

A 2D example can be classified on mental and intuitive thinking bases into three categories by use of fuzzy words. For instance, "disk," "cylinder" and "stick," has different lengths and radius as their common properties. In 2D space they can be described as 3 clusters depending on the relative fuzzy mental values of these dimensions as in Figure 11.

FORMAL CLUSTER METHODS

Mental cluster procedures are not processed by computers, and therefore, it is necessary to develop some methodological procedures for their executions by computers. For this purpose, there are different CL and FL cluster methodologies.

CL K-Means

This cluster approach as suggested by MacQueen (1967) is one of the simplest unsupervised learning algorithms. The procedure follows a simple and easy way to classify a given data set through a certain number of clusters. The number of clusters must be prefixed by the researcher. According to the cluster number and the data, a computer automatically presents the cluster elements and domains. The main idea is to define k number centroids for k different and mutually exclusive clusters. The centroid coordinates are appointed initially in a random manner. In any clustering methodology the following two basic principles should apply.

Figure 11. 2D clustering

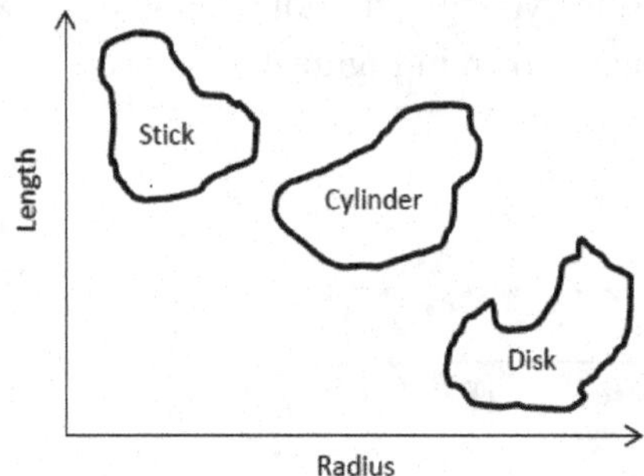

1. Cluster centroids must be as far as possible from each other,
2. Each cluster center must gather all the closest elements.

After the initial cluster centroids' selection, the next step is to take each data point belonging to a given data set and associate it to the nearest centroid. When no point is pending, the first step is completed and the first cluster pattern appears. At this point, one needs to re-calculate new centroids for the available clusters and then a new binding has to be done between the same data set points and the nearest new centroid. As a result one may notice that the new centroids change their location step by step until no more significant changes appear which implies that centroids do not move significantly any more. Here, the significance must be defined objectively through some criterion. For instance, if the last centroid positions are at less than ± 5% relative error distances from the previous centroid locations then the looping process of finding new centroids can be stopped.

All what have been explained in the above paragraph can be repeated theoretically through the minimization of an objective function, F, which is in k-means case a squared error function as,

$$F = \sum_{j=1}^{k} \sum_{i=1}^{n} \left\| x_i^{(j)} - c_j \right\|^2 \tag{5}$$

where $\left\| x_i^{(j)} - c_j \right\|^2$ is the distance measure between a data point $x_i^{(j)}$ and the cluster centroid, c_j. Consideration of Equation (5) leads to the following algorithmic steps for execution on computers.

1. Decide about k cluster centroid locations for the initiation of the algorithm,

2. Calculate the distance of each point to each centroid,
3. Decide for each point as to its belongingness to a certain cluster depending on the minimum distance,
4. Update the centroid locations based on points that belonged to each cluster in the previous step,
5. Renew the belongingness procedure for each point with the updated centroids,
6. Repeat steps 2-5 until the centroids have no longer significant difference from the previous centroid locations within ± 5% error.

The k-means algorithm does not necessarily find the most optimal configuration, corresponding to the global objective function minimum. The algorithm is also significantly sensitive to the initial randomly selected cluster centroids. The k-means algorithm can be run multiple times to reduce this effect. It is a simple algorithm that has been adapted for many problem solutions. This clustering method is dependent entirely on the CL, because each point in the same cluster has the same membership degree as 1 and each cluster is mutually exclusive.

The present classical k-means procedure of cluster analysis does not take into consideration inter-cross among the clusters. The information about the inter cluster number provides additional dimension as to which of the two clusters are in close relationship. This point has not been investigated in the current literature and remains as a research point.

FL K-Means-Standard-Deviations Cluster

CL k-means can be converted to FL case by a simple operation, which allocates different MDs to each element within the clusters. The CL k-means take into consideration the averages of each variable within each cluster,, and hence, the centroid of each cluster is established and after successive iterations, the final cluster centroid locations and members of each cluster are determined crisply. Herein, the simple FL k-means-standard deviations cluster takes into consideration the standard deviation, σ_j, of each cluster (j = 1, 2, . . ., k) as follows.

$$\sigma_j = \sqrt{\frac{1}{n_j}\sum_{i=1}^{n_j}\left\|x_i^{(j)} - c_j\right\|^2} \tag{6}$$

where n_j is the number of elements in the j-th cluster. It is possible to locate on each CL k-means cluster a radial basis function with its peak value as equal to 1 on the top of the centroid and its dispersion coefficient equal to the cluster standard deviation as defined in Equation (6). The picture of such a clustering methodology is shown in Figurc 12 on1D casc with thrcc k-mcans centroid. In 1D each radial basis function appears as the Gaussian MF as in Figure 12 FL k-means-standard-deviations clustering. Each element takes its MD from each cluster according to resulting Gaussian MFs, and hence, if there are k clusters then each element will have theoretically k MDs. The more

Figure 12. Lag-one water level fluctuations and cluster boundaries

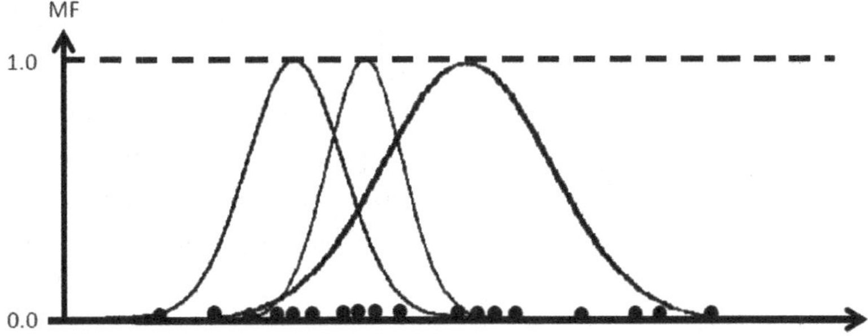

distant is the element to the cluster, the less will be its MD, and hence the MD of each element decreases with distance. Another important point is that the summation of MDs for an element is not equal to 1 necessarily. In order to alleviate this point FL c-means is suggested.

FL C-Means

In the literature, fuzzy c-means (FCM) has been reported as being one of the most promising classification methods. It is an iterative clustering approach, which resembles the well-known k-means technique, but it uses fuzzy MFs instead of crisp values (Bezdek, 1981). FCM partitions the data set $X = x_1, x_2, \ldots, x_n$ into c fuzzy subsets, u_i, where the value $u_i(x_k)$ is the MD of x_k in class i. The values of $u_i(x_k)$ are arranged as a cxn matrix, U. The method approximately minimizes the sum of squared error function defined as,

$$J_m\left(U, V : X\right) = \sum_{i=1}^{c} \sum_{k=1}^{n} \left(u_{ik}\right)^m \left\| x_k - v_i \right\| \quad (7)$$

where $V = v_1, v_2, \ldots, v_c$ is a set of cluster centers and $m > 1$ is a weighting exponent affecting the fuzziness of u. The parameters (U, V) may minimize J_m only if u_{ik} and v_i are defined as,

$$u_{ik} = \left[\sum_{j=1}^{c} \left(\frac{\left\| x_k - v_i \right\|}{\left\| x_k - v_j \right\|} \right)^{2/(m-1)} \right]^{-1} \quad for \quad all \quad i,\ k \quad (8)$$

where

$$v_i = \frac{\sum_{k=1}^{n} \left(u_{ik}\right)^m x_k}{\sum_{k=1}^{n} \left(u_{ik}\right)^m} \quad for \quad all \quad i \quad (9)$$

The stop criteria for the method is determined by $E_t \leq \varepsilon$ where,

$$E_t = \sum_{i=1}^{c} \left\| v_{i,t+1} - v_{i,k} \right\| \quad for \quad all \quad t \quad (10)$$

In practical studies, it is sufficient to take $\varepsilon = 0.05$. The method contains the following iteration steps.

1. Initialize U_0,
2. Choose c, m and ε,
3. Compute all c cluster centers $v_{i,0}$,
4. Compute all cxn memberships $u_{ik,t}$ and update all c cluster centers $v_{i,t+1}$,
5. Compute E_t, and
6. If $E_t \leq \varepsilon$ then stops; else return to step 3.

When the stop criterion is fulfilled a fuzzy output is available. Each data has its MD in each cluster, which represents the fuzzy behavior of this algorithm. To do that, one simply has to build an appropriate matrix named U whose factors are numbers between 0 and 1, and represent the MD between data and centers of clusters.

On the other hand, there are many research works in the literature that are related to cluster analysis. For instance, an algorithm is presented for the analysis of multivariate data along with some experimental results by Sammon (1969). The algorithm is based upon a point mapping of N L-dimensional vectors from the L-space to a lower-dimensional space such that the inherent data "structure" is approximately preserved. Lee et al. (1976) presented a method for the sequential mapping of points in a high-dimensional space onto a plane hence reducing a multi-dimensional cluster down to 2D. Whenever a new point is mapped, its distances to two points previously mapped are exactly preserved. On the resulting map, 2M - 3 of the original distances can be exactly preserved. The mapping is based on the distances of a minimal spanning tree constructed from the points. All of the distances on the minimal spanning tree are preserved exactly.

Many clustering models define good clusters as extremes of objective functions as exampled in the previous section. Optimization of these models is often done using an alternating optimization (AO) algorithm driven by necessary conditions for local extremes. Runkler and Bezdek (1999) abandon the objective function model in favor of a generalized model called alternating cluster estimation (ACE), which uses alternating iteration architecture, but membership and prototype functions are selected directly by the user. Virtually every clustering model can be realized as an instance of ACE. Out of a large variety of possible instances of non-AO models, they presented two examples.

1. An algorithm with a dynamically changing prototype function that extracts representative data,
2. A computationally efficient algorithm with hyper-conic MFs that allows easy extraction of MFs.

They have also illustrated these non-AO instances on three problems.

1. Simple clustering of plane data where they have shown that creating an unmatched ACE algorithm overcomes some problems of fuzzy c-means (FCM-AO) and possibility c-means (PCM-AO),
2. Functional approximation by clustering on a simple artificial data set,
3. Functional approximation on a 12-input 1-output real world data set. ACE models work pretty well in all three cases.

As mentioned by Runkler (2003), the objective functions for non-linear projection and clustering can be combined and lead to the definition of fuzzy non-linear projection. Conventional non-linear projection preserves topologies well, hut produces bad results for multiple manifolds. Conventional clustering can discover complex cluster shapes, but the geometry has to be specified in advance. Fuzzy non-linear projection avoids these drawbacks of projection and clustering methods.

Bezdek and Hathaway (1987) suggested the conventional (or hard) c-means algorithm as a widely used method for finding hard partitioning of objects represented by particular observations in some data set. Although the approach generally produces good hard partitioning for the case when are directly available, it cannot be applied when information about the objects to be partitioned is available only through a matrix A of pairwise squared distance. They presented an approach which produces hard c-means clustering directly from A without reference to the feature vectors. Their approach is illustrated by a simple numerical example. Finally, they have pointed out that the same algorithm can be extended to the family of fuzzy c-means functions.

Improved FL Clustering

Çelikyilmaz and Türkşen (2008) introduced two new criterions for validation of results obtained from recent novel-clustering algorithm, improved fuzzy clustering (IFC) to be used to find patterns in regression and classification type datasets, separately. IFC algorithm calculates membership values that are used as additional predictors to form fuzzy decision functions for each cluster. Proposed validity criterions are based on the ratio of compactness to separability of clusters. The optimum compactness of a cluster is represented with average distances between every object and cluster centers, and total estimation error from their fuzzy decision functions. The separability is based on a conditional ratio between the similarities between cluster representatives and similarities between fuzzy decision surfaces of each cluster. The performance of the proposed validity criterions are compared to other structurally similar cluster validity indexes using datasets from different domains. The results indicate that the new cluster validity functions are useful criterions when selecting parameters of IFC models.

Cluster validity index (CVI) measures (Fukuyama & Sugeno, 1989; Xie & Beni, 1991; Pal & Bezdek, 1995) have been proposed to validate the underlying assumptions of the number of clusters, mainly for FCM (Bezdek, 1981) clustering approach. Later, many variations of these functions are introduced, e.g., (Bouguessa et al., 2006; Dave, 1996; Kim et al., 2003; Kim & Ramakrishna, 2005; Wu & Yang, 2005a, b), have been extended. The main characteristics of these CVIs are that they all use either within cluster, viz., compactness, or between cluster distances, viz., separability, or both as a way of assessing the clustering schema (Kim et al., 2003). Base on the way the compactness and separability are coupled, the CVI measures are generally classified into ratio or summation-type measures (Çelikyilmaz & Türkşen, 2008).

Çelikyilmaz and Türkşen (2008) developed two new validity criterions is introduced to measure the optimum number of clusters, denoted with c*, using two different versions of IFC. The new ratio-type validity criterions measure the ratio between the compactness and separability of the clusters. Since IFC is a new type of hybrid-clustering method, which in a way uses structures from two separate clustering algorithms during optimization, viz., fuzzy clustering types, i.e. FCM (Bezdek, 1981) and FCRM (Hathaway & Bezdek, 1993) in a novel way, and utilizes fuzzy functions (FFs), the new CVI is designed to validate two different concepts. The compactness couples within cluster distances and c number of regression/classification functions errors between the actual and estimated output values/class labels. The separability, on the other hand, will determine the structure of the clusters by measuring the ratio between the cluster center distances and the angle between their fuzzy decision surfaces.

Cluster Regression Model

The cluster regression model for dealing with non-stationary especially is developed by Şen et al. (1999) especially for shifting means or trend identification. The basis of this model is the combination of transition probability between successive clusters and classical regression technique.

Classical regression analysis has several assumptions about the normality and independence of the residuals. Furthermore, an implied assumption that skips from the considerations in most regression line applications is that the scatter diagram should have the points distributed uniformly around a line. Unfortunately, this assumption is often overlooked, especially if the scatter diagram is not plotted. Uniform scatter of the points with homoscedasticity assumption along the line is possible if the original records are homogeneous and steady with no clusters, shifts, trends or seasonality. On the other hand, if level shifts exist through time then the scatter diagram is bound to include clusters of points along the regression line. Confirmation of such clusters is obvious in Figure 13, which shows the lake level lag-one scatter diagram for monthly records from Lake Van, Turkey.

The following conclusions are possible from interpretation of the scatter diagram.

1. The lag-one scatter diagram indicates an overall straight-line relationship between the successive data occurrences. Existence of such a straight line corresponds to the first order serial autocorrelation coefficient in the time series. Hence, data persistence is preserved by this straight line.
2. The scatter of points around the straight-line is confined within a narrow band, which implies that the prediction of subsequent data values cannot be very different from the current data level provided that there are no shifts in the data.
3. There are different cluster regions along the straight-line. Such clusters are not expected in the classical regression approach but the existence of them renders the classical regression analysis into a cluster regression analysis. Separate clusters correspond to different data features.

4. Classical regression analysis provides a basis for predicting data values relative to current data, but in the cluster regression line approach, reliable predictions are only possible provided that the probability of cluster occurrences are taken into consideration. Herein, the questions arise as to which cluster is to be taken in future predictions? Should future predictions remain within the same cluster? Any transition from one cluster to another means a shift or sharp trend transitions within the data structure. It is, therefore, necessary to know the transitional probabilities among various clusters. The cluster regression depicts not only the serial autocorrelation coefficient but also the influence domain of each cluster as in Figure 13 along the horizontal axis as A, B, C and D. The influence domains help to calculate the transitional probabilities between the clusters from the original records.
5. For any current cluster, it is possible to estimate future normal data values by using the regression line equation. For reliable estimations through cluster regression, the following steps are necessary:
    a. In order to decide initially which domain of influence (A, B, C or D) should be taken into consideration, a uniform distribution function is considered that assumes random values between 0 and 400 cm.
    b. Generate a uniformly distributed random number and, accordingly, decide about the next cluster by considering influence domains. For instance, if the uniformly distributed random number is 272 then from Figure 13 influence domain, C will be the current cluster.
    c. Generate another uniformly distributed random number and if the level remains within the same cluster then use the regression equation for estimation. Otherwise, take the average data value in the new cluster. The new value will be adopted as the midpoint of the cluster domains in Figure 13. A better estimation might be based on the random variable generation again from a uniform distribution confined within the variation domain of each cluster. Furthermore, the value found in this manner will be added to a random residual value. This will then give the basis of the subsequent estimations within the same cluster domain.

The cluster regression approach has been presented herein to the recorded water level fluctuations of the Lake Van, Turkey (Şen et al., 1999). For this purpose, various lag scatter points of the successive levels are first plotted in Figures 13-15.

In these figures there are straight lines and the transition boundaries between clusters of A, B, C and D is given in Table 1 in addition to the boundaries of each cluster at different lags up to 9.

Here, A is considered as a "low" lake-level cluster, where only transitions from "low" level to "low" level are allowed. B and C refer to "lower-medium" and "upper medium" level clusters and, finally, D is the cluster that includes "highest" levels only. It is obvious from Table 1 that the transition limits between A and B, and B and C are practically constant on average for all lags and equal to 129 and 219, respectively. However, the upper limit transition between C-D increases with the increase in the lag value. The difference between the first and ninth lags has a relative error percentage of 100´(308)285)/308=7.4 which may be regarded as small for practical purposes.

The scatter diagrams in Figures 13-15 yield the following specific interpretations for Lake Van level fluctuations.

Figure 13. Lag-one scatter diagram

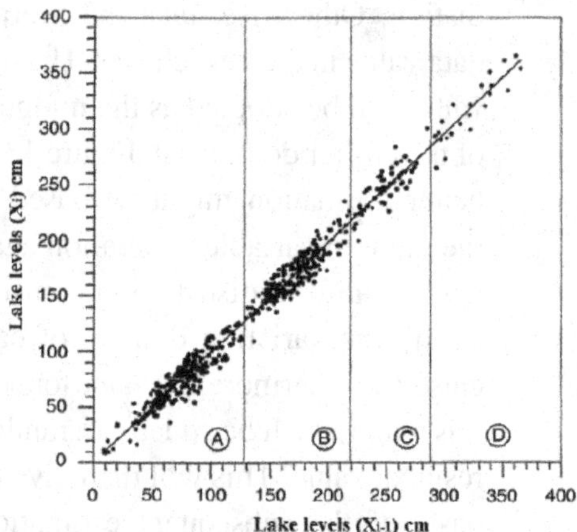

Figure 14. Lag-two water level fluctuations and cluster boundaries

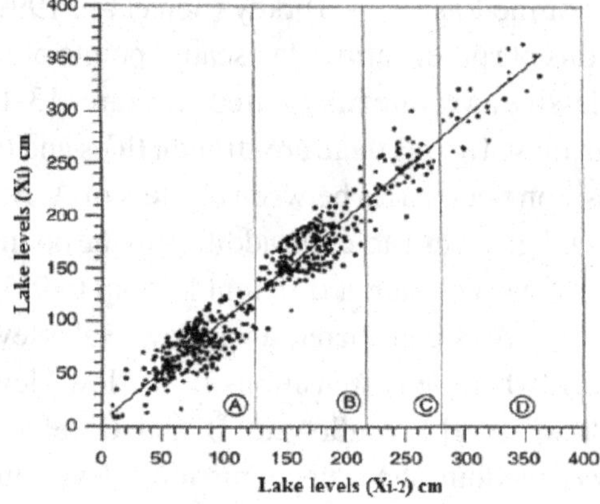

Figure 15. Lag-three water level fluctuations and cluster boundaries

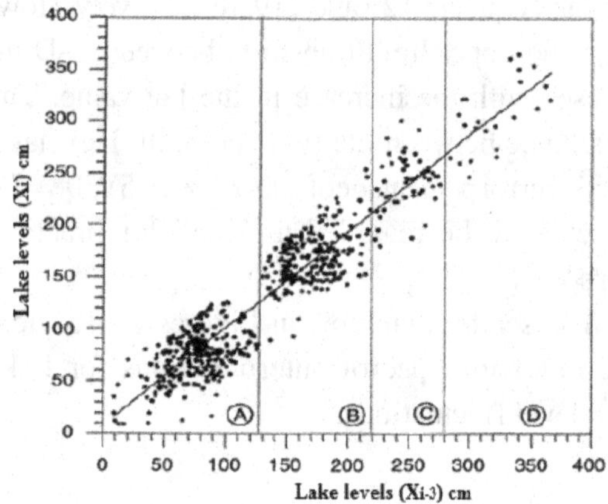

1. The scatter diagrams have four clusters with the densest point concentration in cluster A that represents "low" data value following "low" data. Extreme value fluctuations have the least frequency of occurrences in cluster D.
2. Irrespective of the lag value, points in the scatter diagram deviate from the regression line within a narrow band. This indicates that once the data value is within a certain cluster it will remain within this cluster with comparatively very high probability as will be argued later in this work. Furthermore, the transitions between the clusters are expected to take place rather rarely and in fact between the adjacent clusters only.
3. In none of the scatter diagrams is transition of data value possible from one cluster to another non-adjacent one. This may be confirmed from the calculated transition matrix elements because there are no elements except along the main and the two off diagonals.

Herein, only lag-one regression line will be considered to model the data values by considering transitional probabilities between adjacent clusters. The monthly level time series data for Lake Van from 1944 to 1994 yield lag-one transition probability matrix, [M] as follows

$$[M] = \begin{matrix} & A & B & C & D \\ A & & & & \\ B & & & & \\ C & & & & \\ D & & & & \end{matrix}\begin{bmatrix} 291 & 2 & 0 & 0 \\ 1 & 233 & 4 & 0 \\ 0 & 3 & 54 & 2 \\ 0 & 0 & 1 & 20 \end{bmatrix}$$

The diagonal values in this matrix are the numbers of transitions within each cluster. For instance, there are 291 transitions from low values to low values within cluster A. In the same matrix, inter-cluster transitions occur rather rarely along the o€ diagonals, such as 4 transitions from clus-

Table 1. Cluster regression boundaries and coefficients

Lag	Trans-Boundary Values			Regression Coefficients	
	A - B	B - C	C - D	a	b
1	130	220	>285	0.985	1.459
2	125	218	>280	0.960	4.564
3	129	215	>280	0930	8.239
4	130	219	>281	0.901	11.725
5	128	222	>280	0.878	14.486
6	128	212	>287	0.362	16.293
7	130	221	>296	0.353	17.114
8	132	225	>302	0.852	16.835
9	131	222	>308	0.858	15.532
Average	129	219			

ter B to C. In classical stochastic processes the calculation of transition matrix elements are based on the fundamental assumption that the process is time reversible. This is equivalent to saying that transitions as $A \rightarrow B$ is the same as $B \rightarrow A$.

Consequently, the resulting matrix must be symmetrical. However, in the proposed method of cluster regression technique only one way transitions along the time axis toward future is allowed. This means that the transition along the time axis is irreversible. As a result of this fact the transition matrix is not symmetrical. Accordingly, the above matrix in is not symmetric, the transition from C to B is not equal to 4 but 3. Zero values next to the off diagonals indicate that the data values can move only to adjacent clusters. Hence, the possible transitions are ABCD only. For instance, transition to cluster C is possible 4 times from B, 54 times from previous C and only once from D with no transition from A, (hence a total of 59 transitions). Columnar values show transition to the cluster considered from other clusters and the transition probabilities can be calculated after dividing each value in the column by the column total. Hence, the transition probability matrix [P] becomes from above matrix expression as

$$[P] = \begin{matrix} A \\ B \\ C \\ D \end{matrix} \overset{\begin{matrix} A & \quad B & \quad C & \quad D \end{matrix}}{\begin{bmatrix} 0.9932 & 0.0068 & 0 & 0 \\ 0.0042 & 0.9790 & 0.0168 & 0 \\ 0 & 0.0508 & 0.9152 & 0.0339 \\ 0 & 0 & 0.0476 & 0.9524 \end{bmatrix}}$$

The linear regression line that relates two successive data values, namely, Wi and Wi-1, can be obtained from the cluster scatter diagram in Figure 1 as

$$W_i = 0.9858W_{i-1} + 1.45918 + \varepsilon_i \tag{11}$$

in which ε_i signifies the vertical random deviations from the regression line. Theoretically, these random deviations should have a Gaussian distribution function for the validity of the regression line and Figure 16 indicates that they are normally distributed.

In order to adopt Equation (11) estimations with the cluster scatters, it is essential to take into account the following steps.

1. Because the most frequently occurring data values are confined in cluster A, the initial state $_{W_0}$ is selected randomly from the actual data values in this cluster.

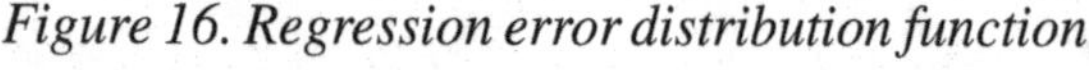

Figure 16. Regression error distribution function

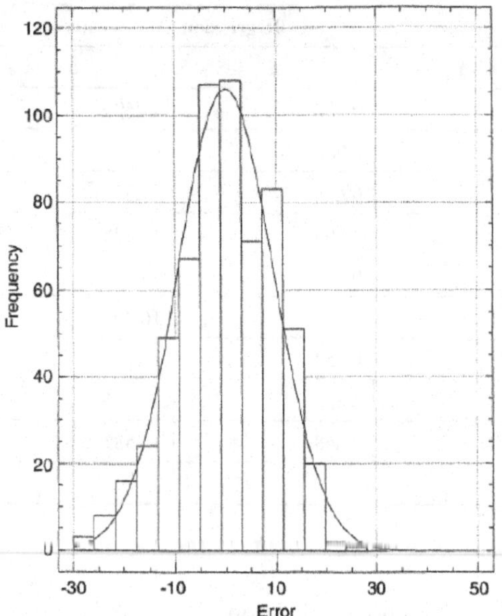

2. Decision whether there is transition to the next cluster is achieved through the transition probabilities given in the above matrix of [P]. The transitions occur according to the following rules.
   a. Transition to cluster A is possible only from cluster B or the value remains within the same cluster. From the transition matrix these have probabilities as 0.9932 and 0.0042 and their summation is equal to 1.0. In order to decide which one of these two clusters will be effective in the next time step, it is necessary to generate a uniform random number, ξ_i, which varies between zero and one. If $\xi_i < 0.9932$ then the data value will remain within cluster A, otherwise for $0.9932 < \xi_i < 1.0$ a transition occurs from cluster A to B. In the former case, after generating a normally distributed random number, ε_i, the new water level value is generated by the use of the cluster regression model in Equation (11). However, in the latter case, water level will be selected randomly from the range of water levels for cluster, B.
   b. At any instant, transition to cluster B may take place from two adjacent clusters (A or C). The transitional probabilities from A and C are 0.0068 and 0.0508, respectively, with complementary probability of 0.9790 remaining within cluster B. Now the decision of transition to B will have three independent regions of the uniform distribution, namely, if $0 < \xi_i < 0.0068$ then a transition occurs from A to B or when $0.0068 < \xi_i < 0.9858$ water level remains within cluster B and finally, for $0.9858 < \xi_i, < 1.0$ a transition occurs from C to B. If the data value remains within cluster B, a normal variate is generated as ε_i and the regression expression in Equation (3) is used to predict the next water level. In the transition cases, data value is depicted randomly from the available levels.
3. Transitions to cluster C show a similar mechanism to cluster B with different transition probabilities but the same generating mechanism.
4. Finally, transition to cluster D is possible only from cluster C, in addition to remaining in the same cluster. The application of all these procedures and steps to data value variations result in the development of the synthetic transition matrix $[M_s]$.

$$[M_s] = \begin{array}{c} A \\ B \\ C \\ D \end{array} \overset{\begin{array}{cccc} A & B & C & D \end{array}}{\begin{bmatrix} 287 & 2 & 0 & 0 \\ 1 & 230 & 3 & 0 \\ 0 & 4 & 56 & 2 \\ 0 & 0 & 1 & 19 \end{bmatrix}}$$

Comparison of corresponding elements between the two matrices of [M] and [M_S] shows that they differ by less than 5% relative error. This indicates that the preservation of transition numbers as probabilities in the predicted data values are indistinguishable from the actual data. The synthetic cluster scatter diagram obtained from the use of matrix [P] and Equation (1) is shown in Figure 17 where the regression line has the form as

$$W_i = 0.978W_{i-1} + 1.47 + \varepsilon_i \qquad (12)$$

Again comparison of this expression with Equation (11) shows that the corresponding coefficients vary by less than 5% relative error. In other words, the autocorrelation coefficient in the prediction of water levels is preserved in spite of shifts in the original data.

INNOVATIVE FUZZY TREND CLUSTERING

Trend analysis became very significant in the last three decades due to interest whether there are increasing tendency in the meteorological, economic, social event occurrences so as to make quantitative conclusions about the overall long-term behaviors. The main purpose of this section is to present basic views and interpretations in a relativistic trend analysis procedure, where each specific sub-group of the whole is compared with its past pattern. Herein, "low," "medium" and "high" categories are considered as individual groups and their positions are evaluated as to whether there are significant trends. In this manner, rather than a holistic and absolute trend approach, partial and relativistic trend assessments are presented leading to fuzzy ingredients (Şen, 2012a).

Trend Detection by Relative Clustering Approach

Trend analysis in various disciplines is one of the major tasks for identifying long-term steady tendencies. The literature is full of many applications in different parts of the world, but they all provide absolute time trends that may be embedded within the given time series. In general, either a moving average procedure is applied for trend identification or by classical calculations Mann-Kendall (Mann, 1965; Kendall, 1944) trend test analysis is applied for trend start and existence identification; trend slope calculation Sen (1968). These methodologies look for holistic and absolute trends without any distinction between "low," "medium" and "high" clusters in the trend search. This section suggests relativistic trend analysis in the sense that trends are sought with respect to some baseline and few clusters within time series. This method can be developed along two but similar directions as the "serial trend" and "cross trend" analyses.

All the classical trend tests have the following basic ingredients in their applications and their existence does not provide a fruitful floor for significant trend identification.

Figure 17. Synthetic lag-one water level fluctuations

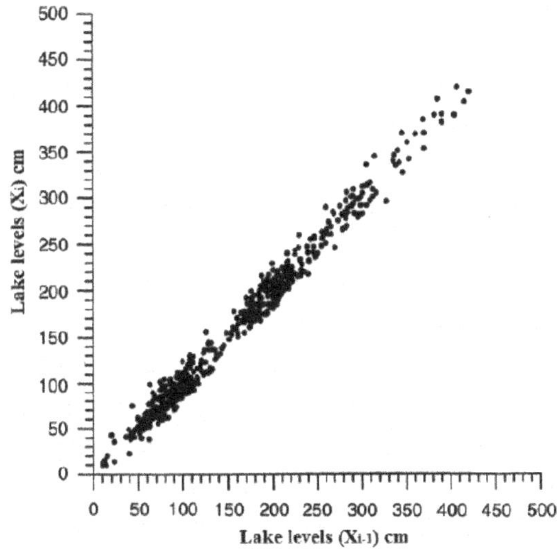

1. They search for monotonic trend component in a holistic manner without any distinction between low and high values,
2. The search is in the absolute time domain, which takes into account real time sequence of the series, and hence the serial correlation coefficient becomes important,
3. The correlation structure of any given series is assumed independent or rendered to independent form, if possible,
4. It is not possible to look for non-linear trends,
5. The results are affected by finite length time series.

Fuzziness in Trend Analysis

Natural, social and economic phenomena evolve by time and the main question is whether they have on the average the same level of variation or there are intervals (clusters) during which steady increases or decreases take place. Everybody in daily life tries to compare the present day weather conditions with respect to previous intervals in a fuzzy manner. They are not concerned with absolute time but their reasoning are based on relativistic bases, where one period is compared with other either for the assessment of present conditions as to what is the increment or decrement or for future estimations on verbal grounds. In this reasoning experience (similar to past records) plays the major role and one is not interested on holistic absolute values or changes but rather changes with respect to previous experience and hence relativistic comparisons become important. Likewise, better and finer interpretations, suggestions and conclusions can be obtained by considering segments of series.

The basis of the approach rests on the fact that if two time series are identical to each other, their plot against each other shows scatter of points along 1:1 (45°) line on the Cartesian coordinate system as in Figure 18. In the figure, there are 25 data points, which come from a non-normal probability distribution function. Whatever the time series are whether trend free or with monotonic trends, all fall on the 1:1 line when plotted. There is no distinction whether the time series are non-normally distributed, having small sample lengths or possess serial correlations. One important conclusion from Figure 18a is that data values sort themselves in ascending (or descending) order along the 1:1 line. This idea will also be used in the trend identification procedure proposed in this paper (Şen, 2012b). The same 25 data points are added with increasing and decreasing trends separately and then they are ordered and plotted against the original (trend free) time series, which is also sorted in ascending order. The results are shown in Figures 18b and 18c, respectively, for increasing and decreasing trends. It is obvious that in the case of increasing (decreasing) monotonic trend, the scatter of the points falls above (below) the 1:1 line. For any trial with non-normal, small sample and serially correlated time series, similar scatter diagrams are obtained for increasing and decreasing trends.

The next question is how could one identify the existing trend in a given time series with respect to the idea of 1:1 line? The answer appears as a plot of the first half of the time series against the second half according to the abovementioned idea. In Figures 19, the same time series are used, this time by considering two-halves and the sorting procedure. It becomes obvious that monotone increasing (decreasing) trend in the given time series fall above (below) the 1:1 line.

On the other hand, it is also possible to have time series with half plots similar to Figure 19 as in Figure 20, where there are scatter of points on both sides of 1:1 line. In Figure 20a "low" ("high") values are "more" ("less") in the first half than the next half, whereas in Figure 20b the opposite situation occurs. These cases correspond to non-monotonic trends where within the same time series there are increasing and decreasing trends at different scales even hidden ones.

The applications of the methodology proposed are presented for different annual runoff and rainfall series recorded at various locations in

Figure 18 a) Trendless time series, b) increasing trend, c) decreasing trend

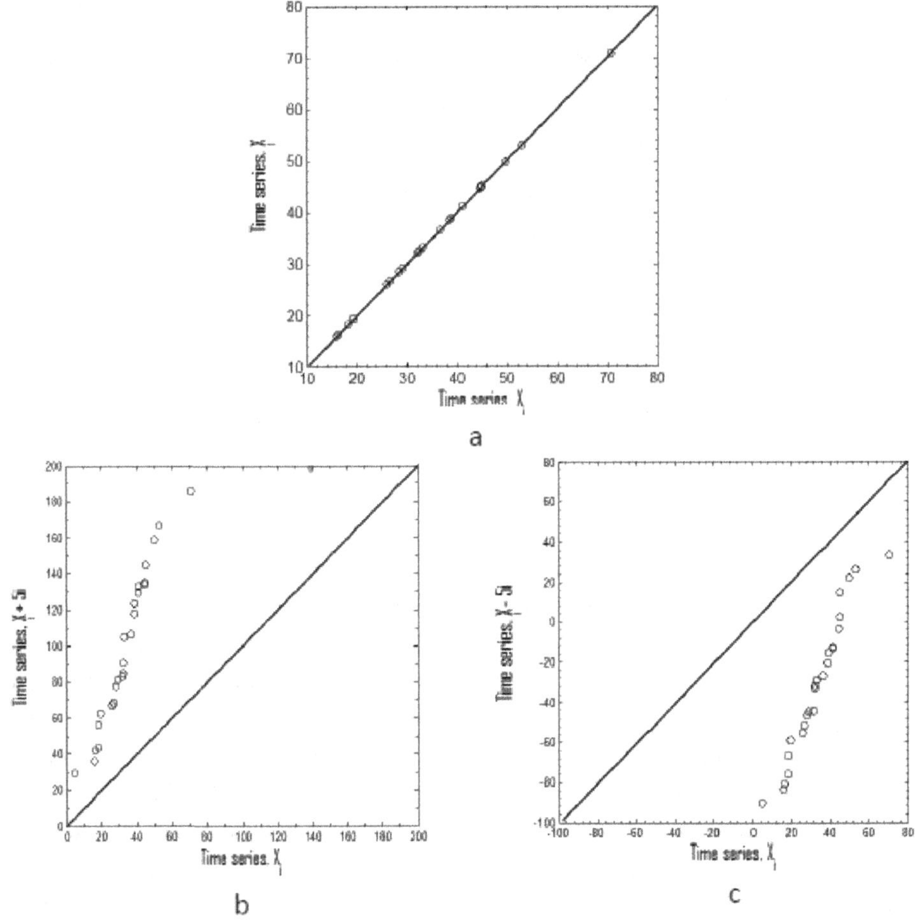

Figure 19. Time series halves with monotonic trends a) increasing, b) decreasing

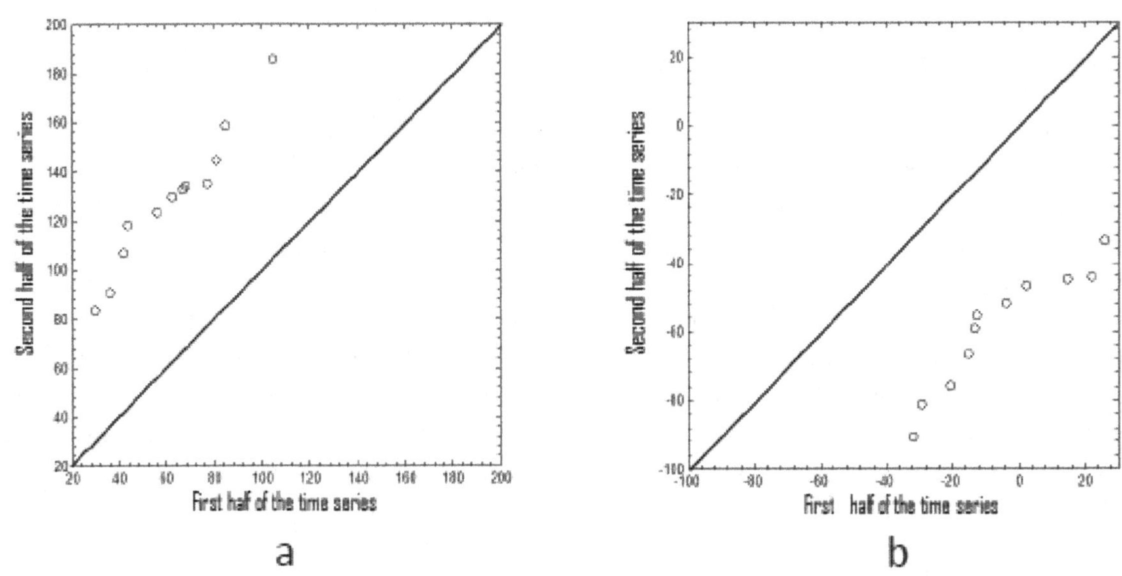

Figure 20. Time series halves with non-monotonic trends a) increasing, b) decreasing

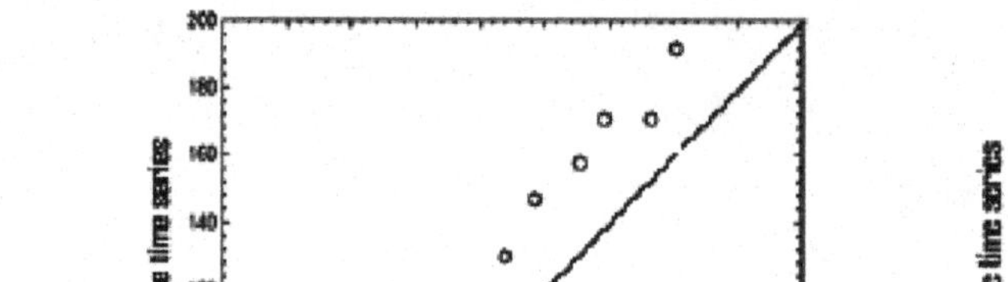

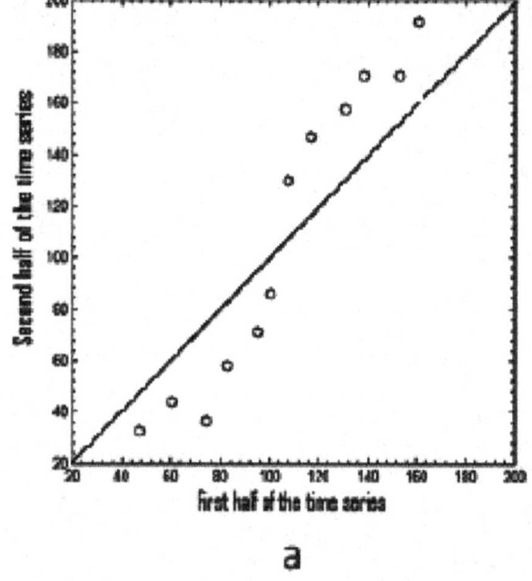

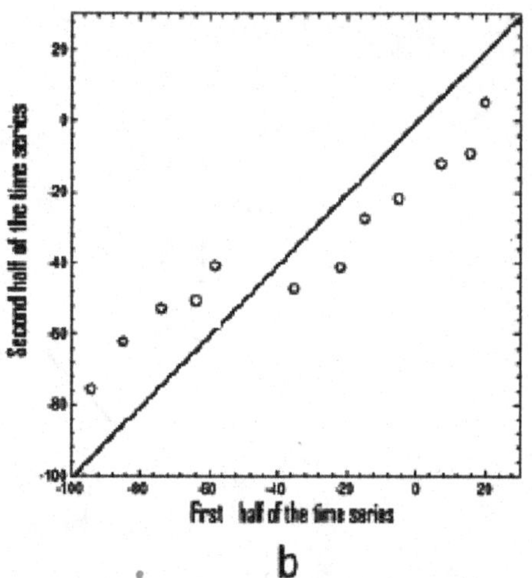

Turkey in addition to annual Danube river flows. Aslantas and Menzelet Dams are in the southern Turkey on Ceyhan River that confluences into the Mediterranean Sea. Cizre streamflow station is on the Tigris River right at the border between Turkey and Iraq. Danube annual streamflow records are from Orshava station in Romania. Figures 21a and 21b are from two hydrological catchments in Turkey, each reflecting annual flows from 1954 to 2003. In the interpretation of these figures it is better to think of the annual flows in three clusters as low, middle and high flows. In order to make a detailed interpretation, the scatter diagram on 1:1 line graphs are divided into three verbal clusters as 'Low,' 'Medium,' and 'High.'

In Figure 21a, "low" flows represent points on the increasing trend upper triangle, which means that there is an increase in the "low" flows during the second half of the historic record (1979-2003) with respect to the first half (1954-1978). In the medium cluster, there is almost no trend and finally, the "high" cluster indicates decreasing trend. All these explanations imply that the annual flow series have a composition of various trend patterns. Prior to the application of the methodology presented in this paper, all the data are checked for homogeneity, and therefore, there is no dam or other man-made effects.

The annual flow scatter diagram between two halves of Menzelet station are shown in Figure 21b, where the "low" flows have slight increasing components within the "low" flow cluster "low" and "high" values. The "medium" flow cluster is trend free because the scatter of points concentrate around 1:1 line. In the "high" cluster a decreasing trend component is valid. At this station there is a decrease in the "high" flow values; and hence, in the future, water stress is more likely to appear.

In Figure 21c, "low" and "high" clusters indicate decreasing trends, whereas the "medium" cluster is trend free. Comparatively "high" flow trends have shorter duration than in the "low" cluster portion. Most of the duration is occupied by "medium" cluster flows with no significant trend component. Furthermore, the "low" and "high" flows have decreases in the (1971-2003) duration compared to (1938-1970). This also gives warning that, at this station, droughts and floods are bound to increase in the future.

Finally, Danube river annual flows do not have any significant trend in the "low" flow cluster, which includes all the annual flows less than about 5750 m^3/sec (Figure 21d). "Medium" flows have some decreasing trend and "high" flow cluster has slightly significant increasing level.

Figure 21. Various 1:1 plots a) Aslantas Dam, b) Menzelet Dam, c) Cizre Station, e) Danube River

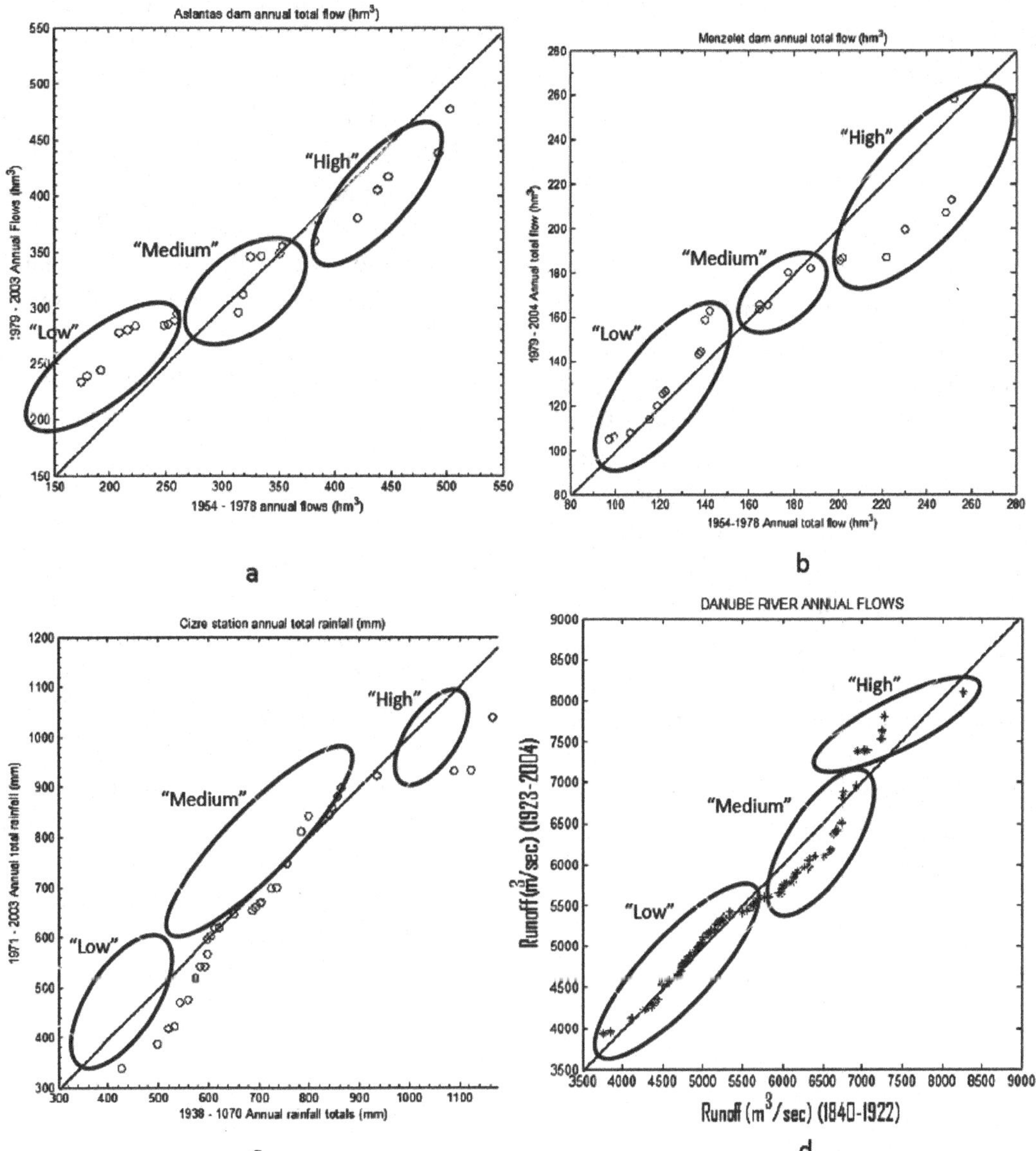

Based on the above, the following important points can be summarized about the proposed methodology.

1. If scatter points on the first quadrant of the Cartesian coordinate system fall on another straight line parallel to 1:1 line, then there is a monotonic increasing (decreasing) trend depending on the fall of the scatter points onto the upper (lower) triangular area of the scatter region,
2. The closer the scatter points are to the 1:1 line, the weaker the trend magnitude (slope),
3. In the case of non-monotonic trends (i.e. composition of various trends in the time series), the scatter points take their position on a curve.

Relative Trend Methodology

The fundamentals of this trend identification are given by Şen (2012b). Any time series trend does not suffer from the standardization procedure. If the given time series, X_i (i = 1, 2, . ., n), has n measurements then its standardized sequence can be obtained as,

$$x_i = \frac{X_i - \overline{X}}{S_X} \tag{13}$$

where $\overline{X}$ and S_X are the arithmetic mean and standard deviation values of the given series. This transformation results in a new dimensionless series with zero mean and unit standard deviation, hence it is possible to compare any two series even though they may be expressed in different units. In the relativistic trend search analysis a certain portions of this series are compared with some other non-overlapping parts. The part that is adapted as basic is referred to as baseline, similar to 30-year baseline (1960-1990) in the climatological studies. Hence, in the relativistic approach at least two segments of the same (or different) series are compared with each other and then one can suggest interpretive statements about the changes with respect to the baseline. The best template for such a comparison is the Cartesian coordinate system box as in Figure 22.

According to this figure the variation domain is divided into 16 squares each with a verbal specification as in Table 2. The third column includes pairwise fuzzy specifications for each cell in the figure.

Such a partition provides the following important interpretation facilities for any researcher in comparison of two standardized time series.

1. One can specify, for any given base cluster and another cluster, the verbal attachment to the data,
2. It is possible to classify verbally a group of data according to their cluster specification,
3. Different clusters of data can be compared as to their neighborship or relative position to each other and hence verbal interpretations are possible,
4. If the scatter points appear along the NL-NL, NM-NM, PM-PM and PH-PH clusters then the two series are closely related to each other, if they are two different physical series. If they are parts of the same series then it implies that there is not trend component within the series,

Figure 22. Scatter template

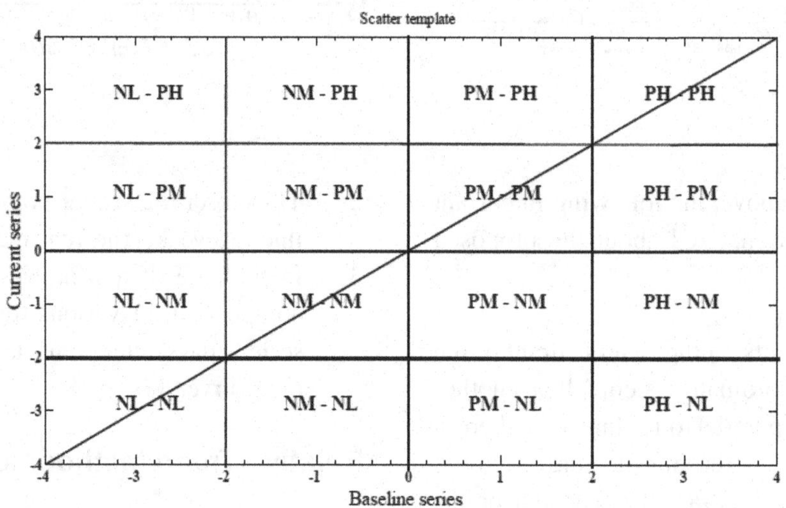

Table 2. Sub-area verbal specifications

Number	Symbol	Verbal Specification of Clusters
1	NL-NL	"Negative Low" – "Negative Low"
2	NM-NL	"Negative Medium" – "Negative Low"
3	PM-NL	"Positive Medium" - "Negative Low"
4	PH-NL	"Positive High" – "Negative Low"
5	NL-NM	"Negative Low" – "Negative Medium"
6	NM-NM	"Negative Medium" – "Negative Medium"
7	PM-NM	"Positive Medium" – "Negative Medium"
8	PH-NM	"Positive High" – "Negative Medium"
9	NL-PM	"Negative Low" – "Positive Medium"
10	NM-PM	"Negative Medium" – "Positive Medium"
11	PM-PM	"Positive Medium" – "Positive Medium"
12	PH-PM	"Positive High" – "Positive Medium"
13	NL-PH	"Negative Low" – "Positive High"
14	NM-PH	"Negative Medium" – "Positive High"
15	PM-PH	"Positive Medium" – "Positive High"
16	PH-PH	"Positive High" – "Positive High"

5. If the scatter of points appear along the NL-PH, NM-PM, PM-NM and PH-NL clusters then these two series are negatively related to each other.

Moreover, as shown in Figure 23 the same variation domain can be divided into two equal triangles, which are separated by 45° line. This template helps to identify relative trends with their increasing or decreasing tendencies not only as a straight-line but also as any curvy trend. Additionally, sequences of linear or curly sub-trends can be identified qualitatively.

It has been mentioned by Şen (2012b) that in the increasing and decreasing regions in Figure 23, if the plot indicates a parallel line to 45° line then there is a monochromatic trend. Otherwise, in the case of any curvy or broken straight-line appearance of the scatter points implies non-monochromatic trend.

The study area is the northeastern part of Turkey where Istanbul is located between two continents as in Figure 24. This is the most industrialized region of Turkey and it presents an example about the trend behavior between the two continents, Europe and Asia.

Although there are many meteorology stations in the area only 10 of them are considered in this study. The meteorology station locations are shown in Figure 18 with their specific features in Table 3. The records are available from 1930 to 2006.

Although it is possible to detect a set of non-overlapping 10-year, 15-year, 20-year, 25-year and any duration clusters, at the maximum length 76/2 = 38-year length, herein the relativistic trend identification is performed for 30-year duration. This leads to two 30-year non-overlapping sub-series as 1931-1960 and 1961-1990 durations. On the horizontal axis are the ascending order sorted precipitation values from the first duration versus the other duration ordered precipitation values on the vertical axis. The European 6 meteorology stations' trend scatter diagrams are shown in Figure 25.

Figure 23. Relativistic trend analysis boxes

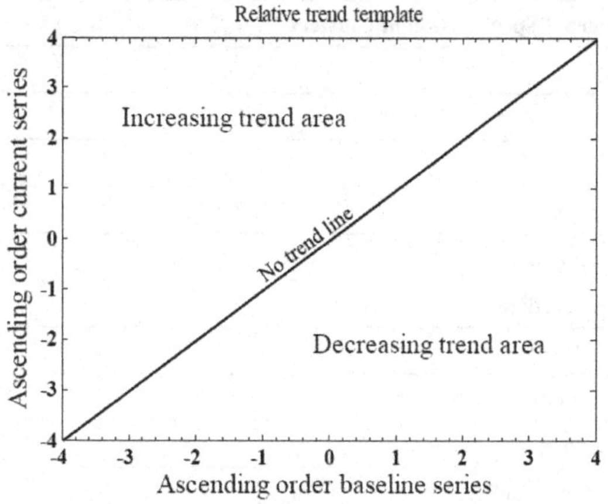

All the graphs show scatters around 45° line, which may lead to the following interpretations for each station.

1. At Florya station all scatter point lie within two sub-areas, namely, NM-NM and PH-PM, which implies that there are not extreme lower and higher precipitations during the whole 60 year duration. Most of the scatter points are slightly below the 45° line hence there is a very slightly decreasing monochromatic trend NM-NM and PM-PM regions, although there was a single year that had very extreme position within PM-PH sub-area,
2. Kilyos station has scatter points within three sub-areas, where the points within the PM-PM sub-area imply very slightly increase in 1961-1990 high precipitation events relative to high values during the previous period, 1931-1960. As for the lower precipitation values there is a sharp decreasing trend,
3. There are three active sub-areas at Corlu station as for the relative trend occurrences are concerned. These are sub-areas NM-NM, PM-NM and PM-PM. IN general there are trends at high, medium and low precipitation ranges in the forms of monochromatic neutral, decreasing and increasing trends, respectively,
4. The scatter diagram at Edirne is quite distinctive from the previous stations, in that four sub-areas are active and increasing non-monochromatic trend at low precipitation group, whereas a transitional trend takes

Figure 24. Study area and meteorology station locations

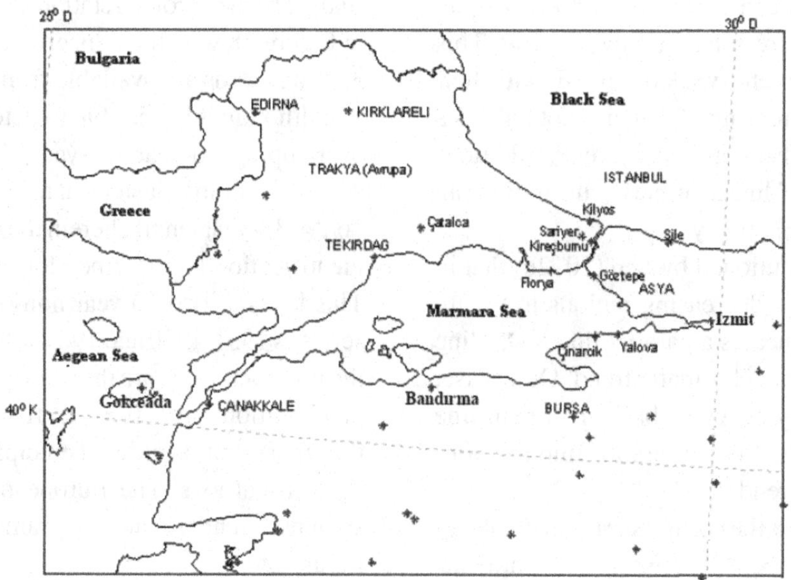

Table 3. Rainfall time series locations

Continent	Station						
	Name	Number	Latitude (N)	Longitude (E)	Statistical Values		
					Mean (mm)	St. Dev. (mm)	Maximum (mm)
EUROPE	Florya	17636	40° 59'	28° 47'	596	199.85	935.60
	Kilyos	17059	41° 15'	29° 02'	573	376.81	1229.80
	Çorlu	17054	41° 09'	27° 49'	516	195.78	970.30
	Edirne	17050	41° 41'	26° 33'	592	135.47	1127.40
	Tekirdag	17110	40° 11'	25° 54	620	133.47	990.30
	Kırklareli	17052	41° 44'	27° 13'	564	133.48	990.30
ASIA	Göztepe	17062	40° 58'	29° 05'	681	118.00	1046.80
	Şile	17610	41° 10'	29° 36'	720	323.34	1696.80
	İzmit	17066	40° 46'	29° 56'	777	151.01	1180.80
	Çanakkale	17112	40° 08'	26° 24'	671	133.24	977.90
	Bursa	17116	40° 13'	29° 00'	692	145.67	1061.30
	Bandırma	17114	40° 41'	29° 23	698	142.98	1086.20

place from the increase to decrease for medium ranges, but again non-monochromatic decreasing trend is valid for high precipitation values,

5. The scatter points are confined to two sub-areas at Tekirdag station with slightly increasing, transitional (from increase to decrease) and another transitional (from decrease to increase) at low, medium and high precipitation ranges, respectively,
6. Kirklareli station has more or less similar behavior to Tekirdağ, because they are neighboring stations with very slight differences in morphology, topography and atmospheric environmental effects.

EARTHQUAKE VISUAL DATA AND FUZZY CLUSTER ASSESSMENT

Expert views and experience play significant role in any preliminary assessment of an event through linguistic statements, principles and rule-of-thumb, which do not require involved mathematical formulations. For the preliminary assessment of any building against potential earthquake vulnerability either the features of the concerned buildings can be checked against a set of empirical rules or an expert is invited for linguistic appreciation of the overall situation. Any expert bases the final conclusion onto a set of previously experienced rules and principles. As will be explained shortly later in this section, various earthquake assessment intensity scales are suggested by different researchers and they become a commonly used and internationally recognized criterion in any earthquake damage assessment irrespective of time and space (Kramer, 1996). These scales are Modified Mercalli Intensity (MMI), Rossi-Forel Intensity (RI), Japanese Meteorological Agency (JMA) and Medvedev–Spoonheuer–Karnik (MSK) intensities (Coburn & Spence, 1992). Each one of these scales are expressed in terms of fuzzy words in proper sentences (statements) such as "low," "moderate," "severe," "high," "more," "almost," etc., (Şen, 2010b).

Figure 25. European meteorology station trend templates

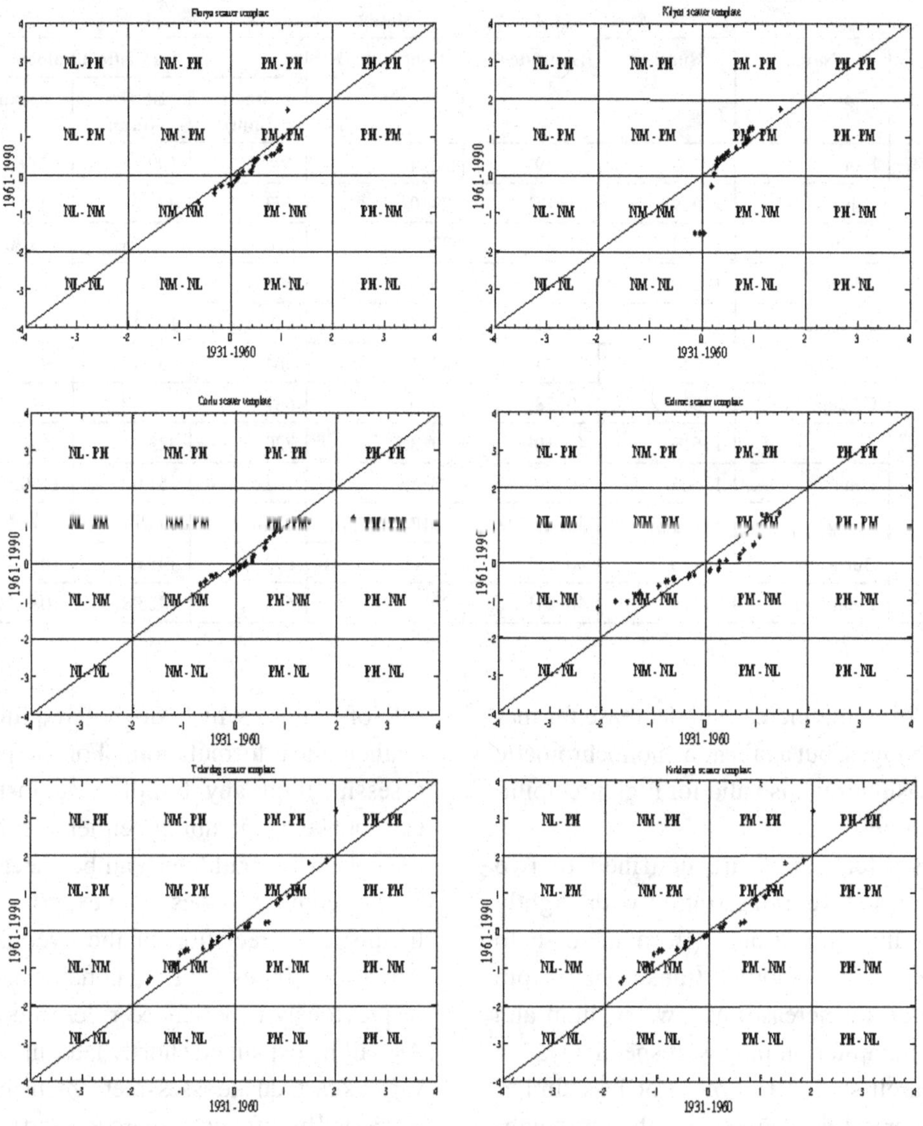

The content of each sentence implies logical rules, which constitute the foundation of fuzzy system modeling and inference procedures. In comprehensive decisions an expert's heuristic knowledge or empirical information is used frequently for better conclusions. Complexity and uncertainty complicate a reasonable judgment by considering multi-criteria for the building behavior (Hong et al., 2003). Uncertainty stems mainly from sources such as the lack of the incomplete data availability, vagueness, linguistic expert view, etc. Such complexities, uncertainties, complications and vagueness can be dealt with fuzzy logic principles and inference systems (Kiszka et al., 1985b; Klir & Folger, 1988; Zadeh, 1973). Besides, they are based on a set of classical logic inference method, which requires ''white'' or ''black'' information ignoring any type of uncertainty. Improvements can be made to existing dataset and in areas of uncertainty for the earthquake behavior characterization by considering an expert fuzzy logic approach, which evaluates ''grey'' information. Especially, damage to buildings and distribution systems in a city will affect the whole post-earthquake recovery operation. It is, therefore, necessary to have pre-earthquake potential models for the rapid assessment of existing buildings leading to rational and logical scenarios, which could provide basic and reliable information about the possible hazard categorization. Fuzzy logic and inference systems are used in civil engineering structures and structural concrete frame analysis (Shiraishi et al., 2005; Stemberk & Kruis, 2005).

It is the main purpose of this section to develop and apply a fuzzy logic model (FLM) only for rapid screening stage of buildings against earthquake danger. At this stage, model inputs are visual factors that should be taken into consideration in any earthquake assessment of a reinforced building and majority of them include linguistic data. All the factors are converted into fuzzy sets (linguistic variables), MFs (simple mathematical expressions), fuzzy-rules and then fuzzy inference system (FIS) is used for the categorization of each building into a few of the five hazard categories, which are ''without,'' ''light,'' ''moderate,'' ''heavy,'' and ''complete'' damages. For the application of the FLM, software is developed by Delphi programming language and its application is presented for 1249 buildings in the pilot study area of Zeytinburnu quarter in Istanbul, Turkey (Şen, 2010b).

Earthquake Intensity Scales

In the FL modeling of building damage scaling, there is an attempt of soft transition between neighboring clusters of hazard. The final result of scaling is achieved accordingly to five classes of decreasing vulnerability as ''complete,'' ''heavy,'' ''moderate,'' slight'' and ''without'' hazard clusters. The first three categories are important for taking immediate action during pre-earthquake period.

The way that buildings respond to earthquake is expressed by their vulnerability. For instance, if two building groups are subjected to exactly the same earthquake then one group may perform better than the other, which means than the buildings that are less damaged have lower earthquake vulnerability than the ones that are more damaged. Likewise, the buildings that are ''without'' or ''slight'' damage are more earthquake resistant. Various intensity scales are based on the performance of different building types. These scales define building classes by type of construction as simple attempt to express the vulnerability of buildings. One essential feature in the vulnerability assessments is the degree of available details in defining building types, damage grades and quantities. Such availability is always incomplete, vague and uncertain, i.e., fuzzy. In a very simple intensity scale, all damage to buildings of a particular type would be grouped together irrespective of the strength the building. This would be easy to use, but might give very different results in the region where different types of buildings are present. The FL modeling incorporates a compromise, in which a simple differentiation in the resistance of buildings to earthquake is also taken into consideration. Macro-seismic intensity is a subjective measure of the severity of earthquake effects at a particular location. It is defined according to an index scale, each level having a qualitative description of earthquake effects based on human perceptions, effects on construction and on natural surroundings. A widely used scale, the Modified Mercalli Intensity (MMI) scale alludes specifically to the level of response of various aspects of systems. The MMI scale is presented in Table 4 in detail where one can see many fuzzy descriptive words such as ''few,'' ''very few,'' ''favorable,'' ''slight,'' ''many,'' ''poorly,'' ''greatly,'' ''heavy,'' etc. In fact this table is based on expert view and it includes many rules which are convenient for fuzzy inferences.

At the lower intensity levels (up to VI), the effects are unlikely to be damaging to intact com-

Table 4. MMI scale clusters

MMI	Linguistic Descriptions
1. Instrumental	Generally not felt by people unless in favorable conditions.
2. Weak	Felt only by a few people at rest, especially on the upper floors of buildings. Delicately suspended objects may swing.
3. Slight	Felt quite noticeably by people indoors, especially on the upper floors of buildings. Many do not recognize it as an earthquake. Standing motor cars may rock slightly. Vibration similar to the passing of a truck. Duration estimated.
4. Moderate	Felt indoors by many people, outdoors by few people during the day. At night, some awaken. Dishes, windows, doors disturbed; walls make cracking sound. Sensation like heavy truck striking building. Standing motor cars rock noticeably. Dishes and windows rattle alarmingly.
5. Rather Strong	Felt inside by most, may not be felt by some outside in non-favorable conditions. Dishes and windows may break and large bells will ring. Vibrations like large train passing close to house.
6. Strong	Felt by all; many frightened and run outdoors, walk unsteadily. Windows, dishes, glassware broken; books fall off shelves; some heavy furniture moved or overturned; a few instances of fallen plaster. Damage slight.
7. Very Strong	Difficult to stand; furniture broken; damage negligible in building of good design and construction; slight to moderate in well built ordinary structures; considerable damage in poorly built or badly designed structures; some chimneys broken. Noticed by people driving motor cars.
8. Destructive	Damage slight in specially designed structures; considerable in ordinary substantial buildings with partial collapse. Damage great in poorly built structures. Fall of chimneys, factory stacks, columns, monuments, walls. Heavy furniture moved.
9. Violent	General panic; damage considerable in specially designed structures, well designed frame structures thrown out of plumb. Damage great in substantial buildings, with partial collapse. Buildings shifted off foundations.
10. Intense	Some well-built wooden structures destroyed; most masonry and frame structures destroyed with foundation. Rails bent slightly. Large landslides.
11. Extreme	Few, if any masonry structures remain standing. Bridges destroyed. Rails bent greatly. Numerous landslides, cracks and deformation of the ground.
12. Catastrophic	Total destruction – Everything is destroyed. Lines of sight and level distorted. Objects thrown into the air. The ground moves in waves or ripples. Large amounts of rock move position. Landscape altered, or leveled by several meters. In some cases, even the routes of rivers are changed.

ponents of the building system significant damage is associated with levels of VII or more.

Categorization of the buildings according to their earthquake resistant design can be achieved under the light of this scale, but the following significant points remain without answer.

1. This scale does not provide opportunity to distinguish between the buildings in the same group. For instance, a group of buildings in scale XII is assumed to have the same behavior without differentiation,
2. It is not possible to consider a given building in two or three of these scale (categories), since each scale is considered mutually exclusive and independent from others,
3. The overall grading of each building as a distinctive number is not possible, but only observed effects are expressed linguistically,
4. Different constituents of the damage factors cannot be identified, and therefore, the expert cannot know the contribution of each element,
5. The planner is not capable of drawing iso-damage maps, because different numbers are not attached to the buildings. All these points are avoided by modeling the earthquake damage of buildings according to FLM as presented in this paper.

Using the damage definitions of 1998 European Macro-seismic Scale (EMS) Grunthal, 1998 a general picture of damage under exposure to these intensity levels can be gained. For the vulnerability cluster where the general reinforced concrete multistory building stock in Istanbul is located, EMS-1998 provides the following damage definitions. Intensity VII: A "few" buildings sustain "moderate" damage. Intensity VIII: "Many" buildings suffer "moderate" damage; a "few" receive substantial to "heavy" damage. Intensity X: "Many" buildings suffer substantial to "heavy" damage; a "few" sustain "very heavy" damage. Herein, "few" is a fuzzy word and it describes less than 20% and "many" describes 20–60%. There is considerable uncertainty in the form of fuzziness associated with macro-seismic intensity levels and the compilation of intensity maps. Caution should therefore be exercised in the use of intensity maps for the definition of the variation in earthquake hazard from place to place or their use as a basis for the estimation of future losses. However, in the absence of instrumental data, micro-seismic data (linguistic) is often the best available (Zadeh, 1973). Various different intensity scales exist, each with its own qualitative descriptions of earthquake effects at different intensity levels.

In any earthquake assessment scale the measure of the damage degree is made through the qualitative fuzzy terms such as "few," "many," "most," etc., which reflect important uncertainties and statistical elements. However, any attempt to present the scale as a series of graphs showing exact percentages would be impossible, because the definition of these terms numerically is not very easy. Although, one can use crisp quantitative numerical values, such as 0–20%, 20–60% and 60–100% for "few," "many," and "most," respectively, there is a sharp transition between neighboring sets, which are mutually exclusive. However, FL model provides a better approach where there is possibility for compromise by using mutually inclusive categorizations with distinctive building hazard degrees.

Herein FL model is presented for the screening stage, where there are eight input variables with one hazard categorization as output (Figure 26). Few of these variables have numerical values, but the others are all in linguistic forms. However, in the classical modeling the inputs Ss, Ce, Ws, Pe and Hse are quantified as 1 implying existence (yes, white) and 0 as nonexistence (no, black) of the effect according to the crisp two-valued logic. In this case, there is no distinction between grey say "little," "medium" and "big" quantities.

For instance, if three buildings have cantilever extensions of 15 cm, 50 cm or 1 m, they are all quantified as 1. In the FLM, each one of the input variables are fuzzified into at least three fuzzy sets and attached membership functions (MFs) as "no," "low," "medium" and "yes." Hence a big distinction is obtained from the two-valued crisp logic (0 or 1, "white" or "black"). In Figure 27 are the MFs for storey number on the horizontal axis versus membership degrees (MDs) on the vertical axis.

In Istanbul, the most vulnerable group is found to be medium rise (4–7 stories) reinforced concrete frame buildings, which are cast in situ reinforced concrete frame buildings with non-reinforced masonry infill walls designed on the basis of outdated codes and generally suffering from re inforcement corrosion problems. In the majority of buildings, ground floor space is reserved for shops and irregular plan shapes are common due to irregular land lots and urban congestion. A distinction was made between buildings with four or more story and those with three or fewer story based on building damage statistics (Sucuoglu & Yilmaz, 2001). As shown in Figure 28, the first category of buildings suffered considerably more damage as a result of the Kocaeli and Duzce earthquakes in 1999 than the second category.

Five of the input variables namely, Ss, Ce, Ws, Pe and Hse are represented with five MFs as shown in Figure 29 where the variables are considered to have values between 0 and 1.

Four fuzzy sets are attached as "No, N," "Low, L," "Medium, M," and "Yes, Y." Weak storey

Figure 26. The overall structure of the model

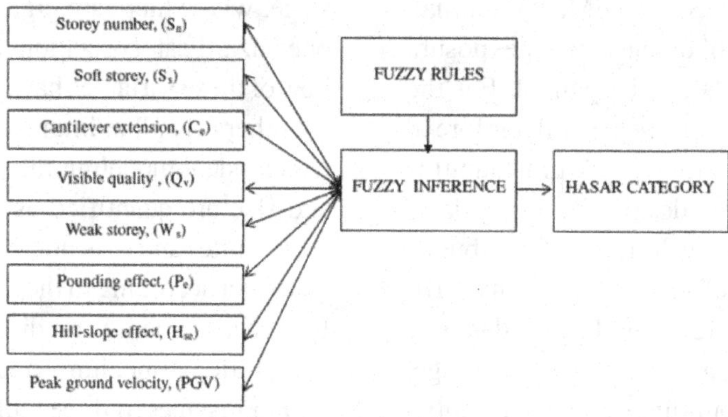

Figure 27. Storey number MFs

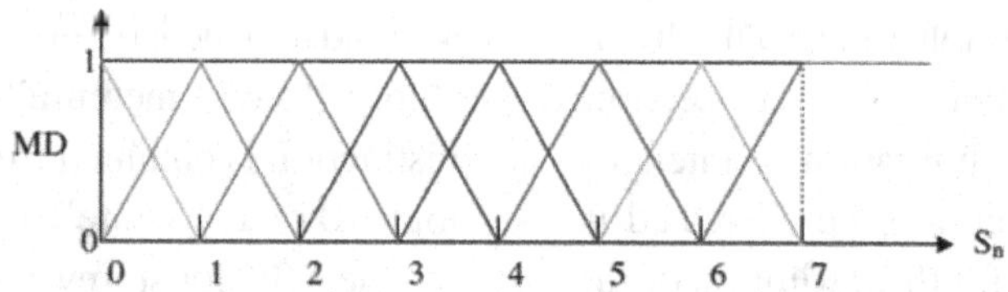

Figure 28. Building damage rates in Düzce according to building height

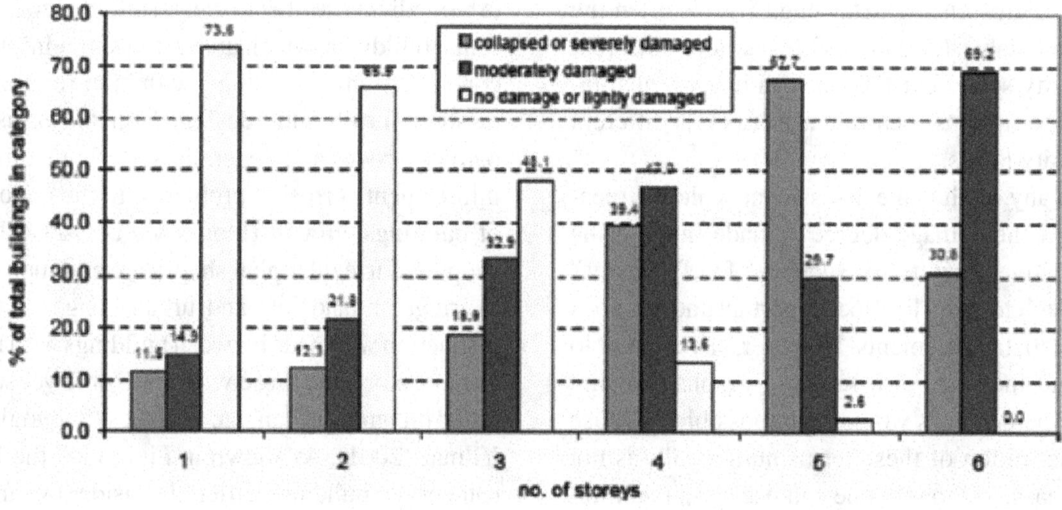

failure was extensive at schools and public buildings. Insufficient gaps between columns and non-structural elements caused large shear forces to be induced on the short columns (weak storey). The stiffening (shortening) of similar columns impose large shear and rotation demands at the plastic hinges in these shorter columns. Weak stories are usually found where vertical disconti-

Figure 29. S_s, C_e, W_s, P_e and MFs

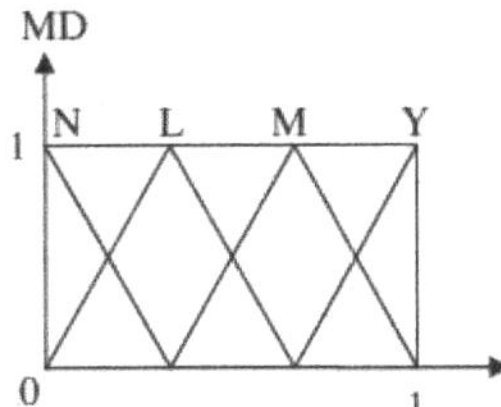

nuities exist, or where member size or reinforcement has been reduced. The result of a weak story is a concentration of inelastic activity that may result in the partial or total collapse of the story. Soft story condition commonly occurs in buildings with open fronts at ground floor or with particularly tall first stories. Soft stories usually are revealed by an abrupt change in inter-storey drift. Although a comparison of the stiffnesses in adjacent stories is the direct approach, a simple first step might be to compare the interstory drifts. Eurocode 8 specifies that there should not be significant difference in the lateral stiffness of individual stories and at any storey the maximum displacement in the direction of the seismic forces should not exceed the average storey displacement by more than 20% (Grunthal, 1998). Buildings may impact each other, or pound, during an earthquake. Building pounding can alter the dynamic response of both the buildings, and impart additional inertial loads on both structures. There is a potential for extensive damage and possible collapse. According to FEMA 310, in order to avoid pounding, the building shall not be located closer than 4% of the height to an adjacent (FEMA, 1999).

Hillside slopes liable to slide during an earthquake should be avoided and only stable slopes should be chosen to locate the building. Also it will be preferable to have several blocks on terraces than have one large block with footings at very different elevations. Figure 30 is the visual building quality input variable MFs as ''Good, G,'' ''Medium, M,'' ''Bad, B,'' and ''Very bad, VB.''

The micro zoning studies (Sucuoglu and Yilmaz, 2001) have provided point peak ground velocity (PGV) numerical values at any desired locations, which are fuzzified into three MFs as ''low, L,'' ''Medium, M'' and ''High, H,'' which are shown in Figure 31.

Finally, five MFs for the building hazard categorization are given in Figure 32, where hazard categories are ''without,'' W, ''slight,'' S, ''moderate,'' M, ''heavy,'' H, and ''complete,'' C hazards. After the aforementioned explanations the logical rules of each variable with the building grade are presented and their fuzzification can be accomplished by considering fuzzy words for input variables and hazard categorizations.

According to these hazard MFs, some of the bilateral descriptions in terms of fuzzy rule bases are presented in Figure 33, where the valid rule domains are shaded. By considering fundamental pairwise associations as in Figure 27 it is possible to develop a joint rule base for the earthquake resistant building categorization.

FL model includes combined fuzzy-rules, which relate the combination of the input variables by ''AND'' connectivity to output fuzzy sets and among the rules ''OR'' connectivity is valid. Dur-

Figure 30. Visible building quality MFs

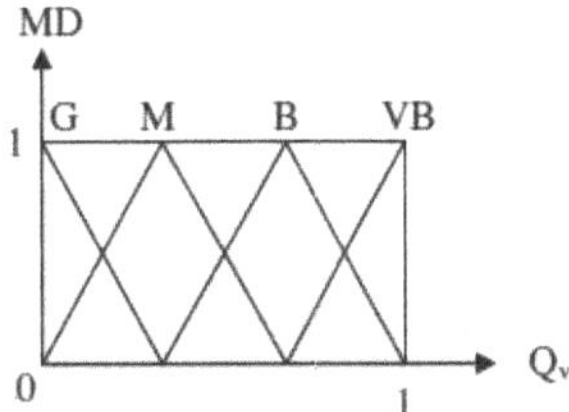

Figure 31. PGV MFs

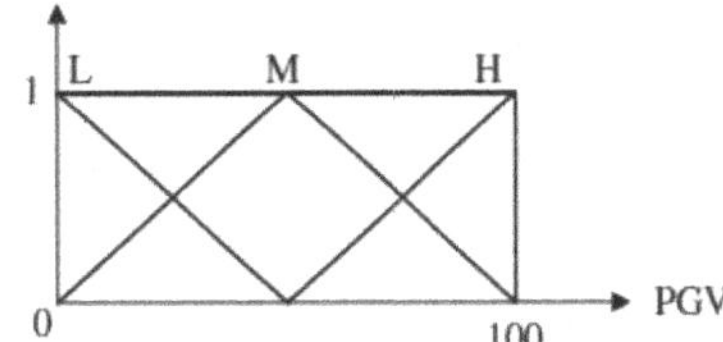

Figure 32. Earthquake hazard cluster MFs

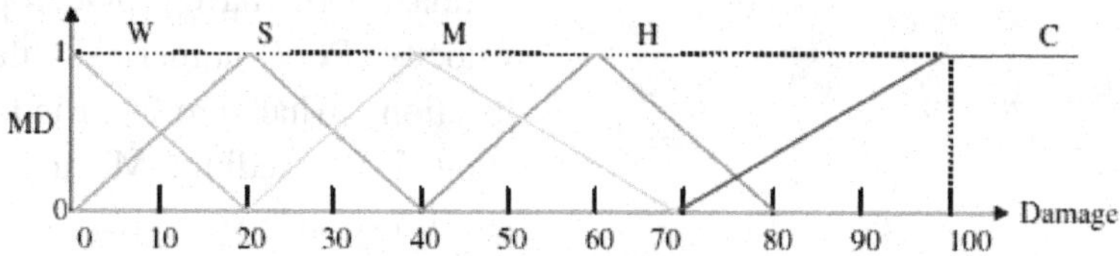

Figure 33. Bilateral fuzzy associations a) S_n, b) S_e, H_e, W_s, P_e, H_{se}, Q_v and c) PGV

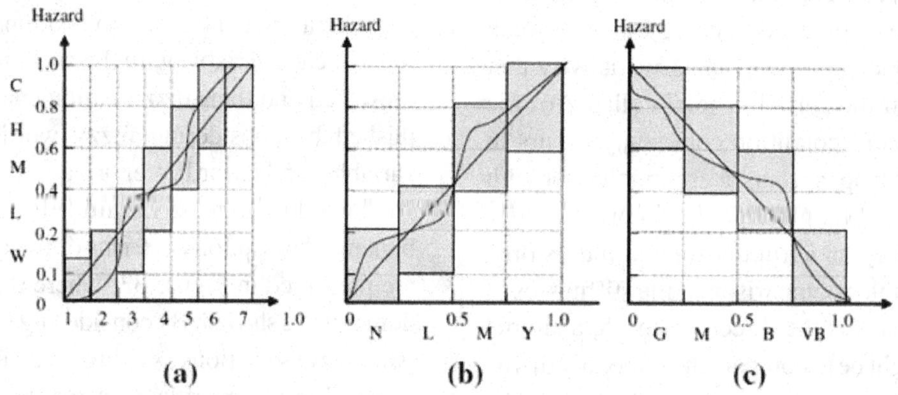

ing the course of this study although there are 4x4x4x4x4x3 = 12,288 such rules for each storey, thousands of these are not logically valid and finally 1344 rules are remained to identify the building damage class. Few of the combined fuzzy-rules are,

```
IF Sn is L AND Ss is L AND Ws is L
AND He is L AND Pe is L AND Hse is L
AND Qv is VB
AND  PGV is H THEN Damage is CD.
IF Sn is M AND Ss is M AND Ws is M
AND He is M AND Pe is M AND Hse is M
AND Qv is M
AND PGV is M THEN Damage is MD.
IF Sn is Y AND Ss is Y AND Wc is Y
AND He is Y AND Pe is Y AND Hse is Y
AND Qv is VB
AND PGV is L THEN Damage is MD.
```

Each fuzzy rule implies a logical association between the fuzzy sets of input variables and the output fuzzy set of categorization. In a way, each rule implies partial association between the input variables set and the hazard categories. Such a logical association is not available in any rapid visual screening procedure presented into literature so far. The elegancy of the FL model lies in the partial association representations by a set of fuzzy-rules, which reflect linguistic expert views in addition to numerical data associations. The execution of the fuzzy rule set is achieved according to the following steps for each building (Mamdani, 1974).

1. The input variables (eight factors) of the building are introduced to each one of the 1344 rules and the ones triggered (fired) are identified.

2. The triggered rules have eight input MDs and the overall premise part MD is adopted according to the minimization (ANDing) operation of the fuzzy sets and hence the representative (MD)r is calculated for each triggered rule.
3. The same (MD) is carried on the consequent (output, after THEN) part of each rule, and accordingly, the valid fuzzy hazard sets are obtained as the consequent of each triggered rule.
4. The set of triggered rules is composed with maximization (ORing) operation, and finally the hazard categorization of the building is obtained.
5. The previous steps are applied to each building in sequence, and finally, hazard categories of all the buildings are obtained.

The distinctions of the FL model from other available rapid visual screening methods are as follows:

1. FL model approach provides not only the possible partial associations between the input and output variables, but additionally between the input variables also.
2. Each building has at least few hazard categories with different MDs. Hence, there will be distinctions among the buildings even though they are within the same group.
3. There is no need for a 'cut-off' value determination for the final categorization of the buildings into two decision categories as in the classical approaches.
4. Since each building has different MDs, it is possible to make iso-hazard maps for each hazard category. Five hazard categorizations are adopted, and hence there will be five distinctive iso-hazard maps each for ''without,'' ''slight,'' ''moderate,'' ''heavy'' and ''complete'' hazard categories.
5. It is not necessary to have all the information in numerical form but each fuzzy rule digests also linguistic data.
6. It is possible to identify which fuzzy-rules are effective for a given building and accordingly the building may be reinforced to the worst earthquake hazard category.

FUTURE DIRECTIONS

It is expected in the future that the clustering algorithms will also take into account the trend analyses in an approximate reasoning manner that conforms to the natural thinking of humanity including fuzzy ingredients. Improvement of fuzzy methodology will depend more on imagination, description and subsequent idea generation, which are all fuzzy concepts that lead to natural solutions without involved mathematical expressions, which require a set of restrictive assumptions. The following research topics may be considered for future research directions.

1. Both k-means and c-means clustering methodologies are based on geometric distances, but it may be possible to make clusters based on a third physical variable concerned with the same phenomenon. A simple guiding idea may be that for precipitation occurrence temperature and humidity play basic role and hence it may be possible to make clusters of precipitation with respect to temperature and humidity,
2. Education system must be dependent on more imaginative, descriptive and production dimensions with linguistic conceptions so as to improve the creative idea generation among the concerned individuals,
3. Search for multi-dimensional data clustering apart from k-means or c-means, simply by grouping the data into at least triple clusters as "minimum," "medium" and "maximum" (or more than three groups) clusters in some

simple manner, say, by intuitive appreciation provided that one is expert in the phenomenon concerned. Of course, such an approach must be laid down as successive steps in the form of an algorithm,

4. In all the cluster analysis after the cluster identification the transition between these clusters in time domain has not been analyzed effectively in the current literature, which appears a new research direction in the future.

CONCLUSION

Fuzzy methodology helps experts to lay down their linguistic, rational and logical thoughts into a system of rule base that generates indistinguishable behavior of the phenomenon under study. This chapter presents the fundamental of fuzzy logic (FL) thinking compared to crisp (two-valued) logic (CL), which requires assumptions, coefficients and a set of equations. FL with its elastic clustering methodology furnishes rods towards linguistic logical propositions in the form of rule base instead of equations, restrictive assumptions and coefficients. After a brief comparative explanation between CL and FL, the significance of clustering methodology is explained with citations from the literature. Later several innovative methodological procedures are explained and some of them are presented through actual FL principles application. Similar to CL k-means, a simple FL k-means-standard–deviations procedure is suggested as a preliminary FL clustering where the summation of membership degrees of each member within different fuzzy sets is not equal to one. The classical fuzzy c-means clustering with the summation of membership degrees equal to one is presented with several other methodologies by many researchers. A new trend of fuzzy functions is also presented with relevant literature. Existing trend analyses require equally spaced (time or space) data, whereas in nature, social and economic subjects there are many unequally spaced data that need trend identification. Such drawbacks can be solved through fuzzy logic modeling without restrictive assumptions. A preliminary innovative example is provided in this chapter towards this goal. Four methodological procedures are suggested, namely, fuzzy logic k-means-standard deviations, cluster regression, relative trend analysis and earthquake clustering. It is also stressed in this chapter that in addition to common sense imagination, description and idea production stages are necessary for effective fuzzy modeling in order to establish rule base and qualitative relationships.

The cluster regression method provides the best regression line in addition to the cluster occurrences and transition probabilities along this line. Its difference from the classical regression approach lies in the appearance of non-overlapping clusters. The cluster regression approach preserves all the statistical parameters in addition to the autocorrelation coefficient, which is a measure of short-term persistence in lake level records. Any shifts in the data do not lead to spurious and unrealistic autocorrelation

REFERENCES

Bezdek, J. C. (1976). Cluster validity with fuzzy sets. *Journal of Cybernetics*, *3*, 58–72. doi:10.1080/01969727308546047.

Bezdek, J. C. (1981). *Pattern recognition with fuzzy objective function algorithms*. New York: Plenium. doi:10.1007/978-1-4757-0450-1.

Bezdek, J. C., & Hathaway, R. J. (1987). Clustering with relational c–means partitions from pairwise distance data. *International Journal of Mathematical Modeling*, *8*, 435–439. doi:10.1016/0270-0255(87)90509-4.

Bouguessa, M., Wang, S., & Sun, H. (2006). An objective approach to cluster validation. *Pattern Recognition Letters*, *27*, 1419–1430. doi:10.1016/j.patrec.2006.01.015.

Box, C. E. P., & Jenkins, G. M. (1970). Time series analysis, forecasting and control: Golden Day. San Francisco, pp. 498.

Celikyilmaz, A., & Türkşen, I. B. (2007). Fuzzy functions with support vector machines. *Information Sciences*, *177*, 5163–5177. doi:10.1016/j.ins.2007.06.022.

Celikyilmaz, A., & Türkşen, I. B. (2008). Validation criteria for enhanced fuzzy clustering. *Pattern Recognition Letters*, *29*, 97–108. doi:10.1016/j.patrec.2007.08.017.

Coburn, A., & Spence, R. (1992). *Earthquake protection*. John Wiley.

Dave, R. N. (1996). Validating fuzzy partition obtained through C-shells clustering. *Pattern Recognition Letters*, *17*, 613–623. doi:10.1016/0167-8655(96)00026-8.

Dimitrov, W. (2000). The consciousness resonance in action. Understanding fuzziness of knowing. *Journal on Hydrolics*, *240*, 90–105.

Dubois, D., & Prade, H. (1988). Representation and combination of uncertainty with belief functions and possibility measures. *Computational Intelligence (Canada)*, *4*(4), 244–264. doi:10.1111/j.1467-8640.1988.tb00279.x.

FEMA. (1999). Earthquake loss estimation methodology HAZUS 99 service release 2: Technical manual. *FEMA*. Retrieved from http://www.fema.gov/hazus

Fukuyama, Y., & Sugeno, M. (1989). A new method of choosing the number of clusters for the fuzzy C-means method. In *Proc. 5th Fuzzy Systems Symposium* (pp. 247–250).

Gelb, A. (1974). *Applied optimal filtering* (p. 382). MIT Press.

Grunthal, G. (1998). *European macro seismic scale 1998* (*Vol. 15*, p. 99). Conseil de l'Europe.

Hathaway, R. J., & Bezdek, J. C. (1993). Switching regression models and fuzzy clustering. *IEEE Transactions on Fuzzy Systems*, *1*(3), 195–203. doi:10.1109/91.236552.

Kendall, M. G. (1975). *Rank correlation methods*. New York: Oxford Univ. Press.

Kim, D.-W., Lee, K. H., & Lee, D. (2003). Fuzzy cluster validation index based on inter-cluster proximity. *Pattern Recognition Letters*, *24*, 2561–2574. doi:10.1016/S0167-8655(03)00101-6.

Kim, M., & Ramakrishna, R. S. (2005). New indices for cluster validity assessment. *Pattern Recognition Letters*, *26*, 2353–2363. doi:10.1016/j.patrec.2005.04.007.

Kiszka, J. B., Kochanska, M. E., & Sliwinska, D. S. (1985a). The influence of some fuzzy implication operators on the accuracy of fuzzy model. Part I. *Fuzzy Sets and Systems*, *15*, 111–128. doi:10.1016/0165-0114(85)90041-7.

Kiszka, J. B., Kochanska, M. E., & Sliwinska, D. S. (1985b). The influence of some fuzzy implication operators on the accuracy of a fuzzy model, Part II. *Fuzzy Sets and Systems*, *15*, 223–240. doi:10.1016/0165-0114(85)90016-8.

Klir, G. J., & Folger, T. A. (1988). *Fuzzy sets, uncertainty, and information. Engle-wood Cliffs*. NJ: Prentice Hall.

Kramer, S. L. (1996). *Geotechnical earthquake engineering*. New Jersey: Prentice Hall.

Lee, R. C. T., Slagle, J. R., & Blum, H. (1976). A triangulation method for the sequential mapping of points from n–space to two–space. *IEEE Transactions on Computers*, *26*(3), 288–292. doi:10.1109/TC.1977.1674822.

MacQueen, J. (1967). Some methods for classification and analysis of multivariate observations. In L. M. Le Cam and J. Neyman (Ed.), *Proceedings of the Fifth Berkeley Symposium on Mathematical Statistics and Probability* (pp. 281).

Mamdani, E. H. (1974). Application of fuzzy algorithms for simple dynamic plant. *Proceedings of the IEEE*, *121*, 1585–1588.

Mann, H. B. (1945). Nonparametric tests against trend. *Econometrica*, *13*, 245–259. doi:10.2307/1907187.

Pal, N. K., & Bezdek, J. C. (1995). On cluster validity for fuzzy C-means model. *IEEE Transactions on Fuzzy Systems*, *3*(3), 370–379. doi:10.1109/91.413225.

Popper, K. (1952). *The logic of scientific discovery* (p. 479). Routledge Publishing Company.

Ross, T. J. (1995). *Fuzzy logic with engineering applications* (p. 606). McGraw-Hill.

Runkler, T. A. (2003). Fuzzy nonlinear projection. In *IEEE International Conference on Fuzzy Systems*.

Runkler, T. A., & Bezdek, J. C. (1999). Alternating cluster estimation: A new tool for clustering and function approximation. *IEEE Transactions on Fuzzy Systems*, *7*(4), 377–393. doi:10.1109/91.784198.

Russell, B. (1948). *Human knowledge: Its scope and limits*. London: George Allen and Unwin.

Sammon, J. W. (1969). A nonlinear mapping for data structure analysis. *IEEE Transactions on Computers*, *C-18*(5). doi:10.1109/T-C.1969.222678.

Sen, P. K. (1968). Estimates of the regression coefficient based on Kendall's tau. *Journal of the American Statistical Association*, *63*, 1379–1389. doi:10.1080/01621459.1968.10480934.

Şen, Z. (2010a). Fuzzy logic and hydrogeological modeling (pp. 340). Taylor and Francis Group, CRC Press.

Şen, Z. (2010b). Rapid visual earthquake hazard evaluation of existing buildings by fuzzy logic modeling. *Expert Systems with Applications*, *37*, 5653–5660. doi:10.1016/j.eswa.2010.02.046.

Şen, Z. (2011a). Fuzzy philosophy of science and education. *Turkish Journal of Fuzzy Systems*, *2*(2), 77–98.

Şen, Z. (2011b). Supervised fuzzy logic modeling for building earthquake hazard assessment. *Expert Systems with Applications*, *38*, 14564–1457. doi:10.1016/j.eswa.2011.05.026.

Şen, Z. (2012a). An innovative trend analysis methodology. *Journal of Hydrologic Engineering*.

Şen, Z. (2012b). Trend identification simulation and application. *Journal of Hydrologic Engineering*.

Şen, Z., Kadıoğlu, M., & Batur, E. (1999). Cluster regression model and level fluctuation features of Van Lake, Turkey. *Annales Geophysicae*, *17*, 273–279.

Shiraishi, N., Furuta, H., Umano, M., & Kawakami, K. (2005). *Knowledge-based expert system for damage assessment based on fuzzy reasoning. Artificial intelligence tools and techniques for civil and structural engineers* (p. 658). Edinburgh, United Kingdom: B.H.V. Topping, Civil-Comp Press.

Stemberk, P., & Kruis, J. (2005). Fuzzy dynamic structural analysis of 2D frames. In *Proceedings of the tenth international conference on civil structures and environmental engineering* (p. 658). Edinburgh, United Kingdom: B.H.V. Topping, Civil-Comp Press.

Sucuoglu, H., & Yilmaz, T. (2001). Duzce, Turkey: A city hit by two major earthquakes in 1999 within three months. *Seismological Research Letters*, *72*(6), 679–689. doi:10.1785/gssrl.72.6.679.

Wu, K.-L., & Yang, M.-S. (2005a). A cluster validity index for fuzzy clustering. *Pattern Recognition Letters*, *26*(9), 1275–1291. doi:10.1016/j.patrec.2004.11.022.

Wu, K.-L., Yu, J., & Yang, M.-S. (2005b). A novel fuzzy clustering algorithm based on a fuzzy scatter matrix with optimality tests. *Pattern Recognition Letters*, *26*(5), 639–652. doi:10.1016/j.patrec.2004.09.016.

Xie, X. L., & Beni, G. A. (1991). Validity measure for fuzzy clustering. *IEEE Transactions on Pattern and Machine Intelligence*, *3*(8), 841–846. doi:10.1109/34.85677.

Zadeh, L. A. (1965). Fuzzy sets. *Information and Control*, *8*, 338–353. doi:10.1016/S0019-9958(65)90241-X.

Zadeh, L. A. (1973). Fuzzy algorithms. *Information and Control*, *12*, 94–102. doi:10.1016/S0019-9958(68)90211-8.

ADDITIONAL READING

Ahmed, M. N., Yamany, S. M., & Mohamed, N. (2009). A modified fuzzy c-means algorithm for bias field: Estimation and segmentation of MRI data. *IEEE Transactions on Medical Imaging*, *21*(3), 193–199. doi:10.1109/42.996338 PMID:11989844.

Chiang, J., & Hao, P. (2003). A new kernel-based fuzzy clustering approach: Support vector clustering with cell growing. *IEEE Transactions on Fuzzy Systems*, *11*(4), 518–527. doi:10.1109/TFUZZ.2003.814839.

Jain, A. K., & Dubes, R. C. (1988). *Algorithms for clustering data*. NJ: Prentice-Hall.

Liew, A. W., & Yan, H. (2003). An adaptive spatial fuzzy clustering algorithm for 3-D MR image segmentation. *IEEE Transactions on Medical Imaging*, *22*(9), 1063–1075. doi:10.1109/TMI.2003.816956 PMID:12956262.

Pal, N. R., Pal, K., Keller, J. M., & Bezdek, J. C. (2005). A possibilistic fuzzy c-means clustering algorithm. *IEEE Transactions on Fuzzy Systems*, *13*(4), 517–530. doi:10.1109/TFUZZ.2004.840099.

Pal, S. K., & Mitra, S. (1990). Fuzzy dynamic clustering algorithm. *Pattern Recognition Letters*, *11*, 525–535. doi:10.1016/0167-8655(90)90021-S.

Park, H. S., Yoo, S., & Cho, S. (2005). Evolutionary fuzzy clustering algorithm with knowledge-based evaluation and applications for gene expression profiling. *Journal of Computational and Theoretical Nanoscience*, *2*, 1–10. doi:10.1166/jctn.2005.007.

Tolias, Y. A., & Panas, S. M. (1998). *A fuzzy vessel tracking algorithm for retinal images based on fuzzy clustering. Medical Imaging* (pp. 263–273). IEEE Transactions.

Yang, M. S. (1993). A survey of fuzzy clustering. *Mathematical and Computer Modelling*, *18*(11), 1–16. doi:10.1016/0895-7177(93)90202-A.

Yang, M. S., Hwang, P., & Chen, D. (2004). Fuzzy clustering algorithms for mixed feature variables. *Fuzzy Sets and Systems*, *141*, 301–317. doi:10.1016/S0165-0114(03)00072-1.

Zhu, Z., Chung, F., & Wang, S. (2009). Generalized fuzzy c-means clustering algorithm with improved fuzzy partitions. *Cybernetics*, *39*(3), 578–591. PMID:19174354.

Zimmermann, H. J. (1991). *Fuzzy set theory and its applications*. Dordrecht: Kluwer. doi:10.1007/978-94-015-7949-0.

KEY TERMS AND DEFINITIONS

Cluster: It is a part from wholeness as a small group or bunch of something. The components of a cluster are usually connected to each other.

Cluster Regression: The form of regression that allows transitional properties between successive clusters on a scatter diagram.

Fuzziness: Any concept that gives impression of being indistinct quality, incoherent, blurred and without sharp outlines.

Logical Rule: It provides linguistically the relationship between the causes and result most often in "IF…..THEN….." statement, where there are implications of either directly or inversely proportional relationships between the causal and effect variables.

System Identification: It is concerned with the transformation procedure of given inputs' data to output in any modeling system. It is also related to the optimal design of experiments for efficiently generating informative data for fitting such models to actual data.

Trend: It indicates a general direction in which something tends or inclines to move along a line or a curve.

Uncertainty: It has not a clear definition but used in subtly different ways in a number of disciplines. It is a very significant component in the modeling of future event predictions based on the available numerical or vague data.

Chapter 13
Analysing the Performance of a Fuzzy Lane Changing Model Using Data Mining

Sara Moridpour
RMIT University, Australia

ABSTRACT

Heavy vehicles have substantial impact on traffic flow particularly during heavy traffic conditions. Large amount of heavy vehicle lane changing manoeuvres may increase the number of traffic accidents and therefore reduce the freeway safety. Improving road capacity and enhancing traffic safety on freeways has been the motivation to establish heavy vehicle lane restriction strategies to reduce the interaction between heavy vehicles and passenger cars. In previous studies, different heavy vehicle lane restriction strategies have been evaluated using microscopic traffic simulation packages. Microscopic traffic simulation packages generally use a common model to estimate the lane changing of heavy vehicles and passenger cars. The common lane changing models ignore the differences exist in the lane changing behaviour of heavy vehicle and passenger car drivers. An exclusive fuzzy lane changing model for heavy vehicles is developed and presented in this chapter. This fuzzy model can increase the accuracy of simulation models in estimating the macroscopic and microscopic traffic characteristics. The results of this chapter shows that using an exclusive lane changing model for heavy vehicles, results in more reliable evaluation of lane restriction strategies.

INTRODUCTION

There is potential for lane changing manoeuvres to have a substantial impact on macroscopic and microscopic traffic flow characteristics due to the interference effect they have on surrounding vehicles (Hoogendoorn & Bovy, 2001; Daganzo, 2002; Sasoh & Ohara, 2002; Wall & Hounsell, 2005; Laval & Daganzo, 2006).

The interference effects of heavy vehicles' lane changing manoeuvres on surrounding traffic are likely to be greater than when passenger cars execute lane changing manoeuvre. While they account for a minority of traffic stream, heavy

DOI: 10.4018/978-1-4666-4213-3.ch013

Copyright © 2013, IGI Global. Copying or distributing in print or electronic forms without written permission of IGI Global is prohibited.

vehicles have a pronounced effect on traffic flow and produce a disproportionate effect particularly during heavy traffic conditions. Heavy vehicles impose physical and psychological effects on surrounding traffic (Uddin & Ardekani, 2002; Al-Kaisy et al., 2005). These effects are the results of physical characteristics of heavy vehicles (e.g. length and size) and their operational characteristics (e.g. acceleration, deceleration and manoeuvrability). The effect of heavy vehicles' operational characteristics becomes more important under heavy traffic conditions.

The number of heavy vehicles on roadways of the U.S. has increased by 75% over the past three decades and this trend is likely to continue at least over the next decade (Bureau of Transportation Statistics, 2002). Typically, the proportion of heavy vehicles ranges from as low as 2% to as high as 25% of total traffic during the day (Al-Kaisy et al., 2002). According to a series of traffic surveys conducted in December 2004 in Australia, the proportion of heavy vehicles could increase to 30% of total vehicles in the morning peak and 20% in the afternoon peak on some freeways (Conway, 2005).

Despite the increasing number of heavy vehicles on freeways, previous studies have predominantly focused on the behaviour of passenger car drivers. In the previous lane changing models, the differences between heavy vehicles and passenger cars is primarily accounted for through differences in vehicle length, maximum speed and acceleration/deceleration capabilities (Gipps, 1986; Wiedemann & Reiter, 1992; Ahmed, 1999; Hidas, 2005; Toledo, 2009). In other words, heavy vehicles are accommodated in current lane changing models by calibrating the parameters of a general lane changing model for heavy vehicles rather than by incorporating a lane changing model developed specifically for the heavy vehicle drivers. However, heavy vehicle and passenger car drivers have fundamentally different lane changing behaviour (Moridpour et al., 2009; Moridpour, 2010a; Moridpour, 2010b; Moridpour et al., 2012). Understanding heavy vehicle drivers' lane changing behaviour is important due to its implications for the models employed in traffic and transportation policies.

To improve freeway capacity and traffic safety, previous research has examined various lane restriction strategies for heavy vehicles (Al-Kaisy & Hall, 2003; Lord et al., 2005; Siuhi & Mussa, 2007; Adelakun & Cherry, 2009; El-Tantawy, 2009; Yang & Regan, 2009). Due to the large size of heavy vehicles, restricting heavy vehicles to certain lanes can potentially bring psychological benefits for passenger car drivers. To evaluate different lane restriction strategies, previous studies have primarily used microscopic traffic simulations. Although heavy vehicles and their driving behaviour have been the main focus of those studies, microscopic traffic simulation packages are mostly using a general lane changing model to estimate lane changing behaviour of heavy vehicle and passenger car drivers. The parameters of the general lane changing model are calibrated for heavy vehicles and passenger cars, separately (Moridpour, 2010). However, heavy vehicle and passenger car drivers may have fundamentally different lane changing behaviour. Therefore, a lane changing model for heavy vehicle drivers may increase the accuracy of microscopic traffic simulation models in estimating heavy vehicle drivers' lane changing behaviour and enhance the performance of microscopic traffic simulation models.

The broad aim of this chapter is to advance microscopic traffic flow modelling by developing a fuzzy lane changing model for heavy vehicles and analysing the performance of that fuzzy lane changing model using data mining. Consistent with that broad aim, the following objectives have been established.

- Develop a fuzzy lane changing model for heavy vehicle drivers on freeways,

- Validate the heavy vehicle lane changing model and assess its accuracy,
- Evaluate different lane restriction strategies for heavy vehicles using data mining.

This chapter is structured as follows. The next section provides a brief background of the fuzzy logic lane changing models. After that, the trajectory dataset which is used in this chapter will be described. It is followed by comprehensive explanation of the fuzzy lane changing model development for heavy vehicle. Subsequently, different lane restriction strategies are defined and the performance of the fuzzy heavy vehicle lane changing model is macroscopically and microscopically analysed and compared for each strategy. The final two sections summarise the findings and conclusions of this chapter and provide suggestions for future research, respectively.

BACKGROUND

Different approaches taken in lane changing studies can be classified as lane changing assistance models and lane changing decision models. In recent years, many studies have been focused on the scope for lane changing assistance systems to enhance road capacity and road safety (Lygeros et al., 1998; Nagel et al., 1998; Knospe et al., 2002; Hatipoglu et al., 2003; Mar & Lin, 2005). Lane changing assistance models can be classified as either collision prevention models or automation models. Both of these model types consider the steering wheel angle and lateral motions to control the lane changing performance of vehicles. Collision prevention lane changing models are developed to control drivers' lane changing manoeuvres and assist them to execute a safe lane change. The collision prevention models are intended to improve road safety. Automation models are applied to perform the driving tasks either partially or entirely. Many different configurations are defined for models in this category such as lane change or side crash avoidance systems. Those applications involve automotive adjustments to the steering wheel angle of vehicles to control their lateral motion and reduce dangerous lane changing manoeuvres (Lygeros et al., 1998; Nagel et al., 1998; Maerivoet & Moor, 2005; Eidehall et al., 2007; Salvucci & Mandalia, 2007; Doshi & Trivedi, 2008; Kiefer & Hankey, 2008; Li-sheng et al., 2009).

Many studies have related the lane changing decision of drivers to surrounding traffic characteristics and they have produced models which fall into one of two broad categories: rigid mechanistic models and artificial intelligence models (Figure 1). The rigid mechanistic models are those which create a crisp relationship between explanatory variables and dependant variable. In these models the magnitude of the result depends on the exact values of the independent variables. Mechanistic lane changing approaches do not usually incorporate the uncertainties associated with drivers' perceptions and decisions.

Rigid mechanistic models do not incorporate the inconsistencies and uncertainties of drivers' perception and decisions (McDonald et al., 1997). These models are based on crisp variable magnitudes (Das & Bowles, 1999). Most of the tradi tional lane changing models use crisp mathematical equations and conventional logic rules to represent drivers' knowledge of the surrounding traffic and to model the drivers' lane changing decisions. Commonly, random terms are included in these models which capture the variation of the explanatory variables around the mean value of those variables. The random terms are mainly Gumbel or normally distributed (Ahmed, 1999; Choudhury et al., 2007; Toledo, 2009). However, drivers make their decisions based on their imprecise perceptions of the surrounding traffic. In recent years, Artificial Intelligence (AI) based approaches have become popular because they overcome the shortcoming of rigid mecha-

Figure 1. Classification of lane changing decision models based on traffic characteristics

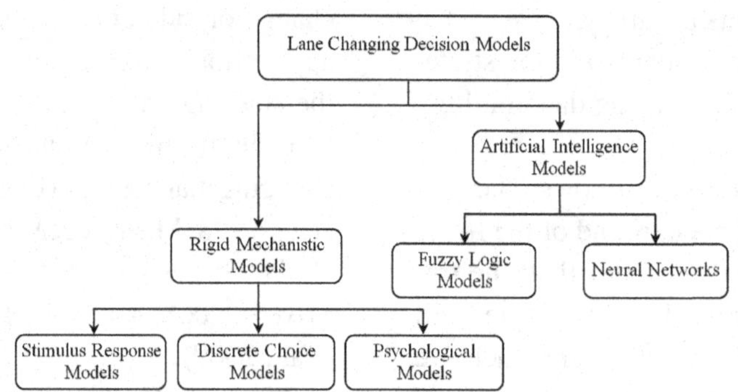

nistic models. One type of artificial intelligence is fuzzy logic models which allow defining uncertainty in the model and therefore, reflect the natural or subjective perception of real variables (Ma, 2004).

Das et al. (1999) proposed a new microscopic simulation methodology based on fuzzy IF-THEN rules and called the software package as Autonomous Agent SIMulation Package (AASIM). The major motivation of using a fuzzy knowledge based approach to model drivers' decisions is that fuzzy models provide an effective means to change highly nonlinear systems into IF-THEN rules. In addition, fuzzy logic is well equipped to handle uncertainties in real world traffic situations. They classified the lane changing manoeuvres as Mandatory Lane Changing (MLC) and Discretionary Lane Changing (DLC). MLC happens when a driver is forced to leave the current lane for instance when merging onto the freeway from an on-ramp or taking an exit off-ramp. DLC is performed when the driver is not satisfied with the driving situation in the current lane and wishes to gain some speed advantage for instance when the driver is obstructed by a slow moving vehicle. To decide when a MLC happens in the microscopic traffic simulation package, the MLC fuzzy rules consider the distance to the approaching exit or merge point and the number of lane changes which are required. When multiple lane changes are required, the probability of making a decision to change lanes increases. The DLC rules of AASIM reflect a binary decision (change lanes or not) which is based upon two explanatory variables. These two explanatory variables are the driver's speed satisfaction level, which is based on the drivers' recent speed history, and the level of congestion in the left or right adjacent lanes. In AASIM, no specific lane changing decision model was considered for each vehicle type. The formulation of driver's speed satisfaction level and congestion level in the left or right adjacent lanes are presented as Equations 1 and 2, respectively. The MLC and the DLC frameworks in AASIM are based on the tactical and operational lane changing decisions of drivers.

$$\sigma_t = (1-\varepsilon)\times\sigma_{t-1} + \varepsilon\times(\frac{v}{v_{\lim}}) \tag{1}$$

where,

$\sigma =$ driver satisfaction,

$v =$ vehicle speed during the current iteration,

$v_{lim} =$ speed limit of freeway,

$\varepsilon =$ learning satisfaction rate.

The driver satisfaction represents the drivers' recent speed history which is updated at each time step. The learning satisfaction rate remains close to unity when the vehicle speed is maintained close to the speed limit and it reduces at lower speeds.

$$c = \frac{\sum_{all\ i} e^{-d_i/\Delta} \times (1 - \frac{v_i}{v_{\lim}})}{\sum_{all\ i} e^{-d_i/\Delta}} \quad (2)$$

where,

c = local lane congestion as seen from a driver's view point,

d_i = distance to the ith vehicle,

Δ = parameter.

The summation in Equation 2 is carried out for all vehicles ahead of a vehicle. In this equation, the quantity $\exp(-d_i / \Delta)$ is a weight associated with the ith vehicle which decreases exponentially with distance.

In AASIM, once the driver decides to execute a lane changing manoeuvre, the next step is to find a suitable gap. The fuzzy rules are based on the adjacent gaps and surrounding vehicles' speeds in the target lane. Then, an acceleration value is calculated which is different from that generated by normal car following rules. If there is an acceptable size of gap in the target lane, the gap finding rules enable the vehicle to speed up or slow down to move closer to the gap. At the same time, the gap finding rules consider the safe headway to the front vehicle in the current lane. The last stage in AASIM lane changing decision model is setting the gap acceptance rules. These rules look for the gaps and speeds of the lead and lag vehicles in the target lane and the distance to the next exit or lane merge (infinite for DLC). The general form of a fuzzy rule which is used in their research is presented below.

j^{th} *rule: IF* I_1 *is* A_{1j} *and ...* I_i *is* A_{ij} *and* I_m *is* A_{mj} *THEN* O *is* B_j (3)

where,

$I = f(I_1, I_2, ..., I_n)$ = input variables,

A_{ij} = fuzzy subsets for input I_j,

O = output,

B_j = fuzzy subsets for output O.

They evaluate the accuracy of AASIM using actual field data. The simulation results were compared with the results from a commercial microscopic traffic simulation package called CORSIM (CORridor SIMulation). The traffic volume and the average speed of a weaving section were estimated for 60 minutes with AASIM and CORSIM. Then, the estimated results were compared to each other and to the field data observations. The results showed the average speeds of the simulated vehicles by AASIM differed from the field observations by less than 4.8 km/hr for each 15 minute time interval. In contrast, the speed differences from CORSIM model were around 16.0 km/hr.

McDonald et al. (1997), Brackstone et al. (1998), and Wu et al. (2003) developed a fuzzy logic motorway simulation model (FLOWSIM) and established fuzzy sets and systems for the model. To model the drivers' tactical and operational lane changing decision, they classified lane changing manoeuvres into two categories: lane changes to the slower lane and lane changes to the faster lane. Lane changes to the slower are mainly performed to prevent disturbing fast moving vehicles which approach from the rear. Lane changes to the faster lane are mainly executed with the aim of gaining speed advantages. Their lane changing decision model to the slower lane uses two variables: pressure from the rear and gap satisfaction in the slower lane. The pressure from the rear is the time headway of the rear vehicle and gap satisfaction is the period of time during which it will be possible for the subject vehicle driver to stay in the gap in the slower lane, without reducing speed. A typical fuzzy rule in the lane changing decision model to the slower lane is given by Equation 4.

IF pressure from rear is Low and gap satisfaction is High, *THEN intention of moving into right lane is Medium* (4)

To establish the lane changing decision model to the faster lane, they defined two variables: overtaking benefit and opportunity. The overtaking benefit is the speed gained when a lane changing manoeuvre to the faster lane is executed. The opportunity reflects the safety and comfort of the lane changing manoeuvre, which is measured by the time headway to the first lag vehicle in the faster lane. The lane changing decision framework which is used in FLOWSIM is a general lane changing decision framework and could be applied for all types of vehicles.

To assess the accuracy of FLOWSIM in estimating the lane changing manoeuvres, the empirical 5 minutes traffic flow counts were used as the simulation inputs. Then, they estimated the number of lane changing manoeuvres and the percentage of lane occupancy for each lane at different traffic flow rates. The estimated results were then compared to the observations in the field data at two steps. First, they used the mean value of the measurements to compare the observed and the estimated measurements. They found the difference between the mean values of the observed and estimated lane changing rates and lane occupancy at different traffic flow rates (5).

$$\textit{Difference} - \textit{of} - \textit{Mean} = (\textit{estimated} - \textit{observed})/\textit{observed} \times 100 \quad (5)$$

The results showed that the differences between the observed and estimated measurements are in the range of 0-11%. To further analyse the results, they statistically tested and compared the distribution of the observed and estimated measurements showing that the overall distribution of the estimated and observed measurements also matches well.

Limitations of the Existing Lane Changing Models

From the foregoing review of the literature, the major limitations of the existing lane changing models become apparent. The literature review has highlighted a number of areas where further research could overcome gaps in existing knowledge. Those areas are presented below:

- Little attention has been paid to a specific lane changing decision model for heavy vehicle drivers. The current lane changing models are principally associated with passenger car drivers and do not explore or attempt to capture the differences which exist between the passenger car and heavy vehicle lane changing patterns.
- Several seconds are required for drivers to complete a lane changing manoeuvre. Heavy vehicle drivers require even greater time for lane changing execution compared to passenger car drivers due to the physical and operational characteristics of heavy vehicles. However, the existing lane changing models mainly focus on drivers' lane changing decision and generally neglect execution of the lane changing manoeuvre. Excluding the lane changing execution, may have a significant impact on estimated

traffic flow characteristics. Considering the lane changing execution may improve the accuracy of lane changing models which subsequently could improve the accuracy of the obtained results from microscopic traffic simulations.

TRAJECTORY DATASET

The trajectory dataset used for model calibration and validation is explained in this section. The dataset provides sufficient heavy vehicle lane changing manoeuvres to support development of a lane changing model. The trajectory dataset used in this study was made available by Cambridge Systematics Incorporated for the Federal Highway Administration (FHWA) as part of Next Generation SIMulation (NGSIM) project. NGSIM captured video images of two highways in California: Hollywood Freeway (US-101) and Berkeley Highway (I-80). Subsequently, a comprehensive vehicle trajectory dataset was developed through processing the video images.

The section of US-101 is 640 meters long and comprises five main lanes and one auxiliary lane. The section includes one on-ramp and one exit off-ramp and there are no lane restrictions applying to heavy vehicles (Cambridge Systematics, 2005a). The data for US-101 was collected from 7:50 to 8:35 AM with a video capture rate of 10 frames per second. The second section considered in this analysis is on I-80. This section is 503 meters long and comprises five main lanes and one auxiliary lane (Cambridge Systematics, 2005b). There is one on-ramp in this section and an exit off-ramp is located downstream of the section. There are no lane restrictions for heavy vehicles in this section of freeway. The data for I-80 were collected from 4:00 to 4:15 PM and 5:00 to 5:30 PM using a video capture rate of 10 frames per second.

The datasets reflect clear weather, good visibility, and dry pavement conditions. Vehicles are classified in the data as automobiles, heavy vehicles and motorcycles. Table 1 shows the traffic composition, along with traffic flow parameters for each study area. In general, extracting the trajectory dataset from video images makes it impossible to capture some physical (e.g. weight) and operational (e.g. power) characteristics of vehicles. The length of vehicles is one of their physical characteristics that can be extracted from video images. Therefore, vehicle length is used to identify heavy vehicles in this research. The vehicles with the length of equal to or greater than 6 meters are classified as heavy vehicles. This classification is consistent with the definition of the heavy vehicles in the trajectory dataset used for this study. Over the time period when the data was captured, the number of heavy vehicle lane changing manoeuvres on US-101 and I 80 were 15 and 27, respectively.

For the time intervals reflected in the data, the traffic flow condition for each site reflects Level of Service (LOS) E. The LOS is a qualitative measure which describes the operational condi-

Table 1. The traffic flow characteristics in each freeway section

Site Name	Automobile		Heavy Vehicle		Motorcycle		Flow (veh/hr)	Speed (m/sec)
	Number	(%)	Number	(%)	Number	(%)		
US-101	5919	97.0	137	2.2	45	0.7	8077	9.7
I-80	5408	95.2	215	3.8	55	1.0	7493	6.6
Total	11327	96.2	352	3.0	100	0.8	7785	8.2

tions within a traffic stream based on service measures such as average speed, travel time, freedom to manoeuvre, traffic interruptions, and comfort and convenience. The trajectory dataset which is used in this study provides information on the subject vehicles and their surrounding traffic characteristics. The subject vehicles are the heavy vehicles which execute the lane changing manoeuvre. The vehicles for which information is available during a lane changing manoeuvre are presented in Figure 2.

The trajectory dataset includes the physical characteristics of each vehicle such as length and width. It is also possible to determine all relevant positions, space gaps, speeds and accelerations/decelerations, at discrete time points throughout the analysis period. The traffic flow characteristics investigated in this study include the speeds of the subject vehicle and each of the surrounding vehicles shown in Figure 2 along with the space gaps and the relative speeds of surrounding vehicles with respect to the subject vehicle.

FUZZY LANE CHANGING MODELS

According to Gipps's lane changing framework (Gipps 1986), a driver's lane changing decision is the result of considering three factors: whether it is possible to change lanes, whether it is necessary to change lanes and whether it is desirable to change lanes. Wiedemann and Reiter (1992) defined a lane changing framework in which a driver's lane changing decision is the result of answering three questions: whether there is a desire to change lanes, whether the present driving situation in the neighbouring lane is favourable and whether the movement to the neighbouring lane is possible. Another framework introduces the lane changing decision process as a sequence of three stages: the decision to consider a lane change, the choice of the target lane and acceptance of a sufficient size gap in the target lane to execute the lane changing manoeuvre (Yang & Koutsopoulos, 1996; Ahmed, 1999). In the previous lane changing studies, the lane changing decision frameworks are mainly based on drivers' desire to change lanes and selection of an appropriate lane to move into as the target lane.

Lane Changing Decision

In this chapter, a lane changing framework is defined which is consistent with the previous lane changing studies. The lane changing behaviour of a driver can be characterized as a sequence of three stages. In the first stage, the drivers are motivated to perform a lane changing manoeuvre. After being motivated to change lanes, the next stage is selection of a lane to change into (the target lane). The final stage of a lane changing manoeuvre is execution of the lane change. The first two stages of the lane changing manoeuvre constitute the lane changing decision. In these two stages, the driver decides about changing lanes and the final stage is associated with executing

Figure 2. Subject vehicle and surrounding vehicles in a lane changing manoeuvre

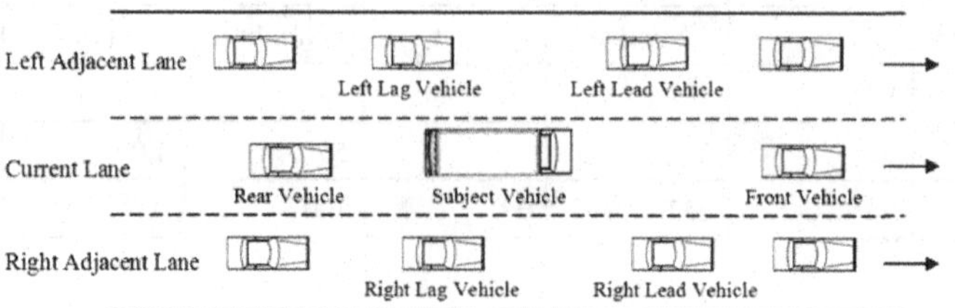

the lane changing manoeuvre. Figure 3 illustrates the general framework developed to structure this research in order to achieve its objectives.

The total numbers of heavy vehicles which performed MLC manoeuvre (either following entry via an on-ramp or to exit at an off-ramp) were relatively small (6 on US-101 and 5 on I-80). This implies that heavy vehicle drivers mainly execute a MLC at distances which are greater than the 500 meter length of the available study areas. The small number of heavy vehicle MLC manoeuvre in the dataset makes it unsuitable for the development of a MLC decision model for heavy vehicle drivers. Drawing on the greater availability of data in the dataset (31 DLC manoeuvres), the emphasis here is therefore on development of a DLC decision model for heavy vehicle drivers.

The DLC decision comprises two stages: motivation to change lanes and selection of the target lane (Moridpour et al., 2008; 2009). In this section, the lane changing decision is defined as an integration of these two stages of lane changing. Therefore, the lane changing decision is defined as the motivation of selecting either the right adjacent lane (slower lane) or the left adjacent lane (faster lane). The motivations for selecting either the slower lane or the faster lane are different. Drivers generally move into the slower lane to prevent obstructing the fast moving vehicles which approach from the rear. However, the aim of moving into the faster lane is generally to gain a speed advantage. Therefore, two separate models are developed in this research for the lane changing decision of heavy vehicle drivers (Moridpour et al., 2009). These two models reflect either Lane Changing to the Slower Lane (LCSL) or Lane Changing to the Faster Lane (LCFL).

In the real world, drivers make their decisions based on their imprecise perceptions of the surrounding traffic (Ma, 2004). Fuzzy logic models have become popular in recent years since they enable uncertainty to be explicitly defined and incorporated in the model. To allow for the uncertainty in drivers' decision, fuzzy logic models are used to model the lane changing decision of heavy vehicle drivers (Zadeh, 1965; 1994). Adaptive Neuro-Fuzzy Inference System (ANFIS) which is an advanced fuzzy inference systems is developed in MATLab and used in this study (Jang & Gulley, 2008). The neural techniques are generally applied to tune the membership function parameters in ANFIS (Chen, 1996). Therefore, the membership function parameters are adjusted and the fuzzy rules are determined by ANFIS in the fuzzy logic heavy vehicle lane changing decision model.

The Fuzzy Sets and Systems for the Lane Changing Decision Model

The characteristics of traffic in the current and target lanes (Figure 2) are considered in the development of the LCSL and LCFL models. These traffic characteristics include: the speeds of the heavy vehicle and the preceding and the following vehicles in the current and target lanes and the space gaps between the heavy vehicle and the preceding and following vehicles in the current and target lanes. The general form of the

Figure 3. Research framework

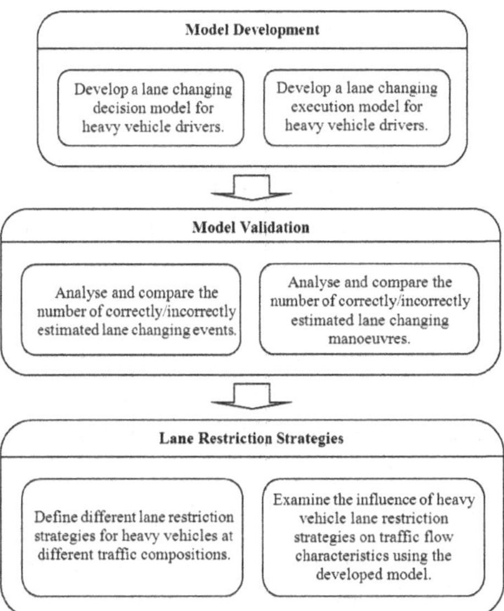

lane changing decision model for heavy vehicle drivers is presented as follows:

$$LC_n(t) = f(\textit{Surrounding Traffic Characteristics}) \quad (6)$$

where,

t = time of observation for heavy vehicle driver n,

$LC_n(t)$ = lane changing decision of the heavy vehicle driver n at time t.

The time of observation (0.5 second time intervals) for each driver/vehicle is the time that traffic characteristics of that vehicle and all surrounding vehicles are measured. The heavy vehicle drivers may move into either the right (slower) lane or the left (faster) lane or they may stay in the current lane at each time step. Their choices can then be reflected as follows:

$$LC_n(t) = [LCSL, LCFL, 0] \quad (7)$$

In this representation, drivers can either change into the slower lane (LCSL), change into the faster lane (LCFL) or stay in the current lane ($LC_n(t) = 0$).

Different combinations of surrounding traffic characteristics were considered in developing the lane changing decision models to the right (slower) lane and to the left (faster) lane. The combinations which resulted in the models being able to most accurately replicate the relevant observed lane changing manoeuvres were selected as the explanatory variables for the LCSL and LCFL models. To confirm the obtained influencing variables on heavy vehicle drivers' lane changing decision, the surrounding traffic characteristics at the time that the heavy vehicle drives change lanes as well as when they do not wish to execute lane changing manoeuvre are analysed. This analysis reveals the influence of surrounding traffic characteristics on the lane changing decision of heavy vehicle drivers.

The explanatory variables likely to motivate the heavy vehicle drivers to move into the slower lane (LCSL model) include: the front space gap, the rear space gap, the lag space gap in the right lane and the average speed of the surrounding vehicles in the current lane. The average speed in the current lane is assumed to be the average speeds of the heavy vehicle and the front and the rear vehicles. The general form of the LCSL model is presented in Equation 8. The drivers may either stay in the current lane, 0, or they may move into the right (slower) lane at each time step.

$$LCSL_n(t) = f(X_n^{LCSL}(t)) \; LCSL_n(t) = [0, 1] \quad (8)$$

where,

$LCSL_n(t)$ = lane changing decision to move into the right (slower) lane for heavy vehicle driver n at time t,

$X_n^{LCSL}(t)$ = vector of the explanatory variables influencing lane changing decision to the right (slower) lane.

The explanatory variables in motivating heavy vehicle drivers to move into the faster lane (LCFL model) include: the front relative speed, the lag relative speed in the left lane and the average speeds of the surrounding vehicles in the current lane and the left lane. The average speed in the adjacent lanes is the average speed of the first two lead and the first two lag vehicles in that lane. In the LCFL which is presented by Equation 9, heavy vehicle drivers may either stay in the current lane, 0, or they may move in to the left (faster) lane at each time step.

$$LCFL_n(t) = f(X_n^{LCFL}(t)) \; LCFL_n(t) = [0, 1] \quad (9)$$

where,

$LCFL_n(t)$ = lane changing decision to move into the left (faster) lane for heavy vehicle driver n at time t,

$X_n^{LCFL}(t)$ = vector of the explanatory variables influencing lane changing decision to the left (faster) lane.

In the previous studies, triangular membership functions were used to develop fuzzy logic car following and lane changing models (McDonald et al., 1997; Brackstone et al., 1998; Das et al., 1999; Wu et al., 2003; Ma, 2004). Similar to the previous studies, the triangular membership functions are used for all fuzzy sets in the heavy vehicle drivers' lane changing decision models developed here. Each explanatory variable consists of several overlapping fuzzy sets. The number of fuzzy sets which could be used for any of the explanatory variables in the lane changing decision model is restricted to drivers' perception capabilities. In a lane changing manoeuvre, a high level of interaction exists between the driver who executes a lane changing manoeuvre and the surrounding traffic. The drivers' lane changing decision is based on the traffic characteristics in the current lane and both adjacent lanes. The drivers have imprecise perception of the surrounding traffic in the current lane and adjacent lanes. To model the drivers' imprecise perception of the surrounding traffic, alternatives of either two or three fuzzy sets are used to represent the explanatory variables. The triangular membership functions for two and three fuzzy sets of the 'Front Relative Speed' variable is illustrated in Figure 4.

The fuzzy set categories for the LCSL model are identified in Table 2. The size of the front space gap reflects the manoeuvrability of heavy vehicles. The larger front space gap implies the lower manoeuvrability and lower speed of heavy vehicles. Therefore, larger front space gaps are observed in front of the heavy vehicles with lower manoeuvrability. In contrast, the vehicles behind may be obstructed by a slow moving heavy vehicle. Heavy vehicle drivers may move into a slower lane to allow following vehicles to increase their speed. The rear space gap may indicate the pressure on the heavy vehicles from the rear. The larger values of the right lag space gap provide the opportunity for heavy vehicle drivers to move into the right lane easily and safely. Finally, the average speed in the current lane indicates the speed difference between the heavy vehicles and the surrounding traffic in that lane. Heavy vehicle drivers are more likely to move into the right (slower) lane, when the speed differences between the heavy vehicle and the surrounding vehicles in the current lane increases.

The fuzzy set categories for the LCFL model are presented in Table 3. The small values of the front speed and consequently the desire to gain speed advantages may motivate the heavy vehicle drivers to move into the faster lane. The small values of the lag vehicle speed in the left lane

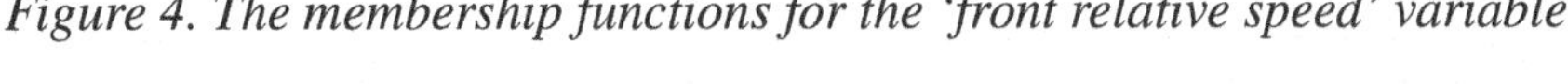
Figure 4. The membership functions for the 'front relative speed' variable

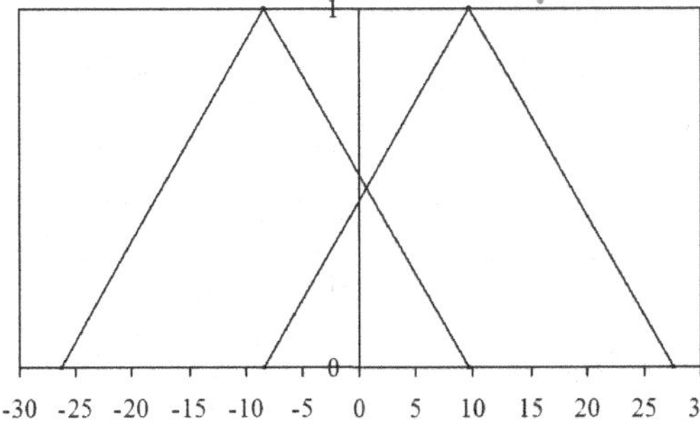

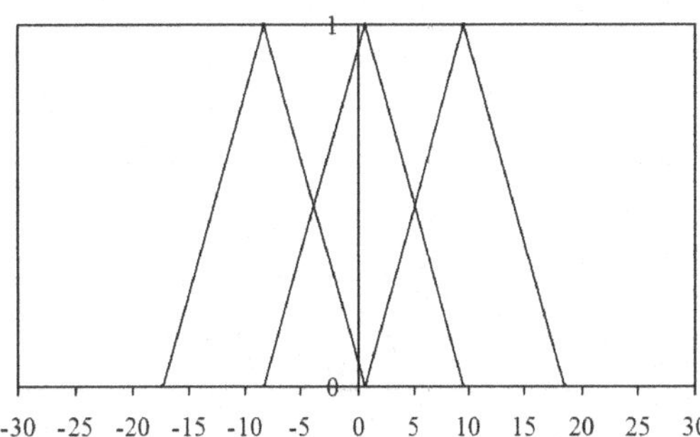

Table 2. Fuzzy set categories for the LCSL model

Front Space Gap	Rear Space Gap	Right Lag Space Gap	Average speed in Current Lane
Two Sets			
Small	Small	Small	Low
Large	Large	Large	High
Three Sets			
Small	Small	Small	Low
Medium	Medium	Medium	Intermediate
Large	Large	Large	High

provide the opportunity for heavy vehicle drivers to execute a safe lane changing manoeuvre. The average speeds in the current lane and the left lane specify the speed difference between the current lane and the left lane. Therefore, the speed advantage of drivers by moving into the left (faster) lane is indicated by these two variables.

The Fuzzy Rule Base of the Lane Changing Decision Model

The fuzzy rule base of the lane changing decision model describes the heavy vehicle drivers' decision to move into either the right or the left lane, based on the above mentioned explanatory variables. Expressed in natural language, typical fuzzy rules for LCSL (Equations 10 and 11) and LCFL (Equations 12 and 13) model with two and three sets are presented using natural language below.

IF (Front Space Gap is Small) and (Rear Space Gap is Small) and (Right Lag Space Gap is Large) and (Average speed in Current Lane is High) THEN (LCSL is Yes). (10)

IF (Front Space Gap is Medium) and (Rear Space Gap is Small) and (Right Lag Space Gap is Medium) and (Average speed in Current Lane is High) THEN (LCSL is Yes). (11)

IF (Front Relative Speed is Low) and (Left Lag Relative Speed is Low) and (Average speed in Current Lane is Low) and (Average speed in Left Lane is High) THEN (LCFL is Yes) (12)

Table 3. Fuzzy set categories for the LCFL model

Front Relative Speed	Left Lag Relative Speed	Average Speed in Current Lane	Average Speed in Left Lane
Two Sets			
Low	Low	Low	Low
High	High	High	High
Three Sets			
Low	Low	Low	Low
Intermediate	Intermediate	Intermediate	Intermediate
High	High	High	High

IF (Front Relative Speed is Low) and (Left Lag Relative Speed is Intermediate) and (Average speed in Current Lane is Low) and (Average speed in Left Lane is High) THEN (LCFL is Yes). (13)

After calibrating the heavy vehicle drivers' lane changing decision model, the accuracy of the calibrated model needs to be examined. To do that, the number of estimated lane changing manoeuvres by the heavy vehicles is compared to the observed number of those manoeuvres from the field data. The estimated error for lane changing manoeuvres is measured by the Root Mean Square Error (RMSE), defined as follows:

$$RMSE = \sqrt{\frac{1}{N+T}\sum_{n=1}^{N}\sum_{t=1}^{T}(LC_{tn}^{obs} - LC_{tn}^{est})} \quad (14)$$

where LC_n^{obs} and LC_n^{est} are the observed and estimated lane change events at time t for manoeuvre n.

The number of observed heavy vehicle lane changing manoeuvres in the trajectory data is insufficient to provide two different datasets for training the model and testing its accuracy. Therefore, the leave-one-out cross-validation method is used to examine the accuracy of the developed model in estimating heavy vehicle drivers' lane changing decision. The leave-one-out cross-validation method uses a single event from the original dataset as the test data with the remaining events used as the training data. Each event is defined as the lane changing decision of a heavy vehicle driver at each 0.5 second time interval. This is repeated such that each event in the sample is used once as the validation data. The advantage of this method is that all events are used for both training and testing and each event is used for testing exactly once (Kwon et al., 2000; Rose et al., 2009).

The leave-one-out cross-validation method is used to examine the accuracy of the developed lane changing decision models in two approaches. In the first approach, a single event is selected as the test data from all events, and the remaining events are selected as the training data. This is repeated for all events and the correctly and the incorrectly estimated events are counted. The correctly estimated events are either the lane changing or non-lane changing events which are estimated correctly by the LCSL and LCFL models (Moridpour et al., 2009). The incorrectly estimated events are either the lane changing events which are estimated as non-lane changing or non-lane changing events that estimated as lane changing events by the LCSL and LCFL models. The error measure under leave-one-out cross-validation (loocv) for individual events is defined by the following equation:

$$RMSE^{loocv} = \sqrt{\frac{1}{N+T}\sum_{n=1}^{N}\sum_{t=1}^{T}(LC_{tn}^{obs} - \hat{LC}_{tn}^{est})} \quad (15)$$

where, $\hat{LC}_{tn}^{est}$ is estimated using all events in the dataset excluding lane changing event at time t for manoeuvre n.

In the second approach, all events which belong to a single manoeuvre are selected as the test data and the remaining manoeuvres are selected as the training data. This is repeated for all manoeuvres and the correctly and the incorrectly estimated manoeuvres are counted to calculate the following error measure.

$$RMSE^{loocv} = \sqrt{\frac{1}{N}\sum_{n=1}^{N}(LC_{n}^{obs} - \hat{LC}_{n}^{est})} \quad (16)$$

where, $\hat{LC}_{n}^{est}$ is estimated using all manoeuvres in the dataset excluding manoeuvre n.

A total of 200 LCSL events (associated with 13 lane changing manoeuvres) and 204 non-lane changing events (associated with 12 non-lane changing manoeuvres) are used to develop the

LCSL model. In addition, 99 LCFL events (8 lane changing manoeuvres) and 102 non-lane changing events (6 non-lane changing manoeuvres) are used to develop the LCFL model. As mentioned earlier, each event is the lane changing decision of a heavy vehicle driver at each 0.5 second time interval. To develop the models it is regarded as appropriate to have a similar number of lane changing and non-lane changing events in the dataset. For each of those manoeuvres, the dataset contains details of the preceding and following vehicles in the current lane and the target lane at each 0.5 second time interval. The leave-one-out cross-validation method is used to examine the accuracy of the developed models in two sections. First, a single event is selected as the validation data from all events, and the remaining events are selected as the training data. This is repeated for all events and the correctly and the incorrectly estimated events are counted. Second, all events which belong to a single manoeuvre (2 events per second) are selected as the validation data and the remaining manoeuvres are selected as the training data. This is repeated for all manoeuvres and the correctly and the incorrectly estimated manoeuvres are counted. The validation results for the LCSL and the LCFL models are presented in Table 4.

This table compares the validation results for the LCSL model and the LCFL model with two and three fuzzy sets. The matrix of estimated events and the matrix of estimated manoeuvres show the results of the leave-one-out cross-validation method for the events and manoeuvres respectively. The matrix interpretation is presented by Equation 17 in Box 1.

In each matrix, the entry on the upper left corner presents the number of correctly estimated lane changes and the entry on the lower right corner represents the correctly estimated number of non-lane changes. The entries on the anti-diagonal represent the number of incorrect estimations. The entry on the upper right corner shows the number of incorrectly estimated lane changes and the entry on the lower left corner is the number of incorrectly estimated non-lane changes. Finally, the sum of two entries on the

Table 4. The validation results for LCSL and LCFL models

Model	Number of Fuzzy Sets	Validation Results			
		Estimated Events	Estimated Manoeuvres	Correctly Estimated Events	Correctly Estimated Manoeuvres
LCSL	2	$\begin{bmatrix} 119 & 81 \\ 57 & 147 \end{bmatrix}$	$\begin{bmatrix} 8 & 5 \\ 7 & 5 \end{bmatrix}$	266 (65.8%)	13 (52.0%)
	3	$\begin{bmatrix} 185 & 15 \\ 14 & 190 \end{bmatrix}$	$\begin{bmatrix} 12 & 1 \\ 1 & 11 \end{bmatrix}$	375 (92.8%)	23 (92.0%)
LCFL	2	$\begin{bmatrix} 90 & 9 \\ 17 & 85 \end{bmatrix}$	$\begin{bmatrix} 6 & 2 \\ 3 & 3 \end{bmatrix}$	175 (87.1%)	9 (64.3%)
	3	$\begin{bmatrix} 99 & 0 \\ 0 & 102 \end{bmatrix}$	$\begin{bmatrix} 8 & 0 \\ 0 & 6 \end{bmatrix}$	201 (100.0%)	14 (100.0%)

Box 1.

$$\begin{array}{ccc} & \multicolumn{2}{c}{Estimated} \\ & Lane\ \text{Changes} & Non-Lane\ Changes \\ Observed\begin{array}{r} Lane\ Changes \\ Non-Lane\ Changes \end{array} & \left(\begin{array}{l} Correctly\ Estimated \\ Lane\ Changes \\ Incorrectly\ Estimated \\ Non-Lane\ Changes \end{array}\right. & \left.\begin{array}{l} Incorrectly\ Estimated \\ Lane\ Changes \\ Correctly\ Estimated \\ Non-Lane\ Changes \end{array}\right) \end{array} \tag{17}$$

diagonal is presented as the correctly estimated observations.

The results from Table 4 shows that the LCFL with 3 fuzzy sets can correctly estimate all lane changing events and lane changing manoeuvres (100%). As mentioned earlier, the number of heavy vehicle lane changing manoeuvres in this research is insufficient to provide two different datasets for calibrating the model and validating its accuracy. Therefore, the same dataset is used for model calibration and validating its accuracy using the leave-one-out cross-validation method. Using the same dataset for model calibration and validation can be the reason of 100% correctly estimating the lane changes (Moridpour et al., 2009). In a comparative sense, the results in Table 4 show that the LCFL model has higher percentage and the LCSL model has lower percentage of accurately estimating the heavy vehicle drivers' lane changing decision. According to the trajectory data, a small proportion of the heavy vehicle drivers, move into the faster lane. Those drivers mainly seek some speed advantages. The speed difference between the current and the left lane and therefore, the desire to move into the faster lane could be modelled by the microscopic traffic characteristics of surrounding vehicles in the current and left lanes. Meanwhile, the trajectory dataset shows that the heavy vehicle drivers mostly move into the slower lane. However, they may have other motivations for moving into the slower lane than only the microscopic traffic flow characteristics in the current and the right lanes. Therefore, it may be possible that the microscopic traffic characteristics of surrounding vehicles in the current and right lanes are insufficient to model the motivation of heavy vehicle drivers for moving into the slower lane. This may justify the higher percentage of accurately estimation in LCFL model and the lower percentage of accurately estimation in LCSL model (Moridpour et al., 2009).

The obtained results from Table 4 show that the models with three fuzzy sets are more accurate than the models with two fuzzy sets. As it was mentioned earlier, increasing the number of fuzzy sets increases the accuracy of the models. However, the number of fuzzy sets is constrained by the drivers' perception capability. Increasing the number of fuzzy sets enhances the model accuracy and meanwhile increases the required time for model development.

Lane Changing Execution

In general, several seconds are required for heavy vehicle drivers to complete a lane changing manoeuvre. This is due to the physical (e.g. length and size) and operational (e.g. acceleration, deceleration and manoeuvrability) characteristics of heavy vehicles. However, the existing lane changing models mainly focus on drivers' lane changing decision and generally neglect execution of the lane changing manoeuvre (Moridpour et al., 2010b). Excluding the lane changing execution, may have a significant impact on estimated traffic flow characteristics, particularly in heavy traffic conditions. Explicitly considering the lane changing execution may improve the accuracy of lane changing models which could subsequently improve the accuracy of the results obtained from microscopic traffic simulations. During a lane changing manoeuvre, interactions occur between the lane changing vehicle and the preceding and the following vehicles in the current and target lanes. The physical and operational characteristics of the lane changing vehicle, as well as their interactions with the surrounding vehicles, may affect their acceleration and deceleration during a lane changing execution. The acceleration/deceleration of the lane changing vehicles may influence the vehicles travelling upstream of the lane changing manoeuvre in either the current or the target lane. Usually, the upstream vehicles may be forced to adjust their speed in line with vehicle that has changed lanes. This may cause speed oscillations in either the current lane or the target lane or may result in flow breakdown in heavy traffic conditions.

Since lane changing execution is an important stage of the lane changing manoeuvre, it is essential to analyse heavy vehicle drivers' acceleration and deceleration behaviour while changing lanes. A review of the literature highlighted that there has been limited prior consideration of drivers' acceleration behaviour during the lane changing manoeuvre. Toledo (2003; 2009) developed a lane changing acceleration/deceleration model which captures the vehicles' acceleration during the lane changing manoeuvre. In his model, the duration of the lane changing manoeuvres is ignored. Therefore, lane changes are reported only at the end of the lane changing manoeuvre when lane changing is completed. Given the limited attention in the literature to lane change execution, it was regarded as important that the speed and acceleration/deceleration of heavy vehicles during their lane changing execution, along with the duration of heavy vehicles' lane changing manoeuvre, be examined in more detail.

According to the results in Table 1, the average speeds in the two sites are considerably different. Therefore, it would be desirable to analyse the lane changing manoeuvres of each site, separately. However, the small number of heavy vehicle lane changes at each site makes it difficult to independently analyse the lane changing manoeuvres of each site (Moridpour et al., 2010c). Therefore, the lane changing manoeuvres of the two sites are considered together for this analysis. The results for all lane changing manoeuvres across the two sites are summarized in Table 5. This table provides a summary of the required time for heavy vehicle drivers to execute a lane changing manoeuvre based on 42 manoeuvres studied in this research. The speed and acceleration of the heavy vehicles during the lane changing manoeuvre are included in the table.

Results show an average of 8 seconds for the lane changing execution of heavy vehicle drivers. In addition, heavy vehicles have small average speeds (8.6 m/sec) during the lane changing manoeuvre. In Table 5, the mean speed is calculated as the average speed of all vehicles at each 0.5 second time intervals during the lane changing execution. To better understand the changes in the speed of heavy vehicles during the lane changing execution, Table 5 also includes summary statistics for the acceleration/deceleration of the heavy vehicles. The heavy vehicles' acceleration is about 0.1 m/sec^2 during the lane change execution.

To better understand the lane changing execution of the heavy vehicle drivers, their speed profile and their acceleration/deceleration behaviour are analysed from the start of the lane changing until the end of the lane changing manoeuvre. To avoid complexity, the following figures are presented based on smoothed trajectory data extracted from all studied manoeuvres at 0.5 second time intervals. The heavy vehicles' speed profile during the lane changing manoeuvre is presented in Figure

Table 5. Summary statistics on heavy vehicle lane changing characteristics

Variable	Mean	Standard Deviation	Minimum	Maximum
Lane Changing Duration (sec)	8.0	3.7	1.6	16.2
Speed* (m/sec)	8.6	0.5	7.4	9.1
Acceleration (m/sec^2)	0.1	0.1	0.0	0.5

* Vehicles' longitudinal speed is considered in this research.

5a. In this figure, time is represented on the X-axis and the average speed of all heavy vehicles during the lane changing execution is represented on the Y-axis. The position of the zero point on the X-axis represents the point in time when the heavy vehicles started to move into the target lane, based on the start of the lateral movement of the of the subject vehicles.

According to Table 5, the minimum lane changing duration time for heavy vehicles is 1.6 seconds. That value is also shown in Figure 5a. This is the minimum required time to complete changing lanes for all studied heavy vehicle lane changing manoeuvres. The average lane changing duration is the average time required for all studied heavy vehicles to complete a lane changing manoeuvre (Figure 5b).

The heavy vehicles' speed shows little variation prior to the start of the lane changing manoeuvre. Summary statistics on heavy vehicles' speed show the mean of 8.7 m/sec and the standard deviation of 0.1 m/sec, from 8 seconds prior to the start of lane changing until the minimum lane changing time. According to the summary statistics and the results from Figure 5a, heavy vehicles' average speed changes little until the minimum lane changing duration time and decreases afterwards. However, this is not due to a decreasing trend in heavy vehicles' speed during the lane changing execution. To better understand the decreasing trend of heavy vehicles' speed in Figure 5a, the relationship between heavy vehicles' average speed during the lane changing execution and their lane changing duration time are presented in Figure 5b. That figure reflects data from the 42 lane changing manoeuvres.

Figure 5b shows that the lane changing duration increases while the heavy vehicle speed decreases. In other words, the heavy vehicles with slower speeds require more time to execute a lane changing manoeuvre. As discussed earlier, Figure 5a shows the heavy vehicles' average speed for all heavy vehicle lane changing manoeuvres. The heavy vehicles with higher speed complete their lane changing manoeuvre in smaller time periods. The remaining heavy vehicles with larger lane changing duration time travel in lower speed. Therefore, the average speed of heavy vehicles decreases while the lane changing duration time increases. This explains the decreasing trend in heavy vehicles' speed after the minimum lane changing duration time shown in Figure 5a. In addition, analysing the speed profiles of the in dividual lane changing manoeuvres showed that heavy vehicles have almost constant speed while changing lanes. Analysing the heavy vehicle drivers' lane changing behaviour shows that heavy vehicles' speed changes little during the lane changing execution in heavy traffic conditions (Table 5 and Figure 5a). In other words, heavy vehicle drivers keep almost constant speed during the lane changing execution. They do not accelerate/decelerate to adjust their speed according to the speed of the surrounding traffic in the target lane. This implies that heavy vehicle drivers may move into the gaps which are alongside the heavy vehicle while performing the lane changing manoeuvre. They do not accelerate/decelerate frequently and

Figure 5. Relationship between heavy vehicles' average speed and lane changing duration

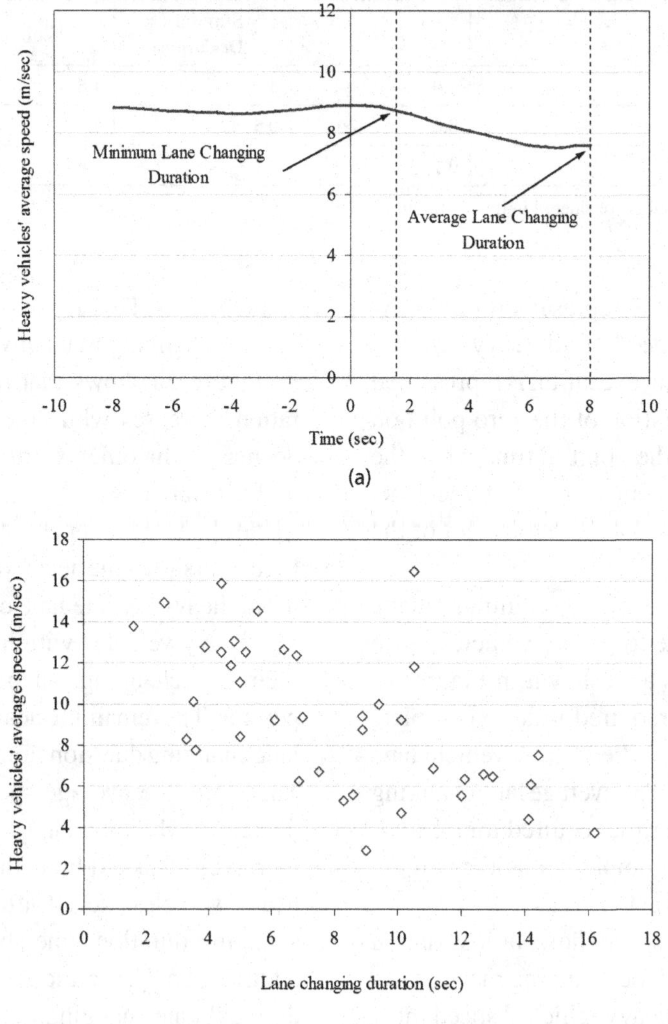

therefore, they may prefer not to move into the gaps which are in front of or behind the heavy vehicle in heavy traffic conditions.

The above analysis highlights that the heavy vehicle drivers usually keep a constant speed and do not accelerate/decelerate frequently when changing lanes. Subsequently, it is not necessary to develop an acceleration/deceleration model for the heavy vehicles during the lane changing manoeuvre. A simple constant speed model could be assumed for the heavy vehicles during the lane changing execution.

Lane Restriction Strategies

In this section, the heavy vehicle lane changing model is used to examine three different lane restriction strategies at different percentages of heavy vehicles. The performance of the heavy vehicle lane restriction strategies are examined macroscopically and microscopically using VISSIM (German abbreviation for 'traffic simulation in cities') microscopic traffic simulation model (PTV, 2007). In the first strategy, heavy vehicles are permitted to use all lanes and no limitation is considered for heavy vehicles. In the second strategy, heavy vehicles are restricted from using the fastest lane. The fastest lane is the lane with the minimum distance to the median. In the third strategy, heavy vehicles are restricted from using the two fastest lanes (the closest two to the median). For each strategy, the percentage of heavy vehicles is increased from 2.2% and 3.8% of the total traffic, respectively in US-101 and I-80 (Table 1) to 30% at different stages (5%, 10%, 15%, 20%, 25%, and 30%). Then, each strategy is evaluated using the VISSIM default model and the heavy vehicle lane changing model. Each strategy is run for 10 times using the VISSIM default model and 10 times using the heavy vehicle lane changing model. The average value of each estimated traffic measurement obtained from 10 times running the model is calculated. The average estimated traffic measurements using the VISSIM model and heavy vehicle lane changing model are considered as the results with the VISSIM default model and the heavy vehicle lane changing model, respectively.

Simulation Results and Discussions

Evaluating the performance of the heavy vehicle lane restriction strategies involves analysing and comparing the macroscopic and microscopic traffic measurements estimated by the VISSIM default model and the heavy vehicle lane changing model. Macroscopic traffic measurements investigated in this research include traffic volumes and the average speeds given by the VISSIM simulation model, whereas the microscopic measure is the number of estimated lane changing manoeuvres of heavy vehicles.

Table 6 present the traffic volumes and the average speeds estimated by the VISSIM default model and the heavy vehicle lane changing model on US-101 and I-80. In this table, the results are presented for individual strategies with different percentages of heavy vehicles. The results demonstrate that estimated traffic flows and average speed (the numbers in brackets) in both freeway sections decreases when the percentage of heavy vehicles increases. The trend is more observed in the traffic flows estimated by the VISSIM default model.

The results in Table 6 highlight the speed benefit of restricting heavy vehicles from entering into faster lanes. The results show that the average speed in both freeway sections decreases when the percentage of heavy vehicles increases. According to the results presented in this table, the estimated average speeds by the heavy vehicle lane changing model are almost similar to the corresponding values estimated by the VISSIM default model. Consistent with previous studies (Cate & Urbanik II, 2003; Siuhi & Mussa, 2007), the results in these tables show minor changes in the macroscopic traffic measurements under different strategies.

Table 7 reports the number of estimated heavy vehicle lane changing manoeuvres on US-101 and I-80. Simulation results show that the number of heavy vehicle lane changing manoeuvres increases when the heavy vehicle percentage increases. In US-101, the estimated number of heavy vehicle lane changes by the heavy vehicle lane changing model is larger than that by the VISSIM default model. However, this is not the case for I-80 in which, the number of heavy vehicle lane changes estimated by the VISSIM default model is considerably larger than the values estimated by the heavy vehicle lane changing model. Comparison of the traffic characteristics at the two sites show that for I-80, the traffic flow rate is lower, the traffic density is higher and the speed is lower than the corresponding values in US-101, respectively (Table 1). This may imply that the VISSIM lane changing model is less accurate in estimating the heavy vehicle lane changing manoeuvres in higher densities and when traffic flow increases. The large number of estimated heavy vehicle lane changing manoeuvres by the VISSIM default model can explain the considerable decreasing trend in the estimated traffic flows using VISSIM model. The large numbers of heavy vehicle lane

Table 6. Estimated traffic volumes (veh) and average speed (m/sec) for different strategies on US-101 & I-80*

Site Name	Lane Changing Decision Model	Strategy Number	Heavy Vehicle Percentage (%)					
			5	10	15	20	25	30
US-101	VISSIM Model	1	5772 (7.1)	5743 (7.0)	5756 (7.0)	5695 (6.9)	5682 (6.8)	5664 (6.8)
		2	5773 (7.7)	5727 (7.7)	5713 (7.7)	5634 (7.6)	5576 (7.5)	5552 (7.5)
		3	5733 (8.8)	5681 (8.7)	5650 (8.7)	5595 (8.6)	5521 (8.6)	5426 (8.6)
	Heavy Vehicle Model	1	5778 (7.0)	5753 (7.0)	5772 (7.0)	5732 (6.9)	5697 (6.9)	5687 (6.9)
		2	5780 (7.6)	5757 (7.6)	5763 (7.6)	5721 (7.6)	5695 (7.5)	5613 (7.5)
		3	5759 (8.6)	5709 (8.6)	5672 (8.6)	5638 (8.5)	5601 (8.5)	5553 (8.4)
I-80	VISSIM Model	1	5077 (6.3)	5041 (6.3)	5017 (6.2)	4970 (6.1)	4964 (6.0)	4953 (5.9)
		2	5069 (7.1)	5002 (7.1)	4998 (7.0)	4962 (6.9)	4938 (6.8)	4925 (6.7)
		3	5059 (7.6)	4994 (7.6)	4976 (7.6)	4921 (7.5)	4907 (7.5)	4886 (7.4)
	Heavy Vehicle Model	1	5084 (6.2)	5069 (6.2)	5034 (6.2)	4992 (6.1)	4965 (6.0)	4958 (6.0)
		2	5072 (7.0)	5057 (7.0)	5021 (6.9)	4974 (6.8)	4953 (6.8)	4931 (6.7)
		3	5043 (7.5)	5029 (7.5)	5003 (7.5)	4983 (7.4)	4942 (7.4)	4926 (7.3)

* The average speeds (m/sec) are shown in brackets.

changing manoeuvres estimated by the VISSIM default model is unrealistic.

The number of heavy vehicle lane changing manoeuvres is a good indicator of the potential for vehicular conflicts (El-Tantawy et al., 2009). Large numbers of heavy vehicle lane changing manoeuvres can increase the number of traffic accidents and potentially reduce the freeway safety. Therefore, adopting the VISSIM default model in safety studies would result in conclusions which are not reliable. The results of Table 7 show that developing an exclusive lane changing model for heavy vehicle drivers could increase the accuracy of the simulation models in microscopically estimating the lane changing manoeuvres of heavy vehicles.

The results obtained from this section shows that using an exclusive lane changing model for heavy vehicles can improve the accuracy of VISSIM model in estimating the traffic flow characteristics. In the traffic with high proportion of heavy vehicles, the estimated values of traffic volume and average speed are more accurate when exclusive fuzzy lane changing model is used for heavy vehicles. Furthermore, the number of heavy vehicle lane changing manoeuvres estimated by the fuzzy lane changing model is more accurate and realistic compared to the corresponding values estimated by the VISSIM default model.

Table 7. Number of heavy vehicle lane changing manoeuvres in different strategies

Site Name	Lane Changing Decision Model	Strategy Number	Heavy Vehicle Percentage (%)					
			5	10	15	20	25	30
US-101	VISSIM Model	1	2	9	12	16	22	26
		2	3	7	17	10	29	26
		3	2	11	17	19	27	29
	Heavy Vehicle Model	1	5	17	25	29	44	42
		2	3	15	18	26	54	41
		3	5	19	31	52	46	56
I-80	VISSIM Model	1	44	81	128	193	231	289
		2	42	107	165	194	282	354
		3	60	111	188	261	336	381
	Heavy Vehicle Model	1	28	38	68	70	93	102
		2	35	43	78	81	101	114
		3	40	65	87	93	107	118

CONCLUSION

The growing number of heavy vehicles on freeways has interested many studies to establish strategies to reduce interactions between heavy vehicles and passenger cars. Many lane restriction strategies for heavy vehicles have been examined using microscopic traffic simulation packages. Those packages mostly use a general lane changing model to estimate the lane changing behaviour of heavy vehicle and passenger car drivers. However, these two groups of drivers have fundamentally different lane changing behaviour. Therefore, there is a major concern in the reliability of those packages when evaluating different lane restriction strategies for heavy vehicles.

This chapter introduced an exclusive heavy vehicle lane changing model and explained the structure. Subsequently, different strategies were defined to restrict the heavy vehicles from using certain lanes. For each strategy, the macroscopic and microscopic traffic measurements of the two freeway sections were analysed, using the VISSIM default lane changing model and the exclusive heavy vehicle lane changing model.

The estimated traffic flows in both freeway sections decreased when the percentage of heavy vehicles increased. The trend was more observed in the traffic flows estimated by the VISSIM default model. This may be due to overestimation of the number of heavy vehicle lane changing manoeuvres by the VISSIM model. The results demonstrated slight difference in the estimated average speeds on both freeway sections when the VISSIM default model and the heavy vehicle lane changing model were adopted. Also, consistent with previous studies, the results showed minor changes in the average speeds under different strategies. However, the VISSIM default model unrealistically overestimated the observed number of heavy vehicle lane changing manoeuvres in high traffic densities. Using the exclusive lane changing model for heavy vehicles enhanced the accuracy of the VISSIM simulation model in microscopically estimating the lane changing manoeuvres of heavy vehicles.

The number of heavy vehicle lane changing manoeuvres is a good indicator of the potential for vehicular conflicts. Large numbers of heavy vehicle lane changing manoeuvres can increase the number of traffic accidents and potentially reduce the freeway safety. Therefore, adopting the VISSIM default model in safety studies would result in conclusions which are not reliable. The results showed that developing an exclusive lane changing model for heavy vehicle drivers could increase the accuracy of the simulation models in microscopically estimating the lane changing manoeuvres of heavy vehicles.

FUTURE RESEARCH DIRECTIONS

The available dataset provides the vehicle trajectory data under heavy traffic conditions. However, heavy vehicle drivers may behave differently under other traffic situations. Further data collection under different traffic conditions is required to ensure comprehensive model development for lane changing behaviour of heavy vehicle drivers. Heavy vehicles comprise a small part of traffic stream. Therefore, a small number of heavy vehicle lane changing manoeuvres exist in the available dataset. Collection and compilation of a larger trajectory dataset for model development is costly and time consuming. However, it would be desirable for model development to be based on a larger sample data. A larger trajectory dataset would enable future research to use separate datasets for model calibration and model validation and thereby increase the confidence in the performance of the model.

While, the proposed lane changing decision model was capable of replicating the DLC decision of heavy vehicle drivers, MLC decisions were ignored due to lack of adequate data. The available datasets were collected on relatively short freeway sections. However, the proposed lane changing decision model should be extended and a MLC decision model should be developed for heavy vehicle drivers. This requires further data collection over longer sections of freeways (1500 to 3000 meters long).

The lane changing model developed here is based on differences between drivers. Differences in the behaviour of individual drivers over time have not been considered. However, the drivers may have dissimilar driving decisions at different times. Further research is required to develop a heavy vehicle lane changing model which captures the differences between drivers as well as the differences for individual drivers over time.

Heavy vehicles impose physical and psychological effects on surrounding traffic. The existence of heavy vehicles may have influence on the car following and lane changing behaviour of the surrounding vehicles. There would be merit in investigating the effect of existence of heavy vehicles on the behaviour of the surrounding traffic, specifically the extent to which the presence of a heavy vehicle induces more lane changing behaviour in the other traffic. Understanding the influence of heavy vehicles on surrounding traffic can increase the accuracy of the microscopic traffic simulation models in estimating the macroscopic and microscopic traffic measurements.

REFERENCES

Adelakun, A., & Cherry, C. (2009). Exploring truck driver perceptions and preferences: Congestion and conflict, managed lanes, and tolls. *Proceeding of the 88th Transportation Research Board Annual Meeting*. Washington, DC. CD-ROM.

Ahmed, K. I. (1999). *Modeling drivers' acceleration and lane changing behavior*. Massachusetts Institute of Technology.

Al-Kaisy, A. F., & Hall, F. L. (2003). Guidelines for estimating capacity at freeway reconstruction zones. *Journal of Transportation Engineering*, *129*(5), 572–577. doi:10.1061/(ASCE)0733-947X(2003)129:5(572).

Al-Kaisy, A. F., Hall, F. L., & Reisman, E. S. (2002). Developing passenger car equivalents for heavy vehicles on freeways during queue discharge flow. *Transportation Research Part A, Policy and Practice*, *36*(8), 725–742. doi:10.1016/S0965-8564(01)00032-5.

Al-Kaisy, A. F., Jung, Y., & Rakha, H. (2005). Developing passenger car equivalency factors for heavy vehicles during congestion. *Journal of Transportation Engineering*, *131*(7), 514–523. doi:10.1061/(ASCE)0733-947X(2005)131:7(514).

Brackstone, M., McDonald, M., & Wu, J. (1998). Lane changing on the motorway: Factors affecting its occurrence, and their implications. *9th International Conference on Road Transport Information and Control*. London, UK.

Bureau of Transportation Statistics. (2002). *US Department of Transportation, National Transportation Statistics BTS02-08*. Washington, DC: US Government Printing Office.

Cambridge Systematics. (2005a). *NGSIM I-80 Data Analysis, Summary Reports. Federal HighWay Administration (FHWA)*. Retrieved from https://camsys.com

Cambridge Systematics. (2005b). *NGSIM US-101 Data Analysis, Summary Reports. Federal HighWay Administration (FHWA)*. Retrieved from https://camsys.com

Cate, M. A., & Urbanik, T., II. (2003). Another view of truck lane restrictions. *Proceeding of the 82th Transportation Research Board Annual Meeting*. Washington, DC., CD-ROM.

Chen, C. H. (1996). *Fuzzy logic and neural network handbook*. McGraw-Hill Companies.

Choudhury, C. F., Ben-Akiva, M. E., Toledo, T., Lee, G., & Rao, A. (2007). Modeling cooperative lane changing and forced merging behavior. *Proceeding of the 86th Transportation Research Board Annual Meeting*. Washington, DC., CD-ROM.

Conway, K. (2005). *Pacific highway upgrade-F3 to Raymond Terrace route (Consultancy Report)*. Maunsell Australia Pty Ltd..

Daganzo, C. F. (2002). A behavioral theory of multi-lane traffic flow part II: Merges and the onset of congestion. *Transportation Research Part B: Methodological*, *36*, 159–169. doi:10.1016/S0191-2615(00)00043-6.

Das, S., & Bowles, B. A. (1999). Simulations of highway chaos using fuzzy logic. *18th International Conference of the North American Fuzzy Information Procecsing Society*. Nafips, New York, U.S.A.

Doshi, A., & Trivedi, M. (2008). A comparative exploration of eye gaze and head motion cues for lane change intent prediction. *IEEE Intelligent Vehicles Symposium* (pp. 49-54). Eindhoven, Netherlands.

Eidehall, A., Pohl, J., Gustafsson, F., & Ekmark, J. (2007). Toward autonomous collision avoidance by steering. *IEEE Transactions on Intelligent Transportation Systems*, *8*(1), 84–94. doi:10.1109/TITS.2006.888606.

El-Tantawy, S., Djavadian, S., Roorda, M. J., & Abdulhai, B. (2009). Safety evaluation of truck lane restriction strategies using microsimulation modeling. *Transportation Research Record. Journal of the Transportation Research Board*, *2099*, 123–131. doi:10.3141/2099-14.

Gipps, P. G. (1986). A model for the structure of lane-changing decisions. *Transportation Research Part B: Methodological*, *20*(5), 403–414. doi:10.1016/0191-2615(86)90012-3.

Hatipoglu, C., Ozguner, U., & Redmill, K. A. (2003). Automated lane change controller design. *IEEE Transactions on Intelligent Transportation Systems*, *4*(1), 13–22. doi:10.1109/TITS.2003.811644.

Hidas, P. (2005). Modelling vehicle interactions in microscopic simulation of merging and weaving. *Transportation Research Part C, Emerging Technologies*, *13*(1), 37–62. doi:10.1016/j.trc.2004.12.003.

Hoogendoorn, S. P., & Bovy, P. H. L. (2001). State-of-the-art of vehicular traffic flow modelling. *Special Issue on Road Traffic Modelling and Control of the Journal of Systems and Control Engineering*, *215*(4), 283–303.

Jang, J. S. R., & Gulley, N. (2008). *Fuzzy logic toolbox for use with MATLAB*. USA: The MathWorks Inc..

Kiefer, R. J., & Hankey, J. M. (2008). Lane change behavior with a side blind zone alert system. *Accident; Analysis and Prevention*, *40*(2), 683–690. doi:10.1016/j.aap.2007.09.018 PMID:18329421.

Knospe, W., Santen, L., Schadschneider, A., & Schreckenberg, M. (2002). A realistic two-lane traffic model for highway traffic. *Journal of Physics. A, Mathematical and General*, *35*(15), 3369–3388. doi:10.1088/0305-4470/35/15/302.

Kwon, J., Coifman, B., & Bickel, P. (2000). Day-to-day travel time trends and travel time prediction from loop detector data. *Transportation Research Record. Journal of the Transportation Research Board*, *1717*, 120–129. doi:10.3141/1717-15.

Laval, J. A., & Daganzo, C. F. (2006). Lane changing in traffic stream. *Transportation Research Part B: Methodological*, *40*(3), 251–264. doi:10.1016/j.trb.2005.04.003.

Li-sheng, J., Wen-ping, F., Ying-nan, Z., Shuang-bin, Y., & Hai-jing, H. (2009). Research on safety lane change model of driver assistant system on highway. *IEEE Intelligent Vehicles Symposium*. Shaanxi, China.

Lord, D., Middleton, D., & Whitacre, J. (2005). Does separating trucks from other traffic improve overall safety? *Transportation Research Record. Journal of the Transportation Research Board*, *1922*, 156–166. doi:10.3141/1922-20.

Lygeros, J., Godbole, D. N., & Sastry, S. (1998). Verified hybrid controllers for automated vehicles. *IEEE Transactions on Automatic Control*, *43*(4), 522–539. doi:10.1109/9.664155.

Ma, X. (2004). *Toward an integrated car-following and lane-changing model based on neural-fuzzy approach*. Helsinki summer workshop.

Maerivoet, S., & Moor, B. D. (2005). Cellular automata models of road traffic. *Physics Reports*, *419*(1), 1–64. doi:10.1016/j.physrep.2005.08.005.

Mar, J., & Lin, H. T. (2005). The car-following and lane-changing collision prevention system based on the cascaded fuzzy inference system. *IEEE Transactions on Vehicular Technology*, *54*(3), 910–924. doi:10.1109/TVT.2005.844655.

McDonald, M., Wu, J., & Brackstone, M. (1997). Development of a fuzzy logic based microscopic motorway simulation model. *Proceeding of the IEEE Conference on Intelligent Transport Systems (ITSC97) Conference* (pp. 82-87). Boston, MA.

Moridpour, S. (2010a). *Modelling heavy vehicle lane changing*. (Ph.D. Thesis). Monash University, Australia.

Moridpour, S., Rose, G., & Sarvi, M. (2009). Modelling the heavy vehicle drivers' lane changing decision under congested traffic conditions. *Journal of Road and Transport Research*, *18*(4), 49–57.

Moridpour, S., Rose, G., & Sarvi, M. (2010b). The effect of surrounding traffic characteristics on lane changing behavior. *Journal of Transportation Engineering*, *136*(11), 937–1055. doi:10.1061/(ASCE)TE.1943-5436.0000165.

Moridpour, S., Sarvi, M., & Rose, G. (2010c). Modeling the lane changing execution of multi class vehicles under heavy traffic conditions. *Transportation Research Record. Journal of the Transportation Research Board*, *2161*, 11–19. doi:10.3141/2161-02.

Moridpour, S., Sarvi, M., Rose, G., & Mazloumi, E. (2012). Lane-changing decision model for heavy vehicle drivers. *Journal of Inteligent Transportation Systems*, *16*(1), 24–35. doi:10.1080/15472450.2012.639640.

Nagel, K., Wolf, D. E., Wagner, P., & Simon, P. (1998). Two-lane traffic rules for cellular automata: A systematic approach. *Physical Review E: Statistical Physics, Plasmas, Fluids, and Related Interdisciplinary Topics*, *58*(2), 1425–1437. doi:10.1103/PhysRevE.58.1425.

PTV. (2007). *VISSIM 5.0 User Manual*. PTV Planung Transport Verkehr AG, Stumpfstra_e 1, D-76131 Karlsruhe, Germany. Retrieved from http://www.vissim.de/

Rose, N., Cowie, C., Gillett, R., & Marks, G. B. (2009). Weighted road density: A simple way of assigning traffic-related air pollution exposure. *Atmospheric Environment*, *43*(32), 5009–5014. doi:10.1016/j.atmosenv.2009.06.049.

Salvucci, D. D., & Mandalia, H. M. (2007). Lane-change detection using a computational driver model. *Human Factors and Ergonomics Society*, *49*(3), 532–542. doi:10.1518/001872007X200157 PMID:17552315.

Sasoh, A., & Ohara, T. (2002). Shock wave relation containing lane change source term for two-lane traffic flow. *Journal of the Physical Society of Japan*, *71*(9), 2339–2347. doi:10.1143/JPSJ.71.2339.

Toledo, T. (2003). *Integrated driving behavior modeling*. Massachusetts Institute of Technology.

Toledo, T., Koutsopoulos, H. N., & Ben-Akiva, M. (2009). Estimation of an integrated driving behavior model. *Transportation Research Part C, Emerging Technologies*, *17*(4), 365–380. doi:10.1016/j.trc.2009.01.005.

Uddin, M. S., & Ardekani, S. A. (2002). An observational study of lane changing on basic freeway segment. *Proceeding of the 81th Transportation Research Board Annual Meeting*. Washington, DC., CD-ROM.

Wall, G. T., & Hounsell, N. B. (2005). Microscopic modelling of motorway diverges. *European Journal of Transport and Infrastructure Research*, *5*(3), 139–158.

Wiedemann, R., & Reiter, U. (1992). *Microscopic traffic simulation the simulation system*. MISSION.

Wu, J., Brackstone, M., & McDonald, M. (2003). The validation of a microscopic simulation model: A methodological case study. *Transportation Research Part C, Emerging Technologies*, *11*(6), 463–479. doi:10.1016/j.trc.2003.05.001.

Yang, C. H., & Regan, A. C. (2009). Prioritization of potential alternative truck management strategies using the analytical hierarchy process. *Proceeding of the 88th Transportation Research Board Annual Meeting*. Washington, DC., CD-ROM.

Yang, Q., & Koutsopoulos, H. N. (1996). A microscopic traffic simulator for evaluation of dynamic traffic management systems. *Transportation Research Part C, Emerging Technologies*, *4*(3), 113–129. doi:10.1016/S0968-090X(96)00006-X.

Zadeh, L. A. (1965). Fuzzy sets. *Information and Control*, *8*, 338–353. doi:10.1016/S0019-9958(65)90241-X.

Zadeh, L. A. (1994). Fuzzy logic, neural networks, and soft computing. *Communications of the ACM, 37*(3), 77–84. doi:10.1145/175247.175255.

ADDITIONAL READING

Ahmed, K. I. (1999). *Modeling drivers' acceleration and lane changing behavior*. Massachusetts Institute of Technology.

Ahmed, K. I., Ben-Akiva, M., Koutsopoulos, H. N., & Mishalani, R. G. (1996). Models of freeway lane changing and gap acceptance behavior. *Proceedings of the 13th International Symposium on the Theory of Traffic Flow and Transportation* (pp. 501-515). Lyon, France.

Choudhury, C. F., Ben-Akiva, M. E., Toledo, T., Lee, G., & Rao, A. (2007). Modeling cooperative lane changing and forced merging behavior. *Proceeding of the 86th Transportation Research Board Annual Meeting*. Washington, DC., CD-ROM.

Das, S., & Bowles, B. A. (1999). Simulations of highway chaos using fuzzy logic. *18th International Conference of the North American Fuzzy Information Processing Society*. Nafips, New York, U.S.A.

Das, S., Bowles, B. A., Houghland, C. R., Hunn, S. J., & Zhang, Y. (1999). Microscopic simulations of freeway traffic flow. *Proceedings of the Thirty-Second Annual Simulation Symposium*. IEEE Computer Society.

El Hadouaj, S., Espié, S., & Drogoul, A. (2000). *To combine reactivity and anticipation: The case of conflicts resolution in a simulated road traffic*. The Second International Workshop on Multi-Agent Based Simulation, Boston, USA.

Espié, S., Saad, F., Schnetzler, B., Bourlier, F., & Djemame, N. (1994). Microscopic traffic simulation and driver behaviour modelling: The ARCHISIM project. The Strategic Highway Research Program and Traffic Safety on Two continents. Lille, France.

Gipps, P. G. (1981). A behavioral car-following model for computer simulation. *Transportation Research Part B: Methodological, 15*, 105–111. doi:10.1016/0191-2615(81)90037-0.

Gipps, P. G. (1986). A model for the structure of lane-changing decisions. *Transportation Research Part B: Methodological, 20*(5), 403–414. doi:10.1016/0191-2615(86)90012-3.

Hidas, P. (2002). Modelling lane changing and merging in microscopic traffic simulation. *Transportation Research Part C, Emerging Technologies, 10*(5-6), 351–371. doi:10.1016/S0968-090X(02)00026-8.

Hidas, P. (2005). Modelling vehicle interactions in microscopic simulation of merging and weaving. *Transportation Research Part C, Emerging Technologies, 13*(1), 37–62. doi:10.1016/j.trc.2004.12.003.

Jin, W. L. (2010). A kinematic wave theory of lane-changing vehicular traffic. *Transportation Research Part B: Methodological, 44*(8-9), 1001–1021. doi:10.1016/j.trb.2009.12.014.

Kiefer, R. J., & Hankey, J. M. (2008). Lane change behavior with a side blind zone alert system. *Accident; Analysis and Prevention, 40*(2), 683–690. doi:10.1016/j.aap.2007.09.018 PMID:18329421.

Laval, J. A., & Daganzo, C. F. (2006). Lane changing in traffic stream. *Transportation Research Part B: Methodological, 40*(3), 251–264. doi:10.1016/j.trb.2005.04.003.

McDonald, M., Wu, J., & Brackstone, M. (1997). Development of a fuzzy logic based microscopic motorway simulation model. *Proceeding of the IEEE Conference on Intelligent Transport Systems (ITSC97) Conference* (pp. 82-87). Boston, MA.

Moridpour, S. (2010a). *Modelling heavy vehicle lane changing*. (Ph.D. Thesis). Monash University, Australia.

Moridpour, S., Rose, G., & Sarvi, M. (2009). Modelling the heavy vehicle drivers' lane changing decision under congested traffic conditions. *Journal of Road and Transport Research*, *18*(4), 49–57.

Moridpour, S., Rose, G., & Sarvi, M. (2010b). The effect of surrounding traffic characteristics on lane changing behavior. *Journal of Transportation Engineering*, *136*(11), 937–1055. doi:10.1061/(ASCE)TE.1943-5436.0000165.

Moridpour, S., Sarvi, M., & Rose, G. (2010c). Modeling the lane changing execution of multi class vehicles under heavy traffic conditions. *Transportation Research Record. Journal of the Transportation Research Board*, *2161*, 11–19. doi:10.3141/2161-02.

Moridpour, S., Sarvi, M., Rose, G., & Mazloumi, E. (2012). Lane-changing decision model for heavy vehicle drivers. *Journal of Inteligent Transportation Systems*, *16*(1), 24–35. doi:10.1080/15472450.2012.639640.

Toledo, T. (2003). *Integrated driving behavior modeling*. Massachusetts Institute of Technology.

Toledo, T., Koutsopoulos, H. N., & Ben-Akiva, M. (2003). Modeling integrated lane-changing behavior. *Proceeding of the 82th Transportation Research Board Annual Meeting*. Washington, DC., CD-ROM.

Toledo, T., Koutsopoulos, H. N., & Ben-Akiva, M. (2009). Estimation of an integrated driving behavior model. *Transportation Research Part C, Emerging Technologies*, *17*(4), 365–380. doi:10.1016/j.trc.2009.01.005.

Transportation Research Board. (2010). *Highway capacity manual (HCM)*. Washington, D.C.: National Research Council.

Uddin, M. S., & Ardekani, S. A. (2002). An observational study of lane changing on basic freeway segment. *Proceeding of the 81th Transportation Research Board Annual Meeting*. Washington, DC., CD-ROM.

Wiedemann, R., & Reiter, U. (1992). *Microscopic traffic simulation the simulation system*. MISSION.

Wu, J., Brackstone, M., & McDonald, M. (2003). The validation of a microscopic simulation model: A methodological case study. *Transportation Research Part C, Emerging Technologies*, *11*(6), 463–479. doi:10.1016/j.trc.2003.05.001.

Yang, Q., & Koutsopoulos, H. N. (1996). A microscopic traffic simulator for evaluation of dynamic traffic management systems. *Transportation Research Part C, Emerging Technologies*, *4*(3), 113–129. doi:10.1016/S0968-090X(96)00006-X.

KEY WORDS AND DEFINITIONS

Driving Behaviour: The general trends of drivers while driving a car which includes their acceleration/deceleration patterns and lane changing.

Fuzzy Models: Models which are based on fuzzy logic approach.

Heavy Vehicles: The vehicles with large size and weight are called heavy vehicles.

Lane Changing: The action of moving from the current lane to either the right or the left adjacent lane.

Lane Restriction: Preventing vehicles from using some certain lanes.

Passenger Cars: Small size vehicles which are privately used by people for their trips.

Traffic Safety: An indicator of the number of accidents in transport system.

Chapter 14
User Segmentation Based on Twitter Data Using Fuzzy Clustering

Başar Öztayşi
Istanbul Technical University, Turkey

Sezi Çevik Onar
Istanbul Technical University, Turkey

ABSTRACT

Social Networking Sites, which create platform for social interactions and sharing are the mostly used internet websites, thus are very important in today's world. The vast usage of social networking sites (SNSs) has effected the business world, new business models are proposed, business process are renewed and companies try to create benefit form these sites. Besides the functional usage of SNSs such as marketing and customer relations, companies can create value by analyzing and mining the data on SNSs. In this paper, a new segmentation approach, using Text Mining and Fuzzy Clustering techniques. Text mining is process of extracting knowledge from large amounts of unstructured data source such as content generated by the SNSs users. Fuzzy clustering is an algorithm for cluster analysis in which the allocation of data points to clusters is fuzzy. In the proposed approach, users self description text are used as an input to the Text Mining process, and Fuzzy Clustering is used to extract knowledge from data. Using the proposed approach, companies can segment their customers based on their comments, ideas or any kind of other unstructered data on SNSs.

INTRODUCTION

Social network sites such as Facebook, Twitter, and Linkedin has gained great attention of internet users and has the highest traffic rankings. Although the social network sites focus on different issues like photo sharing, micro blogging, and professional networking the commonality of these sites is that they enable users with social interactions. In the literature, the social network sites are defined as websites that enables users to create a profile, define a list of other users and share anything with these connections.

DOI: 10.4018/978-1-4666-4213-3.ch014

Copyright © 2013, IGI Global. Copying or distributing in print or electronic forms without written permission of IGI Global is prohibited.

The popularity of SNSs has affected the business models, processes and created new application opportunities. New business models are being developed like social commerce which is the e-commerce applications enhanced by the social applications. Special networks are being formed for crowdsourcing which can be defined as outsourcing tasks to a distributed group of people. Besides these new business models, the business process are also changing with social network technologies, corporate social networks are being used for intra communication and collaboration, Social CRM applications are being used to manage communications with customers through social networks. Marketing efforts are also empowered with social networks, viral marketing has become an important communication tool for advertisement. Human resources processes are also affected by social networks, online job posts and test are popular, and Linkedin is widely used for recruitment.

Besides the functional usage of SNSs, companies can benefit from the data captured from social network sites. There are various tools and methods for social network data analysis, the most popular data mining applications in SNSs are defining a group of people, the topic of that group, recommending systems for individuals and virtual groups and finally sentiment analysis for automatically identifying individual's thoughts about a product, service or idea. While identifying a group and recommending individuals to others are about the connections between the users, profiling a group or understanding someone's opinion about a topic is more about analysis of the content they produce.

The user generated content in the social networks is unstructured and in text format. The term text mining has emerged from the need to analyze and benefit from these kinds of data. Text mining is described as the semi-automated process of extracting patterns, useful information and knowledge from large amounts of unstructured data sources (Turban et al., 2011). While data mining and text mining both have the same purposes of extracting knowledge, the difference comes from the input of text mining, text mining uses a collection of unstructured data file types such as word documents, PDF files, XML files. The initial applications of text mining include analysis of court orders, academic publications, and pattern files; predictions using quarterly financial reports, and automatic prioritization of emails. Text mining is used for various applications such as information extraction, topic tracking, summarization, categorization, clustering and concept Linking, question answering.

Segmentation is the process of dividing the customers into distinct and internally homogeneous groups in order to develop differentiated marketing and communication strategies according to their common charecteristics. In the consumer markets, different types of segmentation can be observed such as, value based, behavioral, loyalty based, and needs and attitudes (Tsiptsis & Chorianopoulos, 2009). Value based segmentation tries to segment the consumers according to their values, behavioral segmentation deals with segmenting the customers according to their behaviors. Loyalty base segmentation on the other hand, focuses on the loyalty level of the customers. And finally needs/attitudes based segmentation groups the customers according to their needs, wants, attitudes, preferences, and perceptions pertaining to the company's services and products. For the last type of segmentation, a market research data is needed to identify the needs and attitudes of the customers. However, with the emergence of SNSs the customers generate data on the web that can be used to identify their needs and attitudes.

The aim of this chapter is to present a novel approach to user segmentation using unstructured data maintained from SNSs. In the proposed approach, text mining techniques are used to convert the unstructured data into structured data and fuzzy clustering is used to extract knowledge from the data. The proposed approach is used in a real world application and the data gathered from an online crowd writing project, BurtonStory is utilized. As the text mining literature proposes, after the data is gathered, it is converted to term document matrix (TDM) and TDM is later used for segmentation using fuzzy cluster analysis. Clustering can be defined as the process of identifying the segments in a set of data so that the objects in a segment are similar to one another, yet dissimilar to data in other segments. The literature provides both crisp and fuzzy clustering techniques. The fuzzy set theory proposed by Zadeh (1965) aims represent uncertainty and vagueness and provide formalized tools for dealing with the imprecision intrinsic to many problems. When compared to crisp methods, fuzzy clustering produce more realistic results since each data object has a membership value to each cluster. Thus in this study, fuzzy C-means clustering is utilized.

The originality of this chapter comes from the usage of text mining and fuzzy techniques to segment users in a social network. The remaining of the chapter is organized as follows; In Section 2, the back ground information about social networks and business applications is given. Section 3 introduces the literature review about the techniques used in the study. In the first part of section 3, Text mining methodology and methods for creating text-document matrix is given, and in the second part fuzzy clustering is depicted. Section 4 contains the details about the real world numerical application and finally the conclusion and further steps are discussed in conclusions.

SOCIAL NETWORKS AND BUSINESS APPLICATIONS

Social media refers to a set of online tools that supports social interaction between users. The term is often used to contrast with more traditional media such as television and books that deliver content to mass populations but do not facilitate the creation or sharing of content by users. With social media, the communication type has changed from monologue to dialog. In practice, it is a catchall phrase intended to describe the many novel online sociotechnical systems that have emerged in recent years, including services like email, discussion forums, blogs, micro blogs, texting, chat, social networking sites, wikis, photo and video sharing sites, review sites, and multiplayer gaming communities.

Social network sites such as Facebook, Twitter, and Linkedin constitute a very important place in social media applications. In the literature, social network sites (SNSs) are defined as, as web-based services that allow individuals to (1) construct a public or semi-public profile within a bounded system, (2) articulate a list of other users with whom they share a connection, and (3) view and traverse their list of connections and those made by others within the system (Boyd & Ellison, 2007).

What makes social network sites unique is not that they allow individuals to meet strangers, but rather that they enable users to articulate and make visible their social networks. This can result in connections between individuals that would not otherwise be made, but that is often not the goal, and these meetings are frequently between "latent ties" (Haythornthwaite, 2005) who share some offline connection. On many of the large SNSs, participants are not necessarily "networking" or looking to meet new people; instead, they are primarily communicating with people who are already a part of their extended social network.

The history of social networks goes back to 1997; SixDegrees.com is the first website that fits the SNS definition given above. From that time to today, there have been great changes in the functionality of SNSs and various sites have established. The researches clearly indicate the popularity of SNSs; US internet users spend a total of 535 billion minutes on Facebook, which more than any other websites (Nielsen, 2011). By

2012, Facebook has 901 million monthly active users, and 300 million photographs uploaded every day, and a total of 125 billion friend connections have been established. Twitter the micro blogging website, which is founded in 2006, has more than 200 million users who create one billion tweets per week (Mosley, 2012). The usage statistics can give insight about text, image and relationship/activity data created the data crated on SNS.

The use of social networking services in an enterprise context presents the potential of having a major impact on the world of business and work (Fraser & Dutta, 2008). Bonchi et al. (2011) identify seven major areas that a company can use social networks as promotion of products and services in online social networks, trend monitoring, mechanisms for interaction with customers, research of new product ideas, creation and follow-up of customer user groups, advertising, sponsoring of interactive content, and finally creation and monitoring of online focus groups. NextMedia (2010) classifies the usage of SNSs for business into two groups, the first one focuses on communications and the second one concentrate on creating benefits by analyzing the data on the social networks.

In the first usage area, the target groups for communication can be listed as employees, customers, potential employees (recruitment process) and potential customers (advertising and marketing). For communications within the company, corporate social networks (CSN) can be used. Since the relationship between members of a social network is flat rather than hierarchal, CSN can maintain a flat relationship between employees and foster collaboration and creativity. Social Customer Relationship Management (CRM) is the term that represents the use of social technology to maintain an effective interaction with customers. Just as with intra company relations, SN can be facilitated to build a better medium for companies to work together with their customers in a more collaborative way. The third area of communication contains the use of social networks for human resource management. With the emergence of social networks, HR practices changed and techniques such as online job posting, recruitment and online testing have become popular applications (Davison et al., 2011; Banyhamdan & Barakat, 2012). Companies can directly get in touch with or investigate the background of the potential employees. The final use of SNs is for marketing and sales purposes. Companies can use SNs to reach potential customers especially using viral marketing. In this application, the company identifies and targets key persons who have the potential to affect its potential customers, sends the advertisement to the key person. If the key person is identified correctly, the ad can reach thousands of people immediately.

Besides the functional usage of the SNSs, the data created in these systems can be analyzed and mined to create value for the companies. The huge amount of data created by SNSs can be analyzed for knowledge extraction using various tools and techniques. Bonchi et al. (2011) investigate the potential use of social network analysis and mining for business applications. The authors specify various processes that social network analysis and mining can be used under 10 process categories (Table 1).

Barbier and Huan (2011) identify the most common data mining applications related to social networking sites as group detection, group profiling, recommender systems and sentiment analysis.

Group detection applications is about finding and identifying a group and is based on analyzing the structure of the network and finding individuals that associate more with each other than with other users. Xu et al. (2012a) aims to detect the appropriate users on SNSs to conduct cost-effective targeted marketing and reputation management. Xu et al. (2012b) propose a method to discover the most influential users using mathematical programming.

The second application, group profiling takes place just after a group is found and deals with finding what the group is about (Tang et al., 2010).

The profiling application is used both for purely scientific interests and for marketing of goods and services. Roy et al. (2012) tries to give insight about people's travel behavior by profiling users based on the ratio between their e-communication and physical travel. Xu and Chau (2007) propose a semi-automated approach that consists of four modules, namely blog spider, information extraction, network analysis, and visualization and identify and analyze hate groups on blogs.

A recommendation system application used in social networks analyzes the data and recommends new friends or new groups to a user. Since the system empowers new relationships between individuals and group, it has a direct effect on the users of the social network. Individuals can find others or groups that interests them. Meo et al. (2011) propose an approach to recommend to a user similar users, resources, and social networks based on both the explicit connections and the implicit connections such as shared interests and behavior. Yu (2012) proposes a dynamic recommendation algorithm based on the competition of multiple component algorithms.

Another important data mining area in the field of social networks is the sentiment analysis which deals with finding out the opinions of people about a topic. This application is closely related to social CRM. For example companies can find out the unsatisfied customers using sentiment analysis and get in connection with them and strengthen the relationship. O'Leary (2012) proposes a sentiment analysis on blogs by extending the use of knowledge from tags, domain specific terms on a blog to capture a richer understanding of mood of blogs.

Li and Wu (2010) propose an algorithm to automatically analyze the emotional polarity of a given text and use K-means clustering and support vector machine to develop unsupervised text mining approach. Sobkowicz et al. (2012) investigate how online opinions emerge, diffuse, and gain momentum and finally propose an opinion formation framework based on content analysis of social media and sociophysical system modeling.

Some other important applications of data mining techniques in social networks can be given as trend analysis (Nohuddin et al., 2010), chat mining (Özyurt & Köse, 2010), and predictive analytics (Boulos et al., 2010). Besides these mentioned applications, a new approach is discussed in the next section.

Table 1. Social network analysis and mining for business processes

Process Category	Process Group
Vision & Strategy	Social Networking
Products & services	Product Recommendations, Social product search
Market & selling	Social CRM, Trend spotting, Product quality, Social marketing, Loyalty programs, Direct marketing, Advertising Influence, Business intelligence, Churn prediction, Reputation monitoring
Delivery Production	Production scheduling
Customer Service	Customer Support
Human Capital	Internal social networking, Professional development, Recruiting
Information Technology	Resource allocation, Information source, Content management
Financial Resources	Customer & product strategies, Customer-product mix, Manage internal controls
External Relationships	Public relations program, Legal and ethical issues, Social networking
Knowledge Management	Knowledge sharing, Strategic KM

METHODOLOGY

Customer segmentation is the process of dividing customers into distinct, meaningful, and homogeneous subgroups based on various attributes and characteristics. Segmentation enables organizations to understand their customers and build differentiated strategies, tailored to their characteristics. Traditionally organizations, tend to use market segmentation schemes that are based on customer demographics and value information, but in today's competitive markets, a more comprehensive approaches are needed (Tsiptsis & Chorianopoulos, 2009). Organizations need to focus on their customers' needs, wants, attitudes, behaviors, preferences, and perceptions to identify the segments. As the segments are identified, the organization can manage and target them more effectively with customized communication messages, offerings, and promotions.

Both in the literature and application, there are various segmentation types and criteria used. Specifically, customers can be segmented according to their value, sociodemographic and life-stage information, and their behavioral, need/attitudinal, and loyalty characteristics. In this chapter, a novel segmentation approach is proposed. Unlike the previous segmentation studies, the proposed approach focuses on users' unstructured data which can be gathered by organizations easily from SNSs. The approach presented in this paper utilizes text mining and fuzzy clustering techniques. Thus in this section, Initially a brief summary is given about Text mining then the application steps are identified and in the later, fuzzy clustering technique, which is used to extract knowledge, is introduced.

Text Mining

At a very high level, the text mining process can be broken down into three consecutive tasks (Figure 1), each of which has specific inputs to generate certain outputs (Turban et al., 2011). If the output of a specific task is not as expected, the researcher can return to the previous task.

Phase 1: Establishing the Corpus

Corpus is a large and structured set of texts that are prepared for further analysis. The purpose of this phase is to collect all of the text files that are relevant to the problem being addressed. The quality and quantity of the documents considered in the corpus is one of the most important elements in text mining projects. In text mining projects, the corpus should be identified and collected using manual or automated techniques such as software programs that periodically collects data from different blogs or searches for relevant news extracts from several websites. The source of data may include HTML files, emails, web blogs or textual documents. As these various types of documents are collected, they should be organized in order to prepare them for the computer processing.

Figure 1. Three tasks of text mining

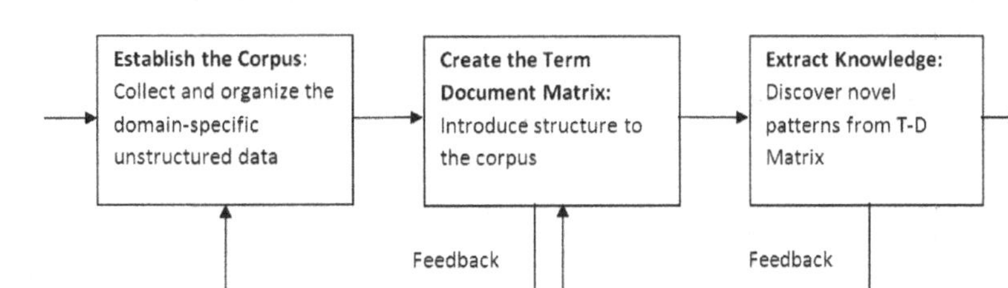

Phase 2: Word Vector Creation

The second phase of the process aims to convert the unstructured data into term-document matrix (TDM) which is a structured representation of the corpus. The TDM is a matrix form in which the documents represented by the rows and terms represented by the columns. A sample TDM is shown in Table 2.

The values in the TDM matrix show the relationships between the terms and the documents such as how frequently a given term occurs in a document (Miner et al., 2012). The relationship between terms and documents can be illustrated with various measures. Converting unstructured data to a TDM matrix, there is an underlying assumption that the meaning of the documents can be represented within the matrix using the measures in the cells. However not all the terms are equally important for characterizing a document, articles and auxiliary verbs have any distinguishing power between the documents and thus they should be excluded from the process. This kind of terms is called "stopterms" and they should be identified before or during this phase. On the other hand there are other specific type of terms that can be identified, the "include terms" defines the predefined terms that are chosen to build the TDM. For the sake of the study the "synonyms," the pairs of terms that are to be treated the same, should be defined. Finally specific phrases can be defined so that the phrase is included as a whole instead of separate words. The phase can be illustrated in Figure 2. Since the success of the text mining process depends on the accuracy of the TDM, the phase includes feedbacks the miner can turn back to previous tasks and renew them for better outcome.

The Measures Used in TDM

The TDM shown in Table 1 consists of raw frequencies; however these values can be normalized to have a more consistent TDM for further analysis. These values can be normalized using the following methods (StatSoft, 2010):

Log frequencies: Log function can be used to transform the raw frequencies. In the formula, tf is the raw term frequency and f(tf) is the result of the log transformation. This transformation is applied to all of the raw frequencies in the TDM where the frequency is greater than zero.

$$f\left(tf\right) = 1 + \log\left(tf\right) for\, tf > 0 \quad (1)$$

Binary frequencies: The transformation shows weather a term is used in a document or not. The transformed values in the TDM matrix are only 1s and 0s, 1s indicating the presence, 0s indicating the absence of the respective terms in the document. This transformation dampens the effect of the raw frequency counts on subsequent computations and analyses.

$$f\left(tf\right) = 1\, for\, tf > 0 \quad (2)$$

Table 2. Sample term-document matrix

	Blog	Artist	Social	Student	Editor
Text1	1		1		
Text2		1			
Text3				2	
Text4					1
Text5			1	1	
Text6		3			1

Figure 2. Tasks of word vector creation (adopted from Miner et al., 2012)

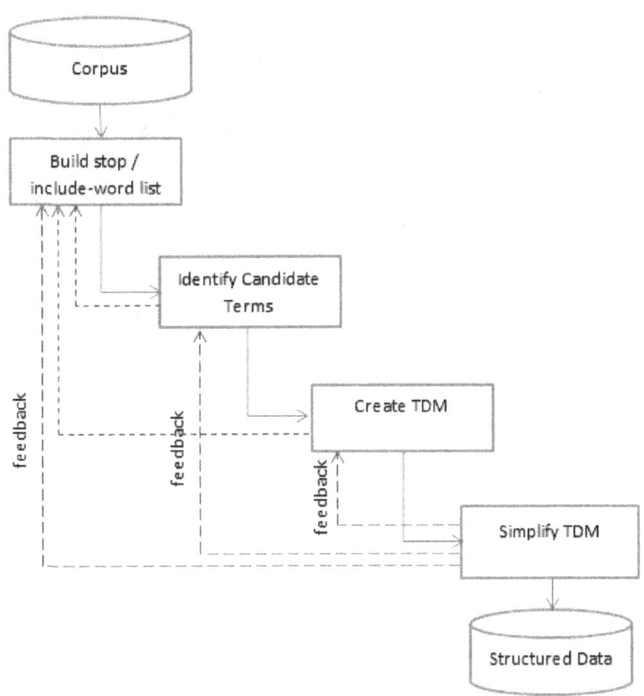

Inverse document frequencies: Analysis based on raw frequencies treat all terms equally important. But in the perspective of knowledge extraction, the importance of a given term in each document is also important. For example, a term such as "know" may occur frequently in all documents, whereas another term, such as "guitar," may appear only a few times. The reason is that "know" can be used in various contexts, whereas guitar is a more semantically focused term that is likely to occur only in documents that deal with music. The equation of idf is given in Equation 3.

$$idf_t = \log_{10} N / df_t \qquad (3)$$

where df is defined to be the number of documents in the collection that contain a term t and N is the number of documents in the corpus. The idf of a rare term is high, whereas the idf of a frequent term is likely to be low.

Term Frequency – Inverse Document Frequency: A common transformation used in TDM is the tf-idf transformation. The transformation is a combination of term frequency and inverse document frequency that produce a composite weight for each term in each document. The tf-idf weighting scheme assigns to term t a weight in document d given by the following formula:

$$tf - idf_{t,d} = \left(1 + \log tf_{t,d}\right) * \log\left(N / df_t\right) \qquad (4)$$

The tf-idf value gets higher values if the term occurs many times within a small number of documents, and gets the lowest value when the term occurs in virtually all documents. When the term occurs fewer times in a document, or occurs in many documents the tf-idf gets medium values.

Dimension Reduction

Depending on the size of the corpus, the TDM can get very large and sparse (most of the cells filled with zeros) which makes it hard, if not impossible, to extract knowledge in the following phase. This problem is called "curse of dimensionality" and dimensionality refers to number of input documents by number of extracted terms. There are two basic approaches to deal with this problem; eliminating the terms and transforming the TDM. In term elimination techniques, the main goal is to ignore the terms with low information value. Depending on the analysis domain and the goal of the text mining application, selected terms are omitted while building the model. This approach also reduces the noise in the data (Albright, 2004).

Transforming the TDM to a simpler matrix is another approach to deal with dimensionality. Singular value decomposition (SVD) is a commonly used method for representing a matrix as a series of linear approximations without losing the underlying meaning-structure of the matrix. SVD is closely related to principal components analysis in that it reduces the overall dimensionality of the input matrix to a lower dimensional space possible (Manning & Schutze, 2002). It allows a very large number of variables to be reduced or summarized to a much smaller and more manageable number of linear combinations that extract the majority of information from the variables.

Phase 3: Extract Knowledge

After the creation of the TDM and dealing with the dimensionality problem, the next task is to extract novel and beneficial patterns from this matrix. The newly formed TDM can be directly used or it can be expanded with other structured data to extract enhanced knowledge In the field of text mining knowledge extraction methods can be categorized in to four which are; classification, clustering, association and trend analysis.

Classification studies deal with assigning the documents into a predetermined set of categories where, for a given set of categories and a collection of text documents, the challenge is to find the correct topic (subject or concept) for each document. In text mining studies, there are two main approaches to text classification which are expert systems and machine learning. With the expert system approach, an expert's knowledge about the categories is transformed into classification rules and these rules are later used to classify the documents. On the other hand with the machine-learning approach, a set of preclassified examples are used in an inductive process in order to build a classifier by "learning" from the examples.

The clustering process deals with grouping an unlabeled collection of objects such as documents, customer comments, web pages, into meaningful clusters without any prior knowledge. Thus, clustering is an unsupervised process which does not use any prior knowledge to guide the process. Clustering is useful in a wide range of applications such as document retrieval and web content searches.

Another type of knowledge extraction application is the association analysis. Association analysis aims to find affinities among different data elements such as events and terms. Association analysis is widely used in retail markets with the name market basket analysis. Association rule generation is about identifying the frequent sets of data elements that go together in a specific context. In text mining, associations refer specifically to the direct relationships between concepts or terms. An association is basically quantified with two basic measures, namely support and confidence are used. Confidence is the percent of documents that include all the concepts in Y within the same subset of those documents that include all the concepts in X. The second measure Support is the percentage of documents that include all the concepts in X and Y. Using specific algorithms, association rules can be identified using these measures.

The last type of knowledge extraction is the trend analysis. Trend analysis attempts to spot a pattern or a trend in the data. In the context of text mining a trend in texts is defined as a topic area that is growing in interest and utility over time

Kontostathis (2003). Different text data sources of the same topic from different time intervals are analyzed and potential different concept distributions are investigated. One of the most important ways of this type of analysis is having two collections from the same source, such as journals and websites, but from different points in time.

Fuzzy Clustering

Basic Definitions

Clustering is the process of partitioning a set of data objects into subsets which are called clusters. Clustering techniques deals with organizing the data such that objects in a cluster are similar to one another, yet dissimilar to objects in other clusters (Han et al., 2011). The term "similarity" should be understood as mathematical similarity and is generally defined by means of a distance norm (Babuska, 2009). In cluster analysis, unsupervised methods that deal with unlabeled data are mostly used. Since the data used by the analysis are unlabeled, there is no error or reward signal to evaluate a potential solution. But still, there are some methods for quantitative evaluation of the results of a clustering algorithm that are called cluster validity (Theodoridis & Koutroumbas, 2008).

There are various clustering algorithms that have been proposed in the literature. These algorithms can be classified according to the formation of clusters; the clusters can be fuzzy or crisp. In crisp clustering, the data is partitioned into a specified number of mutually exclusive subsets. In other words the individual objects either does or does not belong to a cluster. However, in Fuzzy clustering the objects can belong to several clusters simultaneously, with different degrees of membership. Since the results of fuzzy clustering ranges between 0 and 1 in most cases the results are more natural when compared to crisp clustering. This is the case for objects near to the boundaries, crisp partitioning does not make a difference in the membership value of this object, however, in fuzzy clustering they are assigned membership degrees between 0 and 1 indicating their partial membership.

The data used in cluster analysis are gathered from observations each of which consists of n measured variables. An individual observation forms an n-dimensional column vector zk = [z1k, . . ., znk]T, and the dataset that consists of N observations is represented as an n x N matrix. Fuzzy clustering aims to partition the data set Z into a specific number of clusters "c" which is defined before the based on prior knowledge,

$$Z = \begin{bmatrix} z_{11} & z_{12} & \cdots & z_{1N} \\ z_{21} & z_{22} & \cdots & z_{2N} \\ \vdots & \vdots & \vdots & \vdots \\ z_{n1} & z_{n2} & \cdots & z_{nN} \end{bmatrix} \quad (5)$$

As a result of the cluster analysis, the clusters and membership of each data point to these clusters are represented by the partition matrix U. In this matrix, each element μij shows the degree to which element zj belongs to cluster ci In crisp approaches the membership function μij gets the value 0 or 1but in the fuzzy case this value can get any real value in [0, 1].

$$U = \begin{bmatrix} \mu_{11} & \mu_{12} & \cdots & \mu_{1N} \\ \mu_{21} & \mu_{22} & \cdots & \mu_{2N} \\ \vdots & \vdots & \vdots & \vdots \\ \mu_{c1} & \mu_{c2} & \cdots & \mu_{cN} \end{bmatrix} \quad (6)$$

Ruspini (1970) defines the conditions for a fuzzy partition matrix as follows:

$$\mu_{ik} \in [0,1], 1 \le i \le c, 1 \le k \le N, \quad (7a)$$

$$\sum_{i=1}^{c}\mu_{ik} = 1, 1 \le k \le N, \tag{7b}$$

$$0 < \sum_{k=1}^{N}\mu_{ik} < N, 1 \le i \le c \tag{7c}$$

Equation (5b) constrains the sum of each column to 1, and thus the total membership of each zk in Z equals one.

Later possibilistic partition, which is a more general form of fuzzy partition, is proposed by Krishnapuram and Keller (1993). The possibilistic partition is formed by relaxing the constraint (7b). In the fuzzy case, the constraint ensures that the sum of membership values for each observation is equal to 1. However, in the probabilistic partition, this constraint is relaxed and replaced with $\exists i, \mu_{ik} > 0$. The relaxed constraint ensures that each point is assigned to at least one of the fuzzy subsets with a membership greater than zero. The conditions for a possibilistic fuzzy partition matrix are as follows:

The results may differ between fuzzy and probabilistic partition, for example in a case with two clusters (c=2) an outlier observation that is far away from both cluster centers can have a membership equal to 0.5 (so that the sum of the values is equal to one). However, in probabilistic case the membership for the outlier can be lower values showing that it is an outlier.

The Fuzzy C-Means Algorithm

Fuzzy c-means (FCM) is based on minimization of the following objective function:

$$J(Z,U,V) = \sum_{i=1}^{c}\sum_{j=1}^{N}(\grave{\imath}_{ij})^m z_j - v_i^2 \tag{8}$$

where Z is the data set to be partitioned, U is the fuzzy partition matrix, V is the vector of cluster centers. N is the number of observations, c is the number of clusters and μ is the membership value, m is the parameter called fuzzifier, which determines the fuzziness of the resulting clusters. The fuzzifier can get values 1 and more. When m=1 then the clusters are formed in crisp format. In the formula, $z_k - v_i$ shows the distance between observation k and the center of cluster i.

The minimization of the mention objective function represents a nonlinear optimization problem that can be solved by using a variety of methods such as iterative minimization, simulated annealing or genetic algorithms.

The most popular method which is known as fuzzy c-means (FCM) algorithm consists of the following steps (Babuska, 2009).

1. *Initialize* $U=[u_{ij}]$ *matrix,* $U^{(0)}$
2. *At k-step: calculate the centers vectors* $V^{(k)}=[v_i]$ *with* $U^{(k)}$

$$v_i = \frac{\sum_{i=1}^{N}\grave{\imath}_{ij}^m . z_j}{\sum_{i=1}^{N}\grave{\imath}_{ij}^m}$$

3. *Update* $U^{(k)}$, $U^{(k+1)}$

$$\grave{\imath}_{ij} = \frac{1}{\sum_{k=1}^{c}\left(\frac{z_j - v_i}{z_j - v_k}\right)^{\frac{2}{m-1}}}$$

If $U^{(k+1)} - U^{(k)} < \ddot{a}$ then STOP; otherwise return to step 2.

Parameters of the FCM Algorithm

When clustering, the analyzer has to set some important parameters for getting beneficial results from the analysis. While some software packages can enable the user to setup some other parameters, most important parameters are, number of clusters, fuzzifier and termination criteria.

Number of clusters: The number of clusters "c" is the parameter that influences the clustering results most. Before the clustering study, if the analyzer does not have any priori information about the structure of the data, (s)he has to make assumptions about how many clusters can exist within the data. The FCM algorithm then searches for chosen number of clusters. It is expected that when the number of clusters parameter is equal to the number of groups that actually exist in the data, the FCM will identify them correctly. But if this is not the case, misclassifications appear, and the clusters are not correctly separated. Put in another way, the algorithm finds the expected number of clusters regardless of whether they are really thus the validity of the results has to be checked. In the literature validity measures are proposed to assess the goodness of the obtained partition (Bezdek, 1981; Gath & Geva, 1989; Pal & Bezdek, 1995). For the FCM algorithm, the Xie-Beni index (Xie & Beni, 1991) has been found to perform well in practice (Han et al., 2011).

$$X\left(Z;U,V\right)=\frac{\sum_{i=1}^{c}\sum_{j=1}^{N}(\grave{\imath}_{ij})^{m} z_{j} - v_{i}^{2}}{c.\min_{i\neq j} v_{i} - v_{j}^{2}} \qquad (9)$$

This index shows the ratio of the total within-group variance and the separation of the cluster centers. For different number of cluster the best is the one that minimizes the Xie-Beni index.

Another validity measure for FCM is silhouettes values defined by Kaufman and Rousseeuw (1990). The value measures how well each object has been classified by comparing its dissimilarity within its cluster to its dissimilarity with its nearest neighbor (Hintze, 2007). The silhouettes value can range from minus one to one. The values of s (silhouettes) that are close to one show a good classification, if the value is near zero, the object is between clusters two clusters and when the value is close to negative one, it means that the object is poorly classified. Using average silhouette the data miner can understand the most appropriate number of clusters. The ideal number of cluster minimizes the average silhouette.

Fuzziness Parameter (Fuzzifier): The weighting exponent m at the objective function is called the fuzziness parameter of Fuzzifier. As m approaches one from above, the partition becomes crisp and the membership values get values 0 or 1.As m gets higher values, the partition becomes completely fuzzy and the membership values goes to the limit 1/c. These limit properties of are independent of the optimization method used (Pal & Bezdek, 1995). Generally, the value of the fuzzifier is set to two initially.

Termination Criterion: The FCM algorithm does not stop unless the difference between "U" in two consequent iterations is smaller than the termination parameter. The general choice for the criterion is 0.001, however, the value 0.01 works well in most cases, while drastically reducing the computing times.

NUMERICAL APPLICATION: USER SEGMENTATION BASED ON TWITTER DATA

In this section, a real world numerical application of the proposed methodology is represented. In the first subsection, the data gathering and preparation steps are given in the following subsection the details about the analysis are provided. The findings of the study are supplied in the final subsection.

Data Gathering and Preparation

Burtonstory project is a crowd writing project designed by famous film director Tim Burton. The director of the project started the new story of his character "Stainboy" with a sentence and the rest of the story is written by the volunteers via Twitter. Twitter followers sent alternatives for the following sentences and the director selected a suitable one among the alternatives. As a selection is done, it is published and the alternatives for the next sentence are collected. The project ran over Twitter between November 20th and December 6th of 2010. The project was online over burtonstory.com and twitter.com.

Twitter is a microblogging website which users can write messages not longer than 140 characters. All the messages are published on the website so in order to define the messages about a special topic or project a tag is defined. The users use this tag within their messages so that when searched with the tag all the related messages can be reached. In the project "#BurtonStory" is used as a tag to follow the project. The data that is used in this study belongs to the messages sent to the project. The data collection is accomplished on 5th January 2011. A total of 9384 tweets were sent about the project from 2643 Twitter accounts during the project.

The next step in data gathering was about reaching out to the users that sent messages to the project. However there were some messages that carry the specified tag but were not written as a candidate for the project. These kinds of messages were sent for informative purposes. A distinction between contributive and informative messages was done using a set of rules and as a result, 8586 tweets from 2078 accounts were classified as contributive and 798 tweets from 565 accounts as informative. The data used in this study is the self-descriptive text that takes place in the profile of each Twitter account. In order to automatically collect the data, new software is developed. The data about all the users except deleted ones and the users with a security option were reached. As a result, description text of 1366 authors were collected and used for the text mining activities.

Text Mining Process

As defined in Section 3.1, the three steps were followed for the Text mining process and Fuzzy Clustering is used in the knowledge extraction phase. The data about project participant are converted to term-document matrix (TDM) using Rapid Miner 5.02 software. In order to reach an effective TDM, a series of operations are used. The non-letter texts are used for tokenization, stop words and the words shorter than 3 characters are eliminated. Finally, TF-IDF (term frequency–inverse document frequency) matrix is generated with the remaining set of words. As defined earlier, the TF-IDF value increases proportionally to the number of times a word appears in the document, but is offset by the frequency of the word in the corpus, which helps to control for the fact that some words are generally more common than others. A part of the matrix is presented in Figure 3.

The generated TDM is used as an input for the Fuzzy Clustering method. As mentioned earlier, text mining includes feedbacks between the tasks to optimize the results. After the analysis of the first results the non-English text are deleted from the corpus. In order to deal with the dimensional-

Figure 3. A sample part from the created TDM

Row ...	text	artist	academic
388	child artist problem staying artist grow	0.533	0
330	digital media producer photographer artist	0.438	0
242	comic book artist colorist penciler inker	0.433	0
369	editor artist husband father	0.413	0
127	amphibias friend lillypad twitter pond cyber:	0.410	0
129	art culture lover traveler aspirant artist seth	0.400	0
147	artist author musician etc	0.400	0
1351	writer singer actress director artist	0.387	0
1275	vincitrice del concorso letterario streghe vai	0.374	0
476	graphic artist schmuck drunk dad necessa	0.363	0

ity problem, the TDM is reduced and a new TDM is generated using the most popular terms.

For knowledge extraction fuzzy clustering is applied using NCSS 2007/GESS 2006 software. The TDM matrix containing the TF-IDF values and 910 texts is inserted to the software. The K-means techniques is used, as mentioned in Section 3, the most important parameter in the technique is the number of the clusters. NCSS allows users to set a range of cluster numbers and give results about the Silhouette values. In this application, the best Silhouette value is determined for k=4 and the value is determined as 0.186272.

The results of the k-means clustering where k is set to four provide for clusters as shown in Table 3. The clusters are given descriptive names based on the most typical values.

Table 4 presents the resulting centroid table. The centroid of a cluster represents the most typical cases for the cluster. From the table we can see the top three typical word of each cluster.

Findings and Discussion

According to the results of the sample application, four segments are identified among the contributors of the project. According to these results the contributors of the Burtonstory project are as follows:

- **Related Professionals:** These users define themselves as the professionals related with film making. They have a low number of members; nearly 1% of the total users are in this group.
- **Social Media Users:** Can be defined as the users related with social media, blogging and marketing. But do not have a direct relationship with making movies. Social media users have the highest number of users; nearly 45% of all contributors belongs to this segment.
- **Students and Amateurs:** This group is composed of the students from movie related schools and the ones that have a hobby about movies or animations. More than 18% of all users belongs to this segment.
- **Others:** Since the TDM is reduced so that the columns contain the mostly used terms only. As a result, there are some user definitions that do not carry any value in the reduced TDM. This means that these users do not use any of the popular terms. The fourth segment is composed of these users that do not belong to any of the defined clusters and called "others." The group constitutes 35% of all users.

The results show that most of the users that contributed to the project belong to the social media users. This group together with the "Others" group constitutes more than 80% of the total. This shows that most of the contributors of the project do not have any direct relationship with movie making, writing or animation. The remaining 20% of the users are students, amateurs and professionals from related sectors.

Table 3. Descriptive names and number of items in each cluster

Clusters	Descriptive Names	Number of Items
Cluster 1	Students and Amateurs	155
Cluster 2	Related Professionals	13
Cluster 3	Other Professionals	417
Cluster 4	Others	325

Table 4. The typical values of each cluster

Cluster1	Cluster2	Cluster3	Cluster4
Writer	Director	Social	N/A
Love	Film	Media	N/A
Music	Editor	Digital	N/A
Design		Marketing	N/A
Student		Artist	N/A

In the scope of the research, only the four groups and their percentages are defined. However, these results can further be combined with other data sources to create better managerial implications. For example, as the groups are identified, the question can be answered about which group has the highest level of interest (total number of tweets sent) and participation to the story (number of tweets selected) to the project. Similar to this, if the same approach is applied to segment the users of a company's Fan page, the segmentation data can be used to create projects to direct the users to make new purchases or transmit the product advertisement to other users.

FUTURE RESEARCH DIRECTIONS

In this study, a user segmentation approach that uses text mining and fuzzy clustering techniques to cluster the users based on their profile data of SNS is proposed and a real world application is given. The application deals with identifying the "crowd," the participants of the project, in a crowd writing project. As a result, four groups are identified namely; related professionals, social media users, students and amateurs and finally the others. Future studies can focus on combining the segmentation data with the behavioral data of the users such as the number of tweets sent and the number of selected tweets. Combining these two types of data, the link between the segments and their contribution level to the project can be analyzed.

It can be apprised that there are some limitations about the proposed approach. First of all, there is no certainty about the accuracy of the data used; put in another way, the users can write anything to their profile so a segmentation based on this data can be misleading. Another limitation can be identified about the technique used, the ability of the TDM to deal with the ambiguities of languages are questionable. The same terms can be used for different purposes, or different terms can be used to indicate the same meaning. To deal with the first limitation, future researches can aim to develop an automatic system to identify weather an account is fake or not. For the second limitation, the TDM generation steps can be renewed to deal with the ambiguities of the language.

CONCLUSION

Social network sites are widely used all around the world and these sites can be used by companies directly for communications or to generate knowledge form the data generated by the SNSs. In this chapter a novel segmentation approach is proposed. The proposed approach aims to use the unstructured data in the SNSs to define the segments. In all SNSs, which are widely used all around the world, each user has a profile page that they can use to define themselves, using the proposed approach this data can be used to define segments of users. The proposed approach uses text mining and fuzzy clustering techniques to segment the users based on their profile data. As shown in the real world case study, the approach can be used by organizations to segment their customers in the future studies.

REFERENCES

Albright, R. (2004). *Taming text with the SVD*. Retrieved October 5, 2012, from ftp://ftp.sas.com/techsup/download/EMiner/TamingTextwiththeSVD.pdf

Babuska, R. (2009). *Fuzzy and neural control disc course lecture notes*. Retrieved October 5, 2012, from http://www.dcsc.tudelft.nl/~disc_fnc/transp/fncontrol.pdf

Banyhamdan, K., & Barakat, S. (2012). Web 2.0: Internet technology used in human resource recruitment. *American Academic & Scholarly Research Journal, 4*(5).

Barbier, G., & Liu, H. (2011). Data mining in social media. In Aggarwal, C. C. (Ed.), *Social network data analytics* (pp. 327–356). Springer. doi:10.1007/978-1-4419-8462-3_12.

Bonchi, F., Castillo, C., Gionis, A., & Jaimes, A. (2011). Social network analysis and mining for business applications. *ACM Transactions on Intelligent Systems and Technology (TIST), 2*(3).

Boulos, M. N. K., Sanfilippo, A. P., Corley, C. D., & Wheeler, S. (2010). Social Web mining and exploitation for serious applications: Technosocial predictive analytics and related technologies for public health. *Environmental and National Security Surveillance, 100*(1), 16–23.

Boyd, D. M., & Ellison, N. B. (2007). Social network sites: Definition, history, and scholarship. *Journal of Computer-Mediated Communication, 13*(1). doi:10.1111/j.1083-6101.2007.00393.x.

Davison, H. K., Maraist, C., & Bing, M. N. (2011). Friend or foe? The promise and pitfalls of using social networking sites for HR decisions. *Journal of Business and Psychology, 26*(2), 153–159. doi:10.1007/s10869-011-9215-8.

Fraser, M., & Dutta, S. (2008). *Throwing sheep in the boardroom: How online social networking will transform your life, work and world.* Wiley.

Gath, I., & Geva, A. B. (1989). Unsupervised optimal fuzzy clustering. *IEEE Transactions on Pattern Analysis and Machine Intelligence, 11*, 773–781. doi:10.1109/34.192473.

Haythornthwaite, C. (2005). Social networks and Internet connectivity effects. *Information Communication and Society, 8*(2), 125–147. doi:10.1080/13691180500146185.

Hintze, J. L. (2007). *NCSS User Guide IV.* Utah: Kaysville.

Kaufman & Rousseeuw. (1990). *Finding groups in data.* New York: Wiley.

Kontostathis, A., Galitsky, L., Pottenger, W. M., Roy, S., & Phelps, D. J. (2003). *A survey of emerging trend detection in textual data mining*. Springer-Verlag.

Krishnapuram, R., & Keller, J. M. (1993). A possibilistic approach to clustering. *IEEE Transactions on Fuzzy Systems, 1*, 98–110. doi:10.1109/91.227387.

Li, N., & Wu, D. D. (2010). Using text mining and sentiment analysis for online forums hotspot detection and forecast. *Decision Support Systems, 48*(2), 354–368. doi:10.1016/j.dss.2009.09.003.

Manning, C. D., & Schütze, H. (2002). *Foundations of statistical natural language processing* (5th ed.). Cambridge, MA: MIT Press.

Meo, P. D., Nocera, A., Terracina, G., & Ursino, D. (2011). Recommendation of similar users, resources and social networks in a social internetworking scenario. *Information Sciences, 181*(7), 1285–1305. doi:10.1016/j.ins.2010.12.001.

Miner, G., Elder, J. IV, Fast, A., Hill, T., Nisbet, R., & Delen, D. (2012). *Practical text mining and statistical analysis for non-structured text data applications*. Academic Press.

Mosley, R. (2012). Social media analytics: Data mining applied to insurance Twitter posts. *Casualty Actuarial Society E-Forum*, Volume 2. Retrieved October 5, 2012, from http://www.casact.org/pubs/forum/12wforumpt2/Mosley.pdf

Nielsen. (2011). *State of the media: The social media report.* Retrieved October 5, 2012, from http://blog.nielsen.com/nielsenwire/social

Nohuddin, P. N. E., Coenen, F., Christley, R., Setzkorn, C., Patel, Y., & Williams, S. (2010). Finding "interesting" trends in social networks using frequent pattern mining and self organizing maps. *Knowledge-Based Systems, 29*, 104–113. doi:10.1016/j.knosys.2011.07.003.

O'Leary, D. E. (2012). Blog mining-review and extensions: "From each according to his opinion. *Decision Support Systems*, *51*(4), 821–830. doi:10.1016/j.dss.2011.01.016.

Özyurt, Ö., & Köse, C. (2010). Chat mining: Automatically determination of chat conversations' topic in Turkish text based chat mediums. *Expert Systems with Applications*, *37*(12), 8705–8710. doi:10.1016/j.eswa.2010.06.053.

Pal, N. R., & Bezdek, J. C. (1995). On cluster validity for fuzzy c-means model. *IEEE Transactions on Fuzzy Systems*, *3*, 370–379. doi:10.1109/91.413225.

Roy, P., Martínez, A. J., Miscione, G., Zuidgeest, M. H. P., & Maarseveen, M. F. A. M. (2012). Using social network analysis to profile people based on their e-communication and travel balance. *Journal of Transport Geography*, *24*, 111–122. doi:10.1016/j.jtrangeo.2011.09.005.

Ruspini, E. H. (1970). Numerical methods for fuzzy clustering. *Information Sciences*, *2*, 319–350. doi:10.1016/S0020-0255(70)80056-1.

Sobkowicz, P., Kaschesky, M., & Bouchard, G. (2012). Opinion mining in social media: Modeling, simulating, and forecasting political opinions in the web, Social Media in Government. *Selections from the 12th Annual International Conference on Digital Government Research*, *29*(4), 470-479.

StatSoft. (2010). *Statistica data and text miner user manual*. Tulsa, OK: StatSoft, Inc..

Tang, L., Wang, X., & Liu, H. (2010). Understanding emerging social structures — a group profiling approach. *Technical report, School of Computing, Informatics, and Decision Systems Engineering, Arizona State University*. Retrieved October 5, 2012, from http://www.public.asu.edu/~huanliu/papers/groupprofiling.pdf

Theodoridis, S., & Koutroumbas, K. (2008). *Pattern recognition*. Academic Press.

Tsiptsis, K., & Chorianopoulos, A. (2009). *Data mining techniques in CRM inside customer segmentation*. John Wiley & Sons.

Turban, E., Sharda, R., & Delen, D. (2011). *Decision support and business intelligence systems* (9th ed.). Upper Saddle River, NJ: Prentice hall.

Xie, X. L., & Beni, G. (1991). A validity measure for fuzzy clustering. *IEEE Transactions on Pattern Analysis and Machine Intelligence, PAMI*, *13*(8), 841–847. doi:10.1109/34.85677.

Xu, J., & Chau, M. (2007). Mining communities and their relationships in blogs: A study of online hate groups. *International Journal of Human-Computer Studies*, *65*(1), 57–70. doi:10.1016/j.ijhcs.2006.08.009.

Xu, K., Li, J., & Song, Y. (2012b). Identifying valuable customers on social networking sites for profit maximization. *Expert Systems with Applications*, *39*(17), 13009–13018. doi:10.1016/j.eswa.2012.05.098.

Xu, K., Xitong, G., Li, J., Lau, R. Y. K., & Liao, S. S. Y. (2012a). Discovering target groups in social networking sites: An effective method for maximizing joint influential power. *Electronic Commerce Research and Applications*, *11*(4), 318–334. doi:10.1016/j.elerap.2012.01.002.

Yu, S. J. (2012). The dynamic competitive recommendation algorithm in social network services. *Information Sciences*, *197*, 1–14. doi:10.1016/j.ins.2011.10.020.

Zadeh, L. A. (1965). Fuzzy sets. *Information and Control*, *8*, 338–353. doi:10.1016/S0019-9958(65)90241-X.

ADDITIONAL READING

Bonchi, F., Castillo, C., Gionis, A., & Jaimes, A. (2011). Social network analysis and mining for business applications. [TIST]. *ACM Transactions on Intelligent Systems and Technology*, *2*(3), 22–57. doi:10.1145/1961189.1961194.

Delen, D., & Crossland, M. D. (2008). Seeding the survey and analysis of research literature with text mining. *Expert Systems with Applications*, *34*, 1707–1720. doi:10.1016/j.eswa.2007.01.035.

Feldman, R., & Sanger, J. (2007). *The text mining handbook*. Cambridge, MA: MIT Press.

Han, J., Kamber, M., & Pei, J. (2011). *Data mining concepts and techniques*. Elsevier Inc..

Höppner, F., Klawonn, F., Kruse, R., & Runkler, T. (1999). *Fuzzy cluster analysis: Methods for classification, data analysis and image recognition*. John Wiley & Sons.

Miner, G., Elder, J. IV, Fast, A., Hill, T., Nisbet, R., & Delen, D. (2012). *Practical text mining and statistical analysis for non-structured text data applications*. Academic Press.

Miyamoto, S., Ichihashi, H., & Honda, K. (2008). *Algorithms for fuzzy clustering: Methods in c-means clustering with applications. Springer. Alhajj, R. (2012). Social network analysis and mining*. Springer.

Stelzner, M. A. (2012). *Social media marketing industry report how marketers are using social media to grow their businesses*. Retrieved October 5, 2012, from http://www.socialmediaexaminer.com/SocialMediaMarketingIndustryReport2012.pdf

Tsiptsis, K., & Chorianopoulos, A. (2009). *Data mining techniques in CRM inside customer segmentation*. John Wiley & Sons, Ltd..

KEY TERMS AND DEFINITIONS

Fuzzy Clustering: Fuzzy clustering is an algorithm for cluster analysis in which the allocation of data points to clusters is fuzzy.

Segmentation: Segmentation is the process of dividing the customers into distinct and internally homogeneous groups in order to develop differentiated marketing and communication strategies according to their common characteristics.

Social Networking Sites: Social network sites are web-based services that allow individuals to construct a public or semi-public profile, articulate a list of other users with whom they share a connection, and view and traverse their list of connections and those made by others within the system.

Term Document Matrix: Term-document matrix (TDM) is a structured representation of the corpus in which the documents represented by the rows and terms represented by the columns.

Text Mining: Text mining is process of extracting novel knowledge from large amounts of unstructured data source such as pdf files, emails, user comments.

TF-IDF: TF-IDF is a common transformation used in TDM. The transformation is a combination of term frequency and inverse document frequency that produce a composite weight for each term in each document.

Twitter: Twitter is an online social networking and microblogging service that enables its users to send and read text-based messages with a limited number of characters.

Chapter 15
Defining the Factors that Effect User Interest on Social Network News Feeds via Fuzzy Association Rule Mining:
The Case of Sports News

Başar Öztayşi
Istanbul Technical University, Turkey

Sezi Çevik Onar
Istanbul Technical University, Turkey

ABSTRACT

Social networking became one of the main marketing tools in the recent years since it's a faster and cheaper way to reach the customers. Companies can use social networks for efficient communication with their current and potential customers but the value created through the usage of social networks depends on how well the organizations use these tools. Therefore a support system which will enhance the usage of these tools is necessary. Fuzzy Association rule mining (FARM) is a commonly used data mining technique which focuses on discovering the frequent items and association rules in a data set and can be a powerful tool for enhancing the usage of social networks. Therefore the aim of the chapter is to propose a fuzzy association rule mining based methodology which will present the potential of using the FARM techniques in the field of social network analysis. In order to reveal the applicability, an experimental evaluation of the proposed methodology in a sports portal will be presented.

DOI: 10.4018/978-1-4666-4213-3.ch015

Copyright © 2013, IGI Global. Copying or distributing in print or electronic forms without written permission of IGI Global is prohibited.

INTRODUCTION

The number of social network users is increasing dramatically which creates an appealing market for the companies therefore it's expected that most of the companies will be using social media within a few years. Companies can use social networks for efficient communication with their customers and potential customers, for instance news feeds is an option for the companies to push the content to the target audience. Besides its high market potential, the value created through the usage of social networks mainly depends on how well the organizations use these marketing tools. If it's not managed properly the usage of social networks can be a waste of time and energy. Therefore revealing the factors that increase the value created through the social networks is crucial; unfortunately still there is not a proper way to reveal these factors. The objective of this study is to propose a methodology which will reveal the factors that affect the value of social networking usage. In order to reach to this objective the impact created through utilizing news feeds feature of Facebook will be investigated. News Feeds feature, when initially released by Facebook on 2006, was designed for individual uses to gather new information that users post about themselves on their walls. Today, the content that is shared on the Facebook page is automatically posted to the users who liked the page. The content posted on the page can be video, image or a link to another webpage. Although news feeds future is originally designed for individual users, it enables companies to inform customers about the developments in the company and get their direct comments on this information; therefore, it's widely used by the companies as a way of communication with the customers. The users of the social network can do various activities with the posted content, they can simply push the like button indicating that they have a positive attitude towards the content, or they can write their comments with their own words and finally they can share the content with their circle of friends. These three activities can be assumed as indicators of user interest towards the post. These activities are also counted and published with the post content so that the users can see his/her friends who showed interest on the post or which post gets more attention by the general audience.

Fuzzy Association rule mining (FARM) is a commonly used data mining technique which focuses on discovering the frequent items and association rules in a data set. FARM technique can be a useful tool for determining the factors that affect the value of social networking usage. Therefore the aim of the chapter is to present the potential of using the FARM techniques in the field of social network analysis. News feeds feature of social networks will be the subject of the real world example, and the factors that affect the higher user interest will be examined. The results of such a study provide Facebook page owners the information about which type of news to publish and when, in order to generate the highest interest from the users. To the best of our knowledge this will be the first application that uses FARM on social media and news feeds. The remaining of the chapter is organized as follows; in Section 2, the proposed methodology is given. In section 3, a real world numerical application of the proposed methodology in a sports portal is represented. Finally, conclusion and further steps are discussed in conclusions.

LITERATURE REVIEW

In literature various studies focuses on the user interest on social media. These studies can be grouped in to three classes. The first group focuses on finding social media that suits user needs and classified the social media with this objective (Zhu et al., 2012; Kim et al., 2011; Denecke & Nejdl, 2009). Kim et al. (2011) focused on the problem of finding social media suited to user's needs and proposed an approach for understanding user interests that can be exploited to recommender systems by using user-generated tags. Denecke and Nejdl (2009) classified blogs based on their information content via a content analysis.

Second group focuses on the user's motivation and tried to reveal the motivation behind social media user interests (Sashittal et al., 2012; Men & Tsai, 2012; Alikilic & Atabek, 2012). Sashittal et al. (2012) claimed that the motivation behind Facebook usage makes Facebook users poor prospects for advertisers therefore if the advertisement investments on Facebook are not properly made they can be a waste. Ko (2012) tried to reveal the factors effecting continuous usage of social networking sites.

A third study group of researchers, similar with the objective of this study, propose models to capture the user interest in various social media features. Ni et al. (2012) proposed a model to capture the user interest in the "User-Interactive Question Answering" systems with latent topic method. Zhang et al. (2012) tried to reveal the collective behavior of users on blog networks and bulletin board system sites. Authors proposed a method to predict the number of users writing or commenting upon article posts with respect to hot online topics. Zhang and Li (2011) utilized question clustering and trend analysis in order to detect hot topics and reveal the hot topics' trends in community question answering systems. Vries et al. (2012) tried to analyze the drivers for brand post popularity and revealed the number of comments has an effect on this popularity.

Data mining studies are also used to extract knowledge from social networks, these application include group detection, group profiling, recommender systems and sentiment analysis (Barbier & Huan, 2011). Using data mining techniques to detect groups, the individual users are analyzed and the ones that associate more with each other than others are identified as a group. As a group is identified the consequent action is to investigate and understand what is the group about, what is the common interest of the group, this kind of studies are called group profiling and constitutes the second data mining application group (Tang et al., 2010). Barbier et al. (2011) try to understand groups using datamining techniques. Xu et al. (2012) aims to detect the appropriate users on SNSs to conduct cost-effective targeted marketing and reputation management. Roy et al. (2012) try to give insight about people's travel behavior by profiling users based on the ratio between their e-communication and physical travel.

Recommendation systems are initially applied to e-commerce websites for recommending products to users. In a similar perspective, using data mining techniques systems can be built to analyze the data in social networks and recommend friends or groups to individuals. Using the applications users can reach to related groups or friends that they cannot easily reach by themselves. Chen et al. (2009) propose a model that helps users to find new friends on social networks and evaluate four recommender algorithms. Cai et al. (2011) develop a novel neighbour-based collaborative filtering algorithm to predict, for a given user, other users they may like to contact, based on user similarities between them. Similarly, Yu (2012) proposes a dynamic recommendation algorithm based on the competition of multiple component algorithms.

Sentiment analysis represents the applications that deals with understanding the topic and attitude of a user about a specific topic based on the text messages that he/she writes. Using text mining techniques, companies can trace the opinions of their customers based on the entries in the social networks. Using these applications, companies can detect the unsatisfied customers or get the opinions of the customers about new products. Rebelo et al. (2012) propose a new technique for sentiment analysis using link mining techniques to infer opinions of and apply it on Twitter. O'Leary (2012) uses sentiment analysis on blogs by extending the use of knowledge from tags and domain specific terms to apprehend the mood of blogs. Sobkowicz et al. (2012) propose an opinion formation framework based on content analysis of social media and sociophysical system modeling.

METHODOLOGY

Association analysis is a methodology, in the data mining family, which is used for discovering interesting relationships hidden in large data sets. The uncovered relationships can be represented in the form of association rules (Tan et al., 2006). An association rule is defined in the form: X ->Y, where both X and Y are defined as sets of attributes or items; it is interpreted as follows: "for a specified fraction of the existing transactions, particular values of the attributes in set X determine the values of the attributes in set Y as other particular values under a certain confidence" (Kaya & Alhajj, 2005). Besides the crisp association rules, fuzzy association rule mining has received attention in the literature. Fuzzy set theory developed by Zadeh (1965), is concerned with quantifying and reasoning using natural language and thus very suitable to handle quantitative values. As a result, fuzzy mining approaches have been proposed to discover interesting association rules in transaction data with quantitative values (Hong & Lee, 2008). Social networks provide an available medium for capturing and analyzing the user transaction data. Although association rule mining techniques are most suitable for discovering interesting relationships hidden in large data sets, in literature none of the studies that propose models to capture the user interest utilized this method. Studies in literature are more focused on defining the factors that have effect on user interest therefore utilize techniques, such as clustering, but these techniques do not reflect the association rules of these factors. In this chapter, we focus on using fuzzy association rule mining (FARM) in the context of social networks.

The initial objective of association rule mining technique was to solve the so called market basket analysis problem which focuses on revealing the associations among the items purchased together (Agrawal et al., 1993). Fuzzy association rule mining, which incorporates fuzzy sets into rule mining tasks, is commonly used for discovering association rules since it has several advantages (Ho et al., 2012; Taboada et al., 2010; Chen et al., 2010). Fuzzy association rule mining overcomes the sharp boundary problem which refers to the problems such as overestimating or under estimating data while discretizating quantitative values into intervals. Also, it enables the linguistic expression of the mined association rules which easier and understandable for the decision makers. Although various FARM methods are proposed in the literature (Farzandar & Kangavari, 2012; Lin et al., 2012; Palacios et al., 2012; Taboada, 2010; Cock et al., 2005; Kaya & Alhajj, 2005), in this study we'll use the FARM methodology defined by Feil and Abonyi (2008) which have three main phases namely "formation of database," "mining frequent item sets," "generation of fuzzy association rules." The aim of the chapter is to describe fuzzy association rules which will provide Facebook page owners the information about which news to publish and when, in order to generate the highest interest from the users. The flow chart of the proposed model for revealing the factors that affect the value of social networking usage is shown in Figure 1.As a numerical application of the FARM, the news feeds of a sports web portal will be analyzed.

Formation of Database

Step 1: The first phase, formation of database, starts with collecting data.

Step 2: The second step is transformation of quantitative values of attributes into fuzzy sets by the user defined specific membership values.

Figure 1. Flow chart of the proposed model

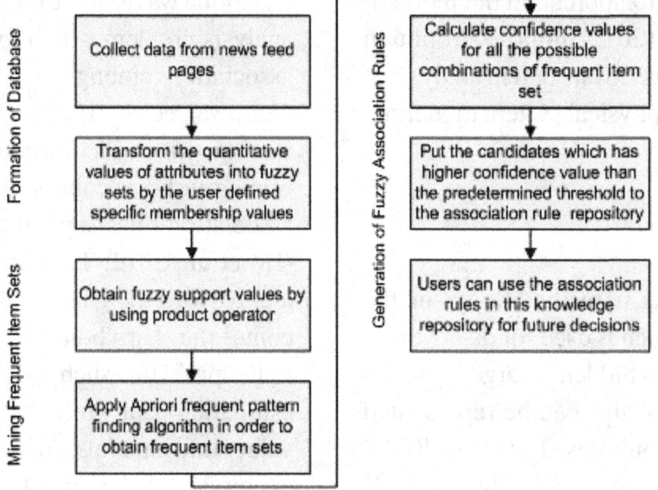

Mining Frequent Item Sets

Step 3: The third step is to obtain fuzzy support values; in order to calculate fuzzy support values the fuzzy product operator is used (Feil & Abonyi, 2008).

Let $Z = \{z_1, \ldots, z_{n+m}\}$ be a set of variables and c_{ij} be an arbitrary fuzzy set associated with attribute z_i in Z. $z_i : c_{i,j}$ denotes a fuzzy item (attribute fuzzy interval pair)and $Z : C$ denotes a fuzzy item set where C refers to a corresponding set of some fuzzy intervals.

$$Z : C = \left[z_{i1} : c_{i1,j} \bigcup \cdots \bigcup z_q : c_{q,j}\right] q \leq n + m \quad (1)$$

In order to calculate fuzzy support values of the fuzzy item sets the following formula is used; in this formula N refers to the number of data points and data point (t_k) of the data set contains value $t_k(z_i)$ for attribute z_i.

$$FSZ : C = \frac{\sum_{k=1}^{N} \prod_{z_i : c_{i,j} \in Z:C} t_k(z_i)}{N} \quad (2)$$

As an example the fuzzy support value of $X : A = [\text{time} : \text{morning} \bigcup \text{shares} : \text{high}]$ item set is calculated via this formula.

Step 4: The fourth step is finding frequent item sets where a frequent item set is defined as item sets whose fuzzy support values are higher than a user defined minimum support threshold. Since the number of candidate itemsets explored is very high an algorithm which reduces this number of candidates is necessary. In this study Apriori algorithm is utilized in order to obtain frequent item sets. The algorithm is a stepwise algorithm which starts with finding the frequent 1 itemsets and iteratively generates new candidates using the frequent items found in the previous iteration (Tan et al., 2006).

Generation of Fuzzy Association Rules

Generation of fuzzy association rules is the process of finding consequents and antecedents of a frequent item set which can be expressed as finding the rules such as if $X : A$ then $Y : B$. A fuzzy association rule is considered as strong when it's both support and confidence values are higher than predetermined thresholds.

Step 5: The first step of generating fuzzy association rules is to calculate confidence values for all the possible combinations of frequent item set. The confidence of the fuzzy association is calculated as follows (Feil & Abonyi, 2008):

$$FC(X : A => Y : B) = \frac{FS(X : A \cup Y : B)}{FSX : A}$$

Step 6: After calculating the confidence values the candidates which has higher confidence values than the predetermined threshold are put to the association rule repository.

Step 7: By applying first six steps the rules such as if a news feed with a "picture" format is published in the "morning" then the shares counts will be "high" can be revealed. This information can be used to increase a portal's shares count by publishing a picture formatted news feed in the morning.

EXPERIMENTAL EVALUATION OF THE PROPOSED APPROACH: SPORTS PORTAL NEWS FEEDS

In this section, a real world numerical application of the proposed methodology in a sports portal is represented. The selected sports portal (SP) is one of the leaders in the sector with more than 300.000 subscribers. SP uses its Facebook page as a proactive way of generating traffic form the subscribers. SP publishes content such as interesting news, match scores, videos on its Facebook page and the subscribers who are interested in the content generally visits SP's portal to read the whole content. As mentioned earlier, subscribers can get socialize by writing comments, liking the content and sharing with their friends. These activities are important because they enable more people to be aware of the news and SP. For the purpose of this application, SP's the news feeds data for the last 6 months is collected.

Figure 2. Fuzzy membership sets for the attributes

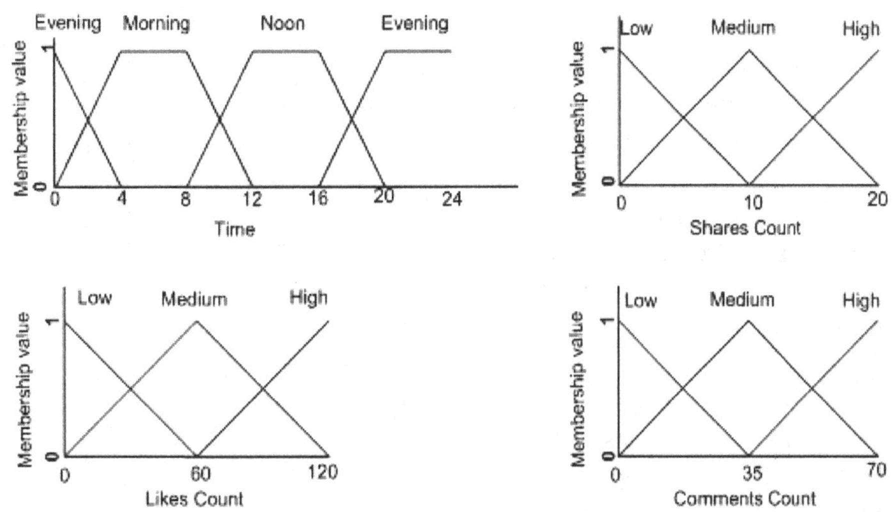

Formation of Database for Sports Portal News Feeds

At this phase, 132 news feed published during the last six months is collected through SP's webpage. The data that will be used are, content type (video, image, and link), publishing time, shares count, likes count, comments count. Content type is a categorical variable, but all the other variables are quantitative.

The content type since a content should either be a video, image or link is a crisp set so it doesn't need to be transformed; but all the other attributes have to be transformed. Publishing time has three classes namely, morning, noon, evening. Shares count, likes count and comments count have three classes namely low, medium and high. The fuzzy membership sets used to transfer the quantitative data in to sets are shown in Figure 2.

Mining Frequent Item Sets for Sports Portal News Feeds

Initially in order to determine the support of each item a single pass over the data set made and with this calculation the fuzzy support values for itemset 1 given in Table 1 is achieved.

According to the Apriori principle, "if an itemset is frequent, then all of its subsets must be frequent." Consequently, the items that have lower support value than the predetermined threshold will be eliminated from the frequent item set. 0.15 is selected as the support threshold value for SP's news feeds by the managers of SP portal. The items except "video format" and "medium shares" have support values higher than this predetermined support threshold therefore all the items other than "video format" and "medium shares" are considered as the frequent 1- item set. By considering every possible combination of attributes from 1-item set, the 2 item set is obtained. The fuzzy support counts for attributes in 2 item sets are given in Table 2. The fuzzy supports which have higher values than the predetermined fuzzy support threshold are shown in bold format.

The frequent 3 item set is calculated with the same Apriori algorithm; the frequent 3 item set and their fuzzy support counts are given in Table 3. None of the candidates of 4 items could satisfy the predetermined fuzzy support count value.

Generating Fuzzy Association Rules for Sports Portal News Feeds

In order to generate fuzzy association rules the confidence values for all the possible combinations of frequent item set is calculated via the formula given in section 2.3. 0.75 is selected as a confidence threshold value. The confidence value of each possible association rule is compared with the predetermined confidence threshold value and the rules with confidence values greater than 75% are kept in the association rule repository.

Findings

The study revealed interesting association rules such as if the shares count is high then the likes count will be high but there is not a reverse as-

Table 1. The fuzzy support values of item set 1

Attributes	Support Values
Link	**0.36**
Photo	**0.55**
Video	0.08
Morning	**0.22**
Noon	**0.48**
Evening	**0.29**
Shares Low	**0.58**
Shares Medium	0.07
Shares High	**0.35**
Likes Low	**0.29**
Likes Medium	**0.23**
Likes High	**0.47**
Comments Low	**0.22**
Comments Medium	**0.41**
Comments High	**0.36**

Table 2. The fuzzy support count for attributes in 2 itemsets

	Link	Photo	Morning	Noon	Evening	Shares Low	Shares High	Likes Low	Likes Medium	Likes High
Morning	0.12	0.09								
Noon	**0.15**	**0.25**								
Evening	0.08	**0.21**								
Shares Low	**0.32**	**0.23**	0.12	**0.30**	**0.15**					
Shares High	0.03	**0.28**	0.09	0.14	0.11					
Likes Low	**0.24**	0.02	0.08	**0.15**	0.05	**0.28**	0.01			
Likes Medium	0.09	0.13	0.02	0.12	0.09	**0.20**	0.01			
Likes High	0.03	**0.41**	0.12	**0.20**	**0.16**	0.10	**0.33**			
Comments Low	0.14	0.04	0.06	0.11	0.05	**0.18**	0.02	0.15	0.05	0.03
Comments Medium	0.13	**0.26**	0.09	**0.18**	0.15	**0.21**	**0.17**	0.08	0.07	**0.26**
Comments High	0.09	**0.26**	0.07	**0.19**	0.10	**0.19**	**0.16**	0.06	0.12	**0.18**

Table 3. The frequent 3 item set and their fuzzy support counts

Attributes			**SupportValues**
Link	Shares Low	Likes Low	**0.23**
Photo	Shares High	Likes High	**0.27**
LikesHigh	Shares High	Comments Medium	**0.16**
LikesHigh	Shares High	Comments High	**0.15**
Photo	Likes High	Noon	**0.16**
Photo	Likes High	Evening	**0.16**
Photo	Likes High	Comments Medium	**0.23**
Photo	Likes High	Comments High	**0.16**

sociation. Also if share count value is high and likes count value is high then the format is photo. Totally 52 association rules are established. By using these association rules decisions such as increasing the number of "photo" format news feeds in order to increase customers' interest can be made. The collection of association rule with confidence value over predetermined confidence threshold is given in Table 4.

CONCLUSION

In this study, the factors that affect the higher user interest on news feeds feature are examined via a methodology based on FARM technique. Interesting relationships between the various factors have been found. The results of such a study provide Facebook page owners the information about which type of news to publish and when,

Table 4. Association rules with confidence value over 0.75

RulesConfidence		RulesConfidence	
If {SharesHigh} then {LikesHigh}	0.94	If {CommentsMedium,SharesHigh} then{LikesHigh}	0.94
If {Link} then {SharesLow }	0.88	If {LikesHigh,CommentsMedium} then{Photo}	0.88
If {Video} then {Noon}	0.86	If {CommentsMedium,LikesHigh} then{Photo}	0.88
If {Photo} then {LikesHigh}	0.74	If {Photo,CommentsMedium} then{LikesHigh}	0.88
If {LikesHigh} then {Photo}	0.86	If {LikesHigh,CommentsHigh} then{Photo}	0.85
If {LikesLow } then {SharesLow }	0.95	If {CommentsHigh,LikesHigh} then{Photo}	0.85
If {LikesMedium} then {SharesLow }	0.88	If {LikesHigh,CommentsHigh} then{SharesHigh}	0.84
If {LikesLow } then {Link}	0.83	If {SharesLow, LikesLow } then{Link}	0.84
If {CommentsLow } then {SharesLow }	0.82	If {LikesLow, SharesLow } then{Link}	0.84
If {SharesHigh} then {Photo}	0.79	If {SharesHigh,LikesHigh} then{Photo}	0.83
If {SharesHigh} then{Photo,LikesHigh}	0.78	If {LikesHigh,SharesHigh} then{Photo}	0.83
If {LikesLow } then{Link,SharesLow }	0.79	If {LikesHigh,Noon} then{Photo}	0.83
If {SharesHigh} then{Photo,LikesHigh}	0.78	If {Noon,LikesHigh} then{Photo}	0.83
If {LikesLow } then{SharesLow, Link}	0.79	If {Photo,Evening} then{LikesHigh}	0.75
If {SharesHigh} then{LikesHigh,Photo}	0.78	If {LikesHigh,Evening } then{Photo}	1.00
If {Photo,SharesHigh} then{LikesHigh}	0.99	If {Photo,SharesHigh} then{LikesHigh}	0.99
If {SharesHigh,Photo} then{LikesHigh}	0.99	If {SharesHigh,CommentsHigh} then{LikesHigh}	0.98
If {LikesLow, Link} then{SharesLow }	0.95	If {Link,LikesLow } then{SharesLow }	0.95
If {CommentsMedium,Photo} then{LikesHigh}	0.88	If {SharesHigh,CommentsMedium} then{LikesHigh}	0.94
If {CommentsHigh,LikesHigh} then{SharesHigh}	0.84	If {LikesHigh,CommentsMedium} then{Photo}	0.88
If {LikesHigh,Evening} then{Photo}	1.00	If {Photo,CommentsMedium} then{LikesHigh}	0.88
If {Evening,LikesHigh} then{Photo}	1.00	If {LikesHigh,CommentsHigh} then{Photo}	0.85
If {SharesHigh,CommentsHigh} then{LikesHigh}	0.98	If {LikesHigh,CommentsHigh} then{SharesHigh}	0.84
If {CommentsHigh,SharesHigh} then{LikesHigh}	0.98	If {SharesLow, LikesLow } then{Link}	0.84
If {Link,LikesLow } then{SharesLow }	0.95	If {SharesHigh,LikesHigh} then{Photo}	0.83
If {SharesHigh,CommentsMedium} then{LikesHigh}	0.94	If {LikesHigh,Noon Memb.} then{Photo}	0.83

in order to generate the highest interest from the users. For instance, the rule "if share count value is low and likes count value is low then the format is link" is revealed. The rule indicates that SP should not publish news in link format if they want to increase customer's interest.

This research provides a systematic way of using the FARM techniques in the field of social network analysis. Using proposed methodology provides a useful support to the decision makers since rules are easy to understand and can be easily be used while designing the relations with the customers. Consequently, with this chapter, the potential of using the FARM techniques in the field of social network analysis have been presented.

In order improve the reliability of the proposed model, as a further research redesigning fuzzy sets and threshold values can be considered. There are various social media features such as "user-interactive question answering systems" and "hot online topics in blog networks and bulletin board system sites." The proposed methodology can be applied to these features. Also, applying the same methodology to the different countries and revealing the cross cultural difference can be an intereresting study.

REFERENCES

Agrawal, R., Imielinski, T., & Swami, A. (1993). Mining association rules between sets of items in large databases. In *SIGMOD '93 Proceedings of the 1993 ACM SIGMOD international conference on Management of data* (pp. 207-216).

Alikilic, O., & Atabek, U. (2012). Social media adoption among Turkish public relations professionals: A survey of practitioners. *Public Relations Review*, *38*(1), 56–63. doi:10.1016/j.pubrev.2011.11.002.

Barbier, G., & Liu, H. (2011). Data mining in social media. In Aggarwal, C. C. (Ed.), *Social network data analytics* (pp. 327–356). doi:10.1007/978-1-4419-8462-3_12.

Barbier, G., Tang, L., & Liu, H. (2011). Understanding online groups through social media. *Wiley interdisciplinary reviews: Data mining and knowledge discovery archive, 1*(4), 330-338.

Cai, X., Bain, M., Krzywicki, A., Wobcke, W., & Kim, Y. S. (2010). In P. Compton and A. Mahidadia (Eds.), Collaborative filtering for people to people recommendation in social networks. AI 2010: Advances in Artificial Intelligence Lecture Notes in Computer Science, 6464, 476-485.

Chen, C.-L., Tseng, F., & Liang, T. (2010). An integration of WordNet and fuzzy association rule mining for multi-label document clustering. *Data & Knowledge Engineering*, *69*(11), 1208–1226. doi:10.1016/j.datak.2010.08.003.

Chen, J., Geyer, W., Dugan, C., Muller, M., & Guy, I. (2009). Make new friends, but keep the old: Recommending people on social networking sites. *CHI '09 Proceedings of the SIGCHI Conference on Human Factors in Computing Systems* (pp. 201-210).

De Cock, M., Cornelis, C., & Kerre, E. E. (2005). Elicitation of fuzzy association rules from positive and negative examples. *Fuzzy Sets and Systems*, *149*(1), 73–85. doi:10.1016/j.fss.2004.07.010.

Denecke, K., & Nejdl, W. (2009). How valuable is medical social media data? Content analysis of the medical web. *Information Sciences*, *179*(12), 1870–1880. doi:10.1016/j.ins.2009.01.025.

Farzandar, Z., & Kangavari, M. (2012). Efficient mining of fuzzy association rules from the pre-processed dataset. *Computing and Informatics*, *31*, 331–347.

Feil, B., & Abonyi, J. (2008). Introduction to fuzzy data mining methods. In Feil, B., & Abonyi, J. (Eds.), *Handbook of research on fuzzy information processing in databases* (pp. 55–95). doi:10.4018/978-1-59904-853-6.ch003.

Ho, G. T. S., Ip, W. H., Wu, C. H., & Tse, Y. K. (2012). Using a fuzzy association rule mining approach to identify the financial data association. *Expert Systems with Applications*, *39*(10), 9054–9063. doi:10.1016/j.eswa.2012.02.047.

Hong,T-P., & Lee, Y-C. (2008). An overview of mining fuzzy association rules. *Fuzzy Sets and Their Extensions: Representation, Aggregation and Models,* 397-410.

Kaya, M., & Alhajj, R. (2005). Genetic algorithm based framework for mining fuzzy association rules. *Fuzzy Sets and Systems*, *152*(3), 587–601. doi:10.1016/j.fss.2004.09.014.

Kim, H., Alghamdi, A., Saddik, A., & Jo, G. (2011). Collaborative user modeling with user-generated tags for social recommender systems. *Expert Systems with Applications*, *38*(7), 8488–8496. doi:10.1016/j.eswa.2011.01.048.

Lin, W.-Y., Su, J.-H., & Tseng, M.-C. (2012). Updating generalized association rules with evolving fuzzy taxonomies. *Soft Computing*, *16*, 1109–1118. doi:10.1007/s00500-011-0786-0.

Men, L., & Tsai, W. (2012). Beyond liking or following: Understanding public engagement on social networking sites in China. *Public Relations Review*.

Ni, X., Lu, Y., Quan, X., Wenyin, L., & Hua, B. (2012). User interest modeling and its application for question recommendation in user-interactive question answering systems. *Information Processing & Management*, *48*(2), 218–233. doi:10.1016/j.ipm.2011.09.002.

O'Leary, D. E. (2012). Blog mining-review and extensions: "From each according to his opinion. *Decision Support Systems*, *51*(4), 821–830. doi:10.1016/j.dss.2011.01.016.

Palacios, A. M., Gacto, M. J., & Alcala-Fdez, J. (2012). Mining fuzzy association rules from low-quality data. *Soft Computing*, *16*, 883–901. doi:10.1007/s00500-011-0775-3.

Rabelo, J. C. B., Prudêncio, R. C. B., & Barros, F. A. (2012). Leveraging relationships in social networks for sentiment analysis. *Proceedings of the 18th Brazilian symposium on Multimedia and the web* (pp.181-188).

Roy, P., Martínez, A. J., Miscione, G., Zuidgeest, M. H. P., & Maarseveen, M. F. A. M. (2012). Using social network analysis to profile people based on their e-communication and travel balance. *Journal of Transport Geography*, *24*, 111–122. doi:10.1016/j.jtrangeo.2011.09.005.

Sashittal, H., Sriramachandramurthy, R., & Hodis, M. (2012). Targeting college students on Facebook? How to stop wasting your money. *Business Horizons*, *55*(5), 495–507. doi:10.1016/j.bushor.2012.05.006.

Sobkowicz, P., Kaschesky, M., & Bouchard, G. (2012). Opinion mining in social media: Modeling, simulating, and forecasting political opinions in the web, Social Media in Government. *Selections from the 12th Annual International Conference on Digital Government Research*, *29*(4), 470-479.

Taboada, K., Mabu, S., Gonzales, E., Shimada, K., & Hirasawa, K. (2010). Mining fuzzy association rules: A general model based on genetic network programming and its applications. *IEEJ Transactions on Electrical and Electronic Engineering*, *5*, 343–354. doi:10.1002/tee.20540.

Tan, P.-N., Steinbach, M., & Kumar, V. (2006). *Introduction to data mining*. Boston, MA: Pearson.

Tang, L., Wang, X., & Liu, H. (2010). *Understanding emerging social structures — a group profiling approach. Technical report*. School of Computing, Informatics, and Decision Systems Engineering, Arizona State University.

Vries, L., Gensler, S., & Leeflang, P. (2012). Popularity of brand posts on brand fan pages: An investigation of the effects of social media marketing. *Journal of Interactive Marketing*, *26*(2), 83–91. doi:10.1016/j.intmar.2012.01.003.

Xu, K., Xitong, G., Li, J., Lau, R. Y. K., & Liao, S. S. Y. (2012). Discovering target groups in social networking sites: An effective method for maximizing joint influential power. *Electronic Commerce Research and Applications*, *11*(4), 318–334. doi:10.1016/j.elerap.2012.01.002.

Yu, S. J. (2012). The dynamic competitive recommendation algorithm in social network services. *Information Sciences*, *197*, 1–14. doi:10.1016/j.ins.2011.10.020.

Zadeh, L. (1965). Fuzzy sets. *Information and Control*, *8*, 38–53. doi:10.1016/S0019-9958(65)90241-X.

Zhang, B., Guan, X., Khan, M., & Zhou, Y. (2012). A time-varying propagation model of hot topic on BBS sites and Blog networks. *Information Sciences*, *187*, 15–32. doi:10.1016/j.ins.2011.09.025.

Zhang, Z., & Li, Q. (2011). QuestionHolic: Hot topic discovery and trend analysis in community question answering systems. *Expert Systems with Applications*, *38*(6), 6848–6855. doi:10.1016/j.eswa.2010.12.052.

Zhu, T., Wang, B., Wu, B., & Zhu, C. (2012). Topic correlation and individual influence analysis in online forums. *Expert Systems with Applications*, *39*(4), 4222–4232. doi:10.1016/j.eswa.2011.09.112.

Compilation of References

Aarthi, S., et al. (2011). Predicting customer demographics in a mobile social network. *International Conference on Advances in Social Networks Analysis and Mining, IEEE Computer Society* (pp. 553 – 554).

Abrol, S., & Khan, L. (2010). TWinner: Understanding news queries with geo-content using Twitter. *Proceedings of the 6th Workshop on Geographic Information Retrieval* (pp. 1-8).

Adelakun, A., & Cherry, C. (2009). Exploring truck driver perceptions and preferences: Congestion and conflict, managed lanes, and tolls. *Proceeding of the 88th Transportation Research Board Annual Meeting*. Washington, DC. CD-ROM.

Aggarwal, C. C., & Yu, P. S. (1998). A new framework for itemset generation. In *Proceedings of the seventeenth ACM SIGACT-SIGMOD-SIGART symposium on Principles of database systems* (PODS '98) (pp. 18-24). ACM.

Aggarwal, C. (2011). *Social network data analytics*. Kluwer Academic Publishers. doi:10.1007/978-1-4419-8462-3.

Agrawal, R., & Psaila, G. (1995). *Active data mining*. In *First International Conference on Knowledge Discovery and Data Mining* (pp. 3-8). ACM press.

Agrawal, R., & Srikant, R. (1994). *Fast algorithms for mining association rules in large data-bases*. In J. B. Bocca, M. Jarke, and C. Zaniolo (Eds.), *International Conference on Very Large Data Bases* (pp. 487-499). Morgan Kaufmann.

Agrawal, R., & Srikant, R. (1995). *Mining generalized association rules*. In *International Conference on Very Large Data Bases* (pp. 407-419). Morgan Kaufmann.

Agrawal, R., Imielinski, T., & Swami, A. (1993). Mining association rules between sets of items in large databases. In *Proceedings of ACM SIGMOD Conference*.

Ahmed, K. I. (1999). *Modeling drivers' acceleration and lane changing behavior*. Massachusetts Institute of Technology.

Ahn, H. et al. (2011). Facilitating cross-selling in a mobile telecom market to develop customer classification model based on hybrid data mining techniques. *Expert Systems with Applications*, *38*, 5005–5012. doi:10.1016/j.eswa.2010.09.150.

Albright, R. (2004). *Taming text with the SVD*. Retrieved October 5, 2012, from ftp://ftp.sas.com/techsup/download/EMiner/TamingTextwiththeSVD.pdf

Alikilic, O., & Atabek, U. (2012). Social media adoption among Turkish public relations professionals: A survey of practitioners. *Public Relations Review*, *38*(1), 56–63. doi:10.1016/j.pubrev.2011.11.002.

Al-Kaisy, A. F., & Hall, F. L. (2003). Guidelines for estimating capacity at freeway reconstruction zones. *Journal of Transportation Engineering*, *129*(5), 572–577. doi:10.1061/(ASCE)0733-947X(2003)129:5(572).

Al-Kaisy, A. F., Hall, F. L., & Reisman, E. S. (2002). Developing passenger car equivalents for heavy vehicles on freeways during queue discharge flow. *Transportation Research Part A, Policy and Practice*, *36*(8), 725–742. doi:10.1016/S0965-8564(01)00032-5.

Al-Kaisy, A. F., Jung, Y., & Rakha, H. (2005). Developing passenger car equivalency factors for heavy vehicles during congestion. *Journal of Transportation Engineering*, *131*(7), 514–523. doi:10.1061/(ASCE)0733-947X(2005)131:7(514).

Al-Khalifa, H. S., & Al-Subaihin, A. A. (2012). *Introducing mobile widgets development in an advanced web technologies course* (pp. 1–4). ACM. doi:10.1145/2380552.2380569.

An Internet Patent Magazine, Social Media/Don't Steal My Avatar! (n.d.). *Website*. Retrieved August 1, 2012, from http://ipwatchdog.com/

Anderson, N., & Technica, A, (2011, January 14). *Tweeters tyrants out of Tunisia: Global Internet at its best*. Retrieved June 23, 2012, from http://www.wired.com/

Apaydin, A., et al. (2010). Semantic image retrieval model for sharing experiences in social networks. *IEEE, Computer Society, 34th Annual IEEE Computer Software and Applications Conference Workshops* (pp. 1–6).

Arroba, J., Grande, J. A., Andujar, J. M., De La Torre, M. L., & Riquelme, J. C. (2007). Application of fuzzy logic and data mining techniques as tools for qualitative interpretation of acid mine drainage processes. *Environmental Geology*, *53*(1), 135–145. doi:10.1007/s00254-006-0627-0.

Asur, S., Huberman, B. A., Szabo, G., & Wang, C. (2011). Trends in social media: Persistence and decay. In *Proceedings of the Fifth International AAAI Conference on Weblogs and Social Media* (pp. 434-437). AAAI press.

Au Keith, W. H., & Chan, C. C. (1999). FARM: A data mining system for discovering fuzzy association rules. *Fuzzy Systems Conference Proceedings, 1999. FUZZ-IEEE '99*, 3, 1217-1222.

Auer, M. R. (n.d.). The policy sciences of social media. *Policy Studies Journal, 39*(4), 709-736.

Babuska, R. (2009). *Fuzzy and neural control disc course lecture notes*. Retrieved October 5, 2012, from http://www.dcsc.tudelft.nl/~disc_fnc/transp/fncontrol.pdf

Backstrom, L., Dwork, C., & Kleinberg, J. (2007). Wherefore art thou r3579x? Anonymized social networks, hidden patterns, and structural steganography. *International Conference on World Wide Web (WWW)*.

Backstrom, L. et al. (2006). Group formation in large social networks: Membership, growth, and evolution. *ACM KDD, 06*, 44–54.

Baldi, M., Baralis, E., & Risso, F. (2005). *Data mining techniques for effective and scalable traffic analysis*. In Proceedings *International Symposium on Integrated Network Management* (pp. 105-118). IEEE press.

Banerjee, N. et al. (2010). Virtual compass: Relative positioning to sense, mobile social interactions. Springer-Verlag Berlin Heidelberg. *Pervasive, LNCS, 6030*, 1–21.

Banking.com. (n.d.). *Social media statistics: By-the-numbers, January,2011*. Retrieved by http://www.banking2020.com/2011/01/24/social-media-statistics-by-the-numbersjanuary-2011 part-ii/

Banyhamdan, K., & Barakat, S. (2012). Web 2.0: Internet technology used in human resource recruitment. *American Academic & Scholarly Research Journal, 4*(5).

Baraldi, A., & Blonda, P. (1999). A survey of fuzzy clustering algorithms for pattern recognition—Part I. *IEEE Transactions on Systems, Man, and Cybernetics. Part B, Cybernetics*, *29*(6), 778–785. doi:10.1109/3477.809032.

Baralis, E., Cagliero, L., Cerquitelli, T., D'Elia, V., & Garza, P. (2010). *Support driven opportunistic aggregation for generalized itemset extraction*. In Proceedings of *The 2010 IEEE Conference on Intelligent Systems* (pp. 102-107). IEEE press.

Baralis, E., Cagliero, L., Cerquitelli, T., Garza, P., & Marchetti, M. (2009). *Context-aware user and service profiling by means of generalized association rules*. In Proceedings *Conference on Knowledge and Engineering Systems* (pp. 50-57). Springer.

Barbier, G., Tang, L., & Liu, H. (2011). Understanding online groups through social media. *Wiley interdisciplinary reviews: Data mining and knowledge discovery archive, 1*(4), 330-338.

Barbier, G., & Liu, H. (2011). *Data mining in social media. Social Network Data Analytics*. Springer.

Baron, S., Spiliopoulou, M., & Gunther, O. (2003). Efficient monitoring of patterns in data mining environments. In Kalinichenko, L., Manthey, R., Thalheim, B., & Wloka, U. (Eds.), *Advances in Databases and Information Systems* (*Vol. 2798*, pp. 253–265). Lecture Notes in Computer ScienceSpringer Berlin Heidelberg. doi:10.1007/978-3-540-39403-7_20.

Barsky, M., Kim, S., Weninger, T., & Han, J. (2011). *Mining flipping correlations from large datasets with taxonomies*. In *Proceedings of the Very Large Data-Base Conference* (VLDB'12) (pp. 370-381). Morgan Kaufmann.

Basile, P., Gendarmi, D., Lanubile, F., & Semeraro, G. (2007). Recommending smart tags in a social bookmarking system. Bridging the Gap between Semantic Web and Web (pp. 22-29).

Beach, A., et al. (2009). Solutions to security and privacy issues in mobile social networking. *IEEE, Computer Society, International Conference on Computational Science and Engineering.*

Beach, A. et al. (2008). WhozThat? Evolving an ecosystem for context-aware mobile social networks. *IEEE Network, 22*(4), 50–55. doi:10.1109/MNET.2008.4579771.

Becker, H., Naaman, M., & Gravano, L. (2011). Beyond trending topics: Real-world event identification on Twitter. In *Proceedings of the Fifth International AAAI Conference on Weblogs and Social Media*. AAAI press.

Bender, M., Crecelius, T., Kacimi, M., Michel, S., Neumann, T., Parreira, J. X., et al. (2008). Exploiting social relations for query expansion and result ranking. *IEEE 24th International Conference on Data Engineering Workshop,* 2, (pp. 501-506). IEEE press.

Benevenuto, F., Magno, G., Rodrigues, T., & Almeida, V. (2010). Detecting spammers on Twitter. In Collaboration, electronic messaging, anti-abuse and spam conference. Redmond.

Benevenuto, F., Rodrigues, T., Cha, M., & Almeida, V. (2011). Characterizing user navigation and interactions in online social networks. In Information Sciences.

Berendt, B. et al. (2002). Towards semantic web mining. Springer-Verlag Berlin Heidelberg. *ISWC 2002. LNCS, 2342*, 264–278.

Berners, T. (2011, May 4). *Long live the Web: A call for continued open standards and neutrality*. Retrieved May 24, 2012, from http://www.scientificamerican.com/

Bernstein, A. et al. (2005). Toward intelligent assistance for a data mining process: An ontology-based approach for cost-sensitive classification. *IEEE Transactions on Knowledge and Data Engineering, 17*(4), 503–519. doi:10.1109/TKDE.2005.67.

Bezdek, J. C. (1976). Cluster validity with fuzzy sets. *Journal of Cybernetics, 3*, 58–72. doi:10.1080/01969727308546047.

Bezdek, J. C. (1981). *Pattern recognition with fuzzy objective function algorithms*. New York: Plenium. doi:10.1007/978-1-4757-0450-1.

Bezdek, J. C., & Hathaway, R. J. (1987). Clustering with relational c–means partitions from pairwise distance data. *International Journal of Mathematical Modeling, 8*, 435–439. doi:10.1016/0270-0255(87)90509-4.

Bezdek, J. C., Keller, J. M., Krishnapuram, R., & Pal, N. (1999). *Fuzzy models and algorithms for pattern recognition and image processing. The Handbooks on Fuzzy Sets*. Dordrecht, Netherlands: Kluwer.

Bhagat, S., Cormode, G., Krishnamurthy, B., & Srivastava, D. (2010). *Prediction promotes privacy in dynamic social networks*. In *Proceedings of the 3rd conference on Online social networks (WOSN)*. CA, USA.

Bhatnagar, V., & Sharma, S. (2010). Challenges in anonymization of social network. *International Conference on Facets of Business Excellence (FOBE)* (pp. 388-396). Delhi, India.

Bhattacharya, S., & Bhatnagar, V. (2012). Fuzzy data mining: A literature survey and classification framework. *International Journal of Networking and Virtual Organisations, 11*(3/4), 382–408. doi:10.1504/IJNVO.2012.048925.

Bhogal, J. et al. (2007). A review of ontology based query expansion. Elsevier. *Information Processing & Management, 43*, 866–886. doi:10.1016/j.ipm.2006.09.003.

Bollen, J., & Mao, H. (2011). Twitter mood as a stock market predictor. *Computer, 44*(10), 91–94. doi:10.1109/MC.2011.323.

Bonch, F. (2011). Influence propagation in social networks: A data mining perspective. *IEEE Intelligent Informatics Bulletin*, 12(1).

Bonchi, F., Castillo, C., Gionis, A., & Jaimes, A. (2011). Social network analysis and mining for business applications. *ACM Transactions on Intelligent Systems and Technology (TIST), 2*(3).

Bonchi, F. et al. (2011). Trajectory anonymity in publishing personal mobility data. *ACM SIGKDD Explorations Newsletter, 13*(1), 30–43. doi:10.1145/2031331.2031336.

Bose, I., & Mahaptra, R. (2001). Business data mining: A machine learning prospective. Elsevier. *Information & Management, 39*, 211–225. doi:10.1016/S0378-7206(01)00091-X.

Bottcher, M., Nauck, D., Ruta, D., & Spott, M. (2007). Towards a framework for change detection in data sets. In Bramer, M., Coenen, F., & Tuson, A. (Eds.), *Research and development in intelligent systems XXIII* (pp. 115–128). Springer London. doi:10.1007/978-1-84628-663-6_9.

Bouchon-Meunier, B., Detyniecki, M., Lesot, M. J., Marsala, C., & Rifqi, M. (2007). Real-World Fuzzy Logic Applications in Data Mining and Information Retrieval. Fuzzy Logic. *Studies in Fuzziness and Soft Computing, 215*, 219–247. doi:10.1007/978-3-540-71258-9_11.

Bouckaert, R. R., Frank, E., Hall, M. A., Holmes, G., Pfahringer, B., Reutemann, P., & Witten, I. H. (2010). WEKA experiences with a java open-source project. *Journal of Machine Learning Research, 11*, 2533–2541.

Bouguessa, M., Wang, S., & Sun, H. (2006). An objective approach to cluster validation. *Pattern Recognition Letters, 27*, 1419–1430. doi:10.1016/j.patrec.2006.01.015.

Boulos, M. N. K., Sanfilippo, A. P., Corley, C. D., & Wheeler, S. (2010). Social Web mining and exploitation for serious applications: Technosocial predictive analytics and related technologies for public health. *Environmental and National Security Surveillance, 100*(1), 16–23.

Bouqata, B., Bensaid, A., Palliam, R., & Gomez Skarmeta, A. F. (2000). Time series prediction using crisp and fuzzy neural networks: A comparative study. *Computational Intelligence for Financial Engineering, 2000. (CIFEr), Proceedings of the IEEE/IAFE/INFORMS 2000 Conference*, 170-173.

Box, C. E. P., & Jenkins, G. M. (1970). Time series analysis, forecasting and control: Golden Day. San Francisco, pp. 498.

Boyd, D. M., & Ellison, N. B. (2007). Social network sites: Definition, history, and scholarship. *Journal of Computer-Mediated Communication, 13*(1), 210–230. doi:10.1111/j.1083-6101.2007.00393.x.

Brackstone, M., McDonald, M., & Wu, J. (1998). Lane changing on the motorway: Factors affecting its occurrence, and their implications. *9th International Conference on Road Transport Information and Control*. London, UK.

Brin, S., Motwani, R., & Silverstein, C. (1997). Beyond market baskets: Generalizing association rules to correlations.[ACM press.]. *SIGMOD Record, 26*(2), 265–276. doi:10.1145/253262.253327.

Brown, D. (2011). *52 Cool facts about social media*. Retrieved October 08, 2012, from www.dannybrown.me

Browne, S. (2010). *Statistics: Social networks will receive 11% of online ad spending in 2011*. Retrieved on August 22, 2012, from http://dannybrown.me/2010/07/03/cool-facts-about-social-media/

Bullying. (n.d.). *Website*. Retrieved May 22, 2012, from http://www.stopbullyingnow.hrsa.gov/

Bureau of Transportation Statistics. (2002). *US Department of Transportation, National Transportation Statistics BTS02-08*. Washington, DC: US Government Printing Office.

Buyya, R. et al. (2009). Cloud computing and emerging IT platforms: Vision, hype, and reality for delivering computing as the 5th utility. Elsevier. *Future Generation Computer Systems, 25*, 599–616. doi:10.1016/j.future.2008.12.001.

Cagliero, L., & Fiori, A. (in press) *Generalized association rule mining from Twitter. Intelligent data analysis.* IOS press.

Cagliero, L., Fiori, A., & Grimaudo, L. (in press). Personalized tag recommendation based on generalized rules. *Transactions on Intelligent Systems and Technology*. ACM press.

Cagliero, L. (2011). Discovering temporal change patterns in the presence of taxonomies.[PrePrints] [. IEEE press.]. *IEEE Transactions on Knowledge and Data Engineering*, 99.

Cagliero, L., & Fiori, A. (in press). News document summarization driven by user-generated content. In *Social media mining and social network analysis: Emerging research*. IGI Global.

Cai, X., Bain, M., Krzywicki, A., Wobcke, W., & Kim, Y. S. (2010). In P. Compton and A. Mahidadia (Eds.), Collaborative filtering for people to people recommendation in social networks. AI 2010: Advances in Artificial Intelligence Lecture Notes in Computer Science, 6464, 476-485.

Cambridge Systematics. (2005). *NGSIM I-80 Data Analysis, Summary Reports. Federal HighWay Administration (FHWA)*. Retrieved from https://camsys.com

Cambridge Systematics. (2005). *NGSIM US-101 Data Analysis, Summary Reports. Federal HighWay Administration (FHWA)*. Retrieved from https://camsys.com

Cantador, I. et al. (2011). Categorising social tags to improve folksonomy-based recommendations. Elseiver. *Web Semantics: Science. Services and Agents on the WWW*, *9*, 1–15. doi:10.1016/j.websem.2010.10.001.

Cao, L. (2010). Domain-driven data mining: Challenges and prospects. *IEEE Transactions on Knowledge and Data Engineering*, *22*(6), 755–769. doi:10.1109/TKDE.2010.32.

Carenini, G., Ng, R. T., & Zhou, X. (2007). Summarizing email conversations with clue words. In *World Wide Web Conference Series* (pp. 91–100).

Castro, F., Vellido, A., Nebot, A., & Mugica, F. (2007). *Applying data mining techniques to e-learning problems. Studies in Computational Intelligence* (pp. 183–221). Springer-Verlag Berlin Heidelberg.

Catanese, S., De Meo, P., Ferrara, E., & Fiumara, G. (2010). *Analyzing the Facebook friendship graph.*

Cate, M. A., & Urbanik, T., II. (2003). Another view of truck lane restrictions. *Proceeding of the 82th Transportation Research Board Annual Meeting*. Washington, DC., CD-ROM.

CBS News. (n.d.). *Bloomers joining social at record rate*. Retrieved November 15, 2010, from http://www.cbsnews.com/

Celikyilmaz, A., & Türkşen, I. B. (2007). Fuzzy functions with support vector machines. *Information Sciences*, *177*, 5163–5177. doi:10.1016/j.ins.2007.06.022.

Celikyilmaz, A., & Türkşen, I. B. (2008). Validation criteria for enhanced fuzzy clustering. *Pattern Recognition Letters*, *29*, 97–108. doi:10.1016/j.patrec.2007.08.017.

Chakrabarti, D., Kumar, R., & Tomkins, A. (2006). Evolutionary clustering. In *Proceedings of the 12th ACM International SIGKDD Conference on Knowledge Discovery and Data Mining* (pp. 554–560).

Chang, Y. J., et al. (2007). A general architecture of mobile social network services. *International Conference on Convergence Information Technology, IEEE Computer Society* (pp. 151 – 156).

Chang, C. T., Lai, J. Z. C., & Jeng, M. D. (2011). A fuzzy k-means clustering algorithm using cluster center displacement. *Journal of Information Science and Engineering*, *27*(3), 995–1009.

Chau, M., Cheng, R., Kao, B., & Ng, J. (2012). *Uncertain data mining: An example in clustering location data*. Retrieved January 13, 2012, from http://www.techrepublic.com/whitepapers/uncertain-data-mining-an-example-in-clustering-location-data/386583

Chen, D., et al. (2009). An efficient algorithms for overlapping community detection in complex networks. *Intelligent Systems GCIS 09 WRI Global Congress*, 1, pp. 244-247.

Chen, G., & Rahman, F. (2008). Analyzing privacy designs of mobile social networking applications. Embedded and ubiquitous computing. *IFIP International Conference*, Vol. 2, pp. 83-88.

Chen, J., Geyer, W., Dugan, C., Muller, M., & Guy, I. (2009). Make new friends, but keep the old: Recommending people on social networking sites. *CHI '09 Proceedings of the SIGCHI Conference on Human Factors in Computing Systems* (pp. 201-210).

Chen, C. H. (1996). *Fuzzy logic and neural network handbook*. McGraw-Hill Companies.

Chen, C. H., Hong, T. P., & Tseng, V. S. (2012). Fuzzy data mining for time-series data. *Applied Soft Computing*, *12*(1), 536–542. doi:10.1016/j.asoc.2011.08.006.

Chen, C.-L., Tseng, F., & Liang, T. (2010). An integration of WordNet and fuzzy association rule mining for multi-label document clustering. *Data & Knowledge Engineering*, *69*(11), 1208–1226. doi:10.1016/j.datak.2010.08.003.

Chen, J., Zaiane, O. R., & Goebel, R. (2009). *Detecting communities in social networks using max-min modularity* (pp. 978–989). SDM.

Chen, L., & Qi, L. (2011). Social opinion mining for supporting buyers' complex decision making: Exploratory user study and algorithm comparison. *Social Network Analysis Mining*, *1*, 301–320. doi:10.1007/s13278-011-0023-y.

Chen, M. S., Han, J., & Yu, P. S. (1996). Data mining: An overview from a database perspective. *IEEE Transactions on Knowledge and Data Engineering*, *8*(6), 866–883. doi:10.1109/69.553155.

Cheong, M., & Lee, V. (2009). Integrating web-based intelligence retrieval and decision-making from the twitter trends knowledge base. In *Proceedings of the Second ACM Workshop on Social Web Search and Mining* (pp. 1-8). ACM press.

Chi, Y., Song, X., Zhou, D., Hino, K., & Tseng, B. L. (2009). On evolutionary spectral clustering. *ACM Transactions on Knowledge Discovery from Data, 3*(4), 17:1-17:30.

Choudhury, C. F., Ben-Akiva, M. E., Toledo, T., Lee, G., & Rao, A. (2007). Modeling cooperative lane changing and forced merging behavior. *Proceeding of the 86th Transportation Research Board Annual Meeting*. Washington, DC., CD-ROM.

Choudhury, T., et al. (2008). The mobile sensing platform: An embedded activity recognition system. *IEEE CS, Activity based Computing, Pervasive computing*.

Chou, L.-D. et al. (2011). Mobile social network services for families with children with developmental disabilities. *IEEE Transactions on Information Technology in Biomedicine*, *15*(4), 585–593. doi:10.1109/TITB.2011.2155663 PMID:21606040.

Clark, J. (1999). XSL transformations (XSLT). *World Wide Web Consortium (W3C)*. Retrieved from http:// www. w3. org/TR/xslt

Clark, J., & DeRose, S. (1999). XML Path Language (XPath) version 1.0 w3c recommendation. *World Wide Web Consortium (W3C)*. Retrieved from http://www. w3.org/TR/1999/REC-xpath-19991116

Clifton, C. (2010). *Encyclopædia Britannica: Definition of data mining*. Retrieved July 2, 2012, from http://www. britannica.com/EBchecked/topic/1056150/data-mining

Coben, P., & Adams, N. (2009). Intelligent data analysis in the 21st century. Springer, Verlag Berlin Heidberg. *LNCS*, *5772*, 1–9.

Coburn, A., & Spence, R. (1992). *Earthquake protection*. John Wiley.

Coenen, F. P., Goulbourne, G., & Leng, P. (2001). Computing association rules using partial totals. Principles of data mining and knowledge discovery.[). SpringerBerlin/ Heidelberg.]. *LNCS*, *2168*, 54–66.

Coffman, T. R., & Marcus, S. E. (2004). Pattern classification in social network analysis: A case study. In *Proc. of IEEE Aerospace Conference*.

Coffman, T., Greenblatt, S., & Marcus, S. (2004). Graph-based technologies for intelligence analysis. *Communications of the ACM*, *47*(3), 45–47. doi:10.1145/971617.971643.

Combe, D., Largeron, C., Egyed-Zsigmond, E., & Grey, M. (2010). *A comparative study of social network analysis tools*. In *International Workshop on Web Intelligence and Virtual Enterprises 2*.

Connecting and engaging with digital consumers. (n.d.). *Website*. Retrieved November 15, 2011, from http://www. blog.nielsen.com/

Conway, K. (2005). *Pacific highway upgrade-F3 to Raymond Terrace route (Consultancy Report)*. Maunsell Australia Pty Ltd..

Create your own blog. (n.d.). *Website*. Retrieved May 23, 2012, from http://www.blogger.com/

Daganzo, C. F. (2002). A behavioral theory of multi-lane traffic flow part II: Merges and the onset of congestion. *Transportation Research Part B: Methodological*, *36*, 159–169. doi:10.1016/S0191-2615(00)00043-6.

Das, S., & Bowles, B. A. (1999). Simulations of highway chaos using fuzzy logic. *18th International Conference of the North American Fuzzy Information Procecsing Society*. Nafips, New York, U.S.A.

Daskalaki, S. et al. (2003). Data mining for decision support on customer insolvency in telecommunications business. Elsevier. *European Journal of Operational Research, 145*, 239–255. doi:10.1016/S0377-2217(02)00532-5.

Data Mining Curriculum. (2006, April 30). *Website*. Retrieved August 21, 2012, from http://www.sigkdd.org/curriculum.php

Data Mining. (n.d.). *Website*. Retrieved June 10, 2012, from http://en.wikipedia.org/wiki/Data_mining

Dave, R. N. (1996). Validating fuzzy partition obtained through C shells clustering. *Pattern Recognition Letters, 17*, 613–623. doi:10.1016/0167-8655(96)00026-8.

Davison, H. K., Maraist, C., & Bing, M. N. (2011). Friend or foe? The promise and pitfalls of using social networking sites for HR decisions. *Journal of Business and Psychology, 26*(2), 153–159. doi:10.1007/s10869-011-9215-8.

De Cock, M., Cornelis, C., & Kerre, E. E. (2005). Elicitation of fuzzy association rules from positive and negative examples. *Fuzzy Sets and Systems, 149*(1), 73–85. doi:10.1016/j.fss.2004.07.010.

De Meo, P., Quattrone, G., & Ursino, D. (2010). A query expansion and user profile enrichment approach to improve the performance of recommender systems operating on a folksonomy. *User Modeling and User-Adapted Interaction, 20*(1), 41–86. doi:10.1007/s11257-010-9072-6.

Deinert, F., & Magedanz, T. (2010). Introducing widget-based IMS client applications. Springer. *Mobile Networks and Applications, 15*, 845–852. doi:10.1007/s11036-010-0239-5.

Deixto. (n.d.). *Website*. Retrieved from http://deixto.com/

Delo, C. (2012). *Startups mining social data take on Facebook AT&T, AmEx, Macy's, Purina warm up to companies targeting ads across the web*. Retrieved by http://adage.com/print/233932

Denecke, K., & Nejdl, W. (2009). How valuable is medical social media data? Content analysis of the medical web. *Information Sciences, 179*(12), 1870–1880. doi:10.1016/j.ins.2009.01.025.

Digital Journalism – How News is sourced with Social Media. (n.d.). *Website*. Retrieved July 5, 2012, from http://www.roymorejon.com

Dikaiakos, M. D. et al. (2009). *Cloud computing distributed internet computing for IT and scientific research* (pp. 10–13). IEEE Computer Society. doi:10.1109/MIC.2009.103.

Dimitrov, W. (2000). The consciousness resonance in action. Understanding fuzziness of knowing. *Journal on Hydrolics, 240*, 90–105.

Ding, Z. et al. (2012). *SeaCloudDM: A database cluster framework for managing and querying massive heterogeneous sensor sampling data*. Springer Science Business Media. doi:10.1007/s11227-012-0762-1.

Djuggler. (n.d.). *Website*. Retrieved from http://www.djuggler.com/

Doan, S., Vo, B.-K., & Collier, N. (2011). An analysis of Twitter messages in the 2011 Tohoku earthquake. In P. Kostkova, M. Szomszor, & D. Fowler (Eds.), *Electronic healthcare: 4th International Conference, eHealth 2011* (pp. 58-66). Málaga, Spain, November 21-23, 2011. Berlin: Springer Berlin Heidelberg.

Dokoohaki, N., & Matskin, M. (2008). Effective design of trust ontologies for improvement in the structure of socio-semantic trust networks. *International Journal on Advances in Intelligent Systems*, 1st (1942-2679): 23–42.

Domingos, P., & Richardson, M. (2001). Mining the network value of customers. *ACM KDD, 01*, 57–66.

Domingue, J. et al. (Eds.). (2011). *Handbook of semantic web technologies* (pp. 468–506). Springer-Verlag Berlin Heidelberg. doi:10.1007/978-3-540-92913-0.

Dominique, H., Joel, D., Abdolreza, E., Selin, S., Nicholas, T., & Heikki, T. (2003). A review of software packages for data mining. *The American Statistician, 57*(4), 290–309. doi:10.1198/0003130032486.

Doshi, A., & Trivedi, M. (2008). A comparative exploration of eye gaze and head motion cues for lane change intent prediction. *IEEE Intelligent Vehicles Symposium* (pp. 49-54). Eindhoven, Netherlands.

Dredze, M., Wallach, H. M., Puller, D., & Pereira, F. (2008). Generating summary keywords for emails using topics. In *Proceedings of the 13th international conference on Intelligent user interfaces* (pp. 199-206).

Duan, D., Li, Y., Li, R., & Lu, Z. (2011). Incremental K-clique clustering in dynamic social networks. *Artificial Intelligence Review*, 1–19.

Dubois, D., & Prade, H. (1988). Representation and combination of uncertainty with belief functions and possibility measures. *Computational Intelligence (Canada)*, *4*(4), 244–264. doi:10.1111/j.1467-8640.1988.tb00279.x.

DuBois, T., Golbeck, J., Kleint, J., & Srinivasan, A. (2009). *Improving recommendation accuracy by clustering social networks with trust*. Recommender Systems & the Social Web.

Duda, R., Hart, P., & Stork, D. (2001). *Pattern classification* (2nd ed.). New York: John Wiley & Sons.

Duncan, J. (1999). *Watts, small worlds. The dynamics of networks between order and randomness*. Princeton: Princeton University Press.

Dustdar, S. et al. (2005). Mining of ad-hoc business processes with TeamLog. Elsevier. *Data & Knowledge Engineering*, *55*, 129–158. doi:10.1016/j.datak.2005.02.002.

Dzeroski, S., & Lavrac, N. (Eds.). (2001). *Relational data mining*. Berlin: Springer. doi:10.1007/978-3-662-04599-2.

Edelman 2010 Trust Barometer Study. (2010). *Website*. Retrieved June 26, 2012, from http://www.edelman.com/trust/2010/

Eidehall, A., Pohl, J., Gustafsson, F., & Ekmark, J. (2007). Toward autonomous collision avoidance by steering. *IEEE Transactions on Intelligent Transportation Systems*, *8*(1), 84–94. doi:10.1109/TITS.2006.888606.

Eleta, I. (2012). *Multilingual use of Twitter: Social networks and language choice. CSCW* (pp. 363–366). Companion.

El-Tantawy, S., Djavadian, S., Roorda, M. J., & Abdulhai, B. (2009). Safety evaluation of truck lane restriction strategies using microsimulation modeling. *Transportation Research Record. Journal of the Transportation Research Board*, *2099*, 123–131. doi:10.3141/2099-14.

Facebook Detox. (n.d.). *Website*. Retrieved May 21, 2012, from http://www.facebookdetox.com

Falkowski, T., Barth, A., & Spiliopoulou, M. (2008). Studying community dynamics with an incremental graph mining algorithm. In *Proc. of the 14th Americas Conference on Information Systems (AMCIS)*. Toronto, Canada.

Farzandar, Z., & Kangavari, M. (2012). Efficient mining of fuzzy association rules from the pre-processed dataset. *Computing and Informatics*, *31*, 331–347.

Fayyad, U., Piatetsky-Shapiro, G., & Smyth, P. (1996). From data mining to knowledge discovery in databases. *AI Magazine*, *17*(3), 37–54.

Fayyad, U., Piatetsky-Shapiro, G., Smyth, P., & Uthurusamy, R. (1996). *Advances in knowledge discovery and data mining*. MIT Press.

Feil, B., & Abonyi, J. (2008). *Introduction to fuzzy data mining methods*. Retrieved November 30, 2011, from http://www.igi-global.com/viewtitlesample.aspx?id=20349

Feil, B., & Abonyi, J. (2008). Introduction to fuzzy data mining methods. In Feil, B., & Abonyi, J. (Eds.), *Handbook of research on fuzzy information processing in databases* (pp. 55–95). doi:10.4018/978-1-59904-853-6.ch003.

Fei-Yue, W. et al. (2007). Social computing: From social informatics to social intelligence. IEEE. *Journal of Intelligent Systems*, *2*, 79–83.

FEMA. (1999). Earthquake loss estimation methodology HAZUS 99 service release 2: Technical manual. *FEMA*. Retrieved from http://www.fema.gov/hazus

Ferguson, R., & Buckingham Shum, S. (2012). *Social learning analytics: Five approaches*. In *Proc. International Conference on Learning Analytics & Knowledge* (pp. 23-33). Vancouver, BC.

Fielding, R. T., & Taylor, R. N. (2002). Principled design of the modern web architecture. *ACM Transactions on Internet Technology*, *2*(2), 115–150. doi:10.1145/514183.514185.

FOMO. The unintended effects of social media addiction. (n.d.). *Website*. Retrieved June 29, 2012, from http://www.nbcnetwork.com/

Francis, L. A. (2006, Winter). Taming text: An introduction to text mining. *Casualty Actuarial Society Forum,* pp. 51–88. Retrieved from http://www.casact.org/pubs/forum/06wforum/06w55.pdf

Fraser, M., & Dutta, S. (2008). *Throwing sheep in the boardroom: How online social networking will transform your life, work and world.* Wiley.

Fukuyama, Y., & Sugeno, M. (1989). A new method of choosing the number of clusters for the fuzzy C-means method. In *Proc. 5th Fuzzy Systems Symposium* (pp. 247–250).

Gladwell, M. (2011, March). Malcolm Gladwell and Clay Shirky on social media and revolution. *Foreign Affairs.* Retrieved June 24, 2012, from http://www.foreignaffairs.com/

Garg, N., & Weber, I. (2008). Personalized tag suggestion for flickr. In *Proceeding of the 17th international conference on World Wide Web* (pp. 1063-1064).

Gartrell, M., et al. (2010). Enhancing group recommendation by incorporating social relationship interactions. *ACM GROUP' 10, Proceeding of the 6th ACM International Conference on Supporting group work*, pp. 97 – 106.

Gasevi, D., et al. (2011). An approach to folksonomy-based ontology maintenance for learning environments. *IEEE Transactions on learning technologies, 4*(4), 301-314.

Gath, I., & Geva, A. B. (1989). Unsupervised optimal fuzzy clustering. *IEEE Transactions on Pattern Analysis and Machine Intelligence, 11*, 773–781. doi:10.1109/34.192473.

Gebremeskel, G. B., et al. (2012). The paradigm integration of computational intelligence performance in cloud computing towards data security. *IEEE Computer Society, 5th International Conference on Information and Computing Science* (pp. 19 – 22).

Gelb, A. (1974). *Applied optimal filtering* (p. 382). MIT Press.

George, A. (2006, September 18). Living online: The end of privacy? *New Scientist, 2569*. Retrieved August 29, 2007, from http://www.newscientist.com/channel/tech/mg19125691.700-living-online-the-end-of-privacy.html

Geser, H. (2006). Is the cell phone undermining the social order?: Understanding mobile technology from a sociological perspective. *Knowledge, Technology & Policy, 19*(1), 8–18. doi:10.1007/s12130-006-1010-x.

Getoor, L. (2005). Link-based classification. Advanced methods for knowledge discovery from complex data (pp. 189-207).

Getoor, L., & Diehl, C. (2005). Link mining: A survey. *SIGKDD Explorations*, *7*(2), 3–12. doi:10.1145/1117454.1117456.

Ghosh, J., & Mukhopadhyay, S. (2011). Studies on fuzzy logic and dispositions for medical diagnosis. *International Journal Computer Technology and Applications*, *2*(5), 1235–1240.

Giannotti, F., & Pedreschi, D. (2008). *Mobility, data mining and privacy: Geographic knowledge discovery* (p. 410). Springer. doi:10.1007/978-3-540-75177-9.

Gipps, P. G. (1986). A model for the structure of lane-changing decisions. *Transportation Research Part B: Methodological*, *20*(5), 403–414. doi:10.1016/0191-2615(86)90012-3.

Goggins, S. P., et al. (2010). Social intelligence in completely online groups: Toward social prosthetics from log data analysis and transformation. *IEEE International Conference on Social Computing/IEEE International Conference on Privacy, Security, Risk and Trust* (pp. 500-507).

Golbeck, J., & Hendler, J. (2006). Filmtrust: Movie recommendations using trust in web-based social networks. In *Proceedings of the IEEE Consumer communications and networking conference*, 42, 43-44. IEEE press.

Golder, S. A., & Macy, M. W. (2011). Diurnal and seasonal mood vary with work, sleep, and daylength across diverse cultures. *Science*, *333*(6051), 1878–1881. doi:10.1126/science.1202775 PMID:21960633.

Goldstein, J., Mittal, V., Carbonell, J., & Kantrowitz, M. (2000). Multi-document summarization by sentence extraction. In *Proceedings of the ANLP/NAACL Workshop on Automatic Summarization* (pp. 40-48).

Gong, S., Qu, Y., & Tian, S. (2010). Summarization using Wikipedia. *Proceedings of Text Analysis Conference.*

Google. (n.d.). *Website*. Retrieved May 21, 2012, from http://www.google.com

Graczyk, M., Lasota, T., & Trawiński, B. (2009). *Comparative analysis of premises valuation models using KEEL, RapidMiner, and WEKA* (pp. 800–812). Computational Collective Intelligence. Semantic Web, Social Networks and Multiagent Systems. doi:10.1007/978-3-642-04441-0_70.

Grob, R. et al. (2009). *Cluestr: Mobile social networking for enhanced group communication* (pp. 81–90). ACM. doi:10.1145/1531674.1531686.

Grunthal, G. (1998). *European macro seismic scale 1998* (*Vol. 15*, p. 99). Conseil de l'Europe.

Guan, Z., Bu, J., Mei, Q., Chen, C., & Wang, C. (2009). Personalized tag recommendation using graph-based ranking on multi-type interrelated objects. In *Proceedings of the 32nd international ACM SIGIR conference on Research and development in information retrieval* (pp. 540-547).

Guo, B., et al. (2011). Living with Internet of things: The emergence of embedded intelligence. *IEEE Computer Society, International Conferences on Internet of Things, and Cyber, Physical and Social Computing* (pp. 297 – 304).

Guo, L., Tan, E., Chen, S., Zhang, X., & Zhao, Y. E. (2009). Analyzing patterns of user content generation in online social networks. In *Proceedings of the 15th ACM SIGKDD international conference on Knowledge discovery and data mining* (pp. 369-378).

Gupta, P., & Bhatnagar, V. (2012). Pros and cons of publishing social network data. In *Proceedings of National Conference on Data Mining and Warehousing* (pp. 422-425).

Gupta, G., Sharma, S., & Bhatnagar, V. (2011). Critical parameters for privacy preservation through anonymization in social networks. *International Journal of Networking and Virtual Organisation, 11*(2), 156–172. doi:10.1504/IJNVO.2012.048327.

Haddadi, H., Mortier, R., & Hand, S. (2012). Privacy analytics. *Computer Communication Review, 42*(2), 94–98. doi:10.1145/2185376.2185390.

Halevy, A., Norvig, P., & Pereira, F. (2009). The unreasonable effectiveness of data. *Communications of the ACM, 24*(2), 812.

Hamasaki, M., Matsuo, Y., Nishimura, T., & Takeda, H. (2009). Ontology extraction by collaborative tagging. In World Wide Web (pp. 427-437).

Hammer, J., Garcia-Molina, H., Cho, J., Aranha, R., & Crespo, A. (1997). Extracting semistructured information from the Web. In *Proceedings of the Workshop on Management of Semistructured Data* (pp. 18-25). Tucson, AZ.

Han, J., Pei, J., & Yin, Y. (2000). Mining frequent patterns without candidate generation. In *Proceedings ACM-SIGMOD International Conference Management of Data* (pp. 1-12). ACM press.

Han, J., Rodriguez, J. C., & Beheshti, M. (2008, December). Diabetes data analysis and prediction model discovery using RapidMiner. In *Future Generation Communication and Networking, 2008. FGCN'08. Second International Conference on* (Vol. 3, pp. 96-99). IEEE.

Hand, D., Mannila, H., & Smyth, P. (2001). *Principles of data mining*. MIT Press.

Han, J., & Fu, Y. (1999). Mining multiple-level association rules in large databases. [IEEE press.]. *IEEE Transactions on Knowledge and Data Engineering, 11*(5), 798–805. doi:10.1109/69.806937.

Han, J., & Kamber, M. (2006). *Data mining: Concepts and techniques. University of Illinois at Urbana-Champaign*. Morgan Kaufmann.

Han, J., Kamber, M., & Pei, J. (2011). *Data mining: Concepts and techniques* (3rd ed.). Morgan Kaufmann.

Hanneman, A., & Riddle, M. (2005). *Introduction to social network methods*. Retrieved January 15, 2012, from http://faculty.ucr.edu/~hanneman/

Harris, K. (2008). Using social networking sites as student engagement tools. *Diverse Issues in Higher Education, 25*(18).

Häsel, M. (2011). Opensocial: An enabler for social applications on the web. *Communications of the ACM, 54*(1), 139–144. doi:10.1145/1866739.1866765.

Hathaway, R. J., & Bezdek, J. C. (1993). Switching regression models and fuzzy clustering. *IEEE Transactions on Fuzzy Systems, 1*(3), 195–203. doi:10.1109/91.236552.

Hatipoglu, C., Ozguner, U., & Redmill, K. A. (2003). Automated lane change controller design. *IEEE Transactions on Intelligent Transportation Systems*, *4*(1), 13–22. doi:10.1109/TITS.2003.811644.

Hay, M., Miklau, G., Jensen, D., Weis, P., & Srivastava, S. (2007). *Anonymizing social networks*. University of Massachusetts Technical Report.

Haythornthwaite, C. (2005). Social networks and Internet connectivity effects. *Information Communication and Society*, *8*(2), 125–147. doi:10.1080/13691180500146185.

Heliumscraper. (n.d.). *Website*. Retrieved from http://www.heliumscraper.com/

Herlocker, J. L., Konstan, J. A., Terveen, L. G., & Riedl, J. T. (2004). Evaluating collaborative filtering recommender systems. [TOIS]. *ACM Transactions on Information Systems*, *22*(1), 5–53. doi:10.1145/963770.963772.

Hernández, C., & Navarro, G. (2012). Compressed representation of web and social networks via dense subgraphs. *Proceedings of SPIRE*, *12*, 264–276.

Heymann, P., Ramage, D., & Garcia-Molina, H. (2008). Social tag prediction. *Proceedings of the 31st annual international ACM SIGIR conference on Research and development in information retrieval* (pp. 531-538). ACM press.

Hidas, P. (2005). Modelling vehicle interactions in microscopic simulation of merging and weaving. *Transportation Research Part C, Emerging Technologies*, *13*(1), 37–62. doi:10.1016/j.trc.2004.12.003.

Hilderman, R. J., & Hamilton, H. J. (2001). *Knowledge discovery and measures of interest*. Kluwer Academic Publishers. doi:10.1007/978-1-4757-3283-2.

Hine, C. (2011). Internet research and unobtrusive methods. *Social research update*, Issue 61. University of Surrey. Retrieved from http://sru.soc.surrey.ac.uk

Hintze, J. L. (2007). *NCSS User Guide IV*. Utah: Kaysville.

Hipp, J., Myka, A., Wirth, R., & Guntzer, U. (1998). A new algorithm for faster mining of generalized rules. In *Proceedings of the 2nd European Symposium on Principles of Data Mining and Knowledge Discovery* (pp. 72–82).

Hipp, J., Guntzer, U., & Gholamreza, N. (2000). Algorithm for association rule mining: A general survey and comparison. *ACM SIGKDD*, *2*(1), 58. doi:10.1145/360402.360421.

Ho, G. T. S., Ip, W. H., Wu, C. H., & Tse, Y. K. (2012). Using a fuzzy association rule mining approach to identify the financial data association. *Expert Systems with Applications*, *39*(10), 9054–9063. doi:10.1016/j.eswa.2012.02.047.

Hong, T-P., & Lee, Y-C. (2008). An overview of mining fuzzy association rules. *Fuzzy Sets and Their Extensions: Representation, Aggregation and Models,* 397-410.

Hoogendoorn, S. P., & Bovy, P. H. L. (2001). State-of-the-art of vehicular traffic flow modelling. *Special Issue on Road Traffic Modelling and Control of the Journal of Systems and Control Engineering*, *215*(4), 283–303.

Hoppner, F., Klawonn, F., Kruse, R., & Runkler, T. (1999). *Fuzzy cluster analysis*. J. Wiley & Sons.

Hotho, A., Jäschke, R., Schmitz, C., & Stumme, G. (2006). BibSonomy: A social bookmark and publication sharing system. In *Proceedings of the Conceptual Structures Tool Interoperability Workshop at the 14th International Conference on Conceptual Structures* (pp. 87-102).

Hotho, A., Jäschke, R., Schmitz, C., & Stumme, G. (2006). Mining association rules in folksonomies. In *Data Science and Classification* (pp. 261–270). Springer Berlin Heidelberg.

Howison, J. et al. (2011). Validity issues in the use of social network analysis with digital trace data. *Journal of the Association for Information Systems*, *12*(12), 767–797.

Hu, J., & Liu, Y. (2006). Designing and realization of intelligent data mining system based on expert knowledge. *IEEE, Management of Innovation and Technology International Conference*, Vol.1, pp. 380 – 383.

Hua, Z. Y., et al. (2010). Discussion of intelligent cloud computing system. IEEE. *Computer Society, International Conference on Web Information Systems and Mining* (pp. 319-322).

Hughes, A. L., Palen, L., Sutton, J., Liu, S. B., & Vieweg, S. (2008, May). Site-seeing in disaster: An examination of on-line social convergence. In *Proceedings of the 5th International ISCRAM Conference*. Washington, DC.

Huhtam, J., Salonen, J., Marttila, J., & Nyk, O. (2010). Context-driven social network visualisation: Case wiki co-creation. In *International Workshop on Knowledge Federation*. Dubrovnik, Croatia.

Huisman, M., & Steglich, C. (2008). Treatment of non-response in longitudinal network studies. *Social Networks*, *30*, 297–309. doi:10.1016/j.socnet.2008.04.004.

Hullermeier, E. (2005). Fuzzy methods in machine learning and data mining: Status and prospects. Elsevier. *Fuzzy Sets and Systems*, *156*(3), 387–406. doi:10.1016/j.fss.2005.05.036.

Humphreys, L. (2008). Mobile social networks and social practice: A case study of dodge ball. *Journal of Computer-Mediated Communication*, *13*, 341–360. doi:10.1111/j.1083-6101.2007.00399.x.

Hura, G. S., & Singhal, M. (2001). *Data and computer communications: Networking and internetworking*. CSR Press. doi:10.1201/9781420041316.

IEEE COMSOC MMTC. (2012). E-Letter. IEEE Communication Society, 7(5).

Inokuchi, A., Washio, T., & Motoda, H. (2000). An Apriori-based algorithm for mining frequent substructures from graph data. In *Proceedings of the 4th European Conference on Principles of Data Mining and Knowledge Discovery* (pp. 13-23).

Investor Relations. (n.d.). *Website*. Retrieved June 25, 2012, from http://investor.fb.com/

Ioannidis, S., et al. (2009). Optimal and scalable distribution of content updates over a mobile social network. IEEE. Communications Society subject matter experts for publication in the IEEE INFOCOM 09 proceedings (pp. 1422-1430).

Is Facebook making us lonely? (2012, May). *The Atlantic*. Retrieved July 13, 2012, from http://www.theatlantic.com/

Jacobs, A. (2009). The pathologies of big data. *ACM Queue; Tomorrow's Computing Today*, *7*(6). doi:10.1145/1563821.1563874.

Jamali, M., & Abolhassani, H. (2006). Different aspects of social network analysis. In *Proceedings of IEEE/WIC/ACM International Conference on Web Intelligence*. Washington, DC, USA.

Jang, J. S. R., & Gulley, N. (2008). *Fuzzy logic toolbox for use with MATLAB*. USA: The MathWorks Inc..

Janjua, N.K., et al. (2012). Semantic information and knowledge integration through argumentative reasoning to support intelligent decision making.

Jensen, D., & Neville, J. (2002). *Data mining in social networks, symposium on dynamic social network modeling and analysis. National Academy of Sciences*. Washington, DC: National Academy Press.

Jensen, D., & Neville, J. (2002). *Data mining in social networks. National Academy of Sciences*. Washington: DC, National Academy Press.

Jones, S. (2005). Facebook: Threats to Privacy. *MIT*. Retrieved May 2012, from http://groups.csail.edu/

Jose, M. M., & Casanovas, M. (2012). *Generalized aggregation operators and fuzzy numbers in a unified model between the weighted average and the OWA operator*. Retrieved May 15, 2012, from http://gandalf.fcee.urv.es/sigef/english/congressos/congres15/039_Merigo_Casanovas.pdf

Joshi, A., & Krishnapuram, R. (1998). Robust fuzzy clustering methods to support web mining. In *Proc. Workshop in Data Mining and Knowledge Discovery, SIGMOD*, 1998, 15, 1-8.

Kadushin, C. (n.d.). *Introduction to social network theory*. Retrieved January 15, 2012, from http://www.communityanalytics.com/Portals/0/Resource_Library/Social%20Network%20Theory_Kadushin.pdf

Kamilaris, A., & Pitsillides, A. (2008). Social networking of the smart home. *IEEE 21st International Symposium on Personal Indoor and Mobile Radio Communications*.

Kandel, A., Gupta, M. M., Bandler, W., & Kiszka, J. B. (1985). Approximate reasoning.[Elsevier.]. *Expert Systems: International Journal of Knowledge Engineering and Neural Networks*, 745–765.

Kantardzic, M. (2003). *Data mining: Concepts, models, methods, and algorithms*. John Wiley & Sons.

Kaplan, A. M. (2012). If you love something, let it go mobile: Mobile marketing and mobile social media 4x4. *Business Horizons*, *55*(2), 129–139. doi:10.1016/j.bushor.2011.10.009.

Kaplan, A. M., & Michael, H. (2010). Users of the world, unite: The challenges and opportunities of social media. *Business Horizons*, *53*(1), 59–68. doi:10.1016/j.bushor.2009.09.003.

Karl, R., Heather, A., & Paul, G. (2010). *2010 Data miner survey – Overcoming data mining's top challenges*.

Kashoob, S., Caverlee, J., & Ding, Y. (2009). A categorical model for discovering latent structure in social annotations. In *Proceedings of the International AAAI Conference on Weblogs and social media* (pp. 27-35).

Kasneci, G., Ramanath, M., Suchanek, F., & Weikum, G. (2009). The YAGO-NAGA approach to knowledge discovery.[ACM press.]. *SIGMOD Record*, *37*(4), 41–47. doi:10.1145/1519103.1519110.

Katzdobler, F.-J., & Filho, H. P. B. (2009). *Knowledge extraction from web*. Retrieved from http://subversion.assembla.com/svn/iskm/FinalDocumentation/FinalReport.pdf

Kaufman & Rousseeuw. (1990). *Finding groups in data*. New York: Wiley.

Kaya, M., & Alhajj, R. (2005). Genetic algorithm based framework for mining fuzzy association rules. *Fuzzy Sets and Systems*, *152*(3), 587–601. doi:10.1016/j.fss.2004.09.014.

Kayastha, N., et al. (2011). Applications, architectures, and protocol design issues for mobile social networks: A survey. *IEEE*, 99(12), pp. 2031-2158.

Keim, D. A. (2001). Visual exploration of large data sets. *Communications of the ACM*, *44*(8), 39–44. doi:10.1145/381641.381656.

Kemp, D. et al. (2012). Corporate social responsibility, mining and "audit culture." Elsevier. *Journal of Cleaner Production*, *24*, 1–10. doi:10.1016/j.jclepro.2011.11.002.

Kendall, M. G. (1975). *Rank correlation methods*. New York: Oxford Univ. Press.

Keogh, E., Lonardi, S., & Ratanamahatana, C. A. (2004). Towards parameter-free data mining. In *Proceedings of the 10th International Conference on Knowledge Discovery and Data Mining (KDD'04)* (pp. 206-215). ACM Press.

Khan, M. S., Coenen, F., Reid, D., Tawfik, H., Patel, R., & Lawson, A. (2010). A sliding windows based dual support framework for discovering emerging trends from temporal data. Research and Development in Intelligent Systems XXVII (pp. 35-48).

Kiefer, R. J., & Hankey, J. M. (2008). Lane change behavior with a side blind zone alert system. *Accident; Analysis and Prevention*, *40*(2), 683–690. doi:10.1016/j.aap.2007.09.018 PMID:18329421.

Kietzmann, J. H., Hermkens, K., McCarthy, I. P., & Silvestre, B. S. (2011). Social media? Get serious! Understanding the functional building blocks of social media. *Business Horizons*, *54*, 241–251. doi:10.1016/j.bushor.2011.01.005.

Kimball, R., Ross, M., & Merz, R. (2002). *The data warehouse toolkit. The complete guide to dimensional modeling*. Wiley.

Kim, D.-W., Lee, K. H., & Lee, D. (2003). Fuzzy cluster validation index based on inter-cluster proximity. *Pattern Recognition Letters*, *24*, 2561–2574. doi:10.1016/S0167-8655(03)00101-6.

Kim, H. K. et al. (2008). Social semantic cloud of tag: Semantic model for social tagging. Springer-Verlag Berlin Heidelberg. *KES-AMSTA, LNAI*, *4953*, 83–92.

Kim, H., Alghamdi, A., Saddik, A., & Jo, G. (2011). Collaborative user modeling with user-generated tags for social recommender systems. *Expert Systems with Applications*, *38*(7), 8488–8496. doi:10.1016/j.eswa.2011.01.048.

Kim, K., McKay, R., & Moon, B. (2010). *Multi-objective evolutionary algorithms for dynamic social network clustering* (pp. 1179–1186). GECCO. doi:10.1145/1830483.1830699.

Kim, M. J. et al. (2011). An intelligent multi –agent model for resource virtualization: Supporting social media service in cloud computing. Springer – Verlag Berlin Heidelberg. *Computer Network Systems and Industrial Eng. SCI*, *365*, 99–111.

Kim, M. S., & Han, J. (2009). *A particle and density based evolutionary clustering method for dynamic networks*. Lyon, France: VLDB.

Kim, M., & Ramakrishna, R. S. (2005). New indices for cluster validity assessment. *Pattern Recognition Letters*, *26*, 2353–2363. doi:10.1016/j.patrec.2005.04.007.

Kim, Y. H., Ahn, S. C., & Kwon, W. H. (2000). Computational complexity of general fuzzy logic control and its simplification for a loop controller. *Fuzzy Sets and Systems*, *111*(2), 215–224. doi:10.1016/S0165-0114(97)00409-0.

Kirkpatrick, D. D. (2011, February 9). Wired and shrewd, young egyptians guide revolt. *The New York Times*. Retrieved June 23, 2012, from http://www.nytimes.com/

Kiszka, J. B., Kochanska, M. E., & Sliwinska, D. S. (1985). The influence of some fuzzy implication operators on the accuracy of fuzzy model. Part I. *Fuzzy Sets and Systems*, *15*, 111–128. doi:10.1016/0165-0114(85)90041-7.

Kiszka, J. B., Kochanska, M. E., & Sliwinska, D. S. (1985). The influence of some fuzzy implication operators on the accuracy of a fuzzy model, Part II. *Fuzzy Sets and Systems*, *15*, 223–240. doi:10.1016/0165-0114(85)90016-8.

Kleinberg, J. M. (2007). *Challenges in mining social network data: Processes, privacy, and paradoxes* (pp. 4–5). KDD. doi:10.1145/1281192.1281195.

Klir, G. J., & Folger, T. A. (1988). *Fuzzy sets, uncertainty, and information. Engle-wood Cliffs*. NJ: Prentice Hall.

Knospe, W., Santen, L., Schadschneider, A., & Schreckenberg, M. (2002). A realistic two-lane traffic model for highway traffic. *Journal of Physics. A, Mathematical and General*, *35*(15), 3369–3388. doi:10.1088/0305-4470/35/15/302.

Kokkoras, F., Lampridou, E., Ntonas, K., & Vlahavas, I. (2008). *Mopis: A multiple opinion summarizer. Artificial Intelligence: Theories* (pp. 110–122). Models and Applications.

Kontostathis, A., Galitsky, L., Pottenger, W. M., Roy, S., & Phelps, D. J. (2003). *A survey of emerging trend detection in textual data mining*. Springer-Verlag.

Koren, Y., Bell, R., & Volinsky, C. (2009). Matrix factorization techniques for recommender systems. *Computer*, *42*(8), 30–37. doi:10.1109/MC.2009.263.

Kornblum, J., & Marklein, M. B. (2006, March 8). What you say online could haunt you. *USA Today*. Retrieved August 29, 2007, from http://www.usatoday.com/tech/news/internetprivacy/2006-03-08-facebook-myspace_x.htm

Korolova, A. et al. (2008). Link privacy in social networks. *ACM, CIKM*, *08*, 1–10.

Kramer, S. L. (1996). *Geotechnical earthquake engineering*. New Jersey: Prentice Hall.

Krestel, R., Fankhauser, P., & Nejdl, W. (2009). Latent Dirichlet allocation for tag recommendation. *Proceedings of the 3rd conference on Recommender systems* (pp. 61-68).

Krishnamurthy, B., & Wills, C. E. (2008). Characterizing privacy in online social networks. In *Proceedings of the Workshop on Online Social Networks in conjunction with ACM SIGCOMM Conference* (pp. 37–42). ACM.

Krishnapuram, R., & Keller, J. M. (1993). A possibilistic approach to clustering. *IEEE Transactions on Fuzzy Systems*, *1*, 98–110. doi:10.1109/91.227387.

Kruse, R., Borgelt, C., & Nauck, D. (1999). Fuzzy data analysis: Challenges and perspectives. *Proc. 8th IEEE International Conference on Fuzzy Systems (FUZZ-IEEE'99, Seoul, Korea)*. IEEE Press.

Kruse, R., Nauck, D., & Borgelt, C. (1999). *Data mining with fuzzy methods: Status and perspectives*. Retrieved December 1, 2011, from http://borgelt.net/papers/dm_fuzzy.pdf

Kudo, T., Maeda, E., & Matsumoto, Y. (2004). An application of boosting to graph classification. *Advances in Neural Information Processing Systems*, *17*, 729–736.

Kumar, R., Novak, J., & Tomkins, A. (2010). Structure and evolution of online social networks. Link mining: Models, algorithms, and applications (pp. 337-357).

Kumar, A. (2011). Reducing data dimensionality using random projections and fuzzy k-means clustering. *International Journal of Intelligent Computing and Cybernetics*, *4*(3), 353–365. doi:10.1108/17563781111160020.

Kuramochi, M., & Karypis, G. (2004). An efficient algorithm for discovering frequent subgraphs. *IEEE Transactions on Knowledge and Data Engineering*, 1038–1051. doi:10.1109/TKDE.2004.33.

Kwon, J., Coifman, B., & Bickel, P. (2000). Day-to-day travel time trends and travel time prediction from loop detector data. *Transportation Research Record. Journal of the Transportation Research Board*, *1717*, 120–129. doi:10.3141/1717-15.

Lal, K., & Mahanti, N. C. (2010). A novel data mining algorithm for semantic web based data cloud.[IJCSS]. *International Journal of Computer Science and Security, 4*(2), 149–164.

Lam, H. Y., & Yeung, D. Y. (2007). A learning approach to spam detection based on social networks. In *Proceedings of the Fourth Conference on Email and Anti-Spam* (pp. 81-94). AIDAA.

Lau, R. Y. K., Song, D., Li, Y., Cheung, T. C. H., & Hao, J. (2009). Toward a fuzzy domain ontology extraction method for adaptive e-learning. *IEEE Transactions on Knowledge and Data Engineering, 21*(6), 800–813. doi:10.1109/TKDE.2008.137.

Laurent, W. (2011). *Business intelligence, governance, and IT strategy*. Retrieved May 21, 2012, from http://williamlaurent.com/biography.htm

Laurent, W. (2011). *Strategic IT planning and business Intelligence*. Retrieved May 23, 2012, from http://williamlaurent.com/

Lauw, H. Ee-Peng, Teck, L., Pang, T.T. (2007). Mining social network from spatio-temporal events. *ACM SIGKDD International Conference on Knowledge Discovery and Data Mining.*

Laval, J. A., & Daganzo, C. F. (2006). Lane changing in traffic stream. *Transportation Research Part B: Methodological, 40*(3), 251–264. doi:10.1016/j.trb.2005.04.003.

Le Grand, B. et al. (2009). Semantic and conceptual context-aware information retrieval. Springer-Verlag Berlin Heidelberg. *SITIS 2006. LNCS, 4879*, 247–258.

Lee, K., Palsetia, D., Narayanan, R., Patwary, M. A., Agrawal, A., & Choudhary, A. N. (2011). Twitter trending topic classification. In ICDM Workshops (pp. 251-58).

Lee, R. C. T., Slagle, J. R., & Blum, H. (1976). A triangulation method for the sequential mapping of points from n–space to two–space. *IEEE Transactions on Computers, 26*(3), 288–292. doi:10.1109/TC.1977.1674822.

Li, C. (2007). Forrester's new social technographics report. *Forrester Research*. Retrieved January 15, 2012, from http://forrester.typepad.com/groundswell/2007/04/forresters_new_html

Li, N., & Chen, G.L. (2009). Multi-layered friendship modeling for location based mobile social networks. *Mobile and Ubiquitous Systems Networking, and Services, 6th International*10.4108/ICST*MobiQuitous2009*, 6828, pp. 1-10.

Li, Q. (2009). An algorithm of quantitative association rule on fuzzy clustering with application to cross-selling in telecom industry. *Computational Sciences and Optimization, 2009. CSO 2009. International Joint Conference*, 1, 759-762.

Li, X., Guo, L., & Zhao, Y. E. (2008). Tag-based social interest discovery. In *Proceeding of the 17th international conference on World Wide Web* (pp. 675-684). ACM press.

Licoppe, C., & Smoreda, Z. (2005). Are social networks technologically embedded? How networks are changing today with changes in communication technology. Elsevier. *Social Networks*, 317–335. doi:10.1016/j.socnet.2004.11.001.

Lin, Y. R., Chi, Y., Zhu, S., Sundaram, H., & Tseng, B. L. (2008). Facetnet: A framework for analyzing communities and their evolutions in dynamic networks. In *Proceeding of WWW '08 Proceedings of the 17th international conference on World Wide Web* (pp. 685-694).

Li, N., & Wu, D. D. (2010). Using text mining and sentiment analysis for online forums hotspot detection and forecast. *Decision Support Systems, 48*(2), 354–368. doi:10.1016/j.dss.2009.09.003.

Lin, W.-Y., Su, J.-H., & Tseng, M.-C. (2012). Updating generalized association rules with evolving fuzzy taxonomies. *Soft Computing, 16*, 1109–1118. doi:10.1007/s00500-011-0786-0.

Lin, Y. R., Chi, Y., Zhu, S., Sundaram, H., & Tseng, B. L. (2009). *Analyzing communities and their evolutions in dynamic social networks. ACM Transactions on Knowledge Discovery from Data, 3(2)*. ACM press.

Li, Q., Wang, J., Chen, Y., & Lin, Z. (n.d.). User comments for news recommendation in forum-based social media. *Information Sciences. Elsevier.*.

Li-sheng, J., Wen-ping, F., Ying-nan, Z., Shuang-bin, Y., & Hai-jing, H. (2009). Research on safety lane change model of driver assistant system on highway. *IEEE Intelligent Vehicles Symposium*. Shaanxi, China.

Liu, B., Ma, Y., & Lee, R. (2001). Analyzing the interestingness of association rules from the temporal dimension. Proceeding of the International Conference on Data Mining (pp. 377-384). IEEE press.

Liu, B. (2007). *Web data mining*. Springer.

Liu, K., Das, K., Grandison, T., & Kargupta, H. (2008). Privacy preserving data analysis on graphs and social networks. In *Next Generation of Data Mining* (pp. 419–437). CRC Press. doi:10.1201/9781420085877.ch21.

Liu, K., & Terzi, E. (2008). *Towards identity anonymization on graphs*. SIGMOD.

Liu, K., & Terzi, E. (2009). *A framework for computing the privacy scores of users in online social networks*. ICDM. doi:10.1109/ICDM.2009.21.

Liu, L., Wang, J., Liu, J., & Zhang, J. (2009). *Privacy preservation in social networks with sensitive edge weights* (pp. 954–965). SDM.

Li, Y., Surendran, A. C., & Shen, D. (2005). Data mining and audience intelligence for advertising pp. (96-99). *SIGKDD Explorations*, *9*(2).

Lopez, J. F., Cuadros, M., Blanco, A., & Concha, A. (2009). Unveiling fuzzy associations between breast cancer prognostic factors and gene expression data. *Database and Expert Systems Application, 2009. DEXA '09. 20th International Workshop*, 338-342.

Lord, D., Middleton, D., & Whitacre, J. (2005). Does separating trucks from other traffic improve overall safety? *Transportation Research Record. Journal of the Transportation Research Board*, *1922*, 156–166. doi:10.3141/1922-20.

Lygeros, J., Godbole, D. N., & Sastry, S. (1998). Verified hybrid controllers for automated vehicles. *IEEE Transactions on Automatic Control*, *43*(4), 522–539. doi:10.1109/9.664155.

Ma, X. (2004). *Toward an integrated car-following and lane-changing model based on neural-fuzzy approach*. Helsinki summer workshop.

Machanavajjhala, A., Gehrke, J., Kifer, D., & Venkitasubramaniam, M. (2006). l-diversity: Privacy beyond k-anonymity. *International Conference on Data Engineering (ICDE)*.

MacQueen, J. (1967). Some methods for classification and analysis of multivariate observations. In L. M. Le Cam and J. Neyman (Ed.), *Proceedings of the Fifth Berkeley Symposium on Mathematical Statistics and Probability* (pp. 281).

Macskassy, S. A. (2012). *Mining dynamic networks: The importance of pre-processing on downstream analytics*. Retrieved August 2012, from http://www.research.rutgers.edu/~sofmac/paper/ecml2012-commper/macskassy-commper2012-preprint.pdf

Maerivoet, S., & Moor, B. D. (2005). Cellular automata models of road traffic. *Physics Reports*, *419*(1), 1–64. doi:10.1016/j.physrep.2005.08.005.

Mamdani, E. H. (1974). Application of fuzzy algorithms for simple dynamic plant. *Proceedings of the IEEE*, *121*, 1585–1588.

Mann, H. B. (1945). Nonparametric tests against trend. *Econometrica*, *13*, 245–259. doi:10.2307/1907187.

Manning, C. D., & Schütze, H. (2002). *Foundations of statistical natural language processing* (5th ed.). Cambridge, MA: MIT Press.

Manyika, J., Chui, M., Brown, B., Bughin, J., Dobbs, R., Roxburgh, C., & Byers, A. (2011). *Big data: The next frontier for innovation, competition, and productivity*. McKinsey Global Institute.

Mar, J., & Lin, H. T. (2005). The car-following and lane-changing collision prevention system based on the cascaded fuzzy inference system. *IEEE Transactions on Vehicular Technology*, *54*(3), 910–924. doi:10.1109/TVT.2005.844655.

Maserrat, H., & Pei, J. (2010). Neighbor query friendly compression of social networks. In *Proceedings of the 16th ACM SIGKDD international conference on Knowledge discovery and data mining* (pp. 533-542).

Mateou, N. H., Hadjiprokopis, A. P., & Andreou, A. S. (2005). Fuzzy influence diagrams: An alternative approach to decision making under uncertainty. *Computational Intelligence for Modelling, Control and Automation, 2005 and International Conference on Intelligent Agents, Web Technologies and Internet Commerce* (1, pp. 58–64).

Mathioudakis, M., & Koudas, N. (2010). TwitterMonitor: Trend detection over the twitter stream. In *Proceedings of the 2010 International conference on Management of data* (pp. 1155-1158). ACM press.

Maximilien, E. M., Grandison, T., Sun, T., Richardson, D., Guo, S., & Liu, K. (2009). Enabling privacy as a fundamental construct for social networks. The *Proceedings of the Workshop on Security and Privacy in Online Social Networking (SPOSN09) at the 2009 IEEE International Conference on Social Computing (SocialCom 09)*. Vancouver, Canada.

McDonald, M., Wu, J., & Brackstone, M. (1997). Development of a fuzzy logic based microscopic motorway simulation model. *Proceeding of the IEEE Conference on Intelligent Transport Systems (ITSC97) Conference* (pp. 82-87). Boston, MA.

McLennan, A., & Howell, G. (2010). *Social networks and the challenge for public relations* (*Vol. 11*). Asia Pacific Public Relations Journal.

Men, L., & Tsai, W. (2012). Beyond liking or following: Understanding public engagement on social networking sites in China. *Public Relations Review*.

Meo, P. D., Nocera, A., Terracina, G., & Ursino, D. (2011). Recommendation of similar users, resources and social networks in a social internetworking scenario. *Information Sciences*, *181*(7), 1285–1305. doi:10.1016/j.ins.2010.12.001.

Miao, Y., & Li, C. (2010). WikiSummarizer - A Wikipedia-based summarization system. In *Proceedings of Text Analysis Conference*.

Miller, H., & Han, J. (Eds.). (2001). *Geographic data mining and knowledge discovery*. London: Taylor & Francis. doi:10.4324/9780203468029.

Miluzzo, E. et al. (2008). *Sensing meets mobile social networks: The design, implementation and evaluation of the cenceme application*. ACM. doi:10.1145/1460412.1460445.

Miner, G., Elder, J. IV, Fast, A., Hill, T., Nisbet, R., & Delen, D. (2012). *Practical text mining and statistical analysis for non-structured text data applications*. Academic Press.

Min, J.-K., & Cho, S.-B. (2011). Mobile human network management and recommendation by probabilistic social mining. *IEEE Transactions on Systems, Man, and Cybernetics. Part B, Cybernetics*, *41*(6), 761–771. PMID:21172755.

Mitra, S., Bagchi, A., & Bandyopadhaya, A. K. (2007). Design of a data model for social network applications. *Journal of Database Management*, *18*(4), 51–79. doi:10.4018/jdm.2007100103.

Mitra, S., Pal, S. K., & Mitra, P. (2002). Data mining in soft computing framework: A survey. *IEEE Transactions on Neural Networks*, *13*(1), 3–14. doi:10.1109/72.977258 PMID:18244404.

Mobasher, B. (2007). Data mining forweb personalization. Springer-Verlag Berlin Heidelberg. *The Adaptive Web, LNCS*, *4321*, 90–135. doi:10.1007/978-3-540-72079-9_3.

Moridpour, S. (2010). *Modelling heavy vehicle lane changing*. (Ph.D. Thesis). Monash University, Australia.

Moridpour, S., Rose, G., & Sarvi, M. (2009). Modelling the heavy vehicle drivers' lane changing decision under congested traffic conditions. *Journal of Road and Transport Research*, *18*(4), 49–57.

Moridpour, S., Rose, G., & Sarvi, M. (2010). The effect of surrounding traffic characteristics on lane changing behavior. *Journal of Transportation Engineering*, *136*(11), 937–1055. doi:10.1061/(ASCE)TE.1943-5436.0000165.

Moridpour, S., Sarvi, M., & Rose, G. (2010). Modeling the lane changing execution of multi class vehicles under heavy traffic conditions. *Transportation Research Record. Journal of the Transportation Research Board*, *2161*, 11–19. doi:10.3141/2161-02.

Moridpour, S., Sarvi, M., Rose, G., & Mazloumi, E. (2012). Lane-changing decision model for heavy vehicle drivers. *Journal of Inteligent Transportation Systems, 16*(1), 24–35. doi:10.1080/15472450.2012.639640.

Morzy, M. (2011). Internet forums: What knowledge can be mined. In Kumar, A. S. (Ed.), *Knowledge discovery practices and emerging applications of data mining: Trends and new domains* (pp. 315–335). IGI Global Publishing.

Mosley, R. (2012). Social media analytics: Data mining applied to insurance Twitter posts. *Casualty Actuarial Society E-Forum*, Volume 2. Retrieved October 5, 2012, from http://www.casact.org/pubs/forum/12wforumpt2/Mosley.pdf

Müller-Prothmann, T. (2006). *Leveraging knowledge communication for innovation. Framework, methods and applications of social network analysis in research and development.* (Dissertation).

Murthy, D., & Longwell, S. A. (in press). Twitter and disasters: The uses of Twitter during the 2010 Pakistan floods. *Information Communication and Society.*

Musolesi, M., & Mascolo, C. (2006). Designing mobility models based on social network theory. *ACM, Mobile Computing and Communications Review, 11*(3).

My Space. (n.d.). *Website.* Retrieved May 21. 2012, from http://www.MySpace.com

Myers, O., et al. (2011). On media memory: Collective memory in a new media age. New York: Palgrave MacMillan. Retrieved from http://www.scientificamerican.com/

Nagel, T., & Duval, E. (2010, September). Muse: Visualizing the origins and connections of institutions based on co-authorship of publications. In *Proceedings of the 2nd International Workshop on Research 2.0. At the 5th European Conference on Technology Enhanced Learning: Sustaining TEL* (pp. 48-52).

Nagel, K., Wolf, D. E., Wagner, P., & Simon, P. (1998). Two-lane traffic rules for cellular automata: A systematic approach. *Physical Review E: Statistical Physics, Plasmas, Fluids, and Related Interdisciplinary Topics, 58*(2), 1425–1437. doi:10.1103/PhysRevE.58.1425.

Nair, P., & Sarasamma, S. T. (2007). *Data mining through fuzzy social network analysis* (pp. 251–255). IEEE Community Society. doi:10.1109/NAFIPS.2007.383846.

Nakhaeizadeh, G. (1998). *Knowledge discovery in databases and data mining. An overview in data mining: Theoretical aspects and applications.* Heidelberg: Physica-Verlag.

Nancy, P., & Geetha Ramani, R. (2011). A comparison on performance of data mining algorithms in classification of social network data (pp. 47-54). *International Journal of Computers and Applications, 32*(8).

Nancy, P., & Geetha Ramani, R. (2012). Frequent pattern mining in social network data (pp. 531-540). *European Journal of Scientific Research, 79*(4).

Nastase, V. (2008). Topic-driven multi-document summarization with encyclopedic knowledge and spreading activation. In *Proceedings of Conference on Empirical Methods on Natural Language Processing* (pp. 763-772).

National Research Council. (2008). *Protecting individual privacy in the struggle against terrorists: A framework for program assessment.* Washington, DC: National Academies Press.

National State Conference of Legislatures. (n.d.). *Issues with cyberbullying and cyber stalking.* Retrieved June 23, 2012, from http://www.Ncsl.org

Newman, M., Barabási, A. L., & Watts, D. J. (2006). *The structure and dynamics of networks (Princeton Studies in Complexity).* Oxford: Princeton University Press.

Newprosoft. (n.d.). *Website.* Retrieved from http://www.newprosoft.com/

Ngai, E. W. T. et al. (2011). The application of data mining techniques in financial fraud detection: A classification framework and an academic review of literature. Elsevier. *Decision Support Systems, 50*, 559–569. doi:10.1016/j.dss.2010.08.006.

Ngai, E. W. T., Xiu, L., & Chau, D. C. K. (2009). Application of data mining techniques in customer relationship management: A literature review and classification. *Expert Systems with Applications, 36*(2), 2592–2602. doi:10.1016/j.eswa.2008.02.021.

Nguyen, N., Dinh, T., Xuan, Y., & Thai, M. (2011). *Adaptive algorithms for detecting community structure in dynamic social networks* (pp. 2282–2290). INFOCOM. doi:10.1109/INFCOM.2011.5935045.

Nielsen. (2011). *State of the media: The social media report*. Retrieved October 5, 2012, from http://blog.nielsen.com/nielsenwire/social

Nikic, V., & Wajda, A. (2006). *Web harvest: Overview*. Retrieved from http://web-harvest.sourceforge.net/overview.php

Nitti, M., et al. (2012). A subjective model for trustworthiness evaluation in the social internet of things. *Personal indoor and mobile radio communications (PIMRC), 2012 IEEE 23rd International Symposium on* (pp.18-23).

Ni, X., Lu, Y., Quan, X., Wenyin, L., & Hua, B. (2012). User interest modeling and its application for question recommendation in user-interactive question answering systems. *Information Processing & Management*, *48*(2), 218–233. doi:10.1016/j.ipm.2011.09.002.

Niyato, D. et al. (2010). *Optimal content transmission policy in publish-subscribe mobile social networks*. IEEE, Communications Society. doi:10.1109/GLOCOM.2010.5683085.

Nohuddin, P. N. E., Coenen, F., Christley, R., Setzkorn, C., Patel, Y., & Williams, S. (2010). Finding "interesting" trends in social networks using frequent pattern mining and self organizing maps. *Knowledge-Based Systems*, *29*, 104–113. doi:10.1016/j.knosys.2011.07.003.

Nohuddin, P., Coenen, F., Christley, R., Setzkorn, C., Patel, Y., & Williams, S. (2012). Finding "interesting" trends in social networks using frequent pattern mining and self organizing maps. *Knowledge-Based Systems*, *29*, 104–113. doi:10.1016/j.knosys.2011.07.003.

Ochoa, S. et al. (2009). Understanding the relationship between requirements and context elements in mobile collaboration. Springer-Verlag Berlin Heidelberg. *Human-Computer Interaction, Part III, HCII. LNCS*, *5612*, 67–76.

O'Leary, D. E. (2012). Blog mining-review and extensions: "From each according to his opinion. *Decision Support Systems*, *51*(4), 821–830. doi:10.1016/j.dss.2011.01.016.

Onkamo, P., & Toivonen, H. (2006). A survey of data mining methods for linkage disequilibrium mapping. *Human Genomics*, *2*(5), 336–340. doi:10.1186/1479-7364-2-5-336 PMID:16595078.

Özyurt, Ö., & Köse, C. (2010). Chat mining: Automatically determination of chat conversations' topic in Turkish text based chat mediums. *Expert Systems with Applications*, *37*(12), 8705–8710. doi:10.1016/j.eswa.2010.06.053.

Pajala, M. (2010). Television as an archive of memory? *Critical Studies in Television*, *2010*, 133–145.

Palacios, A. M., Gacto, M. J., & Alcala-Fdez, J. (2012). Mining fuzzy association rules from low-quality data. *Soft Computing*, *16*, 883–901. doi:10.1007/s00500-011-0775-3.

Palla, G., Barabasi, A. L., & Vicsek, T. (2007). Quantifying social group evolution. *Nature*, *446*(7136), 664–667. doi:10.1038/nature05670 PMID:17410175.

Pal, N. K., & Bezdek, J. C. (1995). On cluster validity for fuzzy C-means model. *IEEE Transactions on Fuzzy Systems*, *3*(3), 370–379. doi:10.1109/91.413225.

Park, H.-S., & Cho, S.-B. (2010). Building mobile social network with semantic relation using Bayesian network-based life-log mining. *IEEE Computer Society, International Conference on Social Computing/IEEE International Conference on Privacy, Security, Risk and Trust* (pp. 401-40).

Pedrycz, W. (1998). Fuzzy set technology in knowledge discovery. *Fuzzy Sets and Systems*, *98*(3), 279–290. doi:10.1016/S0165-0114(96)00377-6.

Pentaho. (n.d.). *Website*. Retrieved from http://www.pentaho.com

Pentland, A. (2007). Automatic mapping and modeling of human networks. Elsevier. *Science Direct. Physica A*, *378*, 59–67. doi:10.1016/j.physa.2006.11.046.

People you may know. (n.d.). *Website*. Retrieved May 23, 2012, from http://blog.twitter.com

Phelan, O., McCarthy, K., & Smyth, B. (2009). Using twitter to recommend real-time topical news. *Proceedings of the third ACM conference on Recommender systems* (pp. 385-388). ACM press.

Phelan, O., McCarthy, K., Bennett, M., & Smyth, B. (2011). Terms of a feather: Content-based news recommendation and discovery using Twitter. In Advances in Information Retrieval (pp. 448—459).

Pietiläinen, A. K. et al. (2009). *MobiClique: Middleware for mobile social networking* (pp. 49–54). ACM.

Ploderer, B. et al. (2010). Collaboration on social network sites: Amateurs, professionals and celebrities. *Computer Supported Cooperative Work*. doi:10.1007/s10606-010-9112-0.

Popper, K. (1952). *The logic of scientific discovery* (p. 479). Routledge Publishing Company.

Pramudiono, I., & Kitsuregawa, M. (2004). FP-tax: Tree structure based generalized association rule mining. In *Proceedings ACM SIGMOD workshop on Research issues in data mining and knowledge discovery* (pp. 60-63). ACM press.

PTV. (2007). *VISSIM 5.0 User Manual*. PTV Planung Transport Verkehr AG, Stumpfstra_e 1, D-76131 Karlsruhe, Germany. Retrieved from http://www.vissim.de/

Pushpa & Shobhag, G. (2012). An efficient method of building the telecom social network for churn prediction.[IJDKP]. *International Journal of Data Mining & Knowledge Management Process*, *2*(3).

Qiu, J., & Lin, Z. (2011). A framework for exploring organizational structure in dynamic social networks. *Decision Support Systems*, *51*(4), 760–771. doi:10.1016/j.dss.2011.01.011.

QL2. (n.d.). *Website*. Retrieved from http://www.ql2.com

Rabelo, J. C. B., Prudêncio, R. C. B., & Barros, F. A. (2012). Leveraging relationships in social networks for sentiment analysis. *Proceedings of the 18th Brazilian symposium on Multimedia and the web* (pp.181-188).

Rahman, A. et al. (2010). Building dynamic social network from sensory data feed. *IEEE Transactions on Instrumentation and Measurement*, *9*(5), 1327–1341. doi:10.1109/TIM.2009.2038307.

Ralf, M., & Markus, R. (2011, September/October). Data mining tools. *Wiley Interdisciplinary Reviews: Data Mining and Knowledge Discovery*, *1*(5), 431–445. doi: 10.1002/widm.24. Retrieved October 21, 201 1, from http://onlinelibrary.wiley.com/doi/10.1002/widm.24/abstract

Rama, J., et al. (2009). An architecture for mobile social networking applications. IEEE Computer Society, 1st International Conference on Computational Intelligence, Communication Systems and Networks.

Rangaswamy, N., & Cutrell, E. (2012). Re-sourceful networks: Notes from a mobile social networking platform in India. *Pacific Affairs*, *85*(3), 587–606. doi:10.5509/2012853587.

Ranjan, J. (2008). Data mining techniques for better decisions in human resource management systems. *International Journal of Business Information Systems*, *3*(5), 464–481. doi:10.1504/IJBIS.2008.018597.

Rawassizadeh, R., Heurix, J., Khosravipour, A., & Min Tjoa. (2011). LiDSec- A lightweight pseudonymization approach for privacy-preserving publishing of textual personal information, ares. In *Sixth International Conference on Availability, Reliability and Security* (pp. 603-608).

Research Survey. (n.d.). *Media Psychology Resource Center*. Retrieved June 24, 2012, from http://mprcenter.org/

Roberto, B., & Mauro, B. (2011, February). *Reactive business intelligence. From data to models to insight.* ISBN 978-88-905795-0-9.

Romsaiyud, W., & Premchaiswadi, W. (2012). Applying mining fuzzy sequential patterns technique to predict the leadership in social networks. *9th International Conference on ICT and Knowledge Engineering (ICT & Knowledge Engineering)* (pp. 134-137).

Rosa, P. M. P., et al. (2012). An ubiquitous mobile multimedia system for events agenda. IEEE. *Wireless Communications and Networking Conference: Mobile and Wireless Networks* (pp. 2103 – 2107).

Rose, N., Cowie, C., Gillett, R., & Marks, G. B. (2009). Weighted road density: A simple way of assigning traffic-related air pollution exposure. *Atmospheric Environment*, *43*(32), 5009–5014. doi:10.1016/j.atmosenv.2009.06.049.

Ross, T. J. (1995). *Fuzzy logic with engineering applications* (p. 606). McGraw-Hill.

Roy, P., Martínez, A. J., Miscione, G., Zuidgeest, M. H. P., & Maarseveen, M. F. A. M. (2012). Using social network analysis to profile people based on their e-communication and travel balance. *Journal of Transport Geography*, *24*, 111–122. doi:10.1016/j.jtrangeo.2011.09.005.

Runkler, T. A. (2003). Fuzzy nonlinear projection. In *IEEE International Conference on Fuzzy Systems*.

Runkler, T. A., & Bezdek, J. C. (1999). Alternating cluster estimation: A new tool for clustering and function approximation. *IEEE Transactions on Fuzzy Systems*, *7*(4), 377–393. doi:10.1109/91.784198.

Ruspini, E. H. (1970). Numerical methods for fuzzy clustering. *Information Sciences*, *2*, 319–350. doi:10.1016/S0020-0255(70)80056-1.

Russell, B. (1948). *Human knowledge: Its scope and limits*. London: George Allen and Unwin.

Salvucci, D. D., & Mandalia, H. M. (2007). Lane-change detection using a computational driver model. *Human Factors and Ergonomics Society*, *49*(3), 532–542. doi:10.1518/001872007X200157 PMID:17552315.

Sammon, J. W. (1969). A nonlinear mapping for data structure analysis. *IEEE Transactions on Computers*, *C-18*(5). doi:10.1109/T-C.1969.222678.

Santoro, N., Quattrociocchi, W., Flocchini, P., Casteigts, A., & Amblard, F. (2011). *Time-varying graphs and social network analysis: Temporal indicators and metrics*. Retrieved August 1, 2011, from http://arxiv.org/abs/1102.0629

Santos, P., Souza, F., Times, V., & Benevenuto, F. (2012). *Towards integrating online social networks and business intelligence*. In *Proceedings of International Conference on Web Based Communities and Social Media*. Lisbon, Portugal.

Sashittal, H., Sriramachandramurthy, R., & Hodis, M. (2012). Targeting college students on Facebook? How to stop wasting your money. *Business Horizons*, *55*(5), 495–507. doi:10.1016/j.bushor.2012.05.006.

Sasoh, A., & Ohara, T. (2002). Shock wave relation containing lane change source term for two-lane traffic flow. *Journal of the Physical Society of Japan*, *71*(9), 2339–2347. doi:10.1143/JPSJ.71.2339.

Savasere, A., Omiecinski, E., & Navathe, S. B. (1998). Mining for strong negative associations in a large database of customer transactions. In *Proceedings of the Fourteenth International Conference on Data Engineering* (ICDE '98) (pp. 494-502). IEEE Computer Society.

Schenkel, R., Crecelius, T., Kacimi, M., Michel, S., Neumann, T., Parreira, J. X., & Weikum, G. (2008). Efficient top-k querying over social-tagging networks. In *Proceedings of the 31st annual international ACM SIGIR conference on Research and development in information retrieval* (pp. 523-530). ACM press.

Schönhofen, P. (2009). Identifying document topics using the Wikipedia category network. *Web Intelligence and Agent Systems*, *7*(2), 195–207.

Scott, J. P. (2000). *Social network analysis: A handbook* (2nd ed.). Thousand Oaks, CA: Sage Publications.

Şen, Z. (2010). Fuzzy logic and hydrogeological modeling (pp. 340). Taylor and Francis Group, CRC Press.

Senator, T. E. (2005). Link mining applications: Progress and challenges. *SIGKDD Explorations*, *7*(2), 76–83. doi:10.1145/1117454.1117465.

Sen, P. K. (1968). Estimates of the regression coefficient based on Kendall's tau. *Journal of the American Statistical Association*, *63*, 1379–1389. doi:10.1080/01621459.1968.10480934.

Şen, Z. (2010). Rapid visual earthquake hazard evaluation of existing buildings by fuzzy logic modeling. *Expert Systems with Applications*, *37*, 5653–5660. doi:10.1016/j.eswa.2010.02.046.

Şen, Z. (2011). Fuzzy philosophy of science and education. *Turkish Journal of Fuzzy Systems*, *2*(2), 77–98.

Şen, Z. (2011). Supervised fuzzy logic modeling for building earthquake hazard assessment. *Expert Systems with Applications*, *38*, 14564–1457. doi:10.1016/j.eswa.2011.05.026.

Şen, Z. (2012). An innovative trend analysis methodology. *Journal of Hydrologic Engineering*.

Şen, Z. (2012). Trend identification simulation and application. *Journal of Hydrologic Engineering*.

Şen, Z., Kadıoğlu, M., & Batur, E. (1999). Cluster regression model and level fluctuation features of Van Lake, Turkey. *Annales Geophysicae*, *17*, 273–279.

Sharma, S., Gupta, P., & Bhatnagar, V. (2012). Anonymisation in social network: A literature survey and classification. *International Journal of Social Network Mining*, *1*(1), 51–66. doi:10.1504/IJSNM.2012.045105.

Shen, Z., & Ma, K.-L. (2008). MobiVis: A visualization system for exploring mobile data. IEEE. *Visualization Symposium, PacificVis. 08*, pp. 175 – 182.

Sheng, V. S., Provost, F., & Ipeirotis, P. G. (2008, August). Get another label? Improving data quality and data mining using multiple, noisy labelers. In *Proceeding of the 14th ACM SIGKDD international conference on Knowledge discovery and data mining* (pp. 614-622). ACM.

Shepitsen, A., Gemmell, J., Mobasher, B., & Burke, R. (2008). Personalized recommendation in social tagging systems using hierarchical clustering. In *Proceedings of the 2008 ACM conference on Recommender systems* (pp. 259-266). ACM press.

Sheta, A. (2006). Software effort estimation and stock market prediction using takagi-sugeno fuzzy models. *IEEE International Conference on Fuzzy System*, pp. 171-178.

Sheth, A., & Ranabahu, A. (2010). *Semantic modeling for cloud, computing, part 1: Semantic and service* (pp. 81–83). IEEE Computer Society.

Shim, J. P. et al. (2011). Past, present, and future of decision support technology. Elsevier. *Decision Support Systems*, *33*, 111–126. doi:10.1016/S0167-9236(01)00139-7.

Shiraishi, N., Furuta, H., Umano, M., & Kawakami, K. (2005). *Knowledge-based expert system for damage assessment based on fuzzy reasoning. Artificial intelligence tools and techniques for civil and structural engineers* (p. 658). Edinburgh, United Kingdom: B.H.V. Topping, Civil-Comp Press.

Sigurbjőrnsson, B., & van Zwol, R. (2008). Flickr tag recommendation based on collective knowledge. In *Proceedings of the 17th international conference on World Wide Web* (pp. 327-336).

Šikšnys, L., et al. (2010). Private and flexible proximity detection in mobile social networks. *IEEE, Computer Society, 11th International Conference on Mobile Data Management.*

Simha, J. B., & Iyengar, S. S. (2006). Fuzzy data mining for customer loyalty analysis. *Information Technology, 2006.ICIT '06. 9th International Conference*, pp. 245–246.

Singh, P. K., Rajput, D. S., & Bhattacharya, M. (2010). An efficient dimension reduction and optimal cluster center initialization technique. *Computational Intelligence and Communication Networks (CICN), 2010 International Conference*, pp. 503–508.

Skillicorn, D., & Talia, D. (2002). Mining large data sets on grids: Issue and prospects. *Computing and Informatics*, *21*, 347–362.

Snow, R., O'Connor, B., Jurafsky, D., & Ng, A. Y. (2008, October). Cheap and fast---but is it good?: Evaluating non-expert annotations for natural language tasks. In *Proceedings of the Conference on Empirical Methods in Natural Language Processing* (pp. 254-263). Association for Computational Linguistics.

Sobkowicz, P., Kaschesky, M., & Bouchard, G. (2012). Opinion mining in social media: Modeling, simulating, and forecasting political opinions in the web, Social Media in Government. *Selections from the 12th Annual International Conference on Digital Government Research*, *29*(4), 470-479.

Social Media and Social Networks. (n.d.). *Website*. Retrieved June 17, 2012, from http://www.socialnomics.net/

Social Media Revolution Video. (2011, June 22). *Website*. Retrieved June 24, 2012, from http://www.youtube.com/

Social Media. (n.d.). *Website*. Retrieved May 22, 2012, from http://en.wikipedia.org/wiki/Social_media

Social media-statistic in Australia Facebook, Blogger, MySpace. (n.d.). *Website*. Retrieved May 24, 2012, from http://www.socialmedianews.com.au/

Social Networking Service. (n.d.). *Website*. Retrieved May 23, 2012, from http://en.wikipedia.org/wiki/Social_networking_service

Song, Y., Zhang, L., & Giles, C. L. (2011). Automatic tag recommendation algorithms for social recommender systems.[ACM press.]. *ACM Transactions on the Web*, *5*(1), 1–31. doi:10.1145/1921591.1921595.

Sopchoke, S., & Kijsirikul, B. (2011). A step towards high quality one-class collaborative filtering using online social relationships. *Advanced Computer Science and Information System (ICACSIS), International Conference on* (pp. 243-248).

Sourceforge. (n.d.). *Website*. Retrieved from http://web-harvest.sourceforge.net/

Spiliopoulou, M., Ntoutsi, I., Theodoridis, Y., & Schult, R. (2006). Monic: Modeling and monitoring cluster transitions. In *Proceedings of the 12th ACM SIGKDD international conference on Knowledge discovery and data mining* (pp. 706-711). ACM press.

Srinivasan, A., King, R. D., Muggleton, S. H., & Sternberg, M. J. E. (1997). Carcinogenesis predictions using ILP. In *Proc. of the 7th International Workshop on Inductive Logic Programming* (vol. 1297, pp. 273–287). Springer-Verlag.

Sriphaew, K., & Theeramunkong, T. (2002). A new method for finding generalized frequent itemsets in association rule mining. In *Proceedings of the VII International Symposium on Computers and Communications* (pp. 20-26). ACM press.

Sriram, B., Fuhry, D., Demir, E., Ferhatosmanoglu, H., & Demirbas, M. (2010). Short text classification in twitter to improve information filtering. In *Proceeding of the 33rd international ACM SIGIR conference on research and development in information retrieval* (pp. 841-842). ACM press.

StatSoft. (2010). *Statistica data and text miner user manual*. Tulsa, OK: StatSoft, Inc..

Stemberk, P., & Kruis, J. (2005). Fuzzy dynamic structural analysis of 2D frames. In *Proceedings of the tenth international conference on civil structures and environmental engineering* (p. 658). Edinburgh, United Kingdom: B.H.V. Topping, Civil-Comp Press.

Strnad, D., & Guid, N. (2010). A fuzzy-genetic decision support system for project team formation. *Applied Soft Computing*, *10*(4), 1178–1187. doi:10.1016/j.asoc.2009.08.032.

Students Addicted to Social Media – New UM Study. (n.d.). *Website*. Retrieved June, 24, 2012, from http://www.newsdesk.umd.edu/

Su, M. Y., Lin, C. Y., Chien, S. W., & Hsu, H. C. (2011). Genetic-fuzzy association rules for network intrusion detection systems. *Fuzzy Systems (FUZZ), 2011 IEEE International Conference*, 2046–2052.

Suchanek, F. M., Kasneci, G., & Weikum, G. (2008). Yago: A large ontology from wikipedia and wordnet. *Web Semantics: Science. Services and Agents on the World Wide Web*, *6*(3), 203–217. doi:10.1016/j.websem.2008.06.001.

Sucuoglu, H., & Yilmaz, T. (2001). Duzce, Turkey: A city hit by two major earthquakes in 1999 within three months. *Seismological Research Letters*, *72*(6), 679–689. doi:10.1785/gssrl.72.6.679.

Sun, J., Faloutsos, C., Papadimitriou, S., & Yu, P. S. (2007). GraphScope: Parameter-free mining of large time-evolving graphs. In *Proceedings of the 13th ACM SIGKDD international conference on Knowledge discovery and data mining* (pp. 687-696). ACM press.

Sun, X., Sun, L., & Wang, H. (2011). *Extended k-anonymity models against sensitive attribute disclosure. Presented at* (pp. 526–535). Computer Communications.

Surma, J., & Furmanek, A. (2011). Data mining in on-line social network for marketing response analysis. *IEEE International Conference on Privacy, Security, Risk, and Trust, and IEEE International Conference on Social Computing.*

Sweeney, L. (2002). k-anonymity: A model for protecting privacy. *International Journal on Uncertainty, Fuzziness and Knowledge-based Systems, 10*(5), 557–570. doi:10.1142/S0218488502001648.

Symeonidis, P., Nanopoulos, A., & Manolopoulos, Y. (2008). Tag recommendations based on tensor dimensionality reduction. In *Proceedings of the ACM conference on Recommender systems,* pp. 43-50.

Taboada, K., Mabu, S., Gonzales, E., Shimada, K., & Hirasawa, K. (2010). Mining fuzzy association rules: A general model based on genetic network programming and its applications. *IEEJ Transactions on Electrical and Electronic Engineering, 5*, 343–354. doi:10.1002/tee.20540.

Takaffoli, M., Sangi, F., Fagnan, J., & Za¨ıane, O. (2010, September). A framework for analyzing dynamic social networks. *Applications of Social network Analysis (ASNA).*

Tan, P. N., Kumar, V., & Srivastava, J. (2000). Indirect association: Mining higher order dependencies in data. In *Proceedings of the 4th European Conference on Principles of Data Mining and Knowledge Discovery* (PKDD'00) (pp. 632-637). Springer-Verlag.

Tan, P. N., Kumar, V., & Srivastava, J. (2002). Selecting the right interestingness measure for association patterns. In *ACM SIGKDD International Conference on Knowledge Discovery and Data Mining* (KDD'02) (pp. 32-41). ACM press.

Tang, J., Musolesi, M., Mascolo, C., Latora, V., & Nicosia, V. (2010). Analysing information flows and key mediators through temporal centrality metrics. In *Proceedings of the 3rd Workshop on Social Network Systems.* ACM.

Tang, L., & Liu, H. (2009). Relation learning via latent social dimensions. In *Proceedings of the 15th ACM SIGKDD international conference on Knowledge discovery and data mining* (pp. 817-826).

Tang, L., Wang, X., & Liu, H. (2010). Understanding emerging social structures — a group profiling approach. *Technical report, School of Computing, Informatics, and Decision Systems Engineering, Arizona State University.* Retrieved October 5, 2012, from http://www.public.asu.edu/~huanliu/papers/groupprofiling.pdf

Tang, J., Musolesi, M., Mascolo, C., & Latora, V. (2009). Temporal distance metrics for social network analysis. *WOSN, 2009,* 31–36. doi:10.1145/1592665.1592674.

Tang, L., & Liu, H. (2010). Toward predicting collective behavior via social dimension extraction. *IEEE Intelligent Systems, 25*(4), 19–25. doi:10.1109/MIS.2010.36.

Tan, P. N., Steinbach, M., & Kumar, V. (2006). *Introduction to data mining*. Pearson Addison Wesley.

Tao, Y., & Tsu, M. (2009). Mining frequent itemsets in time-varying data streams. In *Proceedings of the XVIII Conference on Information and Knowledge Management* (pp. 1521-1524). ACM press.

Teneyuca, D. (2011). Internet cloud security: The illusion of inclusion. Elsevier. *Information Security Technical Report, 16*, 102–107. doi:10.1016/j.istr.2011.08.005.

Theodoridis, S., & Koutroumbas, K. (2008). *Pattern recognition.* Academic Press.

Time spent on Facebook 700 Percent, but MySpace.com still tops for video according Nielson MySpace connecting and engaging with digital consumers. (2011, November 15). Retrieved from http://www.blog.nielsen.com/

Toledo, T. (2003). *Integrated driving behavior modeling*. Massachusetts Institute of Technology.

Toledo, T., Koutsopoulos, H. N., & Ben-Akiva, M. (2009). Estimation of an integrated driving behavior model. *Transportation Research Part C, Emerging Technologies, 17*(4), 365–380. doi:10.1016/j.trc.2009.01.005.

Top 100 Social Media Colleges- Student Advisor. (n.d.). *Website.* Retrieved May 24, 2012, from http://www.studentadvisor.com/

Tsiptsis, K., & Chorianopoulos, A. (2009). *Data mining techniques in CRM inside customer segmentation.* John Wiley & Sons.

Turban, E., Sharda, R., & Delen, D. (2011). *Decision support and business intelligence systems* (9th ed.). Upper Saddle River, NJ: Prentice hall.

Twitter. (n.d.). *Website.* Retrieved from https://dev.twitter.com/, http://developers.facebook.com/

Uddin, M. S., & Ardekani, S. A. (2002). An observational study of lane changing on basic freeway segment. *Proceeding of the 81th Transportation Research Board Annual Meeting*. Washington, DC., CD-ROM.

United State Patent and Trademark Office. (n.d.). *USPTO search on published patent applications mentioning, social media*. Retrieved May 29, 2012, from http://appft.uspto.gov

US Department of Justice. (n.d.). *A report to Congress, cyber stalking: A new challenge for law enforcement and industry: Report to congress*.

Vaidehi, V., Monica, S., Mohamed Sheik, S., Deepika, M., & Sangeetha, S. (2008). A prediction system based on fuzzy logic. *Proceedings of the World Congress on Engineering and Computer Science 2008 WCECS 2008*.

Van Wel, L., & Royakkers, L. (2004). Ethical issues in web data mining. *Ethics and Information Technology*, *6*(2), 129–140. doi:10.1023/B:ETIN.0000047476.05912.3d.

Venture Beat. (n.d.). *Tech, people, money, digital*. Retrieved April 24, 2012, from http://digital.venturebeat.com/2010/02/10/54-of-us-internet-users-on-facebook-27-on-myspace/trackback/

Verlinde, H., De Cock, M., & Boute, R. (2006). Fuzzy versus quantitative association rules: A fair data-driven comparison. *IEEE Transactions on Systems, Man, and cybernatics—Part-B. Cybernatics*, *36*(3), 679–684.

Vries, L., Gensler, S., & Leeflang, P. (2012). Popularity of brand posts on brand fan pages: An investigation of the effects of social media marketing. *Journal of Interactive Marketing*, *26*(2), 83–91. doi:10.1016/j.intmar.2012.01.003.

Wall, G. T., & Hounsell, N. B. (2005). Microscopic modelling of motorway diverges. *European Journal of Transport and Infrastructure Research*, *5*(3), 139–158.

Wang, C., Satuluri, V., & Parthasarathy, S. (2007). Local probabilistic models for link prediction. In *Data Mining, 2007. ICDM 2007. Seventh IEEE International Conference on* (pp. 322-331).

Wang, D., & Li, T. (2010). Document update summarization using incremental hierarchical clustering. In *Proceedings of the 19th ACM international conference on Information and knowledge management* (pp. 279–288). ACM press.

Wang, D., Zhu, S., Li, T., Chi, Y., & Gong, Y. (2011). Integrating document clustering and multidocument summarization. ACM Transactions on Knowledge Discovery from Data, 5(3), 14:1-14:26. ACM press.

Wang, F. (2010). Application of multidimensional association rule techniques in manufacturing resource planning system. *Fuzzy Systems and Knowledge Discovery (FSKD), 2010 Seventh International Conference,* 3, 1433–1437.

Wang, J., Li, Q., Chen, Y. P., Liu, J., Zhang, C., & Lin, Z. (2010). News recommendation in forum-based social media. In *Proceedings of the Twenty-Fourth AAAI Conference on Artificial Intelligence* (pp. 1449-1454). AAAI press.

Wang, W., & Man, H. (2009). Exploring social relations for the intrusion detection in ad hoc networks. *Proc. of SPIE*, Vol. 7344.

Wang, Y. (2010). *SocConnect: A social networking aggregator and recommender*. Retrieved August 2012, from http://library.usask.ca/theses/available/etd-11292010-112405/unrestricted/yuan_thesis.pdf

Wang, J., Li, Q., Chen, Y. P., & Lin, Z. (2010). User comments for news recommendation in forum-based social media. In *Information Sciences* (pp. 4929–4939). Elsevier.

Wang, L. X. (1995). Design and analysis of fuzzy identifiers of nonlinear dynamic systems. *IEEE Transactions on Automatic Control*, *40*(1), 11–23. doi:10.1109/9.362903.

Wang, P., Hu, J., Zeng, H. J., & Chen, Z. (2009). Using Wikipedia knowledge to improve text classification. *Knowledge and Information Systems*, *19*(3), 265–281. doi:10.1007/s10115-008-0152-4.

Wassermann, S., & Faust, K. (1994). *Social network analysis: Methods and applications*. Cambridge: Cambridge University Press. doi:10.1017/CBO9780511815478.

West, A. et al. (2011). *Trust in collaborative web applications: Future generation computer systems*. Elsevier.

White, J., Matthews, J., & Stacy, J. (2012). Coalmine: An experience in building a system for social media analytics. In proceedings of SPIE.

Wiedemann, R., & Reiter, U. (1992). *Microscopic traffic simulation the simulation system*. MISSION.

Wolfe, A. P., & Jensen, D. (2004). Playing multiple roles: Discovering overlapping roles in social networks. In *ICML-04 Workshop on Statistical Relational Learning and its Connections to Other Fields*.

Wu, X., Zhang, L., & Yu, Y. (2006). Exploring social annotations for the semantic web. *Proceedings of the 15th International Conference on the World Wide Web* (pp. 417-426).

Wu, J., Brackstone, M., & McDonald, M. (2003). The validation of a microscopic simulation model: A methodological case study. *Transportation Research Part C, Emerging Technologies*, *11*(6), 463–479. doi:10.1016/j.trc.2003.05.001.

Wu, K.-L., & Yang, M.-S. (2005). A cluster validity index for fuzzy clustering. *Pattern Recognition Letters*, *26*(9), 1275–1291. doi:10.1016/j.patrec.2004.11.022.

Wu, K.-L., Yu, J., & Yang, M.-S. (2005). A novel fuzzy clustering algorithm based on a fuzzy scatter matrix with optimality tests. *Pattern Recognition Letters*, *26*(5), 639–652. doi:10.1016/j.patrec.2004.09.016.

Wu, T., Chen, Y., & Han, J. (2010). Re-examination of interestingness measures in pattern mining: A unified framework.[ACM press.]. *Data Mining and Knowledge Discovery*, 21.

Xie, X. L., & Beni, G. (1991). A validity measure for fuzzy clustering. *IEEE Transactions on Pattern Analysis and Machine Intelligence, PAMI*, *13*(8), 841–847. doi:10.1109/34.85677.

Xue, Y., Zhang, C., Zhou, C., Lin, X., & Li, Q. (2008). An effective news recommendation in social media based on users' preference. In *Proceedings of the 2008 International Workshop on Education Technology and Training & 2008 International Workshop on Geoscience and Remote Sensing*, 1, 627-631.

Xue, Y., Zhang, C., Zhou, C., Lin, X., & Lin, Q. (2009). An effective news recommendation in social media based on users' preference. In *International Workshop on Education Technology and Training* (pp. 627-631). IEEE Computer Society.

Xu, J., & Chau, M. (2007). Mining communities and their relationships in blogs: A study of online hate groups. *International Journal of Human-Computer Studies*, *65*(1), 57–70. doi:10.1016/j.ijhcs.2006.08.009.

Xu, K., Li, J., & Song, Y. (2012). Identifying valuable customers on social networking sites for profit maximization. *Expert Systems with Applications*, *39*(17), 13009–13018. doi:10.1016/j.eswa.2012.05.098.

Xu, K., Xitong, G., Li, J., Lau, R. Y. K., & Liao, S. S. Y. (2012). Discovering target groups in social networking sites: An effective method for maximizing joint influential power. *Electronic Commerce Research and Applications*, *11*(4), 318–334. doi:10.1016/j.elerap.2012.01.002.

Xu, M. et al. (2009). Cloud computing boosts business intelligence of telecommunication industry. Springer Verlag Berlin Heidelberg, *CloudCom. LNCS*, *5931*, 224–231.

Yager, R. R. (1988). On ordered weighted averaging aggregation operators in multi-criteria decision making. *IEEE Transactions on Systems, Man and Cybernetics. Part: B*, *18*, 183–190.

Yang, C. H., & Regan, A. C. (2009). Prioritization of potential alternative truck management strategies using the analytical hierarchy process. *Proceeding of the 88th Transportation Research Board Annual Meeting*. Washington, DC., CD-ROM.

Yang, L., Liu, F., Kizza, J. M., & Ege, R. K. (2009, March). Discovering topics from dark websites. In Computational Intelligence in Cyber Security, 2009. CICS'09 (pp. 175-179). IEEE.

Yang, X., et al. (2010). K-means based clustering on mobile usage for social network analysis purpose. IEEE. *Advanced Information Management and Service 6th International Conference Proceeding, MPI-QMUL Inf. Syst. Res. Centre*.

Yang, Z., Cai, K., Tang, J., Zhang, L., Su, Z., & Li, J. (2011). Social context summarization. *International ACM SIGIR Conference on Research and Development in Information Retrieval* (pp. 255-264). ACM press.

Yang, Q., & Koutsopoulos, H. N. (1996). A microscopic traffic simulator for evaluation of dynamic traffic management systems. *Transportation Research Part C, Emerging Technologies*, *4*(3), 113–129. doi:10.1016/S0968-090X(96)00006-X.

Yao, Y. Y. et al. (2001). Web intelligence (WI) research challenges and trends in the new information age. Springer-Verlag Berlin Heidelberg. *WI 2001. LNAI*, *2198*, 1–17.

Yeh, P. Z. et al. (2009). *Towards a technology platform for building corporate radar applications that mine the web for business insight* (pp. 477–484). IEEE. doi:10.1109/ICTAI.2009.106.

Yin, R. M. (2007). Tagcrawler: A Web crawler focused on data extraction from collaborative tagging communities. (Unpublished thesis). University of British Columbia, Canada.

Yin, Z., Li, R., Mei, Q., & Han, J. (2009). Exploring social tagging graph for web object classification. *Proceedings of the 15th ACM SIGKDD international conference on Knowledge discovery and data mining* (pp. 957-966). ACM press.

Ying, X., & Wu, X. (2008). Randomizing social networks: A spectrum preserving approach. *SIAM International Conference on Data Mining (SDM)* (pp. 739–750).

Ying, X., Pan, K., Wu, X., & Guo, L. (2009). Comparisons of randomization and k-degree anonymization schemes for privacy preserving social network publishing. *The 3rd SNA-KDD Workshop* (pp. 1–10).

YongYeol, et al. (2007). Analysis of topological characteristics of huge online social networking services. *ACM*, pp. 835 – 844.

Yoo, S., Yang, Y., Lin, F., & Moon, I. C. (2009). Mining social networks for personalized email prioritization. *Proceedings of the 15th ACM SIGKDD international conference on Knowledge discovery and data mining* (pp. 967-976). ACM press.

Yu, G. (2007). Social network analysis based on BSP clustering algorithm. *Communications of the IIMA*, *7*(4).

Yu, S. J. (2012). The dynamic competitive recommendation algorithm in social network services. *Information Sciences*, *197*, 1–14. doi:10.1016/j.ins.2011.10.020.

Zadeh, L. A. (1984). A computational theory of dispositions. *Proceedings of the 22nd annual meeting on Association for Computational Linguistics*, pp. 312-318.

Zadeh, L. A. (1994). Fuzzy logic: Issues, contentions and perspectives. *Acoustics, Speech, and Signal Processing, 1994. ICASSP-94., 1994 IEEE International Conference*, 6, 183.

Zadeh, L. A. (1965). Fuzzy sets. *Information and Control*, *8*, 338–353. doi:10.1016/S0019-9958(65)90241-X.

Zadeh, L. A. (1973). Fuzzy algorithms. *Information and Control*, *12*, 94–102. doi:10.1016/S0019-9958(68)90211-8.

Zadeh, L. A. (1975). The concept of a linguistic variable and its application to approximate reasoning-I. *Information Sciences*, *8*(3), 199–249. doi:10.1016/0020-0255(75)90036-5.

Zadeh, L. A. (1984). Making computers think like people. *IEEE Spectrum Magazine*, *8*, 26–32.

Zadeh, L. A. (1989). Knowledge representation in fuzzy logic. *IEEE Transactions on Knowledge and Data Engineering*, *1*(1), 89–100. doi:10.1109/69.43406.

Zadeh, L. A. (1994). Fuzzy logic, neural networks, and soft computing. *Communications of the ACM*, *37*(3), 77–84. doi:10.1145/175247.175255.

Zernik, J. (2010). Data mining as a civic duty – Online public prisoners' registration systems. *International Journal on Social Media: Monitoring, Measurement, Mining*, 1, 84–96. Retrieved from http://www.scribd.com/doc/38328591/

Zernik, J. (2010). Data mining of online judicial records of the networked US federal courts. *International Journal on Social Media: Monitoring, Measurement, Mining*, 1, 69–83. Retrieved from http://www.scribd.com/doc/38328585/

Zhang, H., et al. (2009). Personalized intelligent search engine based on web data mining. *Proceedings of the 2009 International Workshop on Information Security and Application* (pp. 584-587).

Zhang, B., Guan, X., Khan, M., & Zhou, Y. (2012). A time-varying propagation model of hot topic on BBS sites and Blog networks. *Information Sciences, 187*, 15–32. doi:10.1016/j.ins.2011.09.025.

Zhang, X. et al. (2011). Towards an elastic application model for augmenting the computing capabilities of mobile devices with cloud computing. Springer. *Mobile Networks and Applications, 16*, 270–284. doi:10.1007/s11036-011-0305-7.

Zhang, Z., & Li, Q. (2011). QuestionHolic: Hot topic discovery and trend analysis in community question answering systems. *Expert Systems with Applications, 38*(6), 6848–6855. doi:10.1016/j.eswa.2010.12.052.

Zhao, X., & Okamoto, T. (2008). A device-independent system architecture for adaptive mobile learning. *8th IEEE International Conference on Advanced Learning Technologies* (pp. 23-25).

Zheleva, E., & Getoor, L. (2007). Preserving the privacy of sensitive relationships in graph data. PinKDD (pp. 153–171).

Zhenyu, W., et al. (2010). Towards cloud and terminal collaborative mobile social network service. IEEE. *International Conference on Social Computing, on Privacy, Security, Risk and Trust.*

Zhong, N. (2003). *Toward web intelligence. Springer -Verlag Berlin Heidelberg. AWIC* (pp. 1–14). LNAI.

Zhou, B., & Pei, J. (2008). Preserving privacy in social networks against neighborhood attacks. *IEEE 24th International Conference on Data Engineering* (pp. 506–515).

Zhou, B., & Pei, J. (2010). *The k-anonymity and l-diversity approaches for privacy preservation in social networks against neighborhood attacks. Knowledge and Information Systems*. London: Springer-Verlag.

Zhu, J., Wang, C., He, X., Bu, J., Chen, C., Shang, S., et al. (2009). Tag-oriented document summarization. *Proceedings of the 18th international ACM conference on World Wide Web Conference* (pp. 1195—1196). ACM press.

Zhu, T., Wang, B., Wu, B., & Zhu, C. (2012). Topic correlation and individual influence analysis in online forums. *Expert Systems with Applications, 39*(4), 4222–4232. doi:10.1016/j.eswa.2011.09.112.

Ziegler, G., Farkas, C., & Lorincz, A. (2009). A framework for anonymous but accountable self-organizing communities. *Information and Software Technology, 48*, 726–744. doi:10.1016/j.infsof.2005.08.007.

Zimmerman, H. J. (1985). *Fuzzy set theory and its applications*. Boston: Kluwer Nijhoff Publishing.

Ziv, N. D., & Mulloth, B. (2006). An exploration on mobile social networking: Dodgeball as a case in point. *IEEE Computer Society, Proceedings of the International Conference on Mobile Business (ICMB'06).*

About the Contributors

Vishal Bhatnagar received the B-Tech degree in Computer-Science and Engineering from Nagpur University in Nagpur, India in 1999 and the M-Tech in Information-Technology from Punjabi University, Patiala, India in 2005 and PhD from Shobhit University in 2010.Vishal Bhatnagar is Associate Professor in Computer-Science and Engineering department at Ambedkar Institute of Advanced Communication Technologies and Research (Govt. of Delhi), GGSIPU, Delhi, India. His research interests include Database, Advance Database, Data warehouse and Data mining. He has been in teaching for more than eight years. He has guided under-graduate and post-graduate students in various research projects of databases and data mining.

* * *

Sinchan Bhattacharya is doing his B-Tech in Computer Science and Engineering from GGSIPU, Delhi, India. His research interests include database, data warehouse, data mining, and fuzzy data mining. He has to his credit the paper in Inderscience Journal.

Luca Cagliero is a research assistant at the Dipartimento di Automatica e Informatica of the Politecnico di Torino since March 2012. He holds a Master degree in Computer and Communication Networks and a PhD in Computer Engineering from Politecnico di Torino. His current research interests are in the fields of Data Mining and Database Systems. In particular, he has worked on structured and unstructured data mining by means of classification and association rule mining algorithms.

Alessandro Fiori received the European Ph.D. degree from Politecnico di Torino, Italy. He is a project manager at the Institute for Cancer Research and Treatment (IRCC) of Candiolo, Italy since January 2012. His research interests are in the field of data mining, in particular bioinformatics and text mining. His activity is focused on the development of information systems and analysis frameworks oriented to the management and integration of biological and molecular data. His research activities are also devoted to text summarization and social network analysis.

Gebeyehu Belay Gebremeskel received his BSc in Economics in Alemaya University, Ethiopia. His Master's Degree in Computer Science Majoring Advanced Information Technology in London South Bank University, UK, and now Doctoral student in China Chongqing University, College of Computer Science (under Machine Learning Research Group). He is currently doing his research on Data Mining and Intelligent Agents integrated with Business Intelligence. His research interest includes Machine

Learning, Artificial Intelligence, Multi Agent Systems, and Intelligent Cloud System, Algorithms, Pattern Recognition, Computational Intelligence and others. He published more than 5 refereed papers and solid background in software and giant project planning, development and implementation, and more than three years teaching experience. He is also journal reviewer in three journal publishers.

Luigi Grimaudo received the B.S. Degree in computer engineering from the Universita' Degli Studi Di Palermo, Italy, in 2008 and the M.S. Degree in computer engineering from the Politecnico di Torino, Italy, in 2010. He is currently pursuing a Ph.D. Degree in information and system engineering at DAUIN, Politecnico di Torino, Italy, working with the database and data mining research group. His research interests cover the areas of association rule mining, internet traffic classification, recommendation system and social network analysis.

Alexander Gross is Laboratory Associate in the Social Network Innovation Lab. Alexander serves as the Lab's lead programmer and researcher within the lab's core data mining project. He has published and presented papers on data mining, virtual organizations, and online communities.

Preeti Gupta received the B-Tech degree in Computer-Science and Engineering from Kurukshetra University, Haryana, India in 2001 and M-Tech in Information Security from GGSIPU University, Delhi, India in 2012. She has worked as a lecturer from 2001 to 2005 and is currently working with Government of India as Scientist. Her research interest are network traffic analysis (botnets, social networks), tracking of Cyber attacks/Crimes and Malware Analysis.

Zhongshi HE, full professor, currently Vice Dean of College of Computer Science, post doctor, Doctoral and Master's students' supervisor and also a member of AIPR Professional Committee of China Federation of Computer. He received his B.Sc. and M.Sc. in Applied Mathematics in the college of Mathematics and Statistics, a Doctorate Degree in Computer Software and Theory, in the college of Computer Science, Chongqing University, China and pursued his post doctor research in Witwatersrand University, South Africa. He has conducted and supervised immense research works in the area of Machine Learning, Data Mining, Image Processing, Natural Languages Processing and other related fields. On his own and supervision work, he published more than 60 academic papers, 5 textbooks, and other scientific reports. He is also interested in Artificial Intelligence, Algorithms, Modeling, Bioinformatics and others research fields. In general, he has a strong academic and research background, various Technology Development Awards, teaching Honors and is a highly respected professor.

Gurdeep S. Hura received his B. E. from Jabalpur University (India) in 1972, M. E. from University of Roorkee (India) in 1975 and Ph.D. from University of Roorkee (India) in 1984, respectively. He was on the faculty of REC, Kurukshetra (India) from 1975-1984, a Post Doctoral Fellow in the Department of Computer Science, Concordia University, Montreal, Canada during 1984-1985, Department of Computer Science and Engineering of Wright State University, Dayton, Ohio (USA) from 1984-1992, School of Applied Science, Nanyang Technological University, Singapore from 1992-1998, Department of Computer Science, University of Idaho, Idaho Falls from 1998-2005, Professor and Chair Department of Electrical and Computer Engineering, West Virginia University Institute of Technology, Montgomery, West

Virginia from Jan 2005-July, 2006, Professor and Chair of Department of Mathematics and Computer Science, University of Maryland Eastern Shore from July 2006-Sept 2011 and a Professor in the same department since Oct 2011. He was awarded excellence teaching award in 1991 and 2001 and excellence in advising in 2003. He is an author/co-author of over hundred technical papers, which were published, in International IEEE journals and conferences. He guest edited special issues on "Petri nets and related graph models: Past, Present and Future," 1991, "The Practice of Performance modeling and reliability analysis," 1996, and "Internet: The state of the art," Computer Communication (Elsevier, UK), 1998. He is a senior member of IEEE and was elevated to Fellow of Society for Design and Process Science in 2002. He has organized tutorials on Computer Networks, Modeling and analysis, software engineering, Cyber infrastructure in various International Conferences. He was a General Chairman of IEEE EMS Singapore in 1995. He is co-author of a book on "Data and Computer Communications: Networking and internetworking," CRC Press, 2001. He is CAC ABET Program evaluator. He was a consultant to NEC, Inc, Japan on load balancing aspect of its operating system for parallel machine (2000-2004). He has been listed in Marquis' Who's Who in Midwest, Who's Who in America, Who's Who in Leading Technology, Who's Who in Emerging Leaders of America, and Who's Who in World.

Vineet Kansal has done his bachelor's in Computer Science & Engineering from GB Pant University, Pantnagar. He did master's degree from Indian Institute of Technology, IIT/Delhi, earned doctoral degree also from Indian Institute of Technology, IIT/Delhi in the area of Information Systems. He has been in academics for more than 19 years and is associated to CCS University Meerut, UP Technical University, Lucknow and universities abroad. He has several lectures as guest faculty to various institutes in India and abroad. His research and consulting areas include ERP Systems, IT strategy, IT effectiveness and implementation, teaching effectiveness and system thinking. Dr. Vineet has published several research papers in these areas in international journals and presented papers in international and national conferences. He has conducted several Executive development programs. He is presently Member Advisory Board for MIS Contemporary Management Research (CMR) by ATISR - Academy of Taiwan Information Systems Research, Taiwan and Intellectual society for Socio – Techno welfare (ISST), India serving for scholars around the world of all business, information and computer science fields. He had assignment as external consultant with Ed. CIL, Noida for World Bank project. He has been associated with various professional bodies including ACM, Computer Society of India etc. Bottom of Form.

Manish Kumar received his PhD from Indian Institute of Information Technology, Allahabad, India in Data Management in Wireless Sensor Networks. He is an Assistant Professor at Indian Institute of Information Technology, Allahabad, India. His research interest areas are databases, data management in sensor networks, and data mining.

Sara Moridpour holds a Bachelor of Civil Engineering and Masters degree in Transportation Planning and Engineering from Sharif University of Technology, Tehran, Iran. She also received her PhD degree from Monash University in 2011. She has 5 years of work and research experience in the field of traffic and transport. Her main research interests include on driving behaviour modelling and analysis, micro simulation, transport network modeling.

Dhiraj Murthy is Assistant Professor of Sociology at Bowdoin College, USA. His research interests include social media, Big Data, data mining, virtual organizations, online communities, and digital ethnography. He has recently published his work in Information Communication and Society, Sociology, Media, Culture, & Society, and the Hawaii International Conference on System Sciences. He recently published a book with Polity Press entitled Twitter: Social Communication in the Twitter Age.

Sezi Çevik Onar is an Assistant Professor at Industrial Engineering Department of Istanbul Technical University (ITU) Management Faculty. She earned her B.Sc. in Industrial Engineering and M.Sc. in Engineering Management, both from ITU. She completed her Ph.D. studies at ITU and visited Copenhagen Business School and Eindhoven Technical University during these studies. Her PhD was on strategic options. Her research interests include strategic management, multiple criteria decision making and supply chain management. She took part as a researcher in many private funded projects such as organization design, human resource management system design. Her refereed articles have appeared in a variety of journals including Computers & Industrial Engineering, International Journal of Intelligent Systems and Journal of Enterprise Information Management.

Başar Öztayşi is an instructor and researcher at Industrial Engineering Department of Istanbul Technical University (ITU) Management Faculty. After earning his B.Sc. in Industrial Engineering and receiving M.Sc. in Management Engineering, he finished his Ph.D. in Industrial Engineering program at the Istanbul Technical University Institute of Science and Technology in 2009. The focus of his PhD was on fuzzy measurement and CRM systems. His research interests include data mining, customer relationship management, social networks, and systems design. He refereed articles for a variety of journals including Computers & Industrial Engineering, International Journal of Intelligent Systems and Technovation.

Sunil Pandey, Professor at I.T.S. Ghaziabad, earned his Ph.D in Computer Science, has spent almost 15 years in academia and industry. His area of research includes Database Technologies, Data Warehousing & Data Mining and Object oriented Systems. He has been academically associated with various Universities in India. Dr. Pandey was also been associated with Manipal Group, Manipal as a consultant. Dr. Pandey has organized several National Conferences, Seminars, Faculty Development programs, Students Development Programs and delivered several guest talks at various institutes. He has undertaken and successfully completed many consultancy and training assignments. Dr. Pandey has over 35 Research publications credited to his name in various International, National journals and conferences. He has published three edited volumes of collection of research papers in various themes. He has also chaired technical sessions in various conferences. He has been associated with various professional societies including IEEE, ACM, Indian Science Congress, Computer Society of India, IETE, AIMA etc.

Zekai Şen has obtained B. Sc. and M. Sc Degrees from Technical University of İstanbul, Civil Engineering Faculty, Department of Reinforced Concrete in 1971. His further post-graduate studies were carried out at the University of London, Imperial College of Science and Technology. He was granted Diploma of Imperial College (D.I.C) and M. Sc. in Engineering Hydrology in 1972 and Ph. D.

in stochastic hydrology in 1974. He has published about 300 (Science Citation Indexed) SCI scientific papers in almost 50 different international top journals on various topics. He holds several national and international scientific prizes and the most recent one is given as a team work due to his contribution to "Nobel Peace Prize" through his works in IPCC form 2002-2007 concerning Climate Change. He also holds Science Encouragement and Science Prizes from Science and Technology Center of Turkey. Two of his modeling related books are: *Spatial Modeling Principles in Earth Sciences* (Springer-Verlag, 2009) and *Fuzzy Modeling in Hydrological Sciences* (Taylor and Francis, 2010).

Sanur Sharma received her BTech in Computer-Science and Engineering from GGSIPU, Delhi, India in 2010 and is pursuing MTech in Information Security from Ambedkar Institute of Advanced Communication Technologies and Research, GGSIPU, Delhi, India. Her research interests include database, data warehouse, Data-Mining, and social network analysis. She had her paper accepted in International journal of Social Network Mining (IJSNM) and many more.

Alex Takata was an undergraduate research fellow in the Social Network Innovation Lab. He graduated in 2012 with a double major in Computer Science and Economics. His work in the Lab was focused on social network data mining, visualization, and the development of data mining tools such as Voyeur Server.

Jing Xuan, born in Jinan, capital city of Sandong Province with a Confucian Tradition, develops an ongoing interest in Language. With double bachelor's degrees on Linguistics and Computer Science, Chongqing University, a master's degree on Computational Linguistics, College of Foreign Languages, Chongqing University, and now Doctoral student in Chongqing University, College of Computer Science under Machine Learning research Group majoring Natural Language Processing. Her research interest includes Semantics, Knowledge Web, Corpus, FrameNet, Cloud Computing, others. She is more capable in Chinese and English Languages, including 6 years' English teaching experience, which makes her more capable for her academic career. She believes machines are to facilitate language learning in Corpus Linguistics and also Artificial Intelligence, which gives her strong motive to pursue her career in this research field.

Huazheng Zhu received the B.Sc. degree in mathematical and computer science from Gannan Normal University, Ganzhou in 2008, M.Sc. degree in mathematical and computer science from Guangxi University for Nationalities in 2011. Currently, he is pursuing his PhD degree in computer science, Chongqing University, College of Computer Science, China. His research under Machine Learning research Group, majoring Multi Objective Optimization and Bioinformatics. In addition, he is also interested in Machine Learning, Artificial Intelligence, Algorithms (evolutionary, Genetics, others), Data mining, Image Processing and other related fields.

Index

E

F

G

H

I

K

L

M

N

O

P

Q

R

S

T

U

V

W

X